MW01627455

PICASSO/ASIA

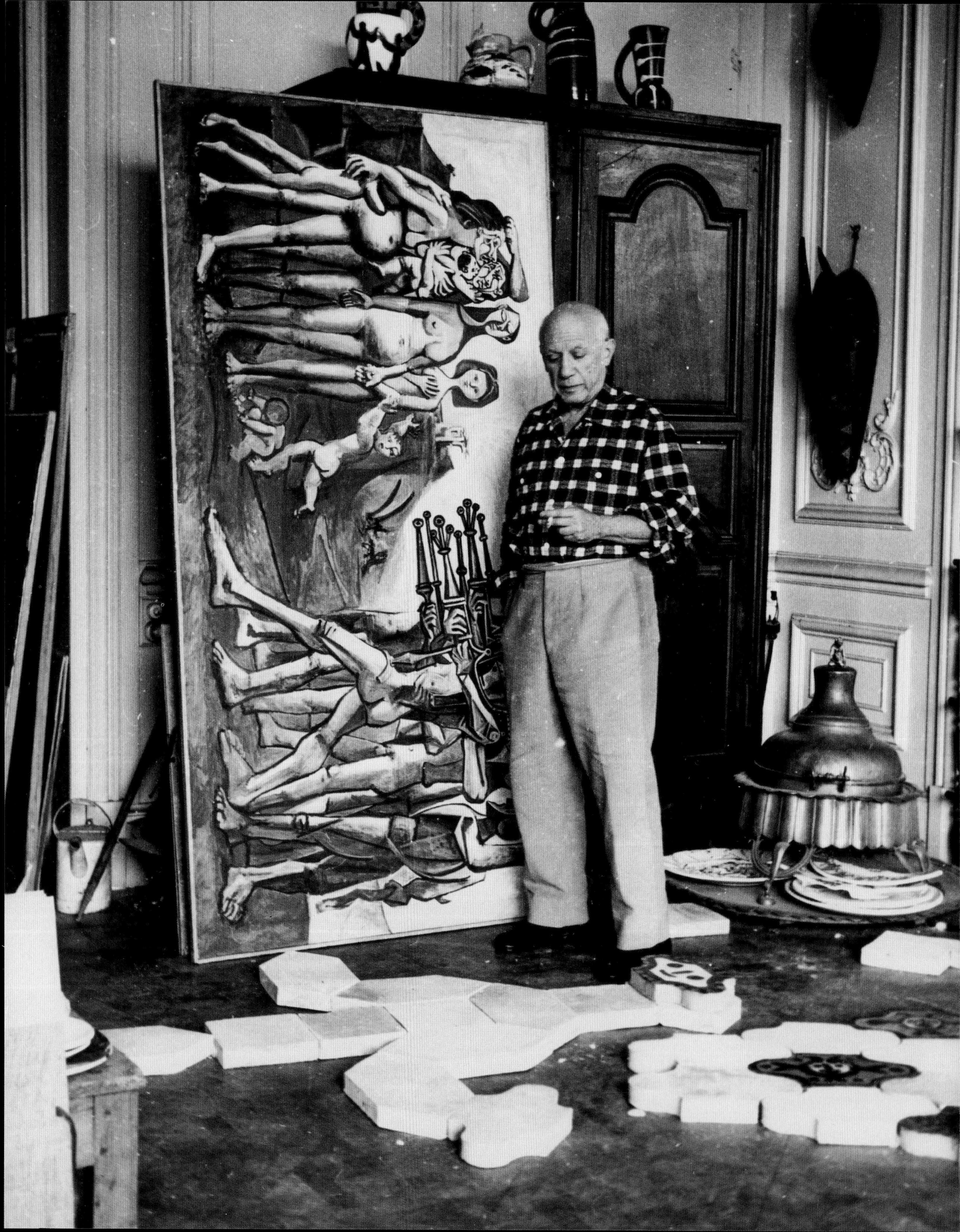

PICASSO/ASIA
A CONVERSATION

Doryun Chong / François Dareau

With 216 illustrations

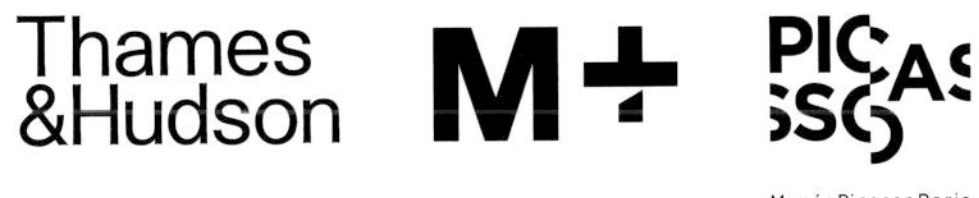

CONTENTS

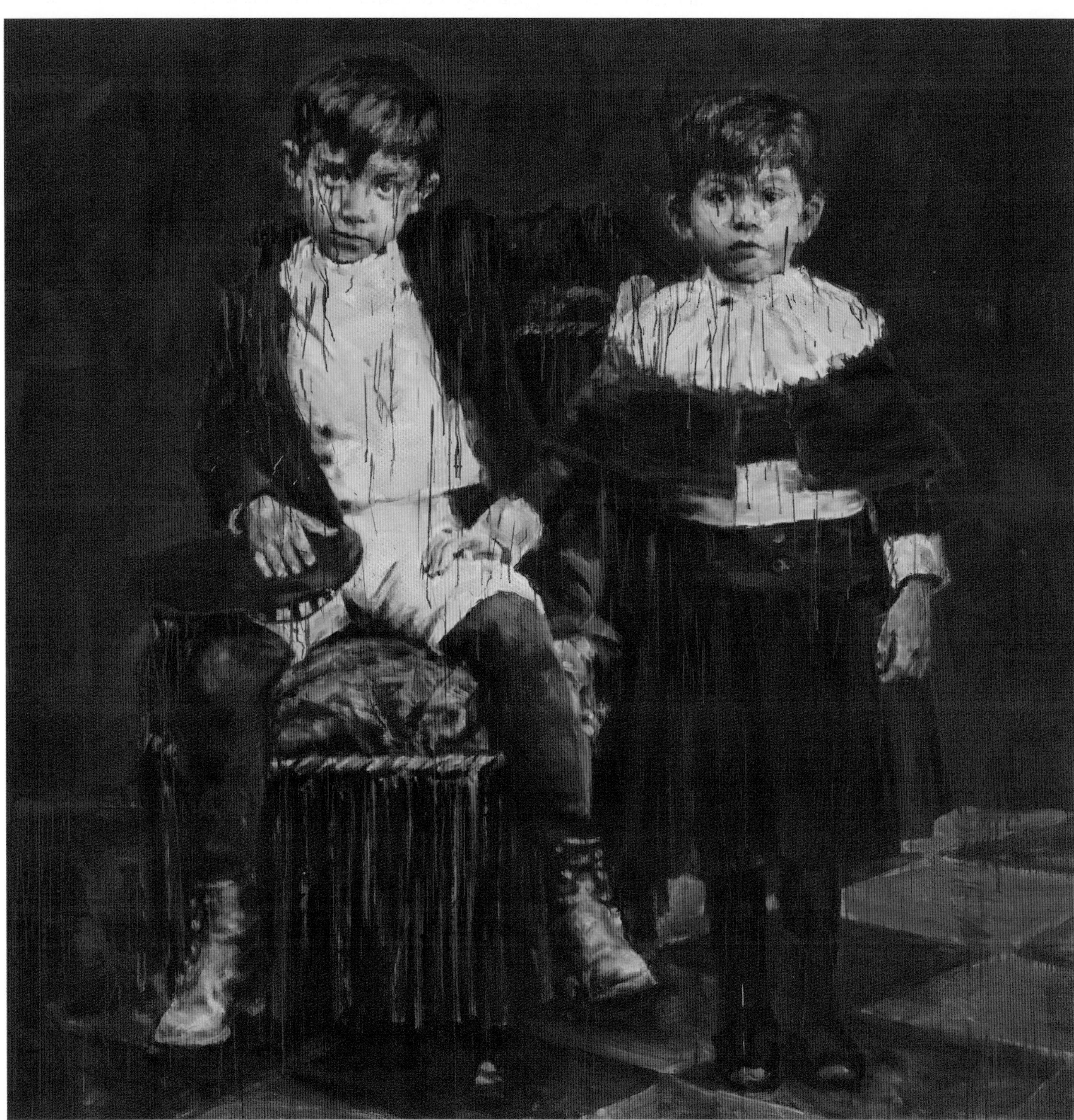

FOREWORD

The Hong Kong Jockey Club Series: Picasso for Asia—A Conversation, the exhibition that occasioned this book, offers a groundbreaking interpretation of the legacy of Pablo Picasso. By placing more than sixty of his masterpieces, on loan from the Musée national Picasso-Paris (MnPP), alongside around eighty works by Asian and Asian-diasporic artists from the M+ Collections, the exhibition presents an unprecedented cross-cultural and intergenerational dialogue—echoing the collaboration between M+ and MnPP, two very different kinds of museums.

The Musée national Picasso-Paris boasts the world's largest collection of works by Picasso. Endowed with works of art from the artist's estate offered as payment to the French state by his heirs, the museum offers a global, comprehensive, and sensitive vision of his career through more than 5,000 works—paintings, sculptures, drawings, engravings, archives, and personal collections. Located in a beautiful seventeenth-century mansion—the Hôtel Salé—in the historic heart of Paris, the museum is both a monographic reference centre and an open, dynamic venue for modern art, focused on the contemporary reception of this key artist of modernity.

M+ is Asia's global museum of contemporary visual culture with a permanent collection encompassing the three disciplines of design and architecture, moving image, and visual art from the twentieth and twenty-first centuries. From its vantage in Hong Kong, the museum surveys international visual culture through an Asian lens. Overlooking the spectacular Victoria Harbour, the landmark M+ building was designed by the Swiss architectural practice Herzog & de Meuron in partnership with TFP Farrells and Arup and was inaugurated in November 2021.

What brought the two museums together on this joint project was a shared interest to explore a unique possibility, an intellectually daring artistic and historical dialogue across times, places, and cultures. With his inimitable artistic languages, Picasso continues to attract audiences from around the world. Asia is no exception to this phenomenon. There have been, however, few critical and thoughtful examinations in Asia of Picasso's towering legacy and wide-reaching influence. Few precedents in the region have grappled with all aspects of the artist's biography, including his troubling chauvinism.

The exhibition and book ask deeply pertinent questions, relevant not only to Asia or to the West, but to the world. Why does Picasso continue to fascinate the public more than a half century after his death? In what ways does his art continue to influence artists of our own times? Are there new meanings in his work for the present, or new sources of relevance for cultural contexts far removed from his own?

Doryun Chong, Artistic Director and Chief Curator at M+, and François Dareau, research fellow at MnPP, co-curated *The Hong Kong Jockey Club Series: Picasso for Asia—A Conversation* and co-edited this publication. Through a sustained, fruitful dialogue, they developed an interpretative framework for examining Picasso's life and career using the archetypes of the modern artist, namely 'genius', 'outsider', 'magician', and 'apprentice'. These archetypes continue to inform how artists are perceived and portrayed in society, and serve as powerful models for how artists fashion and define themselves. And no artist in the modern era has embodied these archetypes more effectively than Picasso.

Dareau's essay in this book explores why this may be the case. Equally important in this 'conversation' is the question of why and how artists located far from the context in which Picasso lived and worked, such as contemporary Asia, may still find Picasso relevant, inspirational, or challenging. Chong's essay proposes different modalities, such as 'homage', 'critique', and 'echo', through which artists of diverse backgrounds have found ways to dialogue with Picasso and his art. Picasso's connections with Asia are not well studied. Though at certain points in

Yan Pei-Ming, *Young Picasso and His Sister—Permanent Rose* (detail; complete work shown overleaf), 2024

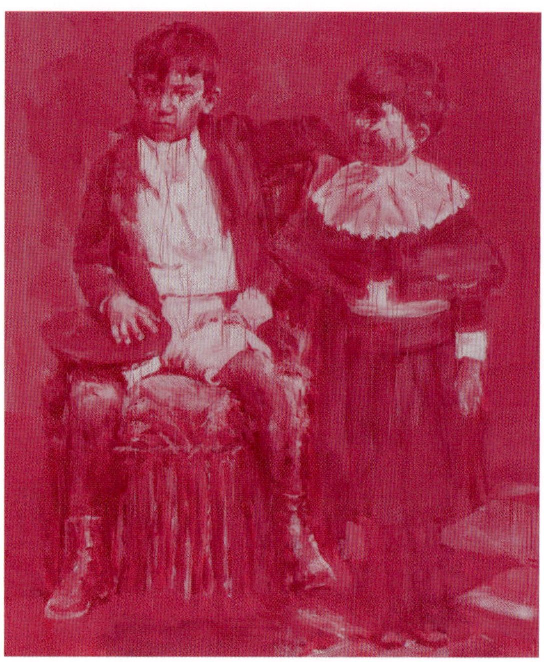
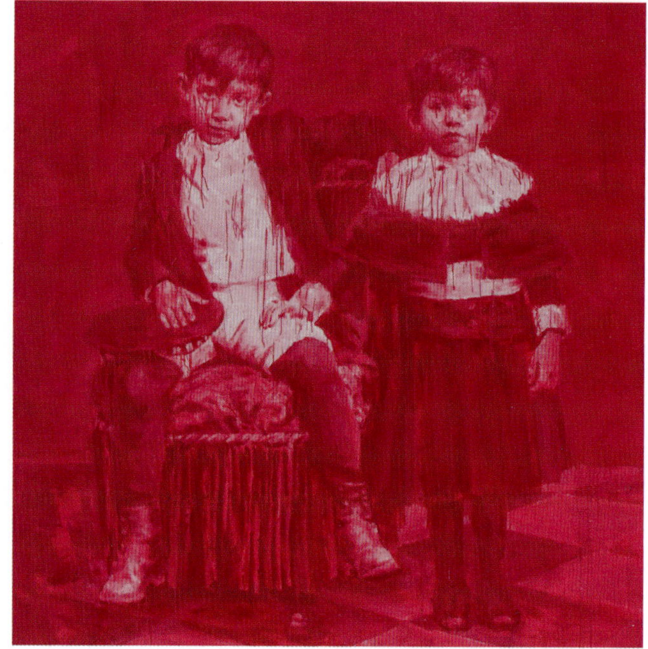

his life he explicitly denied any interest in Asia and rejected influence from the continent's cultural traditions, Asian art and culture had a prominent presence in Picasso's milieu, as the visual chronology in this book makes clear. The conversation that runs through the exhibition and publication avoids perpetuating timeworn binaries such as master and disciples, West and non-West, and original and derivative. By destabilising this inherently hierarchical thinking, and by examining cross-temporal, cross-cultural dialogues through a complex web of inventions and adaptations, the exhibition and the publication can also critically contribute to the study of art since modernity as a history of globalisation, hybridity, and creolisation.

Two artistic examples bear this out. Yan Pei-Ming is internationally renowned for his impactful, often epic-scale portraits of human visages and figures conjured with powerful brushstrokes. He paints ordinary figures, such as his own family members, as well as historic personae, such as politicians and celebrities. Born in Shanghai and trained as a painter in China, Yan moved to France at the age of nineteen to continue his training. His work fully embodies the fusion of East and West: with his large monochromatic canvases, the artist brings the Western tradition of portraiture into a personal and contemporary aesthetic. Fascinated by figures of power, his decision to depict Picasso in several works elevates the Spanish artist—whom he admires—into an artistic pantheon. Yan's diptych *Young Picasso and His Sister—Permanent Rose* takes as its source an early photograph of the artist as a child and his sister, Lola, and revisits the myth of the child prodigy, already gifted with genius. The work embodies the central theme of this exhibition on the image of the artist and Asian re-readings.

Lee Mingwei, a Taiwan-born American artist, is well-known for works that set up intimate relations between the artist and audiences. His *Guernica in Sand*, first realised in 2006, is a floor-based sand painting that recreates Picasso's *Guernica* (1937), the largest painting and the most trenchantly political statement the Spanish artist ever made, now permanently installed in the Museo Reina Sofía in Madrid. Lee leaves a day's work to be done to complete the image in the sand painting when it is presented to audiences. During the exhibition, the artist returns to finish this final piece of the work, while simultaneously inviting audience members to walk on the sand painting, one person at a time, to alter and efface it. Finally, four people

OPPOSITE: Yan Pei-Ming, *Young Picasso and His Sister—Permanent Rose*, 2024

OVERLEAF: Installation view of Lee Mingwei's *Guernica in Sand*, Martin Gropius, Bau, Berlin, 2020

erase the painting by sweeping it with brooms, mixing all the tinctured sands and leaving the painting in a new condition for the rest of the exhibition period. As in many of his powerfully poetic works, with *Guernica in Sand*, Lee combines the late twentieth-century artistic tendency of viewer participation with ritualistic and spiritual elements derived from Buddhist philosophical ideas such as impermanence and karma. By doing so, Lee gives new meanings and life to Picasso's original each time it is reiterated, or reincarnated, around the world.

Yan's painting opens the exhibition, while Lee's painting-performance-participatory event runs parallel to it. In their own distinctive ways, they manifest how Picasso remains a lodestar for contemporary artists. Perhaps more importantly, contemporary artists continually reinvigorate the legacy of Picasso's art by delving into it again and again. We see this clearly in the work of more than two dozen artists hailing from Asia and Asian diasporas included in the exhibition, many of whom are also represented in this book.

We are very proud of this pioneering publication and exhibition, which propose a new methodology and a bold narrative, and which are born of an innovative and inclusive partnership based on a genuine exchange of knowledge, skills, and expertise between our two institutions. We would like to thank Chong and Dareau for sharply curating and steering this rich dialogue with great resonance for both institutions, and for the field of world art history. They were superbly aided by Hester Chan, Curator, Collections, and Annessa Chan and Angela Liu, Curatorial Assistants at M+. For their advice and help, we warmly thank Sébastien Delot, Director of the Scientific and Collections Management, and Johan Popelard, Head of the Collections Department, MnPP. Veronica Castillo, Director, Collection and Exhibition, M+, expertly guided the institutional collaboration, closely working with Julien Sérignac, General Director, and Sophie Daynes-Diallo, Director of Production Management, alongside Clara Gibertoni, Exhibition Manager from MnPP, and Ada Hung, Exhibition Manager from M+.

We thank Manuel Segade, Director of the Museo Reina Sofía, and the Fundación Almine y Bernard Ruiz-Picasso for providing additional loans of key Picasso works to enrich the exhibition. In addition, we thank private lenders Cynthia Hang and Wifredo Lam SDO, the Luis Chan Trust and Hanart TZ, Honus Tandijono, Simon Fujiwara, Esther Schipper Gallery, as well as Studio Haegue Yang, Feng Xi and SPURS Gallery, NANZUKA, Sin Wai Kin, Blindspot Gallery, Zeng Fanzhi Foundation, Atelier Yan Pei-Ming, Nalini Malani, Chung Chi Sam, Simon and Chloe Suen and Yitao Collection, and those who wish to remain anonymous for their support to include their key contemporary artworks in the exhibition.

We thank the exhibition co-presenter, French May Arts Festival. The exhibition is the opening programme of the French May Arts Festival 2025. This show would not have been possible without the generosity of the Title Sponsor, The Hong Kong Jockey Club Charities Trust; the Major Sponsors, Cathay, CC Land, Chubb Life Hong Kong, and HSBC; and the financial support of the Mega Arts and Cultural Events Fund under the Culture, Sports, and Tourism Bureau of the Hong Kong Special Administrative Region Government. Finally, we would like to express our gratitude to all the artists who have participated and added their voices to this substantial new narrative.

Cécile Debray, President, Musée national Picasso-Paris

Suhanya Raffel, Museum Director, M+

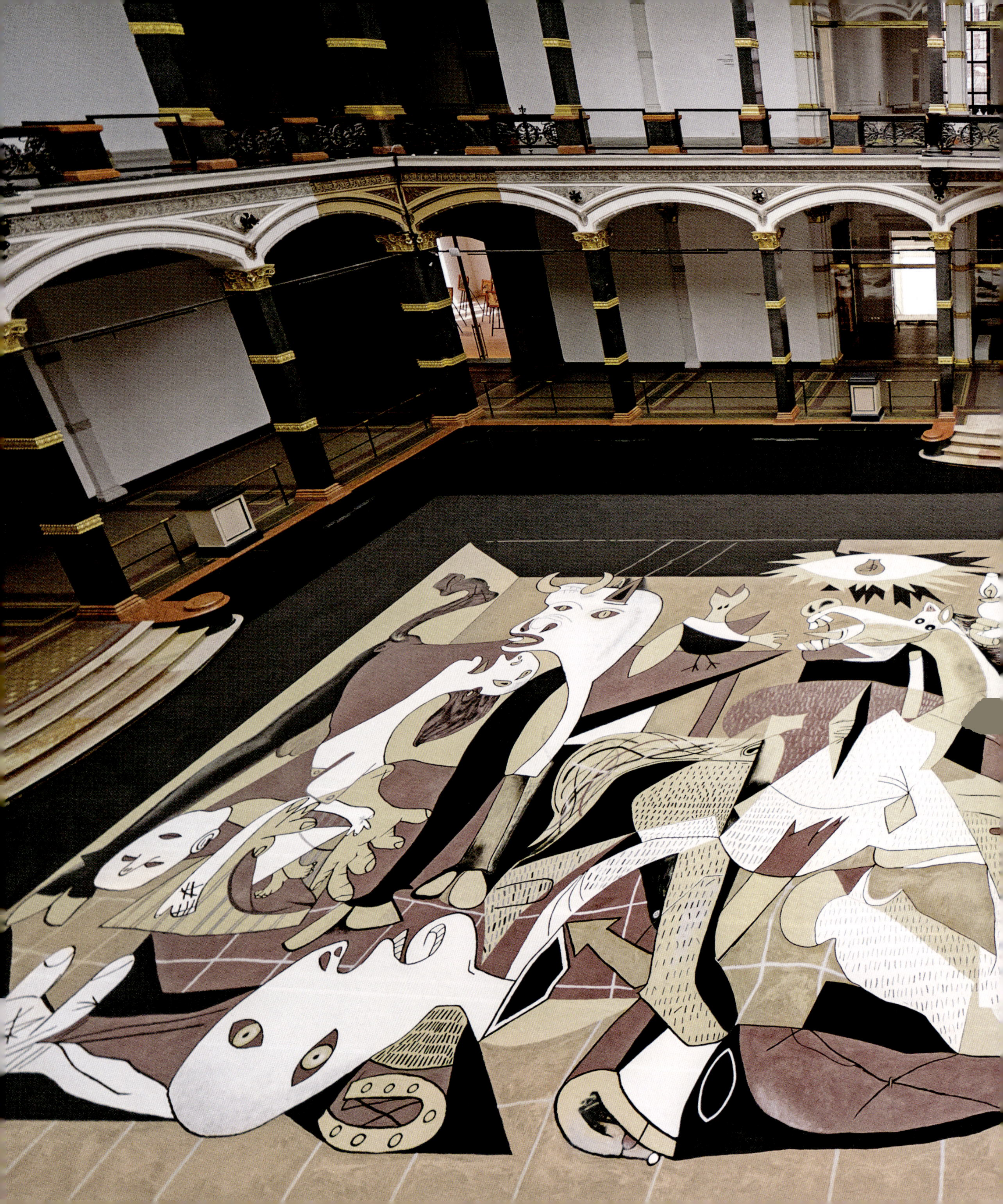

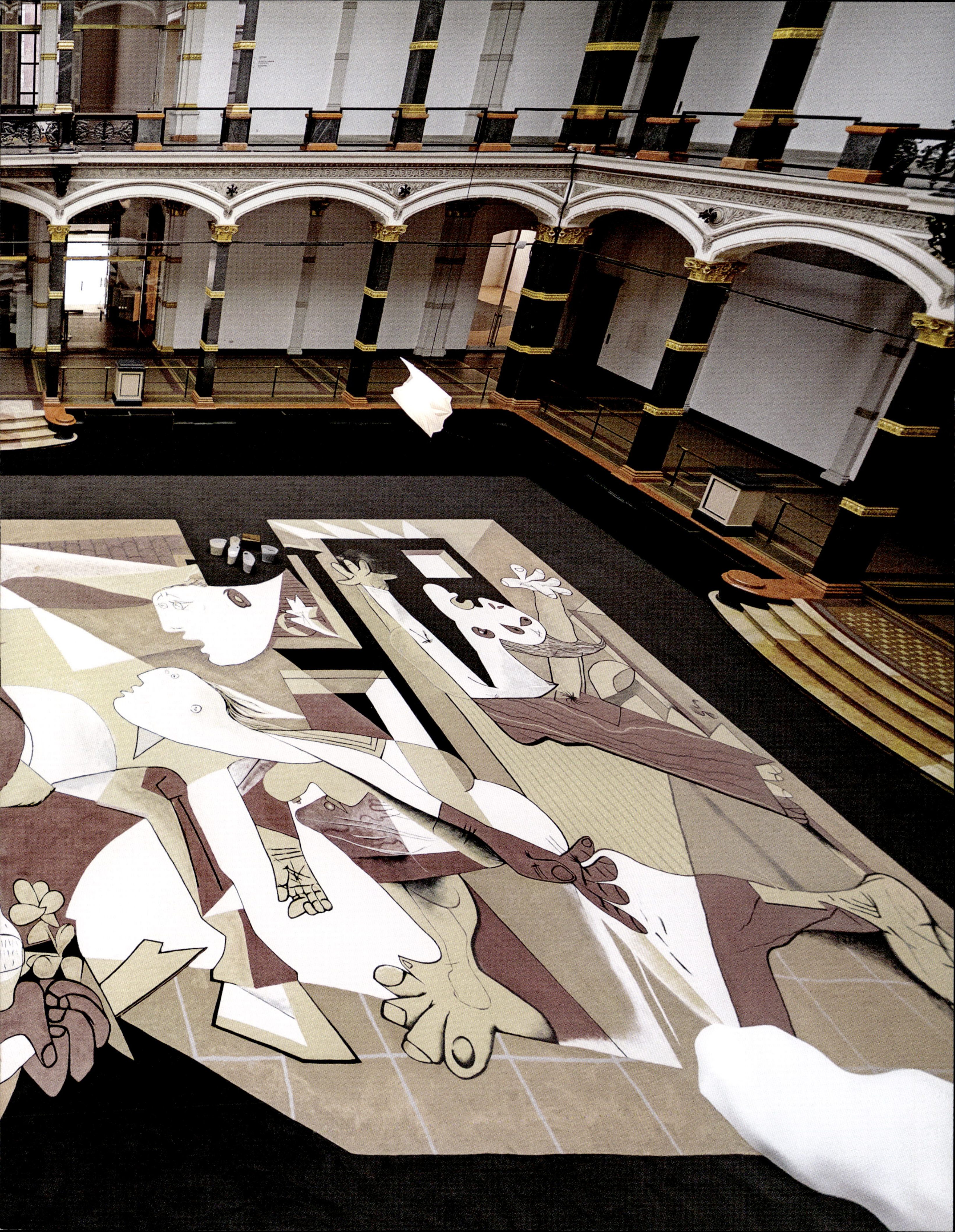

INVENTION

OF A

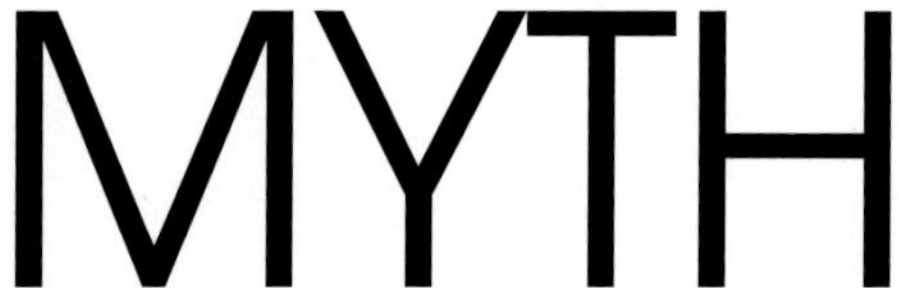

François Dareau

I can see that our epoch is busy constructing an image of itself to cut the ground from beneath the historians' feet.

Jean-Paul Sartre, *War Diaries: Notebooks from a Phony War, 1939–1940*

THE EMBODIMENT OF THE MODERN ARTIST

The history of Western art has been built on a vision that links artists' biographies with their artwork. This historiographical tradition, begun by Pliny the Elder with his *Natural History* in the first century CE, stems mainly from the publication of Giorgio Vasari's *Lives of the Artists* (1550) on the artists of the Italian Renaissance. Vasari's influence glorified our vision of art history, encouraging every era to create its own heroes. In *Legend, Myth, and Magic in the Image of the Artist* (1979), Ernst Kris and Otto Kurz show how these narratives of artists' lives reproduce stereotypical patterns, the earliest expressions of which can be found in ancient Western mythologies. While the myths are based on imaginary narratives and figures, they generally derive from social and cultural realities, which they may then legitimate and maintain: 'Biographical formula and life appear to be linked in two ways. Biographies record typical events, on the one hand, and thereby shape the typical fate of a particular professional class, on the other hand. The practitioner of the vocation to some extent submits to this typical fate or destiny.'[1]

Pablo Picasso is one of the artists who were inspired by these archetypes, before in turn becoming a mythical figure. In his essay on modern mythologies, from Einstein's brain to wrestling, Roland Barthes writes: 'Can everything then be a myth? Yes, I believe so, for the universe is infinitely suggestive. Every object in the world can move from a closed, mute existence to an oral state, open to being appropriated by society, for no law, whether natural or not, forbids speaking about things.'[2] In this way, without us even needing to know his work, Picasso's name has become a commonly used term for evoking the status of the iconoclast artist or that of a master in a given field. French artist Sophie Calle recalls making a drawing as a child that led her grandmother to say that there was 'a Picasso in the family'.[3] We find him as a rhetorical figure in the media, from an article describing painter Zhang Daqian as the 'Chinese Picasso'[4] to a famous chef being called the 'Picasso of gastronomy'.[5] The term has even been used to describe a serial killer as the 'Picasso of crime'.[6]

The particular character of the myth that Picasso established—which can partly explain the significant place that art history grants him—resides in his polymorphic nature, bringing together a wide array of artistic stereotypes that are sometimes contradictory: the child prodigy, the bohemian artist, the iconoclastic revolutionary, the exiled artist, the star, the opportunist, the millionaire, the magician, the monster, the political activist, the artist who scribbles like a child, the artist who has fallen out of fashion, the eternally youthful artist, the genius, and so on. These multiple identities seem at first glance to be irreconcilable in a single lifetime, as biographical narratives have accustomed us to the idea that a life should form a 'consistent and directed whole'.[7] We will examine later the accuracy of the images evoked to describe Picasso, but first let us dismiss the notion that the story of a life, or an artwork, forms a rational whole. Instead, let us keep in mind the words of the filmmaker and novelist Alain Robbe-Grillet, for whom 'reality is discontinuous, composed of elements inexplicably side by side, each of which is unique, all the more difficult to grasp since they arise in an ever-unpredictable fashion, without rhyme or reason, by chance.'[8] We can consider this idea through a painting produced by Picasso in 1920, *Studies* (FIG. 1), in which two heterogeneous styles coexist: late Cubism and classical figuration. This work reminds us that

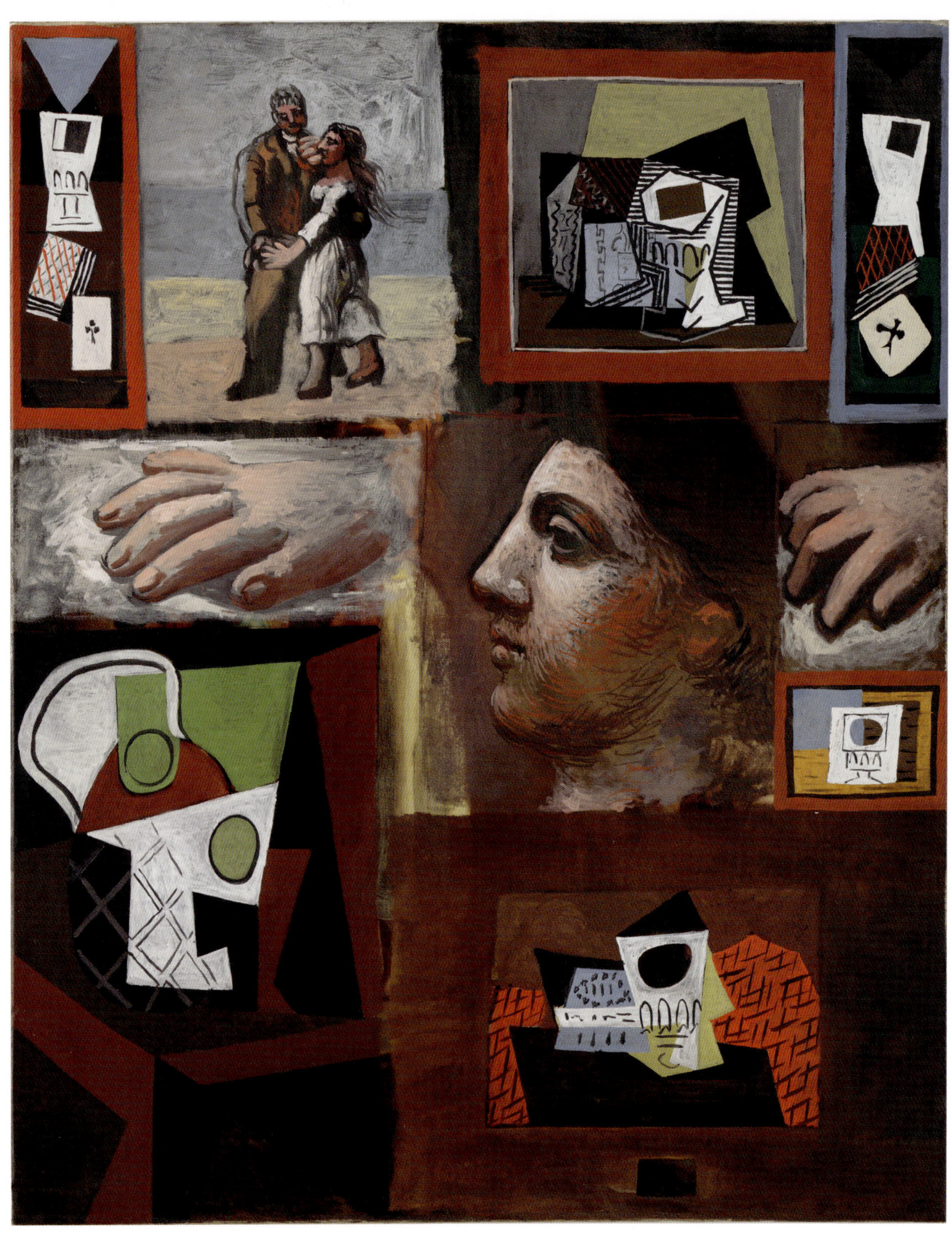

FIG. 1 *Studies*, 1920

the evolution of art is not as linear as we may think, and that one style does not erase another but follows an irregular process characterised by continuities, breaks, returns, and combinations of opposing elements. Let us adopt a different perspective than that of a binary opposition between life and work by using a third way, that of the *figure* of Picasso,[9] which should be distinguished from his real life. We are frequently dealing with this mythical figure, as developed by a variety of sources—artworks, statements, narratives, photographs—coming from others or from the artist himself. Identifying the archetypes that shape Picasso and his oeuvre, and on which he relied, allows us not to be fooled when they make an appearance.

PICASSO: THE MAN AND THE FIGURE

One of the key moments in the creation of Picasso's own mythology occurred as early as 1901, when the artist—born Ruiz-Picasso, from the combination of his parents' surnames—decided to sign his artworks using only his mother's name. Legally maintaining his birth name, his new signature created, to a certain extent, a split. It demonstrated taking control of his image, as this name seemed to him to have a stronger impact: 'It was stranger, more resonant, than "Ruiz" ... And the name a person bears or adopts has its importance.'[10] A self-portrait formalised this change of identity when the words '*Yo Picasso*' (I Picasso) were written on the canvas (FIG. 4). Later, Picasso mostly left it up to others to write about him, with few texts or statements coming directly from the artist. By adopting this strategy of addressing the public through reported speech and quotation, the artist disseminated his ideas while accepting the risk of leaving his interlocutors a margin of interpretation that could lead to misunderstandings and distortions.[11]

Picasso did not seem to be strongly attached to a perfectly faithful transcription of his statements. Christian Zervos, the art critic who undertook in the 1930s to produce a catalogue raisonné of the artist's work, related that when he wanted Picasso to read over his notes, the artist replied: 'You don't need to show them to me. The essential thing in our period of weak morale is to create enthusiasm. How many people have actually read Homer? All the same the whole world talks of him. In this way the Homeric legend is created.'[12] In every statement by Picasso that is reported, we must consider that his words are connected both to himself and to his interlocutor, who inserts part of their own personality. The reference to Homer that the artist slips into his conversation with Zervos is a good example of this, since the art critic, of Greek origin, was a specialist in ancient Mediterranean civilisations. Despite this appropriate caution over the accuracy of the statements attributed to Picasso, there is a consensus on tangible elements, such as the way he expressed himself, described by everyone with whom he conversed—both detractors[13] and defenders—as disjointed and difficult to follow. This fact can help explain Picasso's refusal to write about his art. As he (apparently) told a Catalan journalist: 'People ask me why I don't write. It's very easy to write when you're a writer: words are docile for you, they come to your hands like birds. But if I really wrote a book that was as thick as this, I'd give a dozen bottles of champagne as a prize to anyone who could read more than three lines of it.'[14] In this way, the clarity that we find in the statements attributed to Picasso seems to reveal significant rewriting by those who note down his words.

Many people in Picasso's circle dedicated works and articles to him, starting with his friend the poet Guillaume Apollinaire, who published *The Cubist Painters, Aesthetic Meditations* in 1913. Personal accounts ensued, such as one by the American collector and writer Gertrude Stein, of whom the artist made an emblematic portrait (FIG. 5), and who published her *Picasso* in 1938, in which she recounts the painter's early decades, expresses aesthetic considerations, and recalls her memories of his company; later, in the 1950s, Picasso's friend and secretary Jaime Sabartés published several books about him. The first monographs with encyclopaedic ambitions appeared in the late 1950s, by Antonina Vallentin and Roland Penrose, respectively. Both were authorised by the artist. However, counter-narratives also appeared very early in the literature dedicated to Picasso, especially through the voices of two of his former companions. Fernande Olivier (FIG. 2), a professional model who lived with the artist in the early 1900s, was the first to publish her recollections. She wrote a series of articles that caused a stir in the Paris art world before completing *Picasso and His Friends* in October 1933.[15] Although Olivier makes a few references to art, her account is focused above all on documenting, through anecdotes, her daily life within the circle formed around her and Picasso. The most sensational revelation in the book concerns Picasso's opium consumption, a passage widely reported and commented on in the press at the time.[16] Olivier's portrait of the artist is not dithyrambic, already presenting what Picasso's future literature would complete: a man of 'rather sad, sarcastic, somewhat hypochondriac' character, whose existence was entirely devoted to his art.[17] While Picasso may possibly have tried to prevent the book's publication, he made no official comment.

In the 1960s it was the turn of the painter Françoise Gilot (FIG. 3) to pen the story of the years she spent with Picasso, from 1943 to 1953. First published in the United States, *Life with Picasso* came out in France in 1965. In contrast to his reaction to Olivier's book, Picasso attempted to have Gilot's volume banned, demanding its seizure by a French court. The artist claimed that the book 'has in reality no other goal than to depict him, as a man and from the perspective of his

BELOW: FIG. 2 Portrait of Fernande Olivier in the workshop of the sculptor Ignacio Pinazo Martínez at the Bateau-Lavoir, Paris, 1908

BELOW LEFT: FIG. 3 Lee Miller, *Françoise Gilot drawing in La Galloise's room, Vallauris*, 1953

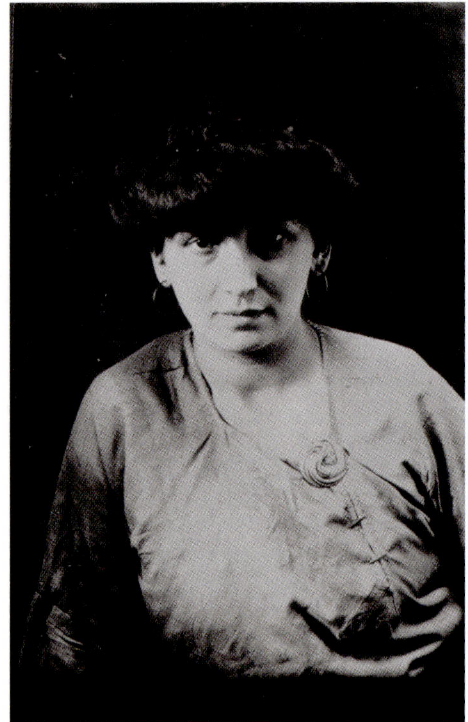

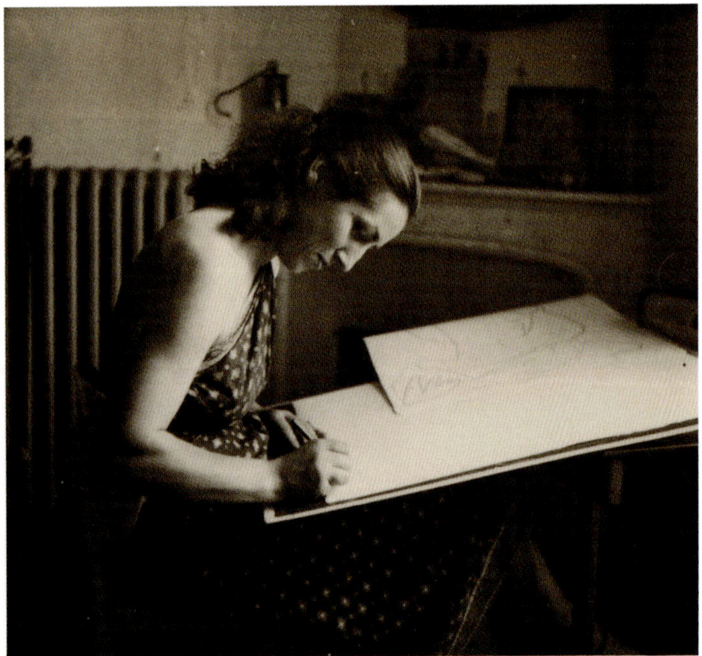

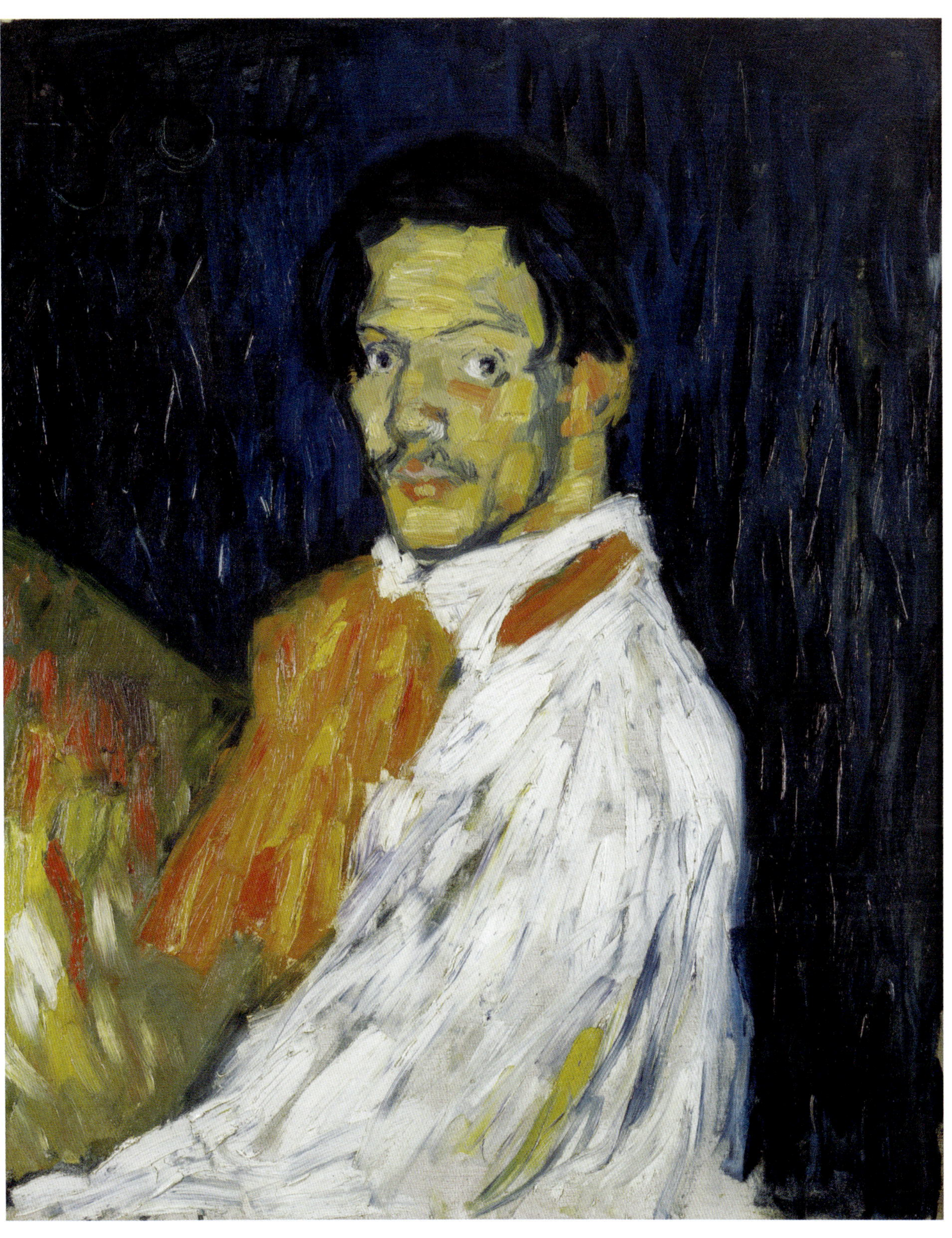

FIG. 4 *I, Picasso*, 1901

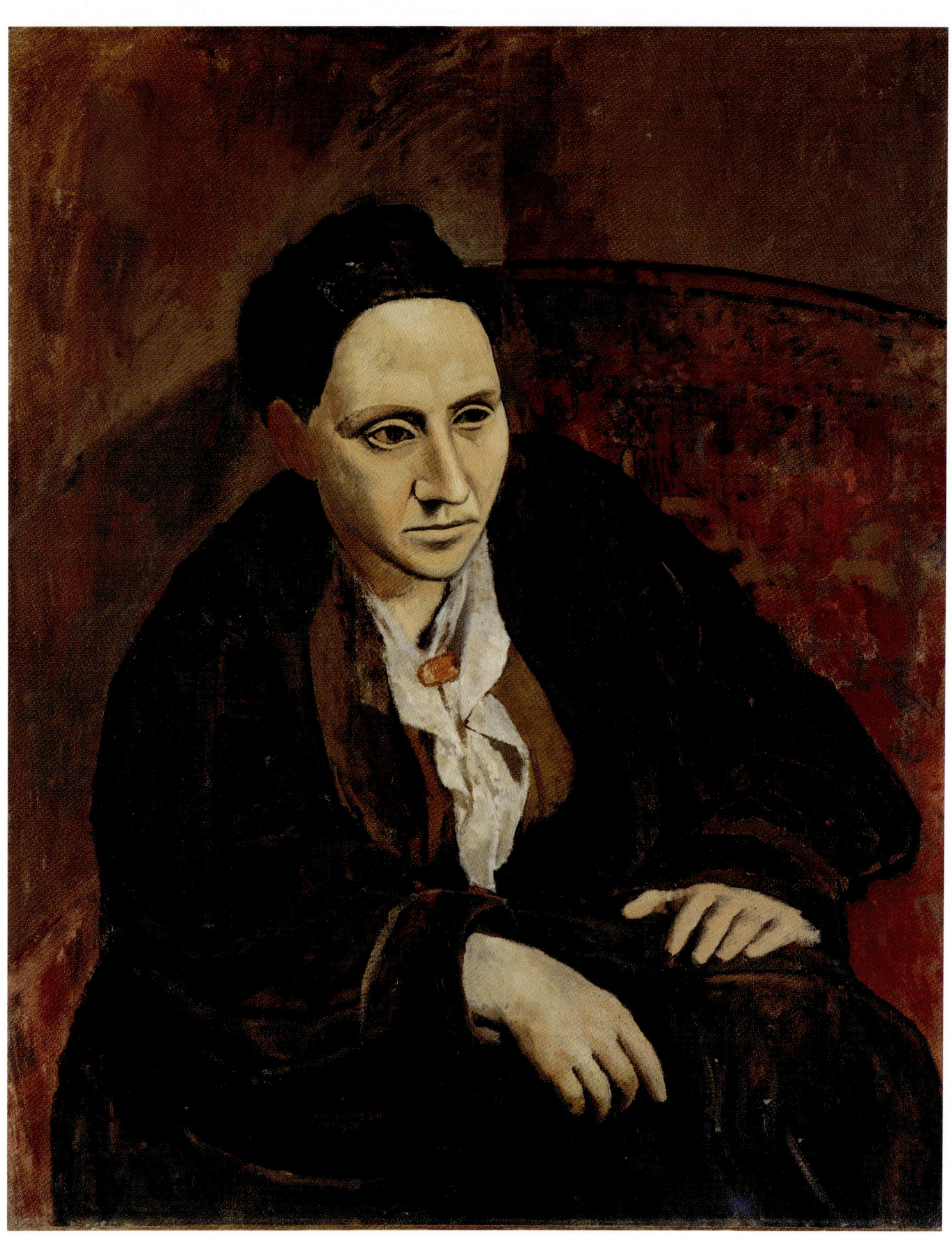

FIG. 5 *Gertrude Stein*, 1905–1906

human relationships, in a systematically unfavourable light and thus damaging both his personality and the consideration that is his due'.[18] Gilot recounts her intimacy with the artist and his violent outbursts, notably when he stubbed out a cigarette on her cheek, leaving a scar.[19] His suit was finally dismissed, with the court deciding that the book, although containing critical and unflattering elements, did not present him only from a negative angle. Ultimately, the court stated that 'while shining a light that is too direct and sometimes distorted on a person may be unbearable to a man of ordinary status, such characteristics are more tolerable for a renowned artist who has never fled publicity and whose physical image—if not his moral being—is unhesitatingly offered to the public eye.'[20] This phrasing reveals the status that Picasso held in the 1960s. While his reputation had been solidly established since the 1930s, it was not until the 1950s that he became a public figure. It was then that his face began to appear in magazines and newspapers around the world, from *Paris Match* to *Life* magazine (FIG. 6). Picasso went along with the photographers' requests, opening the doors of his homes and of his private life. The image of Picasso that we retain today—an old man with a bald head, shirtless or wearing a striped Breton jumper, as seen in a series of photographs by Robert Doisneau—became crystallised (FIG. 7). It did not take long for Doisneau's photographic series to meet with

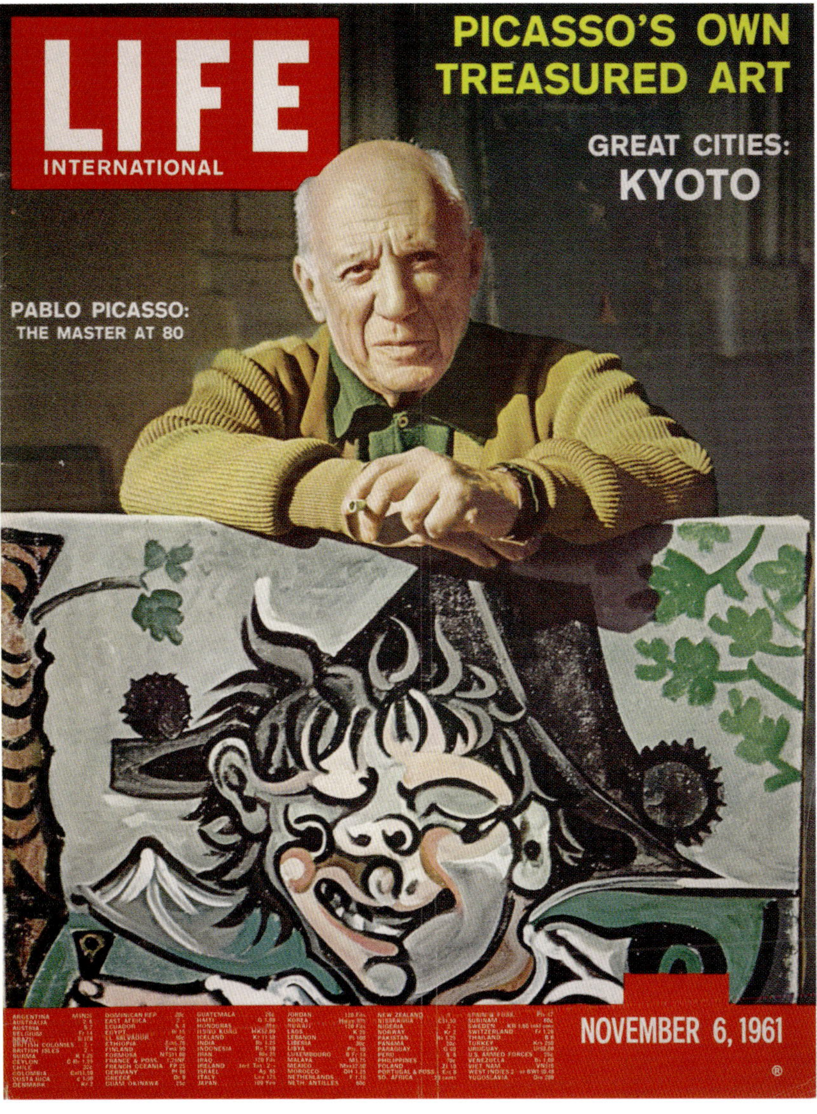

FIG. 6 Picasso on the cover of *Life International* 31, no. 10, 1961

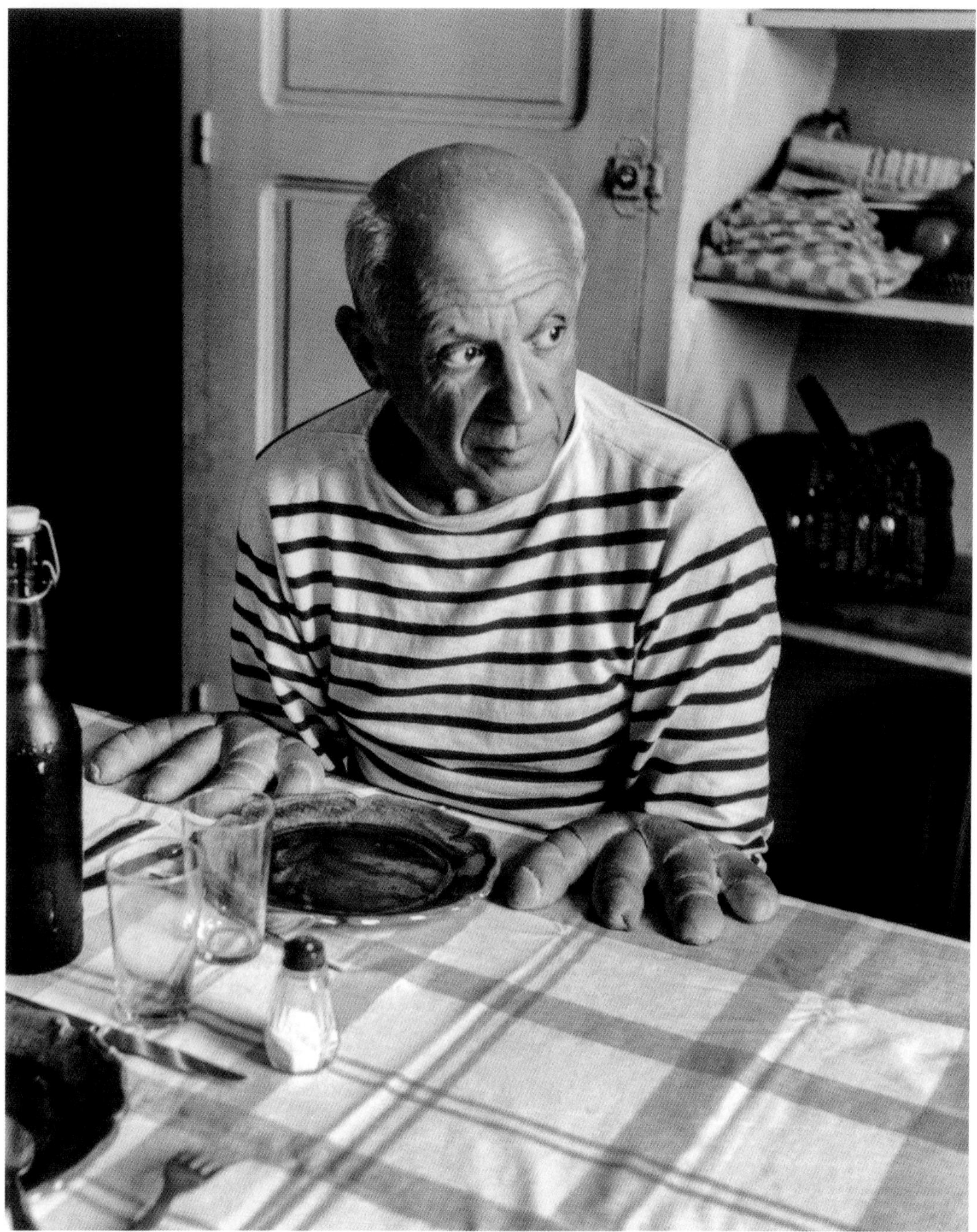

success and wide distribution, from the front of an edition of Gilot's *Life with Picasso* to the cover of *Life* magazine at the end of December 1968, when the famous American weekly devoted a double issue to the painter.

Leaving it up to others to recount his words, Picasso also gave them the responsibility of giving titles to his artworks for exhibitions or publications. This is why most of his artworks have brief, descriptive titles, such as 'Head of ...' ('*Tête de ...*'), 'Bust of ...' ('*Buste de...*'), 'Figure', 'Still Life' ('*Nature-morte*'), and 'Landscape' ('*Paysage*'). The historians' biographical approach gradually led to the inclusion of the model's identity in the titles of artworks where their features were recognisable.[21] As this approach was not uniformly applied, it produces disparities to this day. Even in the collection of the Musée national Picasso-Paris (MnPP), *Portrait of Marie-Thérèse* (FIG. 8) and *Seated Woman with Arms Crossed* (FIG. 10), both from 1937 and artistically very similar, do not

FIG. 7 Robert Doisneau, *Picasso at the table with buns for fingers at La Galloise, Vallauris, in September 1952*, 1952

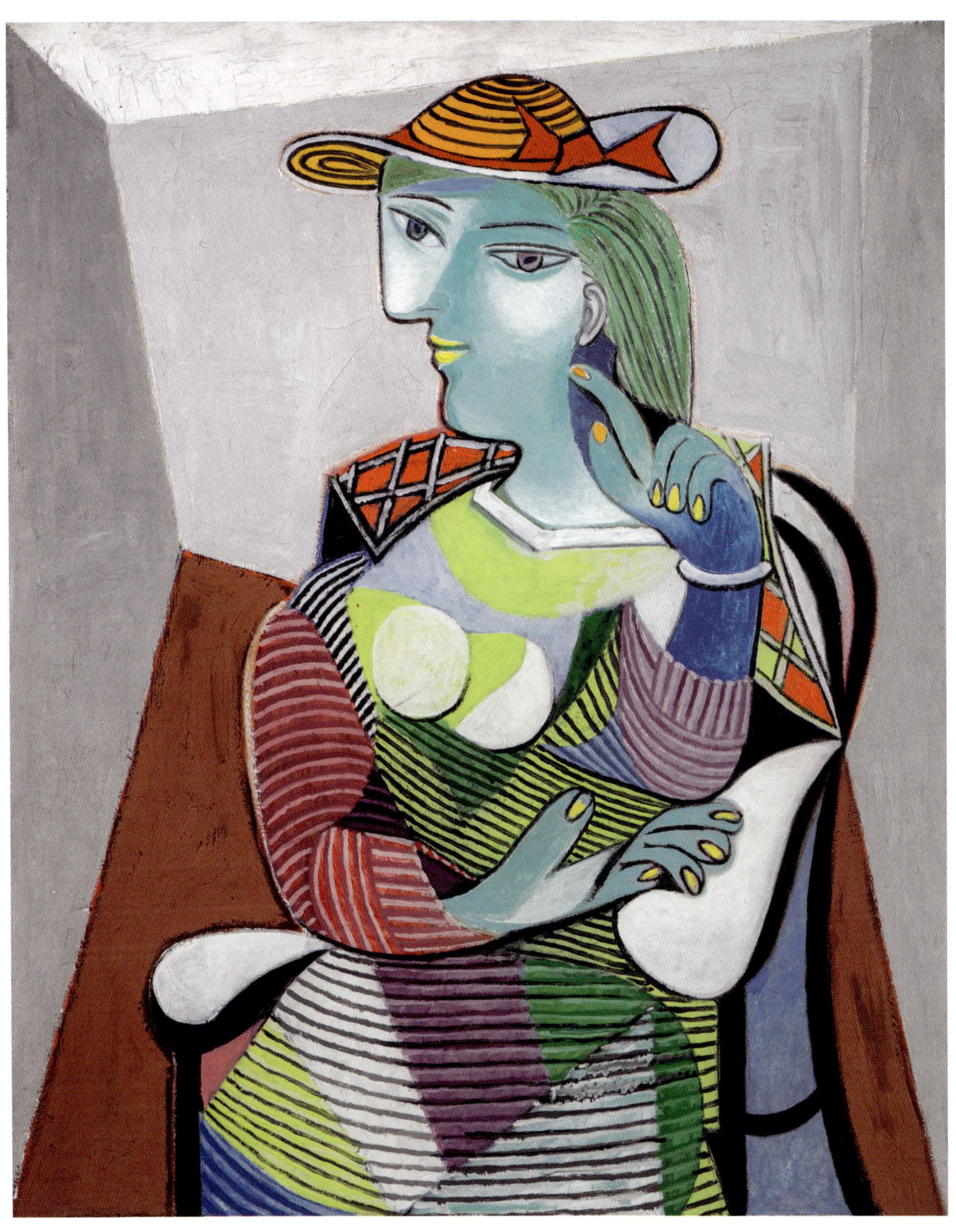

FIG. 8 *Portrait of Marie-Thérèse*, 1937

mention in the same way the name of Marie-Thérèse Walter, his companion and model.[22] Far from trivial, the title of an artwork directly influences our perception. Viewing *Portrait of Marie-Thérèse*, we take into account the affects that link her to the artist, assimilating the model's identity into her representation. This feeling disappears when we are faced with an anonymous figure, as our attention is directed towards the work's artistic qualities.

Over the course of his life, Picasso amassed an enormous archive: private and professional correspondence, journals, newspapers, a personal library, photographs, postcards, invoices, and so on. The archive comprises approximately 200,000 items, and was given by his heirs to the MnPP in 1992 (FIG. 9). Speaking to Brassaï in 1943, the artist explained why he kept such an archive. The photographer quotes him as saying:

It's not enough to know an artist's works. One must also know when he made them, why, how, under what circumstances. No doubt there will some day be a science, called 'the science of man,' perhaps, which will seek above all to get a deeper understanding of man via man-the-creator. I often think of that science, and I want the documentation I leave to posterity to be as complete as possible. That's why I date everything I make.[23]

Together with the other aspects of Picasso's character discussed above, such statements strengthened the hegemony of a biographical reading of his work, which reached its peak in the 1980s,[24] to the point where his oeuvre was segmented by historians into several periods in which each artistic transformation was associated with a change: of companion, of male friendship, of residence, even of pet.[25] Such an approach contributed to the study of his work as a separate discipline, detached from all historical or socio-cultural context, thereby transforming him into an exceptional being.

'GENIUS': THE BIRTH AND DEATH OF A DEMIURGE

Picasso remains inextricably linked to the image of the 'artistic genius'.[26] When his death was announced, on 14 April 1973, praise poured forth from his contemporaries. Salvador Dalí declared that 'Picasso is a genius because he understood everything before the others',[27] while Wifredo Lam paid him an even more emphatic tribute: 'With his work, and the subversive action of his always vigilant mind, always alive with genius, Picasso filled his life and his time with eternity like a god on Earth.'[28] The statements of both artists liken Picasso to the figure of a demiurge, a divine creator ahead of his time or having risen above the ordinary human condition. His obituary in the German weekly *Die Zeit* strengthens this image of the artist as a being endowed with a remarkable talent, which is said to have manifested itself at a very young age, indisputable evidence of his 'genius':

How could one speak of Picasso without pronouncing the word 'genius' ...? The absolutely exceptional quality of his natural gifts finds proof, if any were necessary, in the paintings and studies of the very young Picasso, even during childhood ... He was a child prodigy of painting, a genius of nature, and he remained throughout his life a being who was excessively showered with gifts by the gods with no regard for earthly justice.[29]

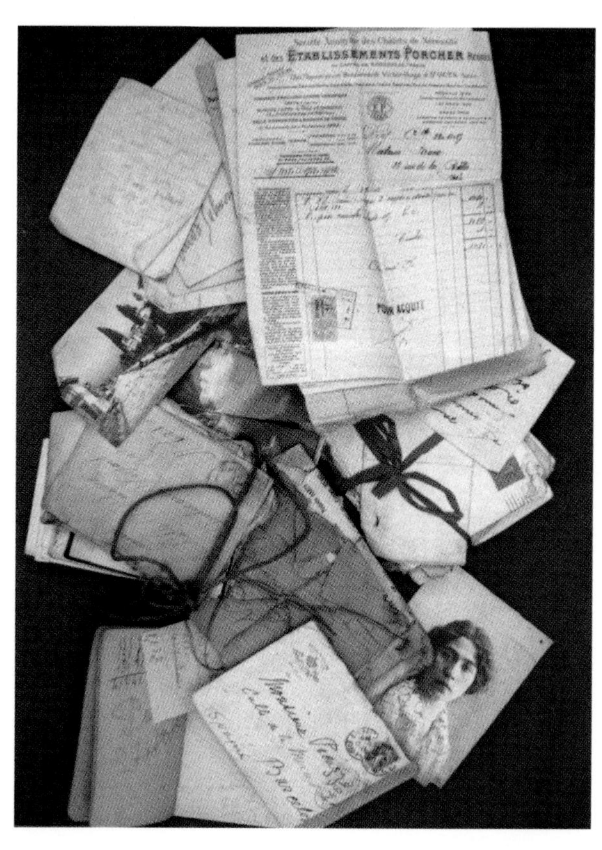

FIG. 9 The archives upon arrival at Musée national Picasso-Paris, 1992

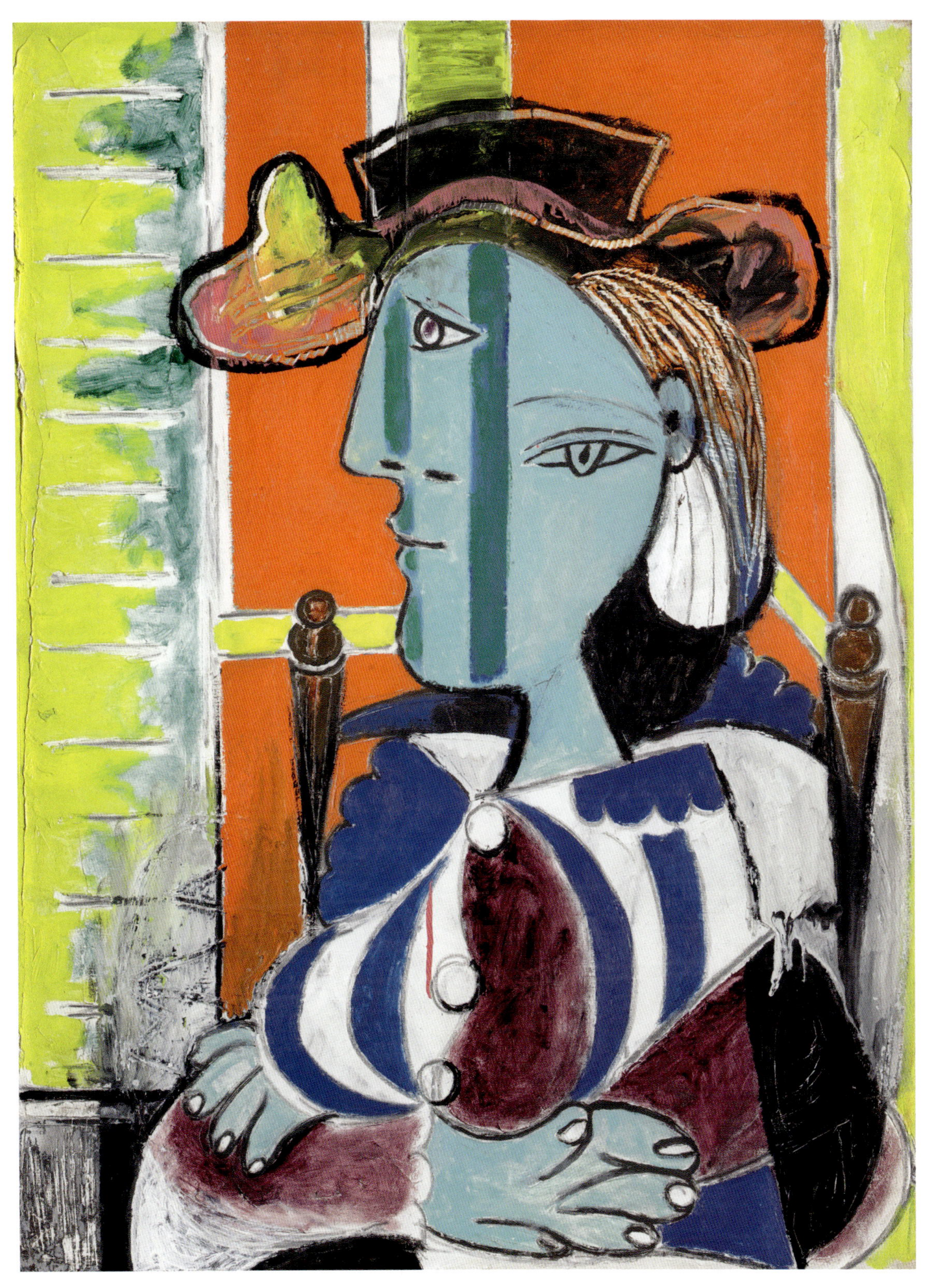

FIG. 10 *Seated Woman with Arms Crossed*, 1937

Although stories of child prodigies are often associated with musicians—the most famous case being that of Mozart—this archetype can also be found in the life stories of painters and sculptors. As Kris and Kurz observe, 'the universal interest in everything reported about the childhood and youth of exceptional persons has deep roots in the human mind.'[30] The writers identify two widespread narrative models. The first emphasises an event or a meeting that radically changes someone's destiny, as in the story told by Vasari about Giotto, who, as a child, was drawing alongside a road and was noticed by the artist Cimabue, who became his teacher. The second narrative model consists of detecting prophetic signs in the available biographical information, as in the case of the young Nicolas Poussin, who was said to have covered his school notebooks with sketches instead of taking notes in his classes.[31] A very similar anecdote can be found in the stories of Picasso's youth; in addition, the artist told poet Max Jacob that he had covered some of the furniture in his family's home with his drawings.[32] While Picasso did not describe any unexpected encounter that had a decisive impact on his vocation as an artist, on various occasions he recounted the following tale: when his youngest sister, Conchita, had diphtheria as a child, he secretly made a pact with God, promising to put down his paintbrushes forever if the little girl's life were spared, but to no avail.[33]

Art historian Linda Nochlin criticises these narratives around the myth of the child prodigy, emphasising historians' neglect of the socio-cultural contexts in which most successful artists develop: 'What is stressed in all these stories is the apparently miraculous, nondetermined, and asocial nature of artistic achievement.'[34] In the case of Picasso, both his gender and the social status of his father, José Ruiz y Blasco—an academic painter, a museum curator, and a teacher at

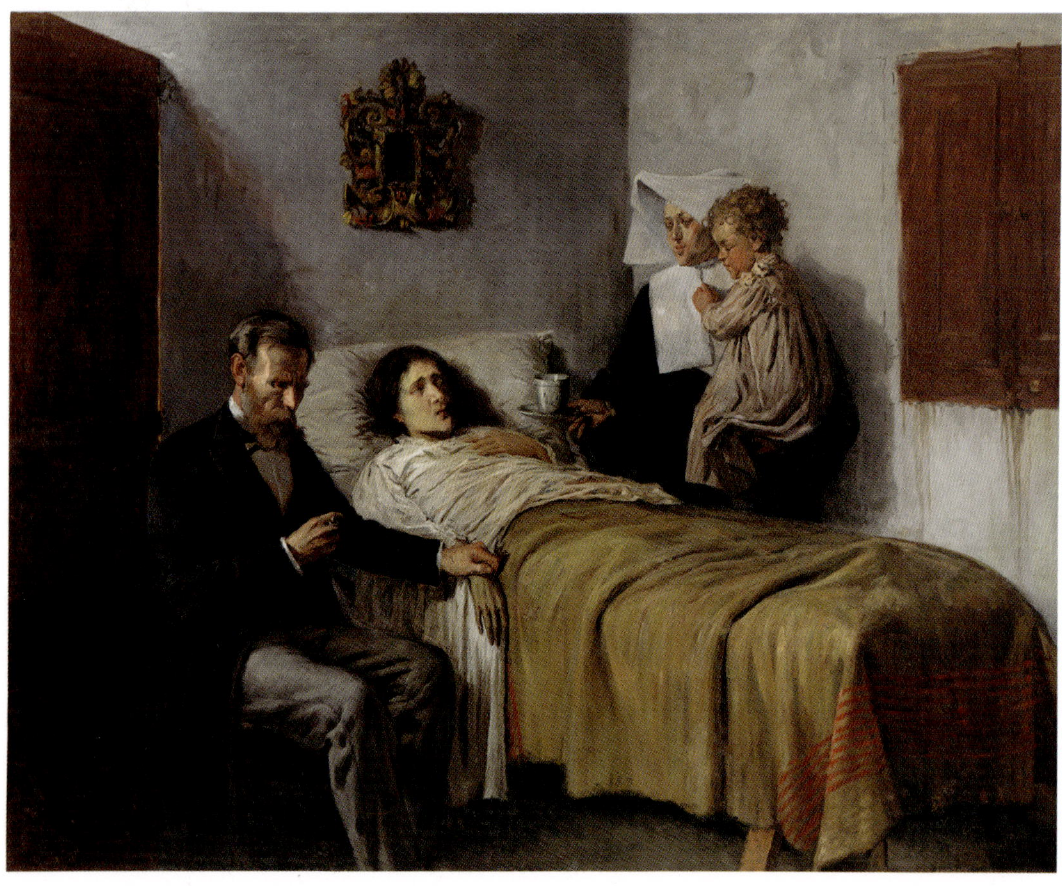

OPPOSITE: FIG. 11 *Science and Charity*, 1897

RIGHT: FIG. 12 *José Ruiz Blasco, Father of the Artist*, 1895

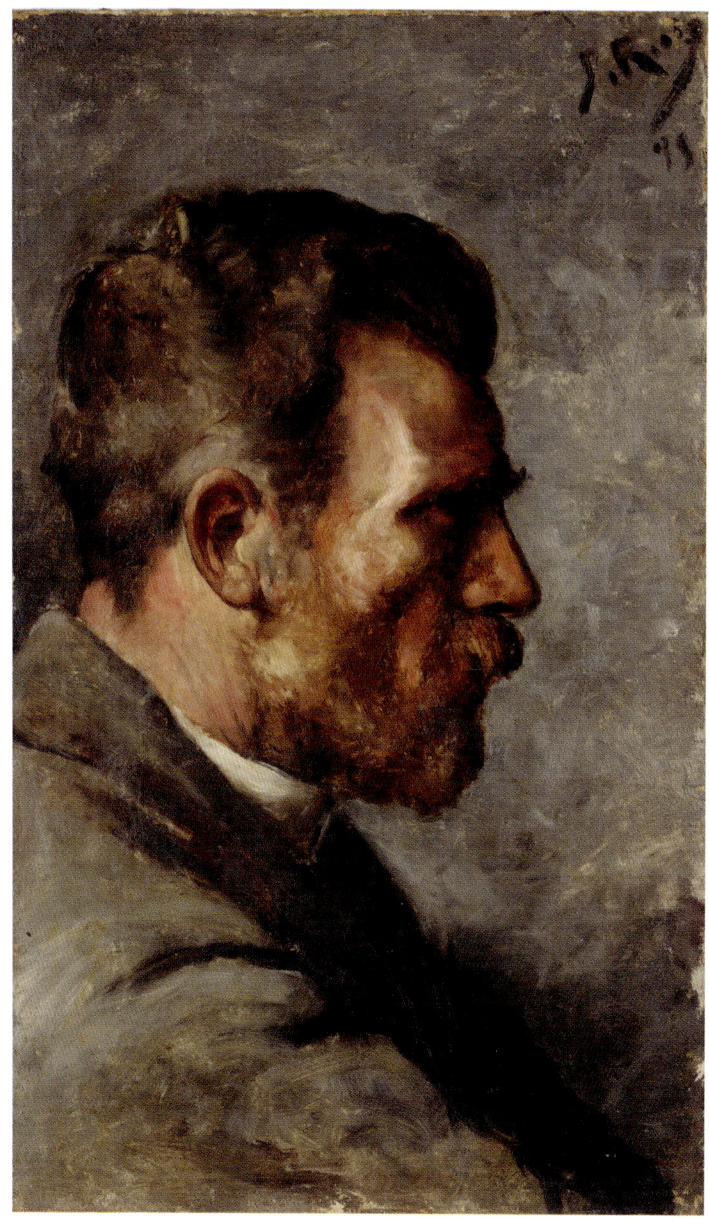

an art academy—allowed him to become familiar at a very young age with Spanish schools of art. Picasso produced dozens of portraits of his father (FIG. 12), depicting him in the role of a doctor in *Science and Charity* (1897; FIG. 11), one of his first accomplished works. In addition to the tales of his youth that he shared with his friends and biographers, Picasso sustained the myth of the child prodigy himself by preserving a significant number of his early artworks. *The Barefoot Girl* (FIG. 14) and *Man with a Cap* (FIG. 15), both from 1895, are among the works that the artist produced as a teenager in A Coruña, in north-western Spain, and which he kept with him until his death. Both works depict marginal figures: a poor girl wearing a traditional Galician costume, and a beggar. Yet we should not try to detect here a harbinger of his future work or the evidence of divine talent; rather, we should consider them as works by a developing artist that inform us about his early sources of inspiration. The iconography and shadow effects place the works in the pure Spanish tradition and refer to its iconic painters, from Francisco de Zurbarán to Francisco Goya. The influence of Diego Velázquez is also evident, especially when we compare *The Barefoot Girl* with Velázquez's portrait *Young Woman* (ca.1650; FIG. 13).[35]

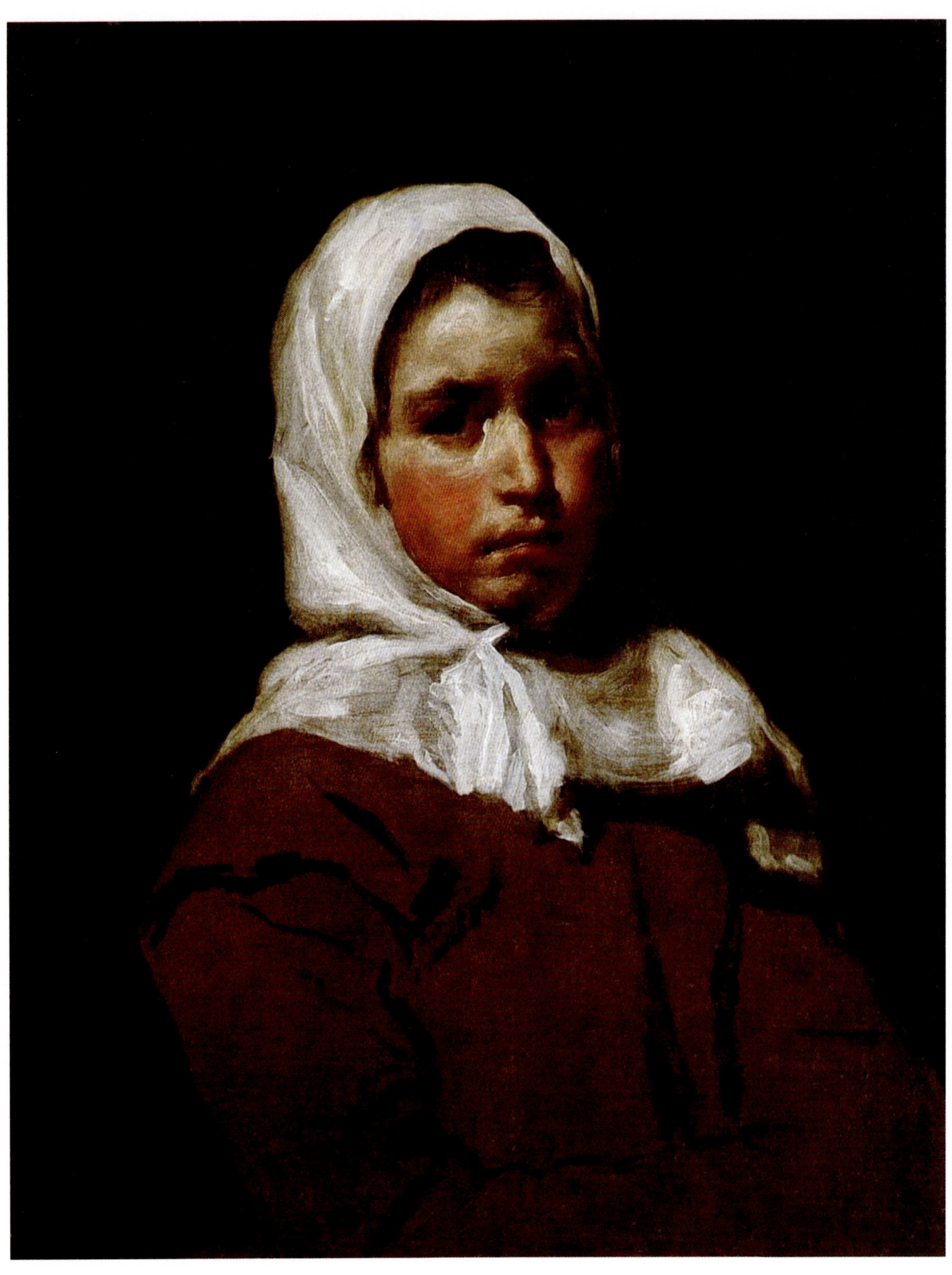

FIG. 13 Diego Velázquez, *Young Woman*, ca.1650

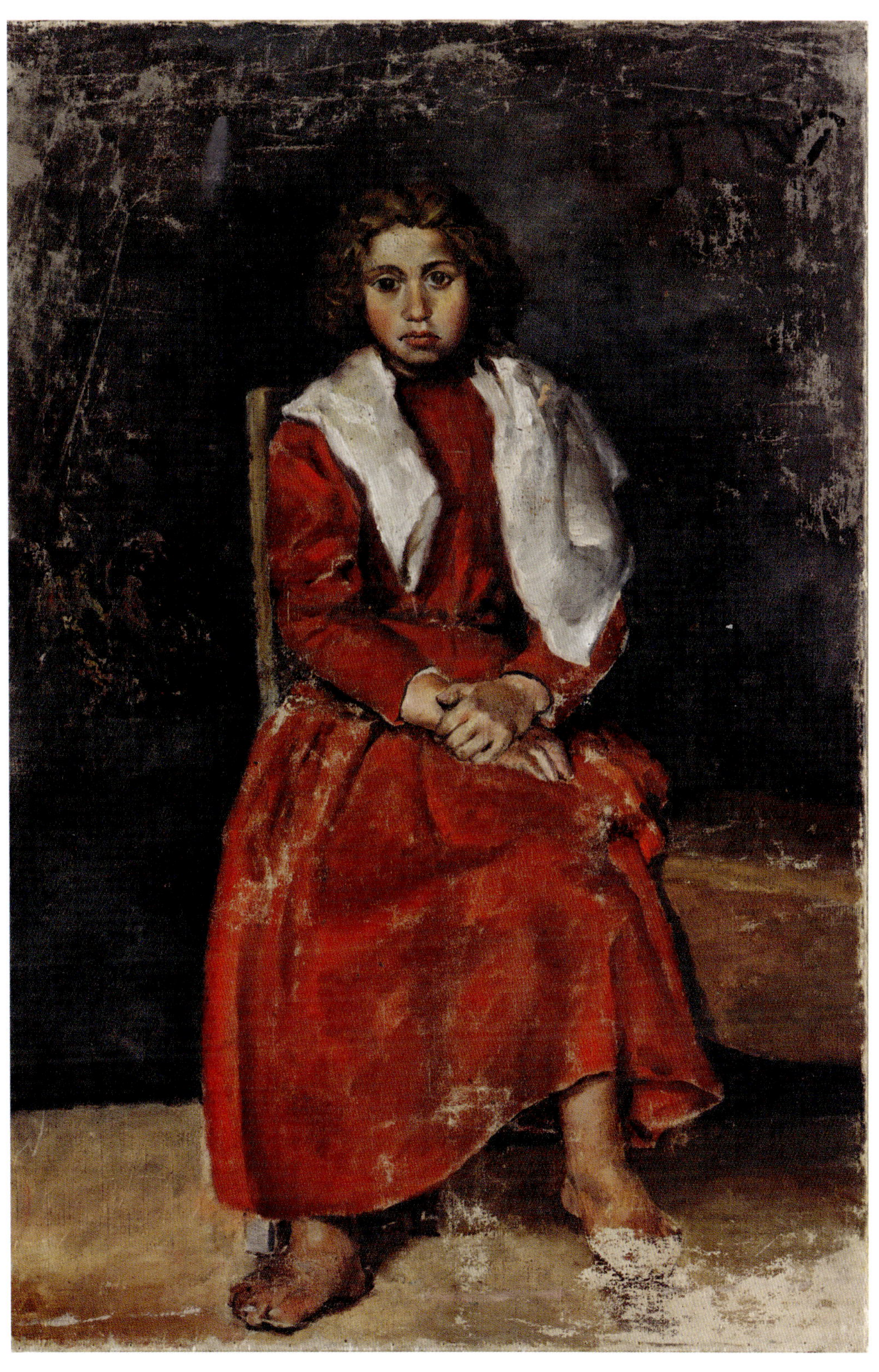

FIG. 14 *The Barefoot Girl*, 1895

FIG. 15 *Man with a Cap*, 1895

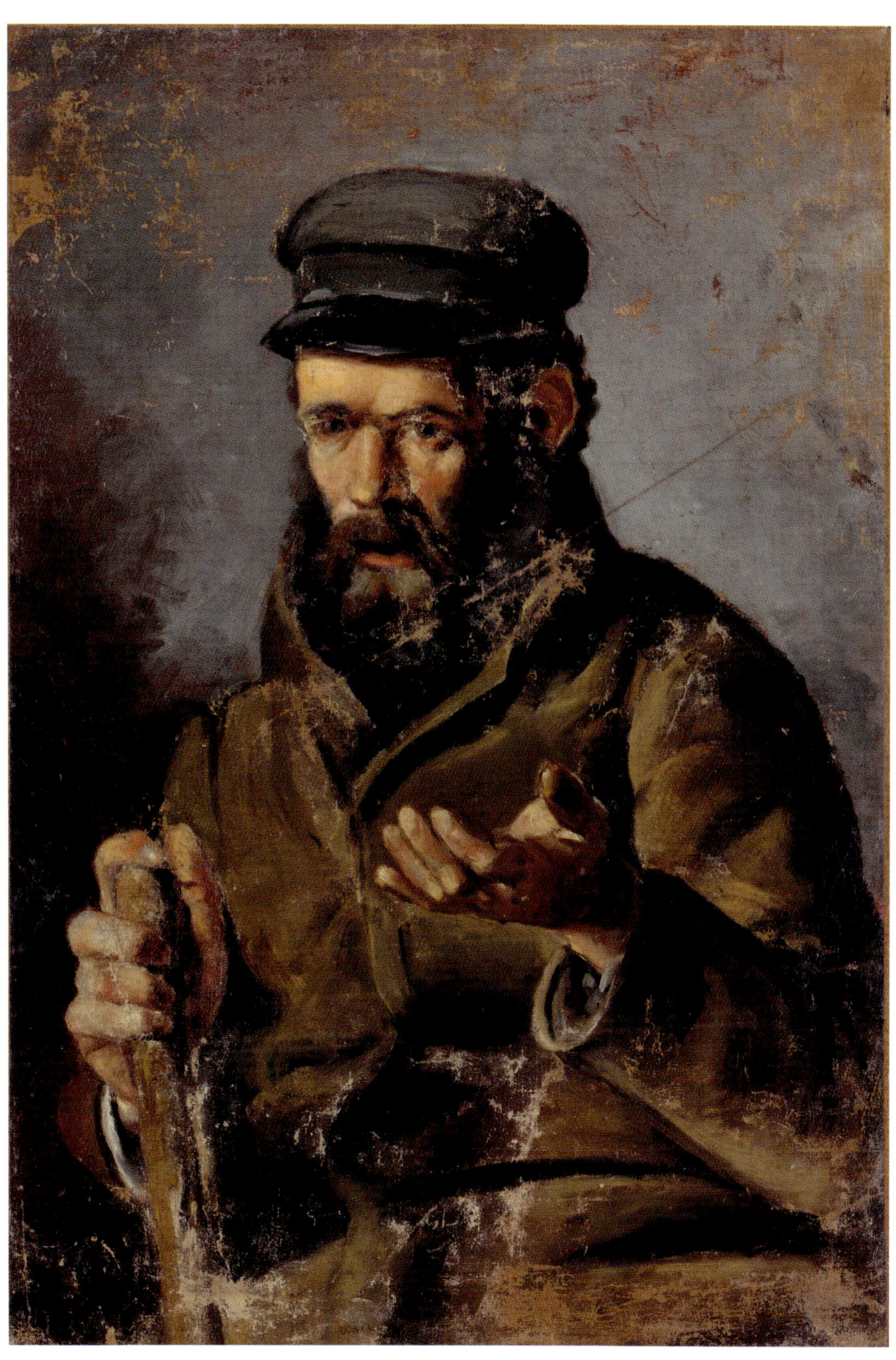

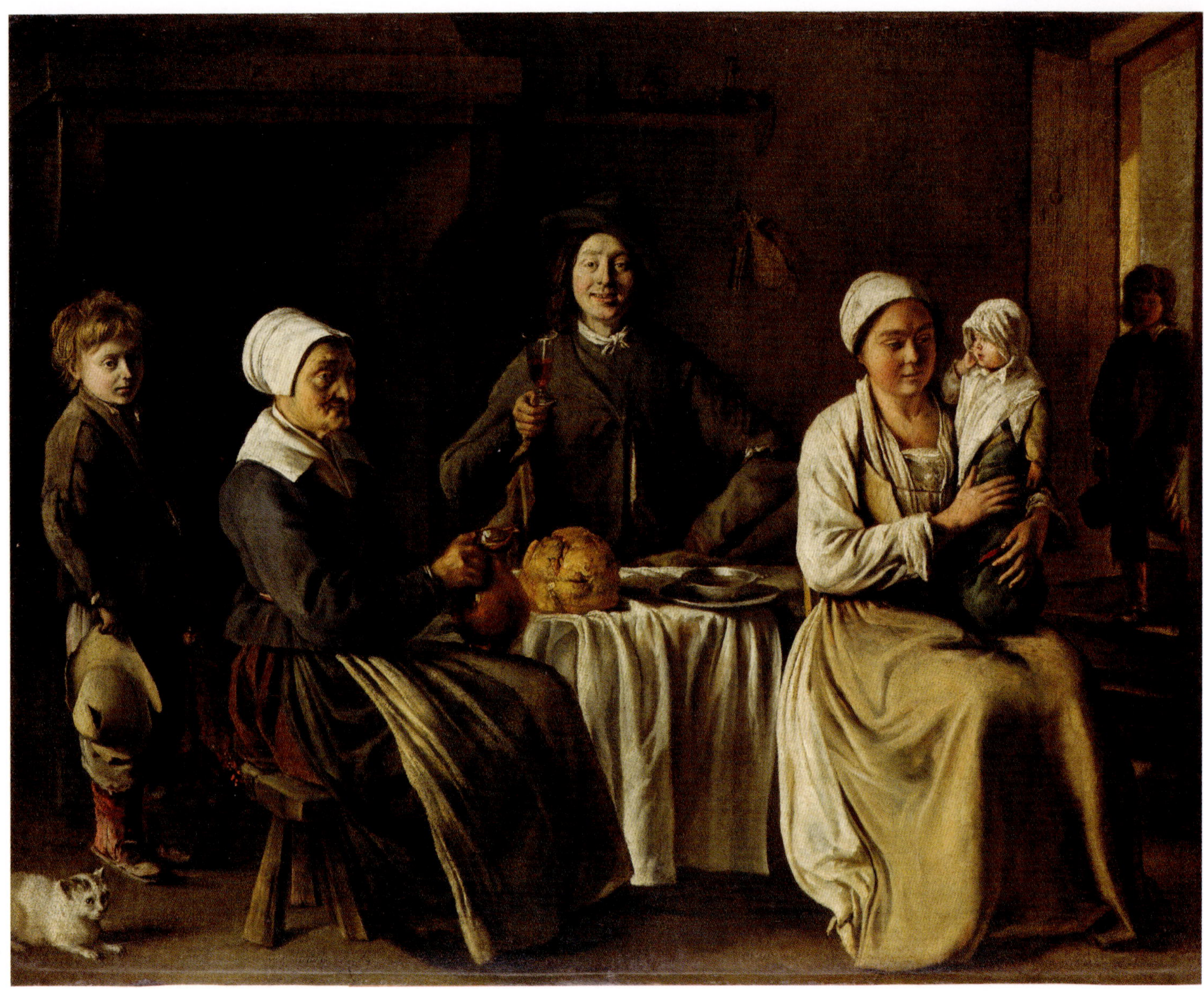

FIG. 16 The Le Nain Brothers, *The Happy Family or The Return from Baptism*, 1642

Picasso expressed very early on his ambition to influence his era and to leave his mark, just like the great names he admired: Velázquez, Goya, Rembrandt, and Manet. He produced several series of works inspired by these artists as a way of establishing himself in the male artistic genealogies so beloved of art historians.[36] This is what he did with *Massacre in Korea* (1951; FIG. 97), which uses the iconography of *The Third of May 1808* (1814; FIG. 100) by Goya and *The Execution of Emperor Maximilian* (1868–1869; FIG. 101) by Manet. Picasso initiated this dialogue with his predecessors at the beginning of his career. In the astonishing *Return from the Baptism after Le Nain* (1917; FIG. 17), he revisited the composition of a painting in the Louvre (FIG. 16) using a Divisionist style, with small coloured dots; later, *Woman with a Stiletto* (1931; FIG. 19) was inspired by Jacques-Louis David's *The Death of Marat* (1793; FIG. 18), which depicts

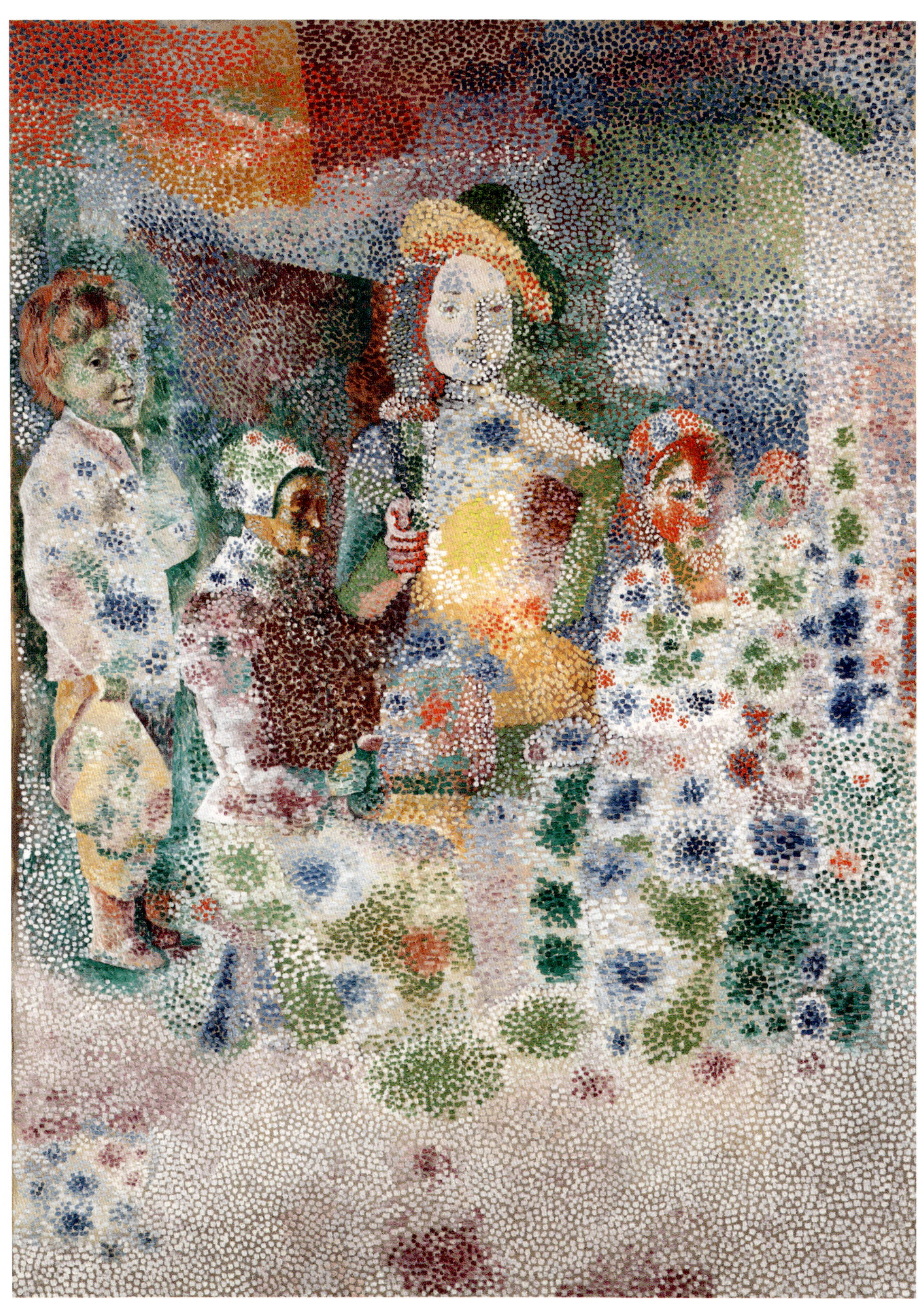

FIG. 17 *Return from the Baptism after Le Nain*, 1917

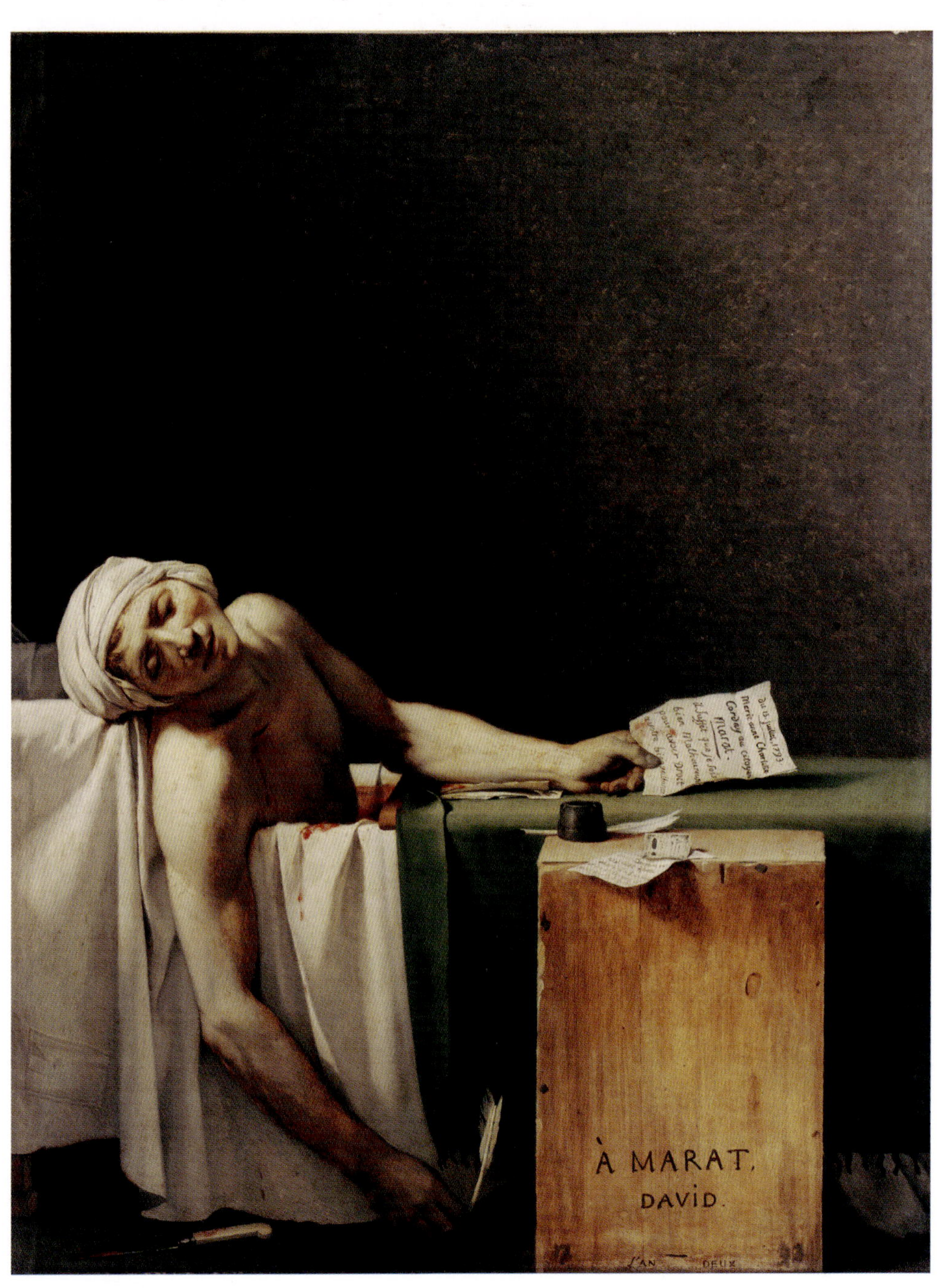

FIG. 18 Jacques-Louis David, *The Death of Marat*, 1793

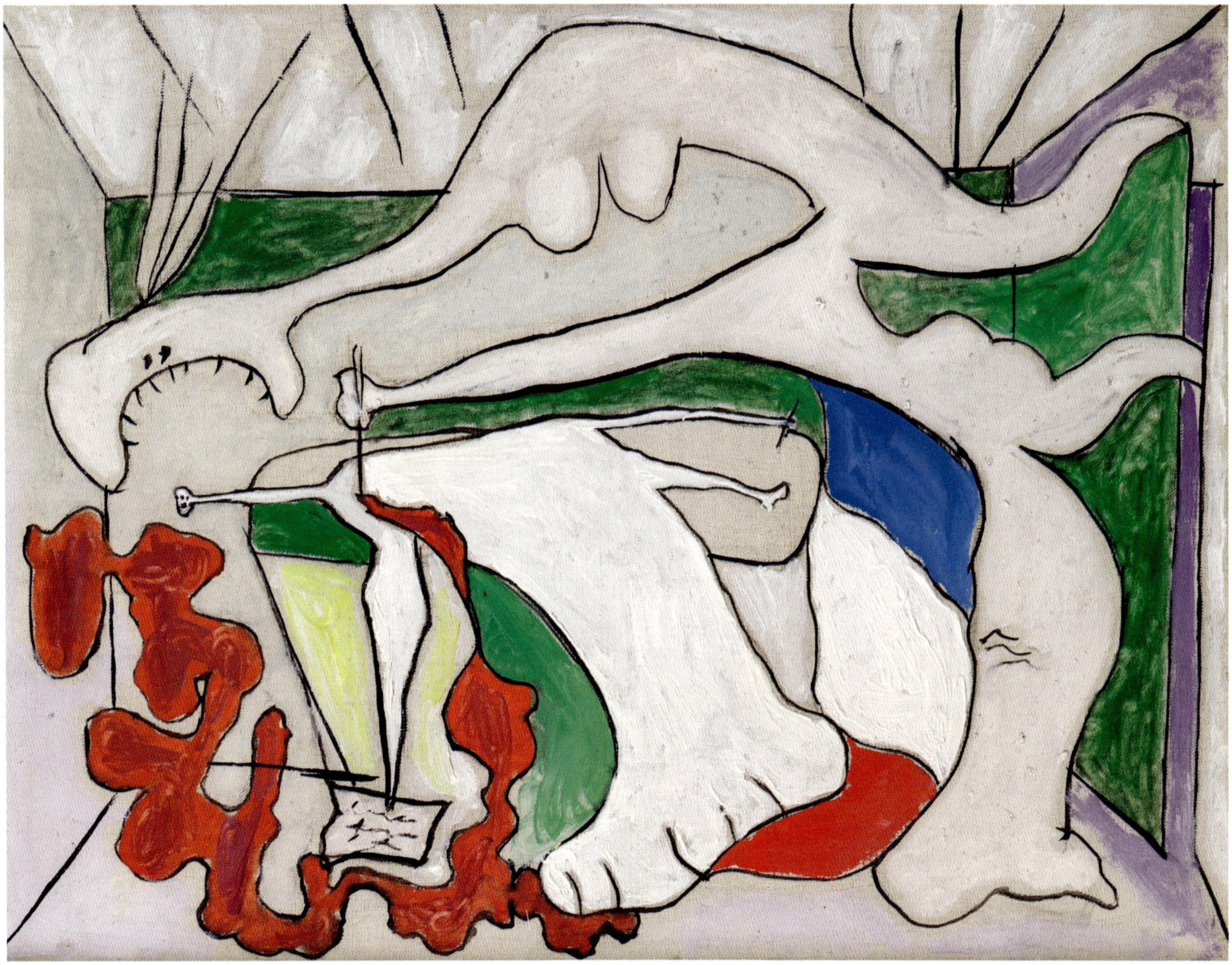

FIG. 19 *Woman with a Stiletto*, 1931

the assassination of a key figure of the French Revolution in his bathtub. During the post-war period these dialogues with his 'masters' increased as Picasso responded directly to major works: *Las Meninas* (1656) by Velázquez (FIGS 20 AND 21), *Le déjeuner sur l'herbe* (1862–1863) by Manet (FIGS 22 AND 23), *Women of Algiers in Their Apartment* (1834) by Delacroix (FIGS 24 AND 25), and *The Abduction of the Sabine Women* (ca.1633–1634) by Poussin (FIGS 26 AND 27). The artist created versions of these works in a number of series of paintings, drawings, engravings, ceramics, and sculptures. In addition to a tribute to the masters, the quantity of artworks produced is perceived by Picasso's biographers as a sign of vigour that would validate his status as a 'genius', with the artist himself associating his practice with an irrepressible surge of energy.[37]

In the 1950s Picasso attributed great importance to constructing an image of himself as the infatigable artist at work, particularly by collaborating with the French filmmaker Henri-Georges Clouzot in his documentary *The Mystery of Picasso* (1956).[38] The director wanted to show what went on in the head of a 'genius' by capturing the creation of an artwork step by step.[39] The goal is announced by the voice-over at the beginning of the film: 'To know what's going on in a painter's head, just follow his hand ... The painter advances, groping like a blind man in the darkness of the white canvas ... For the first time, this daily, private drama of the blind genius will be played out in public.'[40] To achieve his

FIG. 20 Diego Velázquez, *Las Meninas*, 1656

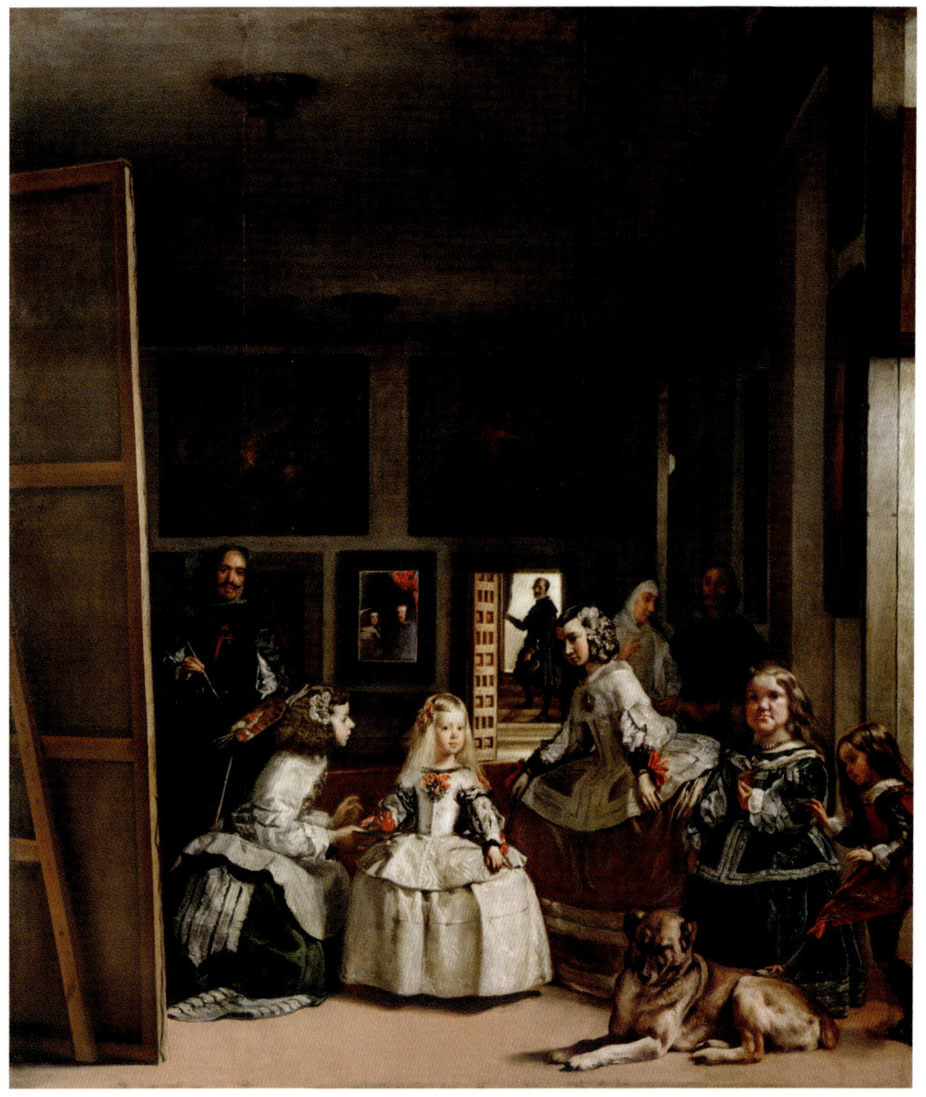

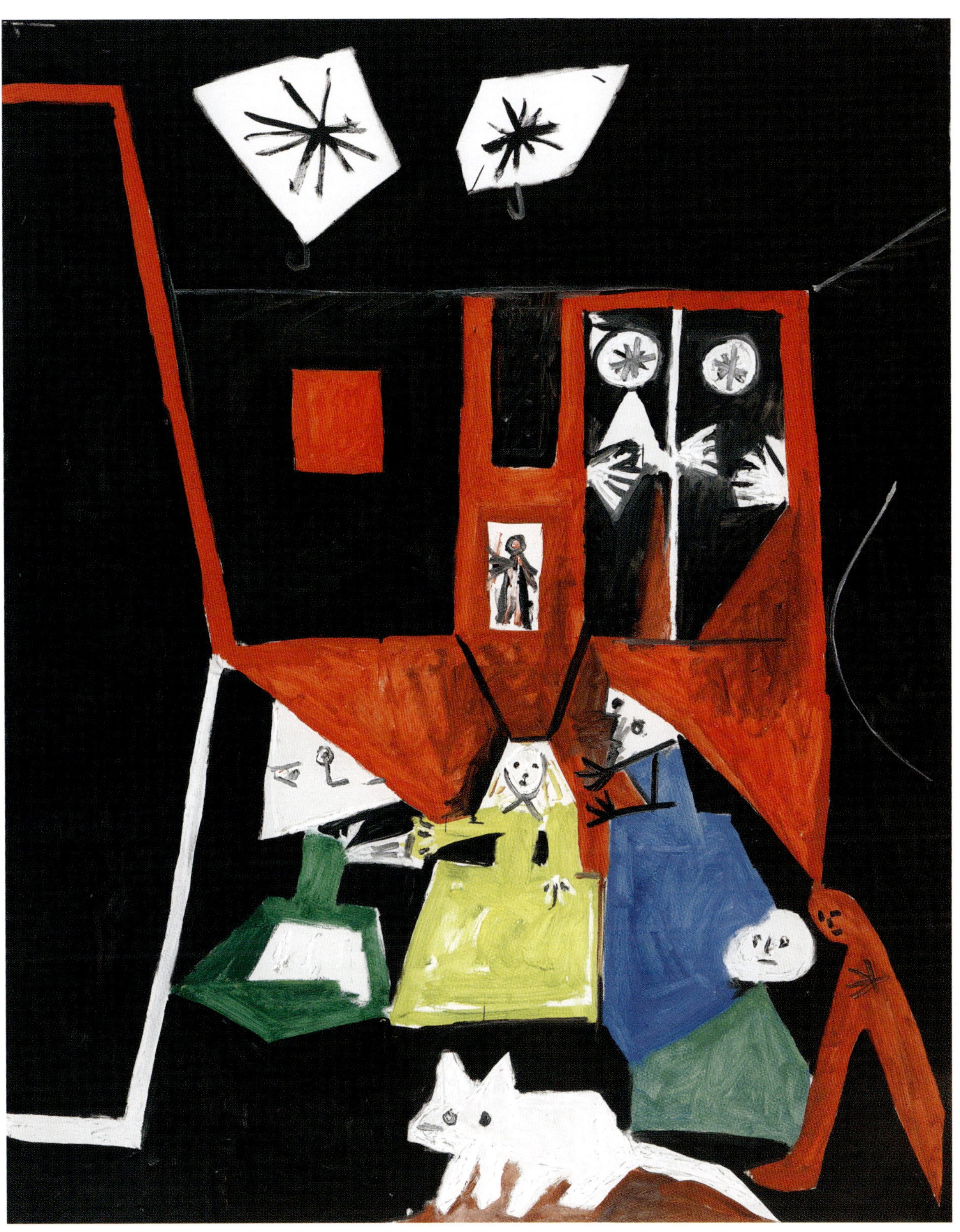

FIG. 21 *Las Meninas*, 1957

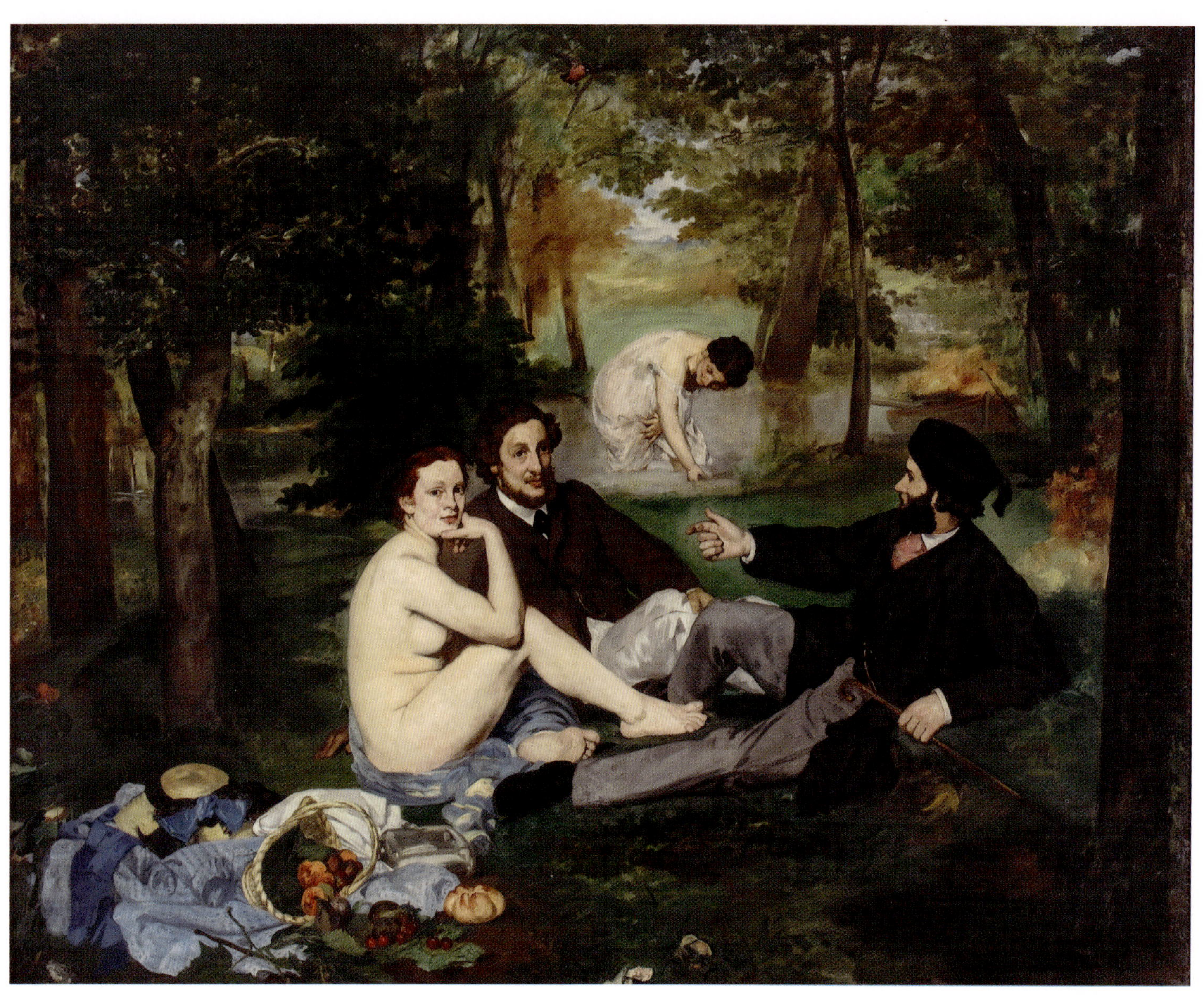

FIG. 22 Édouard Manet, *Le déjeuner sur l'herbe*, 1863

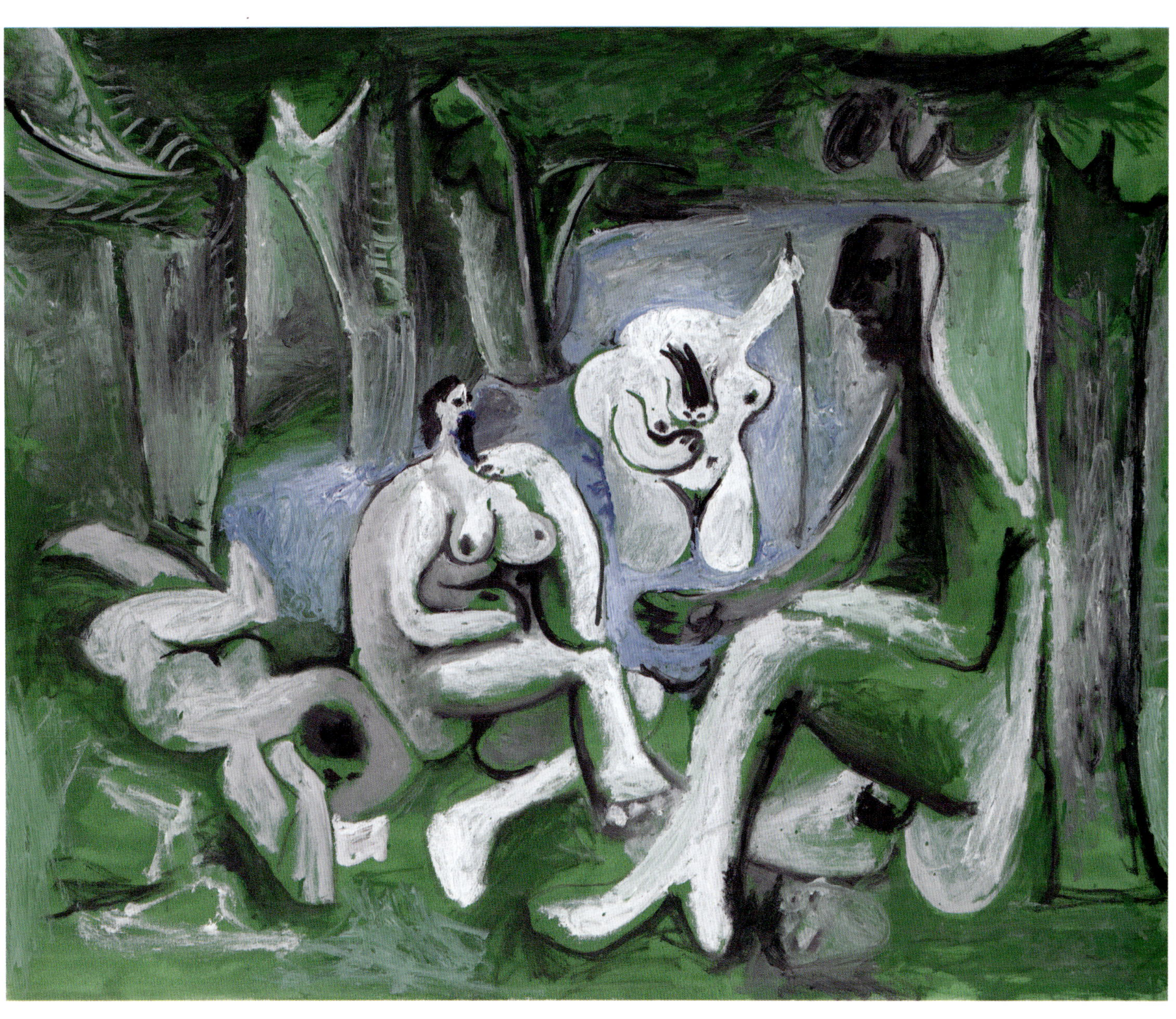

FIG. 23 *The Luncheon on the Grass after Manet*, 1961

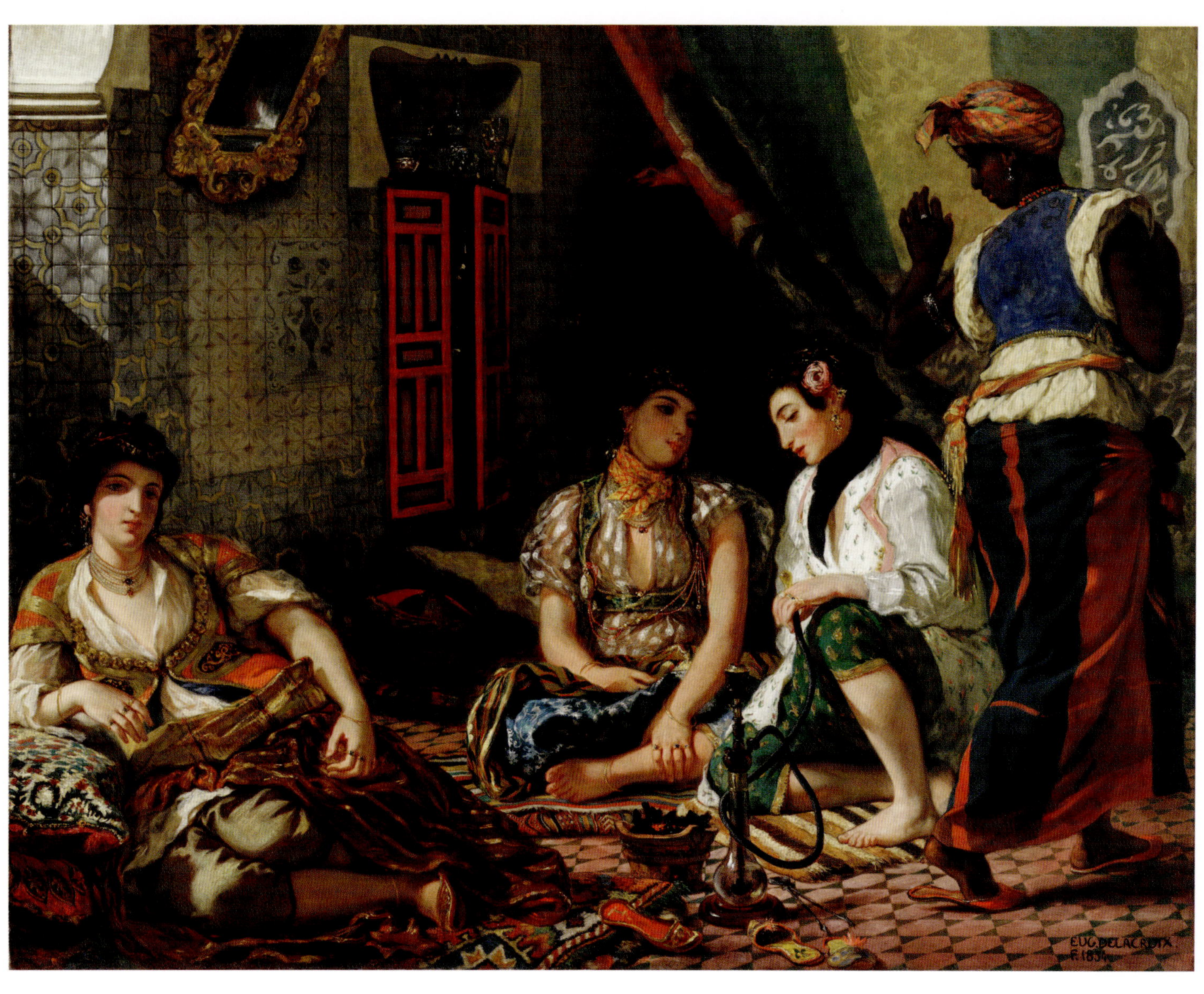

FIG. 24 Eugène Delacroix, *Women of Algiers in Their Apartment*, 1834

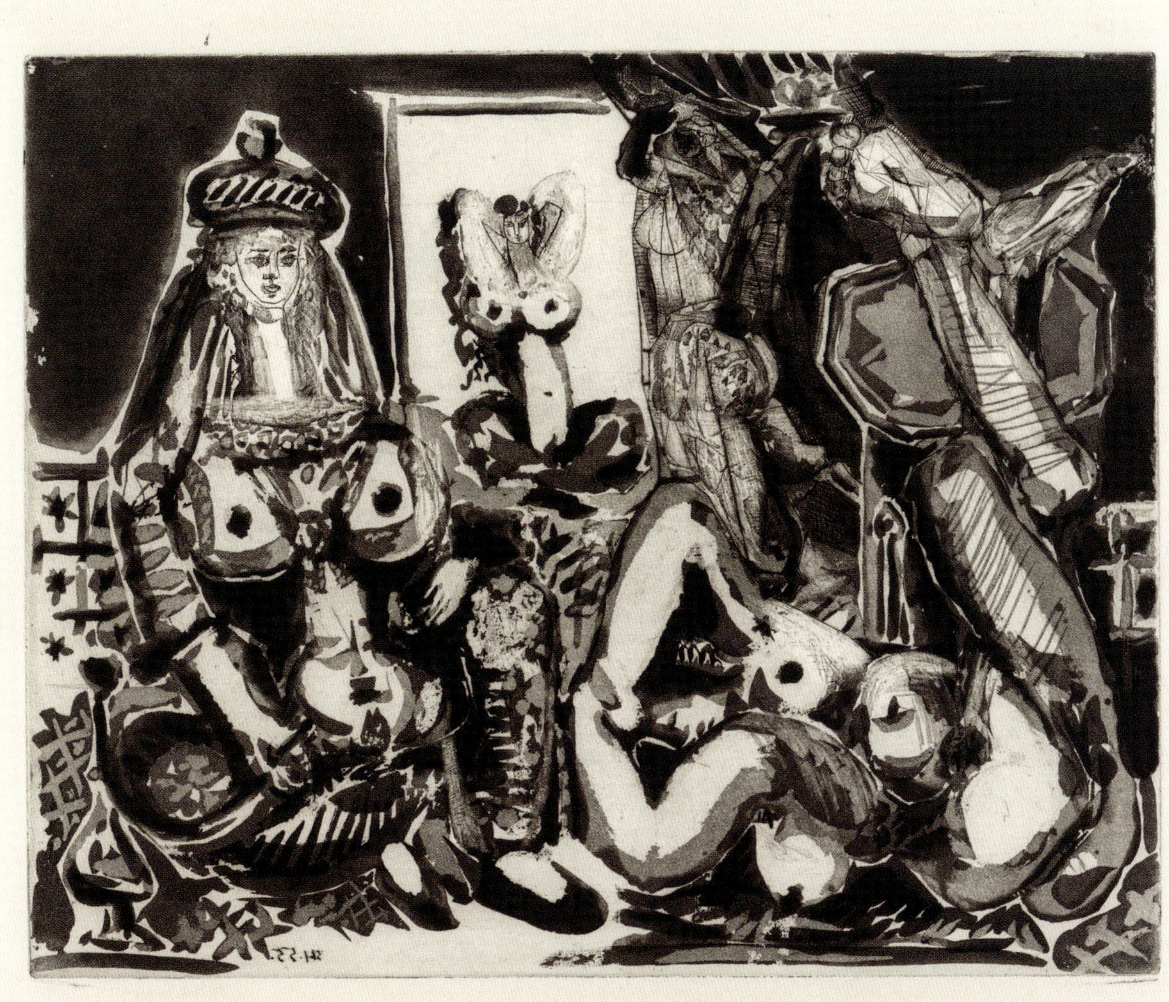

FIG. 25 *Women of Algiers after Delacroix. VIII*, 1955

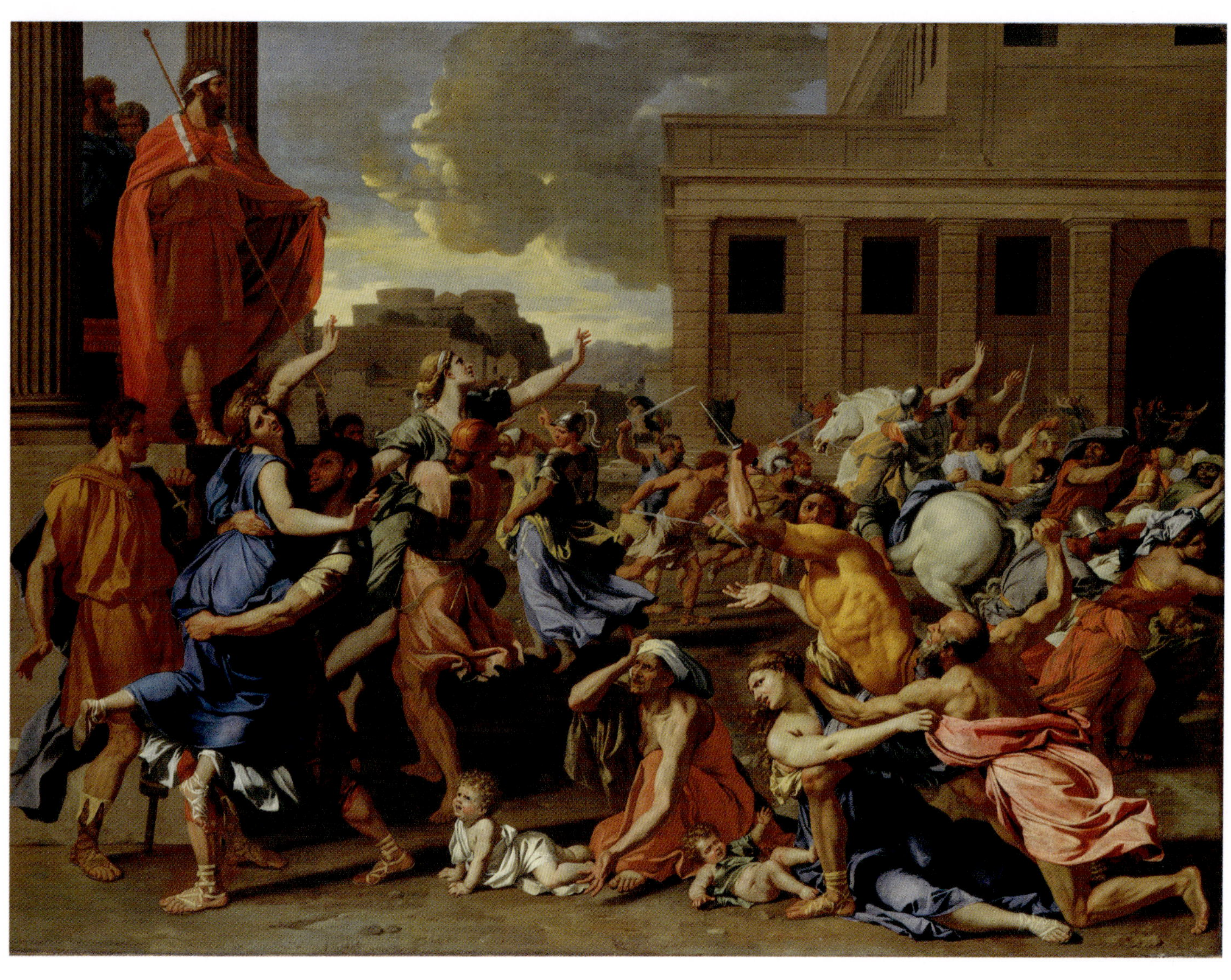

FIG. 26 Nicolas Poussin, *The Abduction of the Sabine Women*, ca.1633–1634

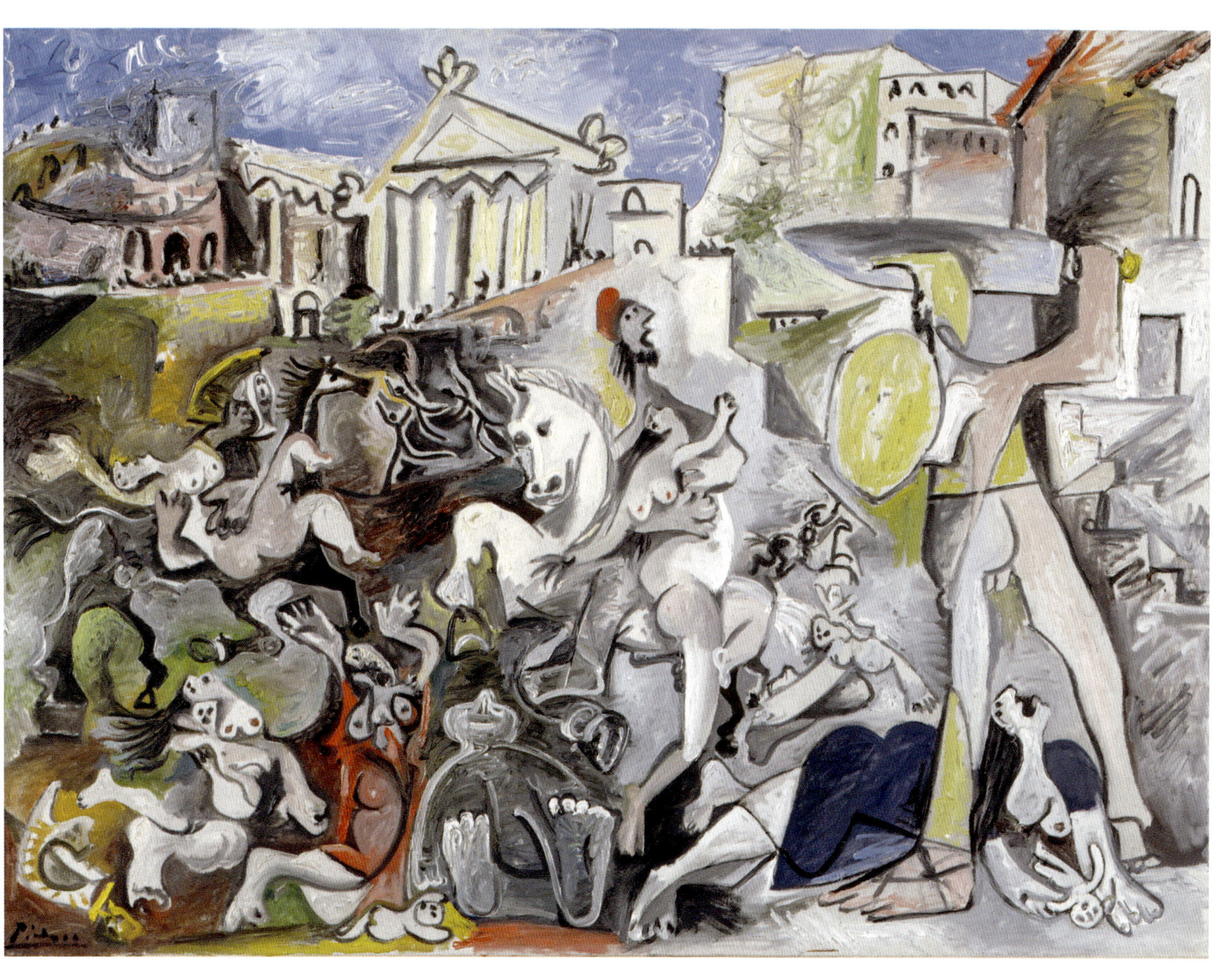

FIG. 27 *The Abduction of the Sabine Women*, 1962

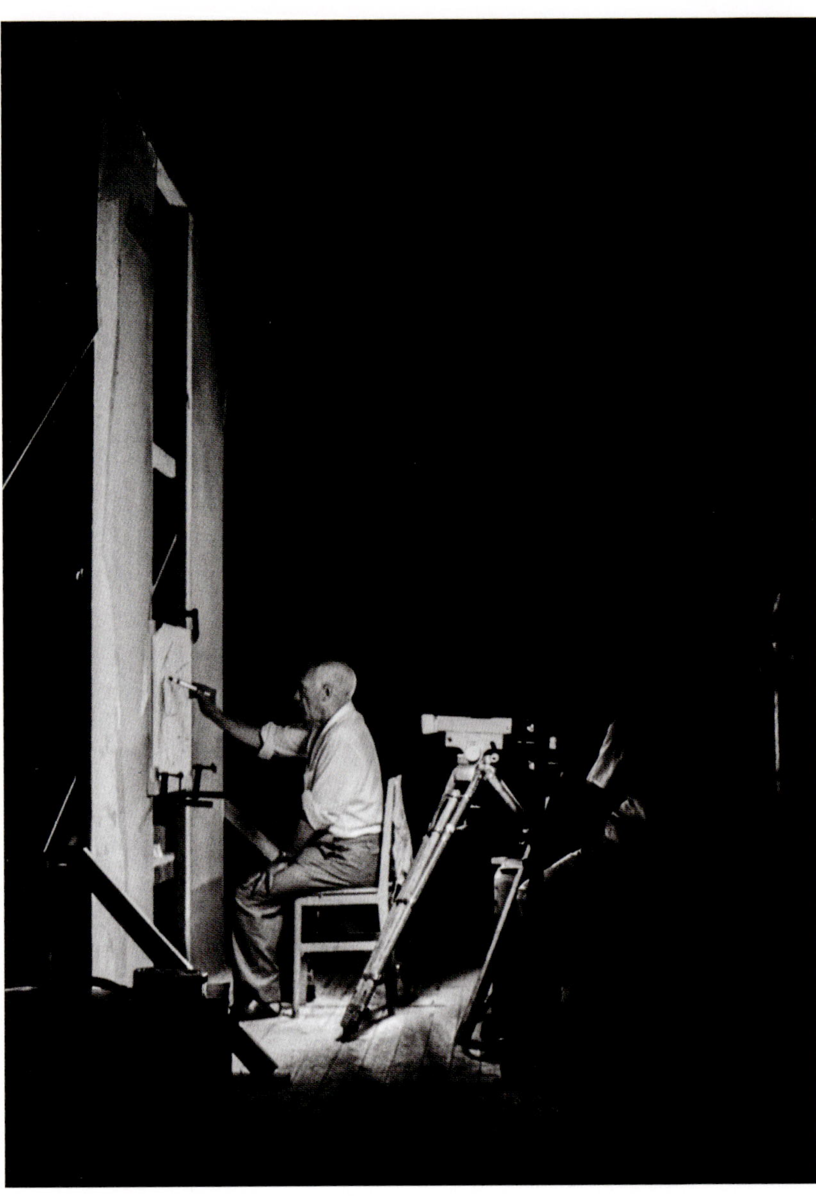

LEFT: FIG. 28 Picasso drawing with a felt-tip pen in the documentary *The Mystery of Picasso* directed by Henri-Georges Clouzot, Victorine studio, Nice, 1955

BELOW: FIG. 29 Installation view of *Picasso 1970–1972, 201 paintings*, 23 May to 23 September 1973, Palais des Papes, Avignon, France

aim, Clouzot placed the camera behind a sheet of paper, and when the artist drew on it with felt-tip pens, the ink went through the paper, giving the viewer the impression that the artist's lines were appearing as if by magic (FIG. 28). Aged seventy-three, Picasso continued to play the role of the virile, bare-chested artist, saying to the director when asked if he felt tired: 'I can continue all night if you want.'

Whether or not this energy was the result of a burning inner force, the artist continued to create during the last months of his life. In 1970 and 1973 two large exhibitions took place at the Palais des Papes in Avignon (FIG. 29), showing his latest artworks: large, colourful canvases with assertively expressive brushstrokes, depicting nudes (FIG. 30) or revisiting the iconography of Spain's Golden Age, inhabited by musketeers (FIG. 31) and matadors (FIG. 32). Reactions were mixed, with two opposing points of view—one celebrating an eternally young artist whose work embraced the issues of his era, the other deploring an aging artist who repeated himself. In the cruel and oft-cited words of collector Douglas Cooper, the works amounted to 'incoherent scrawls done by a frantic old man in death's antechamber'.[41] These critiques of Picasso's last works are part of the controversies that he fuelled throughout his career. One of the paradoxes around the painter, which persists to this

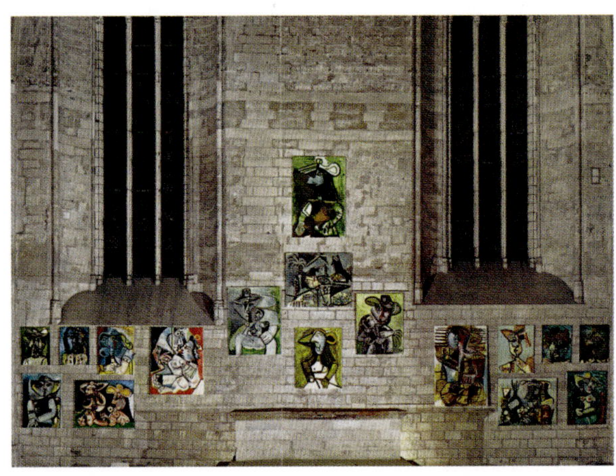

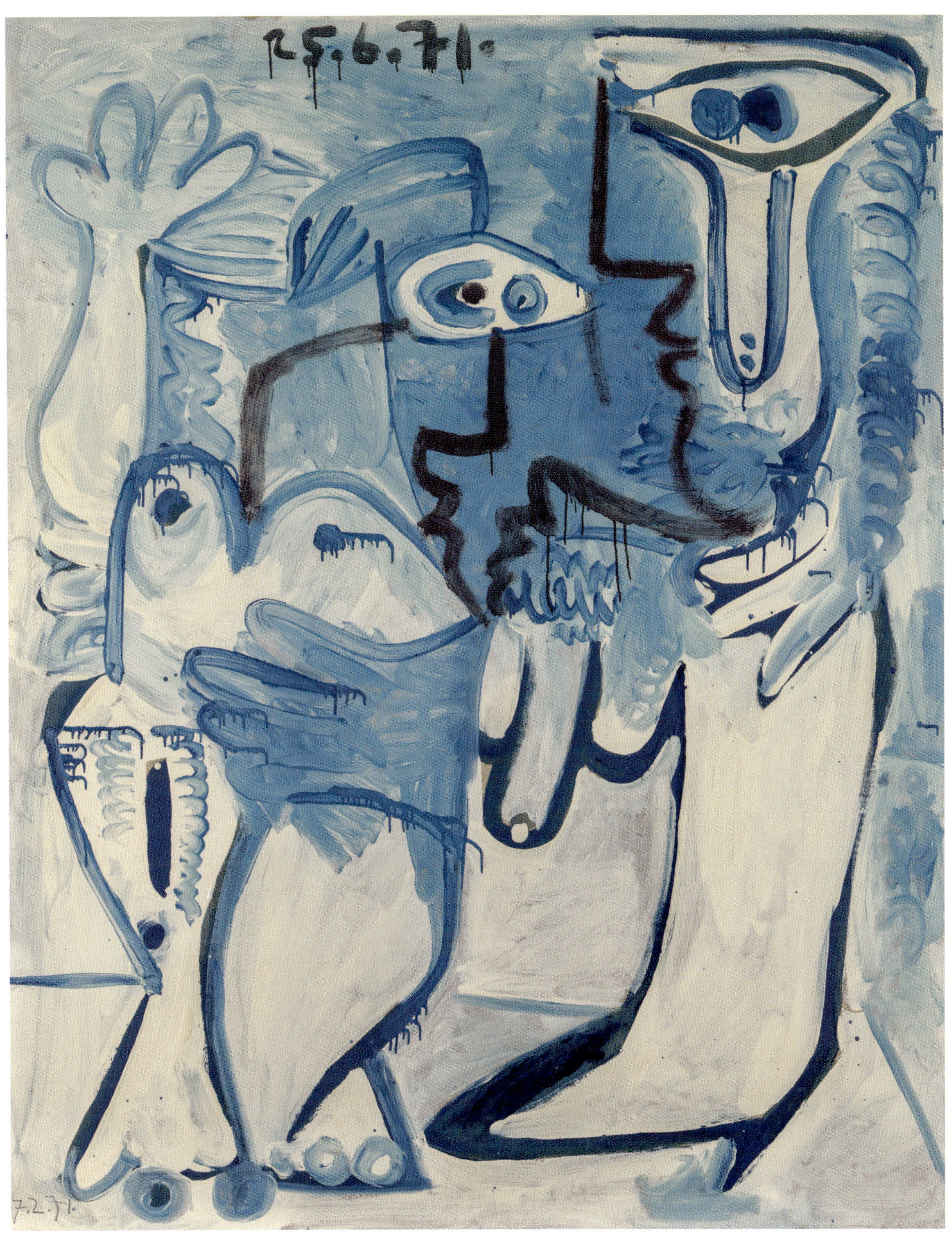

FIG. 30 *Couple*, 1970–1971

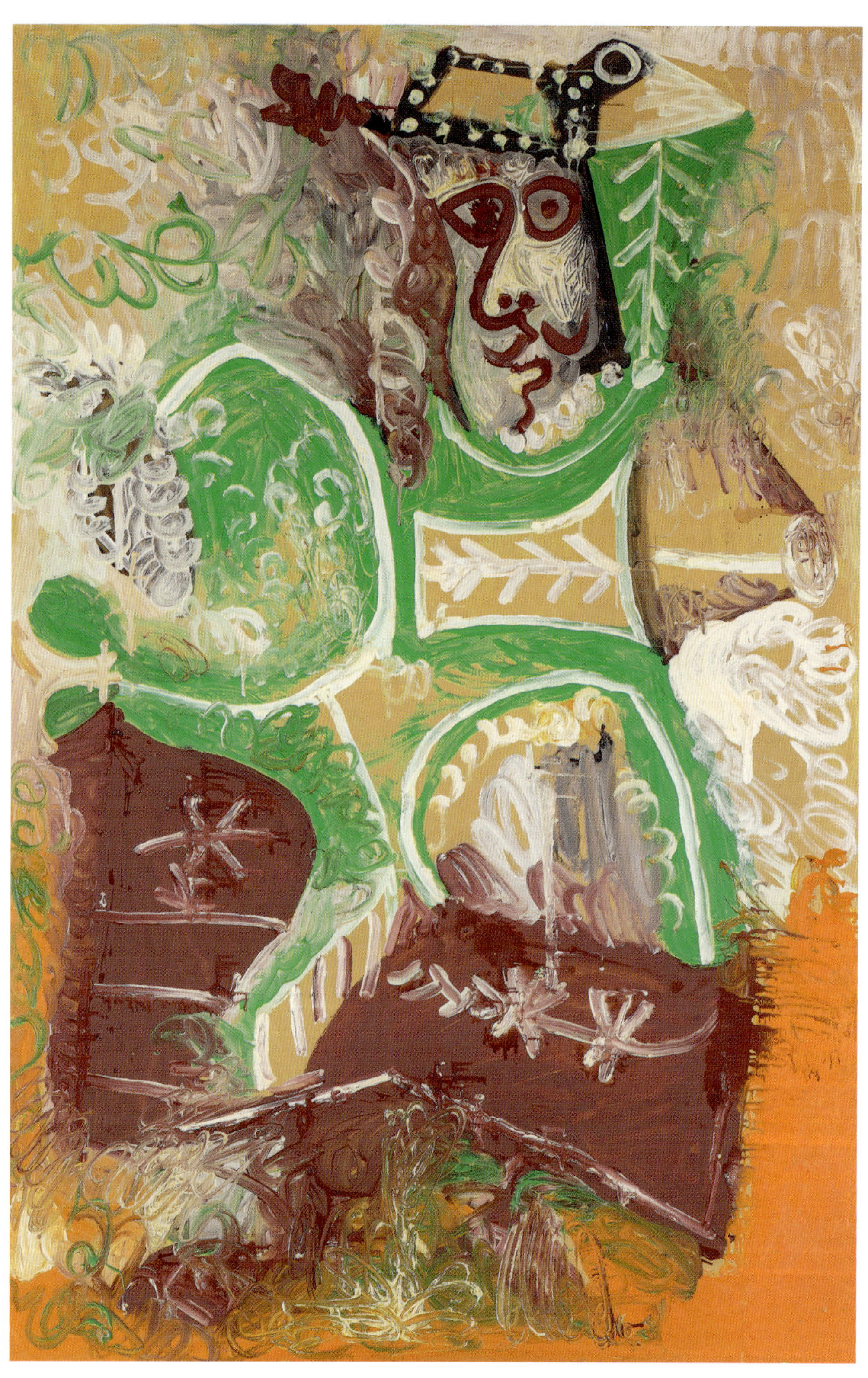

FIG. 31 *The Old Man*, 1970

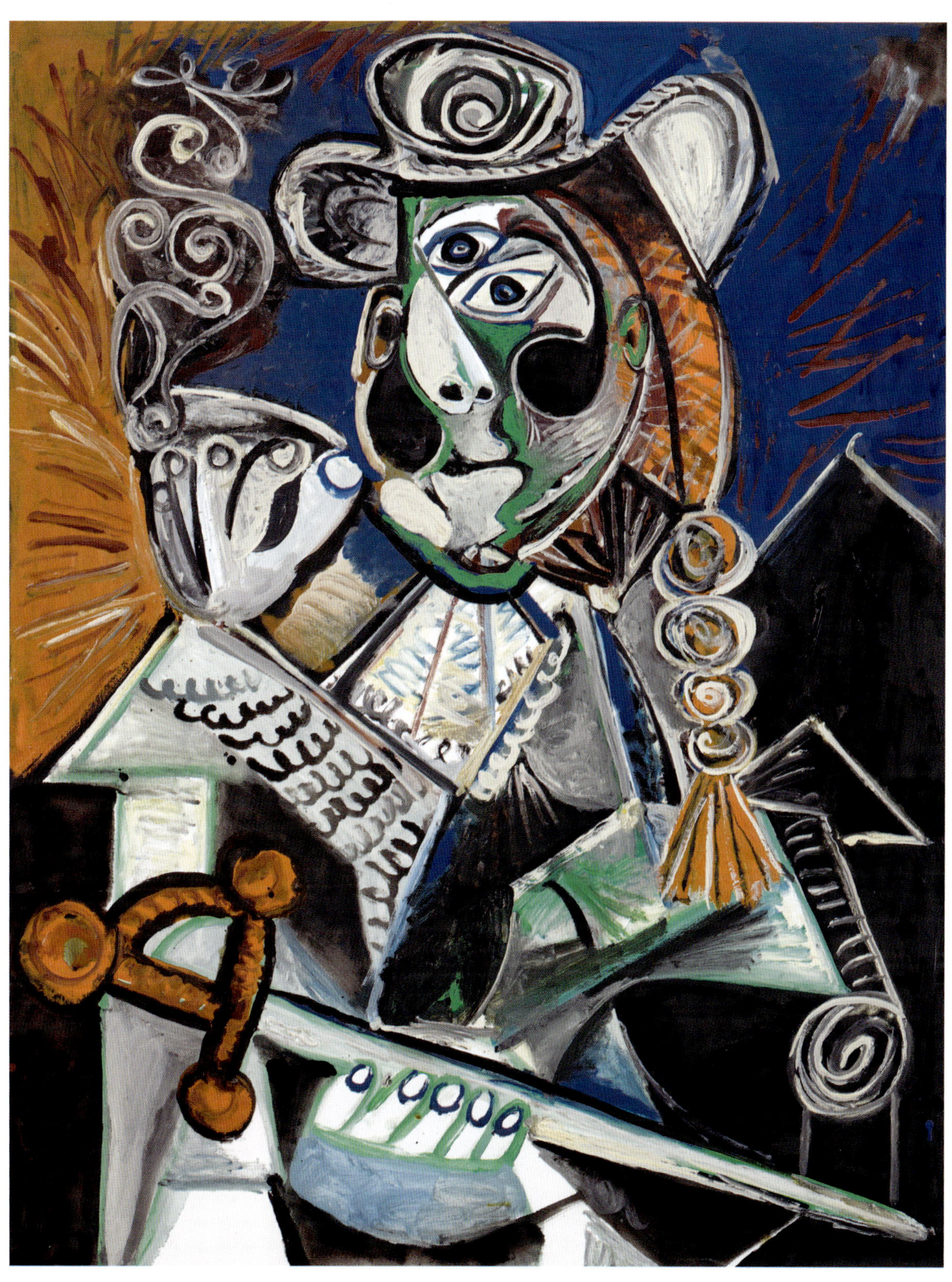

FIG. 32 *The Matador*, 1970

day, is that he was one of the most acclaimed artistic figures of his era, even though his work was often mocked or misunderstood. This brings us to the myth of the visionary, avant-garde artist who can only be understood by like-minded spirits. As of the early twentieth century, Picasso was the embodiment of such a figure, as well as that of another archetype: the bohemian artist.

OUTSIDER: BOHEMIAN AND AVANT-GARDE REVOLUTIONARY

The stereotype of the 'bohemian artist' emerged in the late eighteenth century and crystallised in Paris in the 1830s and 1840s.[42] As historian Michael Wilson explains:

Legends of the artist as a melancholic outsider had distant origins, but it was only from the late eighteenth century that artists self-consciously adopted personas derived from this conception. Subsequently artists, writers and critics all helped to consolidate the image of the rebellious artist-hero, isolated and suffering in his genius, and there are few artists who failed to identify at some level with this mythic figure.[43]

Attracted by this image, Picasso frequented the louche neighbourhoods of Barcelona and then those of Paris, where he first went in 1900, exploring the Montmartre district, the epicentre of this 'bohemian life'. Annexed by the French capital in 1860, this former village had a revolutionary legacy dating to the times of the Paris Commune, which started there in 1871. When he settled in France in 1904, Picasso decided to move to Montmartre. At that time he lived at the Bateau-Lavoir, a former piano factory that had been turned into housing for artists, located just a few steps from the construction site of the basilica of Sacré-Cœur, a redemptive symbol of the insurrection of the Commune that he depicted in one of his paintings (FIG. 33). Following in the footsteps of Théophile Steinlen and Henri de Toulouse-Lautrec, Picasso painted the interiors of iconic local cabarets where people from different walks of life mingled: workers, wine-makers, crooks, artists, merchants, and members of the middle class (FIGS 34 AND 35). Gradually, his interest focused on the most marginal figures, such as beggars, vagabonds, and women in prison, while his colour palette adopted shades of blue. This is what art historians would later call his Blue Period, which lasted from 1901 to 1904 and was marked by frequent trips between Paris and Barcelona. The artist depicted himself in poverty, with a pallid complexion and an emaciated face (FIG. 38). Glorifying his suffering, he took up the romantic image of the tortured, melancholy, frail artist, a heroic figure who is also found at this time in the work of other artists, such as Edvard Munch's *Self-Portrait in Hell* (1903; FIG. 36).

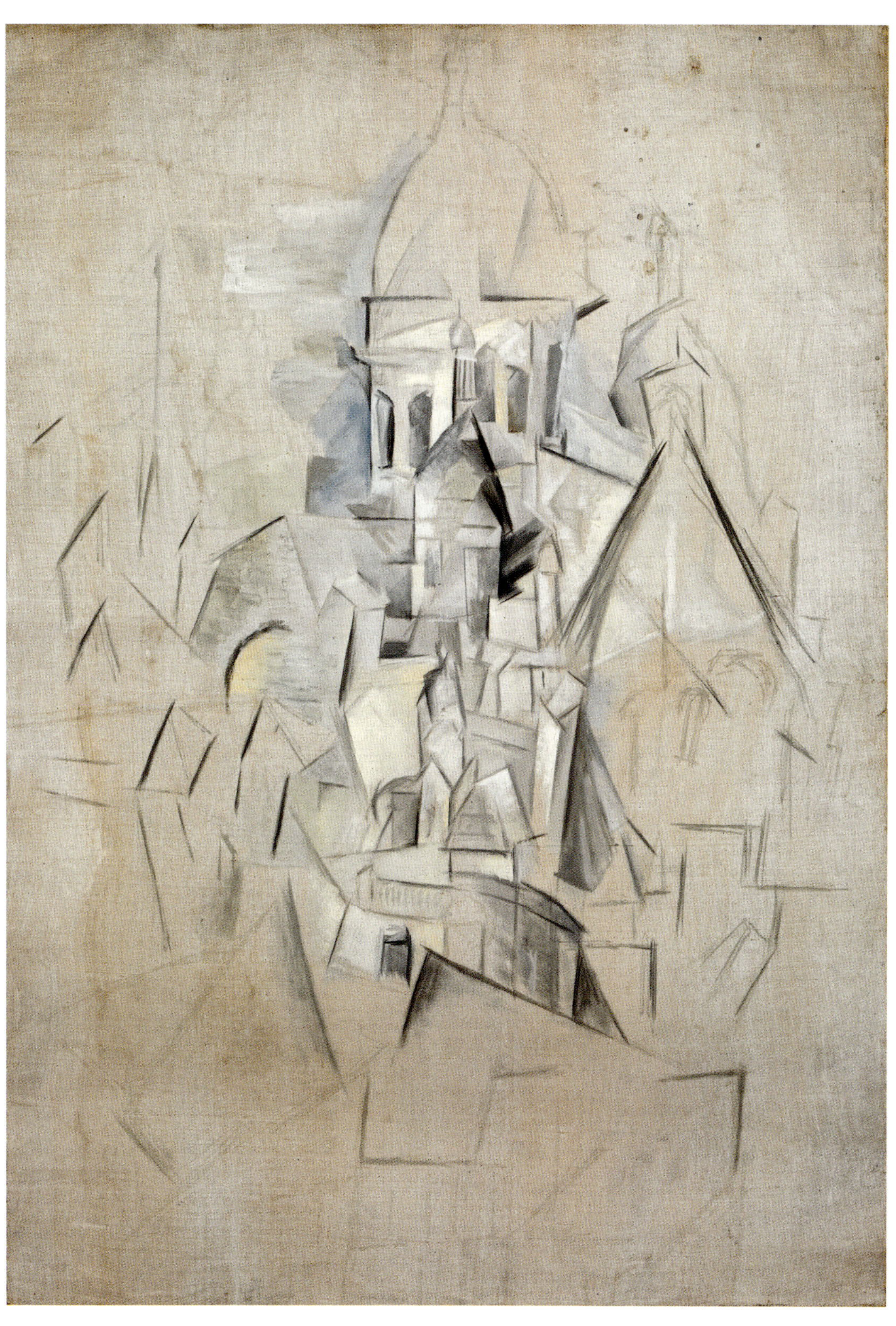

FIG. 33 *Sacré-Cœur*, 1909–1910

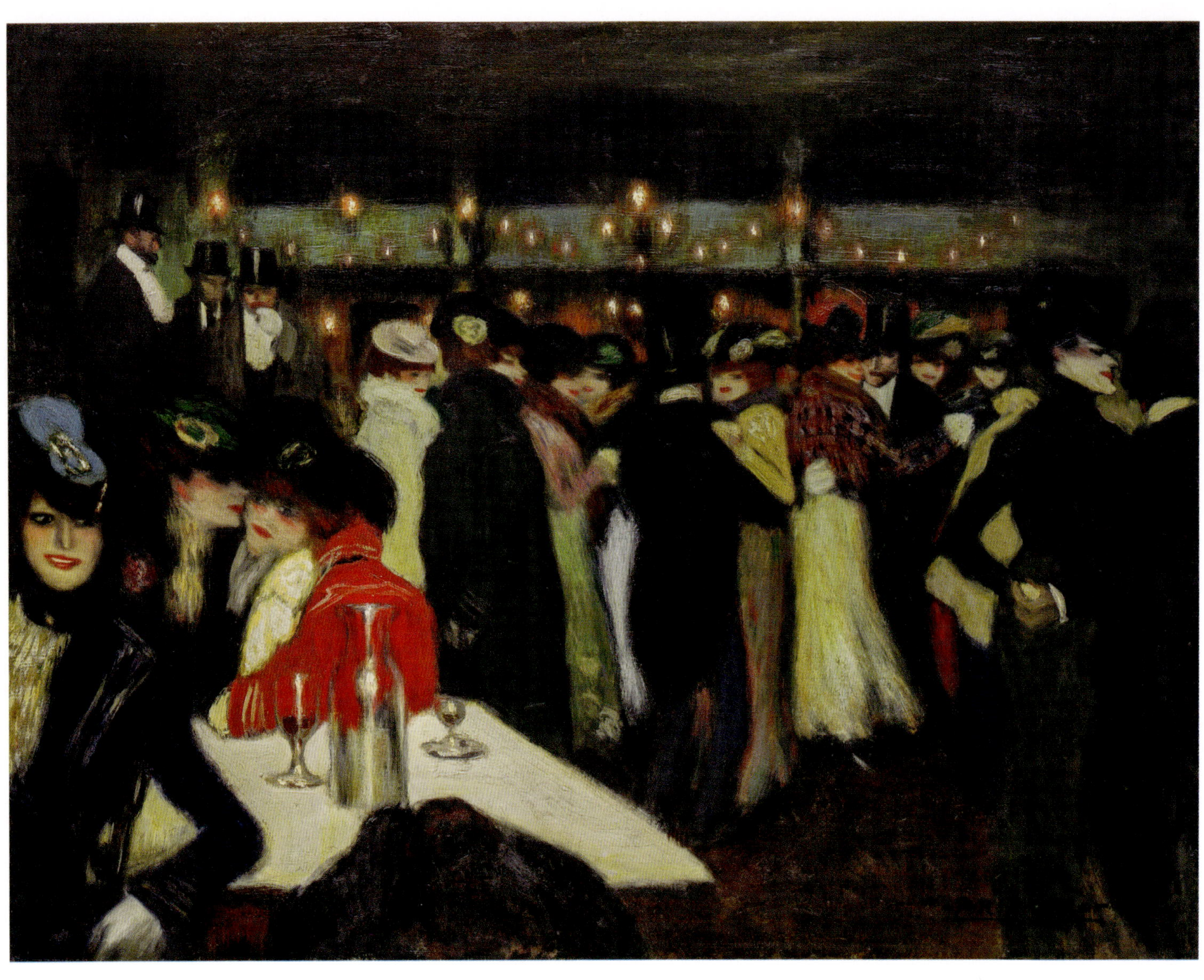

FIG. 34 *Le Moulin de la Galette*, 1900

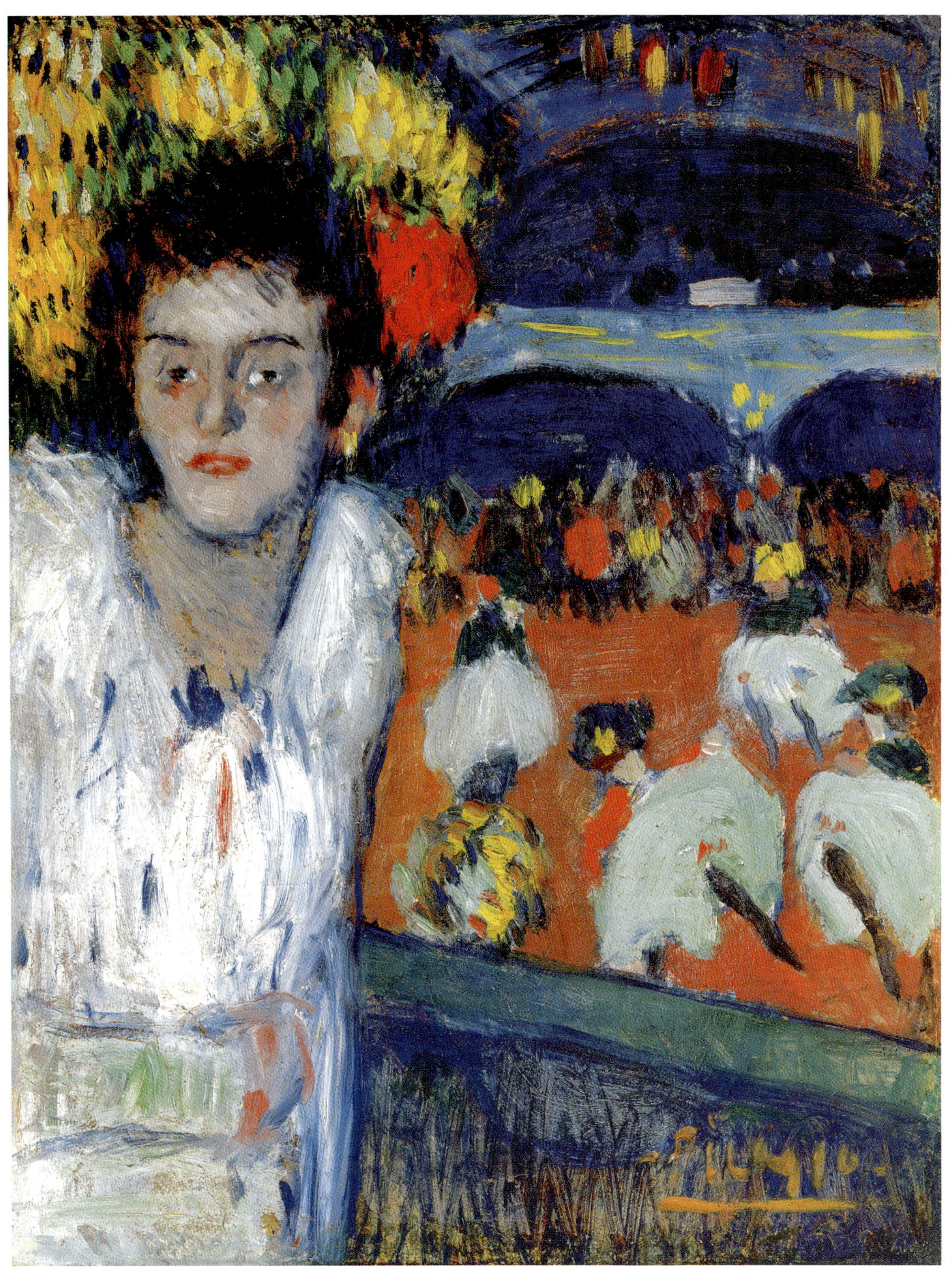

FIG. 35 *At the Moulin Rouge (The Japanese Divan)*, 1901

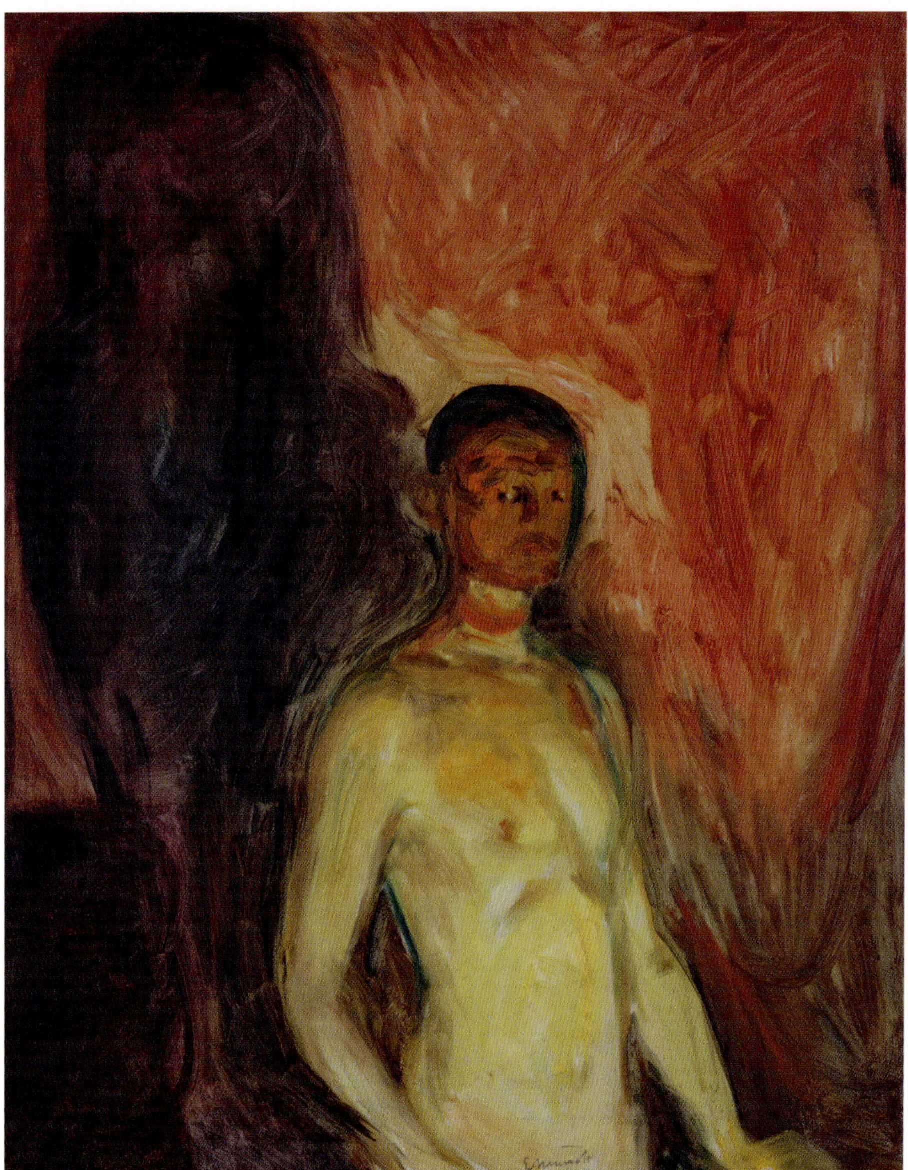

LEFT: FIG. 36 Edvard Munch, *Self-Portrait in Hell*, 1903

BELOW: FIG. 37 The Picasso Room at the Trubetskoy Palace, 1914

OPPOSITE: FIG. 38 *Self-Portrait*, 1901

The work of the Blue Period, followed by that of the Rose Period (1904–1906), which focused on the world of the circus, would attract Picasso's first important collectors, such as Gertrude Stein and her brother Leo, and, a little later, the Russian businessman Sergei Shchukin. It might have been regarded as paradoxical to find the artist's paintings of destitute figures hanging on the walls of lavish interiors (FIG. 37), since the bohemian artist is defined as an anti-academic who is an adversary of the bourgeois world. Here, historian Marilyn Ruth Brown offers a key for interpretation:

The myth of the bohemian in opposition to the bourgeoisie is part of a convenient outlet offered to the bourgeois for their own self-critique ... The bohemianism of the streets does not disappear. It simply is no longer embodied in figures of social otherness, but in sites of exotic memories, which float in the imagination at the intersection of desire and distance, of identification and nostalgia.[44]

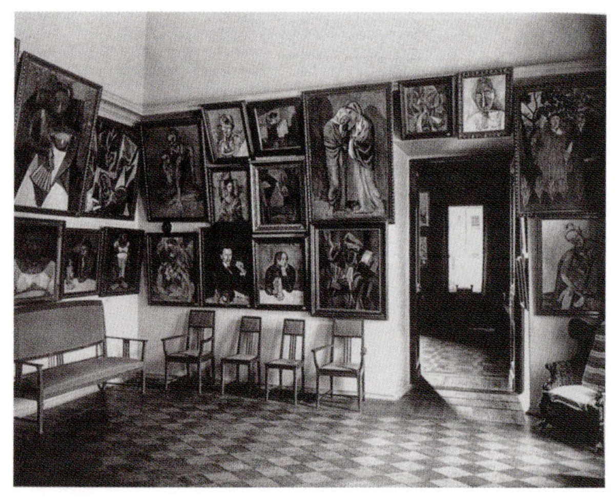

Picasso himself played on this nostalgia when, after becoming wealthy, he stated several times that he would like to become poor again and thus live a 'second youth',[45] or to continue living in disarray in his

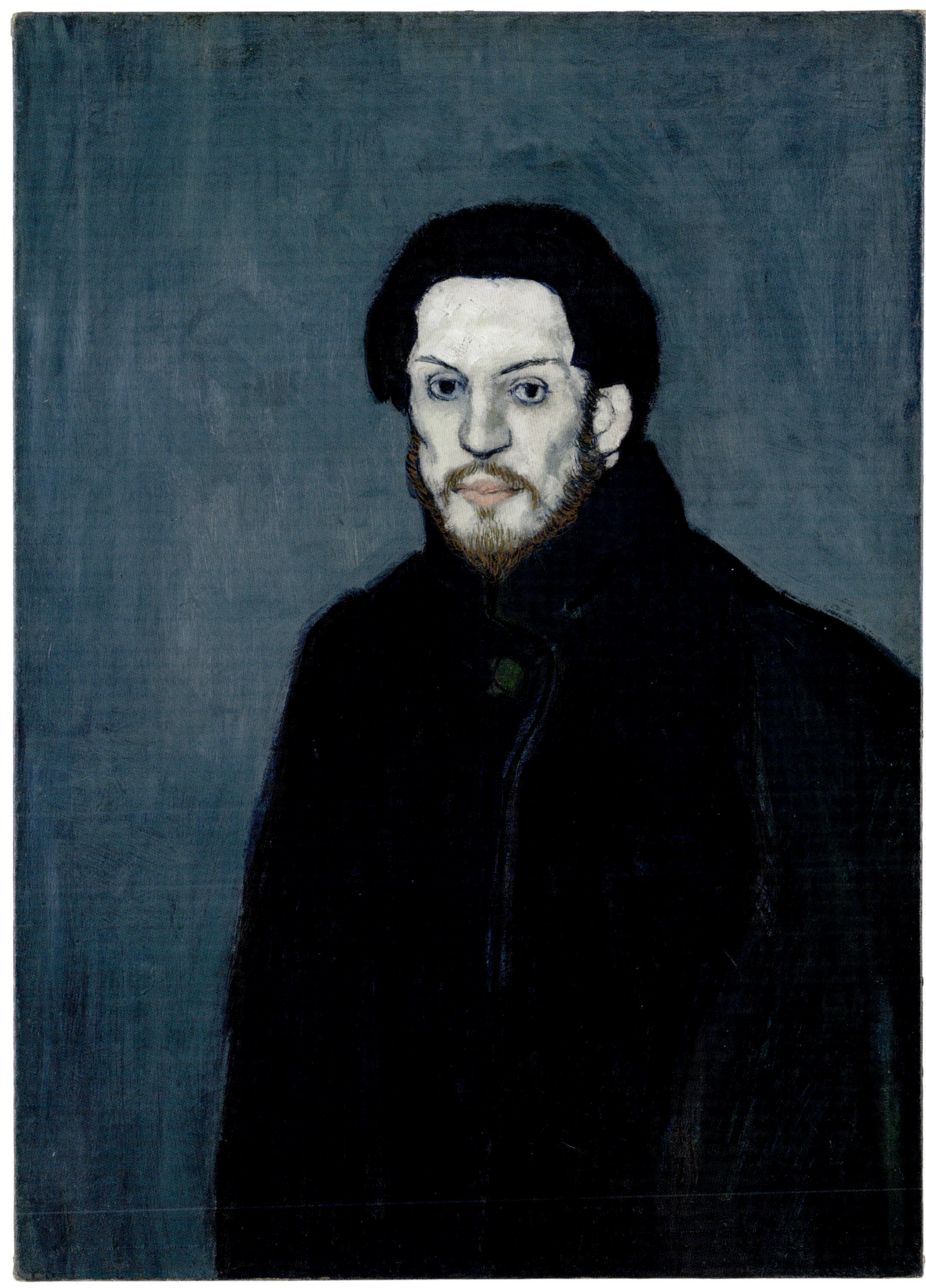

FIG. 39 *Portrait of a Man*, 1902–1903

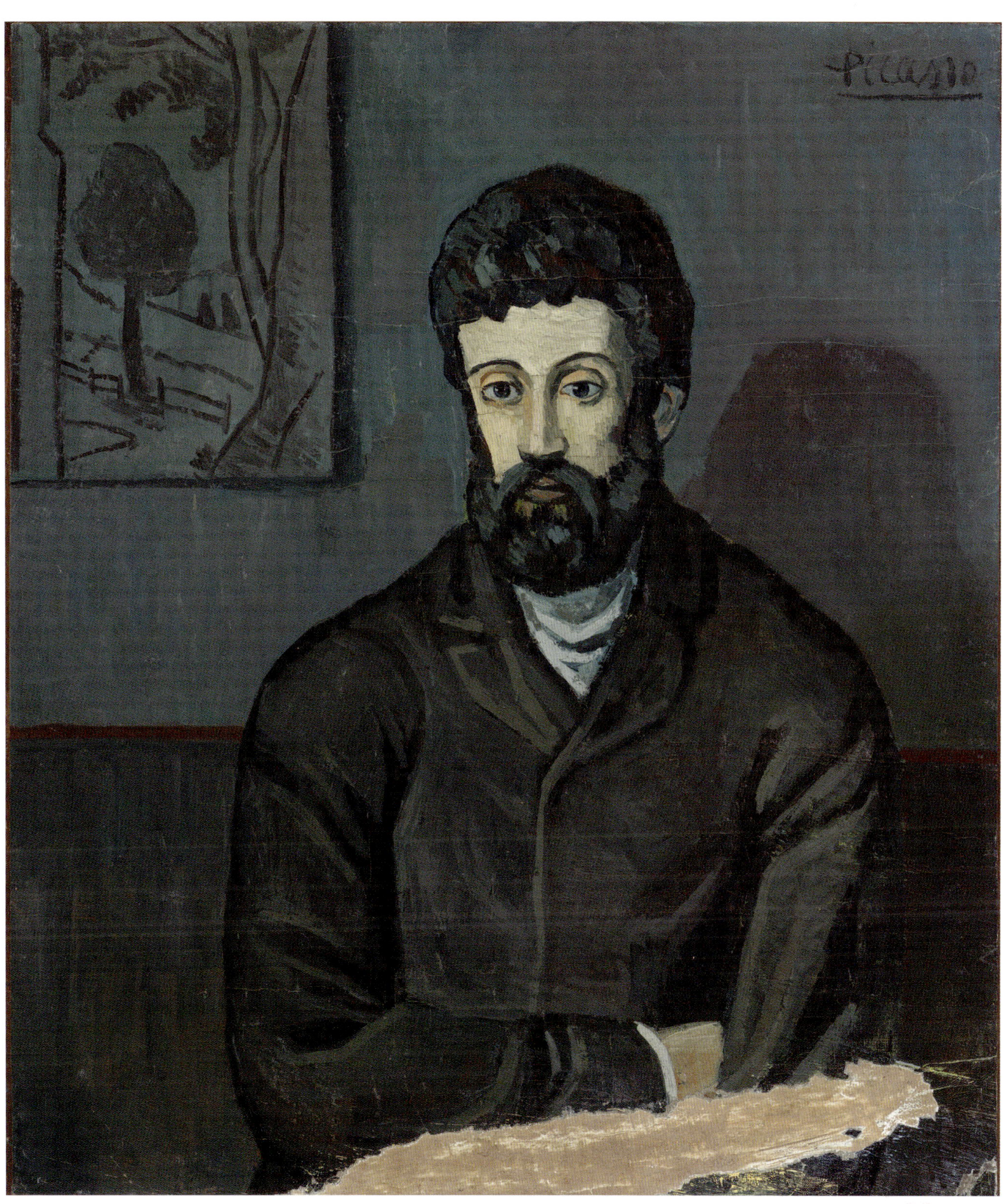
Picasso

luxurious villa in Cannes in the 1950s (FIG. 40). This interest in marginal figures, which is prominent in Picasso's work, did not function, however, as a satirical discourse or a social critique. In any case, that is the reading offered by the art critic Max Raphael in 1933, who stated, 'Very much like Rilke, Picasso looks upon poverty as a heroic thing and elevates it to the power of myth—the myth of "great inner splendour".'[46] The subjects of the Blue and Rose periods leave their social reality for metaphysical, symbolic settings: simple interiors (FIG. 41), the seaside (FIG. 42), deserts (FIG. 43), or even monochrome backgrounds (FIG. 44). They become allegories expressing suffering and solitude (FIG. 45).

While Picasso stood out because of his bohemian way of life that broke with the ordinary, his work remained anchored in a type of tradition. Beginning in 1906, however, his artistic creativity took a radical turn. Inspired by various sources—the work of Paul Cézanne, African and Oceanian sculpture, Iberian art, vernacular architecture—Picasso embarked on a radical simplification of forms. Starting from the observation of reality, his work strayed from mimetic representation and began veering towards schematic figuration. The resulting studies and experiments culminated in the production of his great painting *Les Demoiselles d'Avignon* (1907; FIG. 46). While the artwork relied on the classical iconography of female nudes, its representation turned academic conventions on their head: the bodies are reduced to geometrical figures, and the two faces on the right look more like masks.

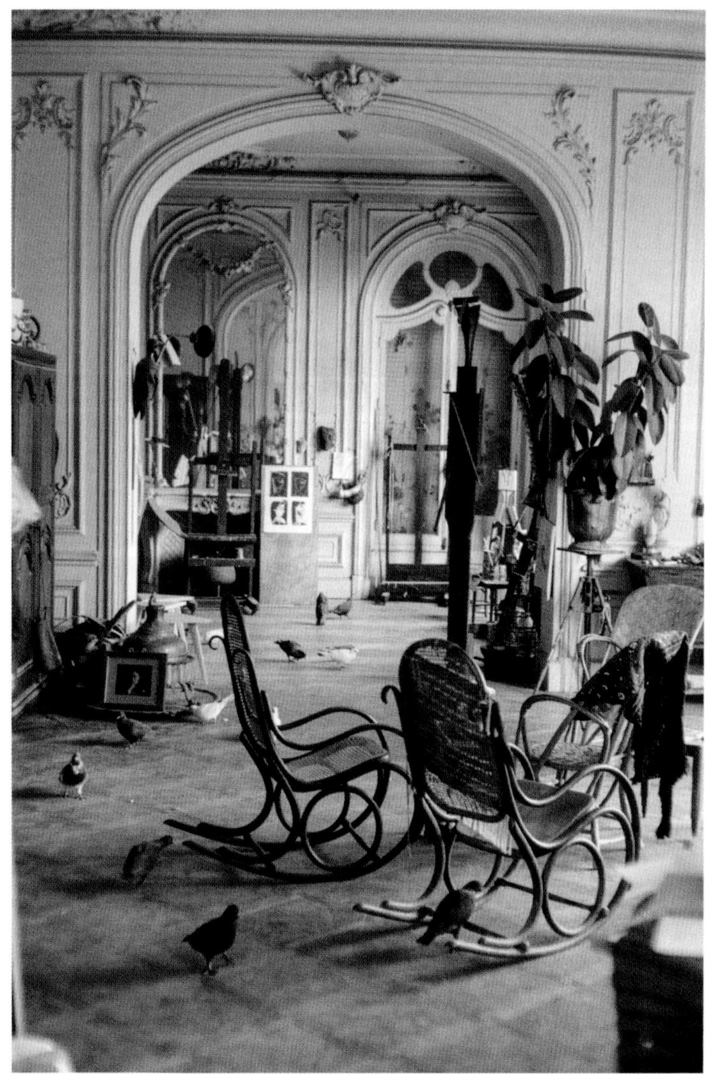

FIG. 40 David Douglas Duncan, *Pigeons in Picasso's living room and studio of La Californie, Cannes, April 1959*, 1959

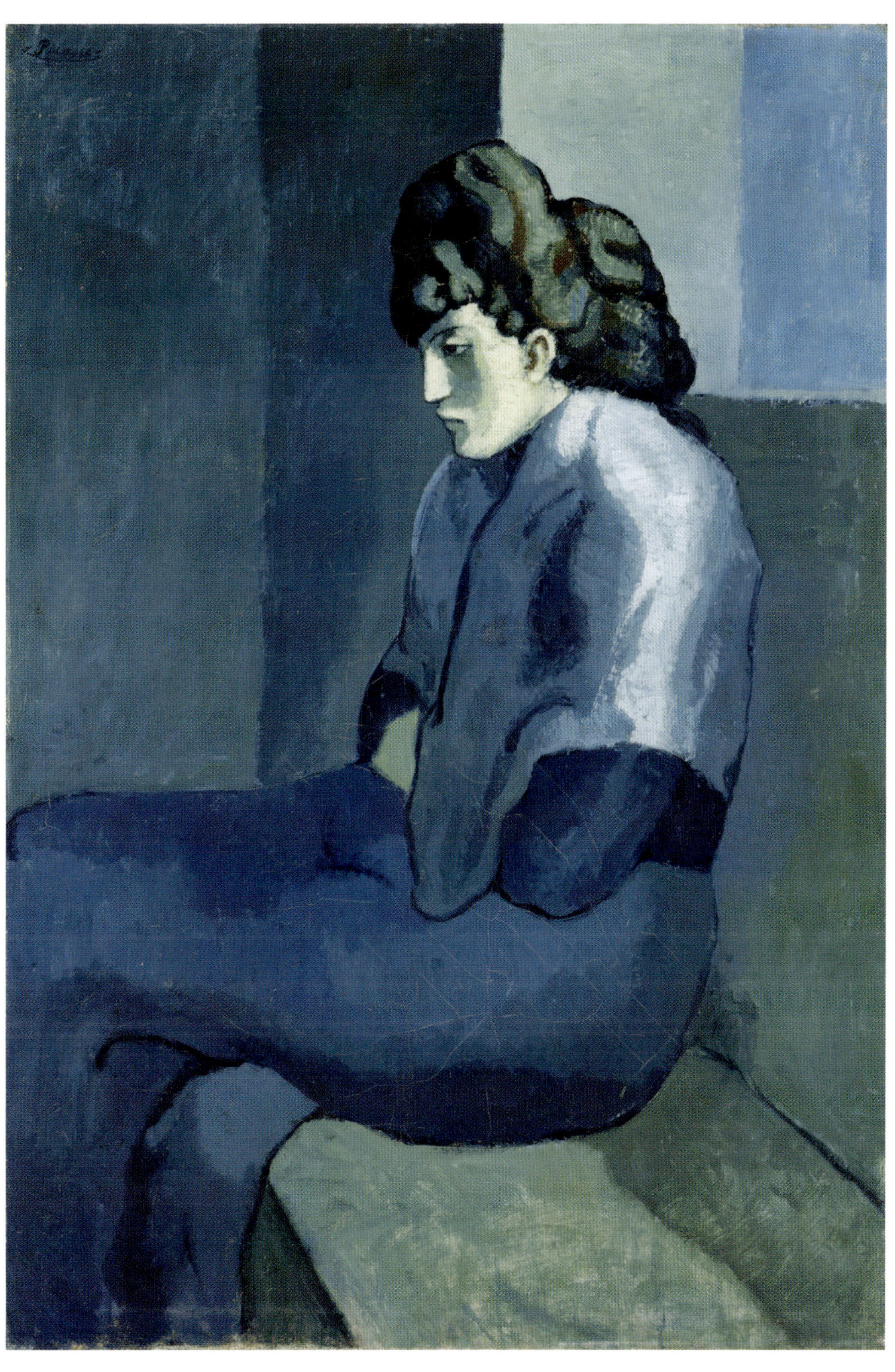

FIG. 41 *Melancholy Woman*, 1902

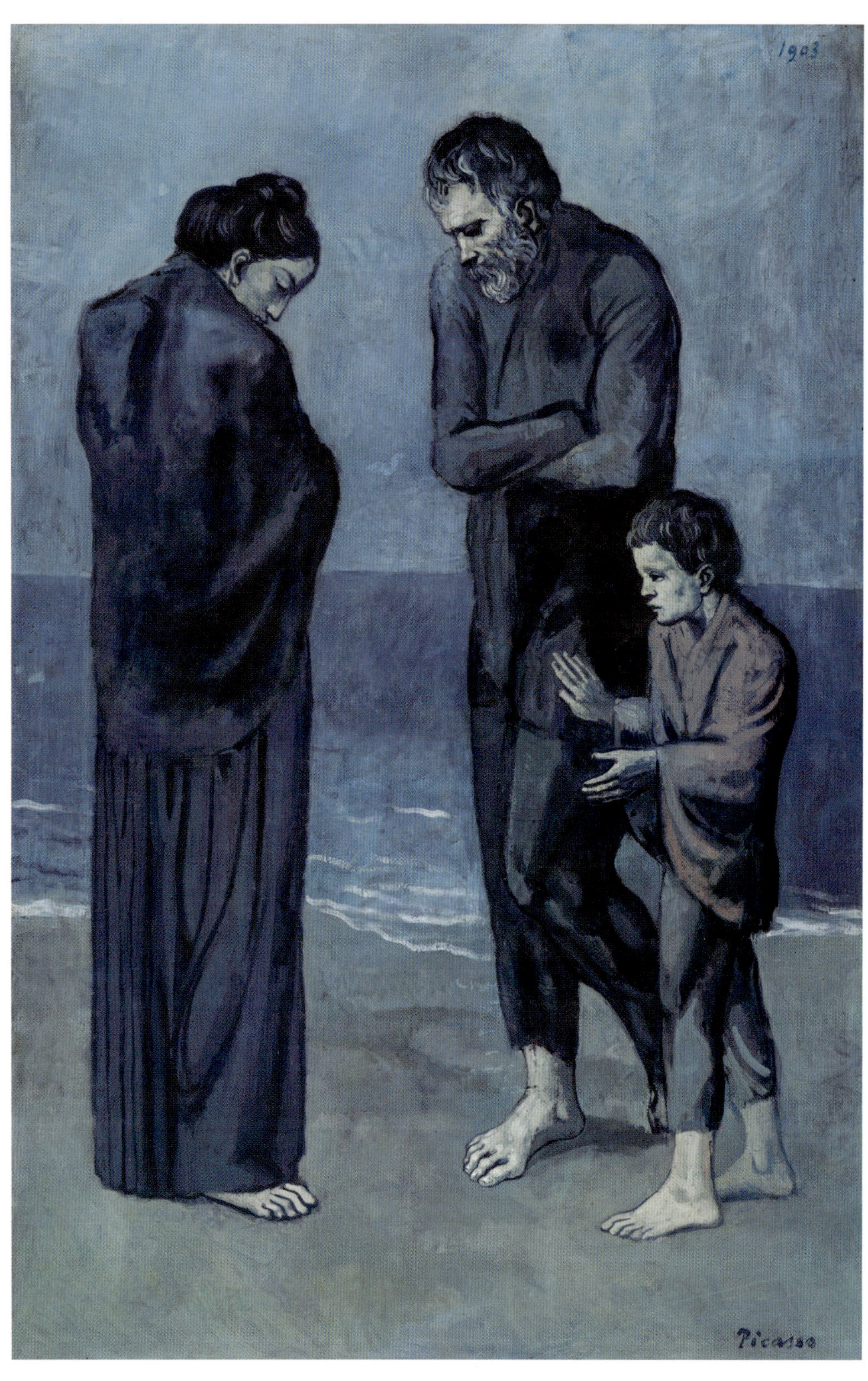

FIG. 42 *The Tragedy*, 1903

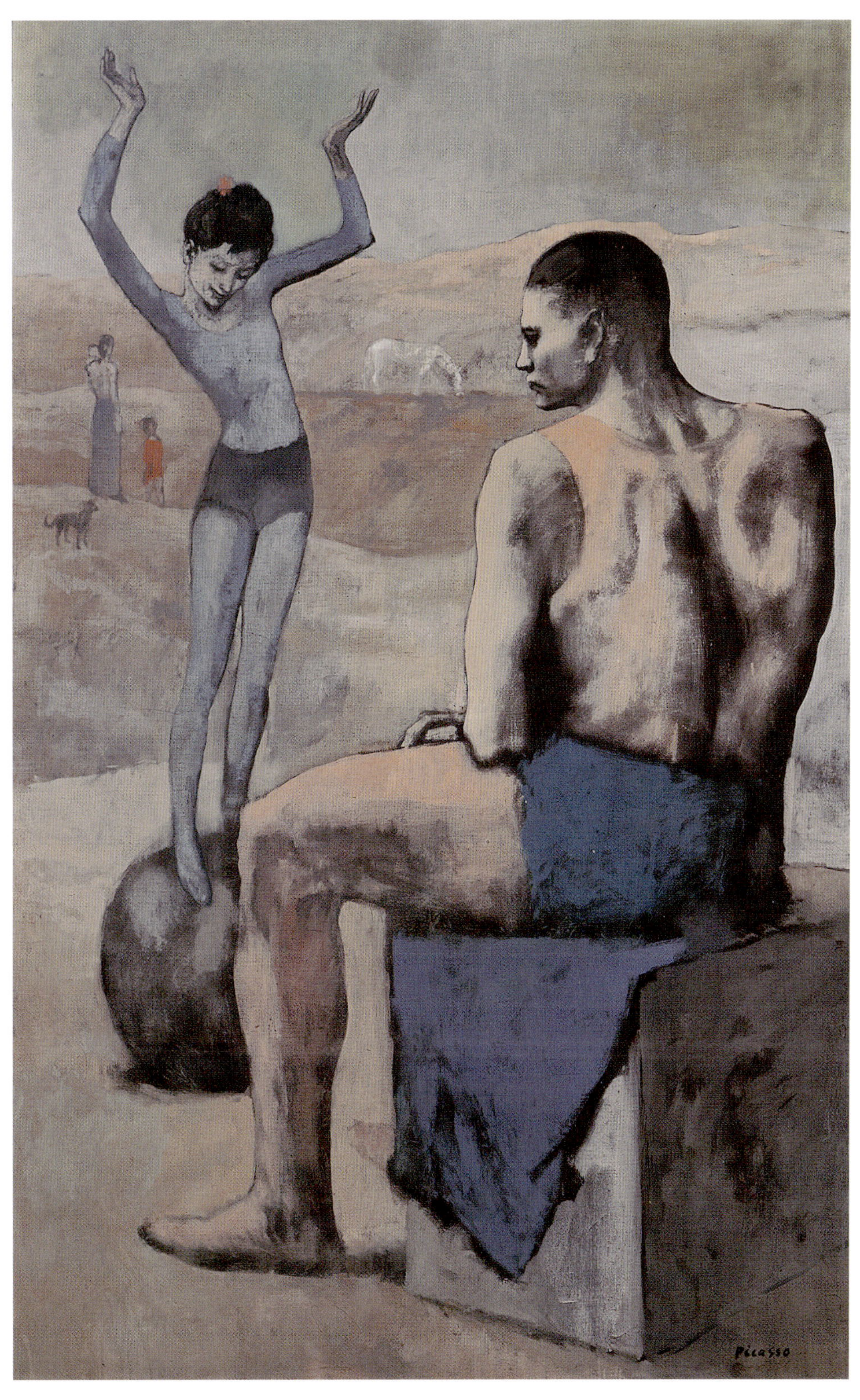

FIG. 43 *Acrobat on a Ball*, 1905

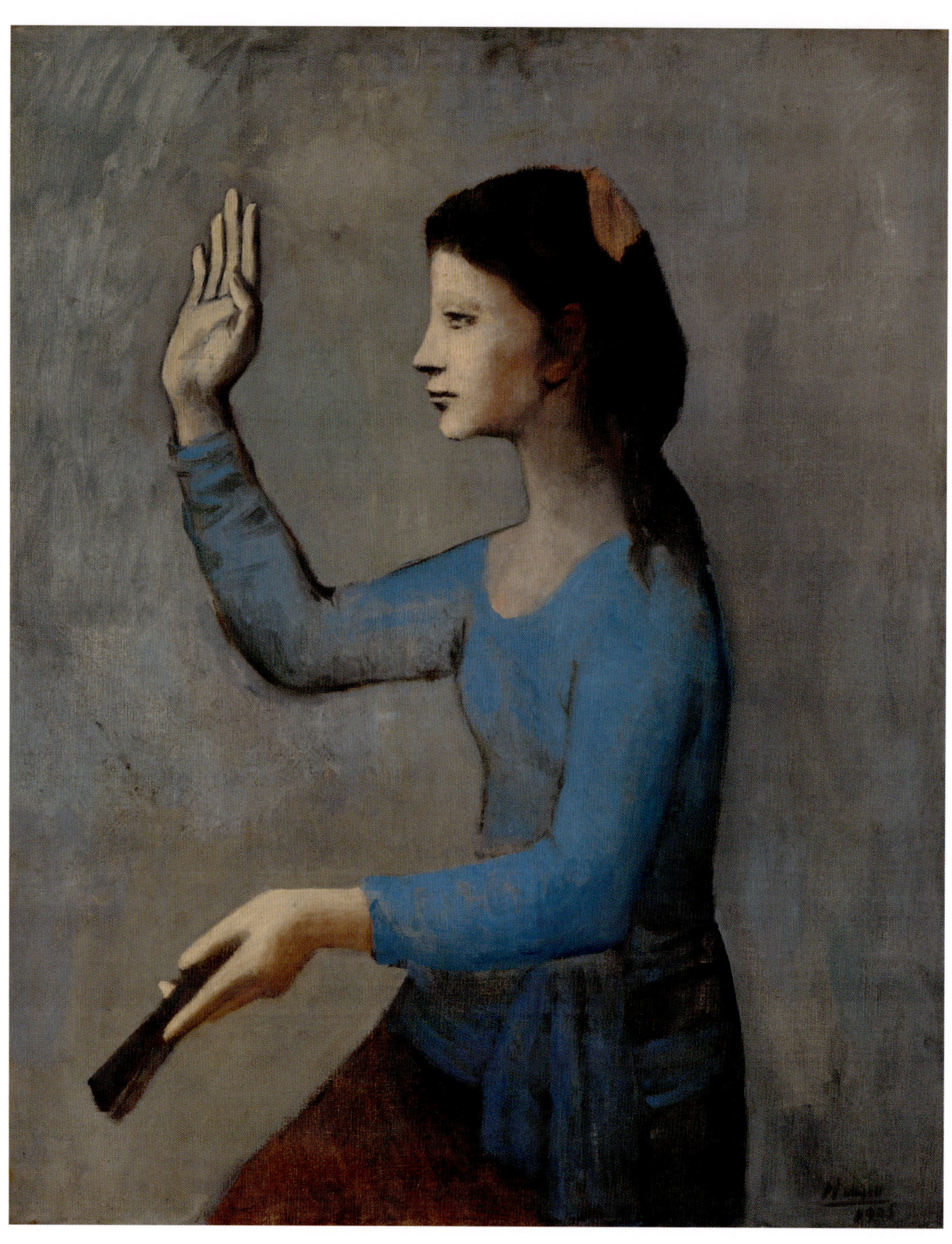

FIG. 44 *Lady with a Fan*, 1905

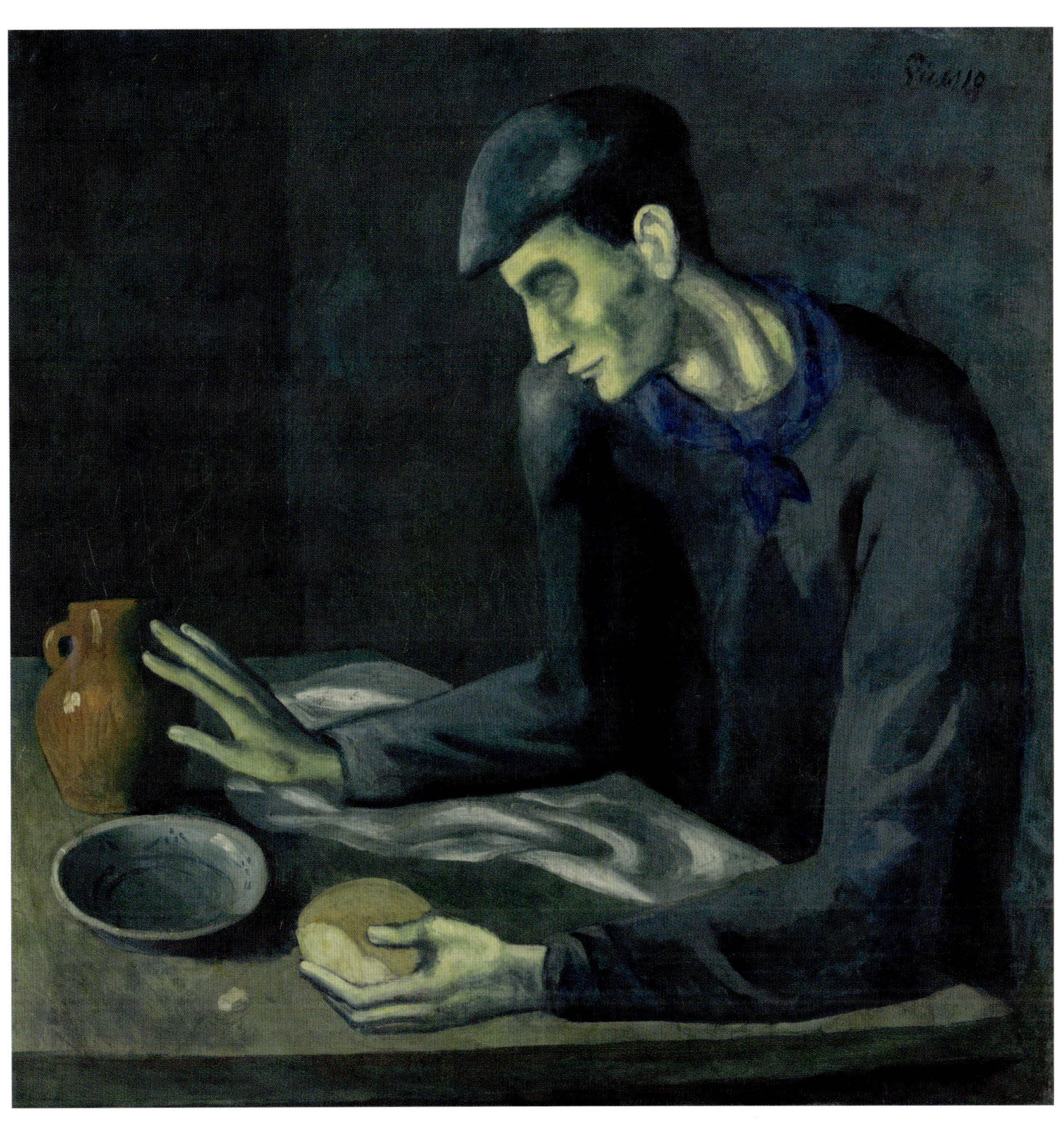

FIG. 45 *The Blind Man's Meal*, 1903

As often, the title did not come from Picasso but from the writer André Salmon, who coined it during the first public exhibition of the painting at the Salon d'Antin, in 1916. The reference to Avignon is not to the city in south-eastern France where Picasso would show his work at the end of his life, but to the Carrer d'Avinyó, a narrow street in Barcelona that was a centre of prostitution at the end of the nineteenth century. Salmon's title could have had the consequence of limiting the interpretation of the artwork to a simple, scandalous depiction of prostitutes. But Linda Nochlin's analysis reveals the artistic issues that concerned Picasso:

The Demoiselles can hardly be said to be, apart from the title, about women at all. As pictorial constructions, its women are neither sexy nor desirable, or even unambiguously feminine in their anatomy. The struggle displayed is not that of a man to dominate women, or of women to seduce a man, but rather the struggle – equally intense – to challenge a tradition of representation in its most important generic manifestation: the nude.[47]

According to available sources, Picasso's work caused strong divisions within his inner circle, and only very few of its members grasped the artist's new direction, the notable exceptions being the art dealer Daniel-Henry Kahnweiler and the French artist Georges Braque. In fact, it was in close collaboration with Braque that Picasso would pursue his interest in form, thus giving rise to the Cubist movement.

The Cubists clearly wanted to make an aesthetic and philosophical break with the art of their time. Their approach consisted of depicting not what one sees of an object, but what one knows about it from different perspectives gathered together. It was a way of deconstructing reality in order to reconstruct it. The first years of Cubism, from 1908 to 1912, are the most difficult to decipher. This is the period referred to as Analytical Cubism, where paintings are constructed of superimposed planes that overlap in varying shades of beige and grey (FIG. 47). Some works, such as *Man with a Mandolin* (1911; FIG. 48), verge on abstraction, a boundary that Picasso refused to cross. As such, he always added something identifiable—a bit of scenery, a piece of clothing, or even a moustache, as in *Man with a Guitar* (1911; FIG. 49)—in order to connect the viewer with reality. The year 1912 saw the start of Synthetic Cubism, in which flat tints of bright colours allowed for strong contrasts. This made the subjects depicted, mostly still lifes (FIG. 50), more easily understood. While the artworks seemed then to settle down and become easier to interpret, practitioners of Synthetic Cubism continued to question academic conventions by integrating paper cutouts and other everyday items into their creations. The first time we see this in Picasso's work is *Still Life with Chair Caning* (1912; FIG. 51), in which the artist incorporates two physical objects: a rope encircling the canvas, and a piece of printed paper imitating the canework of a chair. This aspect of Synthetic Cubism represented a significant development, questioning the traditional role of the artist. The Cubists were the first to incorporate in their art fragments of reality, instead of depicting it with a pencil or brush. Historian Claire Le Thomas has shown how this Cubist innovation partly took inspiration from the popular creative pastimes of the era, including découpage and other handicrafts.[48] By bringing these domestic practices into the art realm, the Cubists established a new paradigm that would give rise to many of the art forms and movements of the twentieth century, from Duchamp's readymades (FIG. 52) to Arte Povera and post-minimalism (FIG. 53).

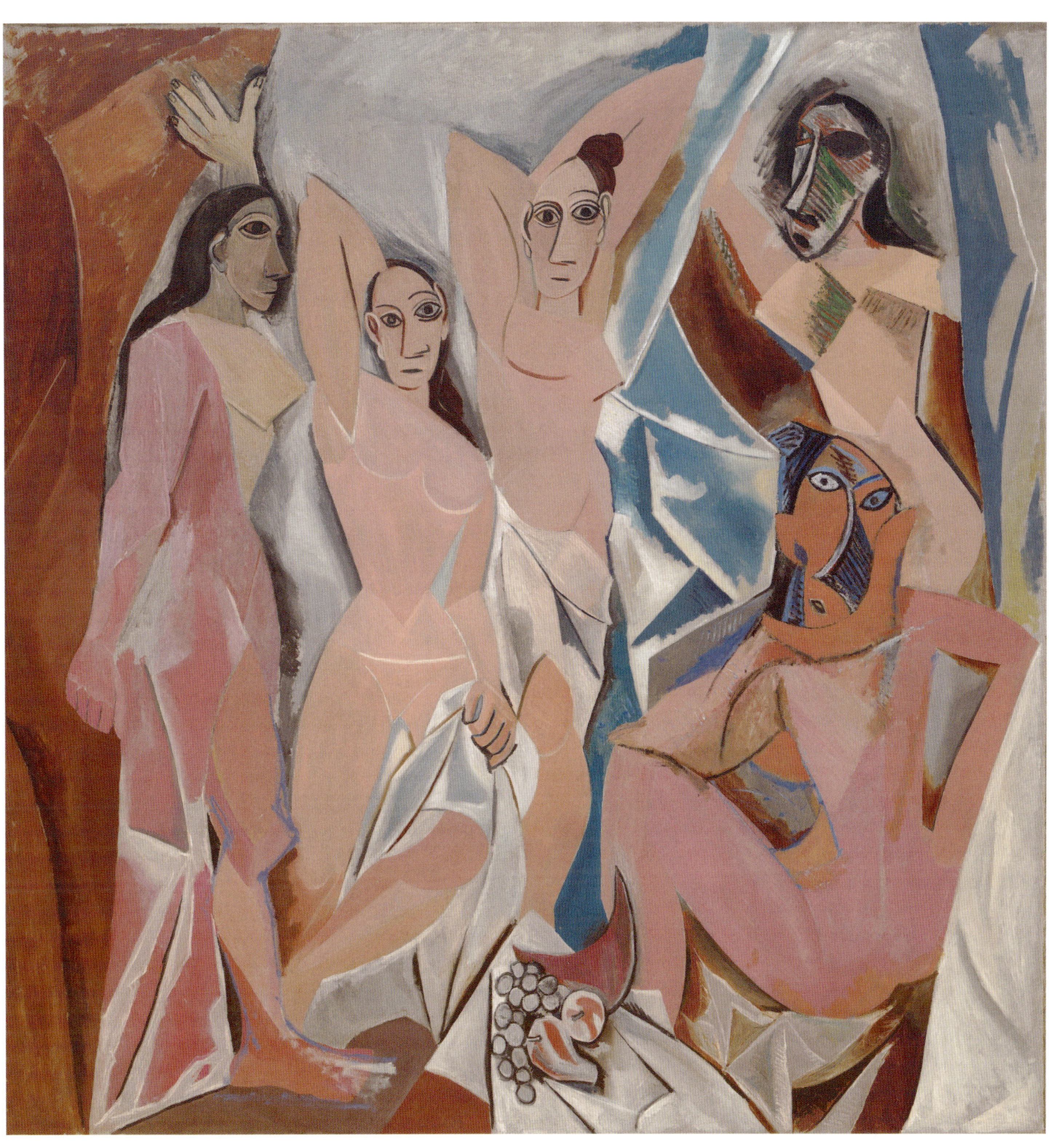

FIG. 46 *Les Demoiselles d'Avignon*, 1907

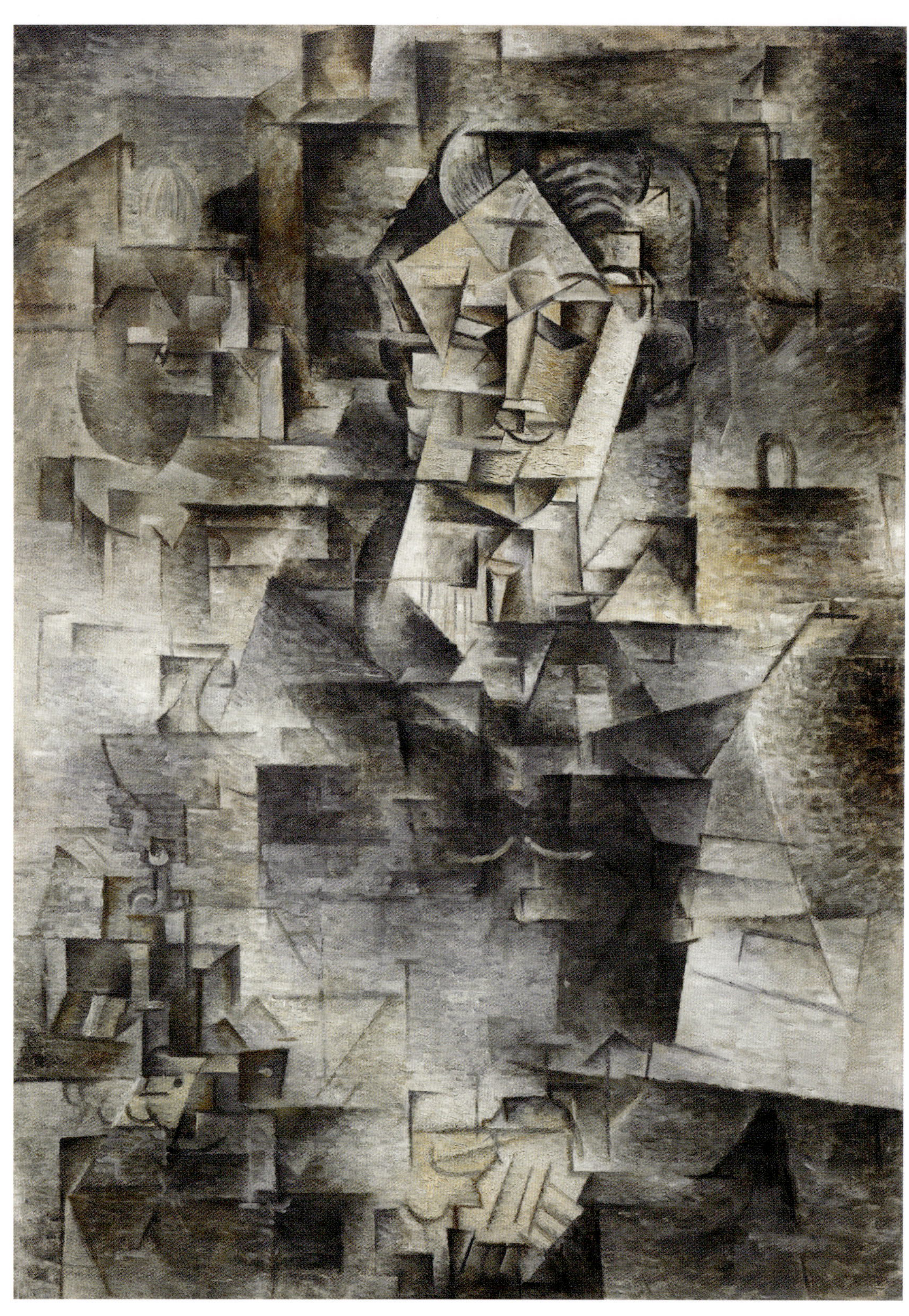

FIG. 47 *Daniel-Henry Kahnweiler*, 1910

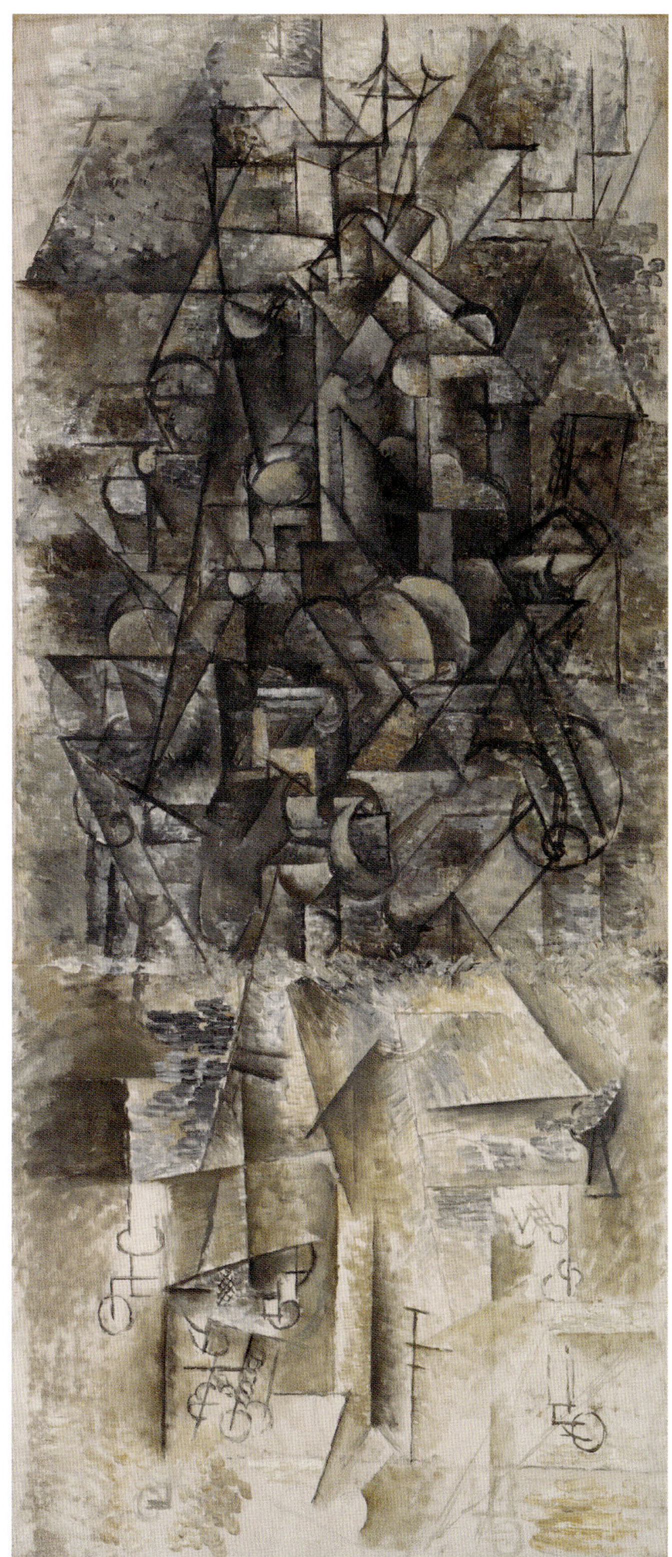

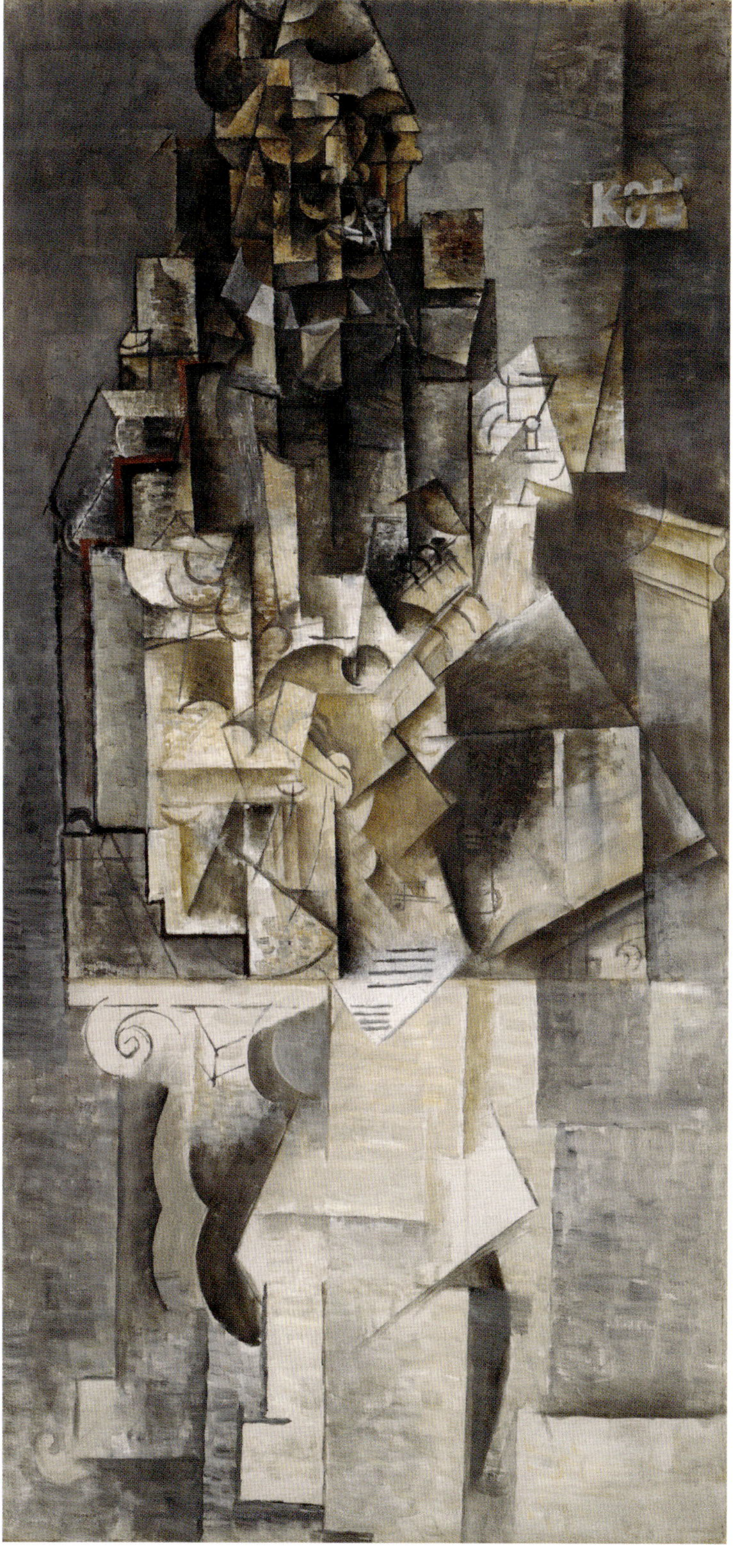

ABOVE LEFT: FIG. 48 *Man with a Mandolin*, 1911

ABOVE RIGHT: FIG. 49 *Man with a Guitar*, 1911

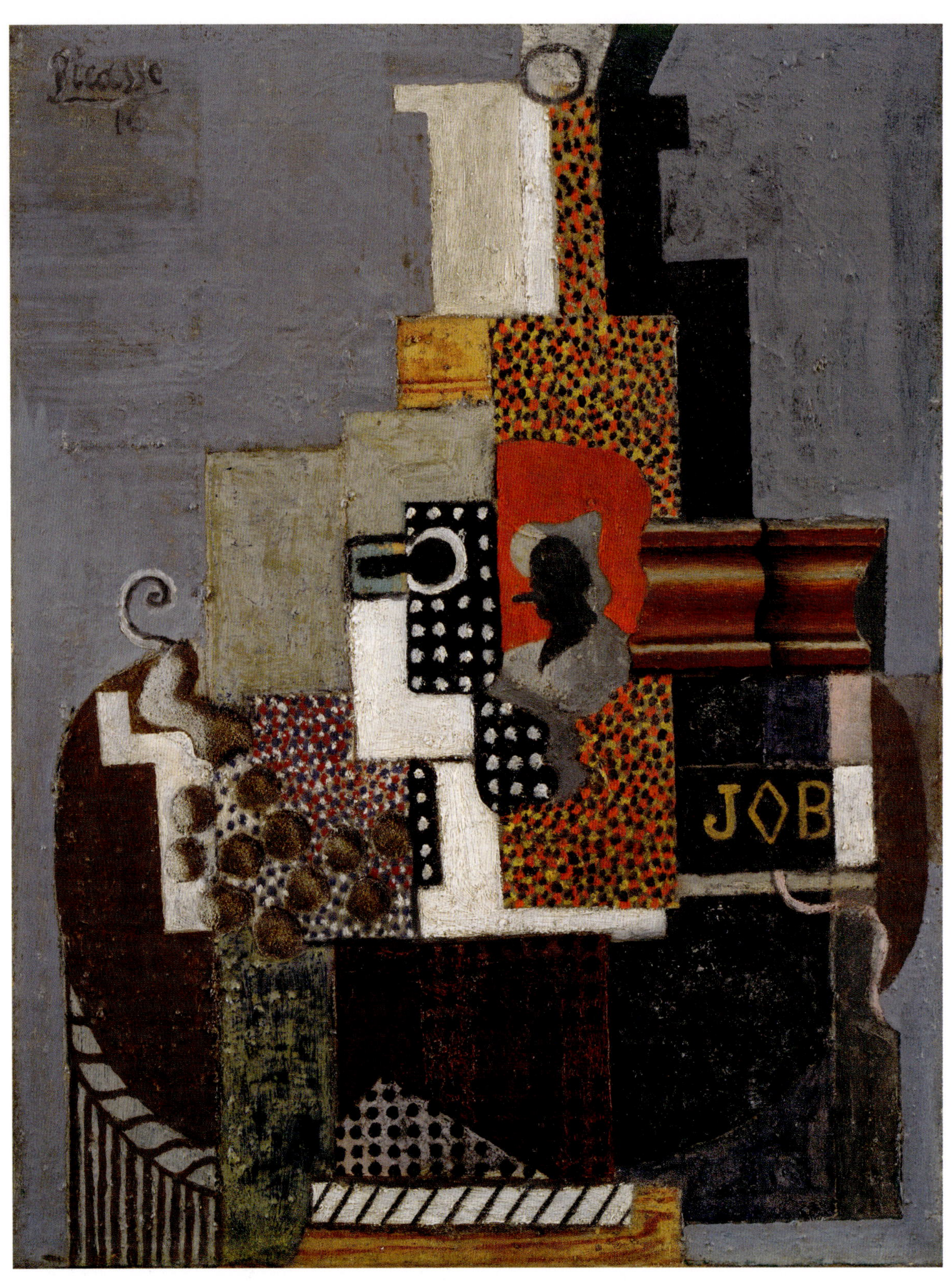

FIG. 50 *Still Life: 'Job'*, 1916

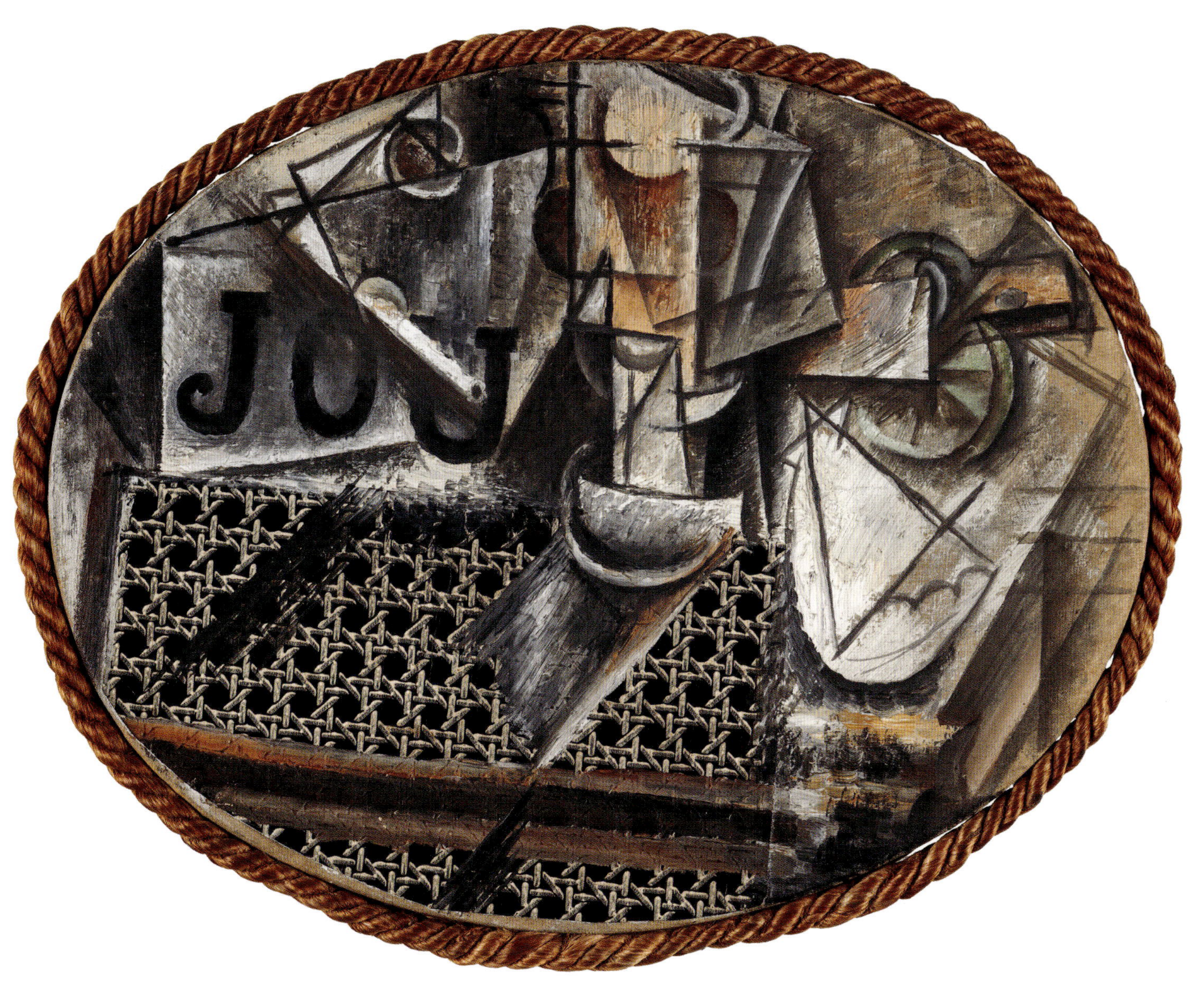

FIG. 51 *Still Life with Chair Caning*, 1912

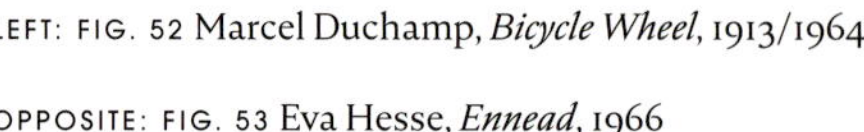
LEFT: FIG. 52 Marcel Duchamp, *Bicycle Wheel*, 1913/1964

OPPOSITE: FIG. 53 Eva Hesse, *Ennead*, 1966

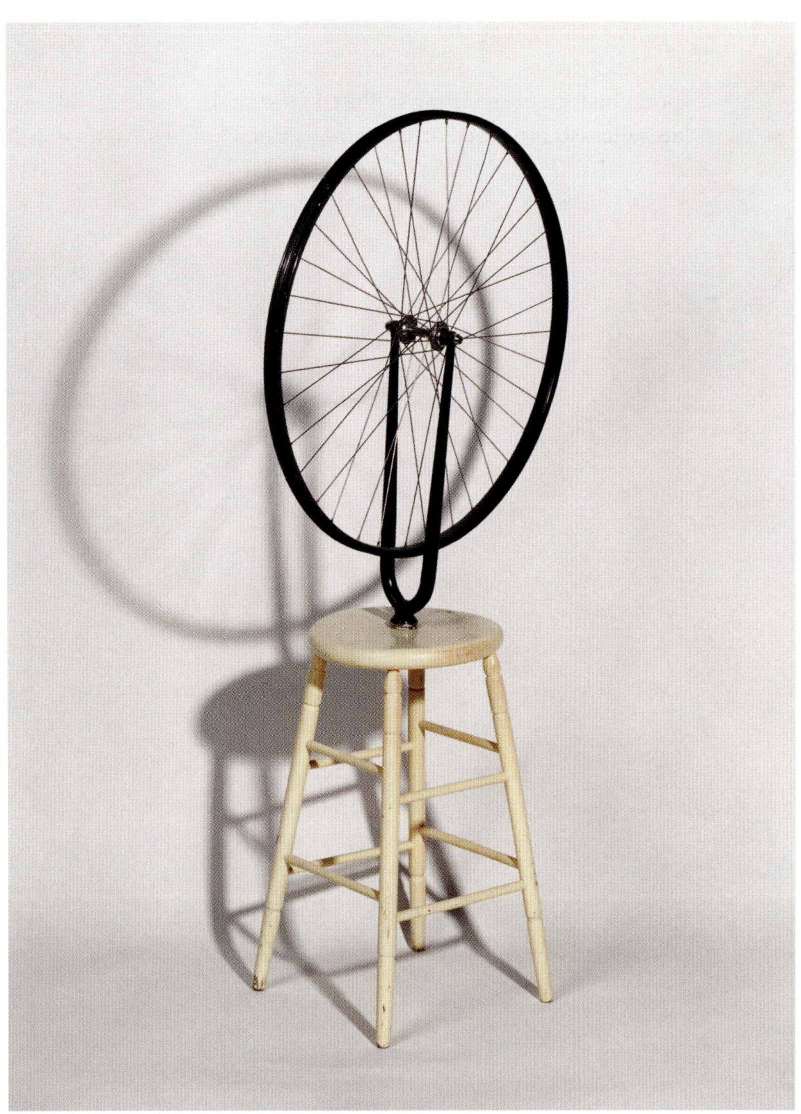

MAGICIAN: TRANSFORMATIONS OF REALITY

Picasso's integration of real objects into his work led the French poet Jean Cocteau, who met the artist in the mid-1910s, to nickname him 'the king of the rag-pickers'. Cocteau compared Picasso to Orpheus, the poet and musician who in ancient mythology charmed wild animals using his seven-stringed lyre:[49]

Picasso is followed by a flock of objects that obey him as the animals obey Orpheus. I would like to depict him in this guise. Each time he enlists an object he causes it to take a shape that makes it unrecognizable in the eyes of habit. Our charmer of objects disguises himself as the king of the rag-pickers and picks up in the streets whatever he finds that can be of use to him. Hardly is the ordinary object in his mitts than it becomes unusual and disconnected from its original meaning to adopt a new one that elevates it into the kingdom of art.[50]

Beginning in 1912, the incorporation of objects became a theme of Picasso's art and can be classified according to two intentions. The first consists in using them while maintaining their original function. This is what he did with scraps of wallpaper or musical scores that he integrated into his earliest collages (FIG. 54). This same spirit can be found in his work as a sculptor, especially in his *Glass of Absinthe* (1914; FIG. 55) where he integrates an authentic absinthe spoon instead of sculpting it like the rest of the piece. A few years later Picasso produced other compositions made of small objects arranged on the back of the frame, creating different kinds of sketches or fantastic dioramas (FIGS 56–58). The artist covered them with sand to make the different materials uniform, but perhaps also with the goal of giving them a more enigmatic dimension. This unusual series of works belongs to the artistic explorations that Picasso conducted as of the mid-1920s, alongside the emergence of the Surrealist movement. Although Picasso was not officially part of the group, he shared with them an interest in psychoanalysis and the unconscious. The paintings he produced at this time present bodies resembling ectoplasms (*Figure and Profile*, 1928; FIG. 59) or which are contorted, as in the melting anatomy of *Large Nude in a Red Armchair* (1929; FIG. 60) or the impossible pose in *The Acrobat* (1930; FIG. 61).[51]

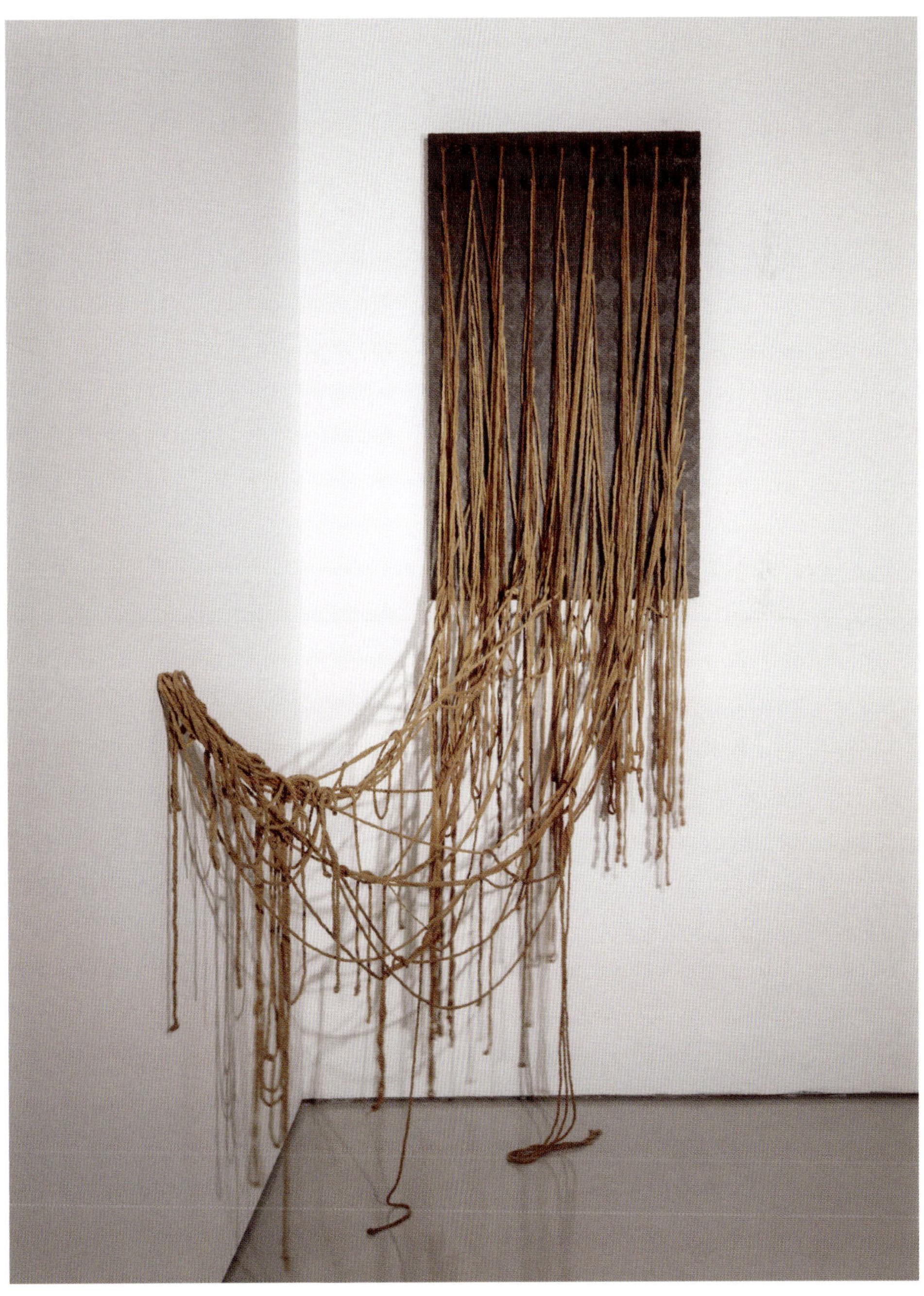

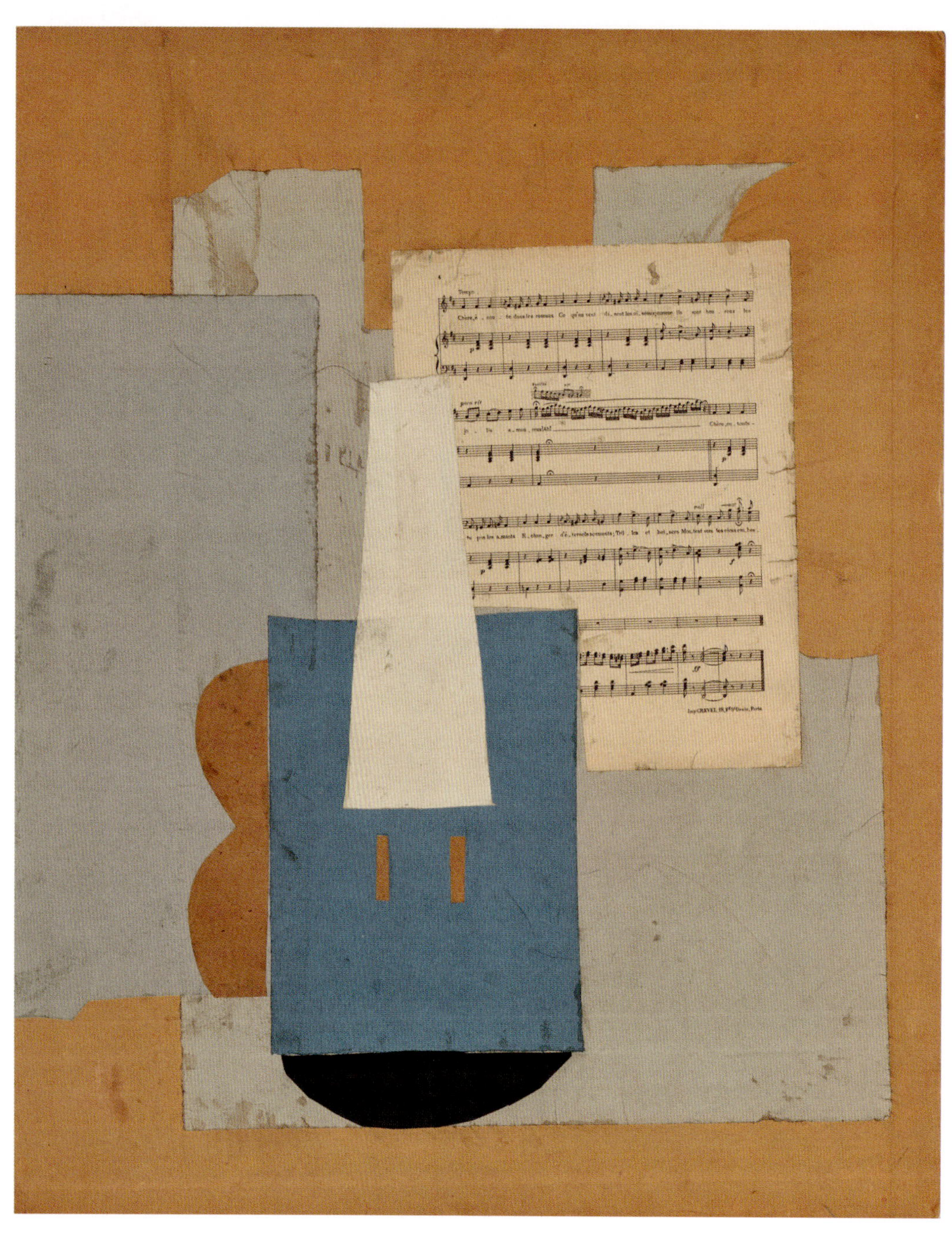

ABOVE: FIG. 54 *Violin and Music Sheet*, 1912

OPPOSITE: FIG. 55 *Glass of Absinthe*, 1914

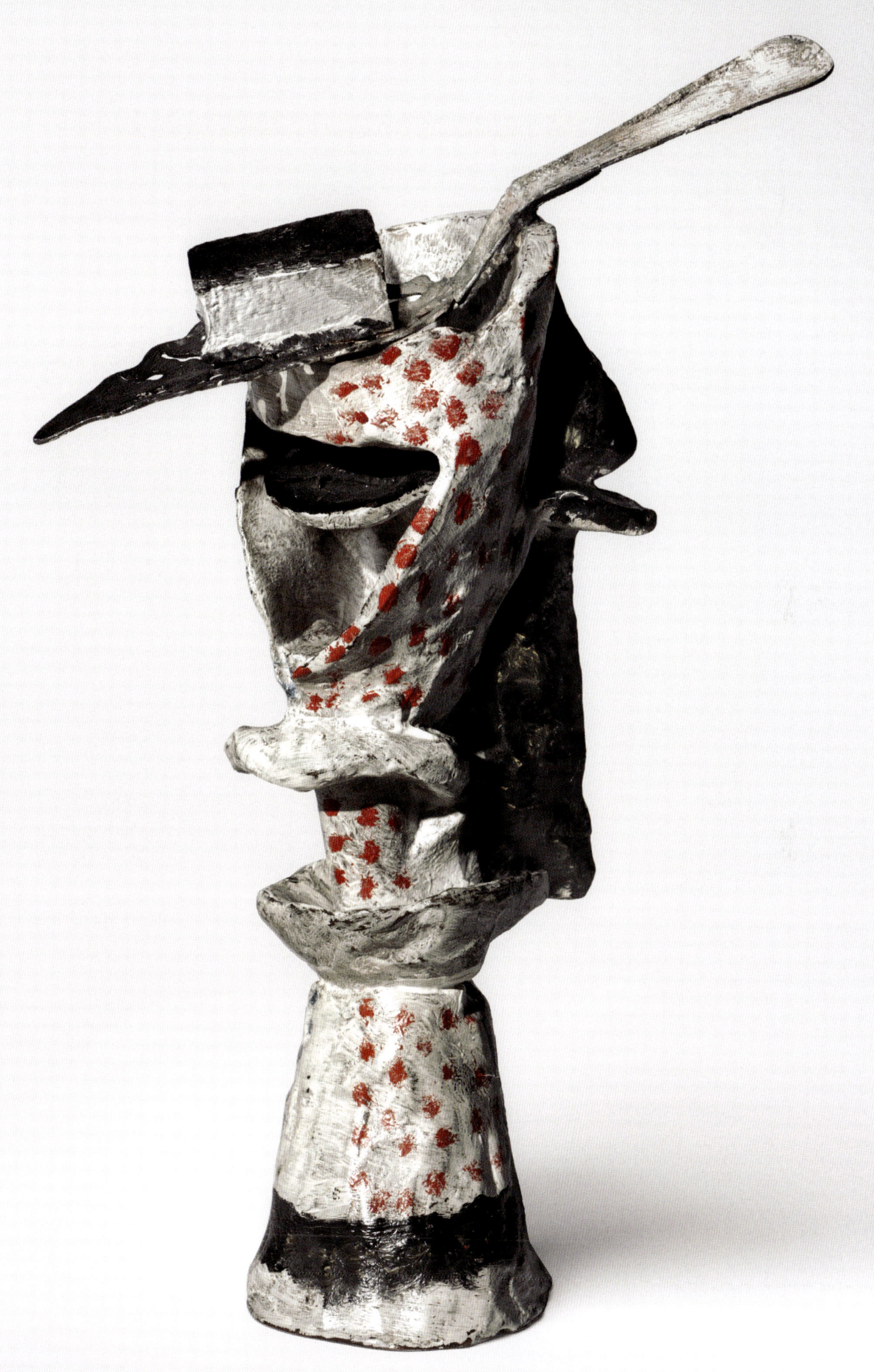

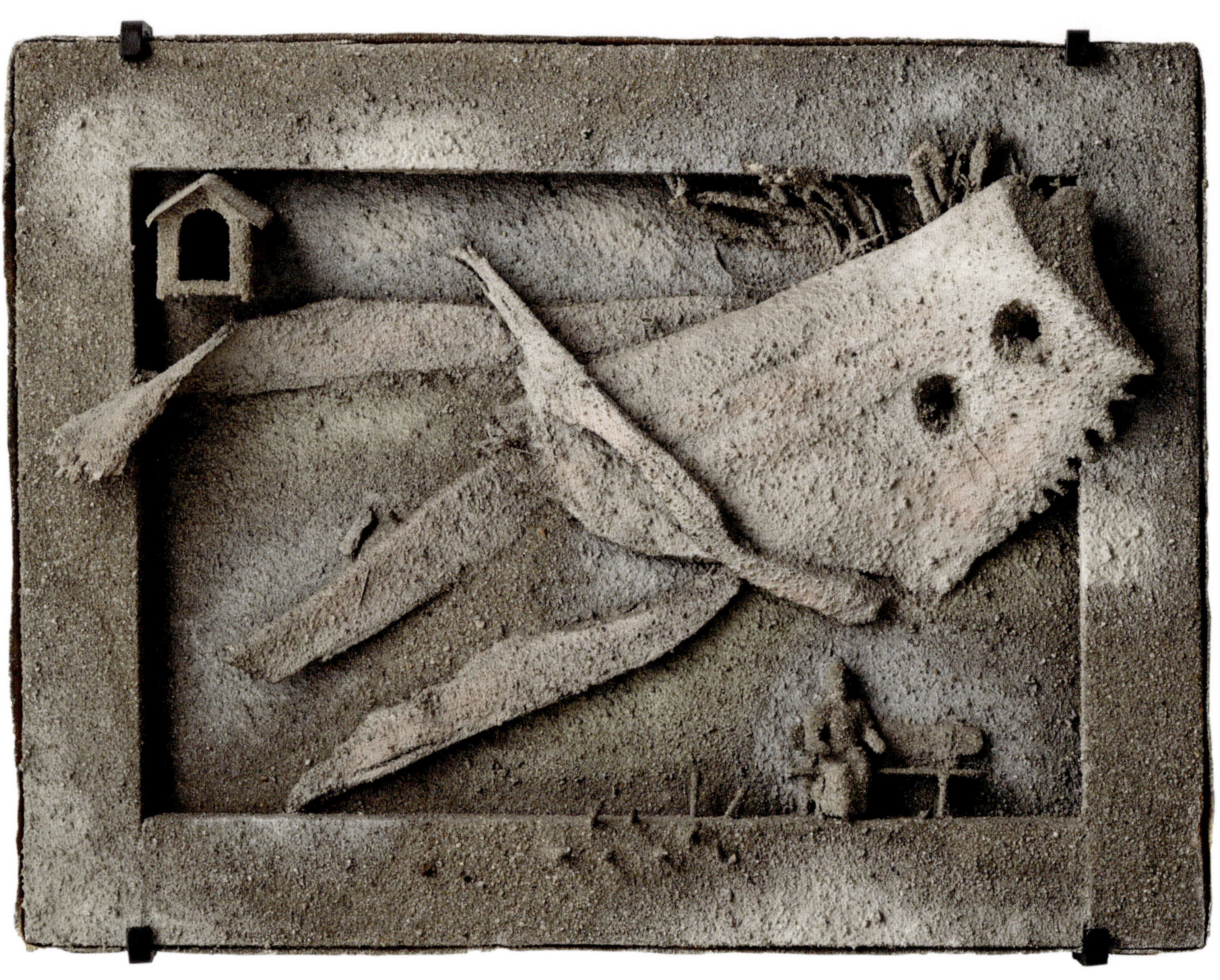

FIG. 56 *Object with Palm Leaf*, 1930

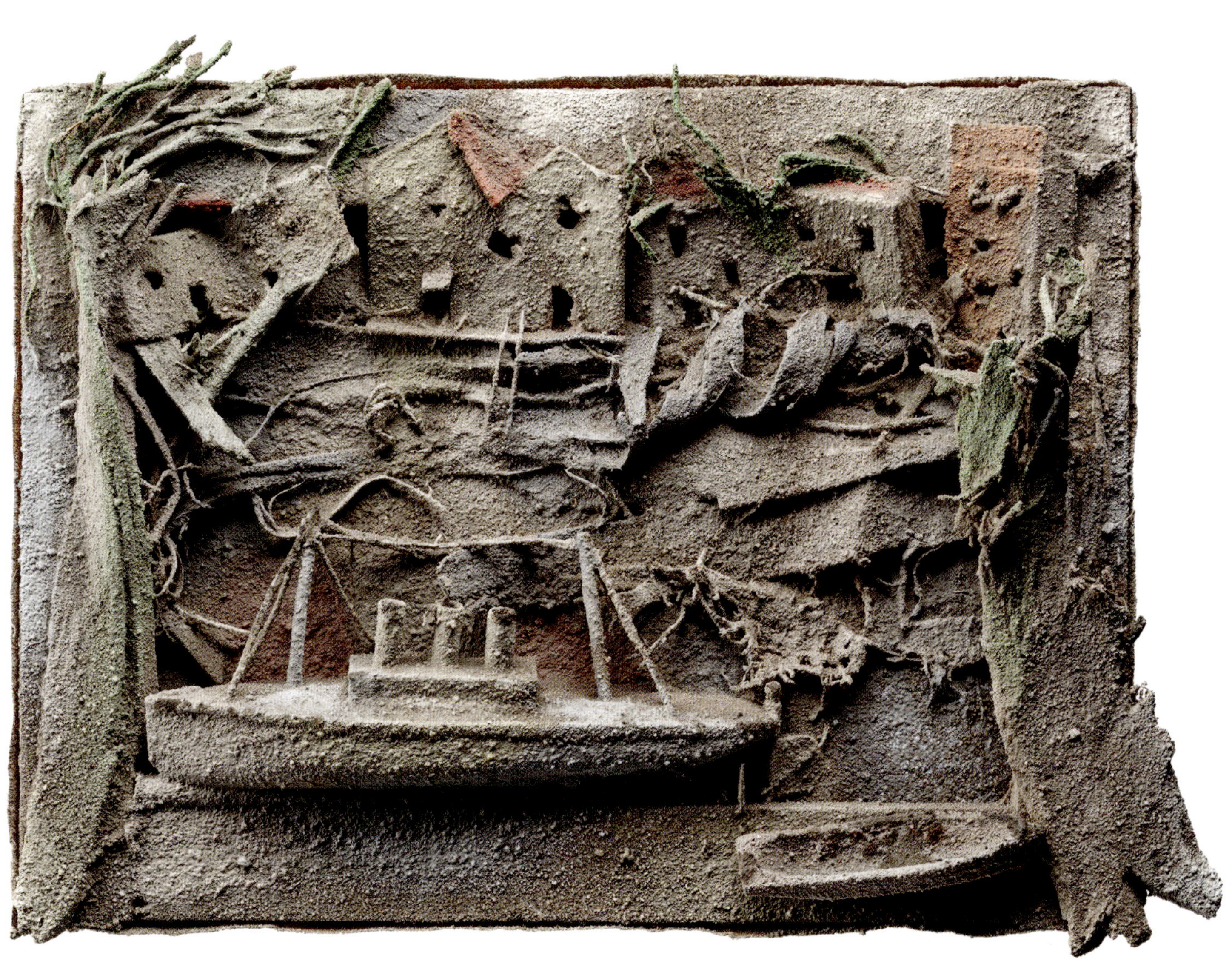

FIG. 57 *Landscape with Boats*, 1930

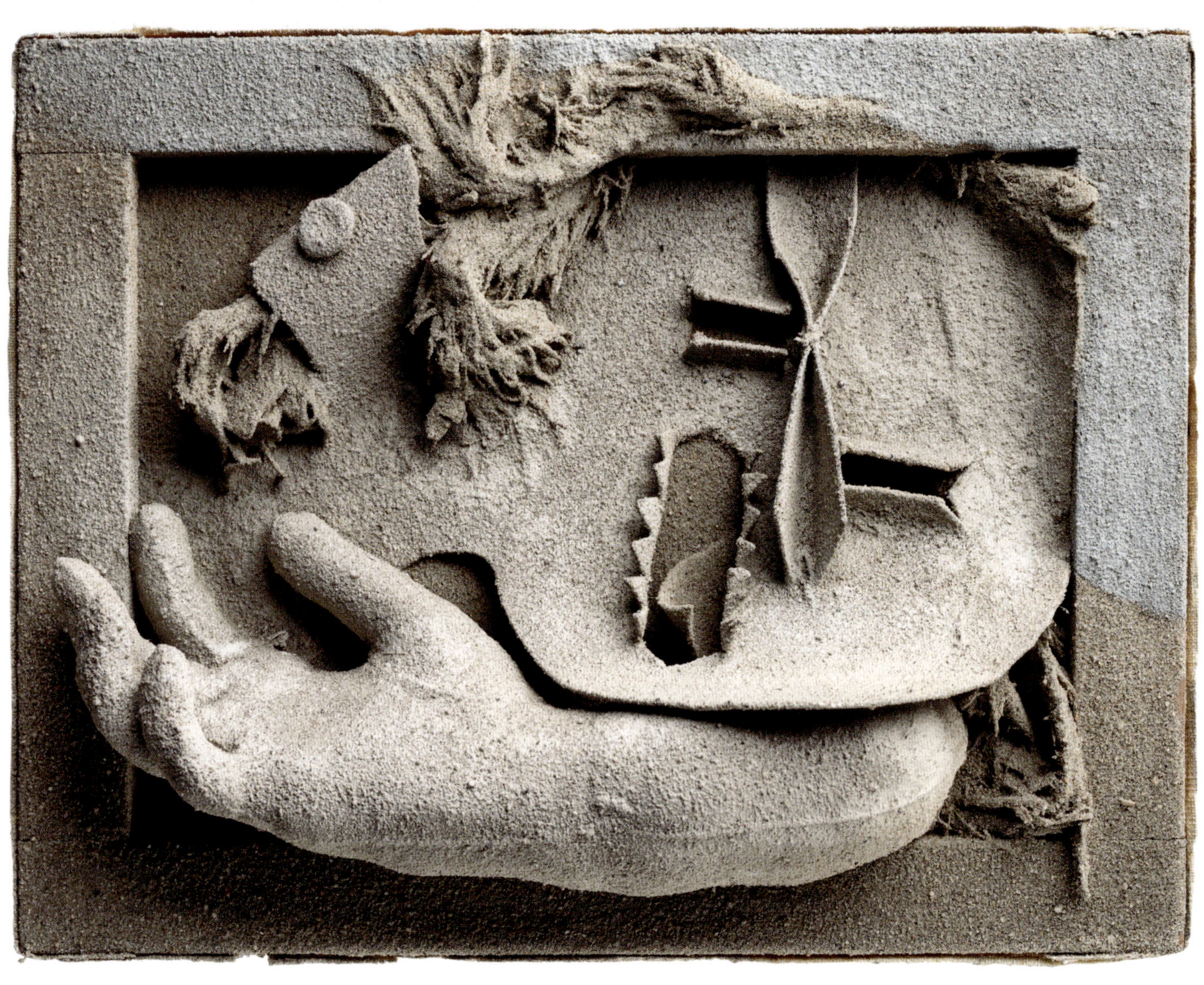

FIG. 58 *Composition with Glove*, 1930

FIG. 59 *Figure and Profile*, 1928

The second intention behind Picasso's use of found objects was to subvert their original function and give them other meanings, a famous example being his *Head of a Bull* (1942; FIG. 63), produced by combining the saddle and handlebars of a bicycle. These subversions began in the Cubist period, as with *Bottle of Bass, Glass, and Newspaper* (1914; FIG. 62), a box of powdered milk transformed into a still life through folding and découpage. At the base of this small sculpture the printed words '*compagnie française du lait*' (French milk company) reveal the former identity of the object. The practice became more frequent starting in the mid-1920s, with Picasso pinning to the canvas ropes, a mop, and nails to create *Guitar* (1926; FIG. 64). A few years later he began a collaboration with the sculptor Julio González, also a Spaniard. As González knew how to weld and work with iron, Picasso was able to produce more ambitious composite sculptures, such as *Head of a Woman* (1929–1930; FIG. 66), made by combining two colanders to suggest a skull. As with the Surrealists during the same period, Picasso's practice was partly

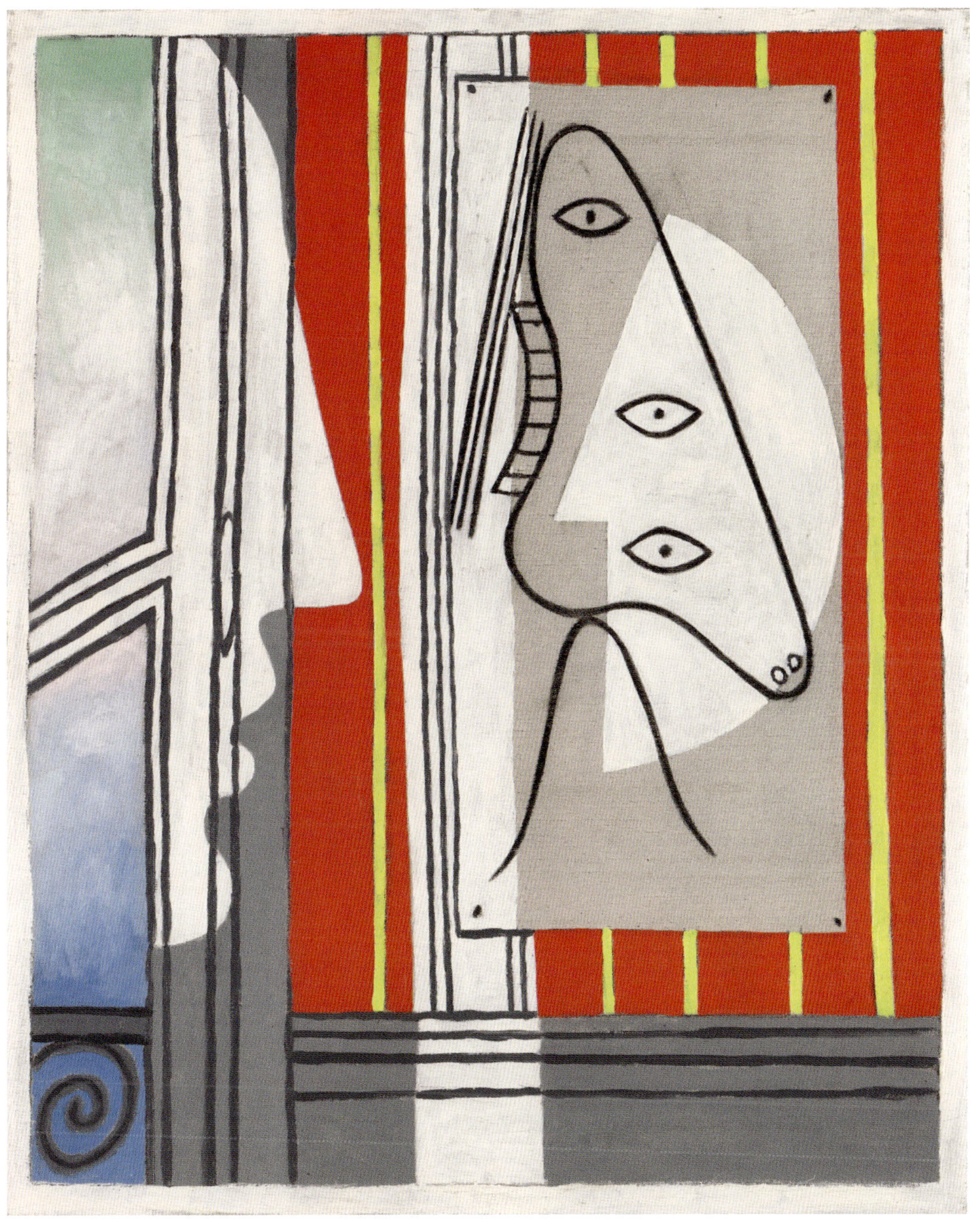

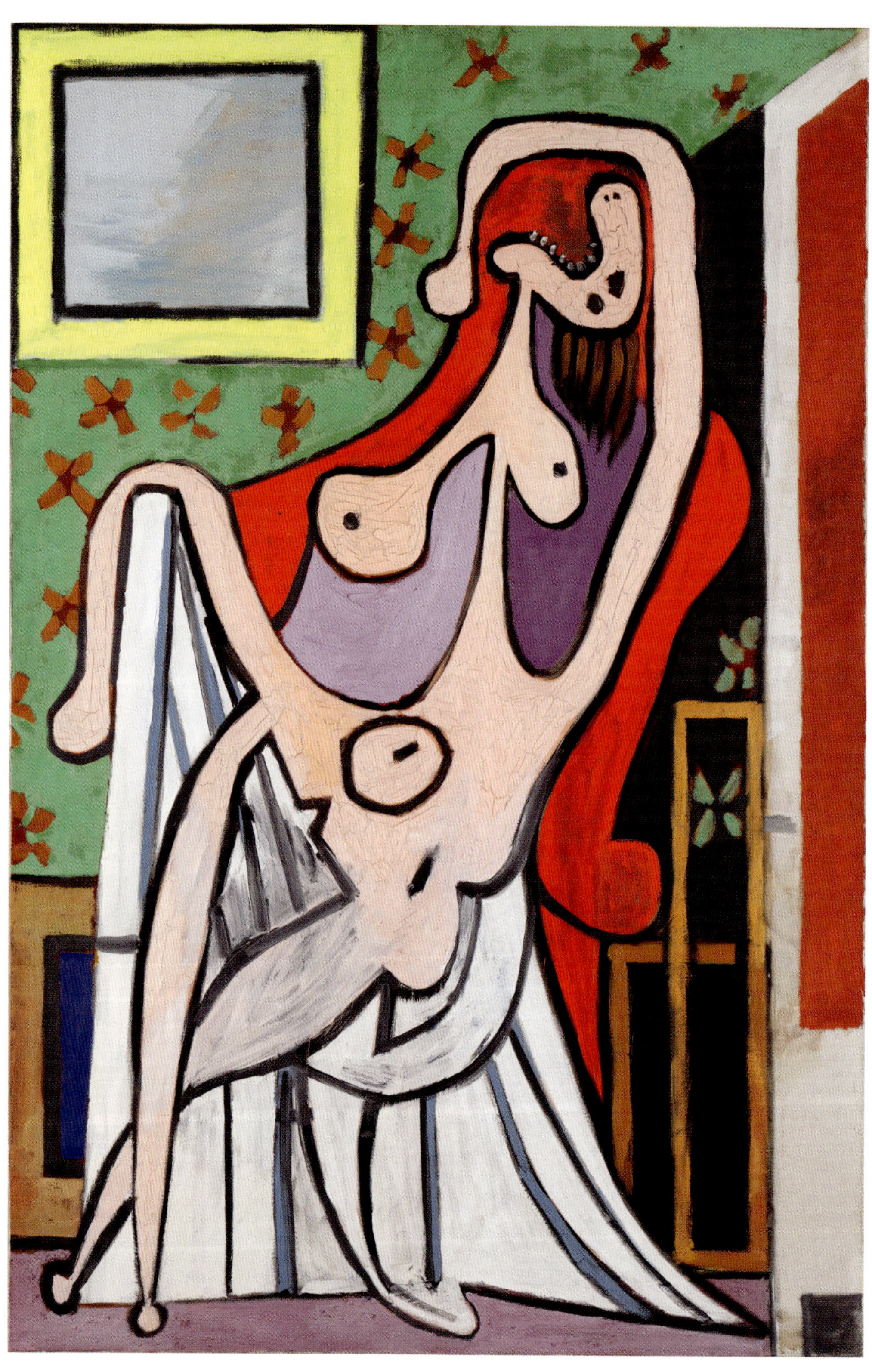

FIG. 60 *Large Nude in a Red Armchair*, 1929

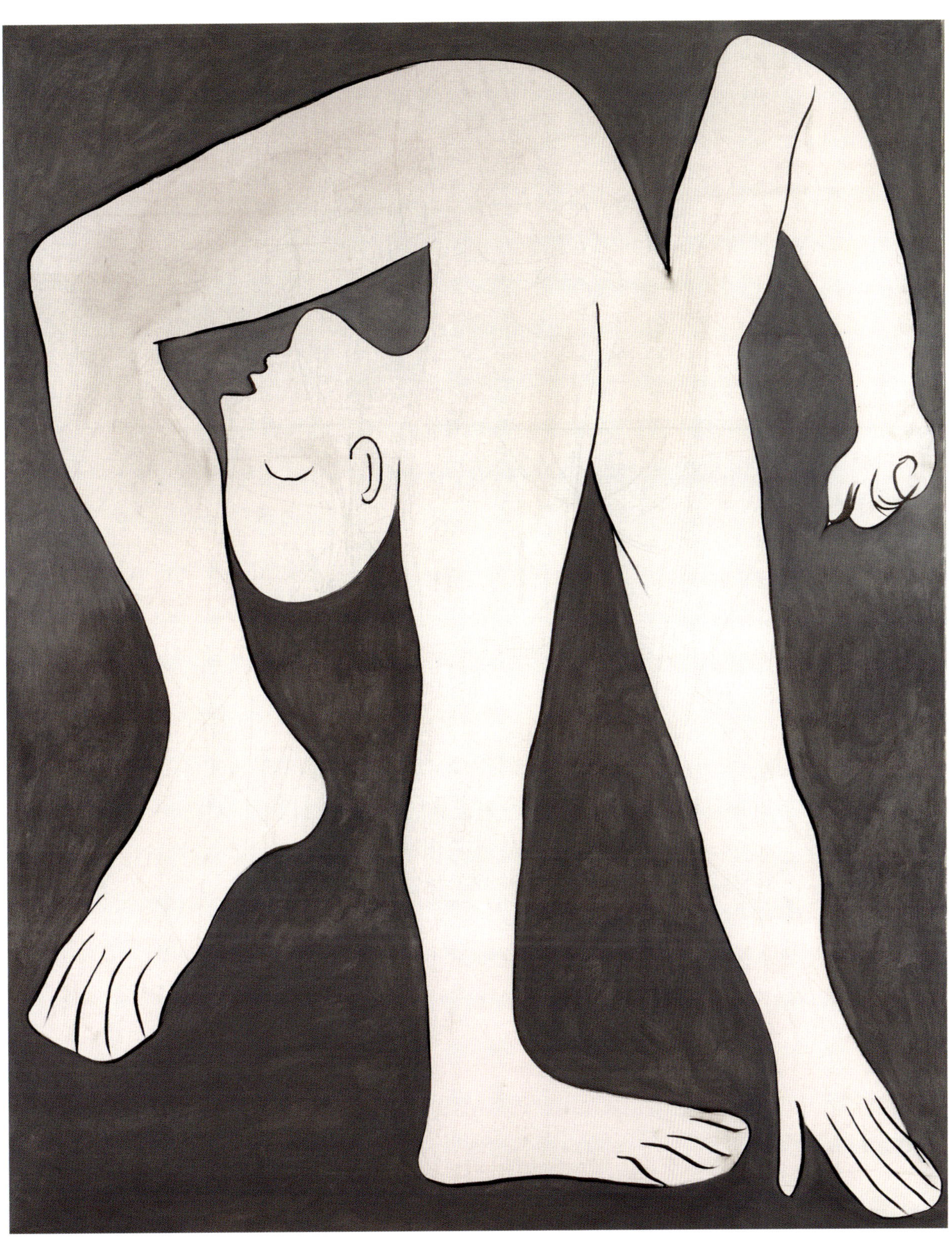

FIG. 61 *The Acrobat*, 1930

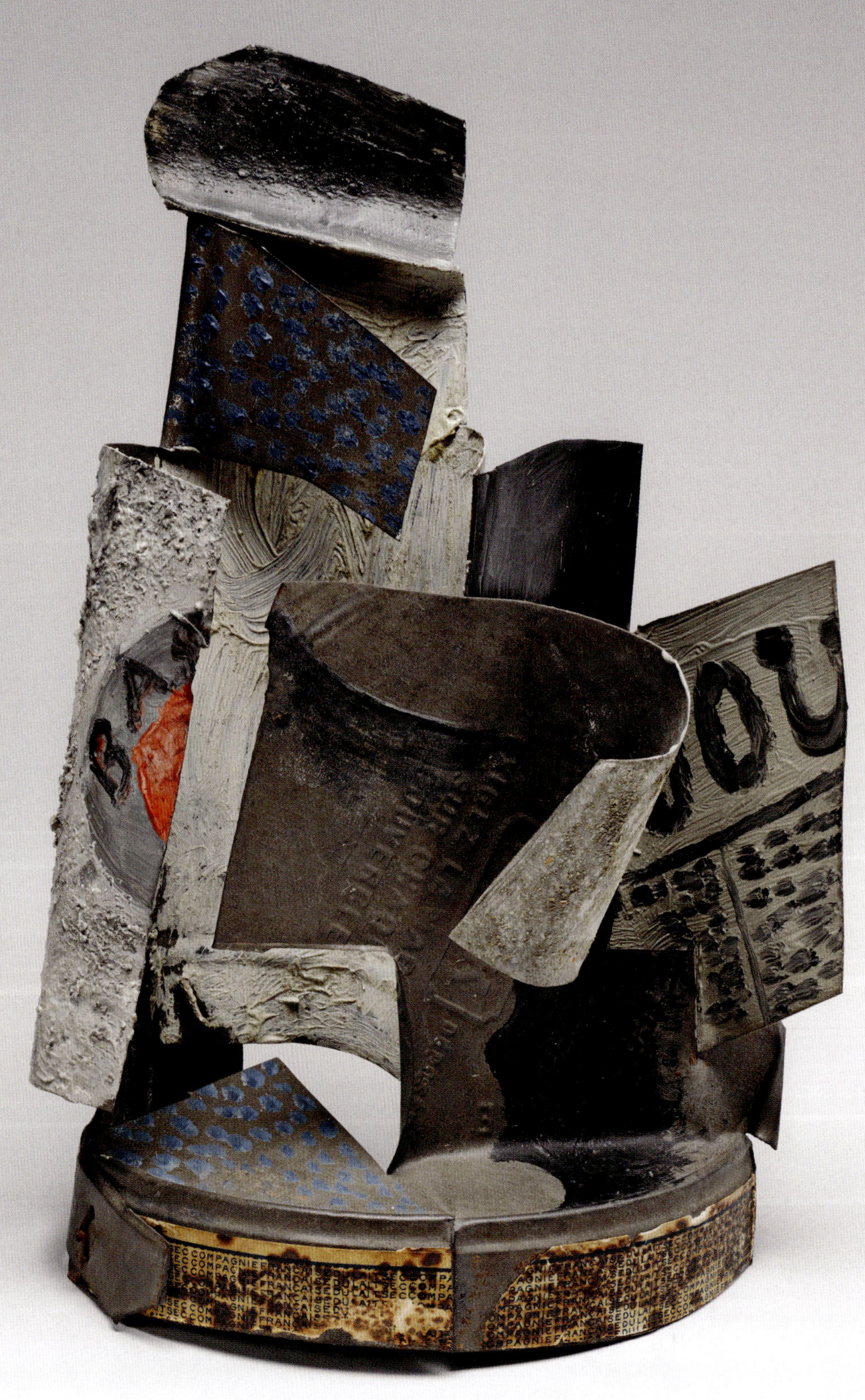
BA
OU

OPPOSITE: FIG. 62 *Bottle of Bass, Glass, and Newspaper*, 1914

BELOW: FIG. 63 *Head of a Bull*, 1942

RIGHT: FIG. 64 *Guitar*, 1926

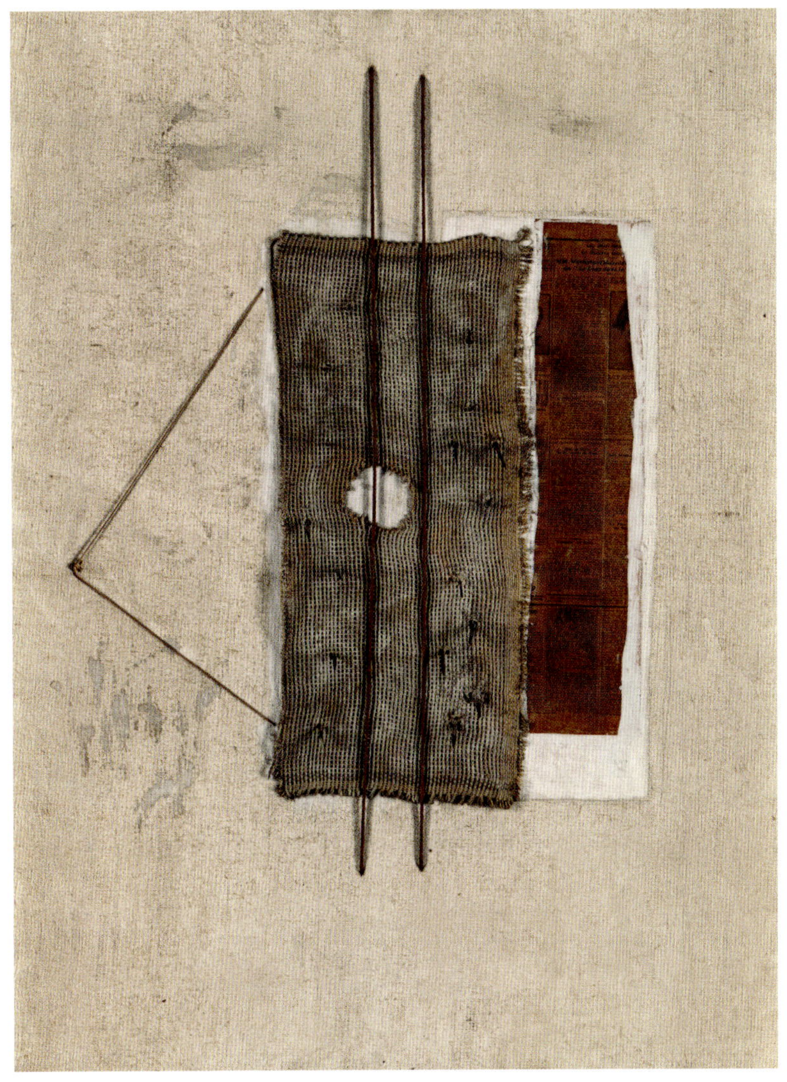

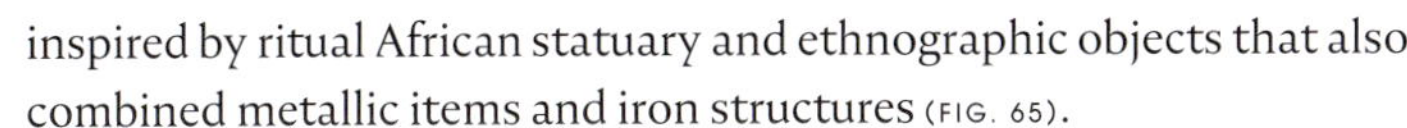

inspired by ritual African statuary and ethnographic objects that also combined metallic items and iron structures (FIG. 65).

The most prolific period of Picasso's sculpture-assemblages phase began in the 1950s, when the artist definitively left Paris to settle in south-eastern France, first in Vallauris in 1948, and then in Cannes in 1955. This is the time of what Werner Spies, who produced the catalogue raisonné of the artist's three-dimensional works, called 'the encyclopaedic sculptures', which combine both intentions discussed above. These are large-scale works in which Picasso incorporated heterogeneous elements—found objects, imprints of materials, and sculpted shapes—which he assembled in plaster on frameworks before producing versions in bronze. As with the use of sand in his relief-paintings of 1930, the bronze lent a uniform appearance to the materials. Thus, the six figures in *The Bathers* (1956; FIG. 164) were originally made from planks of wood, painting frames, bedposts, and broom handles. In *Little Girl Jumping Rope* (1950; FIG. 67), Picasso uses a wicker basket to form the girl's torso and a cake mould to represent the flower at her feet, on which are a real pair of shoes. *The Woman with the Stroller* (1950; FIG. 68) features an actual pram and a metallic stove plate to indicate the upper part of the woman's body. The use of ceramics is one of the constants of this series of 'encyclopaedic sculptures', the child being made of terracotta handles and pots while the mother's skirt is made of a fragment of a kiln. At this time the Spanish artist was a frequent visitor to the Madoura

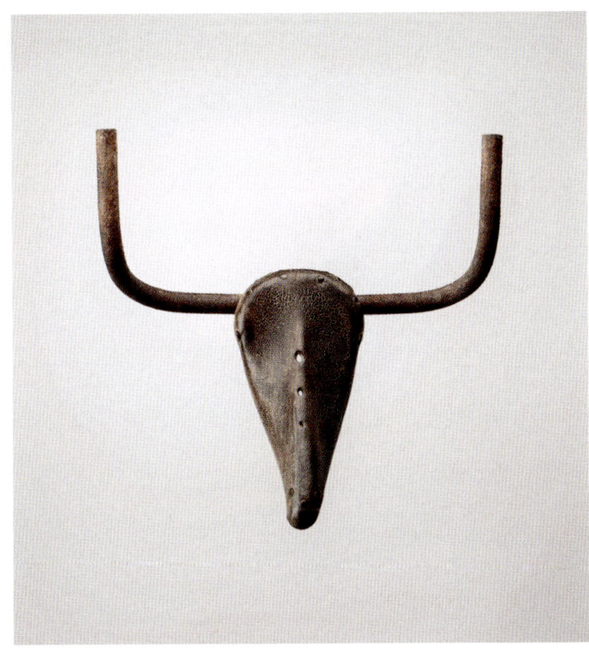

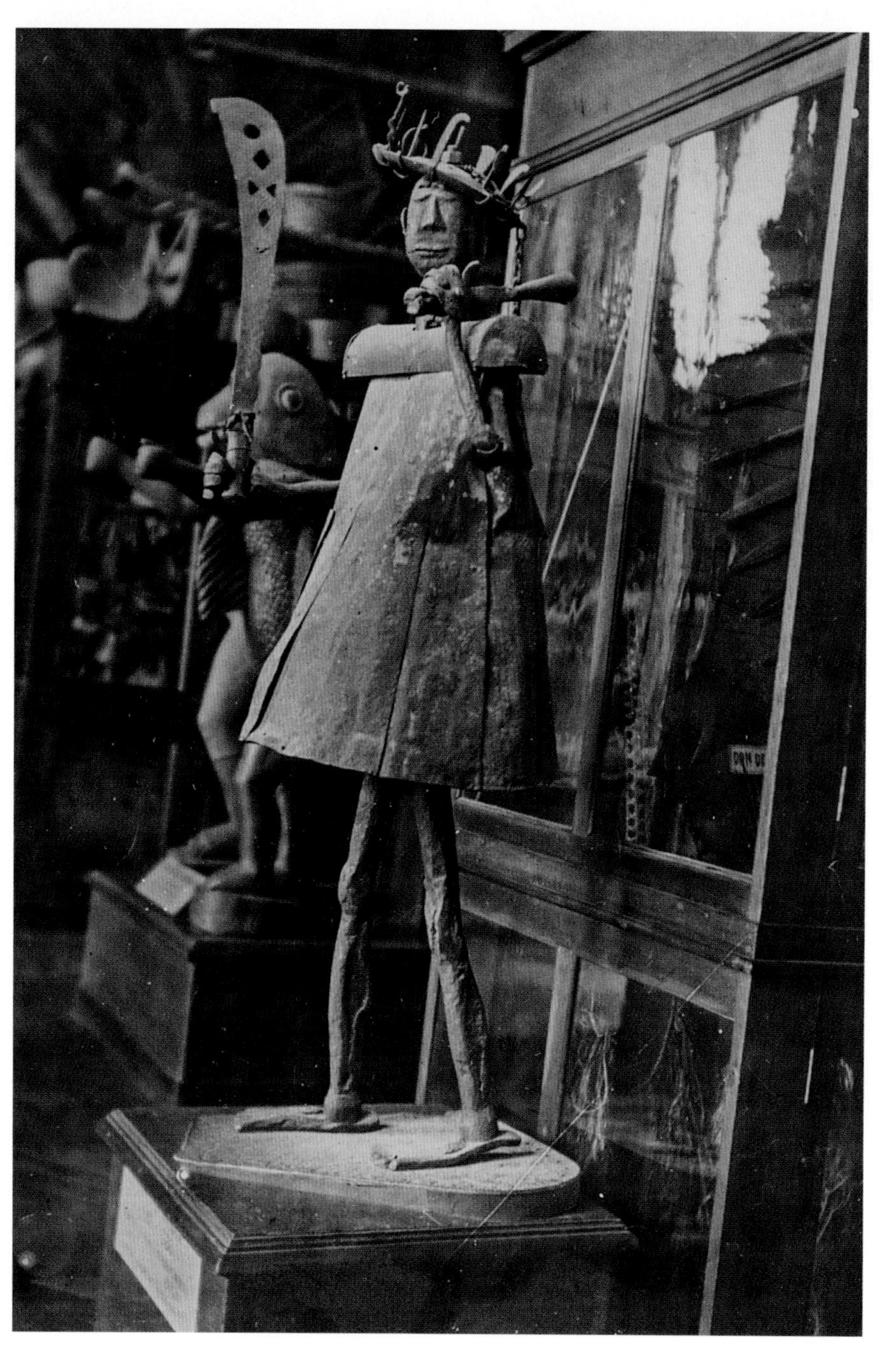

ABOVE: FIG. 65 Iron statue of Ebo, god of war, at the Musée d'Ethnographie du Trocadéro, 1895

OPPOSITE: FIG. 66 *Head of a Woman*, 1929–1930

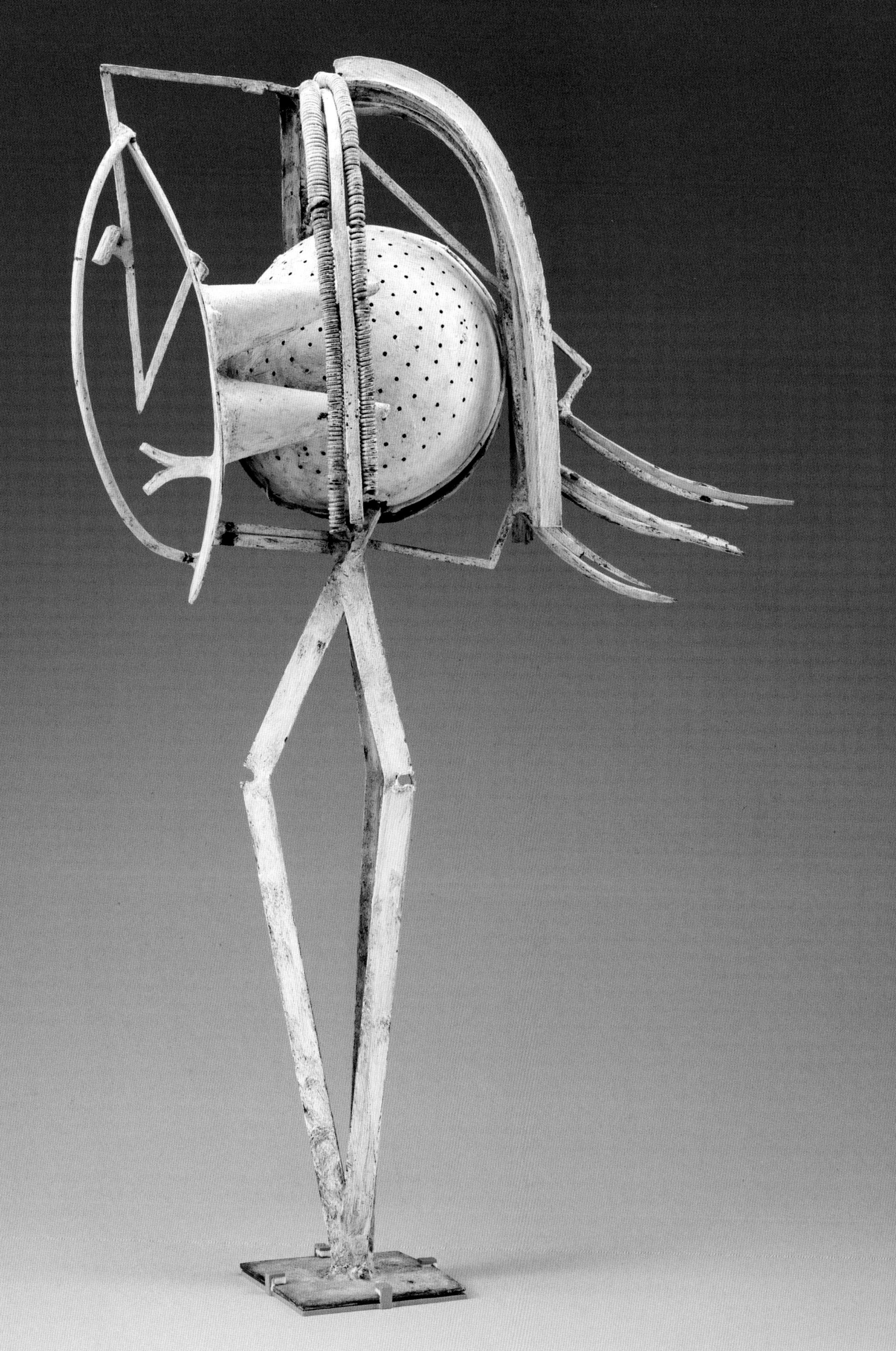

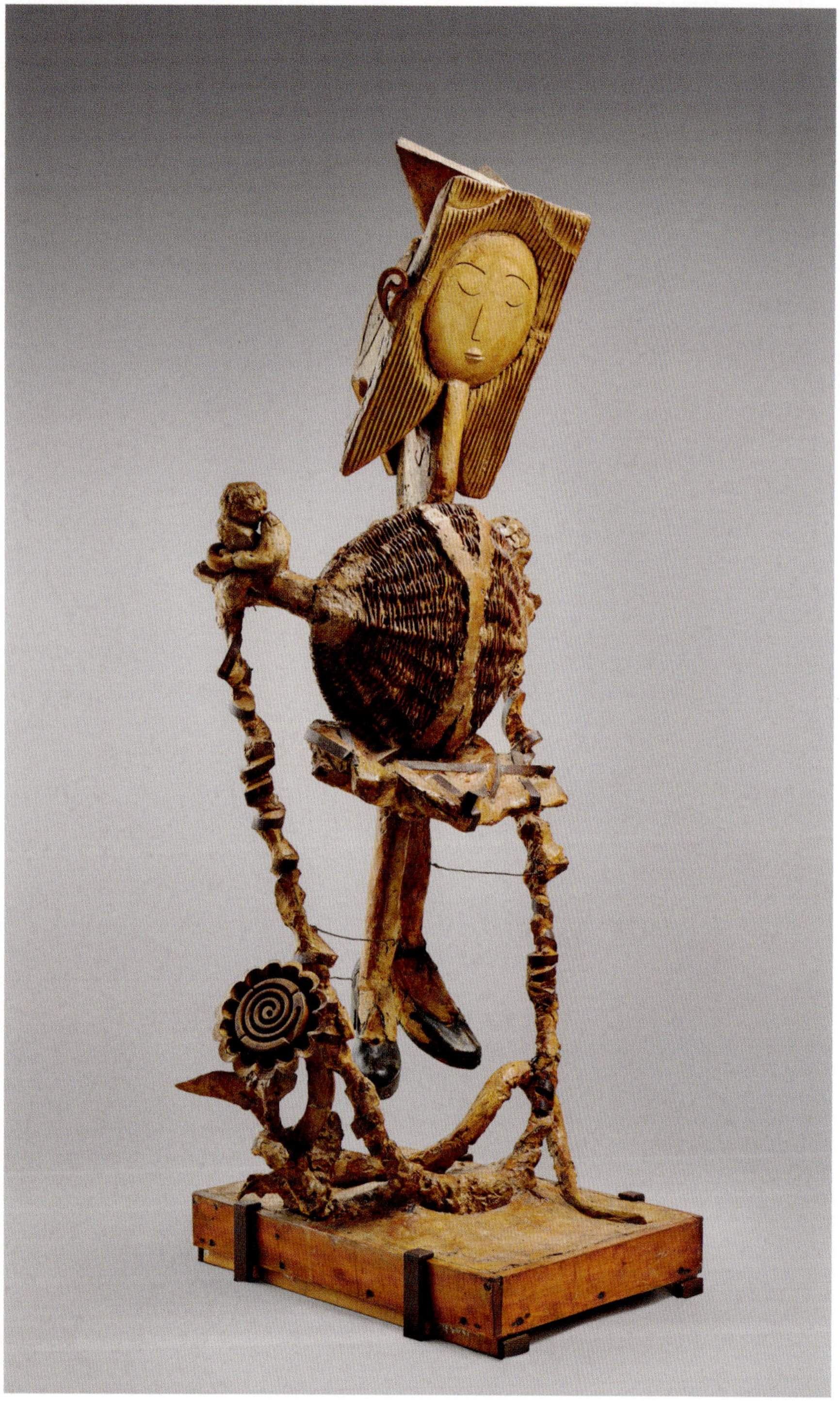

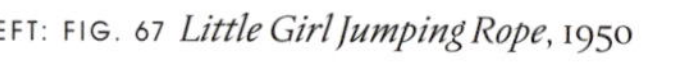

LEFT: FIG. 67 *Little Girl Jumping Rope*, 1950

OPPOSITE: FIG. 68 *The Woman with the Stroller*, 1950

ceramics workshop, founded by the couple Suzanne Douly and Georges Ramié. Picasso met them in 1946, marking the beginning of a fruitful collaboration that allowed him to explore all the artistic possibilities offered by this material. He produced thousands of pieces, playing with dishes, plates (FIG. 69), and bricks, giving shape with a touch of humour to zoomorphic figures (FIG. 70) or parodying Greco-Roman antiquity (FIG. 73). Some of his sculpture-assemblages have close connections to the artistic explorations in which he engaged in the pictorial realm. This is the case with the pair of works both called *Goat Skull, Bottle, and Candle* (1952 and 1951–1953; FIGS 71 AND 72), for which the artist used the same iconography, with the two artistic practices—painting and sculpture—each having an influence on the other.

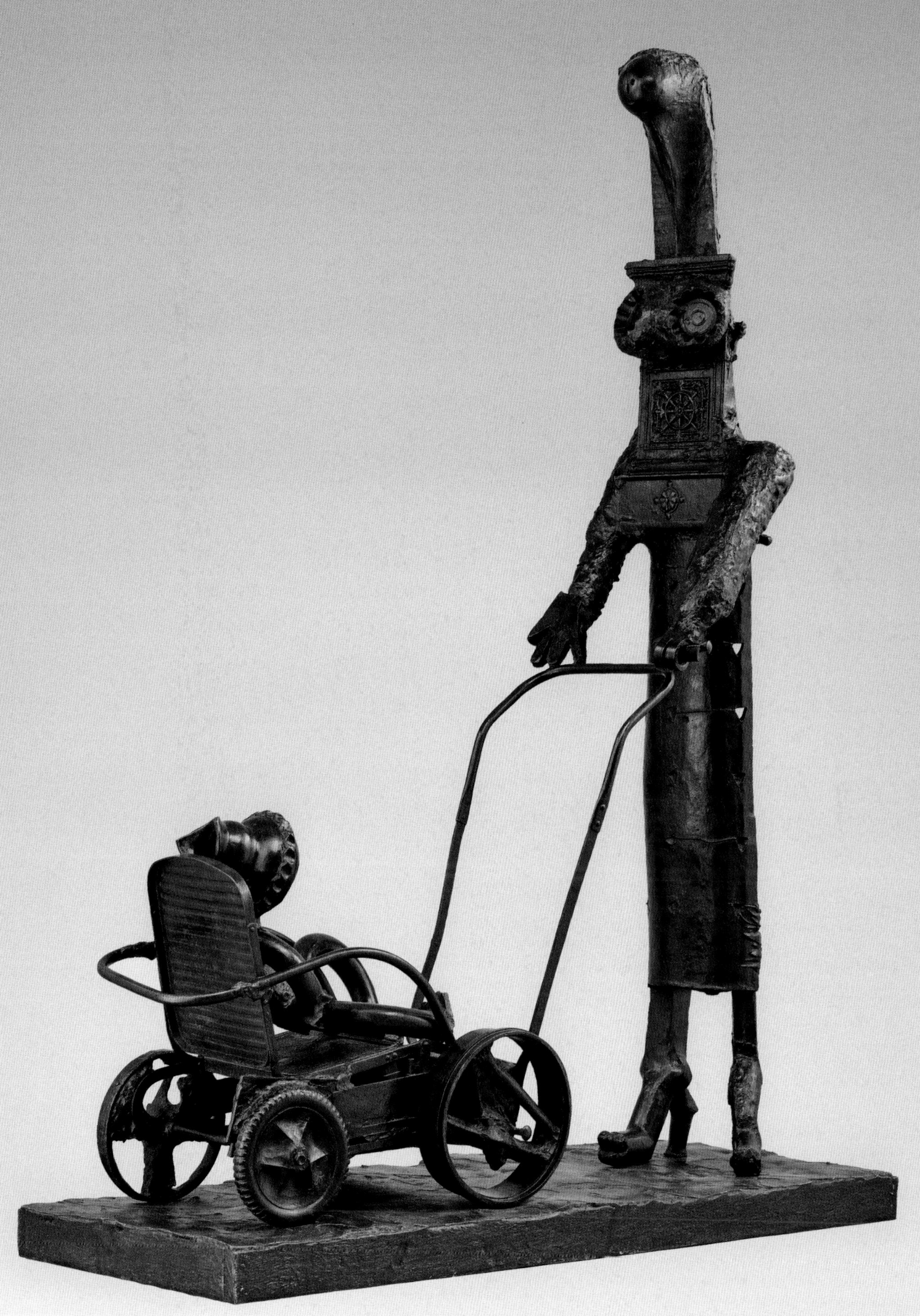

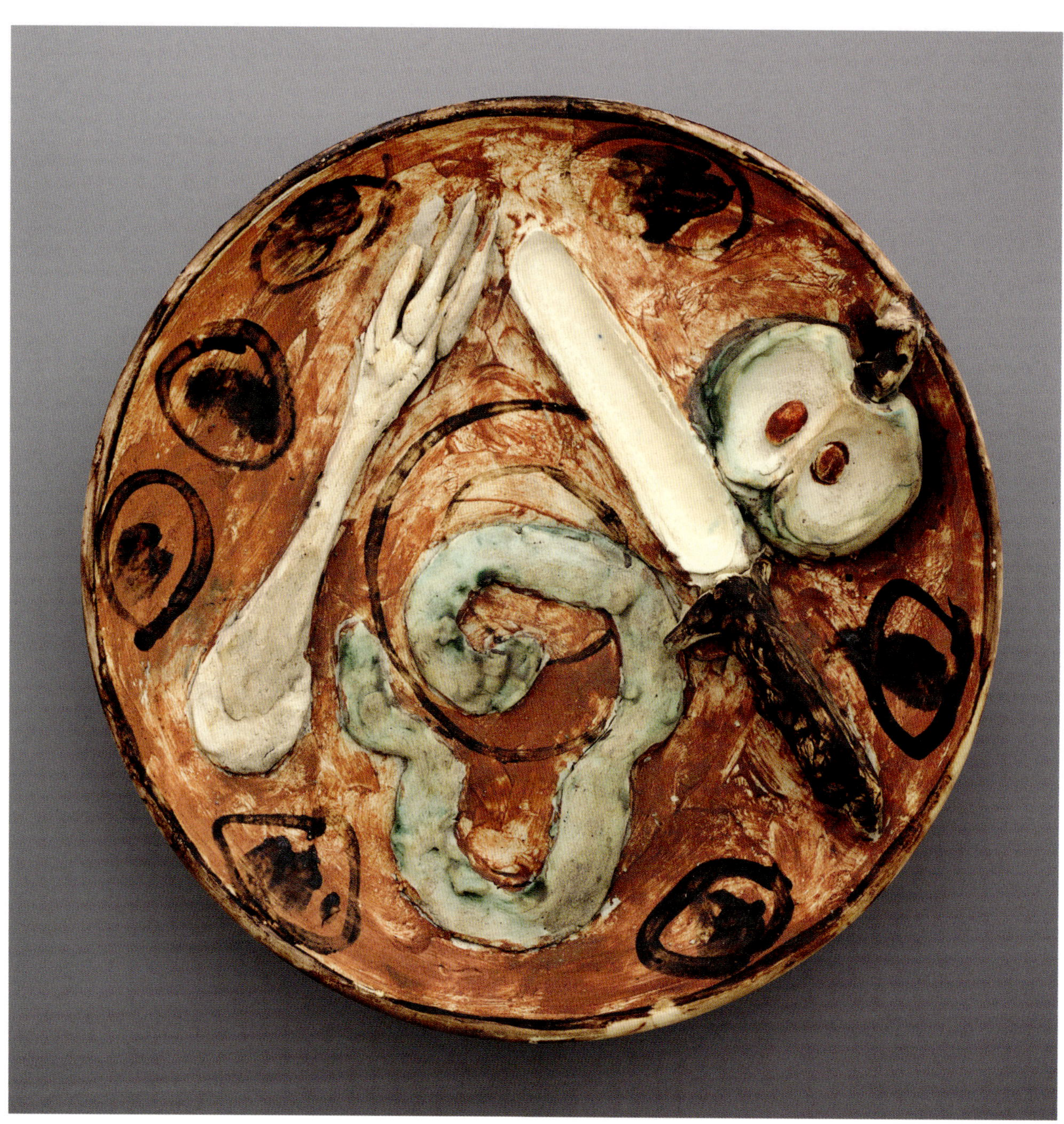

FIG. 69 *Plate with a Knife, Fork, Apple Cut in Two and Peel*, 1947–1948

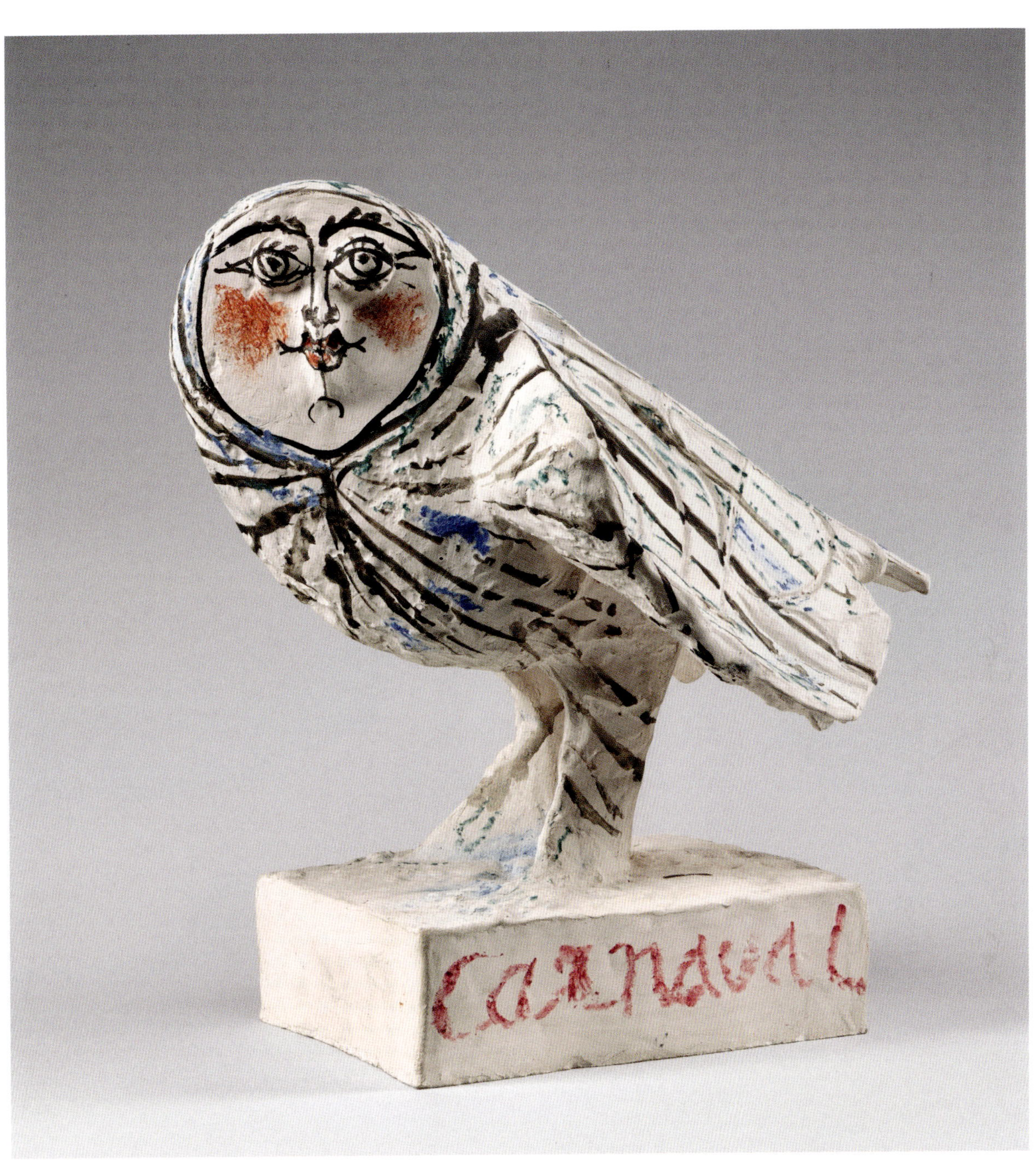

FIG. 70 *Owl with a Woman's Head*, 1951–1953

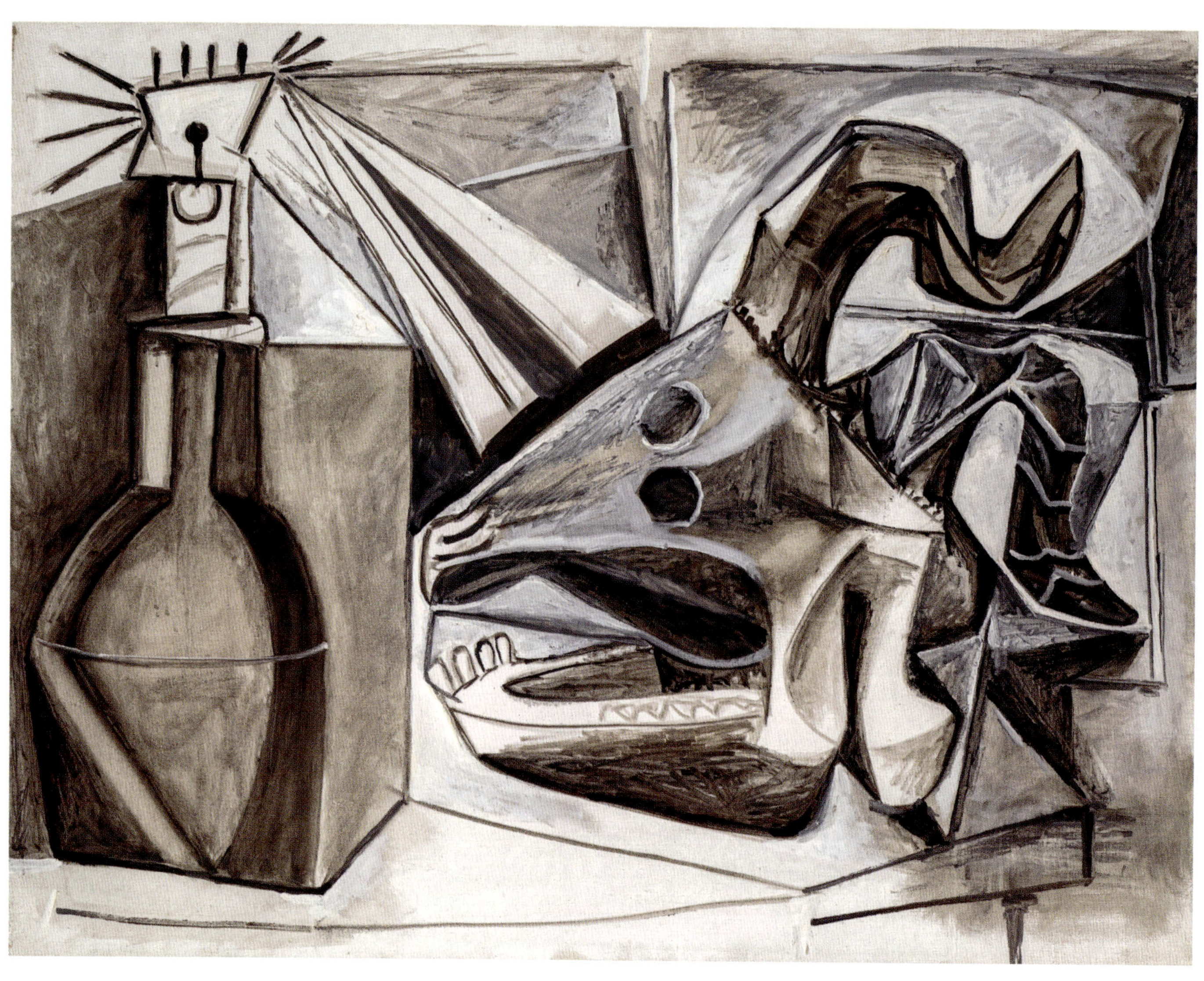

FIG. 71 *Goat Skull, Bottle, and Candle*, 1952

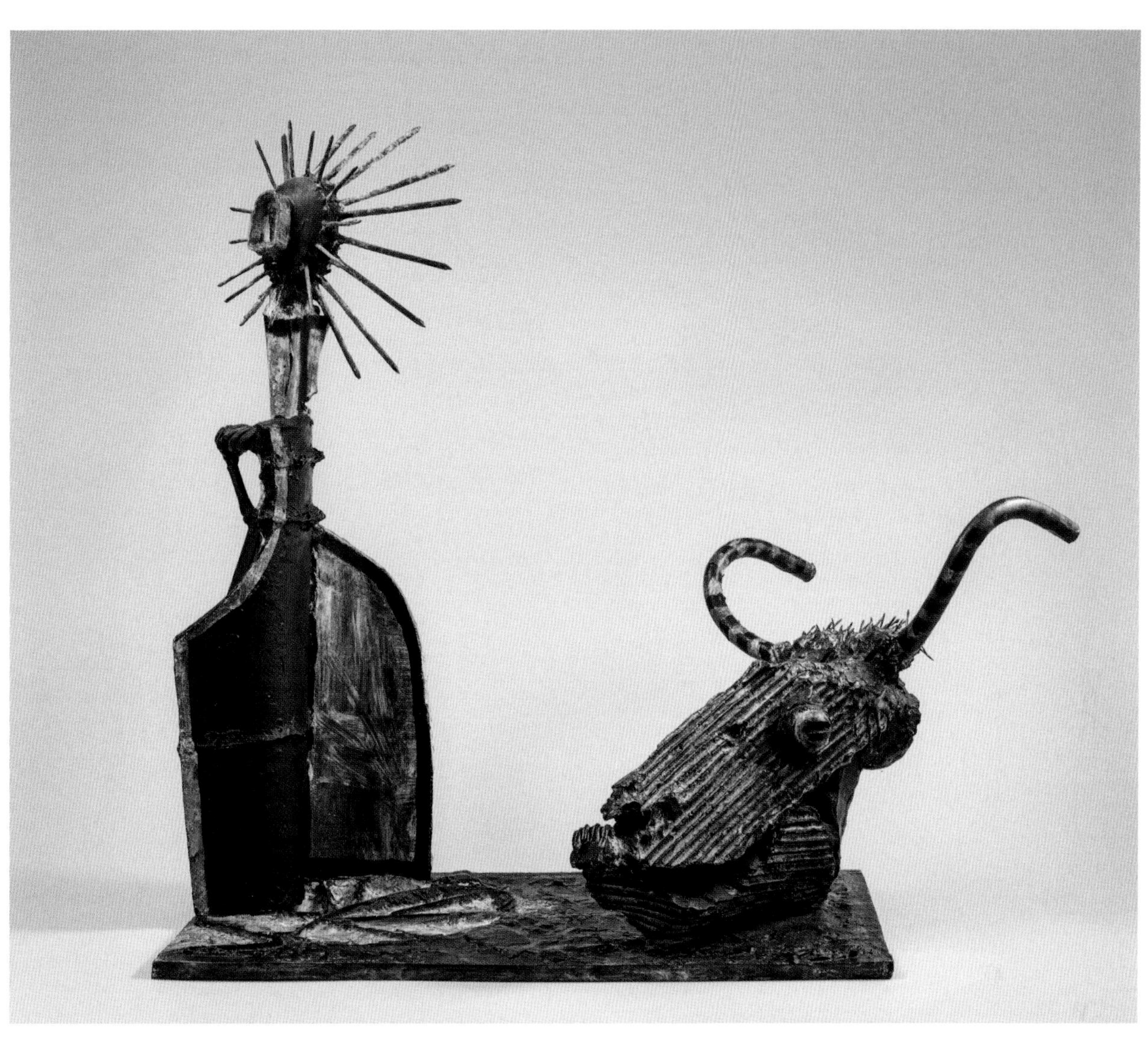

FIG. 72 *Goat Skull, Bottle, and Candle*, 1951–1953

'EVIL MAGICIAN': TRANSGRESSION OF BEAUTY

To complete this portrait of Picasso the magician, who humorously transforms his environment, let us borrow once more the words of Cocteau:

His eye picks up the slightest spectacle. And if you attentively observe his work, you will always recognise the neighbourhood where he lived when he painted one or another canvas, for you find the elements that inattentive people do not notice: chalk drawings on the sidewalks, shop windows, posters, lamps splashed with plaster, garbage can treasures.[52]

We must take into consideration Picasso's subversive intention to introduce into his work the incongruity of the everyday, which he sometimes pushed to the point of bad taste. This is the motivation behind his monumental painting *The Sideboard at Vauvenargues* (1959–1960; FIG. 74), in the centre of which he depicts an ostentatiously decorated sideboard that he owned, about which he declared: 'Some Henri II junk, nothing more. But how beautiful it is!'[53] The transgression in which Picasso engaged in his art thus goes beyond the simple transformation of reality to radically shift academic aesthetic conventions. During an interview with Christian Zervos, the artist stated: 'Art is not the application of a canon of beauty but what the instinct and the brain can conceive beyond any canon.'[54]

The creation of *Les Demoiselles d'Avignon* was surely one of the first stages in this questioning of official canons. In fact, this is how the American art critic Gelett Burgess described his impression of the work when he discovered it in the artist's studio in 1910: 'The terrible pictures loom through the chaos. Monstrous, monolithic women, creatures like Alaskan totem poles, hacked out of solid, brutal colors, frightful, appalling! How little Picasso, with his sense of humor, with his youth and deviltry [*sic*], seems to glory in his crimes!'[55] By comparing the *demoiselles* to totem poles of Alaska, Burgess reminds us of the artist's own shock when he went to the Musée du Trocadéro for the first time. There, he discovered hundreds of African and Oceanian pieces that had been collected or looted during various exploratory missions by European anthropologists. Françoise Gilot reported Picasso's reaction:

Men had made those masks and other objects for a sacred purpose, a magic purpose, as a kind of mediation between themselves and the unknown hostile forces that surrounded them, in order to overcome their fear and horror by giving it form and an image. At that moment I realized that this was what painting was all about. Painting isn't an aesthetic operation; it's a form of magic ...[56]

While the artist seemed to be attracted by the ritual nature of these pieces, claiming a magical dimension for his own creative output, the aesthetic question remains. During the same interview he told Gilot that while being inspired by these pieces, he 'was against what was called beauty in the museums'.[57] In *On Ugliness* (2007), Umberto Eco writes about the reception of the works of avant-garde modernism: '[The public] did not consider them as beautiful portrayals of ugly things but ugly portrayals of reality. In other words, the bourgeoisie was scandalised by the female face as painted by Picasso not because they thought it a faithful reproduction of an ugly woman (nor did Picasso

FIG. 73 *Jug Painted with Fauns*, ca.1951

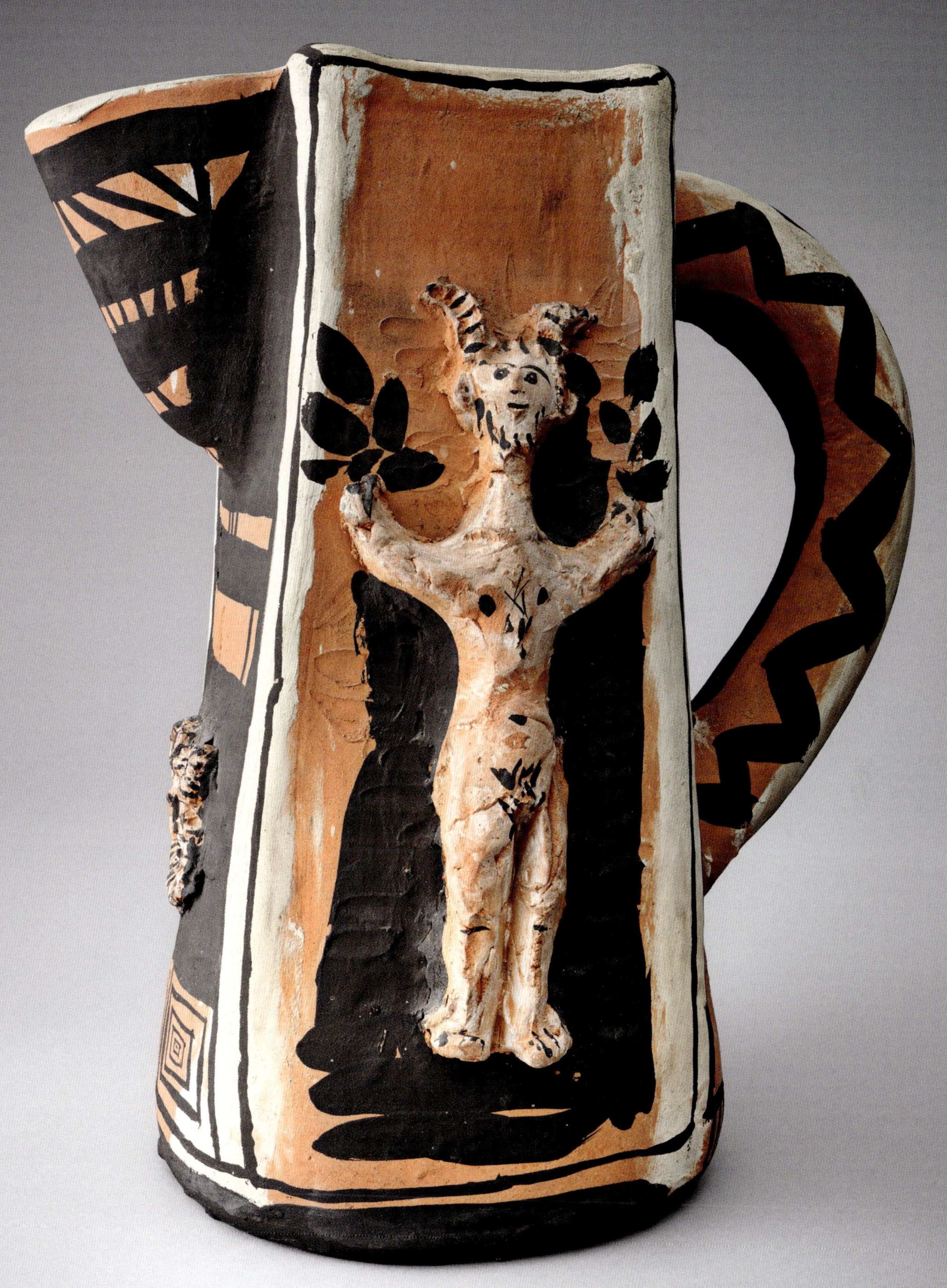

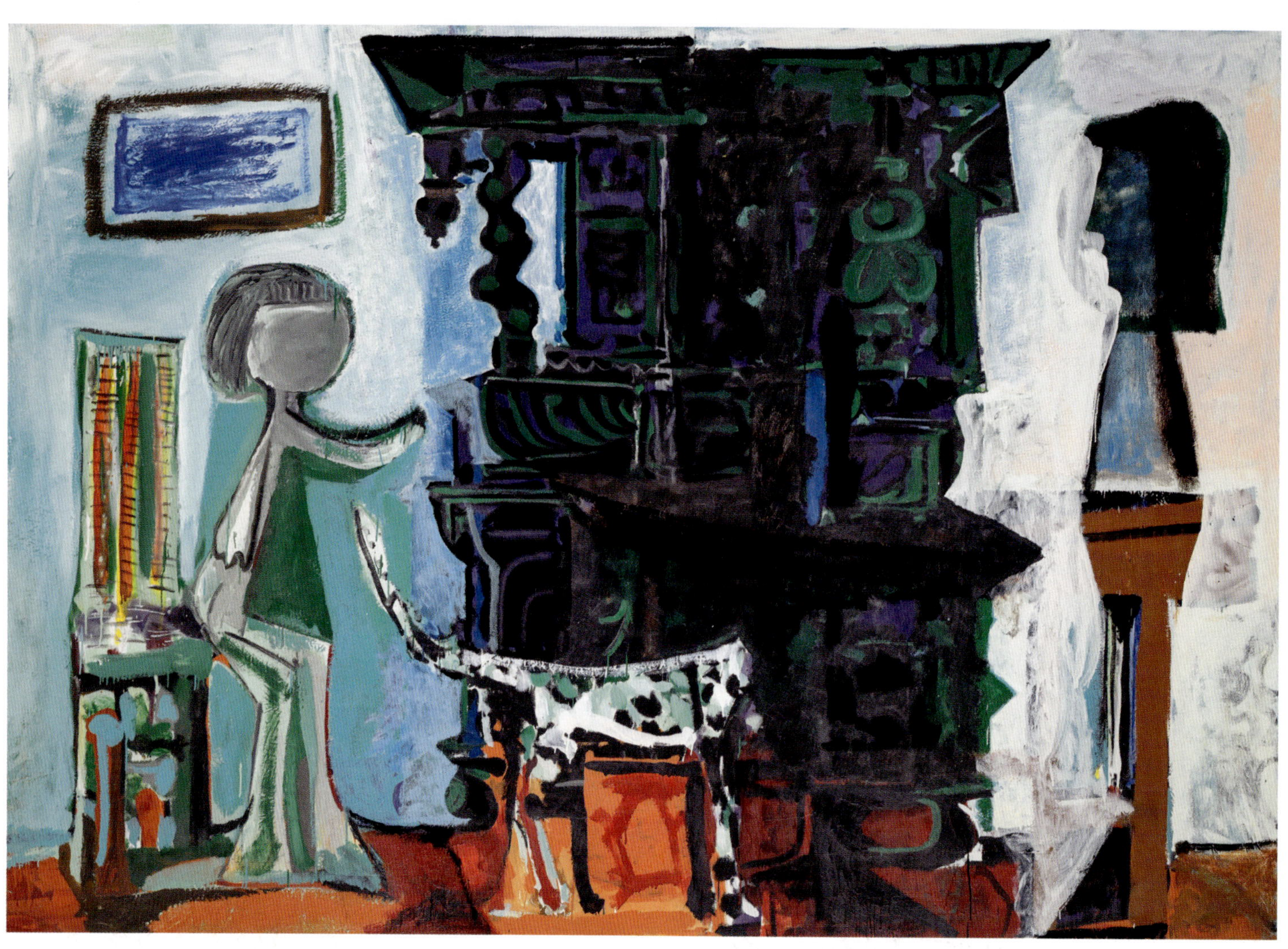

FIG. 74 *The Sideboard at Vauvenargues*, 1959–1960

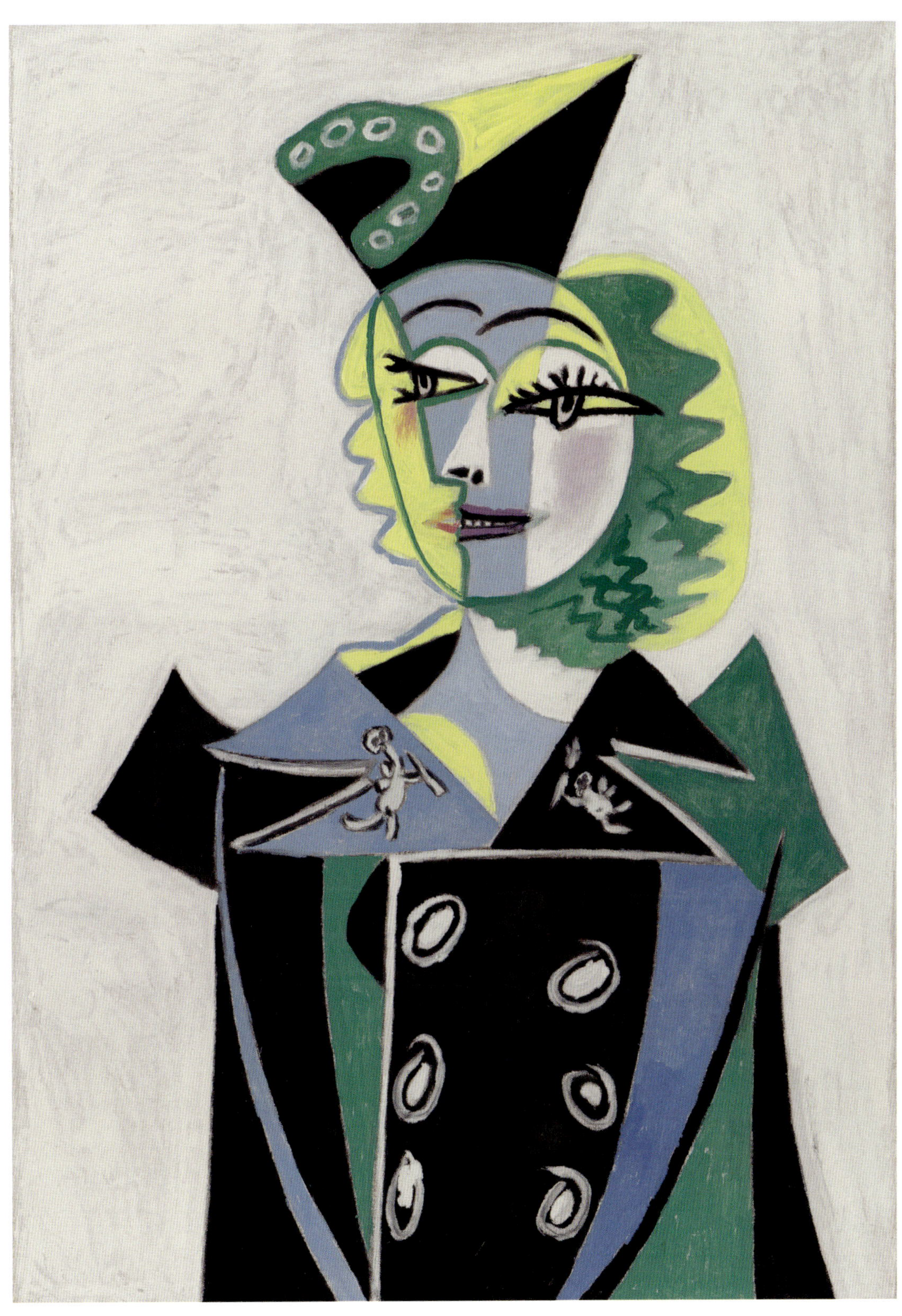

FIG. 75 *Portrait of Nusch Eluard*, 1937

want her to be so) but because they felt that it was an ugly portrayal of a woman' (FIG. 75).[58]

During the first half of the twentieth century the shock caused by this new aesthetic would serve as a catalyst for xenophobic and anti-Semitic discourses. During the First World War Cubism gradually came to be seen in France as an art that was distant from the French tradition. The German nationality of the art dealers who championed it, Daniel-Henry Kahnweiler and Wilhelm Uhde, was used in support of this argument. At the premiere of the ballet *Parade* in 1917, with costumes and sets by Picasso that were inspired by Cubism (FIG. 76), the audience shouted, 'Back to Berlin! Opium smokers! Dirty immigrants!'[59] The attacks on avant-garde art took an even more violent turn as fascist regimes came to power in Europe in the 1930s. The Nazis considered modern art 'degenerate', pathologising the members of

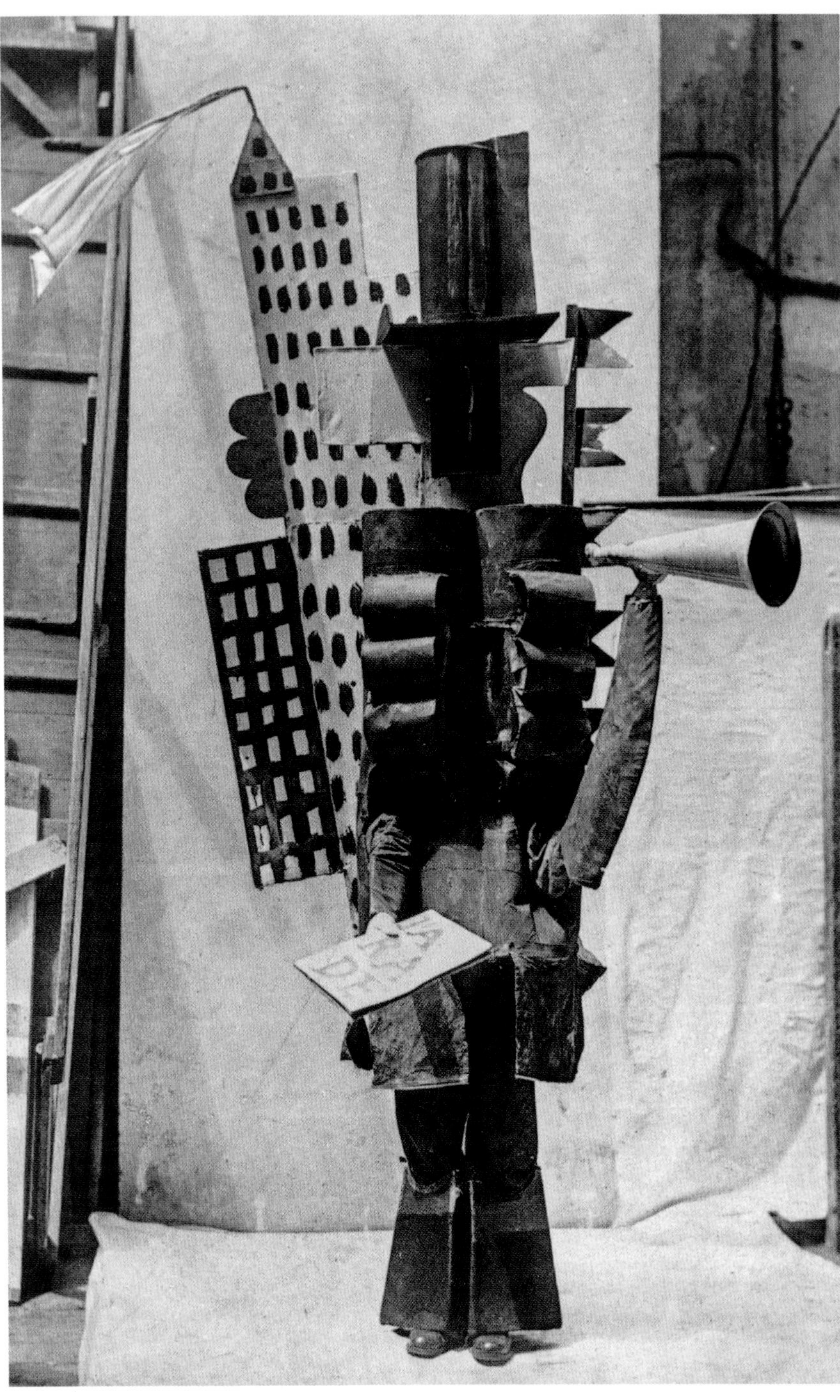

FIG. 76 Costume design by Picasso for the ballet *Parade*, worn by dancer Maximillian Statkiewicz in the role of 'The Manager from New York', 1917

various art movements as sick individuals whose work would be poisonous to 'Aryan' culture. In the face of the myth of the 'purity of Aryan blood' brandished by Nazi Germany, modern art was targeted as the embodiment of artistic perversion from foreign countries and the mixing of different ethnic groups.[60] This was clearly expressed by Alfred Rosenberg, a high-ranking official in the Third Reich, in 1936 when he published *The Myth of the Twentieth Century*, an anti-Semitic and racist screed in which he makes a direct reference to Picasso.[61]

The artist positioned himself as the adversary of fascist and Nazi ideologies, and this stance inspired his masterpiece *Guernica* (1937; FIG. 77), a visual denunciation of the bombing of civilians in the eponymous Basque town by Italian and German aircraft during the Spanish Civil War. Classified as a 'degenerate artist', Picasso nevertheless stayed in Paris during the German occupation, where his celebrity and connections allowed him to be undisturbed by the authorities.[62] In the weeks that followed the liberation of Paris in August 1944, the Salon d'Automne took place, renamed the 'Salon de la Libération' and celebrating artistic creativity and defiance under the Occupation. Picasso had a very significant presence, exhibiting seventy-four paintings and five sculptures. The artist's works continued to perturb some members of the public, who either did not understand them or saw only ugliness. A few months later the writer Michel Leiris published his explanation of the scandal caused by Picasso's work: 'If the painter gives a table, a glass, or a bottle the most absurd shape, it's still acceptable; if he takes on the human face to the extreme point that he does (until the figure, without losing any of its humanity, seems to be a creature from another planet), they will never forgive him.'[63] Indeed, there was widespread criticism from some, accusing Picasso of creating artworks stripped of humanity. In their study, Kris and Kurz remind us that the stereotypical formula of the rejected artist is common to many narratives using the image of the 'evil magician', an inverted reflection of that of the 'mighty creator'.[64] This duality has its origin partly in mythologies where the achievements of humans that rival divine actions find themselves punished by the gods.[65] By presenting the rejection of Picasso's work as a penalty for having violated accepted standards, Leiris depicts the artist as a modern Prometheus.

MYTHOLOGICAL INSPIRATIONS

In the early 1920s many modern artists renewed their interest in figurative and classical subjects in a movement that historians have called the 'Return to Order'. Following the devastation of Europe during the First World War, art was seen as a reference point for rebuilding the continent. Alongside Cubism, which he continued to develop, Picasso was inspired by the myths of the Mediterranean, with numerous paintings presenting robust figures resembling ancient sculptures (FIG. 78). This interest in mythology is also found in the *Vollard Suite*, a collection of 100 copper etchings produced by Picasso between 1930 and 1937, named after the art dealer, Ambroise Vollard, who commissioned them. Several of the etchings take up the theme of the 'sculptor in his studio', where the sculptor assumes the appearance of a young, beardless man with curly hair (FIG. 79) or that of an older bearded man (FIG. 81). Picasso also depicts a sculptor carving marble busts of women that closely resemble those he created during the same period in his new studio in the Château de Boisgeloup (FIG. 80), located some forty

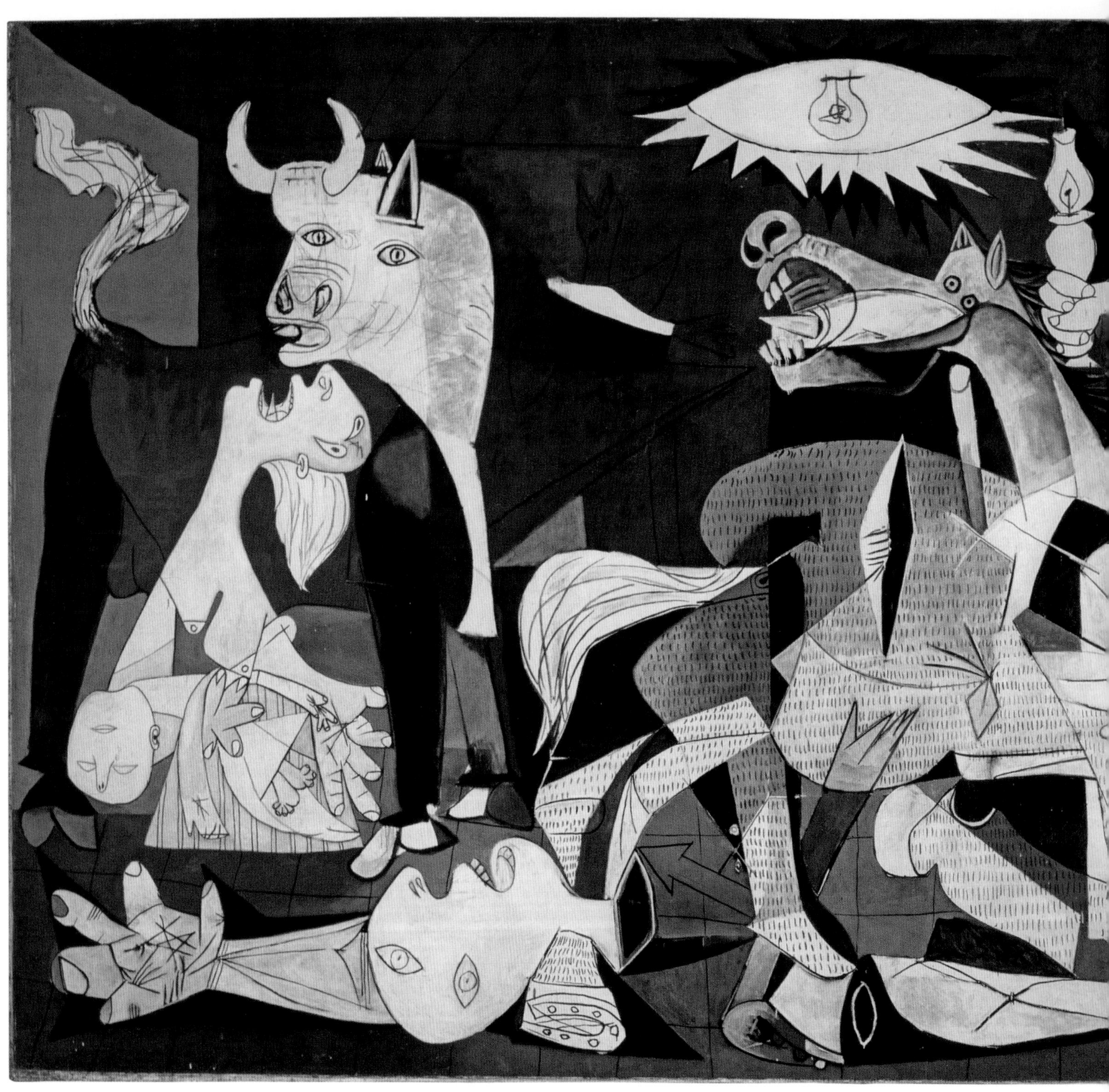

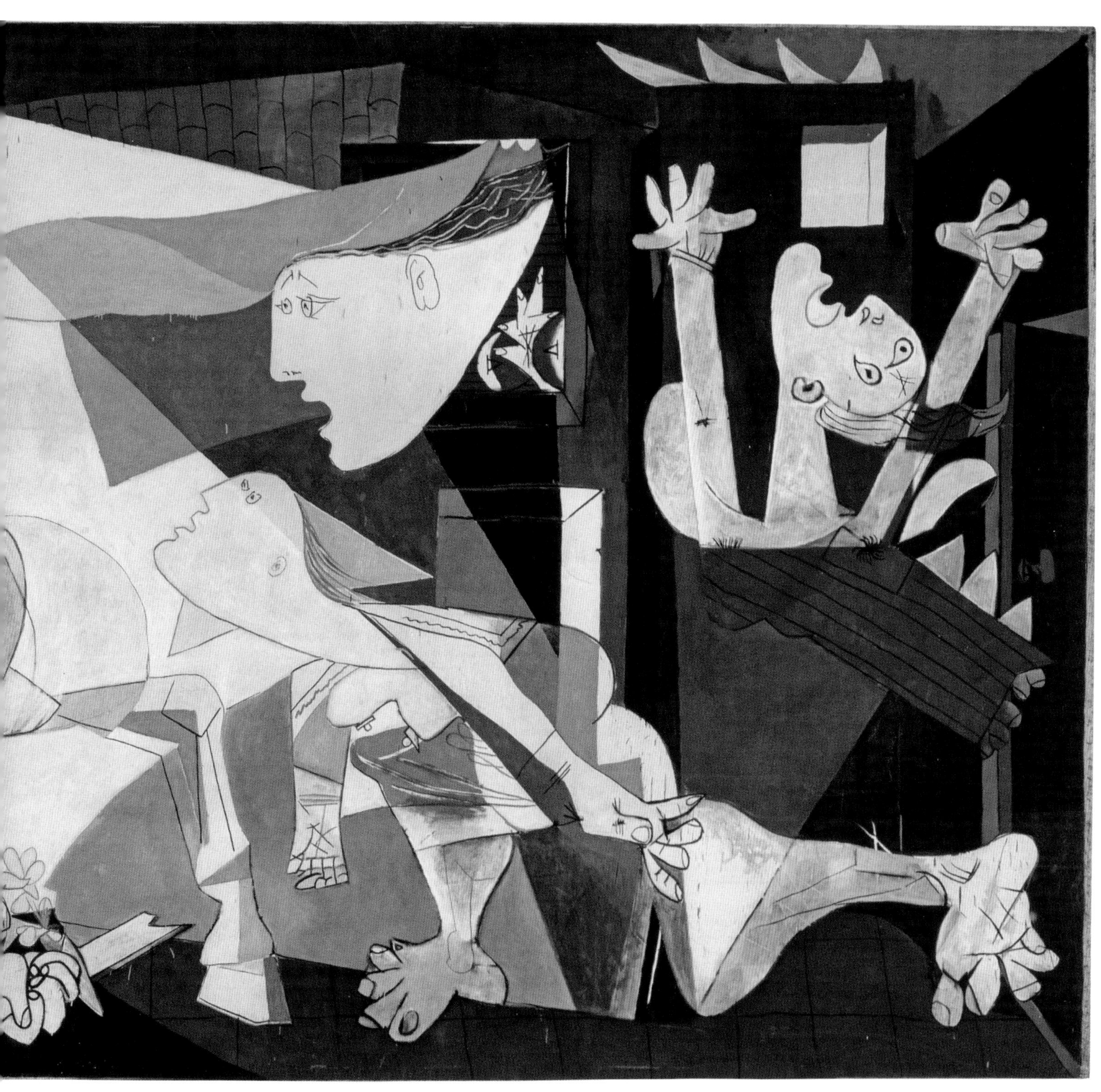

FIG. 77 *Guernica*, 1937

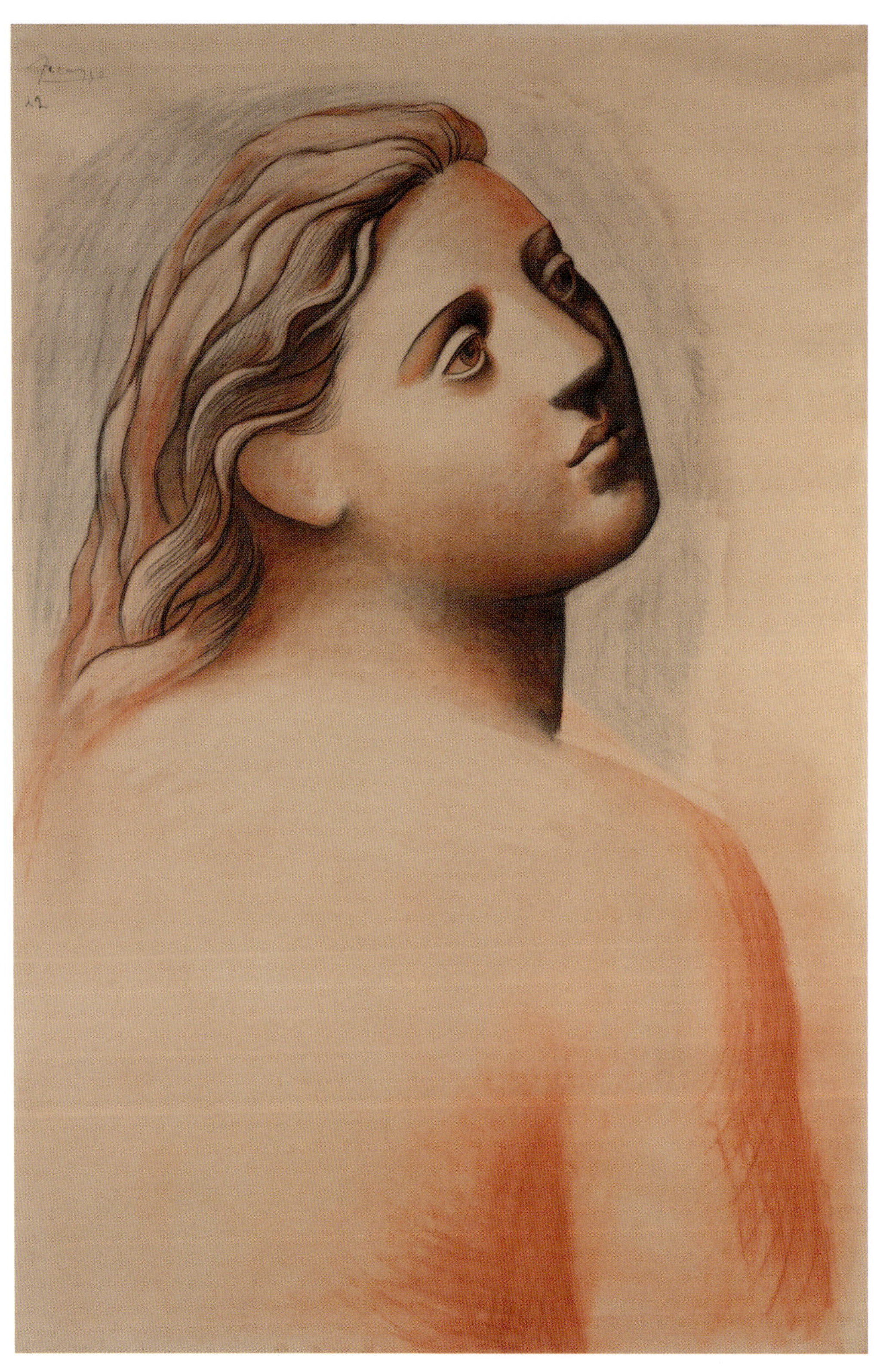

FIG. 78 *Head of a Woman*, 1922

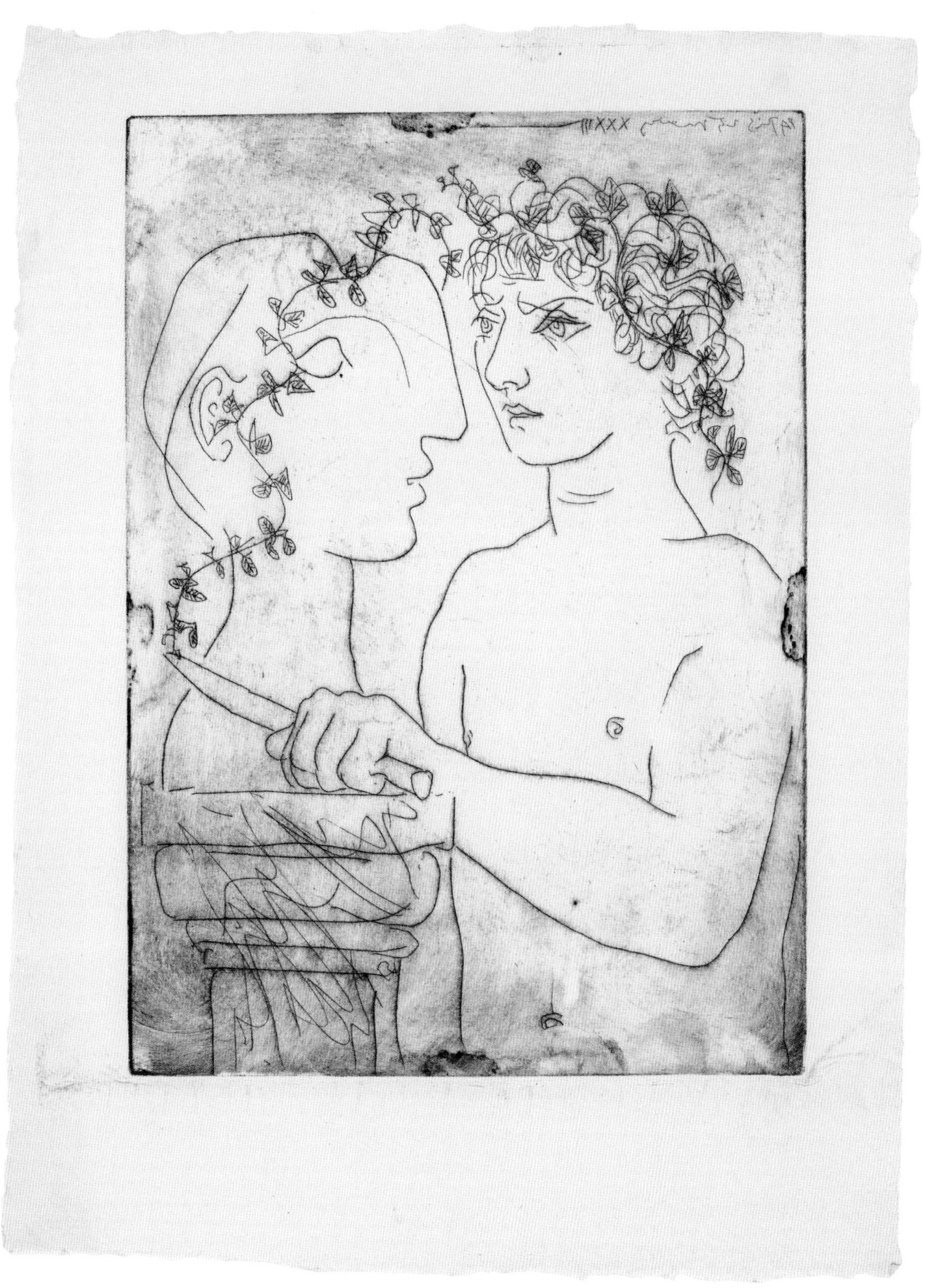

FIG. 79 *Young Sculptor Finishing a Plaster*, 1933

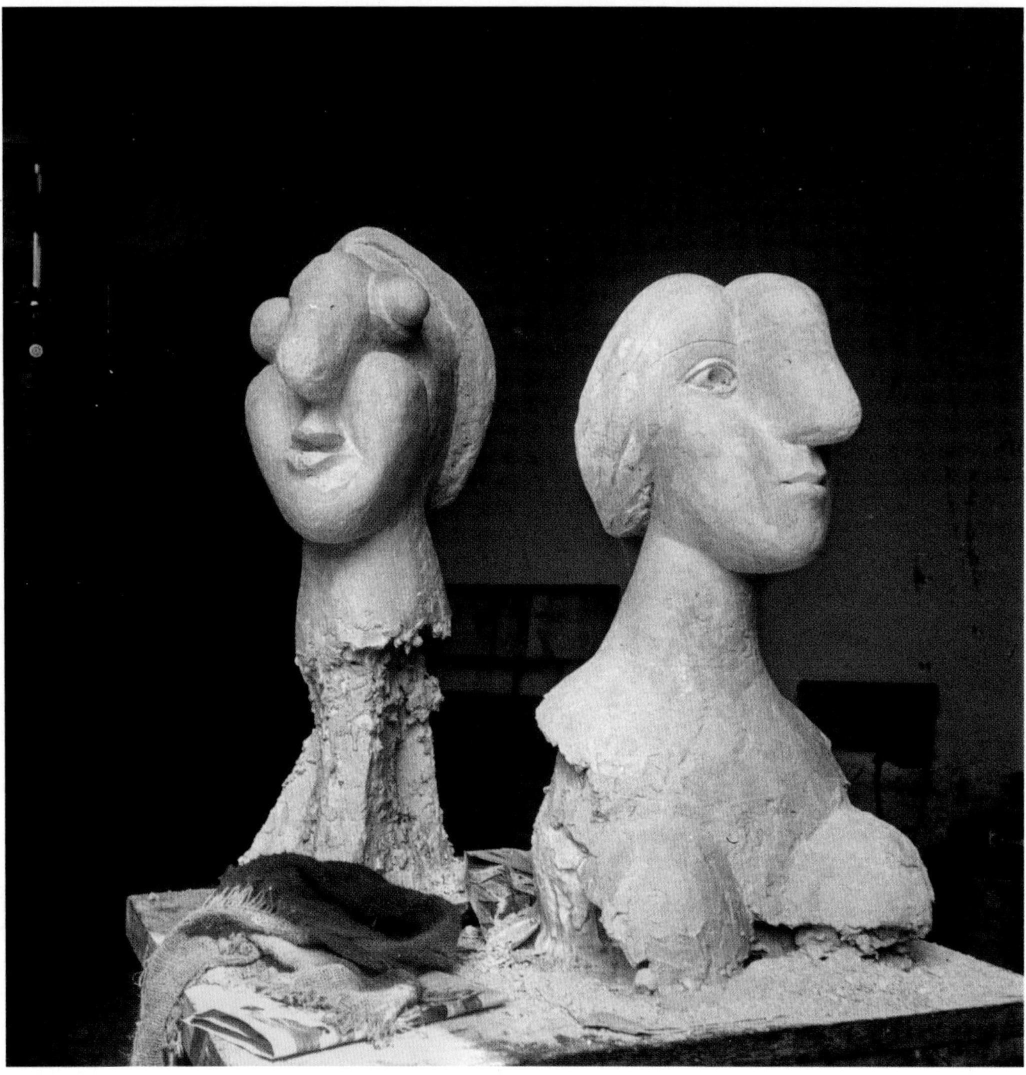

miles to the north-west of Paris. There, he had large spaces that were conducive to making sculptures. However, the artist did not devote himself to the technique of *taille directe* (direct carving), preferring instead to shape his works in plaster before casting them in bronze.[66] In one of his etchings, a sculptor observes the head of a woman he has just sculpted, and which sits on a pedestal as a self-portrait (FIG. 81). Picasso gives the sculpture a halo composed of rays of light, inspiring him to make the following comment: 'While [the figure of the sculptor] is working on it, he's sure it's pure genius.'[67]

At the heart of the *Vollard Suite* is the subject of the relationship between the artist, the artwork, and his or her model. This theme can be found in the ancient Greek myth of Pygmalion, an artist who sculpts in ivory a woman so beautiful that he falls in love with her, causing the goddess Aphrodite to bring her to life. Chronicled by Ovid in *Metamorphoses*, the myth inspired many artists, especially in the late nineteenth century—from Auguste Rodin (*Pygmalion and Galatea*, modelled 1889, carved ca.1908–1909; FIG. 85) to Jean-Léon Gérôme (*Pygmalion and Galatea*, ca.1890; FIG. 84). Picasso's Pygmalion-inspired artwork is *The Sculptor* (1931; FIG. 86), a painting in which a bearded artist stares lovingly at a bust of a woman in his studio. One aspect of this myth—the animation of inert matter—can be found in *Large Still Life with Pedestal Table* (1931; FIG. 83), where a collection of curved shapes seems to evoke the female anatomy. The effect is strengthened by the similarity of these

FIG. 80 Boris Kochno, Picasso's *Head of a Woman* (left) and *Bust of a Woman* (right) in the Boisgeloup studio, Gisors, 1931

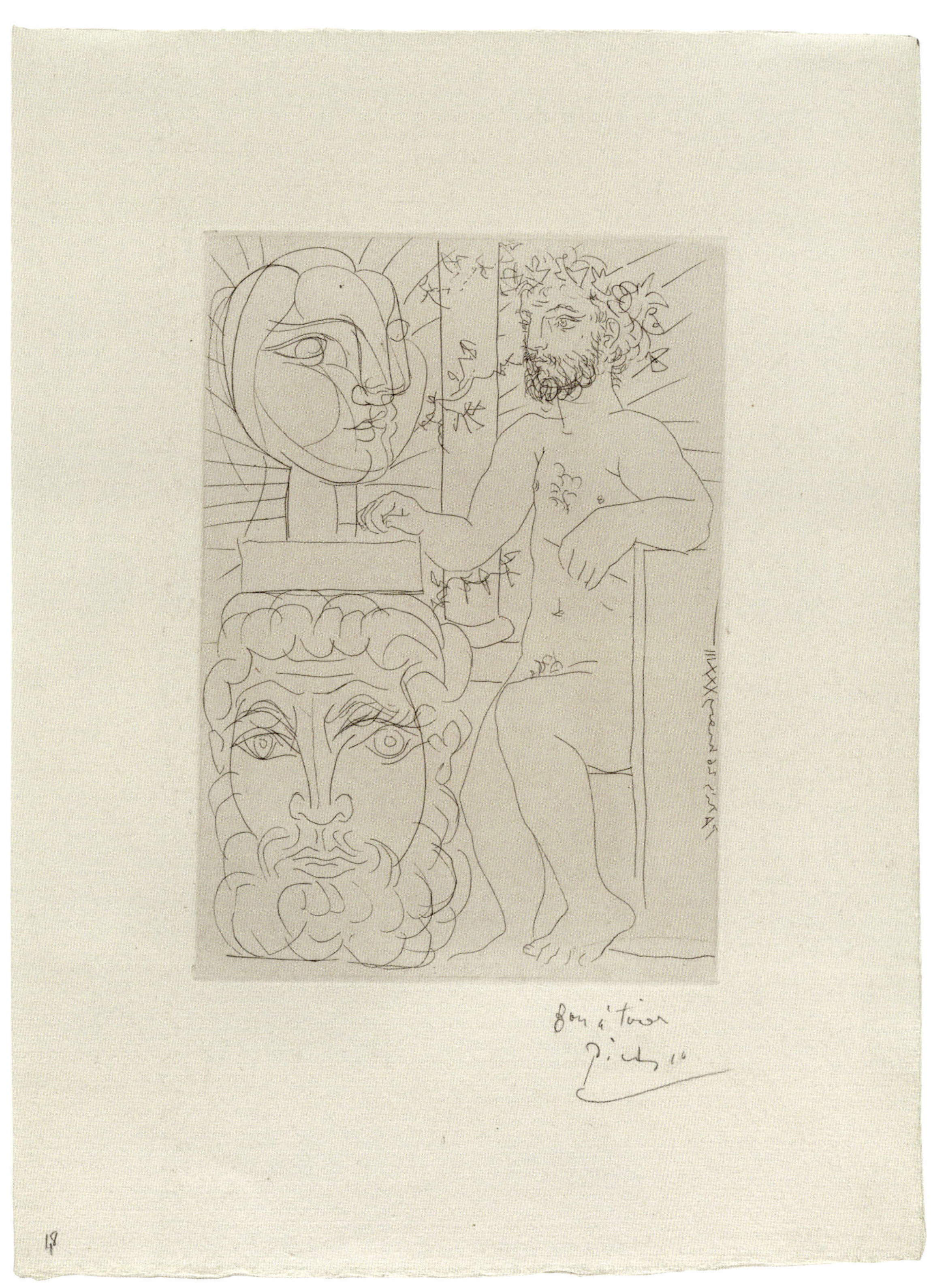

FIG. 81 *Sculptor and His Self-Portrait Serving as a Pedestal for the Head of Marie-Thérèse*, 1933

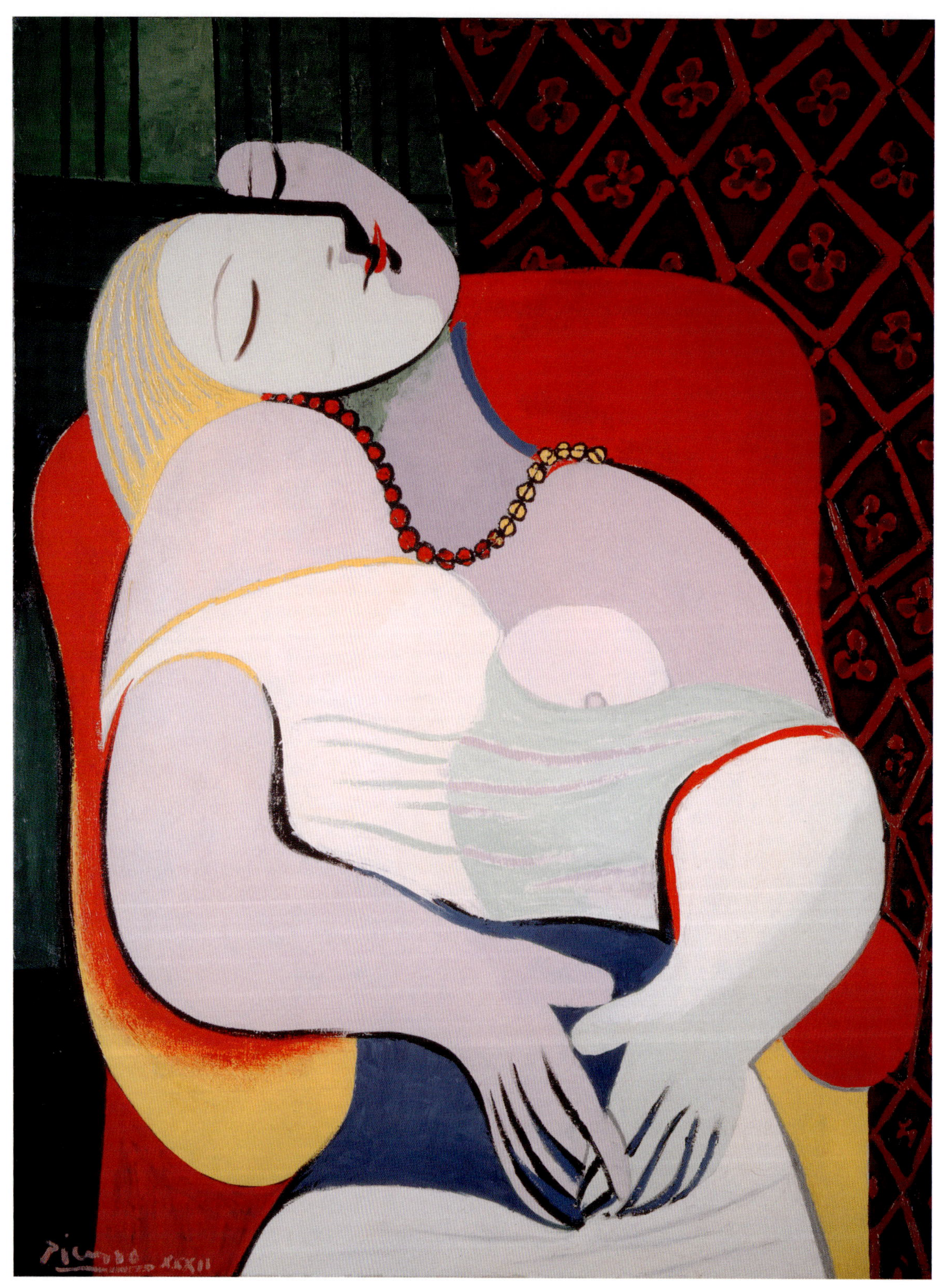

FIG. 82 *The Dream*, 1932

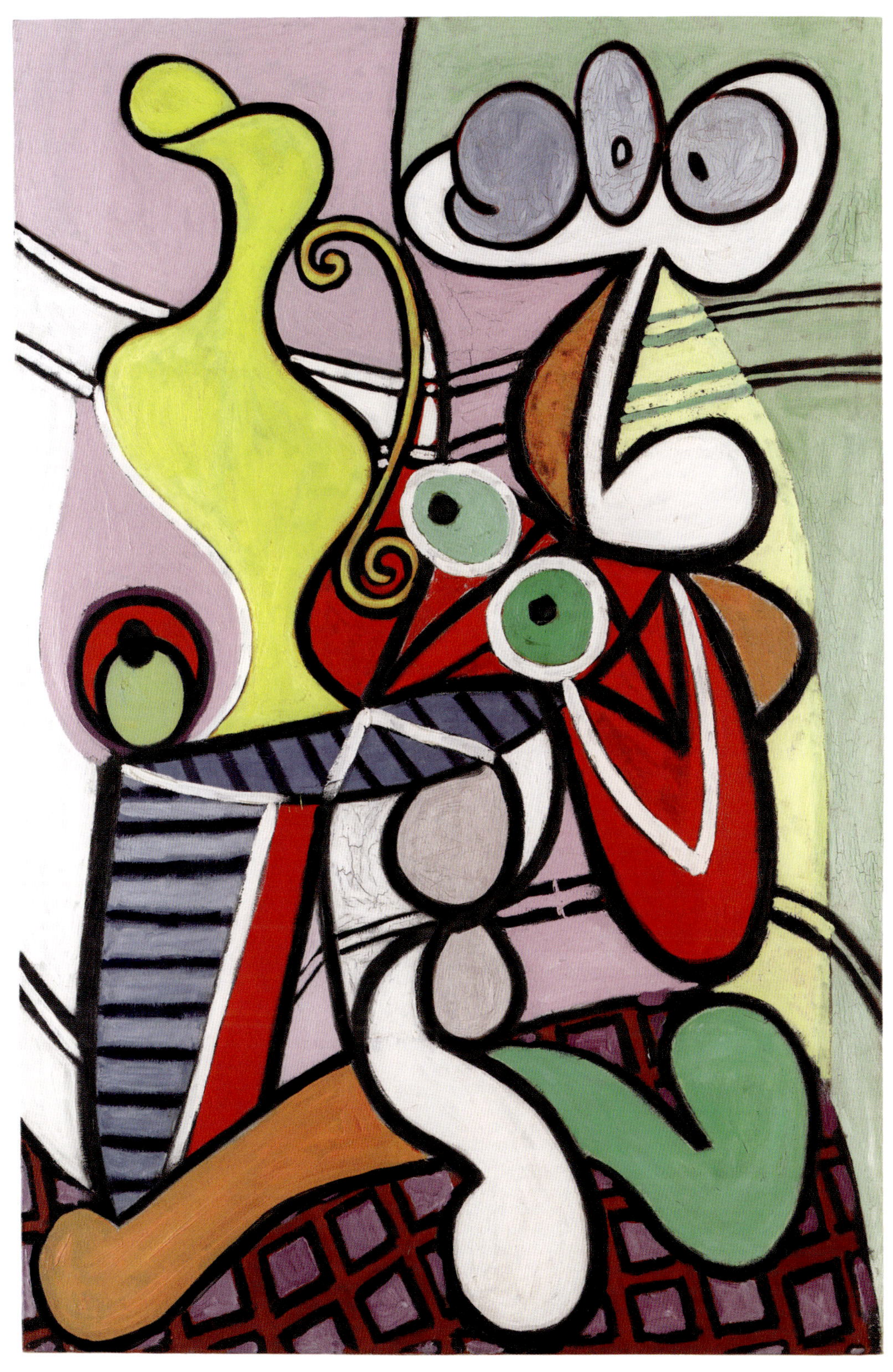

FIG. 83 *Large Still Life with Pedestal Table*, 1931

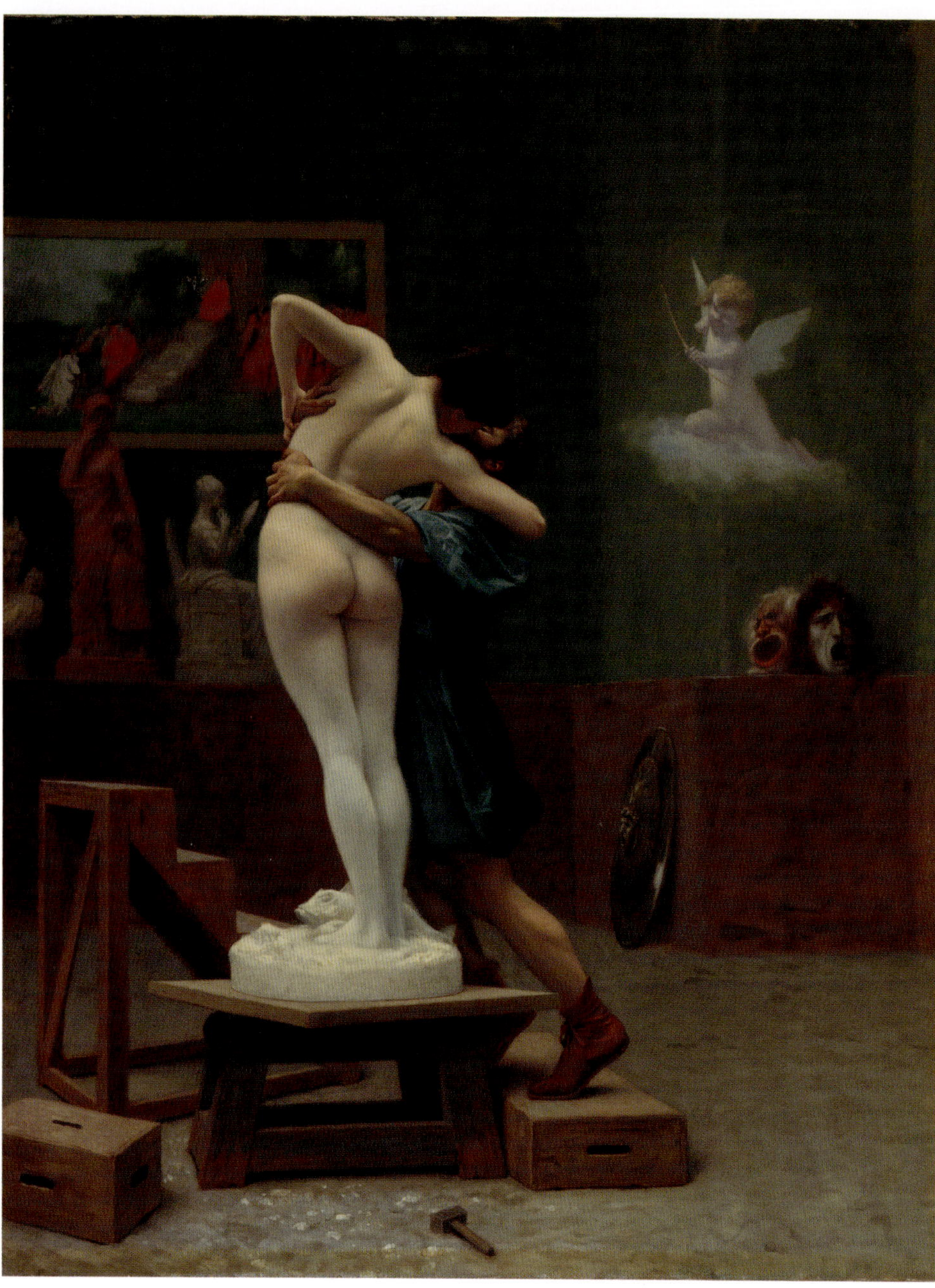

LEFT: FIG. 84 Jean-Léon Gérôme, *Pygmalion and Galatea*, ca.1890

BELOW: FIG. 85 Auguste Rodin, *Pygmalion and Galatea*, modelled 1889, carved ca.1908–1909

paintings' forms and colours, which recall the numerous female figures that the artist painted at this time (FIG. 82). The large size of the canvas, an unusual format for this genre, emphasises the feeling that this is more than simply a still life. Art historian Carol Duncan summarises the trope of Pygmalion as 'the expectation that significant and vital content in all art presupposes the presence of male erotic energy'.[68] Art history is rife with such narratives, combining sexual desire and the creative impulse, in which male artists depict the features of their lovers in their art. One of the most well-known examples is Goya's *The Naked Maja* (1795–1800), which has been interpreted as a portrait of the Duchess of Alba, with whom the artist is thought to have had an affair.

In the *Vollard Suite*, the figure of the minotaur also emerges. In Greek mythology, the minotaur was a part-bull, part-human monster imprisoned in the labyrinth of the palace at Knossos, devouring young men and women. Picasso reworks the original myth to transform the monster into a sexual being desiring women. Picasso himself

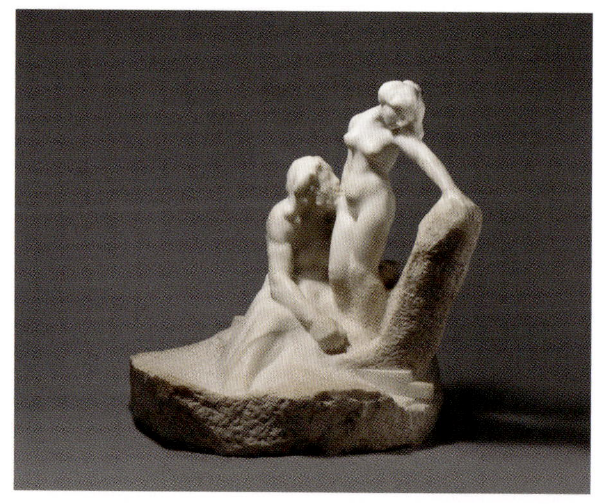

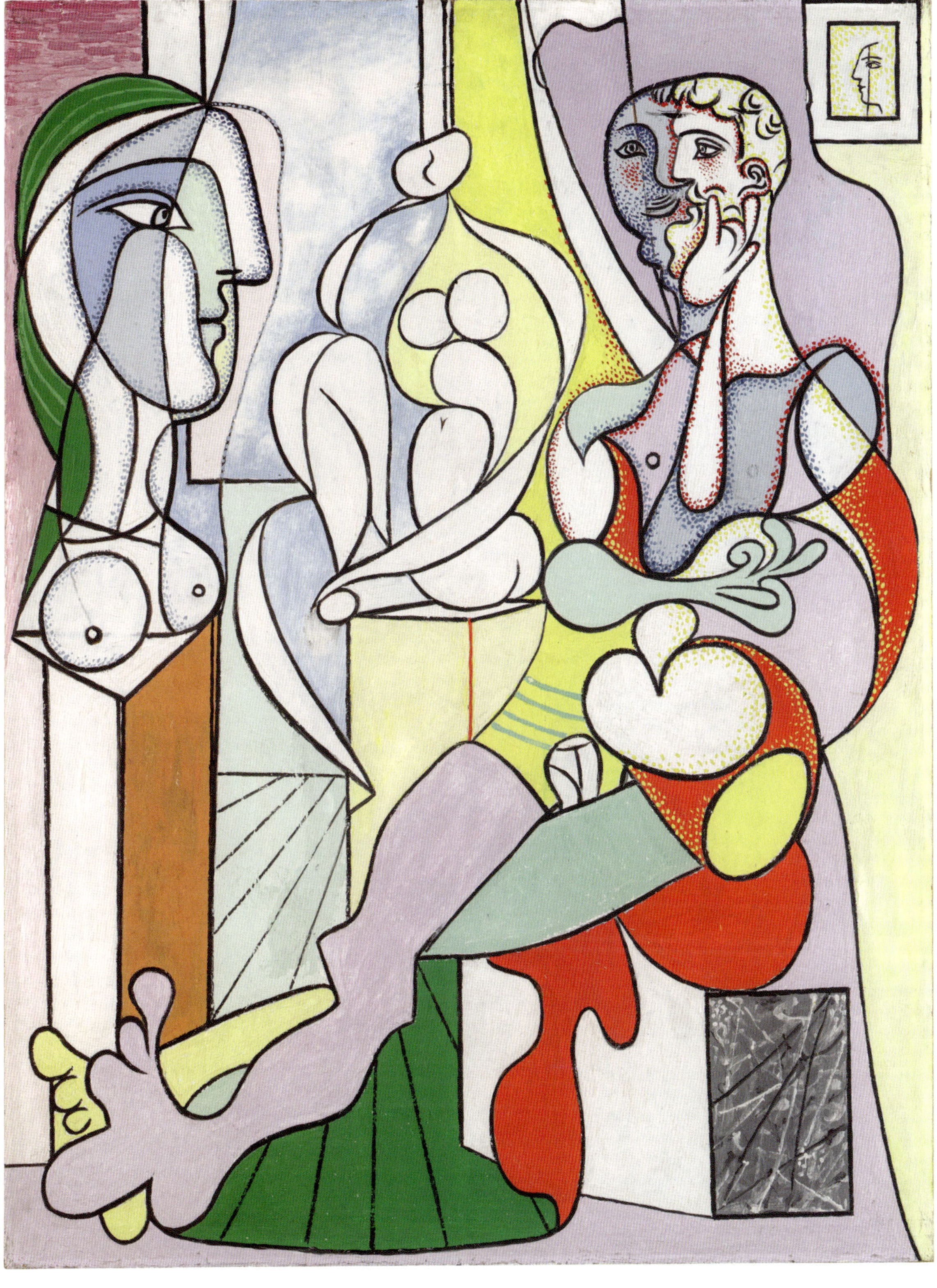

FIG. 86 *The Sculptor*, 1931

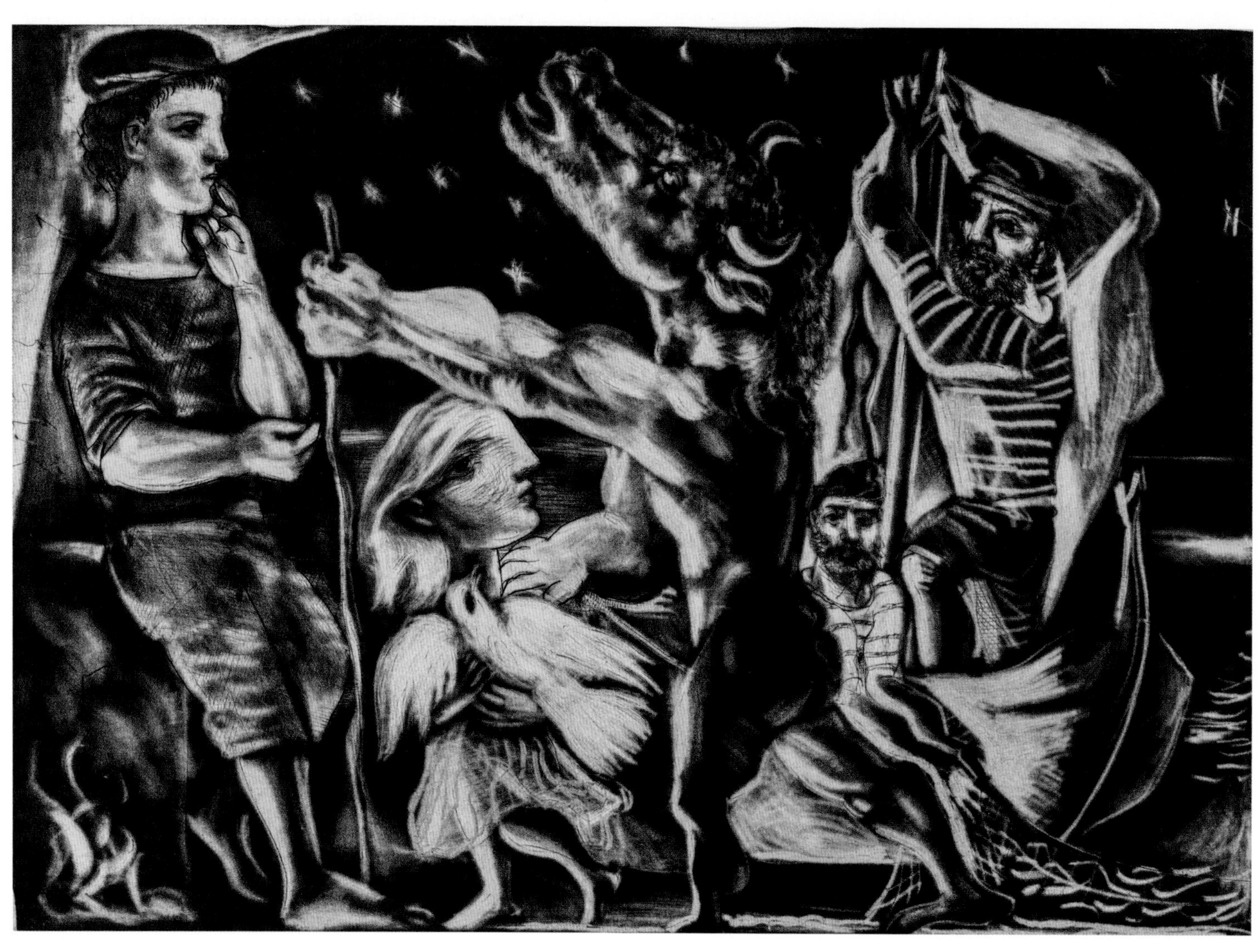

FIG. 87 *Blind Minotaur Guided through a Starry Night by Marie-Thérèse with a Pigeon*, 1934–1935

participated in the identification of the artist with this monstrous figure in statements he made, such as: 'If all the ways I have been along were marked on a map and joined up with a line, it might represent a minotaur.'[69] This self-identification was emphasised by the artist's depictions of the minotaur alongside figures with the features of his companions, as in *Blind Minotaur Guided through a Starry Night by Marie-Thérèse with a Pigeon* (1934–1935; FIG. 87) and *Dora and the Minotaur* (1936; FIG. 89), a colourful drawing in which we recognise Dora Maar (FIG. 88), the Surrealist artist and photographer of whom Picasso made several portraits in the mid-1930s (FIGS 90 AND 91). Minotaurs, fauns, and centaurs are also depicted in numerous scenes of rape and abduction (FIG. 92), recurring subjects in ancient mythology that have been widely illustrated in the history of Western art. Since rape and violence against women have rightly become major topics of debate, these artworks may raise the question of the connections between Picasso's oeuvre and the artist himself, who was portrayed by some in his circle as a violent, abusive man. An artist whose work has been studied mainly from a biographical perspective, the influence of his sexism on his art has remained an unexplored angle. According to Siri Hustvedt: 'Picasso's biographers have cast their subject's misogyny and sadism in various lights, but none of them doubts that his fear, cruelty, and ambivalence [towards women] found their way onto his canvases.'[70] Today, Picasso represents a symbol of the patriarchy at the heart of feminist discourses criticising the protection that the most celebrated male artists receive, and the lack of recognition granted to women. By its variety, his oeuvre allows him to be viewed and discussed from numerous angles while resisting a single-minded interpretation. The angle concerning his sexism thus opens up new perspectives, from the issue of gender[71] to that of historiography,[72] questioning certain outmoded myths.[73]

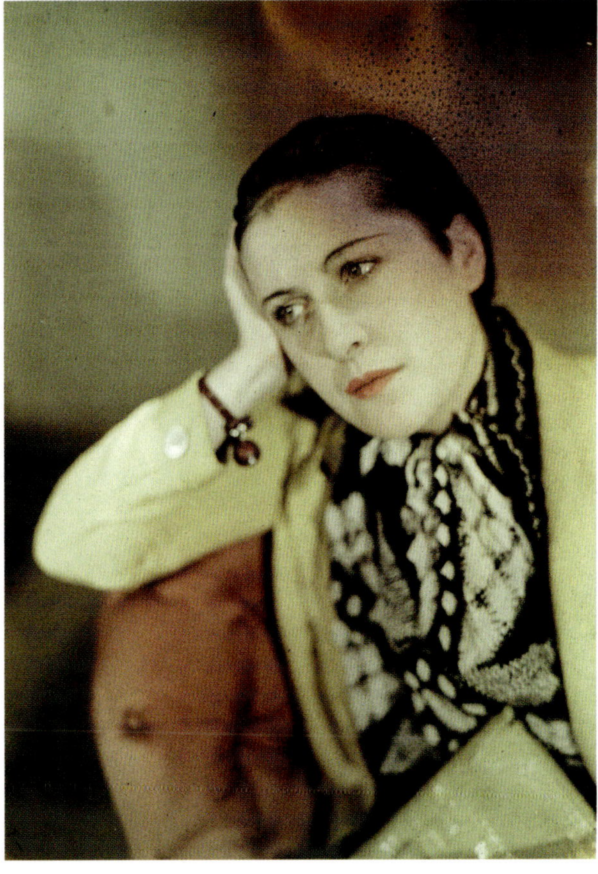

FIG. 88 Dora Maar, *Self-Portrait*, 1935

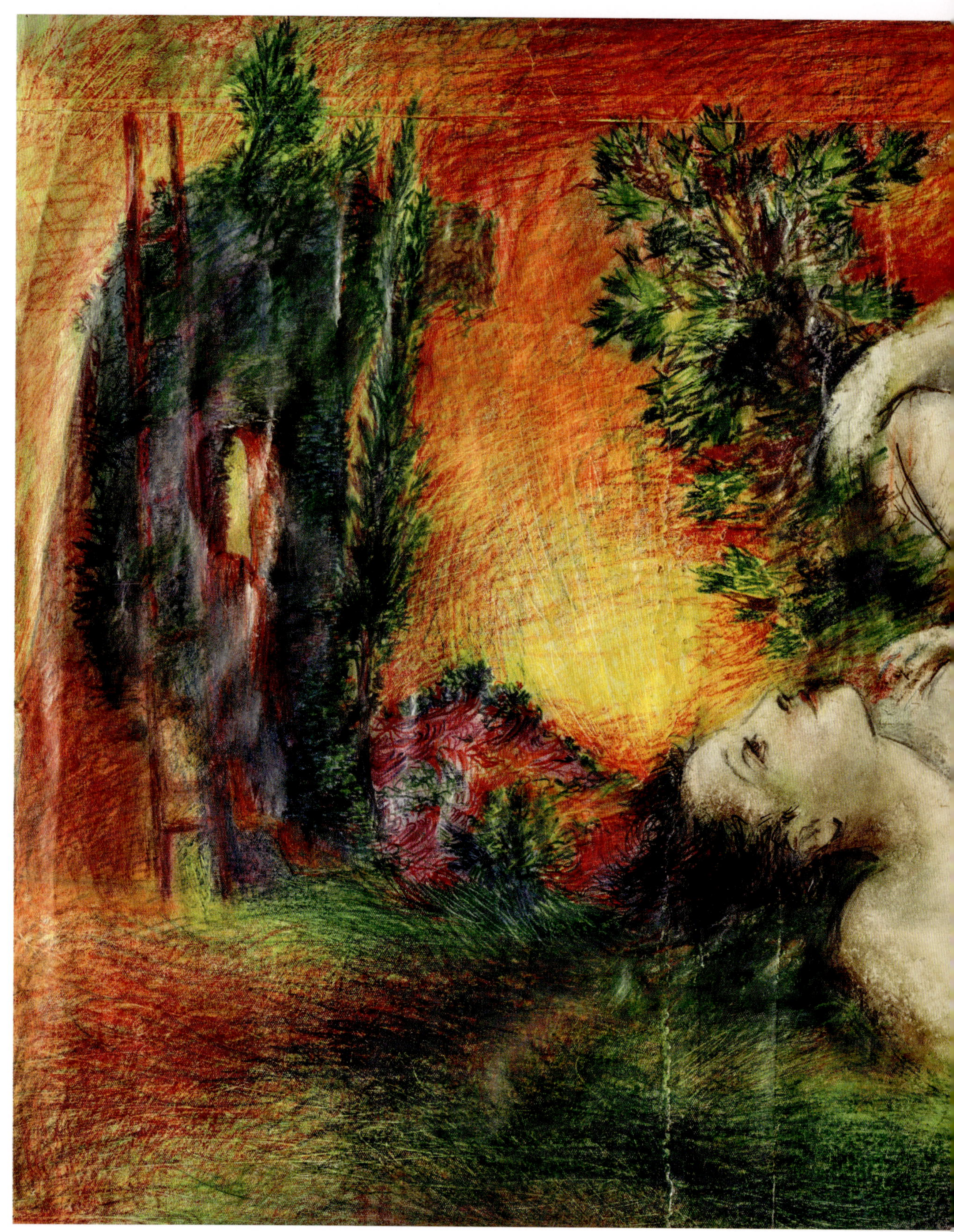

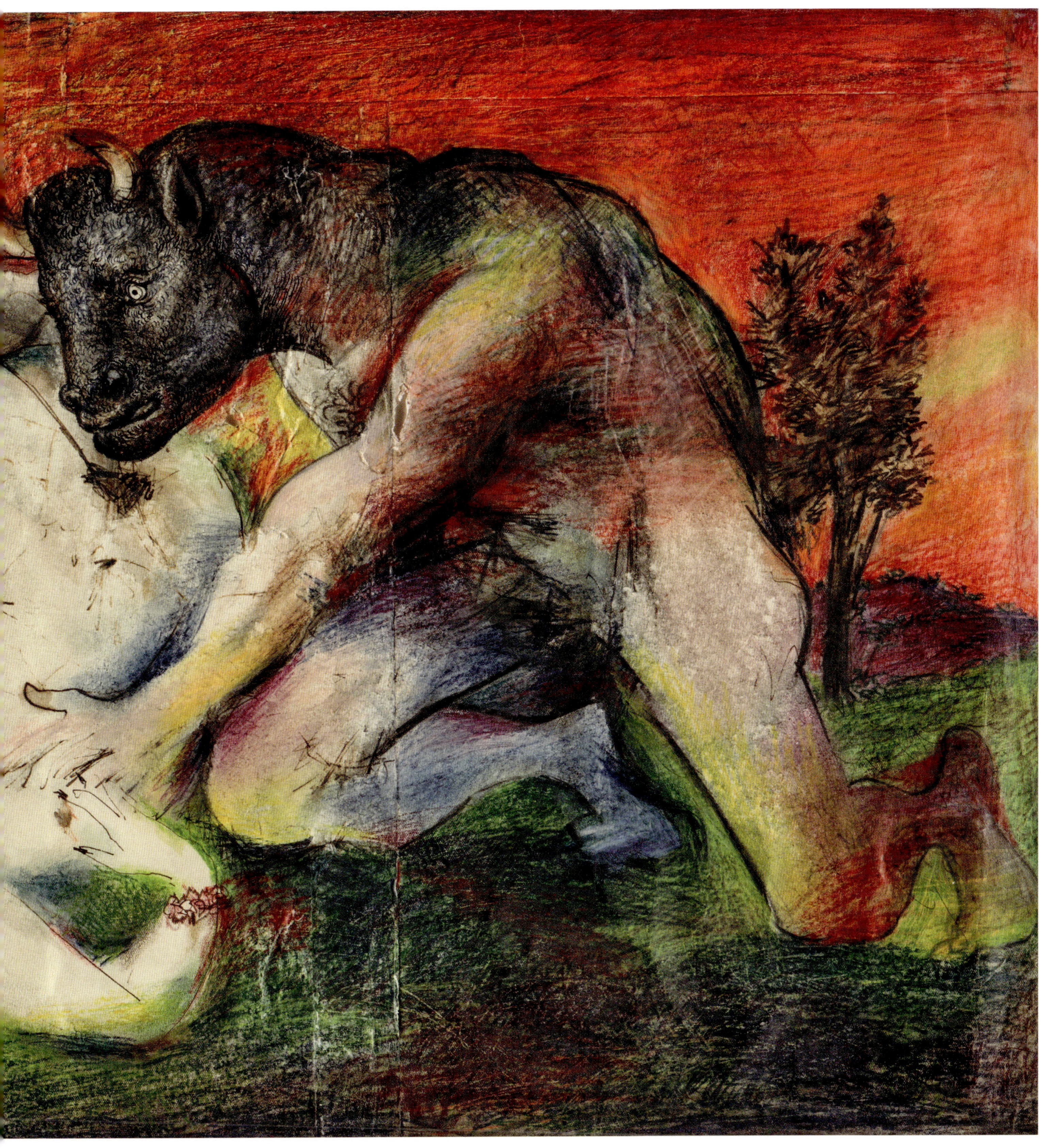

FIG. 89 *Dora and the Minotaur*, 1936

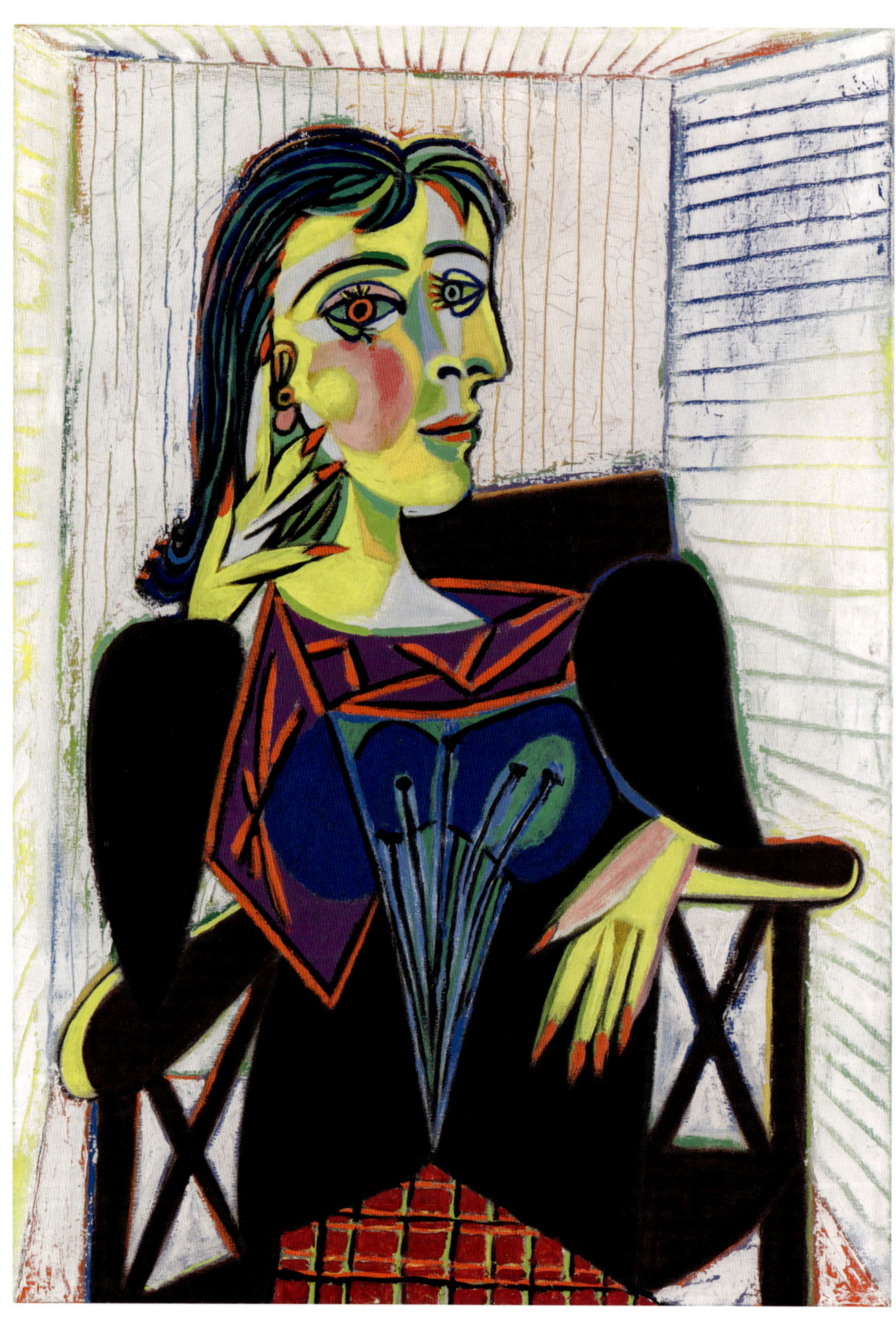

FIG. 90 *Portrait of Dora Maar*, 1937

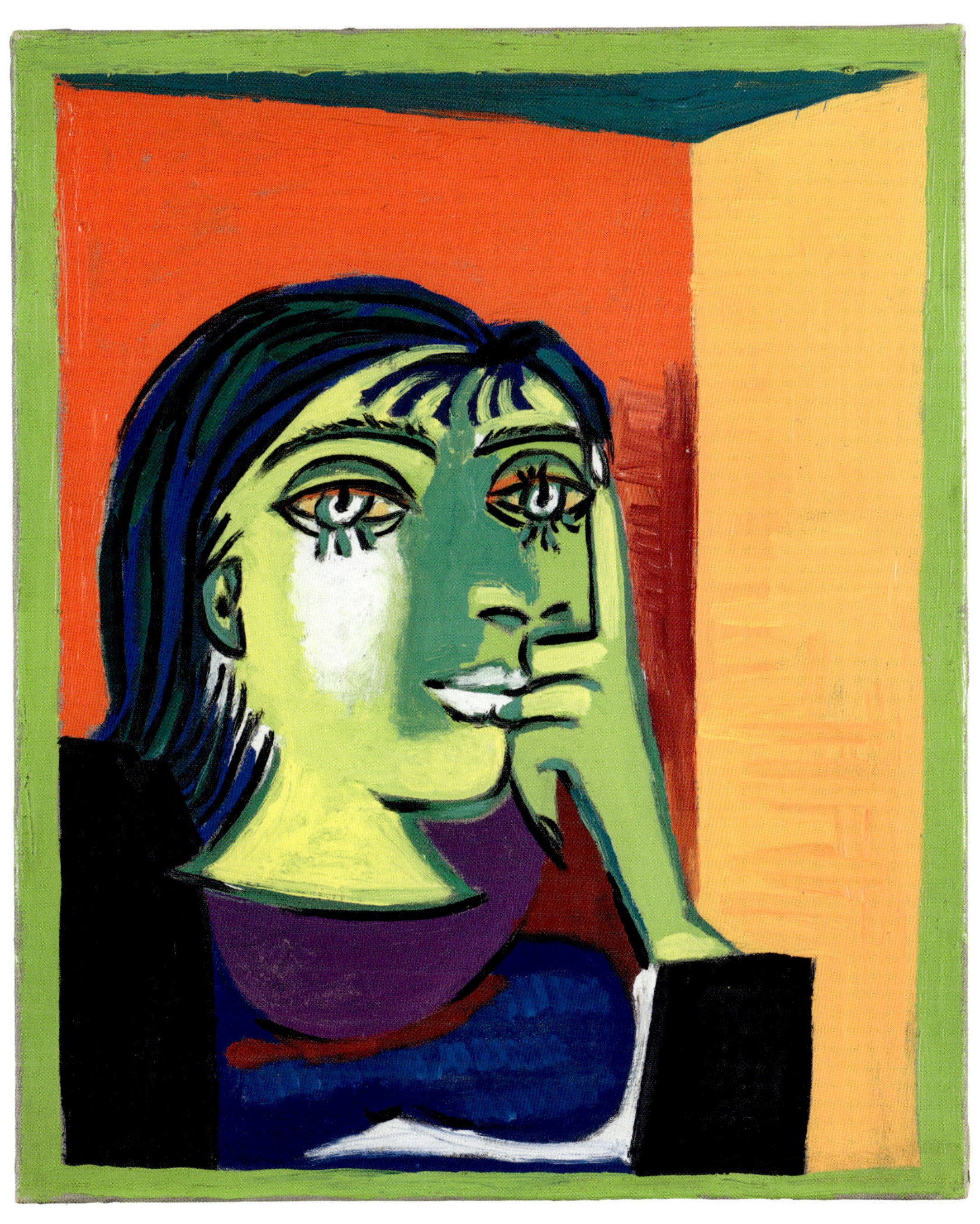

FIG. 91 *Portrait of Dora Maar*, 1937

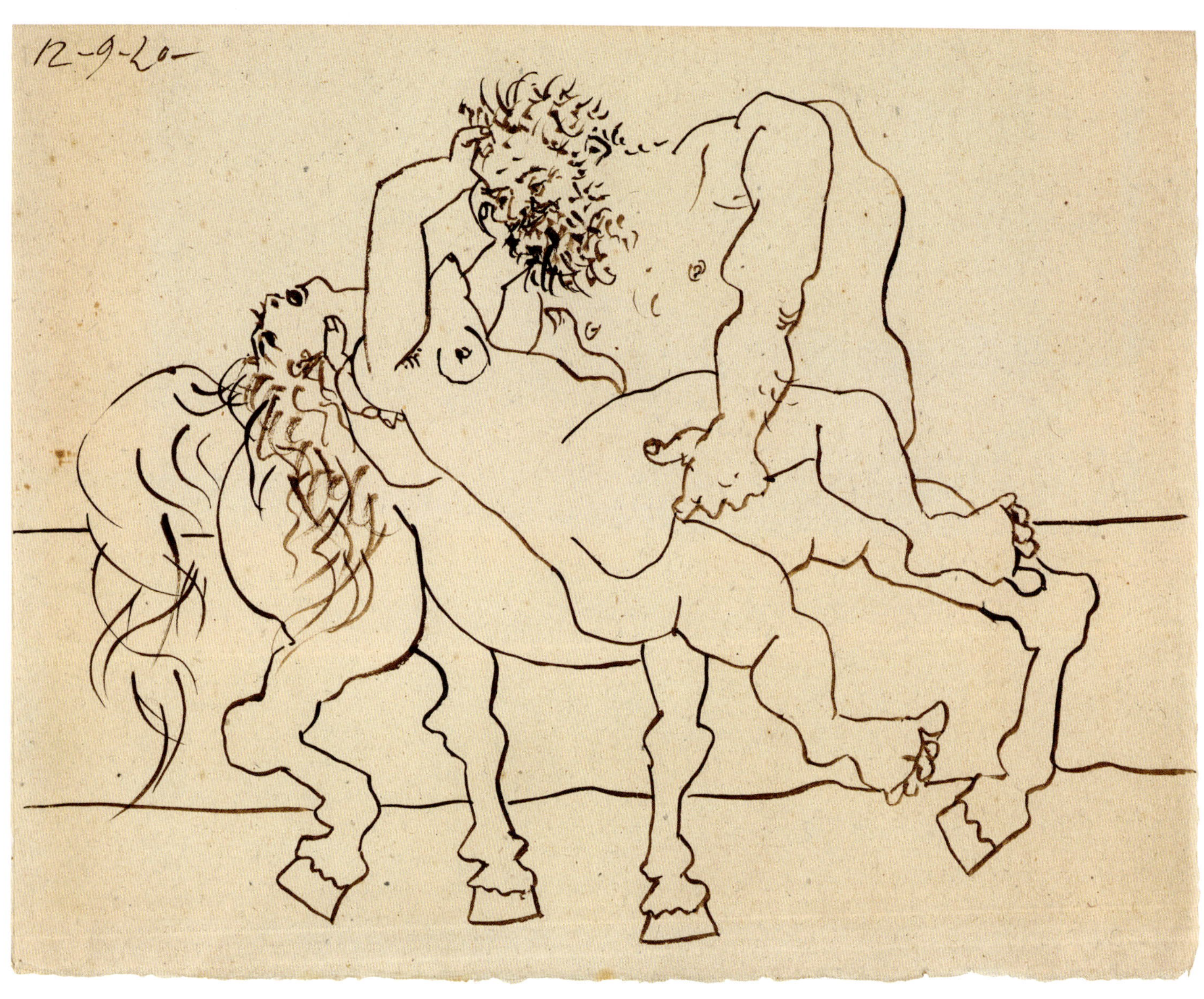

FIG. 92 *Nessus and Déjanire*, 1920

NEW MYTHS

In his book *Radical Picasso: The Use Value of Genius* (2021), C. F. B. Miller writes: 'Picasso's last years coincided with the demise of genius. Already weakened by decades of artistic and ideological critique, having been almost fatally contaminated by its association with the fascist leader cults, the sagging figure of genius, which had bestridden Western aesthetics since the mid-eighteenth century, finally collapsed in the post-modern era.'[74] Miller reminds us that societies draw on myths or dismiss them according to their aspirations. Today, many voices call for the writing of art history based on the figure of the 'genius' to be questioned, criticising the tendency to base sweeping transformations on a few 'great men'. By re-evaluating the place of artists who have hitherto been neglected, including a significant number of women, our knowledge is enriched with new artistic practices and models of representation.

This is the case with the American artist Faith Ringgold, whose multidisciplinary work has been seen in a number of retrospectives, including one at the MnPP shortly before her death, in 2024.[75] Several of her works aim to move beyond the myths around modern artists, including Picasso, and contribute other discourses. Ringgold's works are often narrative, the artist writing in the margins of her works the stories surrounding the images she produces. In *Picasso's Studio* (1991; FIG. 93), Ringgold takes up the conventions of the biographical approach

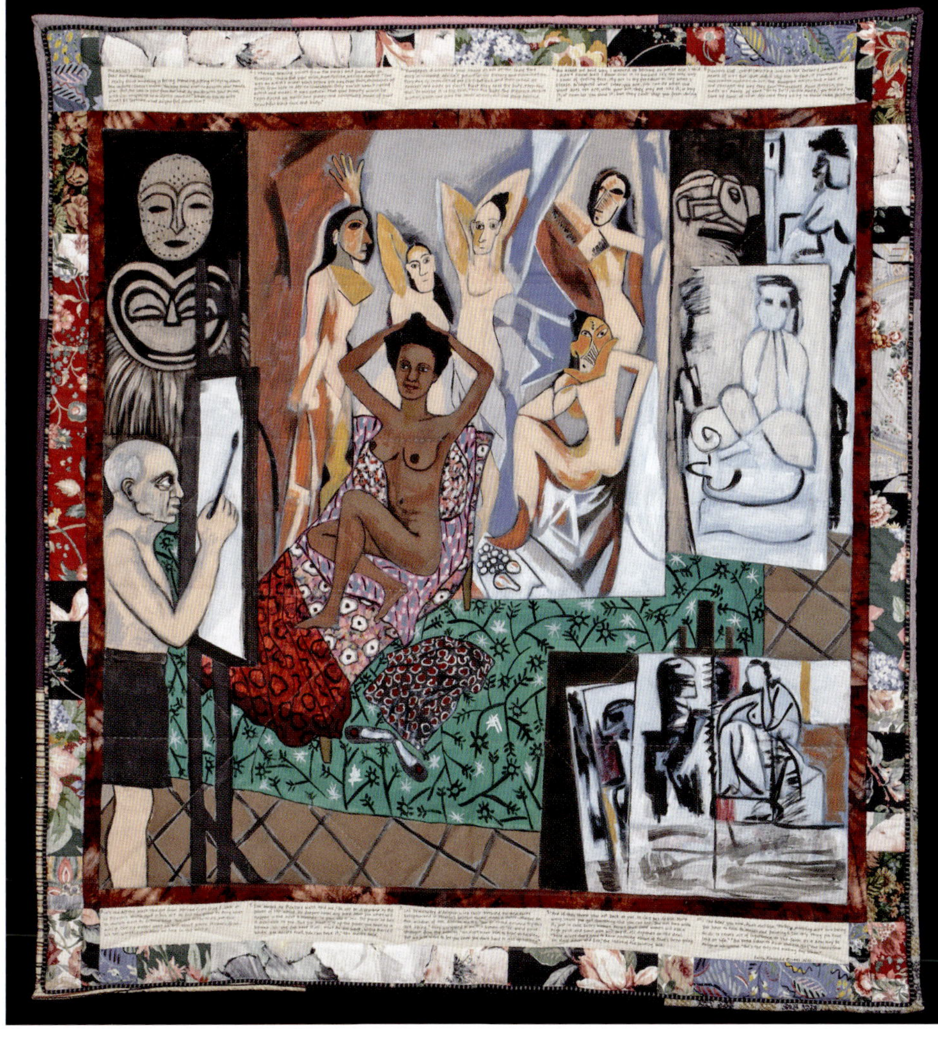

FIG. 93 Faith Ringgold, *Picasso's Studio*, 1991

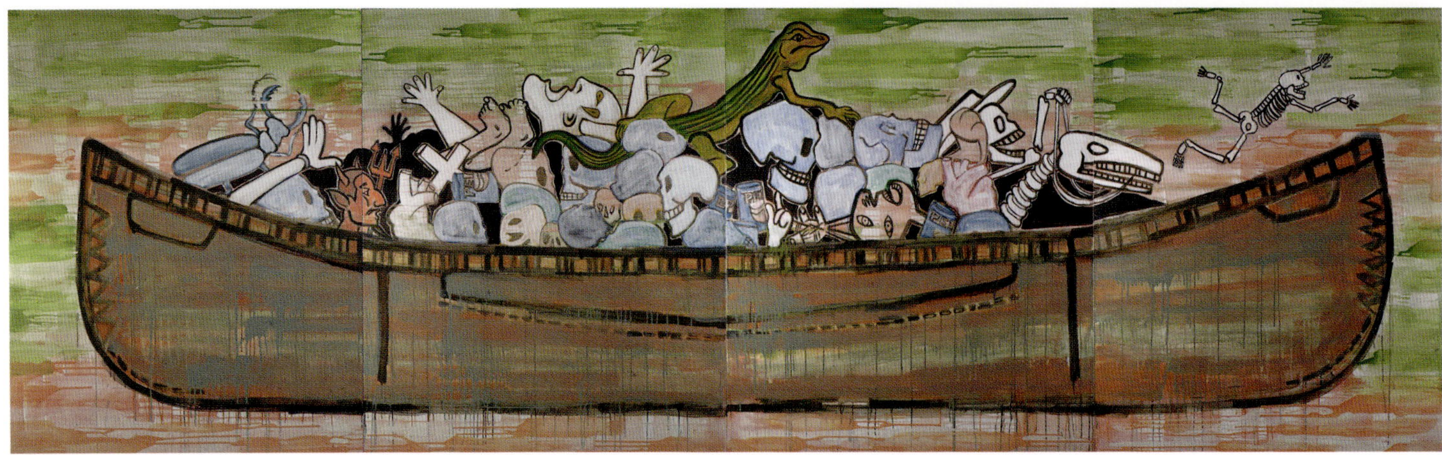

by representing her alter ego in the Spanish painter's studio, which is populated by African masks that begin speaking to her, encouraging her to assert herself as a Black female artist. They add as a warning: 'Do not let yourself be impressed by the artist's power'. Taking up this advice, Ringgold integrates into her artworks the artistic innovations that Picasso helped to establish, making them serve her own vision and her feminist and anti-racist standpoint. Similarly, Native American artist Jaune Quick-to-See Smith uses figures borrowed from *Guernica* in her paintings (FIG. 94) to evoke the massacres of Indigenous populations by colonists in the United States. The approaches of Smith and Ringgold echo the words of Miller: 'The personality cult of Picasso is not worth salvaging. What is, is the material practice, by turns dialectical and deconstructive, that he introduced into the field of vision.'[76] We might add: 'and his artistic commitment to peace'. With *Guernica* and his doves of peace, the artist created powerful symbols that have withstood the passage of time, and which are still used in political demonstrations. From the protests against the American invasion of Iraq in 2003 (FIG. 95) to more recent reactions to the war in Ukraine or the Israeli bombing of Gaza, these symbols continue to embody the political struggles of our time. Through such contemporary resurgences, Picasso's works—and his aesthetic—ultimately transcend their creator, emerging as autonomous objects that anyone can claim, transforming them into mythical images.

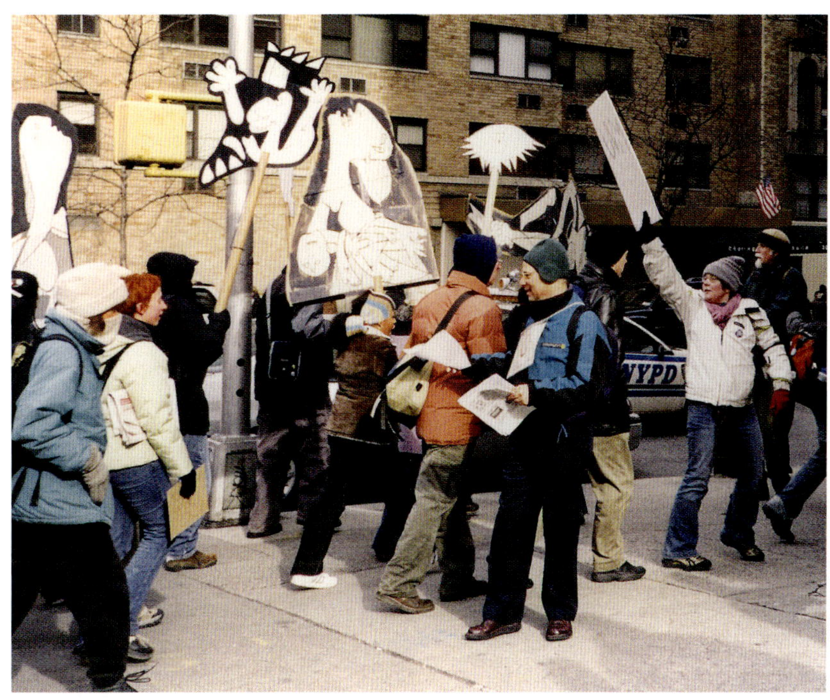

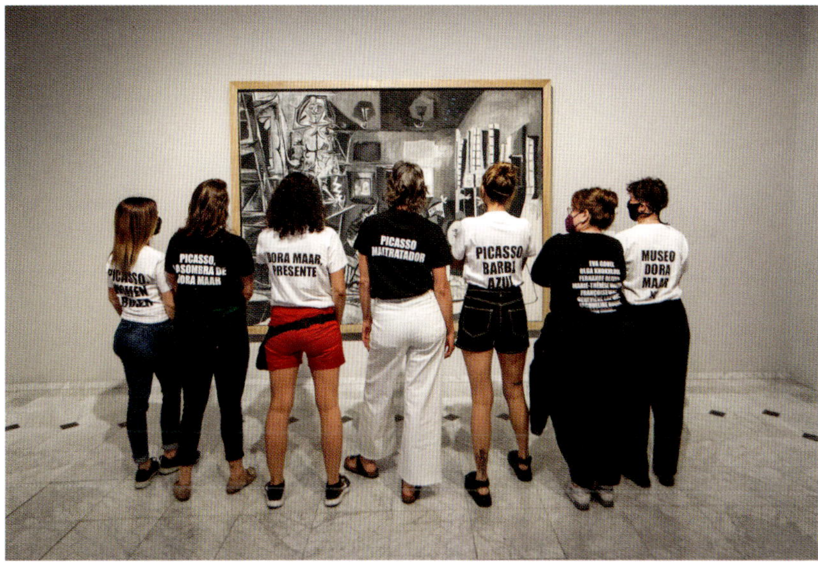

OPPOSITE: FIG. 94 Jaune Quick-to-See Smith, *Trade Canoe for Don Quixote*, 2004

RIGHT TOP: FIG. 95 Anti-Iraq War protest in New York City, 2003

RIGHT BOTTOM: FIG. 96 Maria Llopis and her students at the Picasso Museum in Barcelona, 2021

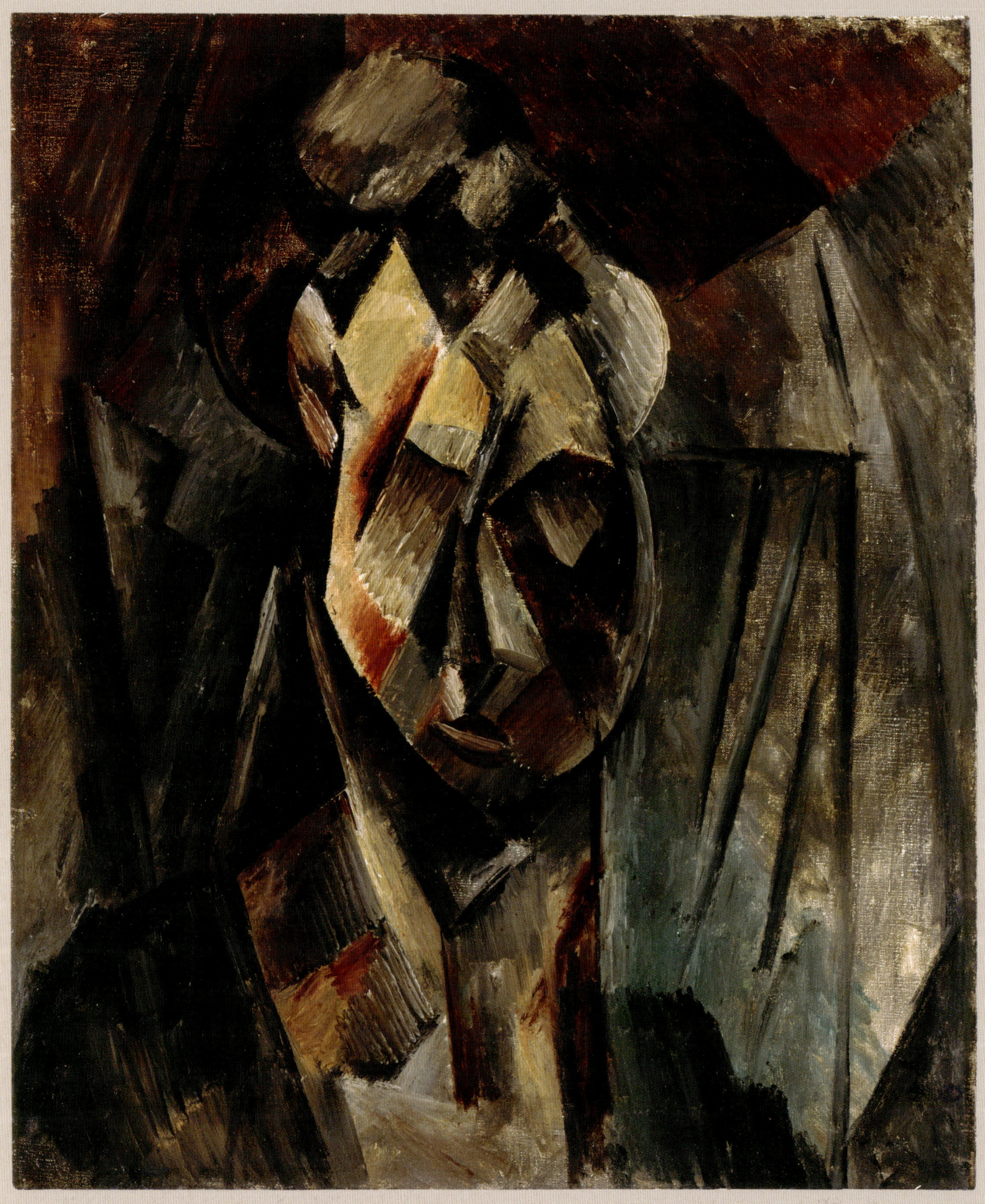

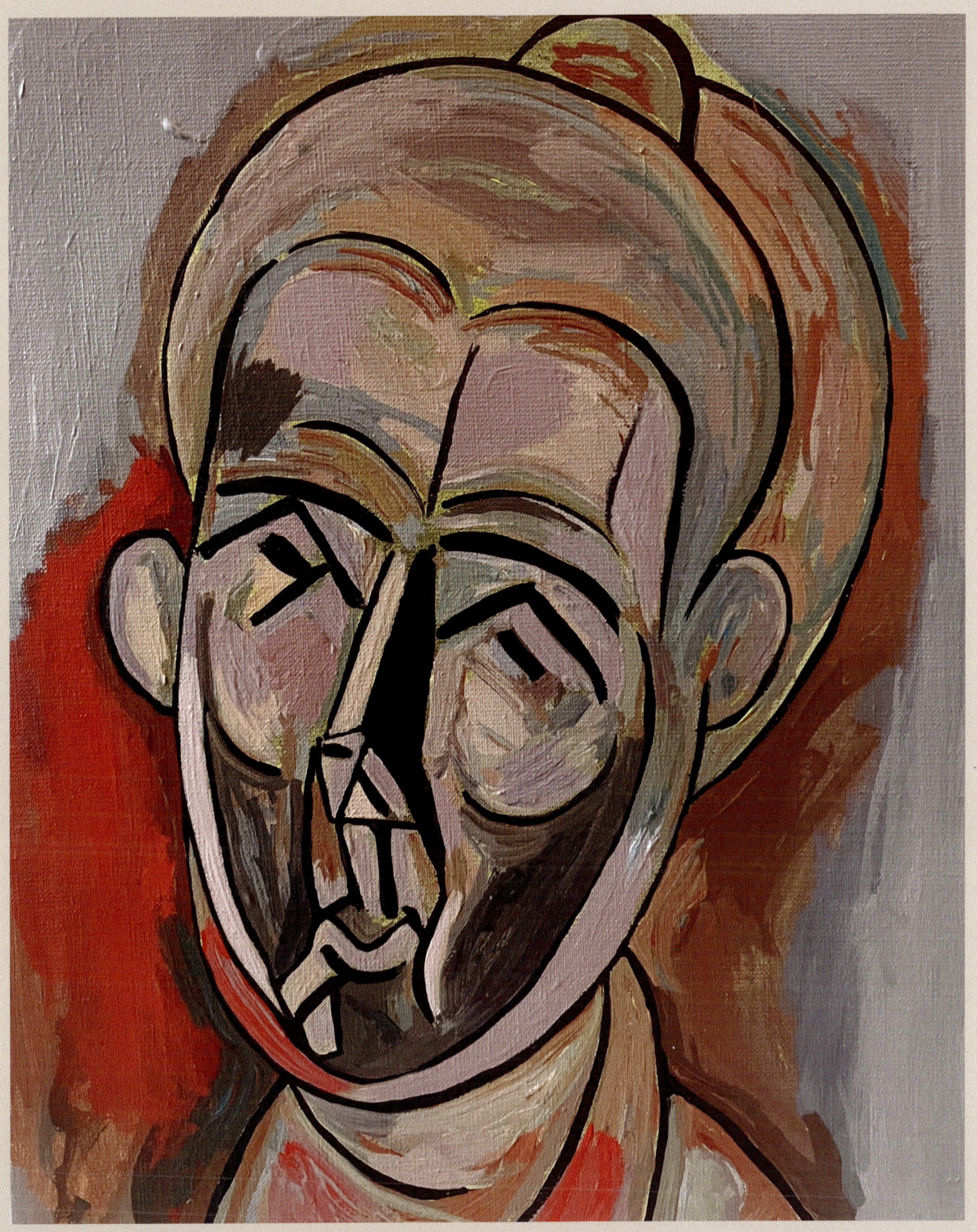

REMAKING

PICASSO

FOR ASIA

Doryun Chong

PICASSO AND ASIA?

Let us begin with the 1951 painting *Massacre in Korea* (FIG. 97) by Pablo Picasso. Started and completed on 18 January by the famously quick-handed artist,[1] the painting depicts a scene of horrifying atrocity unfolding on the Korean peninsula. The Korean War had broken out seven months earlier, on 25 June 1950, when the armies of Soviet Union–backed North Korea crossed the 38th parallel and invaded the United States–backed South Korea. Amid the increasingly tense Cold War, this 'hot' conflict in Korea was a proxy battle in Asia between the great powers.

The sixty-nine-year-old Picasso was following the news from his home in the town of Vallauris in the south of France. The long, horizontally orientated oil-on-plywood painting that he produced features two groups of figures: on the left side, four women with four children, all stripped bare; and on the right, a firing squad of six male figures, also nude except for the metal helmets on their heads. The two women at the far left of the composition wear expressions of extreme anguish and desolation, their visages reminiscent of the women's faces in *Guernica* (1937; FIG. 77), among the best-known works in Picasso's oeuvre. The faces of the two women in the centre-right of *Massacre in Korea* recall those depicted in other well-known paintings by Picasso. One woman has the kind of mask-like face that appears in *Les Demoiselles d'Avignon* (1907; FIG. 46), while the other appears placid, her image likely based on that of Françoise Gilot, Picasso's companion at the time of the painting's creation.

Four children, including two infants, join the group of women. They are variously held in arms, crying out of fear, fleeing in panic, and crouching on the ground playing, heedless of the imminent death descending on them. The image of the child at play recalls the recurring motifs of innocence and joy evident in the artist's portraits of his own children. At the time, Picasso was a father of four: Paulo with his first wife, Olga Khokhlova; Maya with Marie-Thérèse Walter; and, most recently, Claude and Paloma with Gilot, both of whom were born within a few years of the painting.

If the depiction of women and children presents a summary of the quintessential elements of Picasso's portraiture, there are few precedents for the male figures, whose rigidity is atypical of Picasso's work. Five of the six men in the group point their rifles and bayonets, while the figure on the extreme right holds a sword in his right hand and raises it above his head in a classically heroic posture. Their robust, even brutish musculature ironically reminds informed viewers of the 'savage' and 'primitive' bodies of the brazenly exhibitionist women of *Les Demoiselles d'Avignon* while contrasting with the soft roundedness of the women's bodies, in particular those of the two figures who are clearly pregnant. The men are painted in reference to Hellenistic or Roman statues, and Picasso might also have been thinking of scenes of both brotherhood and carnage in Jacques-Louis David's *Oath of the Horatii* (1784; FIG. 98) and *The Intervention of the Sabine Women* (1799; FIG. 99). The former is echoed in *Massacre in Korea* in the massing of the male figures and their forward-lunging postures while the latter is invoked in the men's muscular nudity and their rampage on women.[2] In Picasso's version the men are rendered classical and modern, heroic and robotic, orderly and helter-skelter, all at the same time. Beyond David's late eighteenth-century history paintings, the overall composition of *Massacre in Korea* pays an explicit homage to two examples of

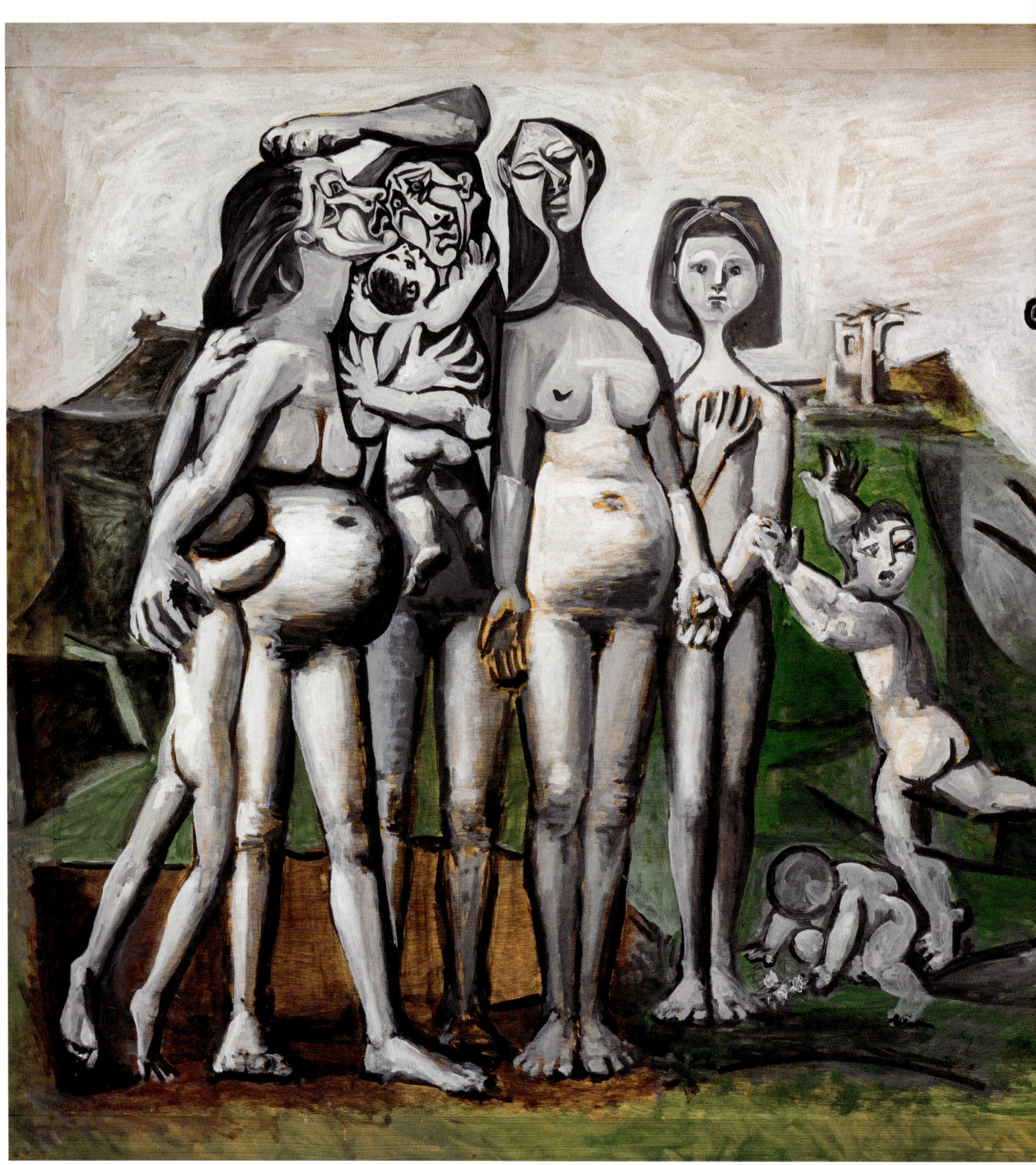

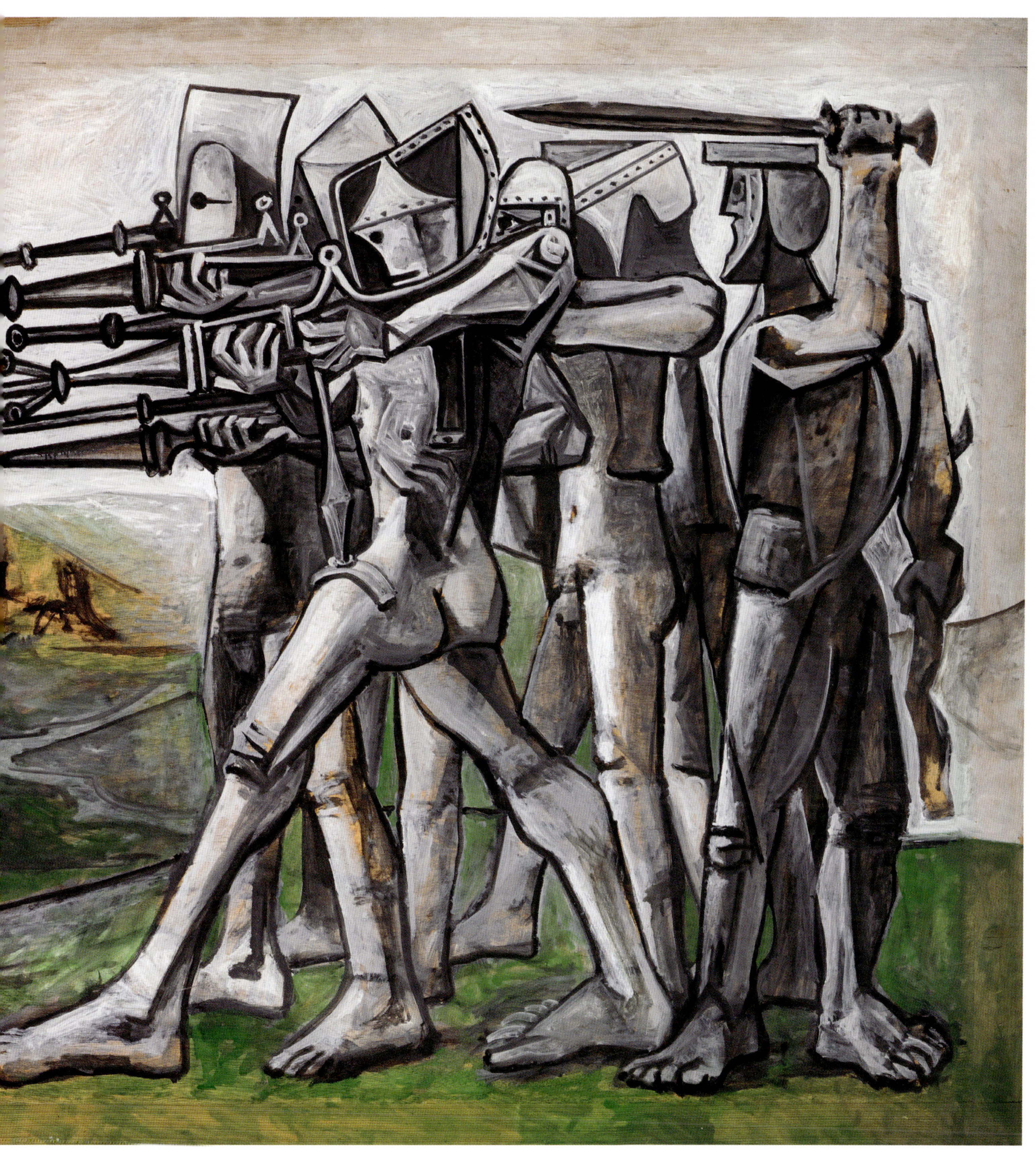

FIG. 97 *Massacre in Korea*, 1951

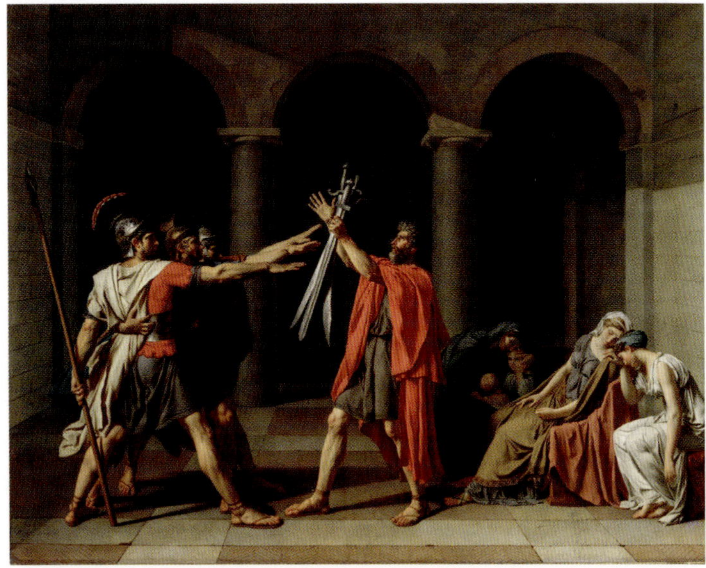

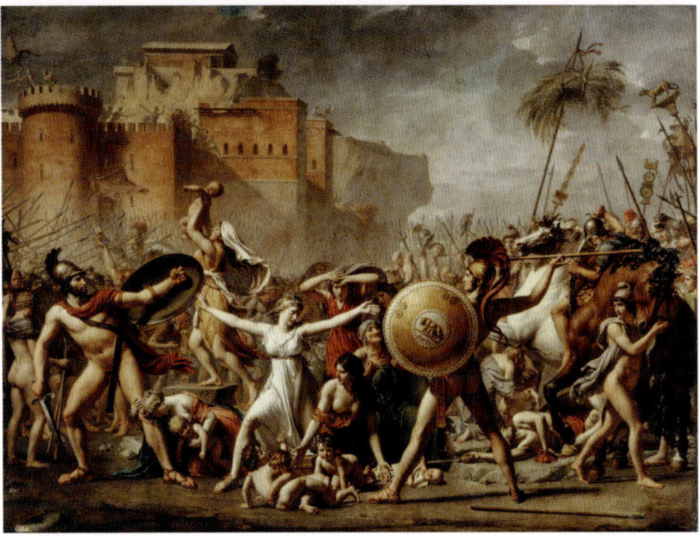

FIG. 98 Jacques-Louis David, *Oath of the Horatii*, 1784

FIG. 99 Jacques-Louis David, *The Intervention of the Sabine Women*, 1799

modern updates on history painting: *The Third of May 1808* (1814; FIG. 100) by Francisco Goya and *The Execution of Emperor Maximilian* (1868–1869; FIG. 101) by Édouard Manet. In other words, Picasso learned from his nineteenth-century predecessors how a painting can be a witness of events unfolding in the present, while from his eighteenth-century artistic ancestors he retained the idea that the present can be put in continuum with legendary events from antiquity.

Massacre in Korea is one of Picasso's few explicitly political paintings, along with *Guernica* and *The Charnel House* (1944–1945; FIG. 102). The former is a searing response to the bombing of the Basque town of the same name perpetrated by the Nazis with cooperation from Franco's fascist regime in the artist's native Spain. The latter, a largely unfinished composition, was painted during the final years of the Second World War and is usually seen as Picasso's response to the Holocaust. Both paintings radiate the profound despair and anger the artist felt towards the cruelties inflicted by the human race upon itself. They are also the bookends to Picasso's war years, which—unlike many of his artist friends and colleagues, who chose to emigrate to the United States—he spent mostly in Paris.

After the war Picasso became increasingly active in left-wing politics. He joined the French Communist Party and publicly advocated

FIG. 100 Francisco Goya, *The Third of May 1808*, 1814

FIG. 101 Édouard Manet, *The Execution of Emperor Maximilian*, 1868–1869

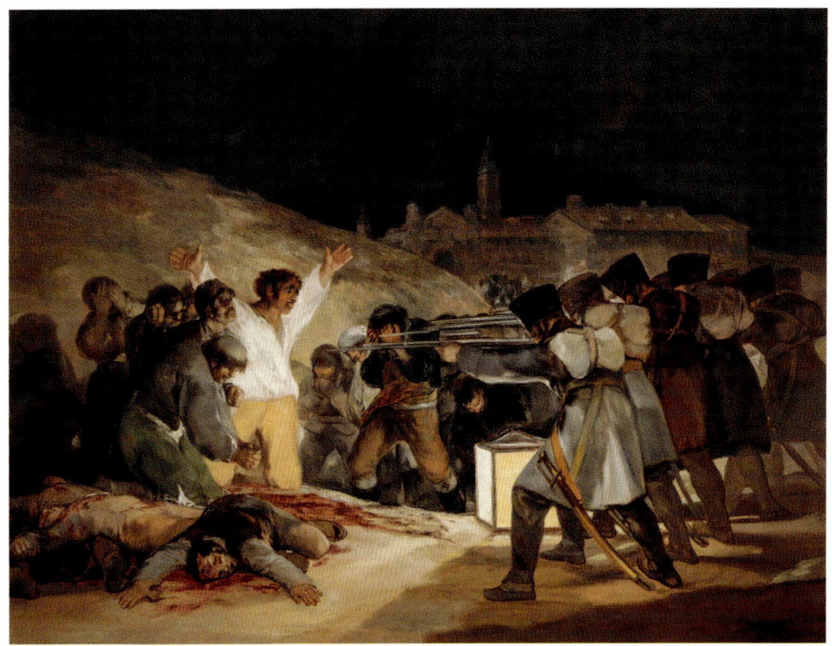

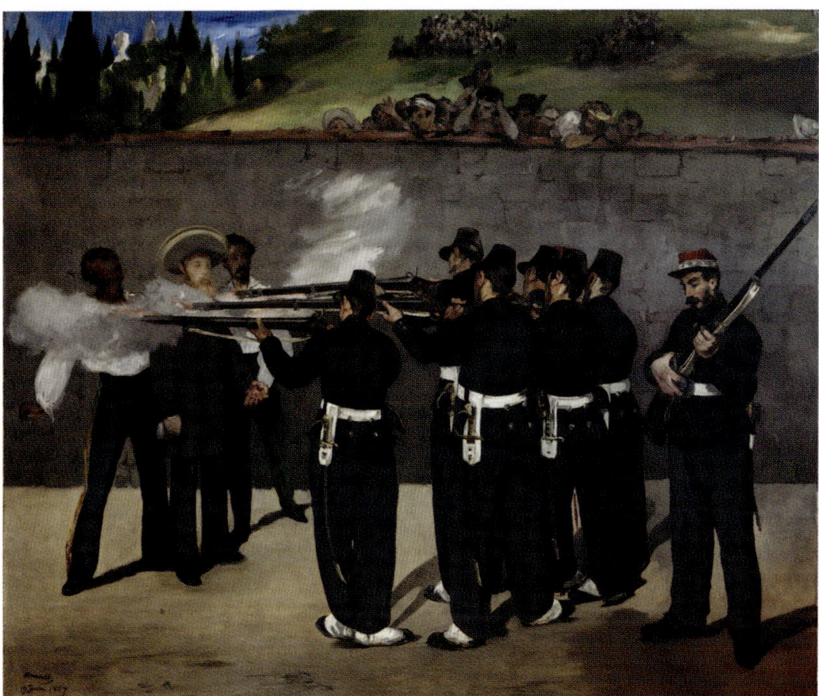

pacifism. Picasso had rarely left France since settling there in 1904, venturing to Spain only a handful of times. Yet in 1948 he attended the first World Congress of Intellectuals in Defense of Peace in Wrocław, Poland. On the same trip he visited Warsaw and Kraków, as well as the site of Auschwitz concentration camp.[3] Two years later, in October 1950, he attended the Second World Peace Congress in Sheffield, England. The poster for the event features his now-famous lithograph *Dove in Flight* (FIG. 103), made in July that year.[4]

It was during this extraordinary period, when Picasso remade himself into a public figure aligned with the peace movement, that he painted *Massacre in Korea*. In the summer of 1950 the North Korean army quickly overwhelmed most of South Korea's territory, only to be pushed back by the US-led UN allied forces in a counterattack that resulted in the loss of its own territory. With help from the People's

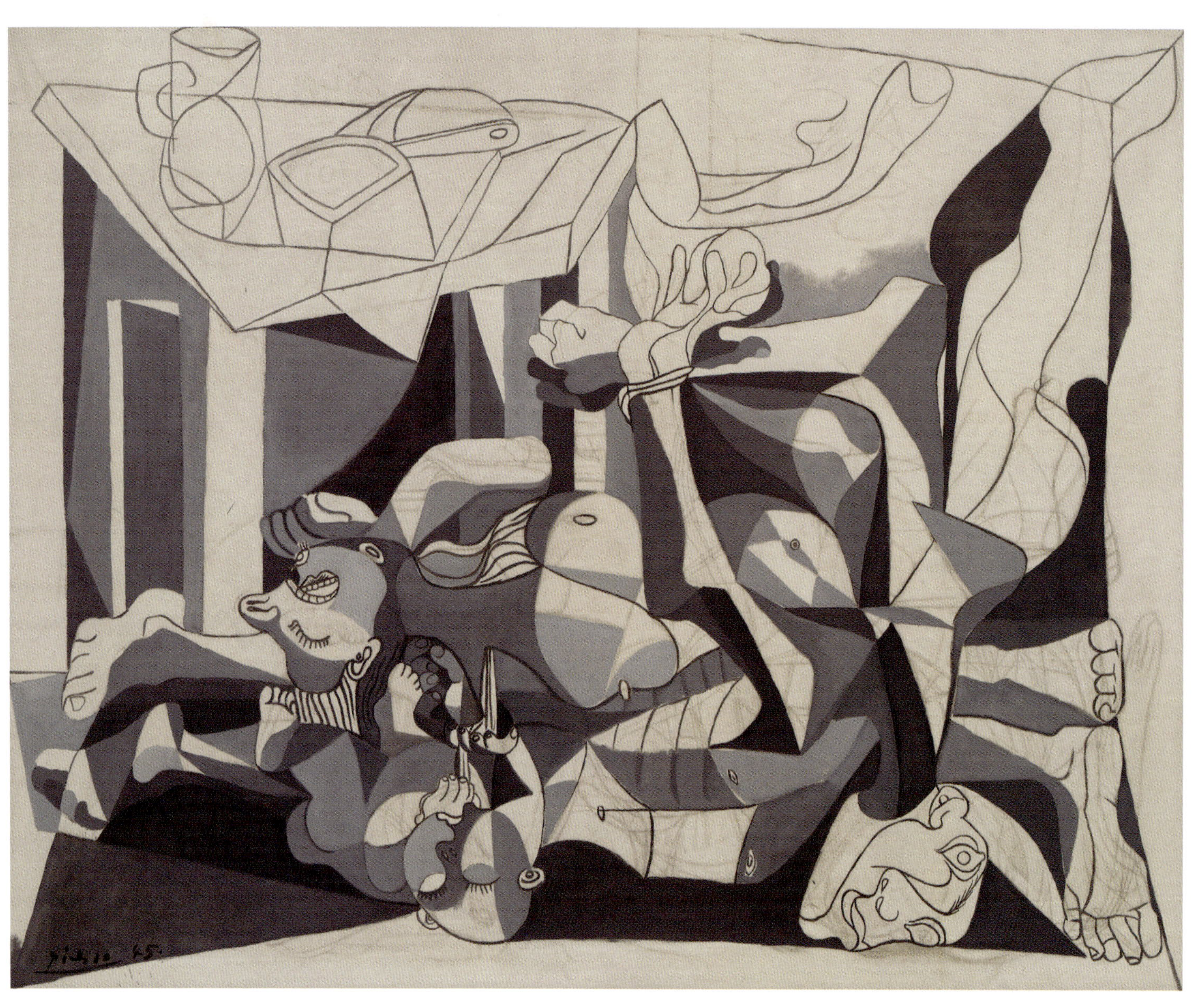

FIG. 102 *The Charnel House*, 1944–1945

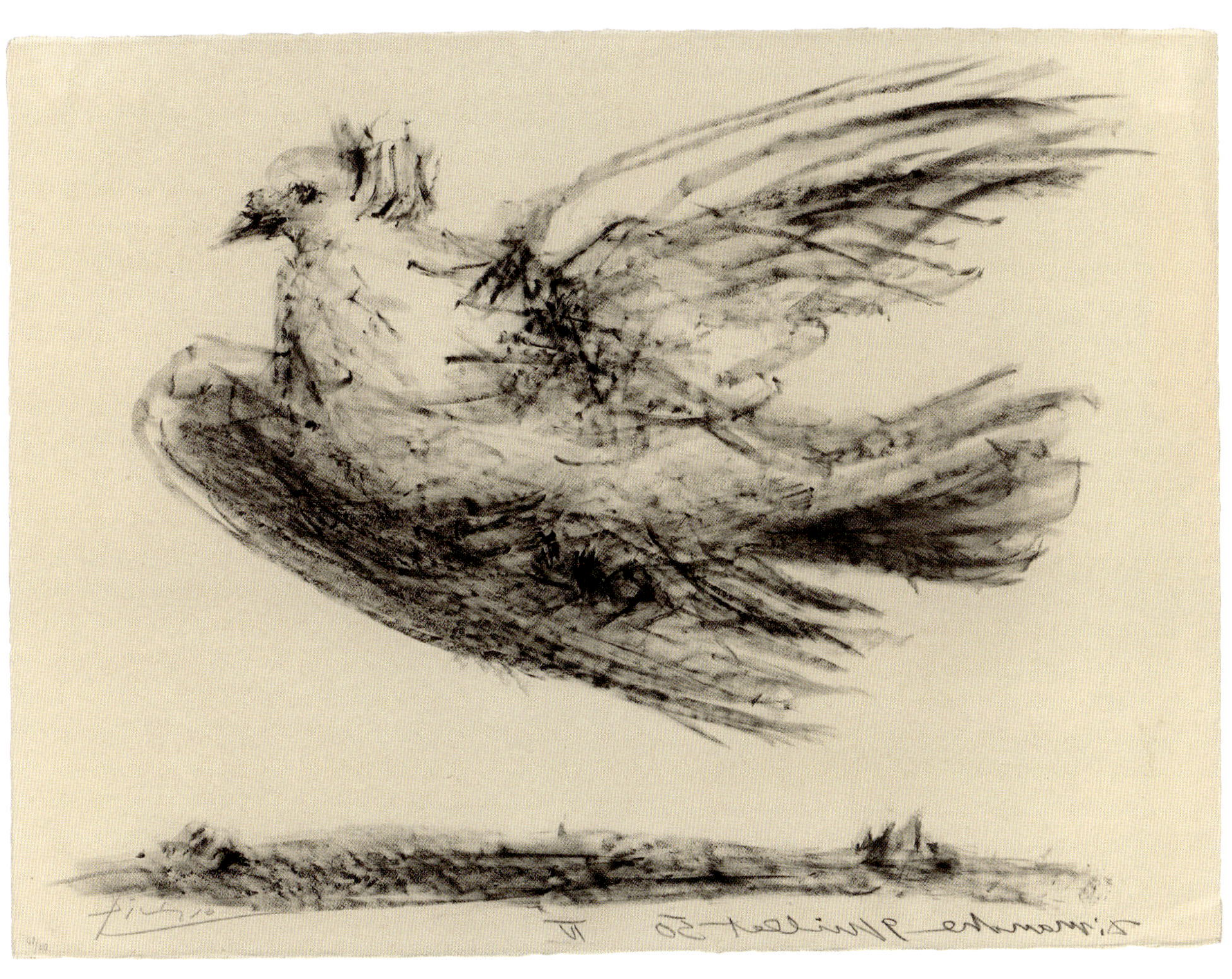

FIG. 103 *Dove in Flight*, 1950

Republic of China (PRC), however, North Korea began to turn the tide by early 1951. A protracted tug-of-war between the two sides would eventually lead to the division of the country that persists to this day.

According to one critic, *Massacre in Korea* is Picasso's effort to be validated by the Communist Party.[5] The same critic also notes: 'Lacking Picasso's usual formal and symbolic ambiguity, *Massacre in Korea* constitutes an uncharacteristically clear depiction of a contemporary event ... Picasso had never taken such pains to respond in the way that the party expected of him as he did in *Massacre in Korea*.'[6] Although the painting is remarkable for its connection to a contemporary world event—a rarity in Picasso's oeuvre—its formal language was not sufficiently realist for the party leaders and it was thus considered a failure. '[When] it was exhibited at the *Salon de Mai* in 1951, the canvas's lack of propagandist detail provided an opportunity for party critics to chide the artist for not showing the obviously American nationality of the aggressors and for portraying an execution instead of the resistance of the Koreans.'[7]

New ideological urgency motivated Picasso to depict political subject matter, even pushing him to work beyond his established, albeit extremely protean styles and iconography. A sense of belonging via political association seems to have driven this foreigner in his own long-adopted country to shift his gaze and interest to an event in a far-away land.[8] Decidedly European—or, to be more precise, Mediterranean—Picasso was at the same time happily ensconced in Provence with Gilot and their young family. Throughout his life the artist gave little credence to sources or traditions outside of his own immediate cultural context, except during a brief, if revolutionary, period of Primitivism, when he looked towards the cultures of Africa, but only via deracinated artefacts looted during France's colonial conquests. *Massacre in Korea* is even more remarkable as a rare example of Picasso engaging with an event happening outside of Europe.

During the late 1930s and 1940s the Museum of Modern Art in New York (MoMA) and its founding director, Alfred H. Barr, led the systematic canonisation of Picasso's art. On the other side of the world, in East Asia, Picasso had been introduced through publications and even several exhibitions in Japan, China, and South Korea. Whereas Picasso's affiliations with Communist parties caused consternation for Barr and MoMA amid an increasingly anti-Communist climate in the United States, 'his leftist tendency', one writer argues, 'was quite generously accepted or was emphasised in Asia while still being an object of disputes. Ultimately, such disputes reinforced the introduction of Picasso's works in the 1940s and 1950s to Asia.'[9] Receptions of Picasso in Asia, especially among artists, may have had a much more far-reaching impact:

Picasso made many artists in Asia think about and render the way of life as an artist, the participation in and responding to political issues, the ways to deliver explosive sentiments metaphorically and symbolically rather than rationally, and the ways to incorporate the mythologies and history of their own countries.[10]

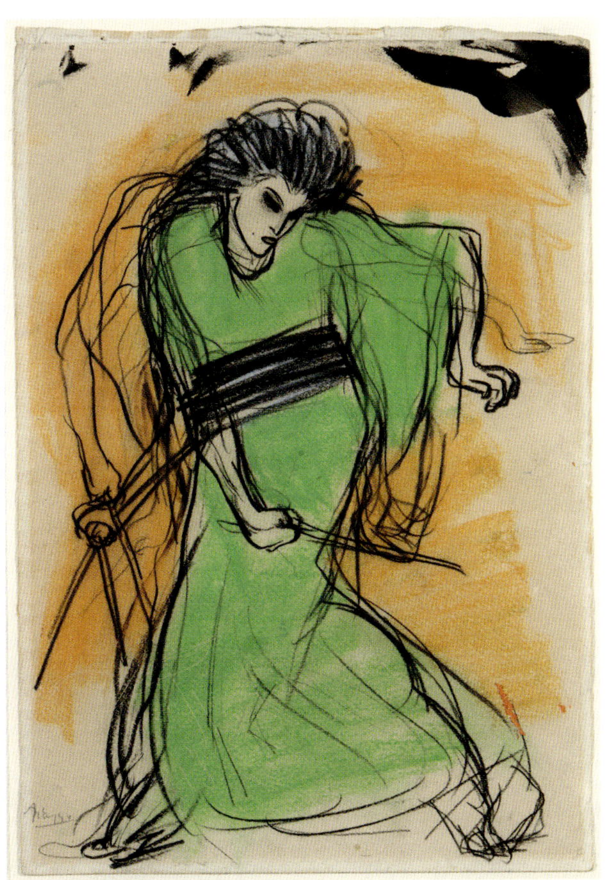

FIG. 104 *The Dancer Sada Yacco*, 1900–1901

ASIA IN PICASSO, PICASSO IN ASIA

It would be difficult to argue that one specific reference to Korea in a work by Picasso, however significant, constitutes a substantial connection between the archetypal Western master and the development of modern art in Asia, a vast and diverse region.[11] Textual evidence points to Picasso's seeming lack of interest in—if not outright dismissal of—Asian art and visual culture. Gertrude Stein, the American expatriate writer who was one of the artist's earliest advocates, relayed Picasso's complaints about her brother Leo making him look at his collection of Japanese *ukiyo-e* woodblock prints.[12] Stein's influential account, however, seems to be contradicted by a recollection of Fernande Olivier. In the 1930s Olivier wrote: '[The Stein family] had a very important collection of Chinese and Japanese prints, which were extremely beautiful. If one felt bored one could always retire into a corner and sitting comfortably in an arm-chair forget oneself in contemplation of these masterpieces.'[13] In another anecdote, Picasso wrote to the poet Guillaume Apollinaire, a close friend of the artist and an early proponent of Cubism, saying: 'My greatest artistic emotions came when I suddenly saw the sublime beauty of the sculptures executed by the anonymous artists of Africa ... I hasten to add that, however, I detest exoticism. I've never liked the Chinese, the Japanese or the Persians.'[14] It is striking that he does not seem to consider his appropriation of African art as a form of exoticism.

A young Picasso's expression of distaste for what he calls 'exoticism' sounds reactionary in its stridency. There is other evidence, however, that he had in fact been exposed to, and even tried his hand at, an iconography inspired by *ukiyo-e*. He depicted the Japanese stage actress Sada Yacco (1901; FIG. 104), whose European tour garnered great acclaim around the turn of the twentieth century, when Picasso was making a name for himself in Barcelona and Paris. Although an isolated work within the artist's oeuvre, *The Dancer Sada Yacco* exemplifies the dominant aesthetic trends of the time. The work of Picasso's predecessors, from whom he both distanced himself and drew influence, had been incontrovertibly transformed by the exposure to the artistic vocabulary that came from *l'Extrême-Orient* (Far East). One writer argues, 'By absorbing and combining certain artistic principles typical of van Gogh, Gauguin, Toulouse-Lautrec or Degas, Picasso incorporated into his own work some of the plastic solutions practised by the *ukiyo-e* masters.'[15] By the early 1900s, however, the four-decade craze for Japanese art and visual culture that spawned Japonisme—the powerful influence of the visual languages of the Far Eastern country on the art, design, and crafts in Europe, especially in France—had already reached an apogee and was beginning to wane. Nonetheless, widespread interest in Japanese and broader Asian arts was certainly behind the founding in Paris of two museums dedicated to Asia: Musée Guimet and Musée Cernuschi (originally called Musée des arts de l'Asie de la Ville de Paris) in 1889 and 1898, respectively. Japan's participation in world's fairs during this time introduced Japanese visual art and culture to members of the public in Europe.[16] Dealers in Japanese art, especially prints, the most prominent of whom was Siegfried Bing in Paris, also played a crucial role.

Leading French artists of the early twentieth century, including Cézanne and Matisse, had been enthralled by Japanese art and other non-Western aesthetic traditions. As a young enterprising artist seeking to distinguish himself, Picasso rejected the older generation's influences, castigating Asian art as merely 'decorative'. One scholar contends

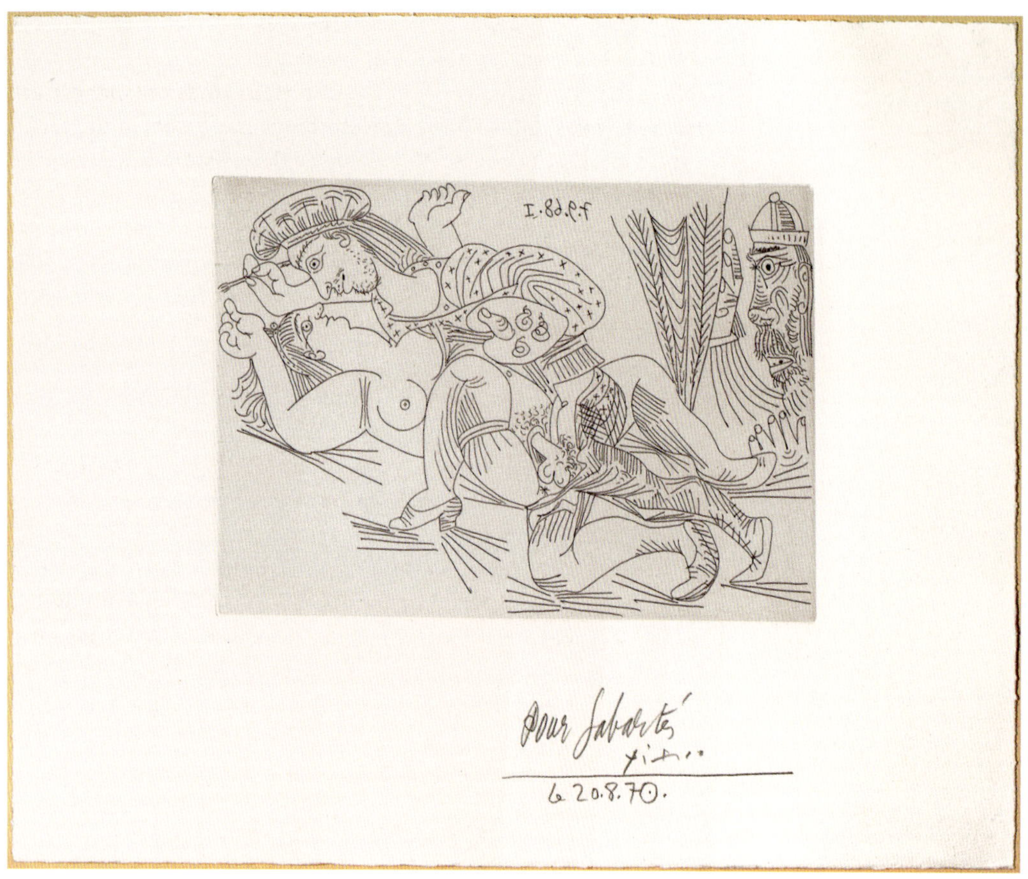

that this rejection is also consistent with the formal experimentation that led Picasso to Cubism, his most radical innovation:

As he concentrated on the transformation of the pictorial space, conceived independently of the objects and figures but inseparably linked to the radiation of forms and the rejection of the 'motif' as the source of painting, how could Picasso not repeatedly express his dislike for exoticism in general and Japanese art in particular? The single focus of Japanese prints and their subtly outlined, delicately coloured surfaces were diametrically opposed to the non-delineated planes, the fusion of space and objects and the multiple points of view which characterized the new pictorial language that Picasso and Braque were beginning to develop.[17]

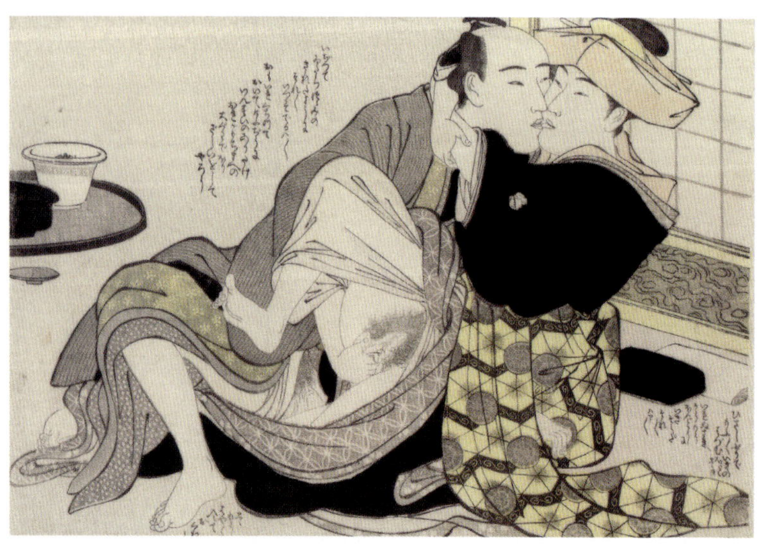

ABOVE: FIG. 105 *Raphael and the Fornarina. XX: The Pope Leaves*, 1968

LEFT: FIG. 106 Katsukawa Shunchō, *Couple Sheltering Behind a Shōji Door*, 1789–1801

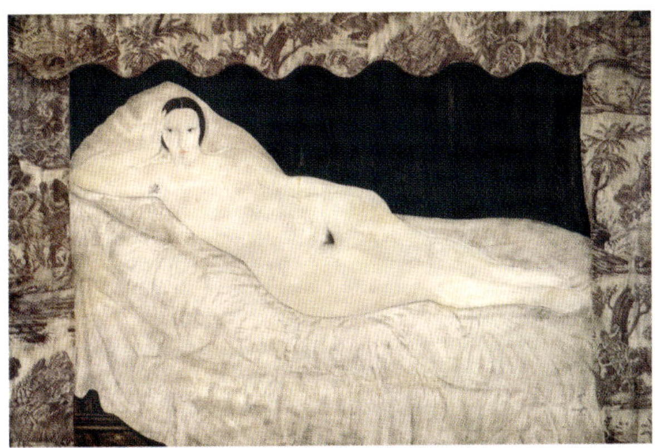

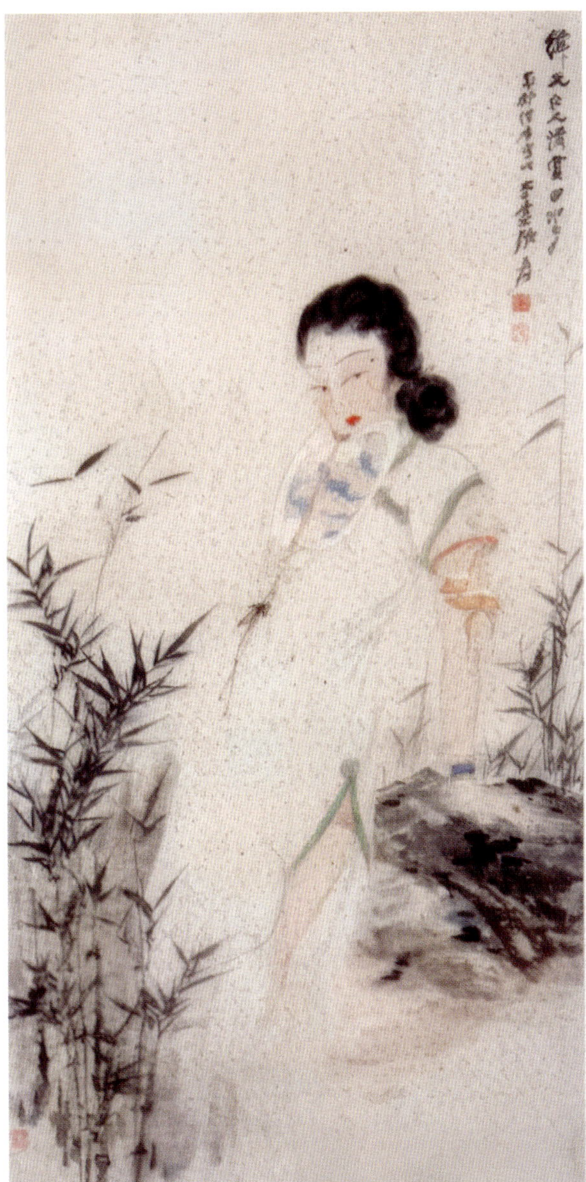

Despite his stated dislike, Picasso kept a group of Japanese prints in his private collection throughout his life. Some of his late works also reflect the unmistakable influence of certain kinds of Japanese art. His *Suite 347* (1968)—named after the number of prints in the series, executed over the course of little more than six months—features various erotic and even pornographic scenes of an amorous couple, based on the story of the Italian Renaissance painter Raphael and his alleged lover La Fornarina. The explicit depictions of copulation and theatrical exaggerations of both male and female genitalia closely recall the unmistakably identifiable characteristics of *shunga* (spring picture) prints (FIG. 106).[18]

Another way Picasso came into contact with Asian art and visual culture was through encounters with important Asian artists who visited Europe and came to pay their respects to the incomparable modern master. Léonard Tsuguharu Foujita (1886–1968; FIG. 107), the Japanese artist who became an integral part of the École de Paris (School of Paris), met Picasso soon after he moved to the French capital in 1913.[19] More than half a century later, in 1956, Chinese ink painter Zhang Daqian, also known as Chang Dai-chien (1899–1983; FIG. 108), made a trip to Nice to meet Picasso, a rendezvous described as a summit between two towering figures in modern art, in the East and in the West (FIG. 109).[20] Both individuals had been made into an archetypal genius but had a nuanced understanding of their lifelong outsider status. In the same way Picasso retained his Spanish citizenship throughout his life while living primarily in France, Zhang led a peripatetic life in the last three decades before his death, moving between countries ranging from Argentina and Brazil to the United States and Taiwan. Picasso

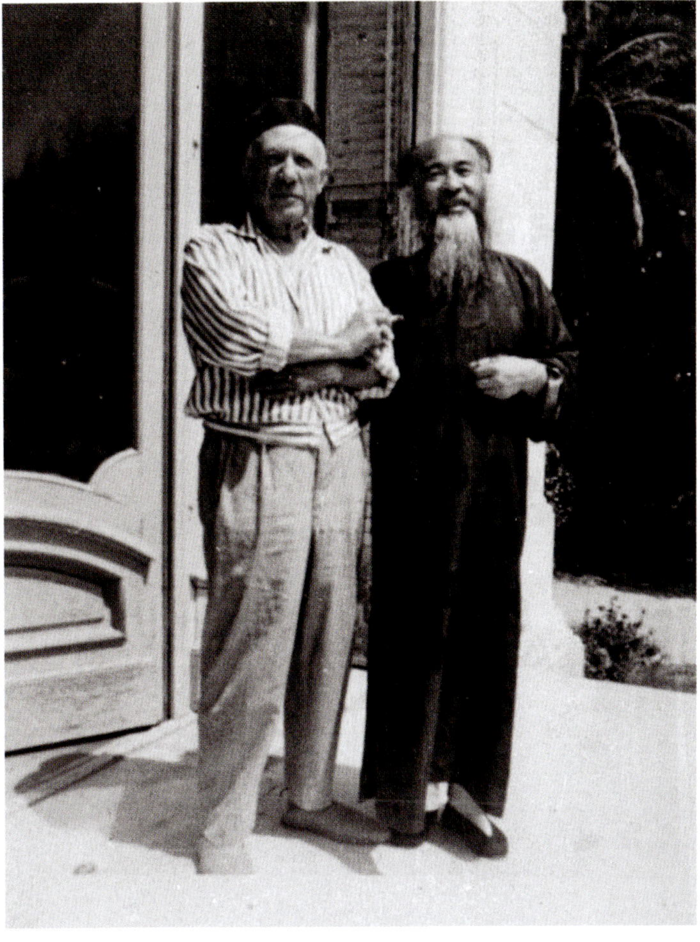

ABOVE TOP: FIG. 107 Léonard Tsuguhara Foujita, *Fujita, Reclining Nude with Toile de Jouy*, 1922

ABOVE: FIG. 108 Zhang Daqian, *Lady Holding a Fan*, 1944

RIGHT: FIG. 109 Pablo Picasso and Zhang Daqian at Villa La Californie, Cannes, 1956

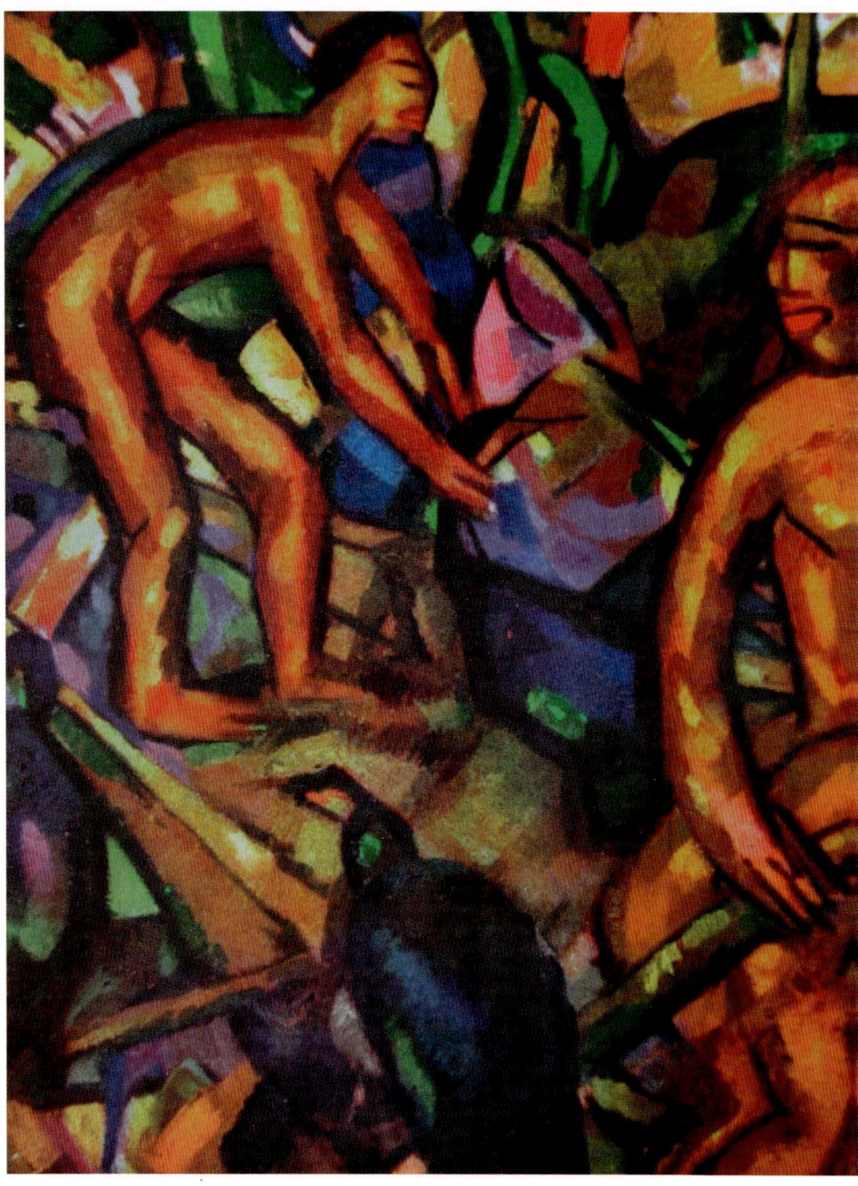

LEFT: FIG. 110 Lin Fengmian, *Composition*, ca.1934

BELOW: FIG. 111 Fang Ganmin, *Melody in Autumn*, 1933

OPPOSITE: FIG. 112 Lin Fengmian, *Still Life*, 1952

may have had encounters with other Asian modern artists that are undocumented or buried in the archives. Paris in the early decades of the twentieth century drew waves of young Asian artists seeking training and immersion in modern art in its indisputable capital. Many of them, unlike Foujita, chose to return to their homelands after their Parisian sojourns, becoming foundational figures in the modern art of their countries of origin.

Alongside the broader modernisation of Chinese culture and society, artistic modernism in China accelerated rapidly with the fall of the Qing dynasty and the establishment of the Republic of China in 1911, the same year in which Picasso and Georges Braque were deeply embroiled in their invention of Cubism. Their artistic revolution was reported in Chinese newspapers, journals, and publications as early as 1912, inspiring aspirants of Western-style art to make their way to Paris. Lin Fengmian (1900–1991), often hailed as the godfather of modern Chinese art, studied drawing and oil painting in the atelier of Fernand Cormon (1845–1924) at the École nationale supérieure des Beaux-Arts. Throughout his life, Lin would attempt to assimilate the essence of Western-style painting, thus creating an original style of his own. After returning to China, he founded the National Academy of Art in Hangzhou, now the

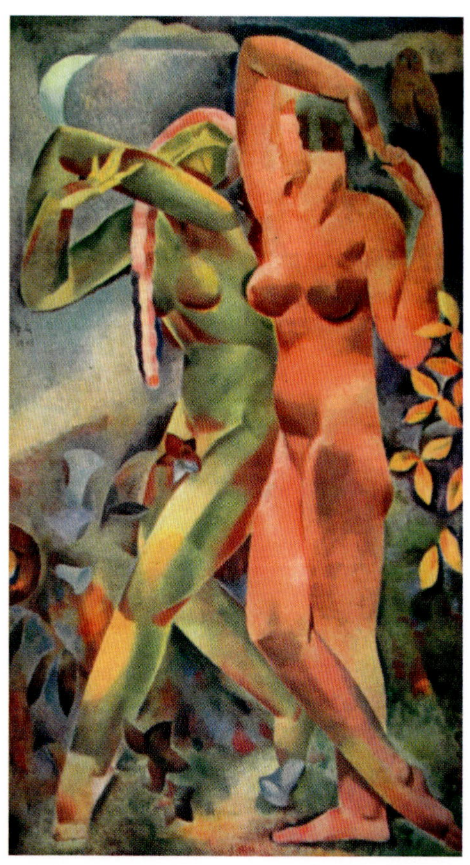

China Academy of Art. None of his works from his time in France are believed to have survived, but *Composition* (ca.1934; FIG. 110), known only through a reproduction in a 1934 issue of *Studio* (Meishu zazhi), shows an intense Fauvism- and Expressionism-influenced palette within a Cubist composition. Also reproduced in the same issue was *Melody in Autumn* (1933; FIG. 111) by Fang Ganmin (1906–1984), another pioneer of oil painting in China, who travelled to France in 1925. After preliminary studies in Lyon, Fang enrolled at the École in Paris in 1927 and returned to China in 1929. There he joined the faculty of Lin Fengmian's academy as a professor in the Western Painting Department. The illustrious list of artists he taught includes such Chinese-born modernist giants as Zao Wou-Ki (1920–2013), Chu Teh-Chun (1920–2014), and Wu Guanzhong (1919–2010). Zao moved to France in 1948, Chu in 1955, and both lived in the country for the rest of their lives. Wu also spent a couple of crucial years in France, from 1947 to 1950. Lin Fengmian continued to practise Cubism, among other diverse styles, in subsequent decades, as can be seen in his *Still Life* (1952; FIG. 112), produced in the early years of the newly established PRC and in the midst of the Korean War.

The modernisation of Japan began in a more wholesale and systematic fashion than that of China, following the forced 'opening' of the country in 1853 by the 'gunboat diplomacy' of the United States and the Meiji Restoration of 1868.[21] As with almost all the country's institutions

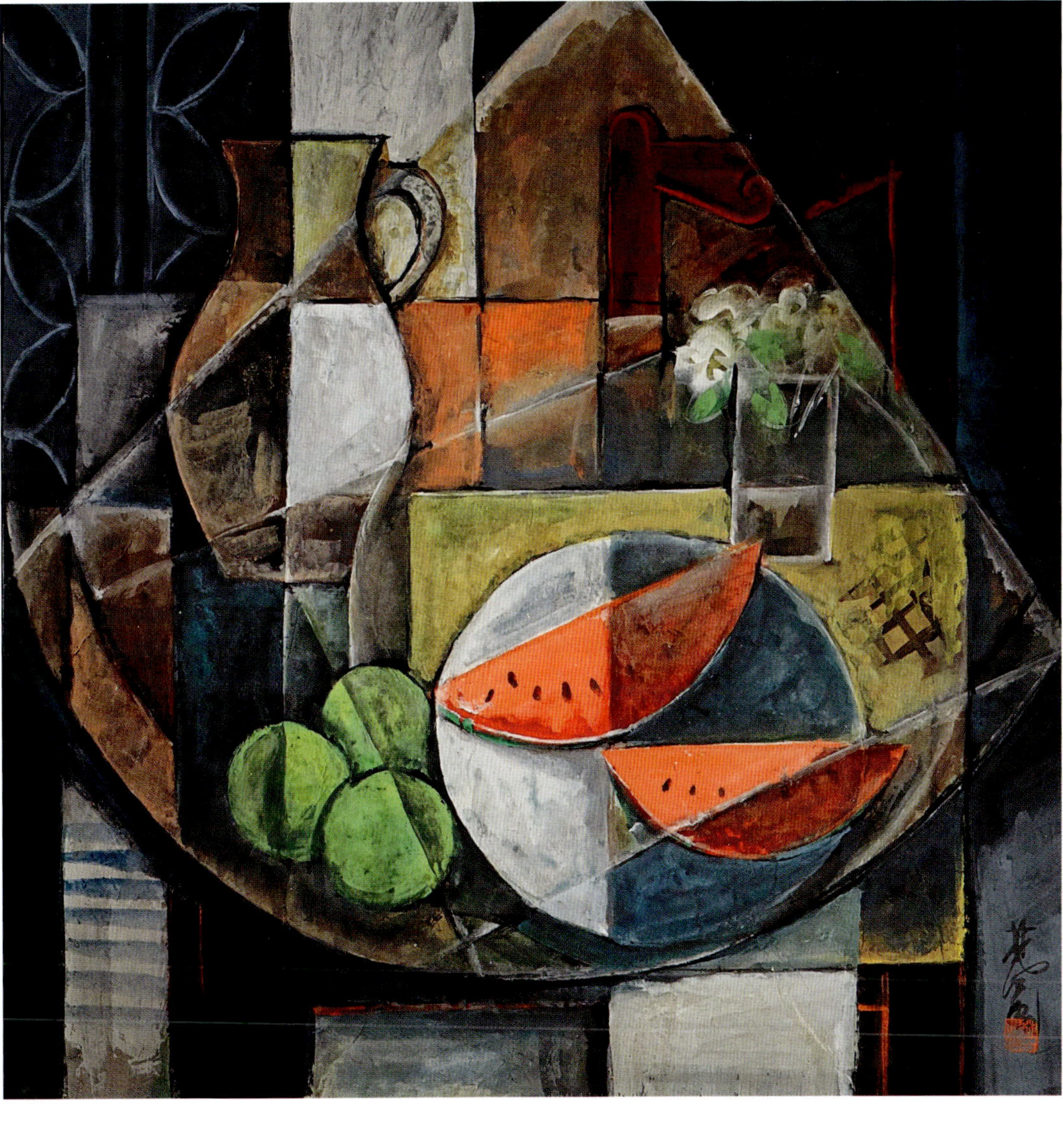

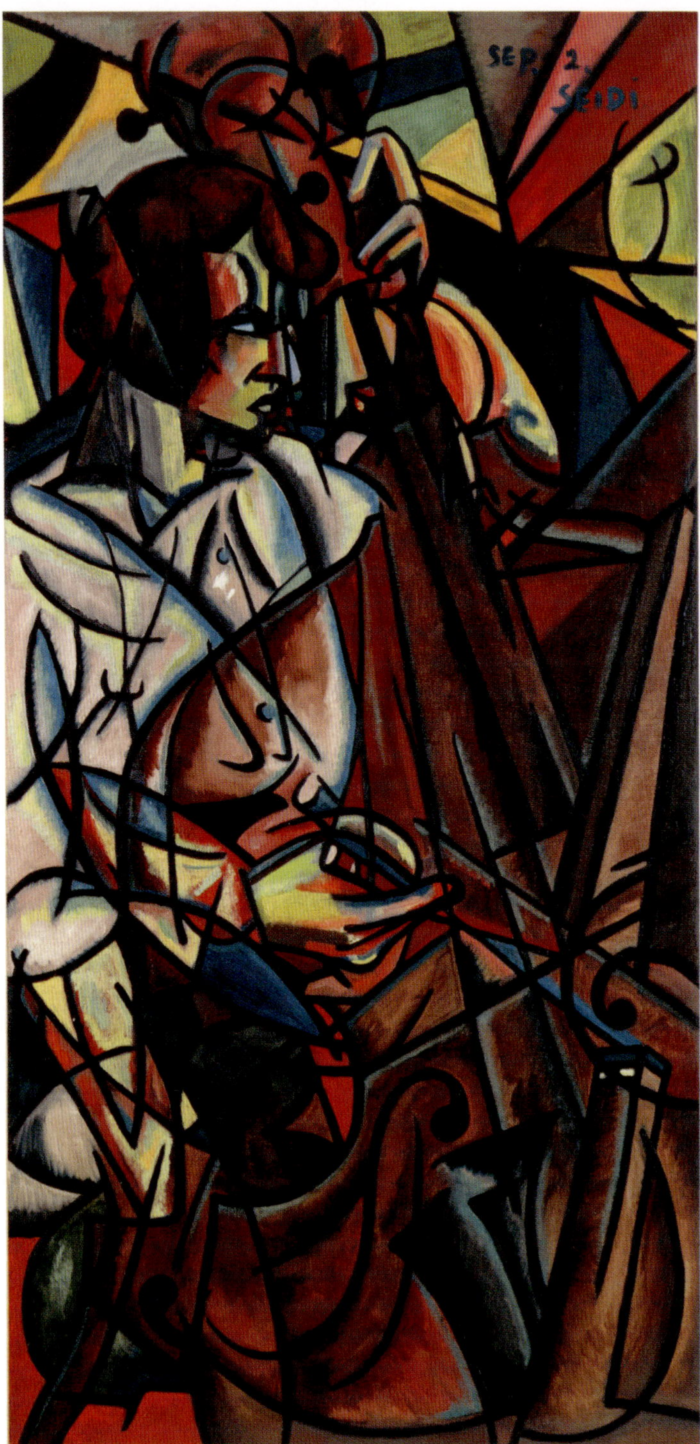

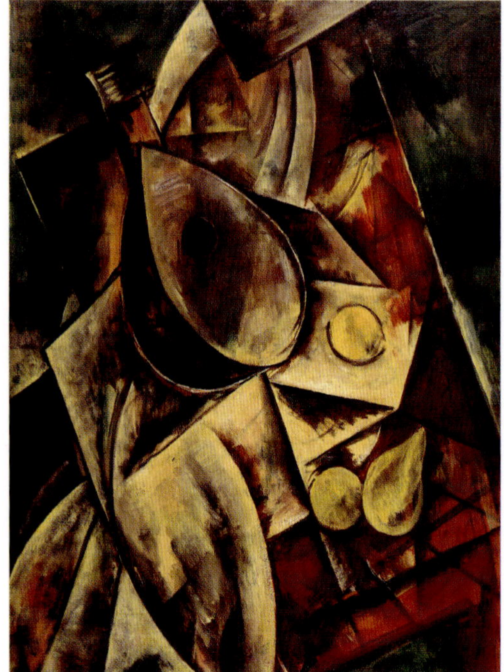

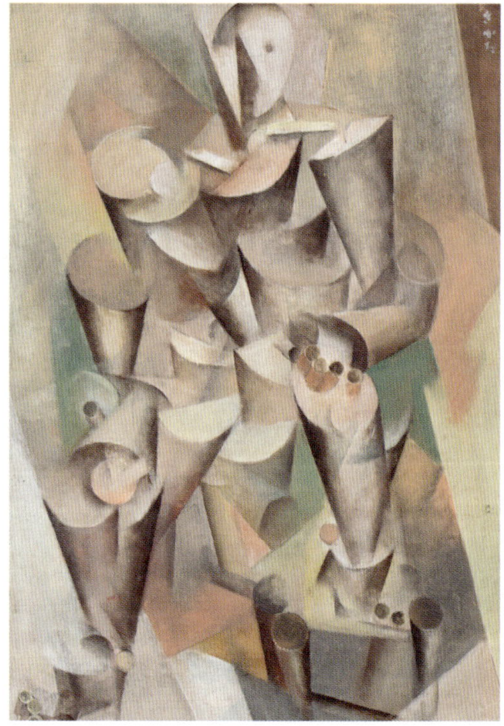

and systems, art education in Japan had already been Westernised by the 1870s, at the same time as the craze for Japonisme began to engulf Paris and other European urban centres. The first generation of Japanese artists to have been trained in Western-style art was already in France by the late nineteenth century. Kuroda Seiki (1866–1924), a name synonymous with the beginning of *yōga* (Western-style painting), was in France from 1884 to 1893, studying under Raphaël Collin and becoming proficient in academic as well as Impressionist styles. Kuroda was the teacher of Foujita before the latter migrated to Paris in 1913. Tokyo was a modern metropolis by then, in sync with other metropolises in the West, and the latest developments in avant-garde art were reported regularly and promptly. Cubism was reported soon after its debut,

LEFT: FIG. 113 Tōgō Seiji, *Playing the Contrabass*, 1915

ABOVE TOP: FIG. 114 Kawaguchi Kigai, *Still Life, Mandolin*, 1927–1931

ABOVE: FIG. 115 Sakata Kazuo, *Cubistic Figure*, 1925

BELOW LEFT: FIG. 116 Yorozu Tetsugorō, *Self-Portrait with Red Eyes*, 1912–1913

BELOW RIGHT: FIG. 117 Yorozu Tetsugorō, *Leaning Woman*, 1917

and artists who lived and trained only in Japan also began to practise this revolutionary style. One of the most celebrated names in modern Japanese art, Tōgō Seiji (1897–1978), was already painting in a Cubist style several years before heading to France, as can be seen in *Playing the Contrabass* (1915; FIG. 113). Staying in the capital of modern art from 1921 to 1928, Tōgō studied the recent and current avant-garde movements, including Futurism and Cubism as well as Dada. Japanese artists such as Kawaguchi Kigai (1892–1966; FIG. 114) and Sakata Kazuo (1889–1956; FIG. 115) arrived in Paris in the 1920s and later studied at the academies established by the Synthetic Cubists André Lhote and Fernand Léger. Sakata even became an assistant at the Académie Moderne established by Léger and Amédée Ozenfant.

There is perhaps no better example of the cosmopolitanism of Tokyo than Yorozu Tetsugorō (1885–1927). Yorozu studied and was active only in Japan. He made a single trip outside the country in 1906 with the intention of settling and studying in the United States, but the effort was in vain. He nonetheless created the most iconic works of avant-garde art in early twentieth-century Japan, naturalising Cubism, Futurism, and Fauvism in the milieu of modern Japanese art (FIGS 116 AND 117).

The divergence in the way in which Picasso was accepted in Japan and the PRC during the Cold War period illustrates the deep ideological divide that existed in the second half of the twentieth century. In the early post-war years Picasso's affiliation with the Communist

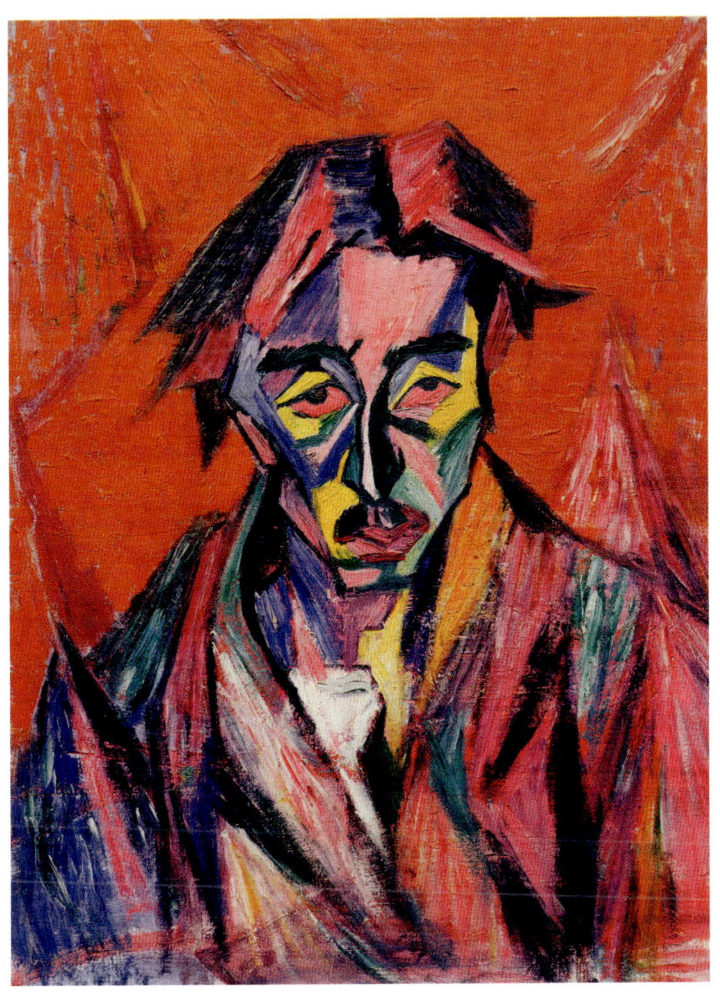

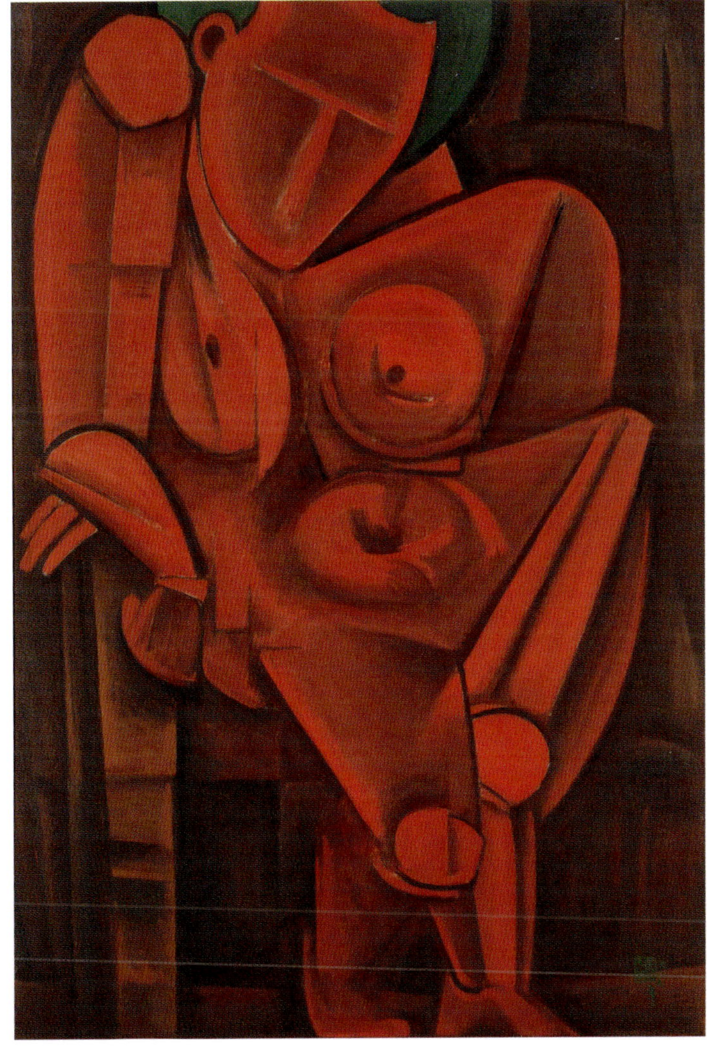

Party drew the attention of the US Federal Bureau of Investigation, which kept a file on the artist. Picasso's political commitments also complicated Barr's attempts to organise a major retrospective of the Spaniard's work at MoMA in 1957.[22] While Picasso's avant-garde artistic vocabulary and personal subject matter were anathema to Socialist Realism, the style officially adopted by the PRC, the artist's membership of the French Communist Party was welcome. Still, the main official art journal, *Meishu*, celebrated Picasso's eightieth birthday, highlighting the artist's work in 'enthusiastically opposing wars of aggression and safeguarding world peace', and even mentioning Cubism—a remarkable concession at a time when adherence to Socialist Realism was strictly enforced.[23]

In 1962 the National Museum of Western Art in Tokyo presented the exhibition *Picasso: Guernica* featuring a tapestry replica of the Picasso masterpiece woven by atelier Jacqueline Dürrbach and supervised by Picasso himself (FIG. 118). The artist's monumental painting had been in the United States since 1939. He requested that MoMA serve as the custodian of the work and not return it to Spain until the end of Franco's dictatorship. The painting travelled throughout America in the early 1940s as part of MoMA's blockbuster *Picasso: Forty Years of His Art*, and then to Europe as part of another travelling exhibition. It also toured Brazil in the early 1950s. From the mid-1950s until the painting's

FIG. 118 Film negative of Jacqueline de la Baume Dürrbach's *Guernica (Tapestry after Pablo Picasso)*, 1955, at *Picasso: Guernica*, 1962

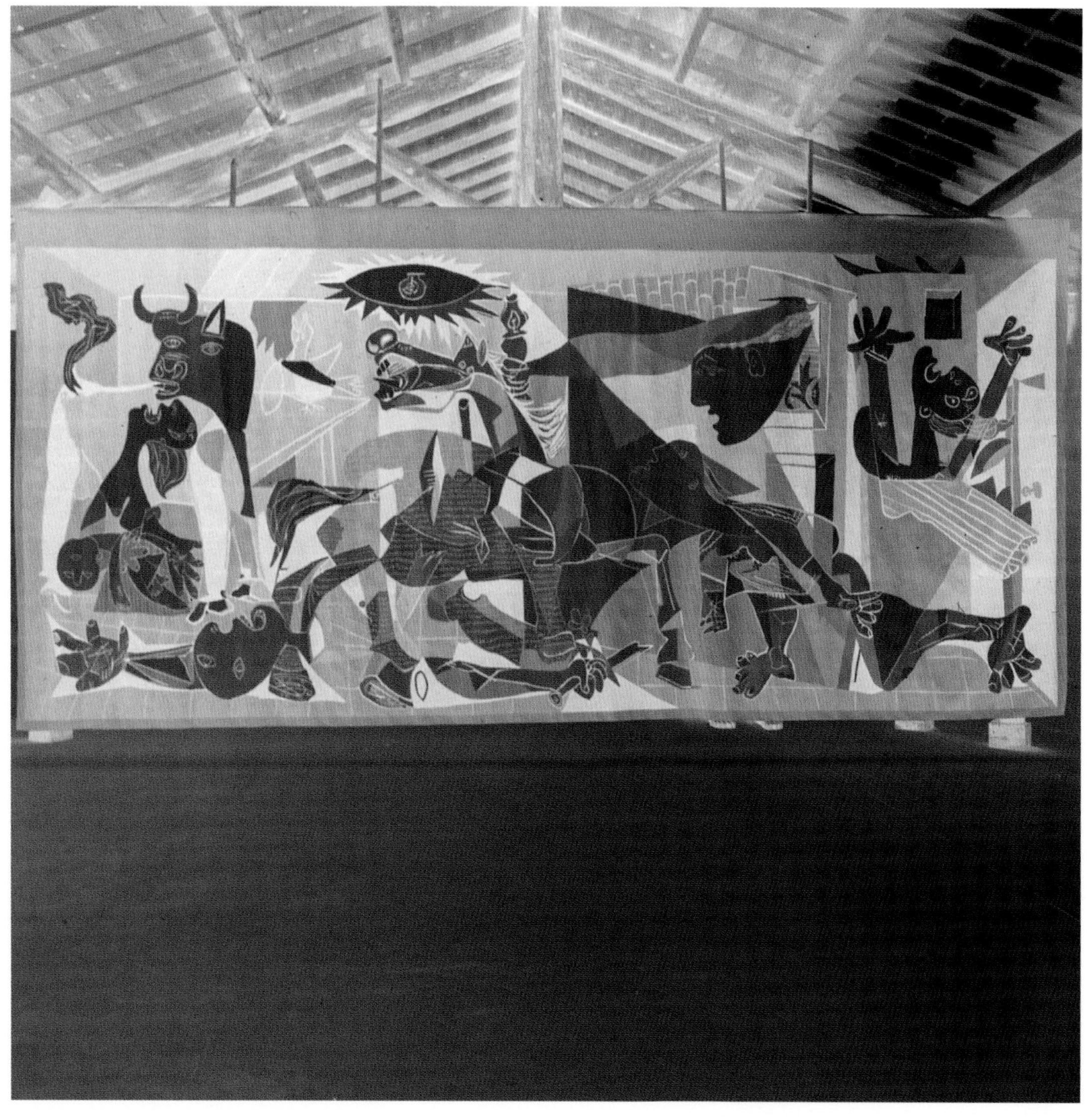

repatriation to Spain in 1981, *Guernica* remained in a dedicated gallery at MoMA—the reason why a tapestry version was presented in lieu of the painting itself, alongside more than sixty paintings, drawings, and prints, in Tokyo in 1962. Just two years later, in 1964, the year Japan hosted the Summer Olympics, the National Museum of Modern Art, Tokyo, held the largest retrospective of Picasso in the country—and likely in all of Asia.[24] Featuring 148 works on loan from dozens of public and private collections in the United States and Europe, including 58 works from the artist's own collection, the exhibition was claimed to '[stand] in its scale second only to the Retrospective Show in Rome, 1955 and in London, 1960', and was described as 'the greatest Picasso Exhibition ever held in Japan, and an epoch-making event in the world of art'.[25]

The accompanying exhibition catalogue features short but glowing introductory essays by the two most important advocates of Picasso's work during his lifetime: Barr and Daniel-Henry Kahnweiler, his long-time dealer. Calling Picasso a 'great artist' as well as a 'great individual' and even a prophet, Barr writes: 'In a world in which social pressures—democratic, collectivist, bourgeois—tend to restrict the freedom of the exceptional individual, Picasso's art assumes a significance far beyond its artistic importance.'[26] In turn, Kahnweiler extols:

There are no more rules for Picasso; only the pure joy of painting remains. Its evolution does not correspond to any preconceived idea. 'I don't look, I find,' he said. He no longer travels. He lives in his large house in Mougins, gets up late, has breakfast around three in the afternoon, like a true Spaniard, dines around eleven in the evening, and works late into the night. We know that he is as great a sculptor, an engraver, and a ceramicist as he is a painter. It is according to circumstances that he practises one or the other of these arts. He is the complete artist as the Renaissance knew him. If, as I think, the plastic arts are not a meaningless game, nor a simple reflection of the external world but rather the creation of this world visible to men, few artists have done as much for this creation as Pablo Picasso. His work continues relentlessly. Your Hokusai signed, towards the end of his life, 'The old man crazy about drawing'. It is with as much right that Picasso could sign: 'The old man crazy about painting.'[27]

In the last decade of his life, Picasso was the world's most famous artist in the eyes of the public. At the same time, he was also considered a has-been by many denizens of the art world, partly because of his lifelong insistence on figuration and intransigent contempt for the abstract (although he may be seen as having had a close encounter with the latter during his most radical Cubist period). With the centre of gravity of the avant-garde now shifted to the 'New World', the École de Paris had long passed the baton to the New York School of Abstract Expressionism and successive movements.

After his youth and the early phase in his career, Picasso had always been a solitary, larger-than-life figure belonging to no movement or collective. He was not immune, however, to devastating revelations and critiques of his art, and his life—two of which came in succession with the publication of Françoise Gilot's memoir *Life with Picasso* (1964) and the influential British art critic and novelist John Berger's *The Success and Failure of Picasso* (1965). The outpouring of bombastic, unabashed erotic portraits of the artist and his amorous models in the late work did not help his reputation within the art establishment. Despite the excesses and failures that characterised his final years,

Picasso was quickly recuperated, and his lasting influence, revisited again and again by generations of artists, has kept his legacy alive for half a century and more. New crops of exhibitions and publications continue to follow, more than fifty years after his death.[28]

If a picture of Picasso's long presence in Asia through his works and ideas has now come into sharper focus, the question here is not so much how his art has influenced artists and attracted public interest. Instead, we should ask why Picasso is, or should be, still relevant in contexts far removed from the places where he lived and the cultures and politics that shaped his work.

PICASSO FOR ASIA (NOW)

In 2003, in response to the atrocities of the Iraq War waged by the United States on the Middle Eastern country following the events of 9/11, the British artist David Hockney painted *The Massacre and the Problems of Depiction* (FIG. 119). The massive watercolour substantially reproduces Picasso's *Massacre in Korea* but adds an unfamiliar image. Hockney appended a separate depiction of a hooded photographer with a large-format camera, placing this sheet directly beneath the updated version of the Picasso composition so that the overall work takes the form of a squat 'T'. The artist states:

[Picasso's Massacre in Korea*] was generally dismissed as propaganda and compared very unfavorably with* Guernica *[1937], and was rarely discussed again. Years later, on seeing it in the Picasso show at* MoMA *[in 1980], I was struck by it. It stayed with me, and I began to see another interpretation. In 1950, images from the Second World War were still vivid and shocking: recovery from the war was just under way, when news of a new conflict far away from Paris arrived ... My point is that his image is a universal one, yet Picasso realized that the photographs were after the event, indeed in a way not telling us the terrible brutal activity of the camps but of the survivors—the few against the terrible number of deaths. So his painting is perhaps a painter's response to the limitations of photography, limitations that are still with us, and need some debate today.*[29]

Thirty years after Picasso's death in 1973, one of the most renowned living British artists (born 1937), who had long expressed his admiration for the Spanish master, readily turned to the controversial *Massacre in Korea* to address the most pressing topic of the time: the brutalities instigated once again by an American military intervention. This time the evidence of wartime horrors was indisputable, unlike the narrative about those caused by Americans during the Korean War. Hockney rehabilitates Picasso's 1951 work by emphasising the 'universal' power of painting to symbolise rather than document, as photography is presumed to do.

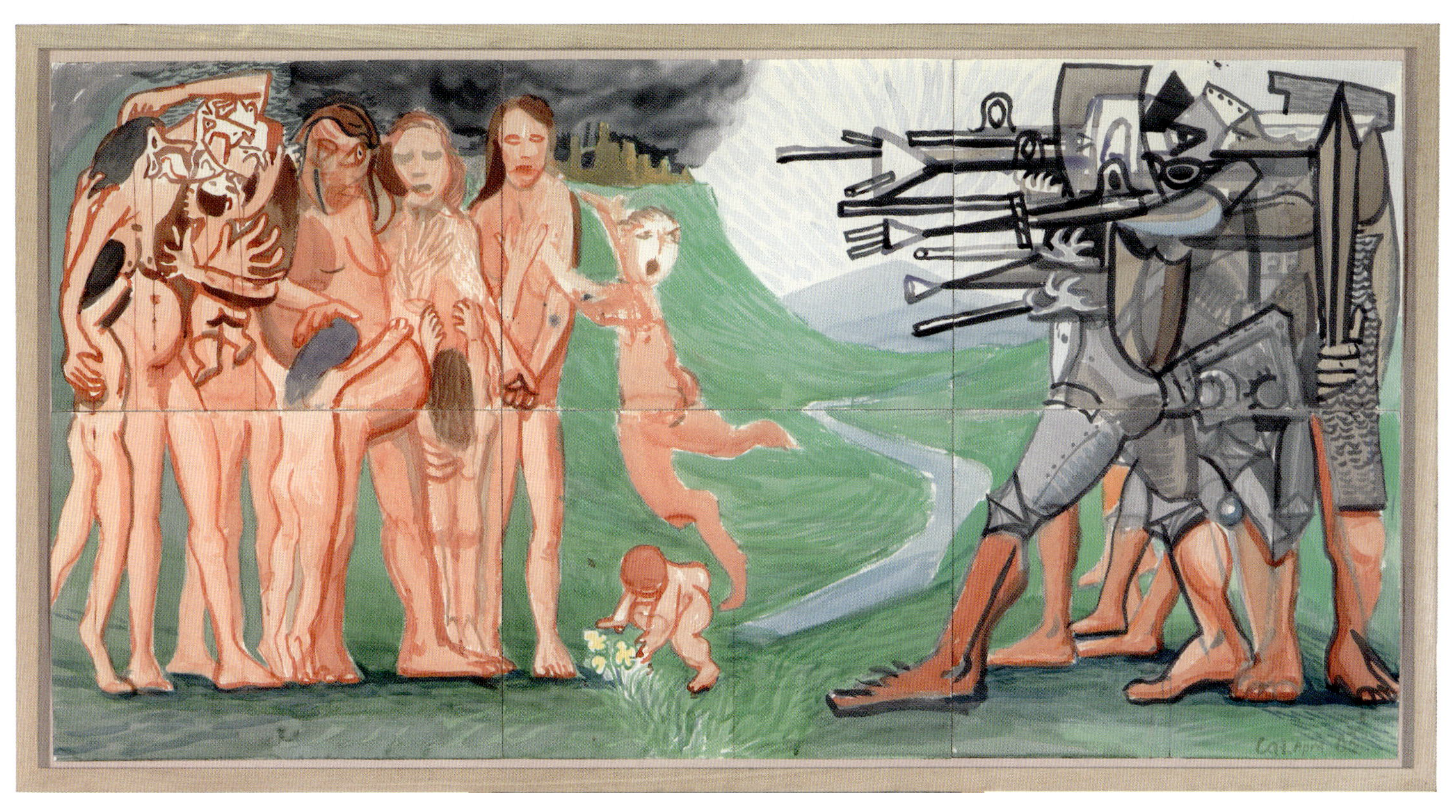

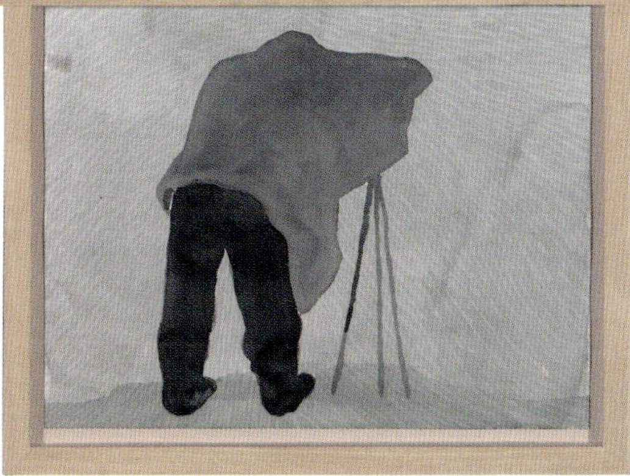

FIG. 119 David Hockney, *The Massacre and the Problems of Depiction*, 2003

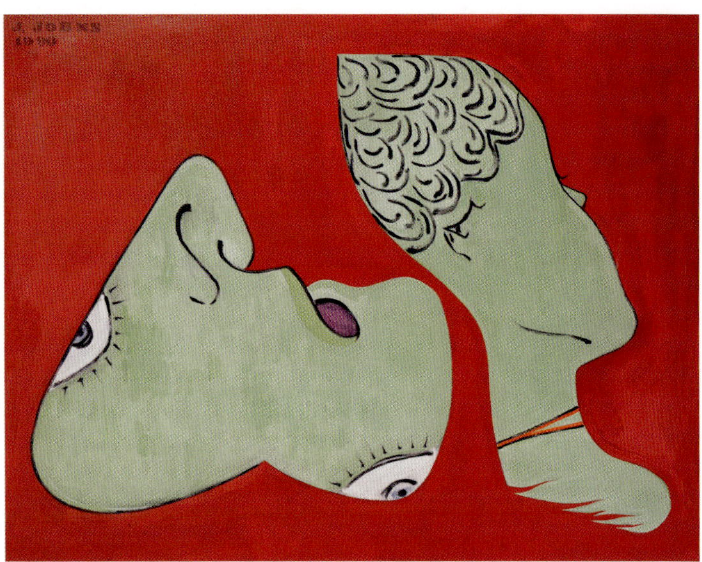

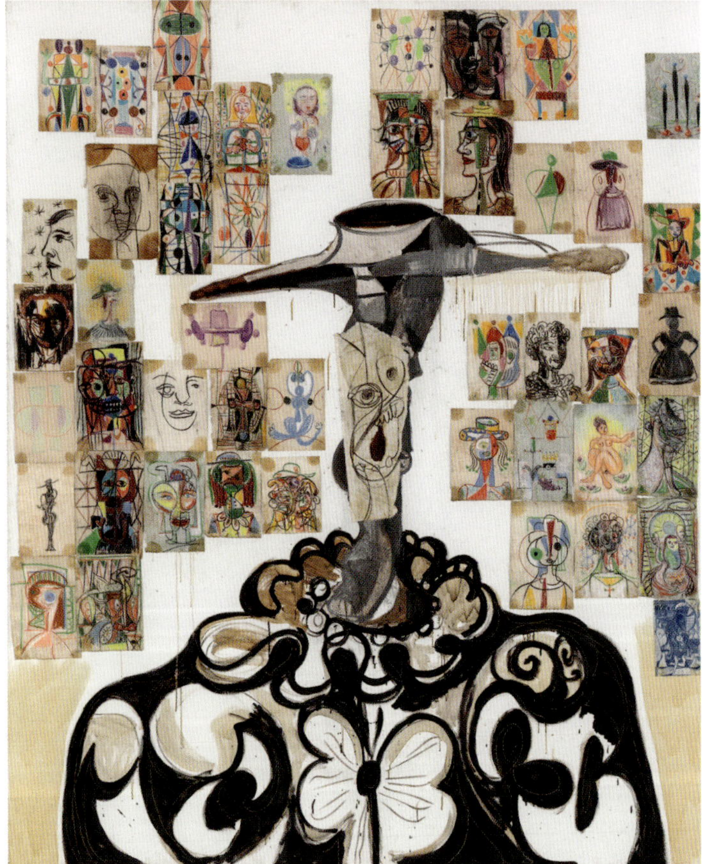

Does Picasso need to be recuperated, or at least revisited? The answer seems a resounding 'yes', at least in the West. Hockney is one of the most senior members in an expansive fellowship of contemporary artists committed to keeping alive the legacy of Picasso's art. Some of the most celebrated contemporary artists have lent their voices to the enduring need to remember and respond to Picasso, from Jasper Johns to Martin Kippenberger and George Condo to Maurizio Cattelan (FIGS 120–122). Lest it appear that the re-engagement of Picasso has happened only in the hands of artists who are white and male, we would do better by remembering examples of African American artists, such as Robert Colescott, Faith Ringgold, and Jean-Michel Basquiat, who have revisited Picasso or taken him to task (FIGS 123 AND 124). There are

LEFT TOP: FIG. 120 Jasper Johns, *Untitled*, 1990

LEFT BOTTOM: FIG. 121 George Condo, *Spanish Head Composition*, 1988

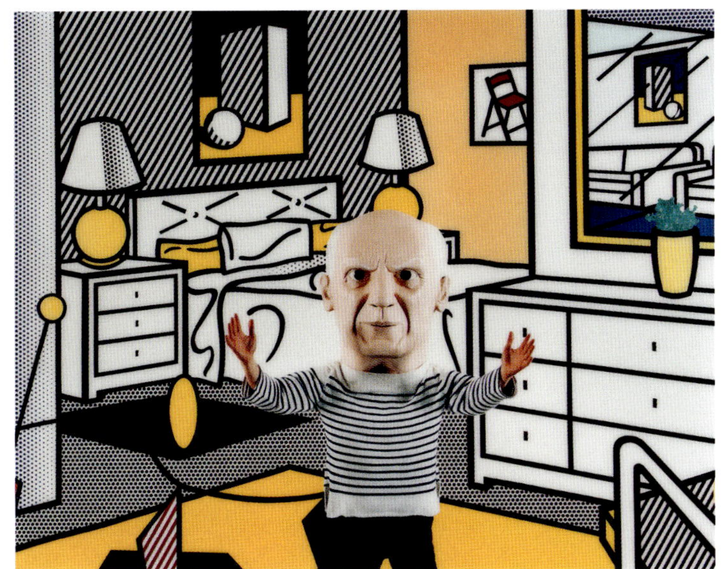

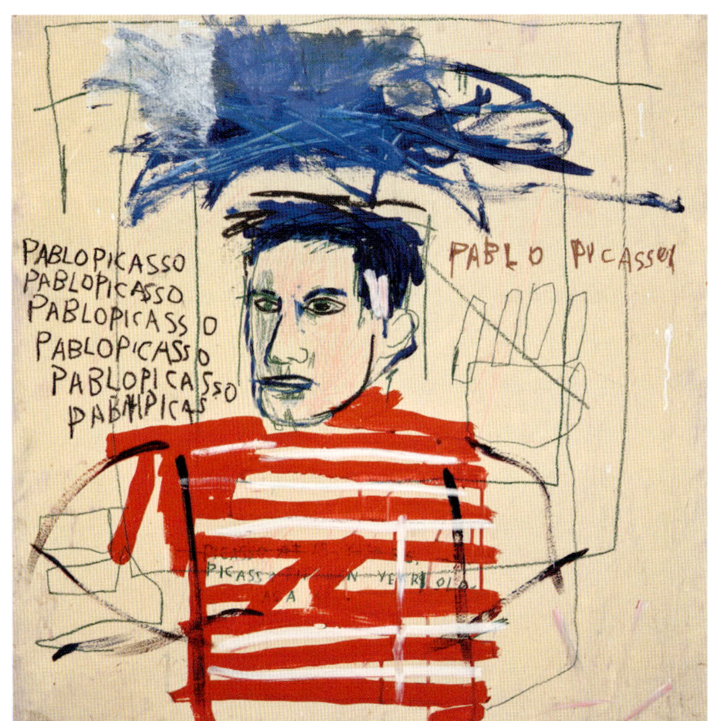

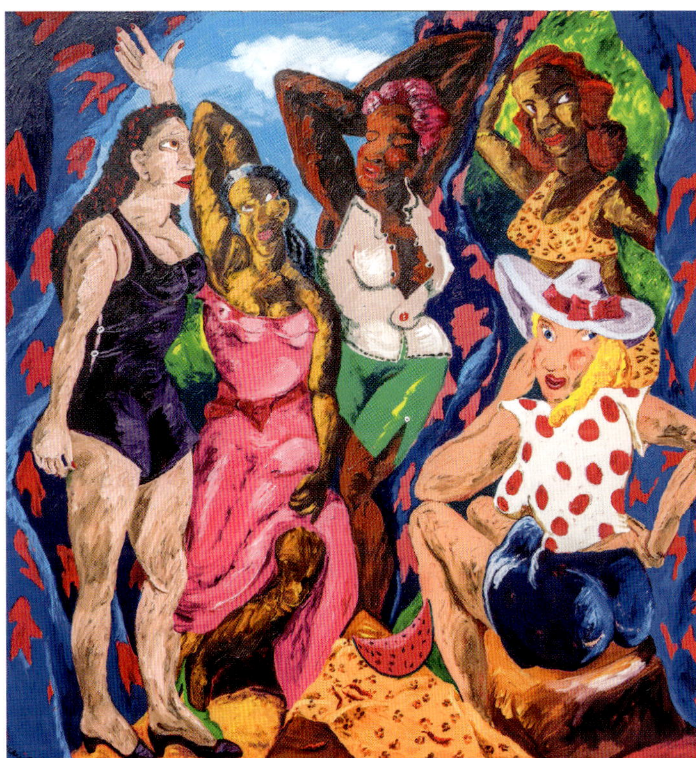

ABOVE: FIG. 122 Maurizio Cattelan, *Untitled*, 1998

RIGHT TOP: FIG. 123 Jean-Michel Basquiat, *Untitled (Pablo Picasso)*, 1984

RIGHT BOTTOM: FIG. 124 Robert Colescott, *Les Demoiselles d'Alabama: Vestidas*, 1985

also examples of non-Western artists who turned to Picasso at critical junctures in their practices, such as Atul Dodiya, Yokoo Tadanori, and Chéri Samba (FIGS 125–127).[30] In the post-feminist, 'Me Too' era, Picasso has been re-envisioned and even strongly criticised—although the myth of genius that took root during the artist's early career and is now more than a century old has proven to be resilient, if not ironclad.[31] Such an unsparing re-evaluation has not exactly proliferated in other parts of the world, including Asia. Rather, Picasso continues to be viewed primarily through blockbuster exhibitions that present him, matter-of-factly, as a monolithic genius.[32] Are there ways in which we can

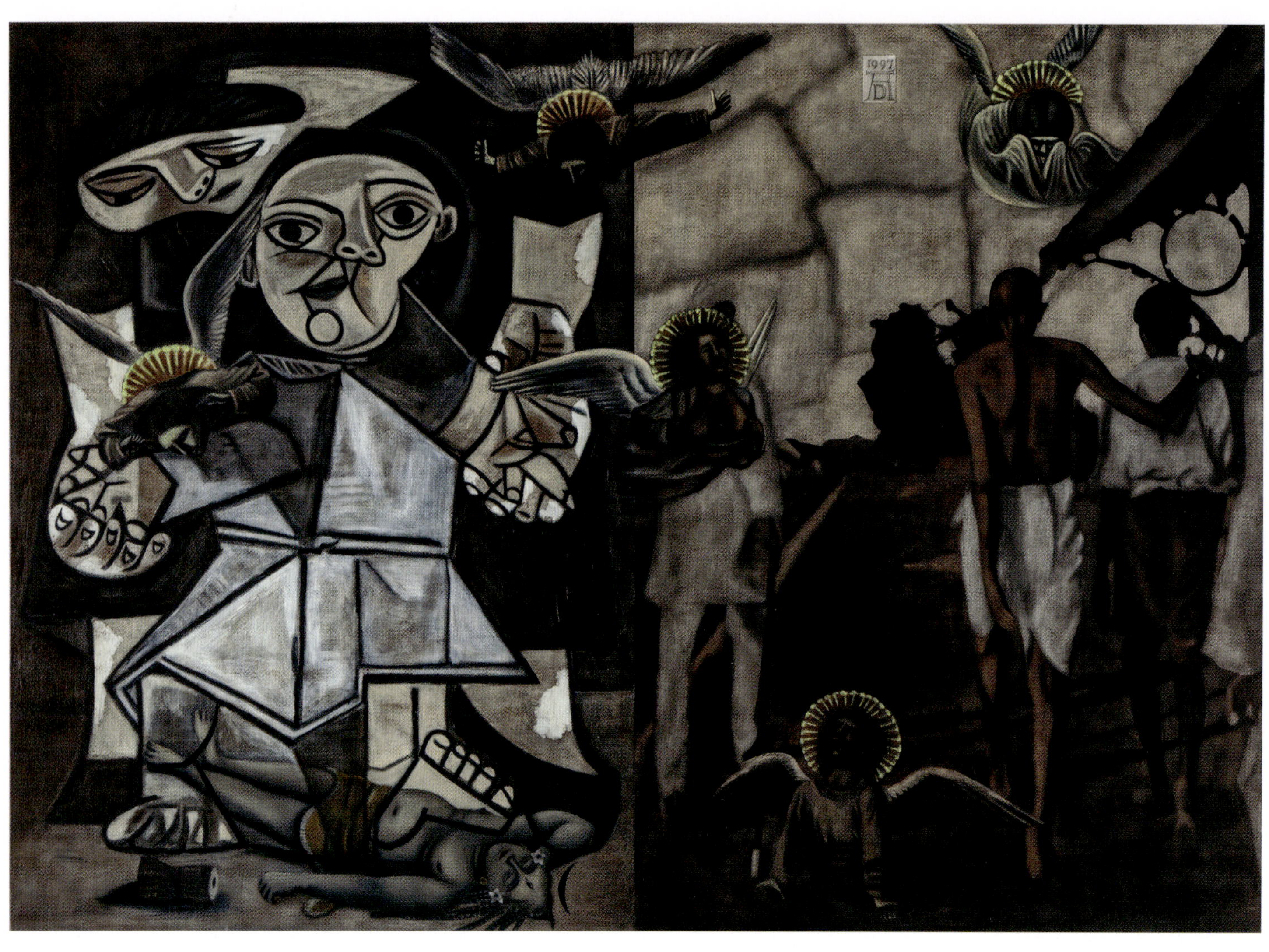

FIG. 125 Atul Dodiya, *Lamentation*, 1997

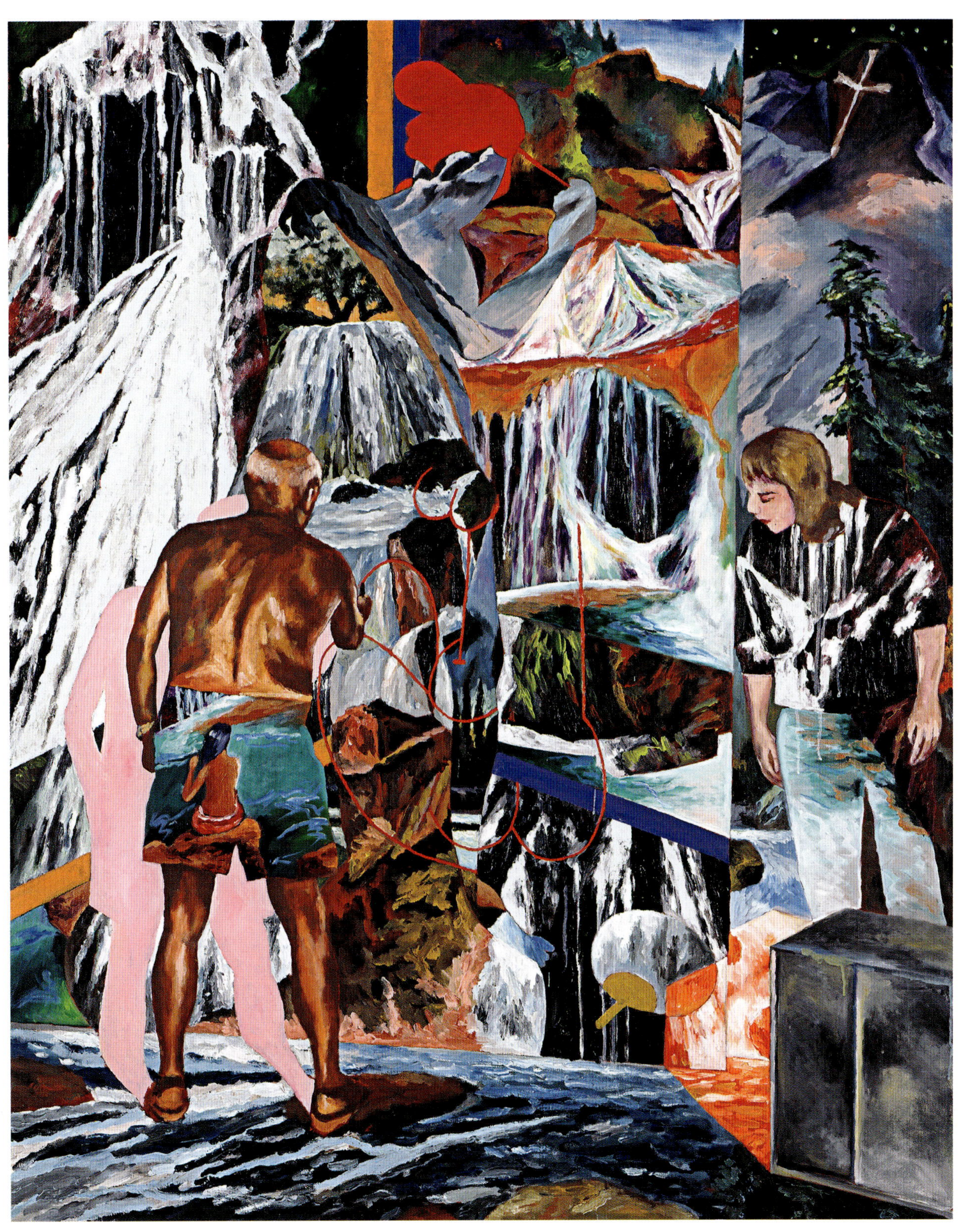

FIG. 126 Yokoo Tadanori, *Marriage of Sympathetic and Parasympathetic Nerves*, 1991

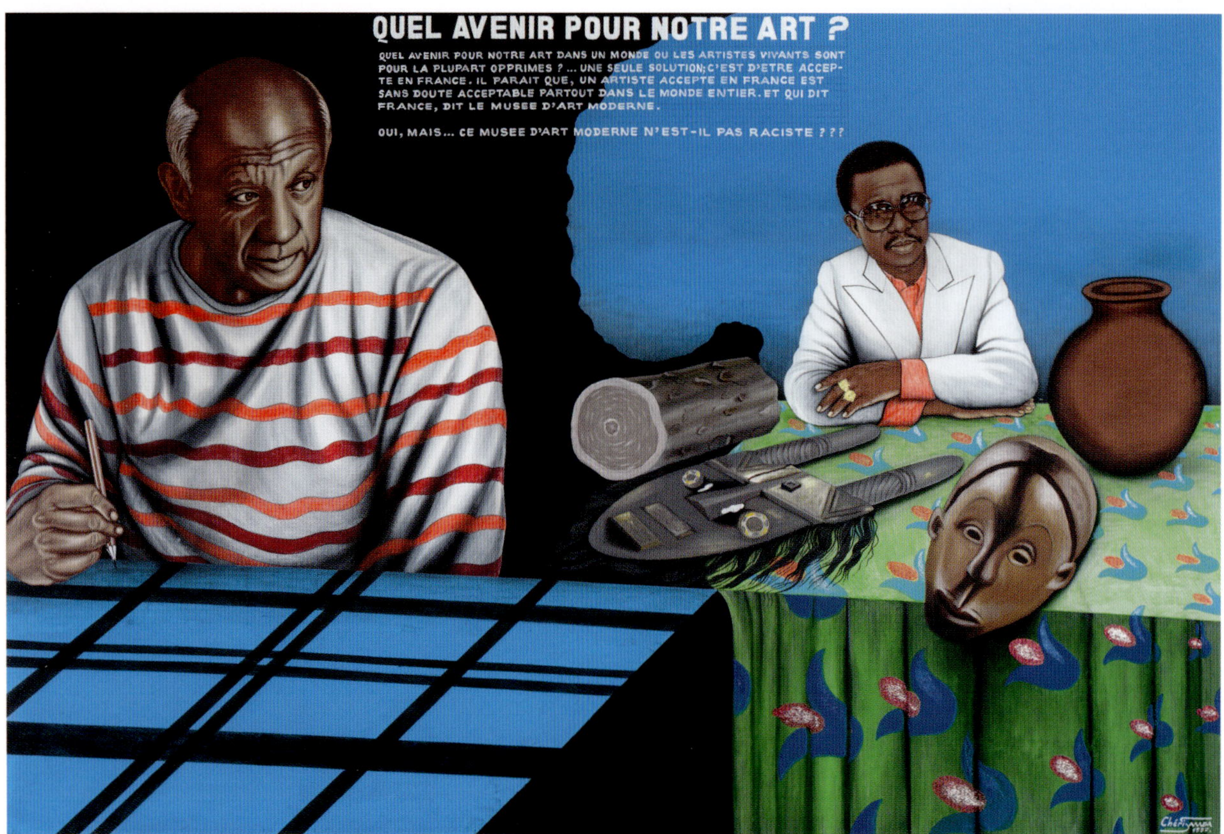

understand Picasso as more than a 'brand', different from other potent and profitable signifiers of classical grandeur, like Versailles, or luxury consumption, like Louis Vuitton, that have originated from the West?

In the last decades of the twentieth century the discourse of globalism grew and evolved, opening up new possibilities in world art history that promise a reconciliation between the still largely Euro-American–centric narrative of modernism and the disparate non-Western national and regional histories of modern art's development.[33] Against this backdrop, more serious reflections are needed on how artistic practices that emerged in places and eras at a remove from Picasso's own can relate to his art and its legacy. Such efforts can also help reconcile the parallel realities of the evolution of progressive, critical artistic practices and the continually uncritical celebration of Picasso the brand. In what follows, five modalities, or possibilities, are proposed for relating more recent artistic practices—specifically based in Asia—to the work of the twentieth-century Western master. Admittedly, the selection of artists discussed here is rather subjective, its purview largely limited to East Asia, with a particular focus on Greater China and Japan. This particular case study, I believe, can be reprised in comparable contexts in other parts of Asia, or other non-Western contexts.

Homage

In 2011, Zeng Fanzhi (born 1964), a celebrated contemporary Chinese painter, made a portrait of Picasso (FIG. 128). Dressed in an oxblood jacket, the subject holds a cigarette and looks directly at the viewer, a fierce gaze shooting out from his famously dark pupils. The background of the unprimed canvas is left unfinished. Picasso's trouser legs fade away from just above the knee, and his greying hair is smudged upwards, as if the Spaniard's irrepressible artistic energy and virility

FIG. 127 Chéri Samba, *What Future For Our Art? (1/3)*, 1997

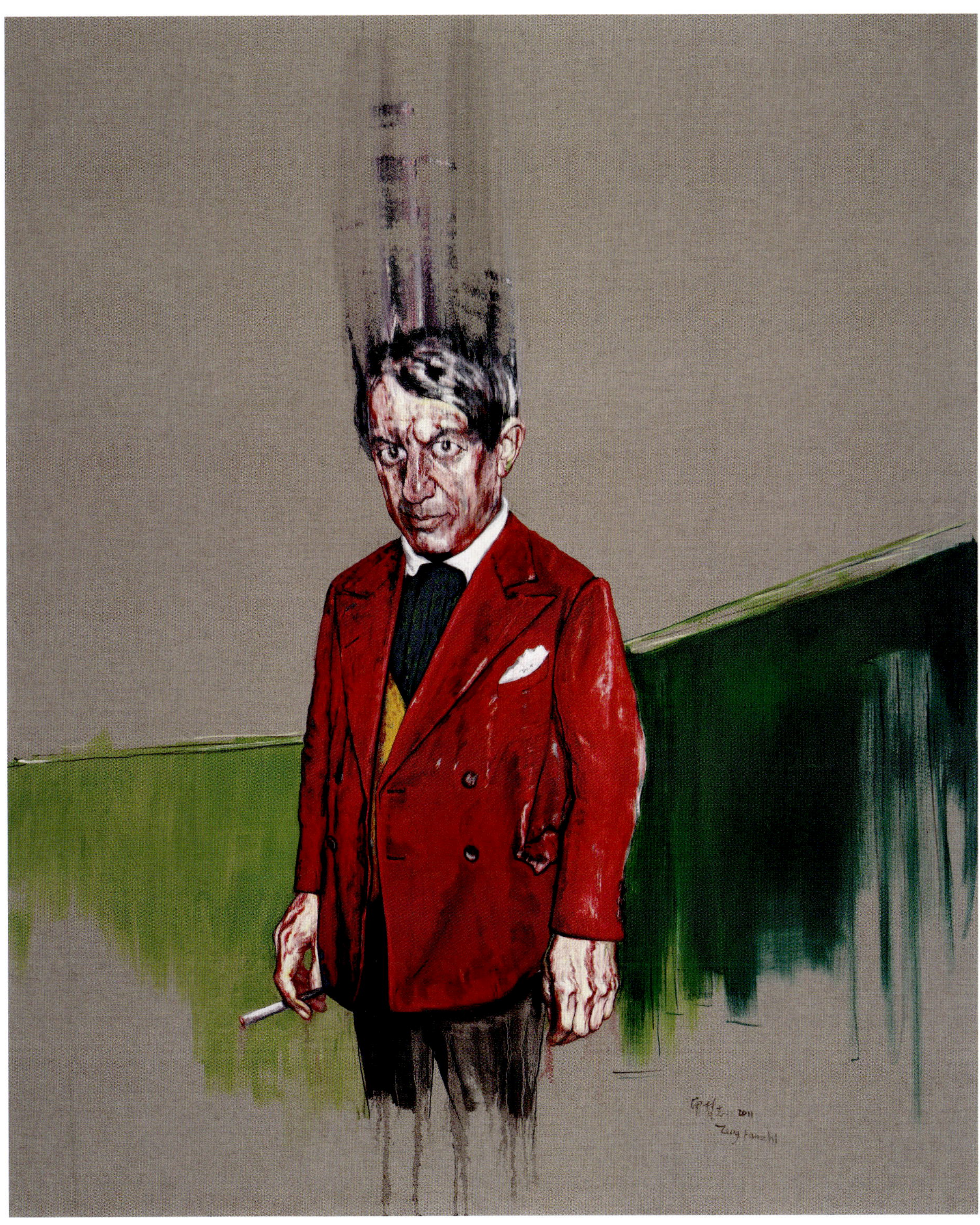

FIG. 128 Zeng Fanzhi, *Picasso*, 2011

were erupting like a geyser from the top of his head. The Picasso in the painting is likely based on a photograph by Brassaï taken in 1932, the year of Picasso's first Parisian retrospective held at Galeries Georges Petit. The artist was in his fifties at the time and at the height of his power and fame. Another portrait by Zeng, from 2012, shows a seated Picasso in 1913, when he was in the midst of his incipient Cubist period (FIG. 129).[34] His gaze is still intense but less severe, and his drab green jacket seems to suggest his position on the threshold between the life of a bohemian in Montmartre and worldwide recognition. A sweep of Zeng's brush gives another eruption of energy from the top of the artist's head.

FIG. 129 Zeng Fanzhi, *Picasso*, 2012

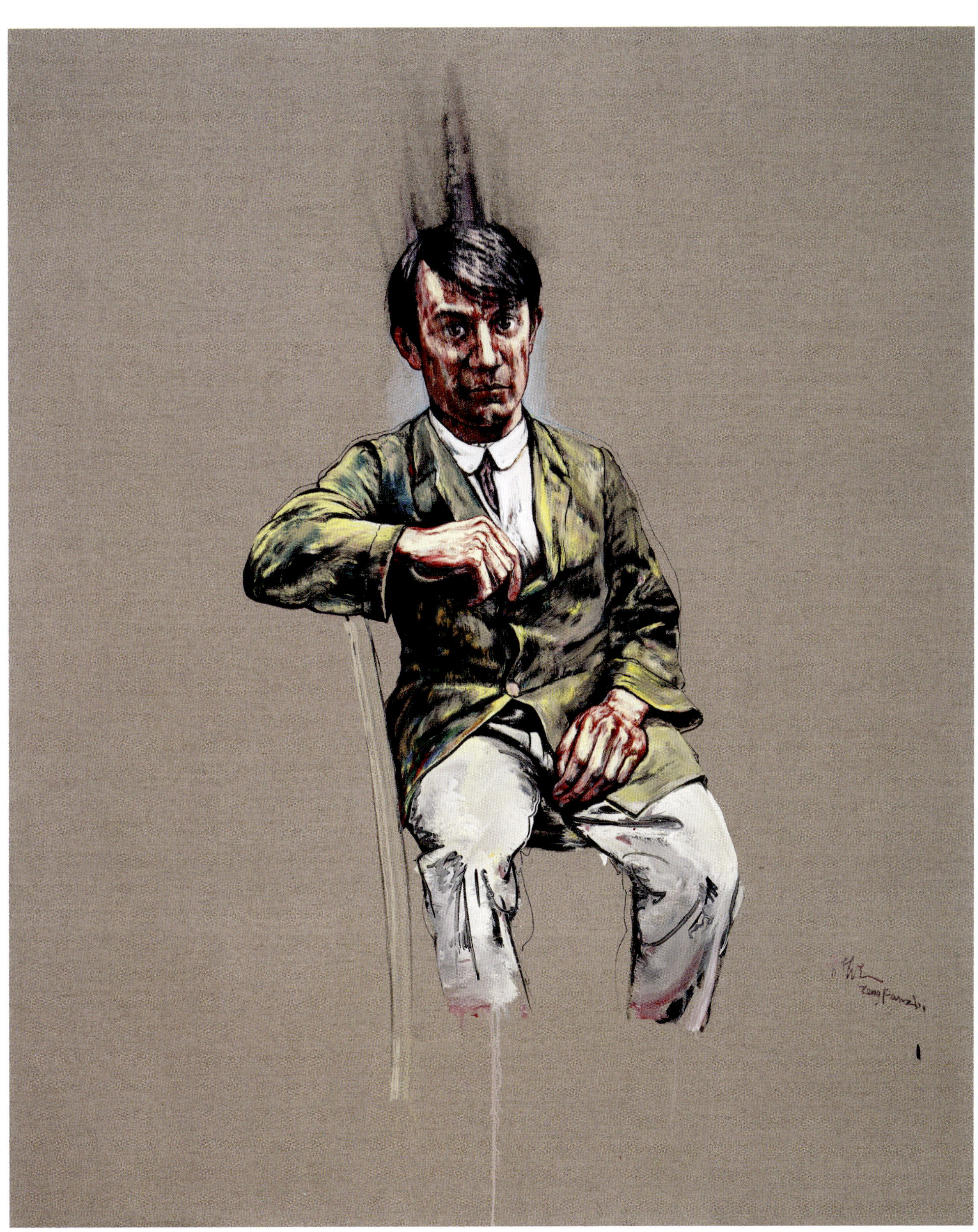

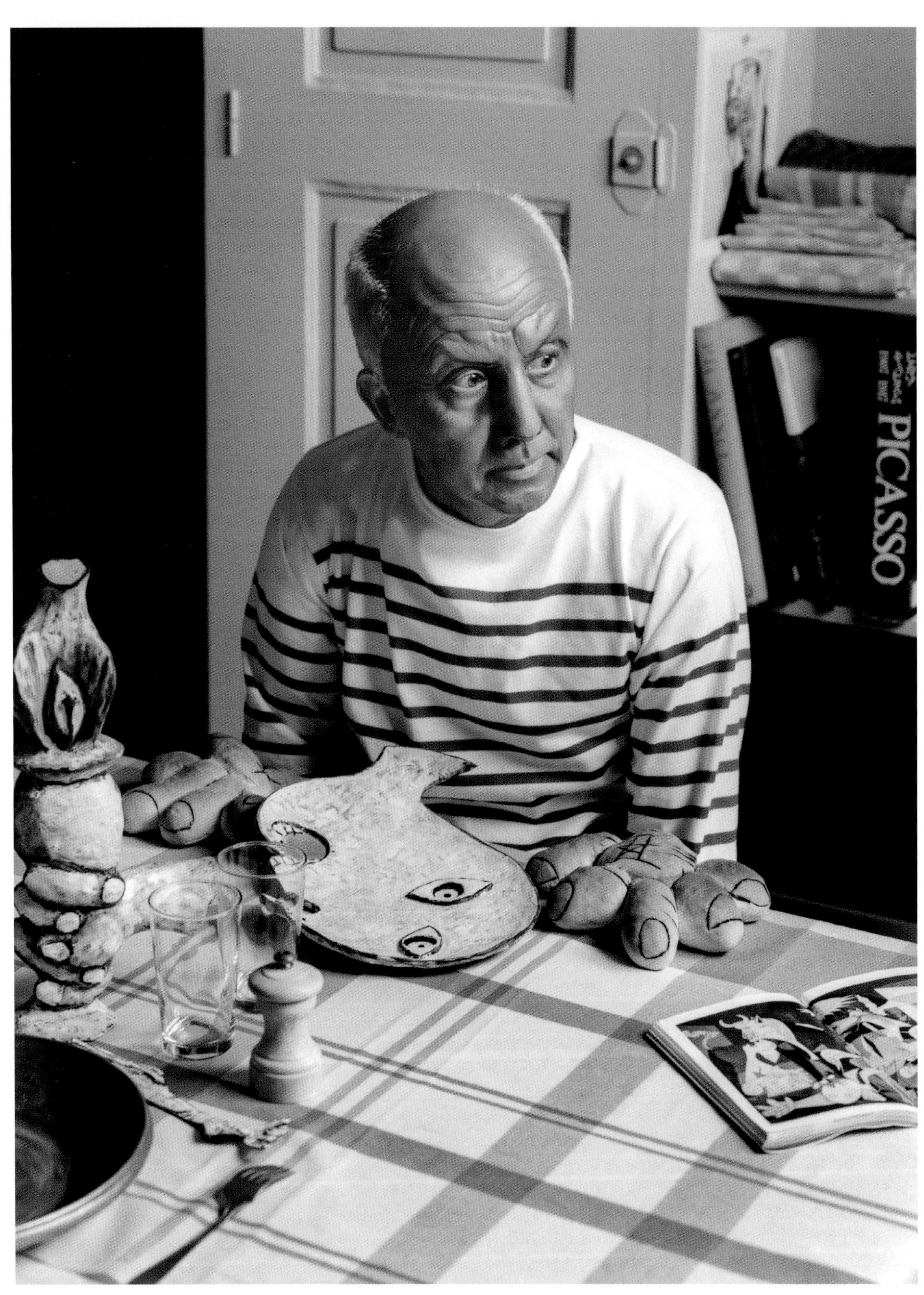

FIG. 130 Yasumasa Morimura, *A Requiem: Theater of Creativity / Self-Portrait as Pablo Picasso*, 2010

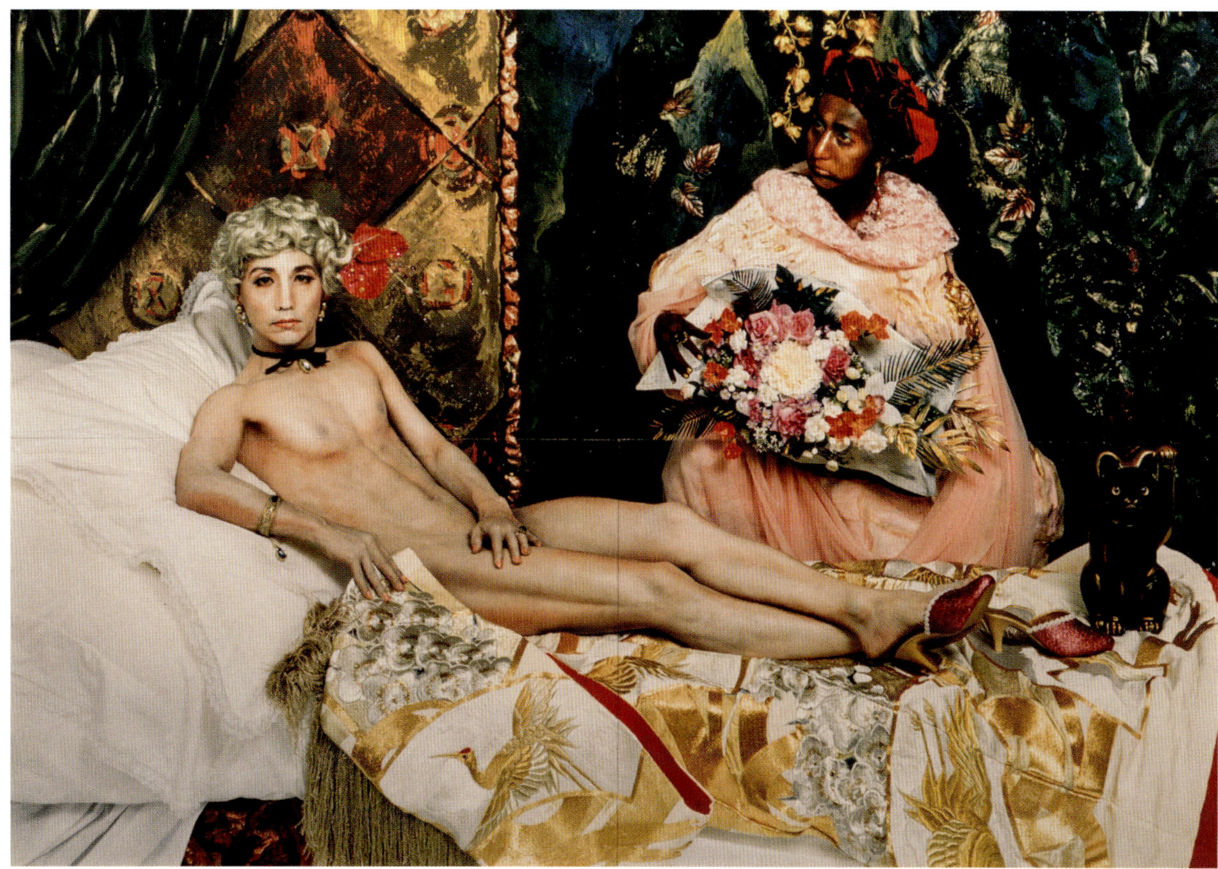

FIG. 131 Yasumasa Morimura, *Portrait (Futago)*, 1989

A year or so before Zeng began engaging with the image of Picasso, Japanese artist Yasumasa Morimura (born 1951) made *A Requiem: Theater of Creativity / Self-Portrait as Pablo Picasso* (2010; FIG. 130), recreating one of the best-known photographic portraits of the artist, by French photographer Robert Doisneau. Morimura came to international attention in the 1990s for staged photographs in which he recreates iconic images of female (and mostly but not exclusively Western) movie actresses and pop stars, such as Brigitte Bardot, Liza Minnelli, and Madonna. Since the mid-1980s Morimura has also recreated historical paintings or photographic portraits with astounding fidelity to detail, while also making witty, 'spot the difference' changes to the originals. In addition to the Picasso portraits, he has also produced versions of Marcel Duchamp as Rrose Sélavy and Manet's Olympia (FIG. 131). An uncanny reproduction of an original image of the then seventy-plus-year-old Spanish painter by an almost sixty-year-old Japanese conceptual artist, *Self-Portrait as Pablo Picasso* includes a couple of clever updates, such as a plate that reproduces the visage of the woman in anguish in *Guernica*.

More recently, another Japanese artist, Tanaami Keiichi (1936–2024), who was active from the 1960s as a visual artist as well as a graphic designer, made paintings based on a group of Picasso originals. The *Pleasure of Picasso* series—begun as a daily practice during the early days of the Covid-19 pandemic in 2020, when the artist found himself in social isolation—comprises more than five hundred pieces. The first paintings in the series are based on *Mother and Child (First Steps)* (1943; FIG. 132). As he quickly and successively iterated the image, Tanaami riffed on the original, modifying the composition and adding new elements. Over the course of Tanaami's series the child mutates into Mickey Mouse and then Minnie Mouse, morphs into a skull, and

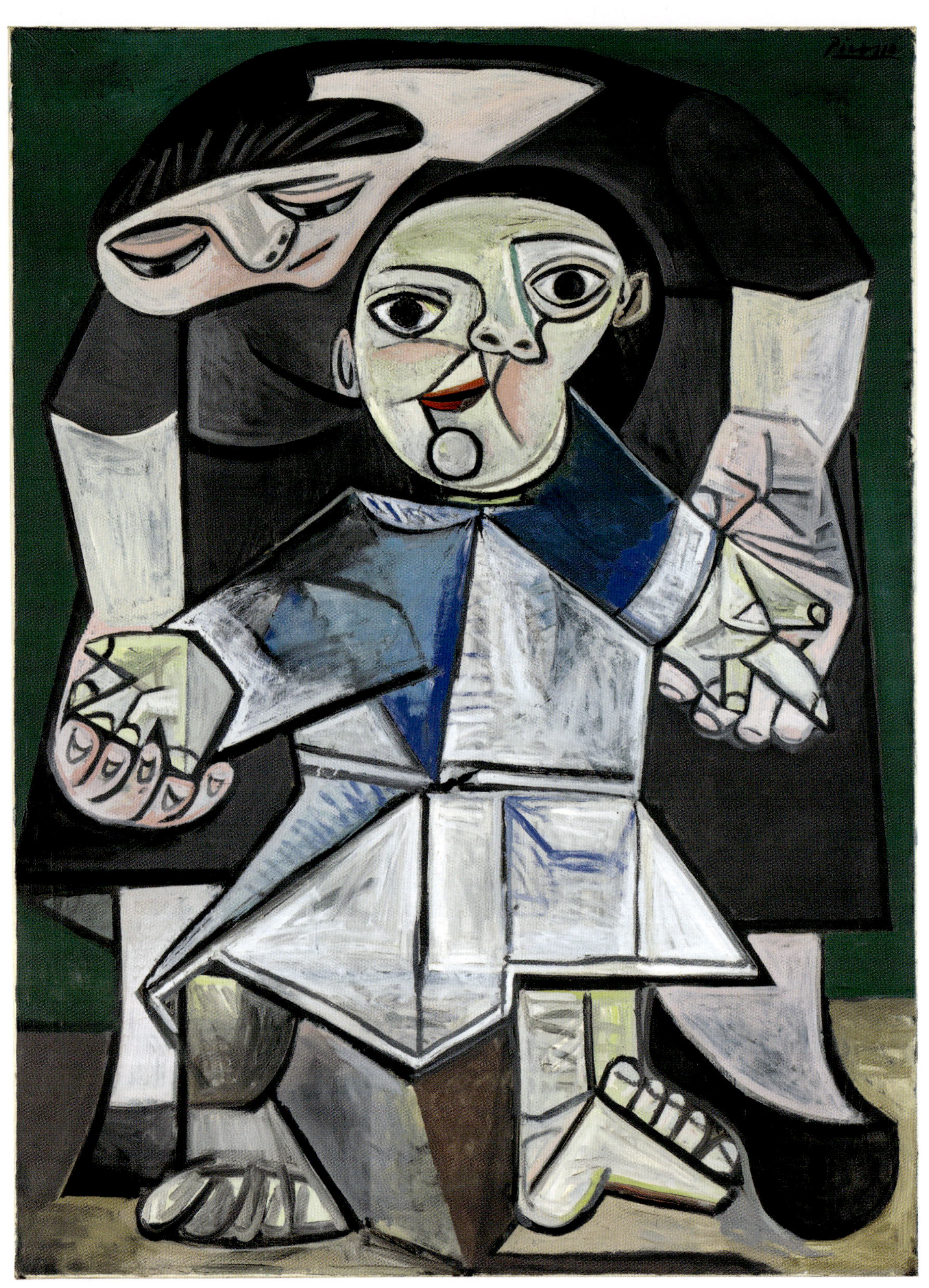

FIG. 132 *Mother and Child (First Steps)*, 1943

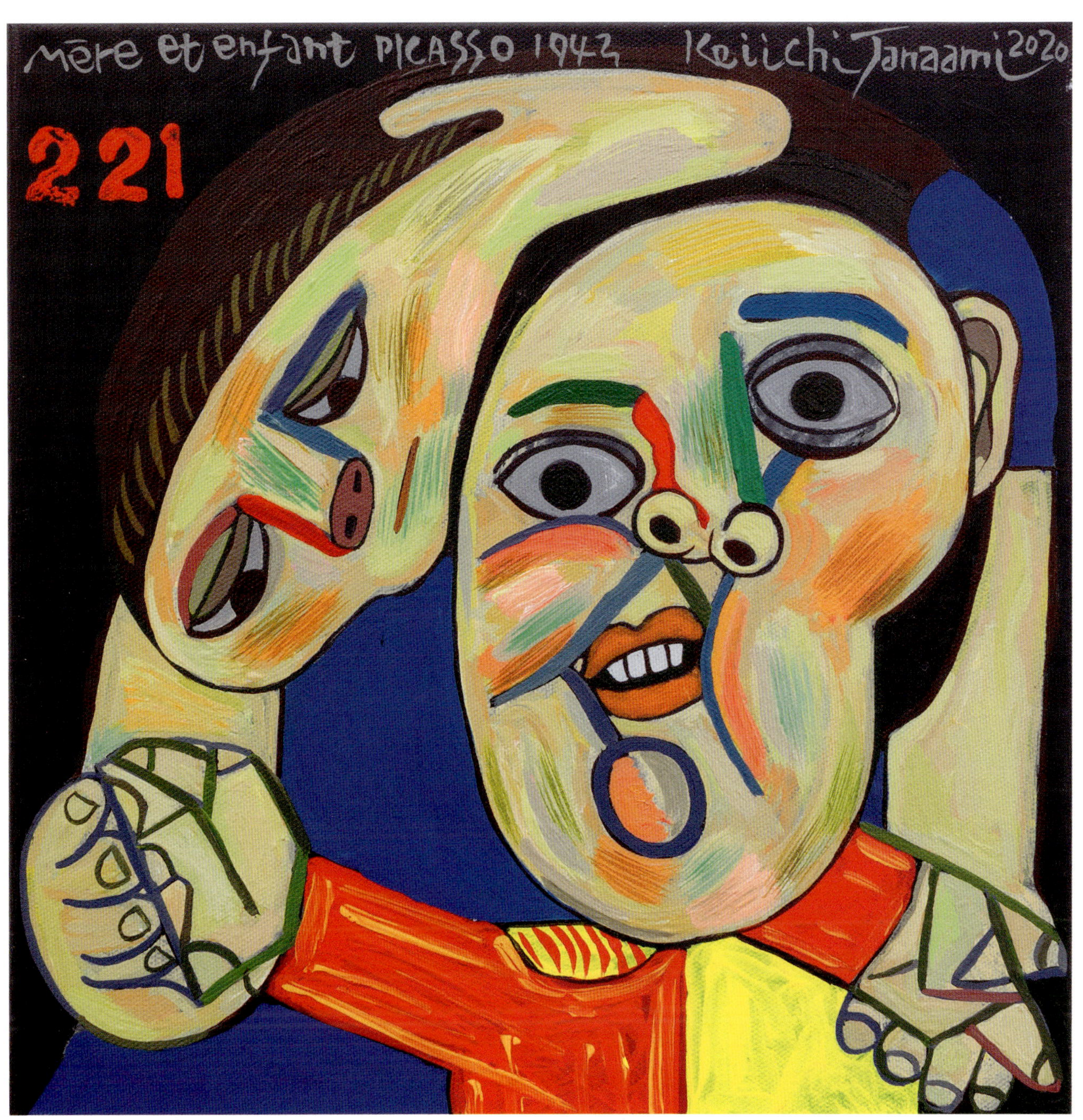

FIG. 133 Tanaami Keiichi, *Pleasure of Picasso–Mother and Child 0221*, 2020

sports a bandana. Soon, Tanaami began working with other Picasso originals, such as the Spanish artist's iconic portraits of women and children, amorous couples, studies for *Les Demoiselles d'Avignon*, and reinterpretations of works by the Old Masters (FIGS 133 AND 134). This new painting project was a necessary diversion for Tanaami during the uncertain, frightening early days of the pandemic and an act of self-reassurance through an elemental mode of art-making. And for Tanaami, it was the archetypal artist Picasso who embodied the very definition of art. The examples of Zeng, Morimura, and Tanaami together evince Picasso's enduring status in Asia today as a paradigmatic artist, a role he has held in the past and in other parts of the world.

Connection

Earlier, I gave examples of the Asian artists who encountered and were directly influenced by Picasso (Foujita); became adherents to Synthetic Cubism, a descendant of Picasso and Braque's revolutionary art form (Lin, Tōgō); or measured their stature against that of the Western master (Zhang). Here, I offer two examples of artists of Asian heritage and from Asian diasporas who formed far closer connections to Picasso within the history of Euro-American modern art in Picasso's own time.

Isamu Noguchi (1904–1988) was a towering modernist whose life and work, as well as the reception of his art, were intertwined with his biracial background and multicultural confluences. Born to a Japanese father and a Scottish American mother in Los Angeles, Noguchi spent his formative years in both Japan and the American Midwest. It was during his first sojourn in Paris that the young artist, who had been

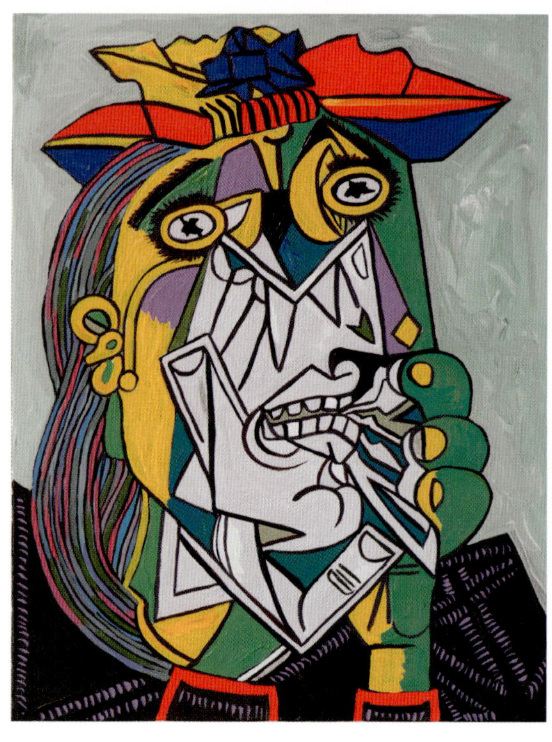

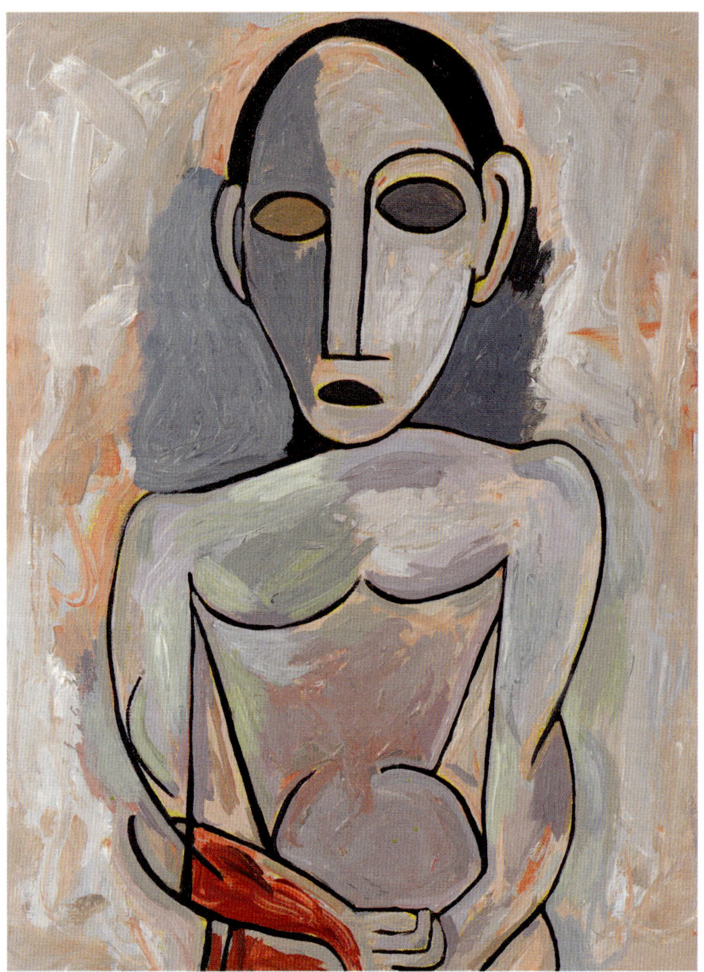

ABOVE: FIG. 134 Tanaami Keiichi, *Pleasure of Picasso–Mother and Child No.057*, 2020–2021

LEFT: FIG. 135 Tanaami Keiichi, *Pleasure of Picasso–Mother and Child No.379*, 2020–2022

BELOW LEFT: FIG. 136 Isamu Noguchi, *Leda*, 1928

BELOW RIGHT: FIG. 137 Constantin Brâncuși, *Bird in Space*, 1932–1940

working as a figurative portrait sculptor in New York, embarked on his journey to the heart of modernism. During a pivotal apprenticeship under Constantin Brâncuși, which lasted from 1927 to 1928, Noguchi made *Leda* (1928; FIG. 136), a work that signals his crucial transition to modernist abstraction. *Leda* clearly demonstrates the influence of Brâncuși's method of distilling figures into essential forms—an approach exemplified by *Bird in Space* (1932–1940; FIG. 137). *Leda* is also reminiscent of Picasso's works of the same period, such as *Figure* (1927; FIG. 140), in which the human body—mostly female—is fantastically and at times violently subjected to plastic manipulations.[35]

Arguably, Noguchi's first great breakthrough to be noted in the history of modern sculpture occurred around the final years of the Second World War, when he began making sculptures of interlocking slate slabs. Different blocks balance one another with their weight, making forms that are alternately noble, humorous, and poignant. The first in the series, *Figure* (1945; FIG. 138), is very much 'Picassoid',[36] as is evident when seen vis-à-vis Picasso's *Figures by the Sea* (1931; FIG. 141) as well as Noguchi's own *Strange Bird* (1945/1971; FIG. 139). This artistic breakthrough for Noguchi came on the heels of his experience of voluntarily entering an internment camp in Arizona for American citizens of Japanese descent—one of ten such camps established in the United States after the Japanese attack on Pearl Harbor. Aiming to improve conditions for the Japanese American community and hold art classes,

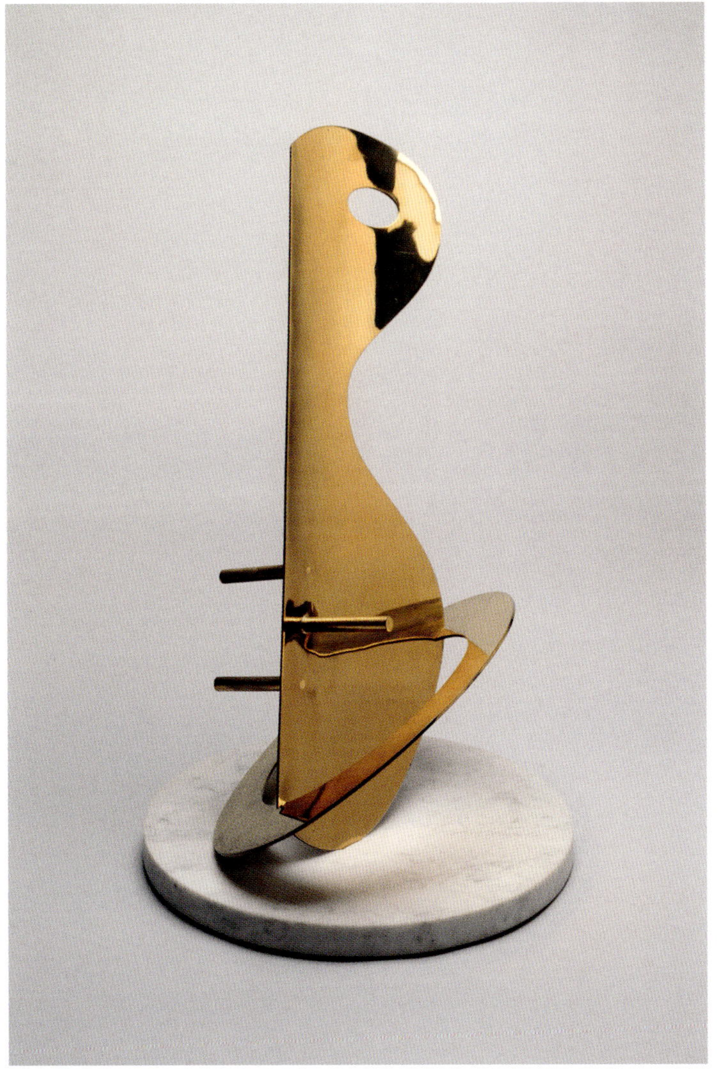

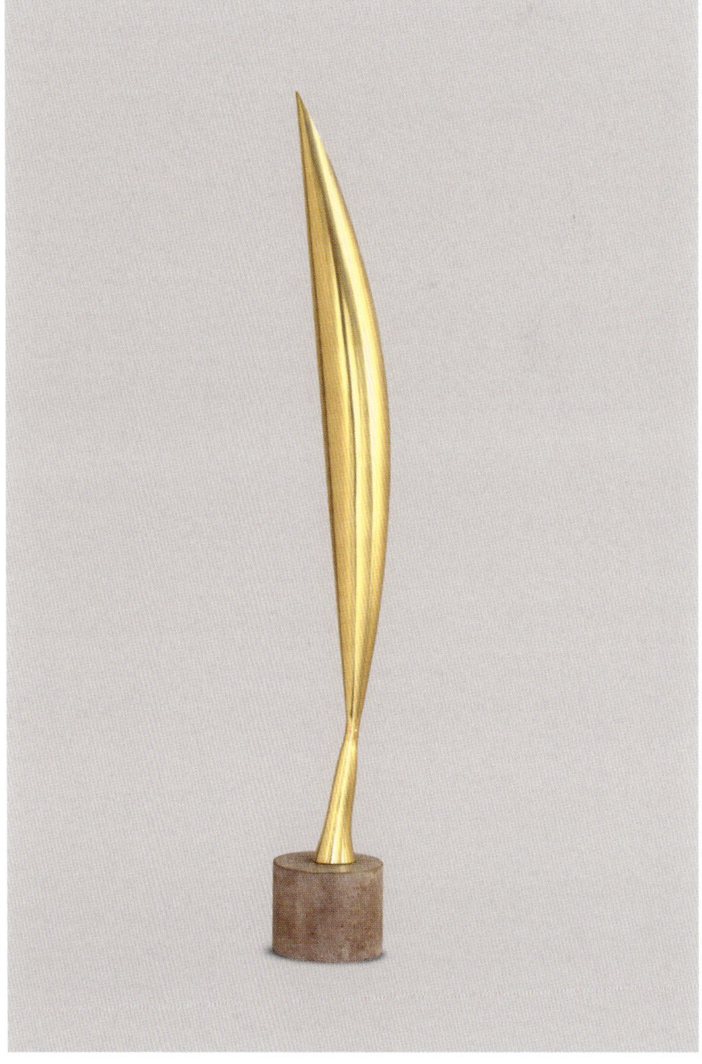

Noguchi stayed for more than half a year. His efforts proved to be in vain, however, and a deeply frustrated Noguchi retreated back to New York. This life-changing experience may have informed the bodily allusions in Noguchi's slate works, which appear delicately interlocked and precariously balanced, and which recall Picasso's work from the late 1920s and early 1930s.

Although there is no known direct connection between Noguchi and Picasso, Noguchi's experience of self-interning mirrors Picasso's choice to stay in Paris during the Nazi occupation of France from 1940 to 1944. By the mid-1950s Noguchi was in league with the Spanish

BELOW: FIG. 138 Isamu Noguchi, *Figure*, 1945

OPPOSITE: FIG. 139 Isamu Noguchi, *Strange Bird*, 1945/1971

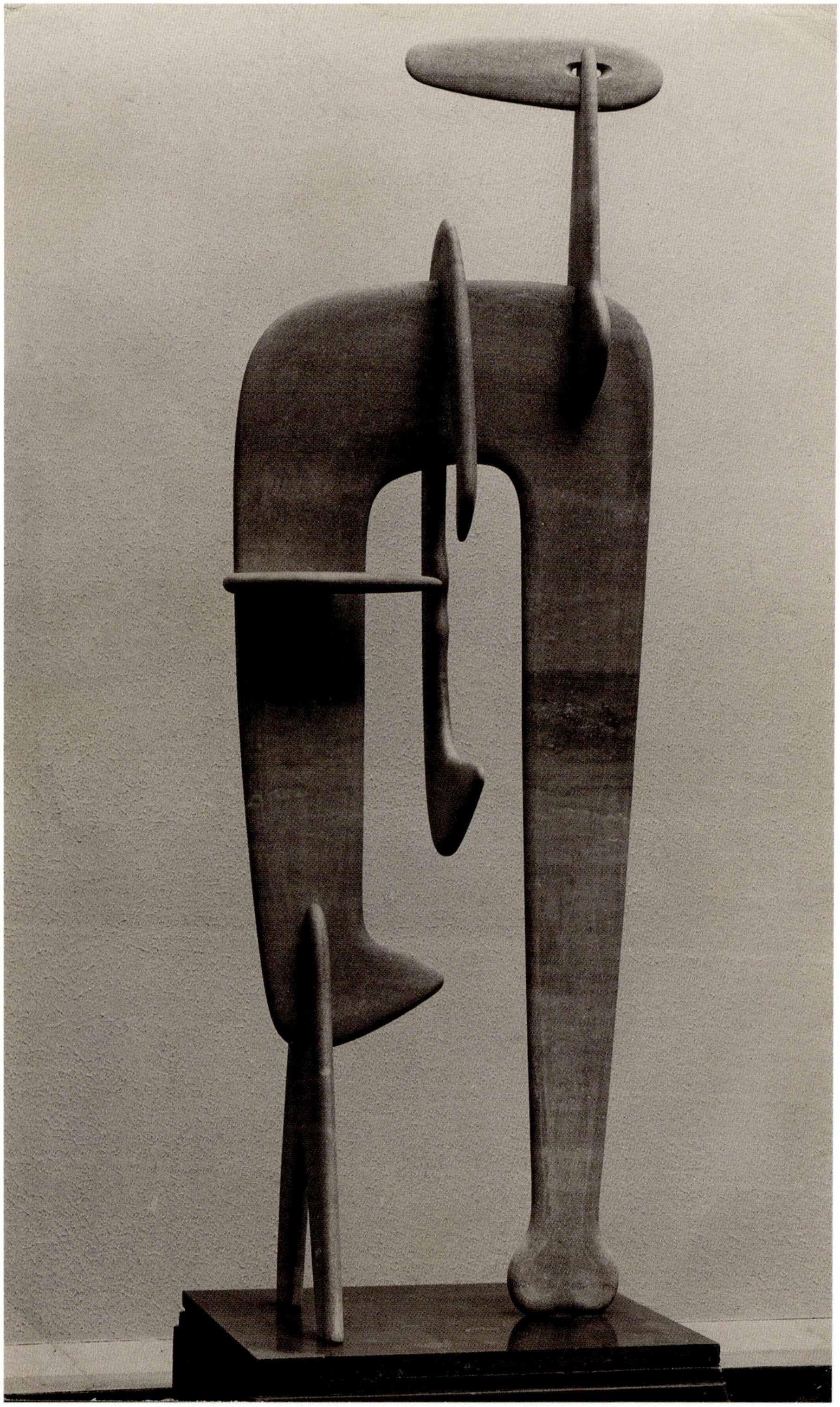

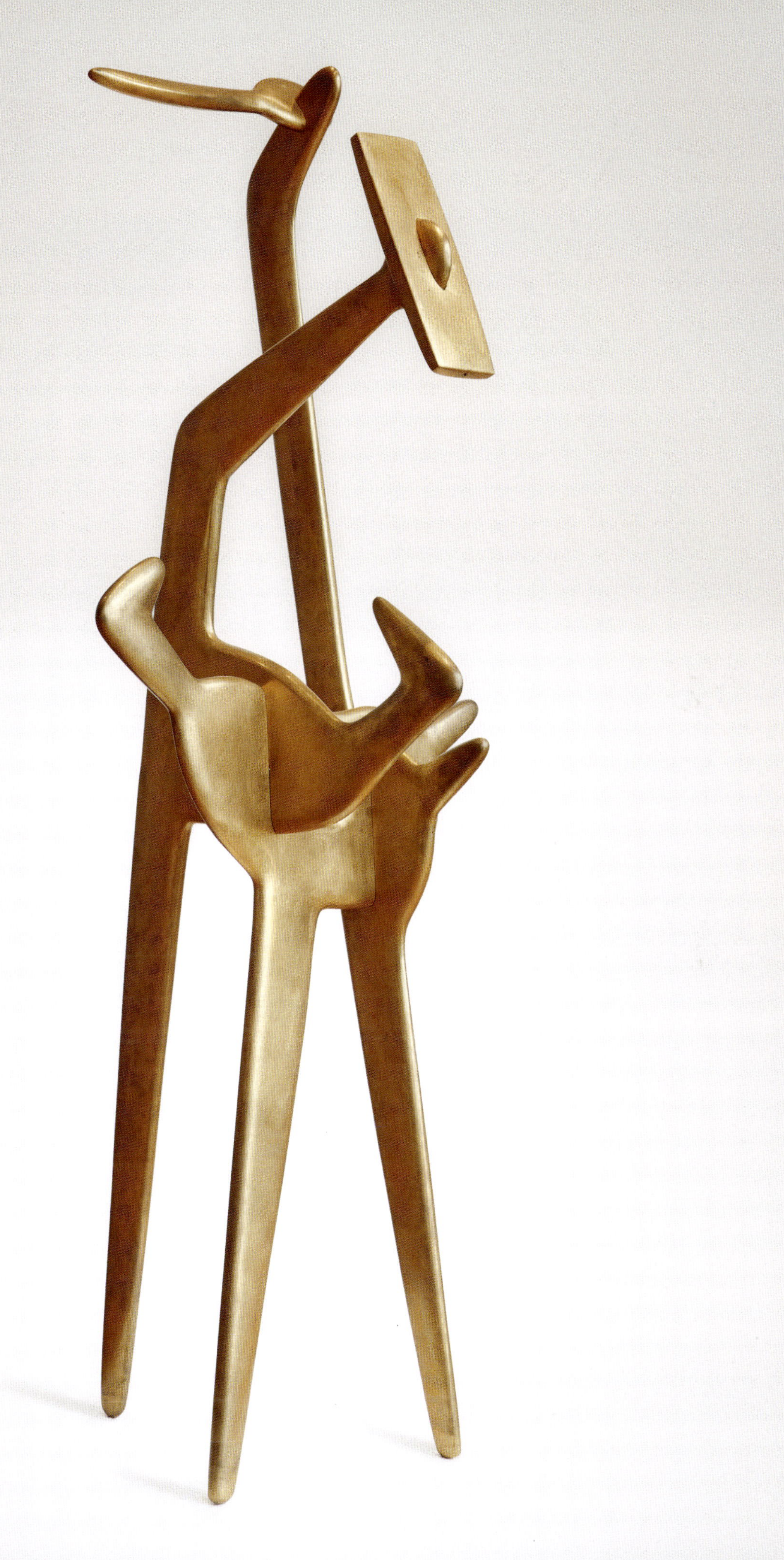

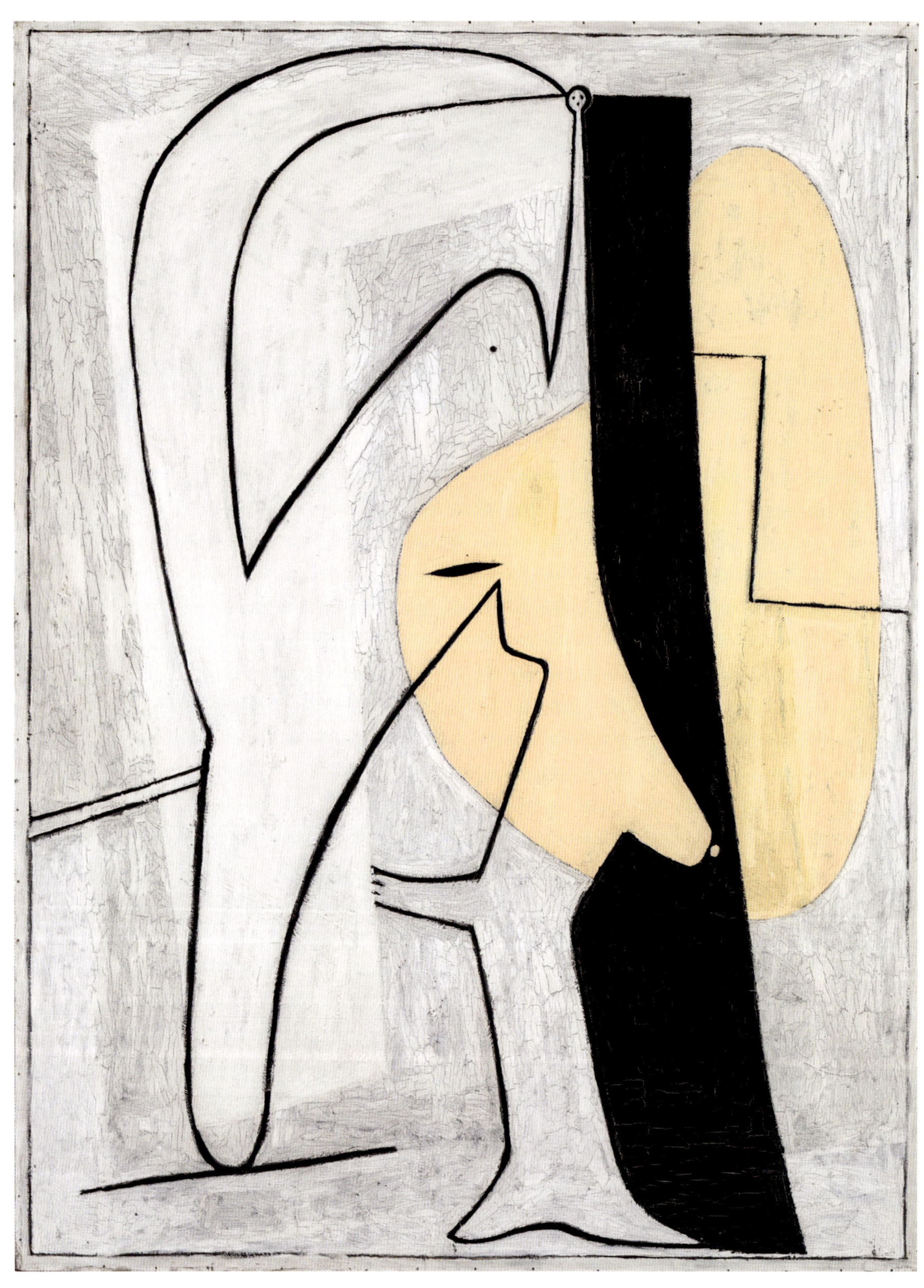

FIG. 140 *Figure*, 1927

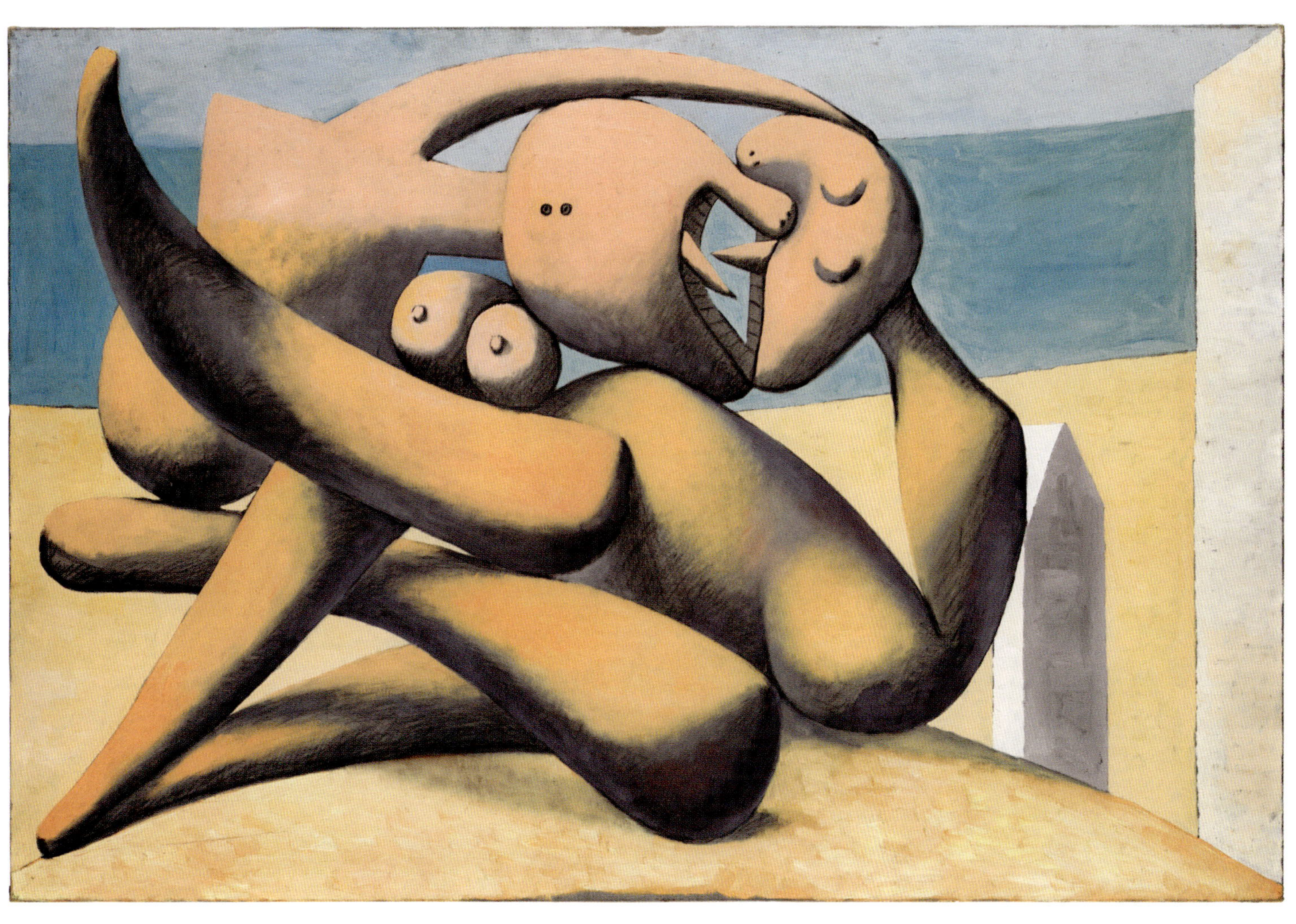

FIG. 141 *Figures by the Sea*, 1931

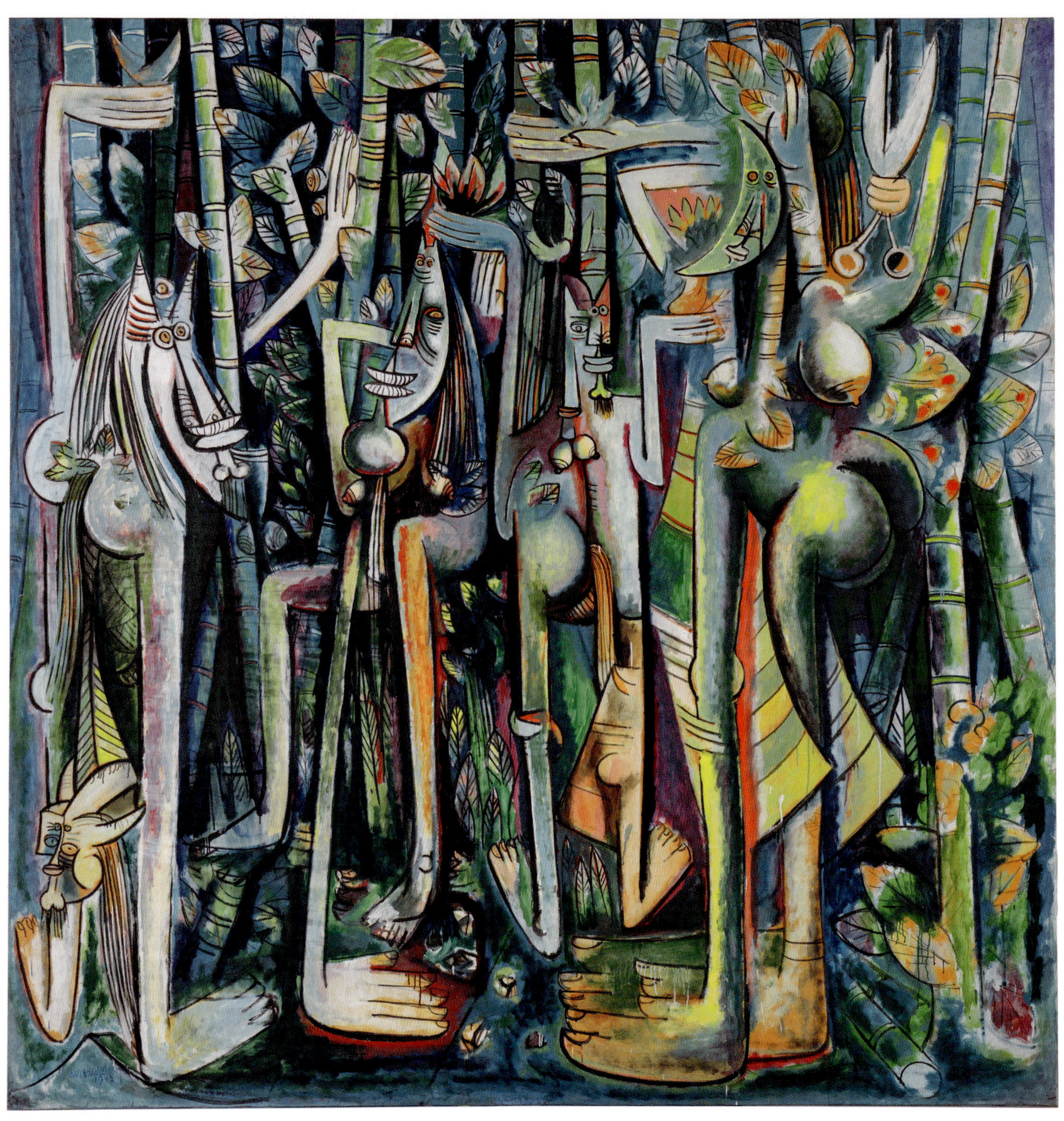

FIG. 142 Wifredo Lam, *The Jungle*, 1943

master, alongside the likes of Henri Matisse, Joan Miró, and Henry Moore, when eleven artists were selected to create works for the new UNESCO headquarters in Paris by a committee that included the building's chief architect, Marcel Breuer.

Another Asian diasporic artist in the sphere of Picasso was Wifredo Lam (1902–1982). Lam was born to a Chinese father who had migrated from Canton to Cuba and an Afro-Cuban mother of Spanish descent. Although he is usually seen as a Latin American artist, he spent long years in Europe, primarily in Spain, France, and Italy. Lam's visit to an exhibition of Picasso's work in 1936 in Madrid was an important turning point in his career. 'I at last understood that a picture is a proposal made to others,' Lam said.[37] He moved to Paris in 1938 and quickly became part of the circle around Picasso. Although the influence from the older artist and the mutual affection between them are undeniable, Lam could not escape an essentialising racial identification by Picasso, who told Michel Leiris, a Surrealist writer and ethnographer who was also a close associate, to bring Lam to the Musée de l'Homme and teach him about African art. Picasso also introduced his 'adopted son' to the art dealer Pierre Loeb, who was 'astonished by Lam's "exotic" figures, to which Picasso replied with deference, and almost envy, "He has the right, he is a negro!" Total freedom, gained by Picasso so painstakingly, seemed to come naturally to Lam.'[38] One of Lam's best-known works, *The Jungle* (1943; FIG. 142), was painted within a couple of years of his return to Cuba during the Second World War after almost twenty years away in Europe. Shown in a solo exhibition at Pierre Matisse's New York gallery in 1944, the work entered the collection of MoMA. A celebrated article by the American poet and critic John Yau, written in 1988, puts a spotlight on the fate that befell the monumental painting:

Wifredo Lam's The Jungle *... hangs in the hallway leading to the museum's coatroom. Its location is telling. The artist's work has been allowed into the museum's lobby, but, like a delivery boy, has been made to stand and hold the package in an inconspicuous passageway near the door. By denying Lam and his work the possibility of going upstairs and conversing with Cézanne, Picasso, Matisse, Jackson Pollock, Morris Louis, and Kenneth Noland (their works are carefully arranged on the walls of the main galleries), the museum relegates both the artist and his work to secondary status.*[39]

Yau takes to task the formalist approach that had by then ossified at MoMA. The museum dogmatically adhered to a single narrative of evolution in predominantly Western modern art that relegated *The Jungle* to a mere homage to Picasso's *Les Demoiselles d'Avignon*. Although the 1938 encounter with Picasso was a crucial turning point for Lam, an even more consequential event in his life, Yau suggests, was his return to Cuba, where he rediscovered his roots and understood the purpose of his art with a renewed social and political consciousness. 'After Lam perceived Picasso to be an artist-colonialist,' writes Yau, 'he defined himself as an artist-restorer, and began demanding parity. He did so by re-appropriating the African gods Picasso first appropriated in 1907, restoring them to their rightful domain. Painting was the only world they could still rule.'[40]

One would be hard-pressed to think of another artist with an ethnic and familial heritage and cosmopolitan cultural experiences as rich and complex as those possessed by Lam. Leiris immediately recognised this, writing that Lam 'seemed predestined to create a "deeply

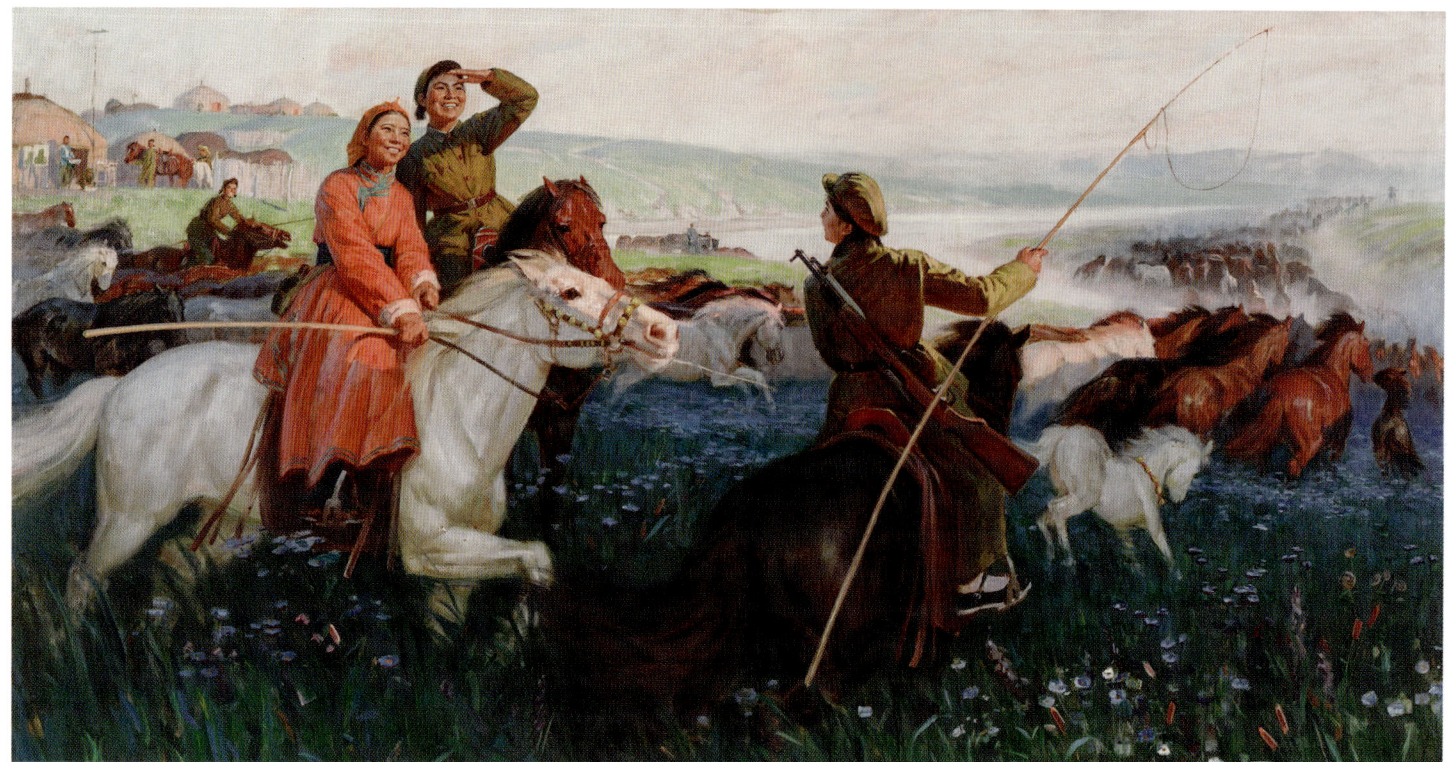

universalist" work where "four worlds [were] united: Asia, Africa, Europe and, by his birthplace, America."'[41] Despite his Chinese-origin family name and paternal lineage, Lam's trajectory was primarily transatlantic rather than transpacific. By reconsidering him as an 'Asian diasporic artist', however, Leiris would make Lam an even more powerful reminder of the exceedingly fertile topography of global modernism, marked by the crisscrossing lines of the travel of people and ideas, genetic mixings, cultural appropriations, colonialisms and decolonising struggles, as well as adoptions, mutations, and naturalisations.

Echo

How might artists working far from Picasso's Europe and in a different era still relate to him and his work? Do they need to or wish to? Many works by artists of later generations based in different parts of the world can generate resonance—like tuning forks—with Picasso's precedents, for reasons of formal resemblance, topical relevance, and spiritual reverberation.[42]

Picasso found the greatest subjects for his art in his immediate environs: people (the women in his life and his children), domestic objects, and his homes and studio spaces. In the first decades of the twentieth century Picasso painted Fernande Olivier, his first live-in lover. He also depicted what he could easily find in their shared living space in Montmartre, the Bateau-Lavoir—a guitar, a vase, a fruit bowl, a table. The crux of the Cubist revolution, however, lay not so much in the easy accessibility of these subjects as Picasso's transformation of them on canvas. More than six decades later, in Beijing, the young artists of the No Name Group jump-started unofficial, underground art—and contemporary art as a whole—in China in the final days of the Cultural Revolution (1966–1976). While official art called for heroic images celebrating the ideals of China's Communist Revolution, No Name Group painters found subjects by turning to mundane objects in their private rooms, the scenes outside their windows, and their

FIG. 143 Guang Tingbo, *I Graze Horse for My Motherland*, 1973

BELOW: FIG. 144 Zheng Ziyan, *Self Portrait*, 1978

BELOW BOTTOM: FIG. 145 Shi Zhenyu, *Drunk*, 1974

BELOW RIGHT: FIG. 146 Wang Aihe, *Portrait of Zhang Wei*, 1974

friends and artistic comrades. This defiance of the diktat of Socialist Realism, the only sanctioned artistic style in the PRC at the time, was in itself a revolutionary artistic act.

The most natural and benign forms of artistic practice, like sketching *en plein air*, could pose risks that the young artists of the No Name Group were nevertheless willing to take. Self-portraits by Zheng Ziyan, Shi Zhenyu, and Tian Shuying show budding knowledge of early Western avant-garde movements such as Post-Impressionism and Fauvism. Similar aesthetic experimentation is evident in Ma Kelu's gentle portraits of other members of the group, including Wang Aihe and Yang Yushu, and Wang painting Zhang Wei (FIGS 144–147). Reminiscent of Picasso's Blue Period depictions of people on the margins of society, these images of young Chinese artists looking contemplative, melancholy, and even depressive were in direct contrast to the rosy faces of the energetically labouring men and women represented in Socialist Realist paintings (FIG. 143).

As artists in Beijing began to reflect a nascent period of reform in the PRC, Luis Chan (1905–1995) was establishing his own identity as an artist in Hong Kong, the entrepôt on the South China Sea under British colonial rule. Chan was an autodidact who learned about a wide range of Western artists and artistic movements through books, compensating for the lack of opportunities to encounter artworks from

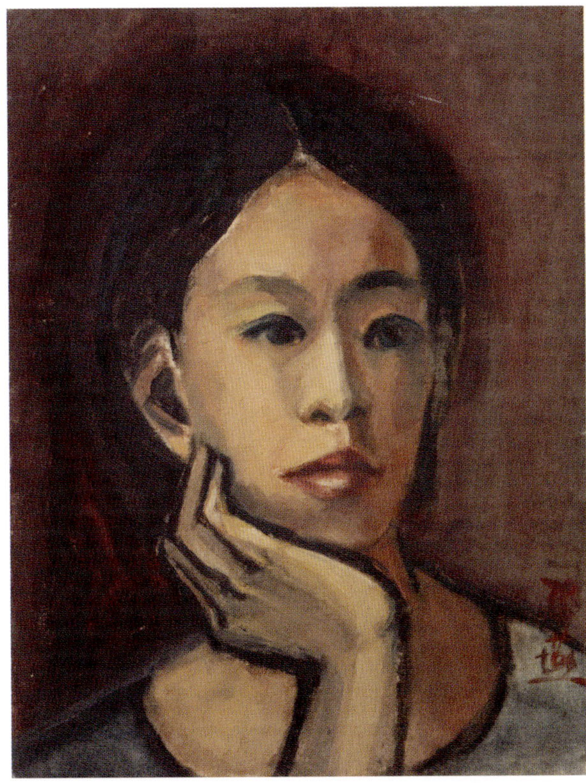

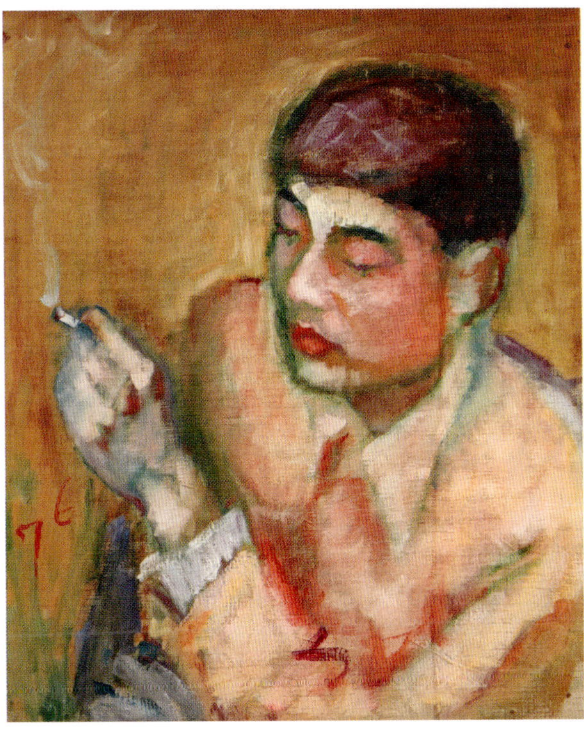

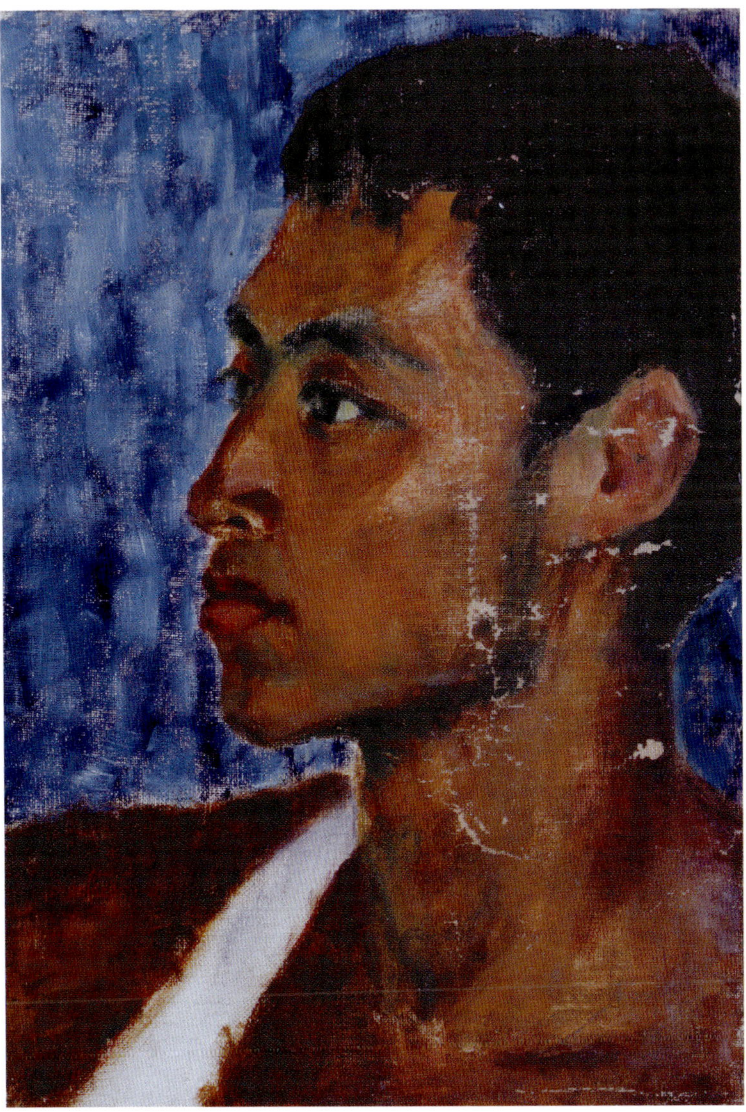

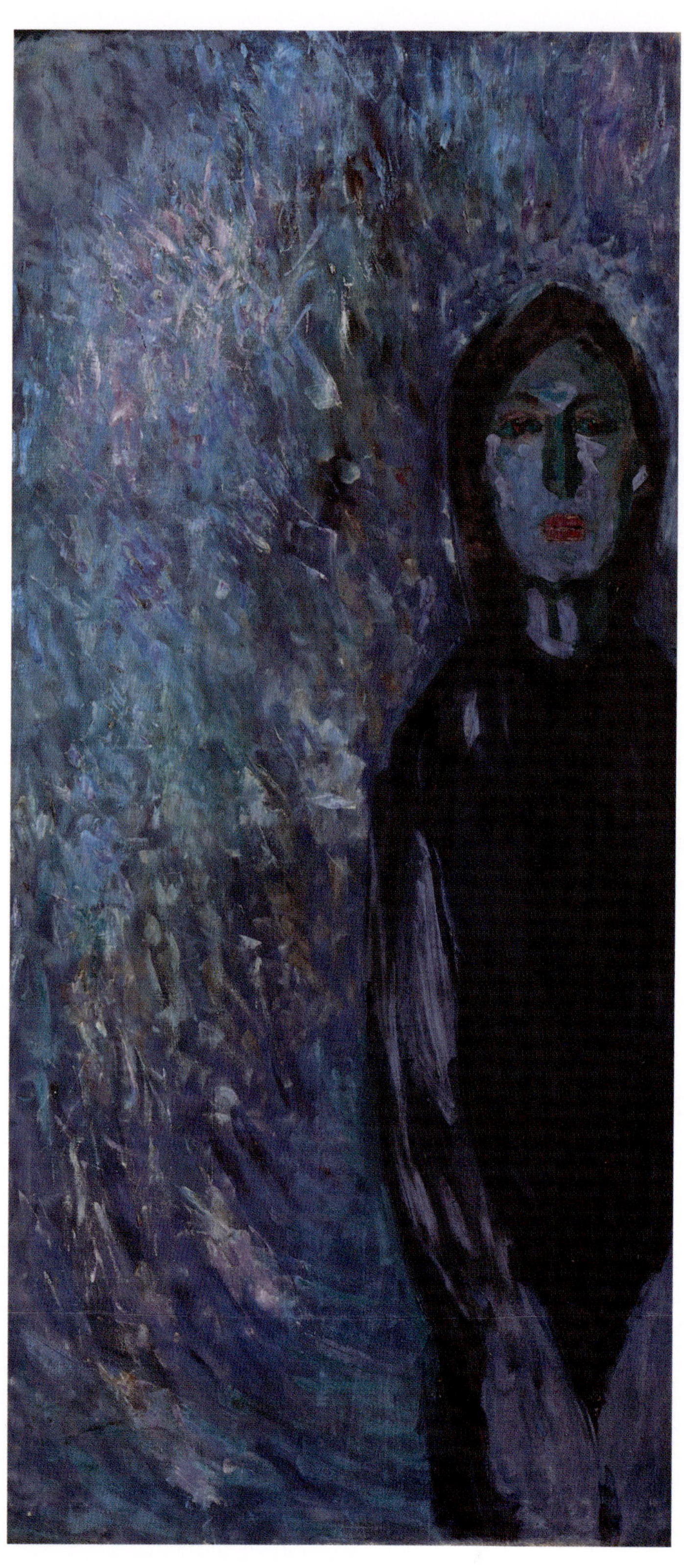

FIG. 147 Wei Hai, *Lady in Blue and Cloves*, 1975

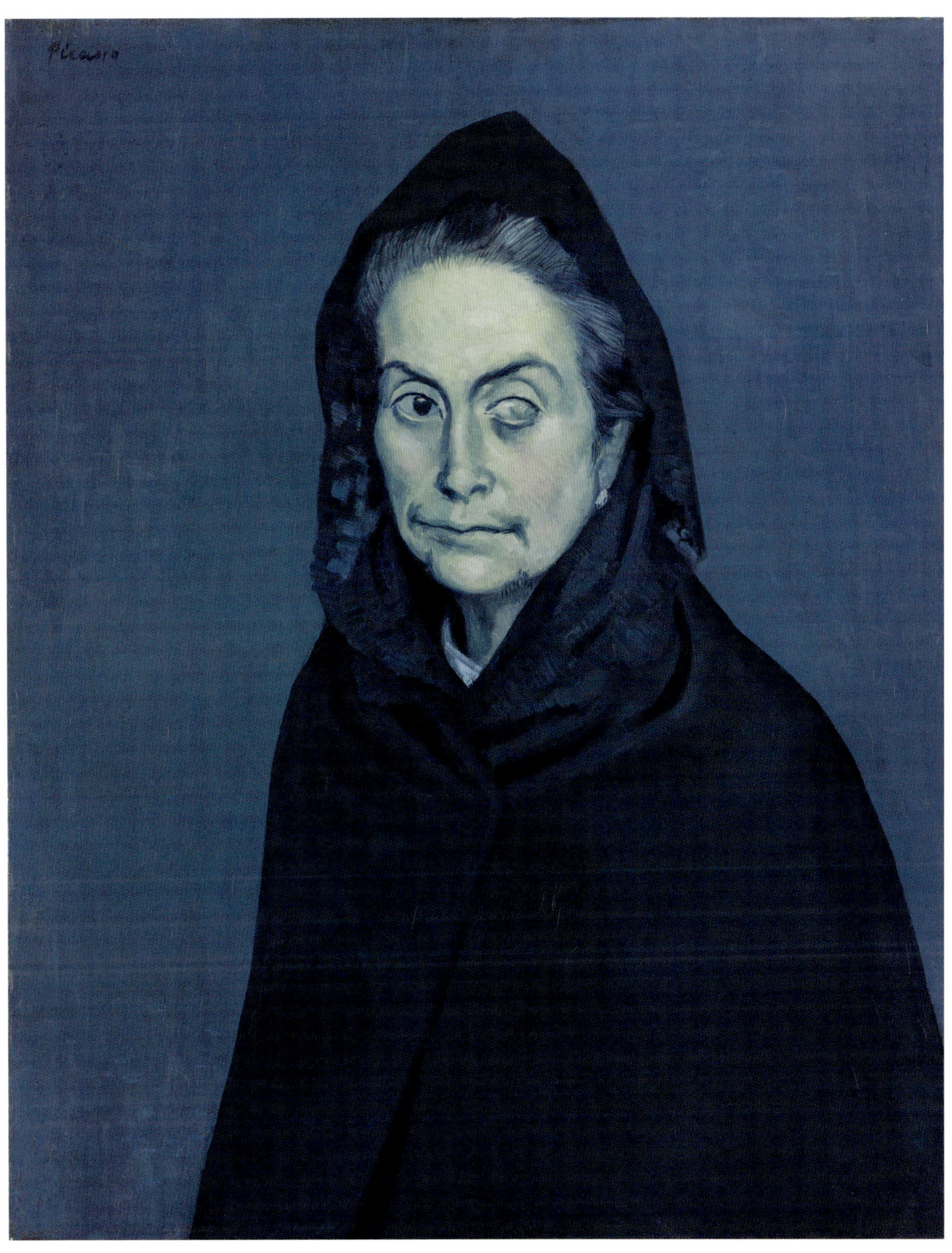

FIG. 148 *Celestina (Woman with a Cloudy Eye)*, 1904

outside Hong Kong in real life. From the 1930s to the mid-1960s he tried his hand at various styles, from watercolour landscape to gestural abstraction, and even had a brief period of Cubist experimentation (FIG. 149). By the late 1960s Chan had arrived at a signature style and iconography: figurative paintings filled with fantastic characters and creatures he observed and imagined in his neighbourhood of Wan Chai. The Hong Kong Island district was known for its vibrant nightlife, with bars catering to tourists and sailors as well as local residents. *Joy of Life* (1969; FIG. 150) typifies Chan's idiosyncratic visual language and depictions of figures that are alternately grotesque and humorous. Many of his ethnically ambiguous subjects appear both Asian and Western. As they merge with one another and into the background of different hues of blue and green, the painting recalls, as much in its palette as in its subject matter, Picasso's Blue Period and Rose Period paintings featuring peripheral, melancholy, and downtrodden figures (FIG. 148).

A natural inheritor of Chan's distinctly Hong Kong art is Firenze Lai (born 1984). Like Chan's works, Lai's paintings are based on her observations of daily life and her reflections on the relationship between people and their surroundings. *The Bone Setting Clinic* (2012; FIG. 151) exemplifies what Lai calls 'situation portraits'. Depicted in exaggerated proportions, with a large lower half and diminutive head, the sole figure in the painting appears to blend into the forlorn interior scene rendered in drab hues. Lai's portraits appear simple, childlike, and whimsical, but deceptively so, revealing depths of possible psychic distress and evoking the anxiety and sense of isolation that plague residents of dense, fast-paced, and alienating urban environments.

Especially in his works from the late 1920s and early 1930s, during the period when the artist was affiliated with Surrealism and its exploration of the unconscious and erotic desire, Picasso's art plastically moulded the human visage and body, remaking them again and again. This artistic language and methodology have resonated across the work of generations of artists, including those in Greater China. Ink painter Irene Chou (1924–2011), also known as Zhou Luyun, was among

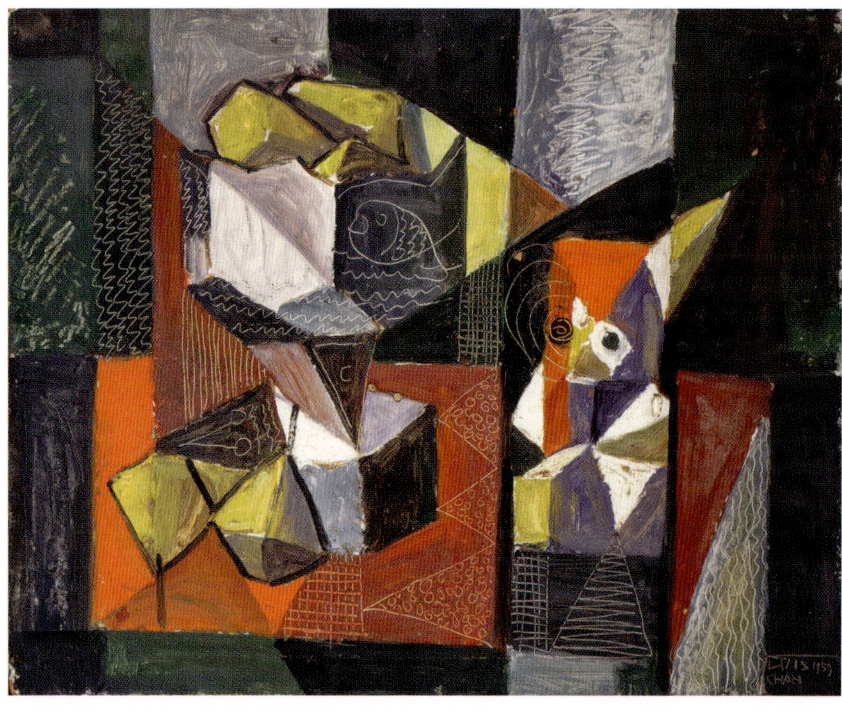

FIG. 149 Luis Chan, *Cubist Sea Shore*, 1959

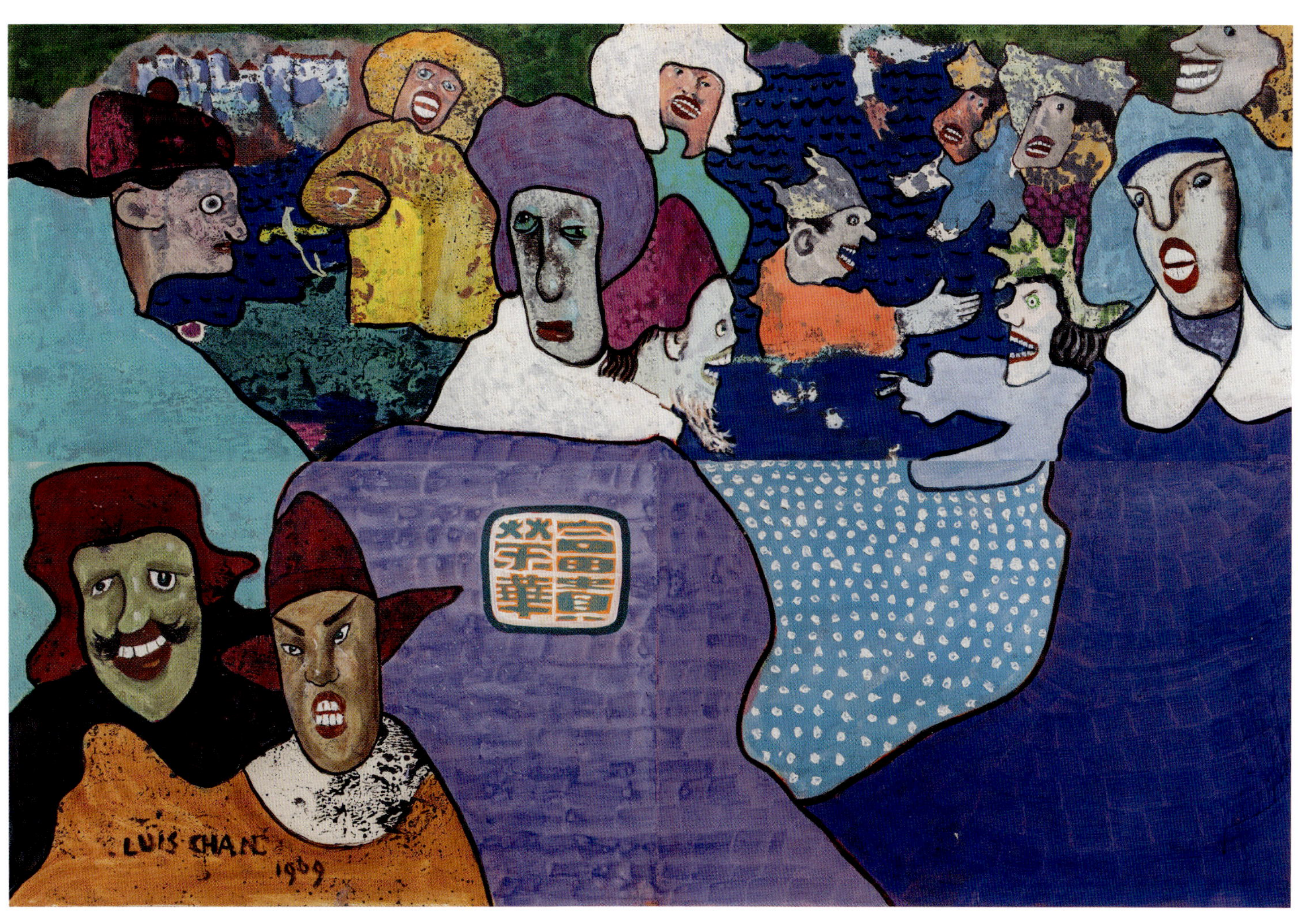

FIG. 150 Luis Chan, *Joy of Life*, 1969

the few female artists in the circle of experimental ink painters that emerged in colonial-era Hong Kong in the 1960s.[43] Deftly working across a spectrum of styles, from figuration to abstraction, Chou conjured images and moods that can be mysterious and sublime, as well as erotic and outright sexual. Made during the 1970s—a dark period in the artist's life, when she lost both her artistic mentor Lui Shou-kwan (1919–1975) and her husband—*Portrait #2* (1970s; FIG. 152) and an untitled work (1970s; FIG. 153) can be loosely categorised as a portrait and a landscape, respectively. The former zooms in on the lower half of a presumably male face that is covered with abundant facial hair. Flowing downwards like a waterfall, and flicking up like dancing flames, the beard is reminiscent of Michelangelo's famous early cinquecento sculpture of Moses ensconced in the Basilica of San Pietro in Vincoli in Rome—a Renaissance-era precursor to Picasso's own authority in the twentieth century. An unusual landscape, the untitled work features undulating, overlapping, wave-like forms in the foreground and receding peaks and a nocturnal halo in the background; in the middle ground are masses of rocky outcrops depicted with exaggerated furrows and folds, at the centre of which is the opening of a cavern blocked by thickets of root-like growths. In its form, the opening in the centre of the composition cannot avoid being seen as the female sex, rather disturbingly obscured, while the beard, the cipher of masculinity and perhaps patriarchy, overflows in unchecked exuberance. Together, they may be seen as simultaneously resonating with and subverting the erotic and sexual drive that is the central motor of Picasso's art.

In the same decade, back in Beijing, Feng Guodong (1948–2005) painted *Body* (1978; FIG. 154). Feng was a self-taught artist, like Luis Chan, but with far less access to Western art owing to the fact that, prior to 1978, mainland China had been closed to the outside world for several decades. For this reason his highly individualistic protean style is a surprising development, especially given that deviations from Socialist Realism in China were still considered suspect. *Body* is dominated by an irregular black form that seems to hang from a laundry line, against the backdrop of a desert-like landscape. A low-slung horizon intersects in places with the black biomorphic form, which features openings that could be an eye and an anus, and indentations that recall the folds of intestinal linings. If this is indeed a 'body', it is a monstrous, mutating part-body, recalling certain forms that Picasso depicted in the early 1930s as well as Salvador Dalí's melting figures. Like his contemporaries in the No Name Group, Feng sought out autonomous expressions, but his search was solitary. This indescribable form is one result of expressing the self in ways that cannot be easily programmed into the sanctioned, dominant practice of Socialist Realism.

FIG. 151 Firenze Lai, *The Bone Setting Clinic*, 2012

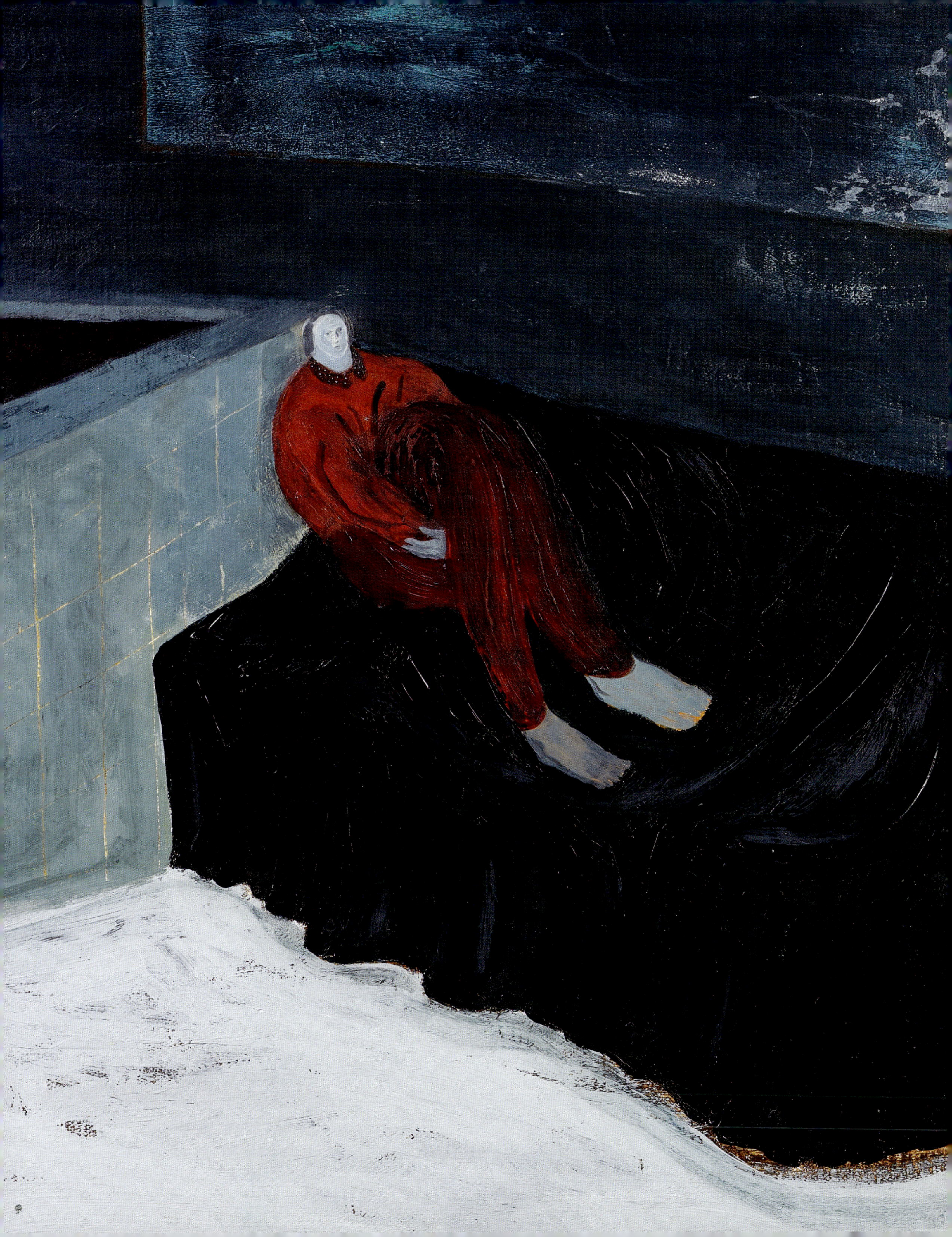

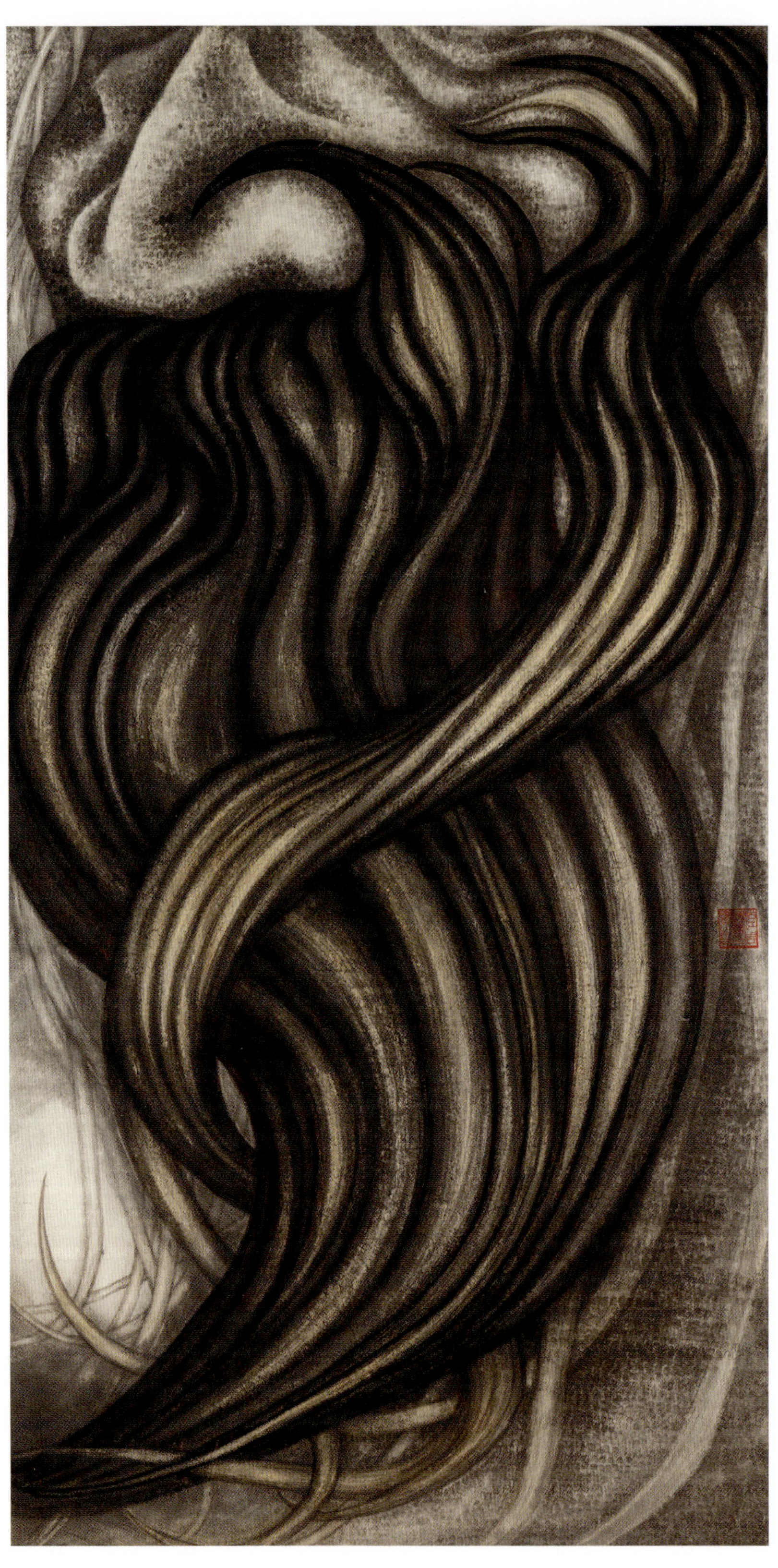

FIG. 152 Irene Chou, *Portrait #2*, 1970s

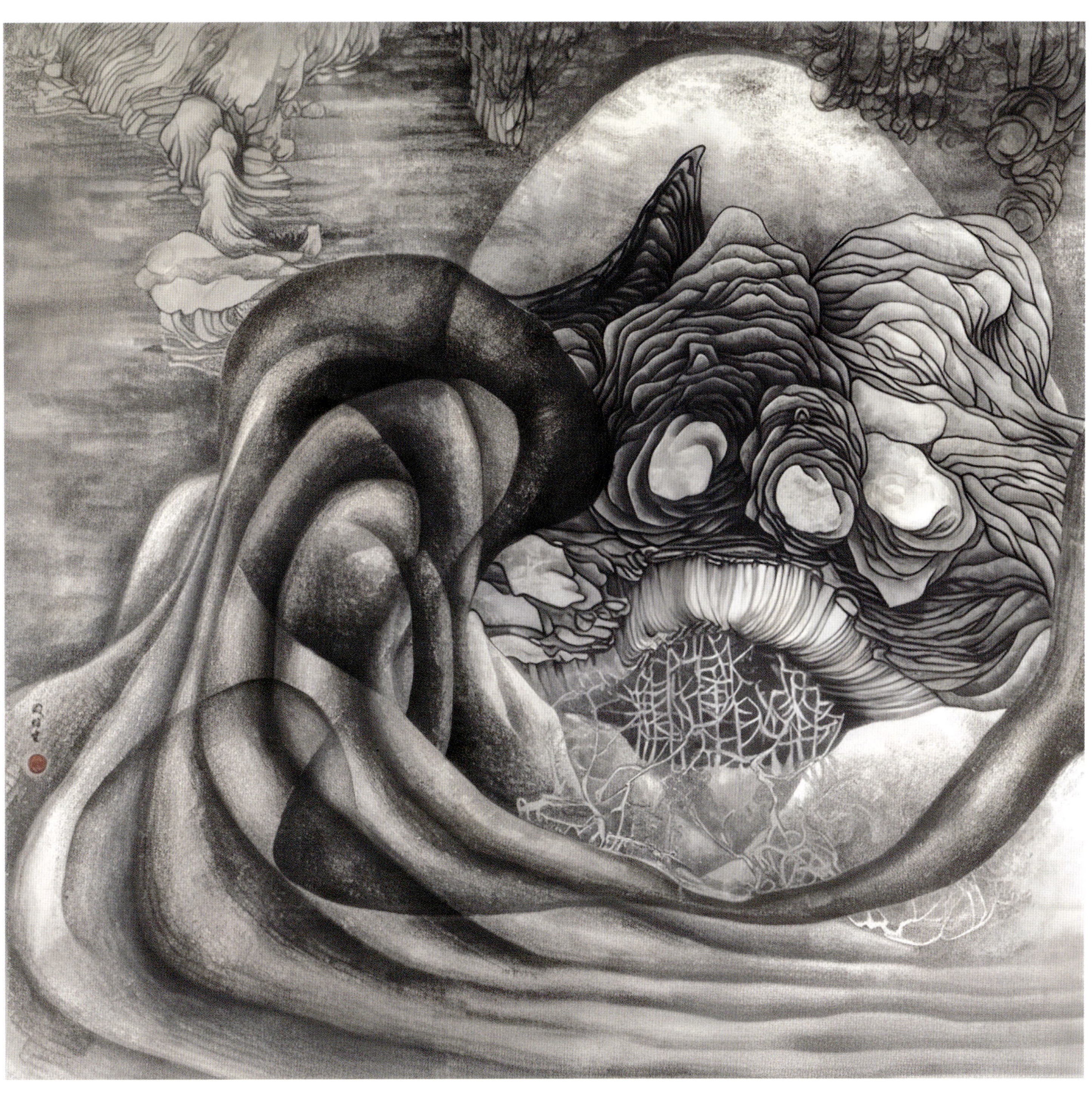

FIG. 153 Irene Chou, untitled, 1970s

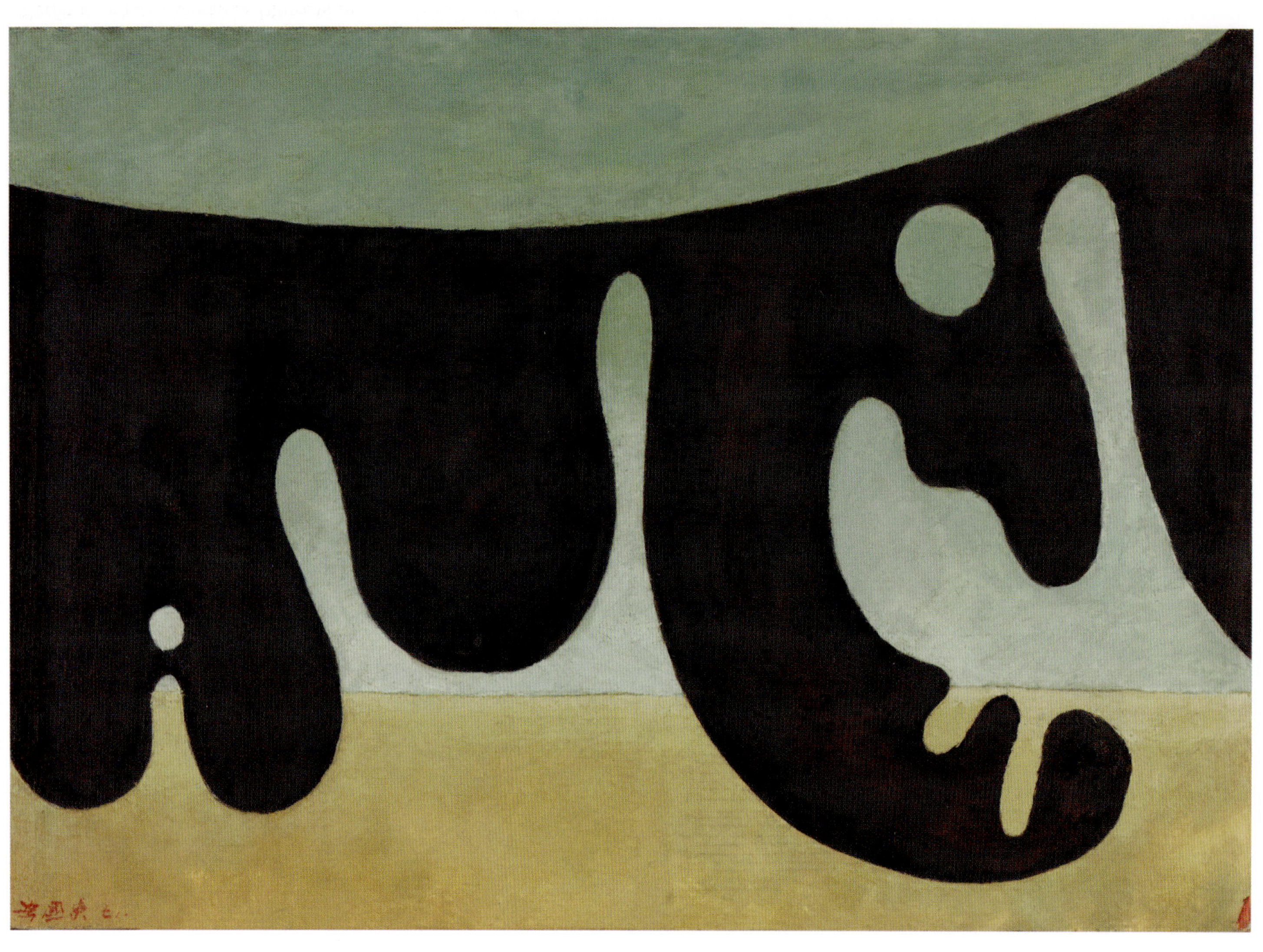

FIG. 154 Feng Guodong, *Body*, 1978

As individualistic as Feng and equally hailed as an 'artist's artist', Gu Dexin (born 1962) is also self-taught and is similarly known for his enigmatic practice and strongly evocative visual language. His 1983 painting *B24* (FIG. 155) features phantasmagorical humanoids, each sporting two or three animal heads, multiple breasts, and the bodies of women—part-human, part-animal monsters. Gu's decision to paint his creations' eyes and breasts on the same side shows the influence of Cubism on his painting. These creatures are seen flying, dancing, and making love. By the end of the 1970s Gu and his fellow artists were able to access at the city library in Beijing the catalogues of major modernist painters, including Vincent van Gogh, Oskar Kokoschka, and Henri Rousseau, as well as Picasso. *B24* demonstrates the impressive outcomes of the creative impulses unleashed by China's opening to the world.

Picasso's work from a career spanning almost eight decades is extensive and varied, but his art is still arguably best known for, and represented by, one genre in particular: portraits of women. Many of them have become icons in the history of modern art and in popular culture, helping to cement the iconicity of the artist himself. In the later twentieth century, during a groundbreaking period for culture in China following the Cultural Revolution, portraiture also played a central role in revolutionising art. After an initial period of cautious yet courageous experimentation, contemporary Chinese art burst onto the global art scene with strong figurative works focused on the human visage and body. One of the most celebrated subjects in contemporary Chinese art from the turn of the millennium is the bald male figure in paintings by Fang Lijun (born 1963). Fang's *1995.2* (1995; FIG. 156) is a head-and-shoulders portrait of a bald man seen from behind. The pink tints of his smooth skin and his clothing contrast with the blue hues of the rippling backdrop and the three identical-looking men, also bald, facing him and the viewer. Because the artist himself is bald, it has often been assumed that his paintings are self-portraits. They are instead expressions of a sceptical, even cynical stance towards recent history marked by the violence of the masses. Fang became closely associated with Cynical Realism, one of the most prominent artistic styles of late twentieth-century Chinese art. Baldness in Chinese culture 'is characteristic of both monks and prisoners, extremes of virtue and vice that neatly encapsulate the ambivalence that Fang seeks to convey'.[44]

All of these artists consciously positioned themselves in the history of modern art, especially that of the West. It is probably safe to assume that they were all aware of Picasso to varying degrees, but the resemblances and resonances of subject, form, and ideas are not meant to suggest that they were influenced by Picasso. What is undeniable is that these artists, working across the twentieth century in Greater China, pursued the goal of modern and contemporary art that could honestly and accurately reflect the turbulent experiences of the time. Examining potential relationships between Picasso's legacy and the diverse practices of contemporary artists, one curator writes: 'the oeuvre of Picasso "resounds" with echo, sometimes deafening and sometimes fainter, in contemporary ears. Whether contemporary with Picasso himself or subsequent to his demise, every period has found new echoes, again and again and for all sorts of reasons, in keeping with the thoughts proposed to us by artists.'[45]

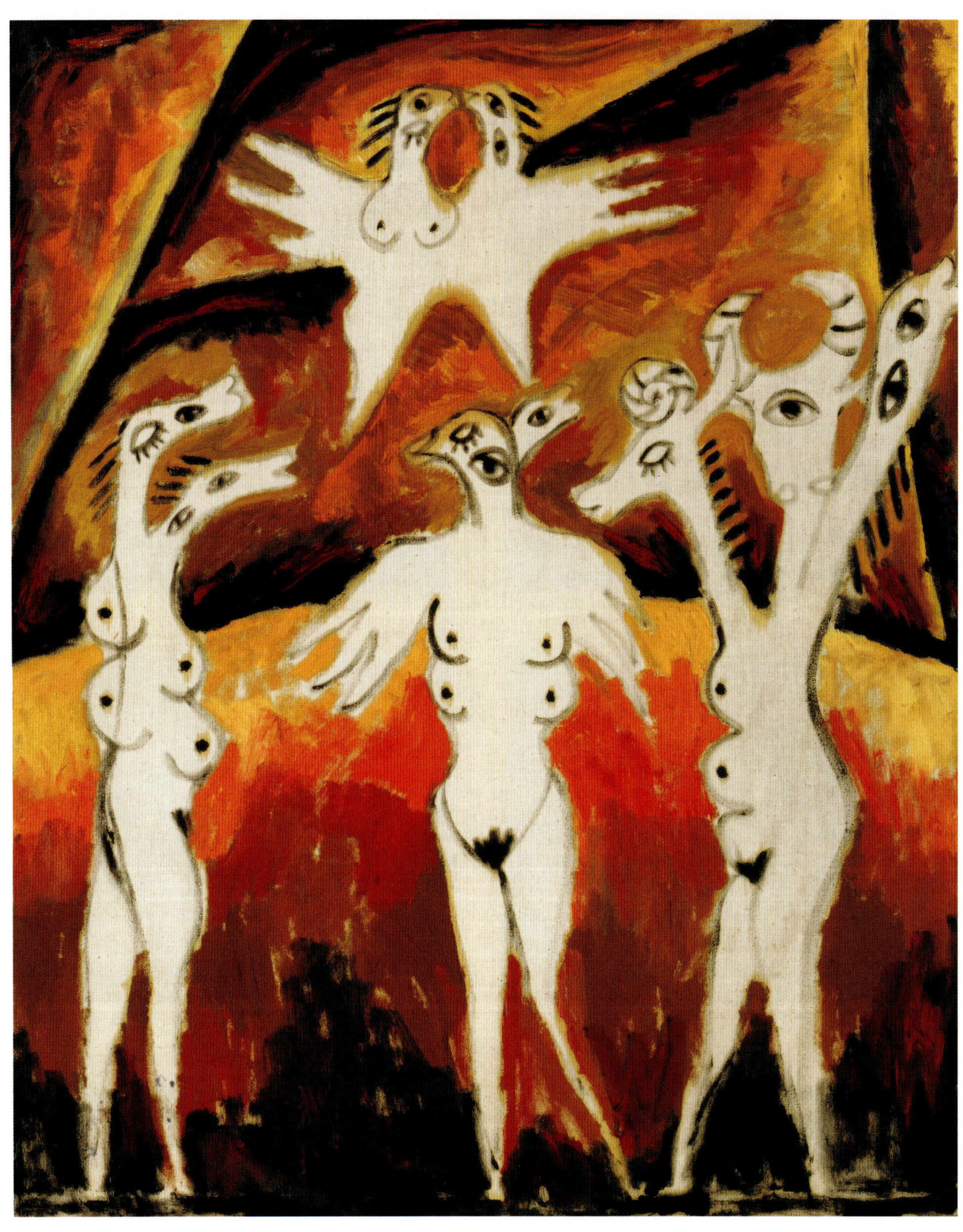

FIG. 155 Gu Dexin, *B24*, 1983

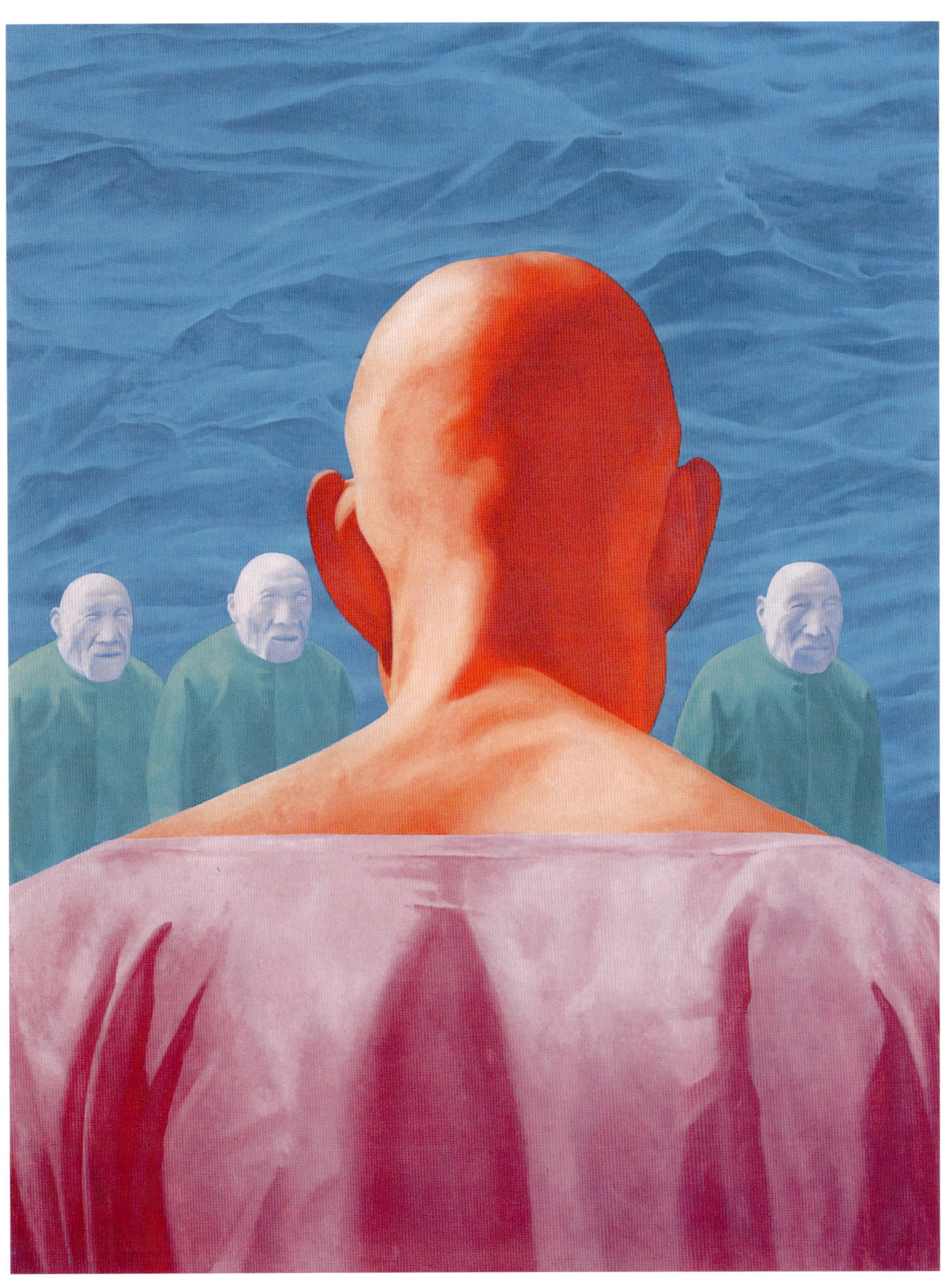

FIG. 156 Fang Lijun, *1995.2*, 1995

Critique

Anyone writing on Picasso today would be remiss not to recognise what we now know about the troubling aspects of his biography, especially his relationship with women, who were also the main subjects of his art. He married twice, divorced once, and lived with five other women, sometimes simultaneously, in multiple households. Two of the seven women, Marie-Thérèse Walter and Jacqueline Roque, committed suicide after his death. There were also others. It is said that only one of them, Françoise Gilot, left and survived Picasso, the man who said to her, 'Woman is a machine for suffering ... For me, there are only two types of women, goddesses and doormats.'[46] Dora Maar, who, like Gilot, was an artist in her own right, famously said, 'After Picasso, only God.'[47] A growing number of books and exhibitions, and even a stand-up comedy act, have begun to expose and excoriate Picasso's philandering and misogyny.[48] Such revisionism, however, does not seem to have curbed the public interest in, if not the appreciation of, Picasso's art in our time. Why Picasso has not been thoroughly reassessed, justifiably humbled, or even 'cancelled' in spite of all the exposés is part of the bigger question of why patriarchy, heteronormativity, and racial supremacy continue to persist despite the cultural critiques and political activism of the past several decades. The enduring attraction of Picasso is also inextricably linked to how we continue to make monsters into geniuses and make ourselves believe that we need the geniuses even if they are monsters.[49]

Without making any direct reference to Picasso, and perhaps without even lending him any mental space, three artists—three women of different generations from across Asia—together demonstrate an ongoing struggle against the patriarchal structure inherent not only in the art world but also in our long-standing cultural narratives and mythology. The art of Akutagawa (Madokoro) Saori (1924–1966), whose brilliant career was cut short by her death at the age of forty-one, was unique in post-war Japan.[50] One of the few female artists to gain recognition at the time, she was lauded for paintings made with a unique wax-dyeing technique. Akutagawa depicted semi-abstract figures: women in various emotional states, and divine figures drawn from Japanese folklore and mythology. Her forceful visual language is marked by confident forms and vibrant palettes. As the title suggests, Akutagawa's 1954 work *God of Spring* (FIG. 157) features a mythological deity. The large C-shaped form sporting two sets of three black fangs and a pair of ferocious red eyes in the upper-left part of the canvas seems precariously balanced on a flat, expanding, and angular geometric shape. The overall composition also alludes to ancient Chinese bronze vessels, or, more fittingly perhaps, to Japanese pottery from the prehistoric Jōmon era (around 14,000 to 300 BCE). Akutagawa admired Mexican muralism, and her exploration of ancient Japanese myths, as well as traditional dye techniques, may have been inspired by a desire to search for a new cultural identity for her nation, which was emerging from the devastations of war and the US-led occupation (1945–1952). The drawings she produced in parallel with her paintings strongly recall the Surrealist automatic drawings that were created in trance-like states. Appearing to have emerged from her unconscious, Akutagawa's works evoke ancient scripts, celestial bodies, monstrous beings, and micro-organisms. She affirmed in her practice that a woman can express the active life of the unconscious and also think broadly about history and mythology, even aspiring to refashion a national cultural identity.

History and mythology, as well as literature and politics, have also been consistent sources of inspiration for Nalini Malani (born

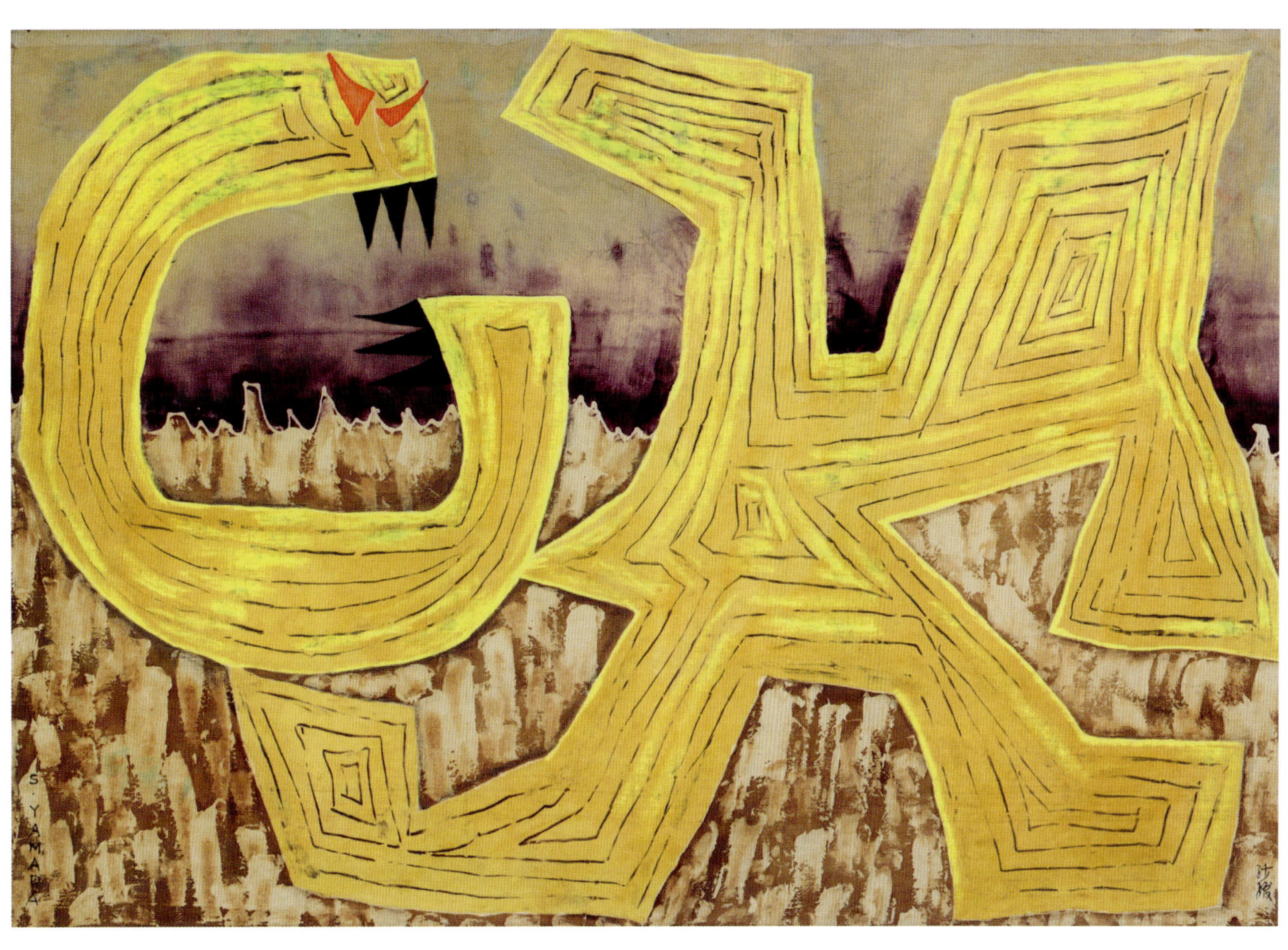

FIG. 157 Madokoro (Akutagawa) Saori, *God of Spring*, 1954

1946). Malani is a pioneering artist who has been working in a wide range of mediums, from printmaking and artist's books to moving image and theatre production. While her practice continues to evolve as she embraces new technologies and ways of working, she retains a steadfast commitment to investigating the effects of war, violence, and the repression of women. Her work magnifies the experiences of the disenfranchised and oppressed by layering motifs from folklore and classical literature with personal narratives that are informed by her early experience as a refugee in post-partition India. Alongside such Hindu goddesses as Sita and Radha, archetypal female figures from the West, including the sorceress Medea from Greek mythology and characters from Lewis Carroll's *Alice's Adventures in Wonderland* (1865), have figured prominently. Another figure from Greek mythology who appears in Malani's art is Cassandra, a truth-teller who is cruelly destined to see but not to be believed. According to Malani, Cassandra is blessed with 'profound insights that individuals have that can be good for the future of humankind [but which] are not paid heed to and we continue in the direction of death and destruction'.[51] In Malani's video play *In Search of Vanished Blood* (2012; FIG. 158), the character of Cassandra appeals to humanity against extremism and self-destruction; however, as in the original myth, she is tragically ignored and castigated by others. In addition to such rich, iconographic references as Goya's *The Disasters of War* series, Malani draws from a range of literary references, including Christa Wolf's 1983 novel *Cassandra*, an Urdu poem by Agha Shahid Ali, and texts by Heiner Müller, Samuel Beckett, and the Indian activist and writer Mahasweta Devi.

Raised under the PRC's one-child policy, Pixy Liao (born 1979) grew up feeling the weight of familial responsibilities and societal expectations. Liao moved to the United States in her late twenties and met Moro, a younger man from Japan who would become her muse, collaborator, and life partner. In her staged photographs featuring Moro and, at times, herself, Liao explores the possibilities of modern relationships and romance. Although her bold, often humorous images

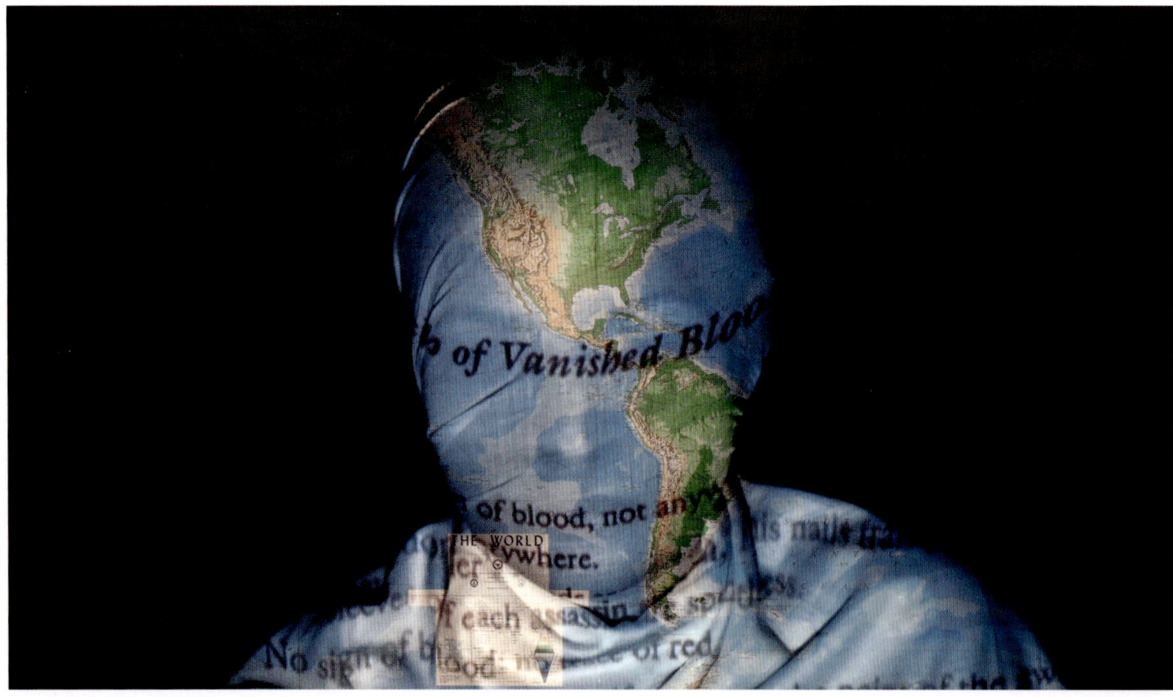

FIG. 158 Nalini Malani, *In Search of Vanished Blood*, 2012

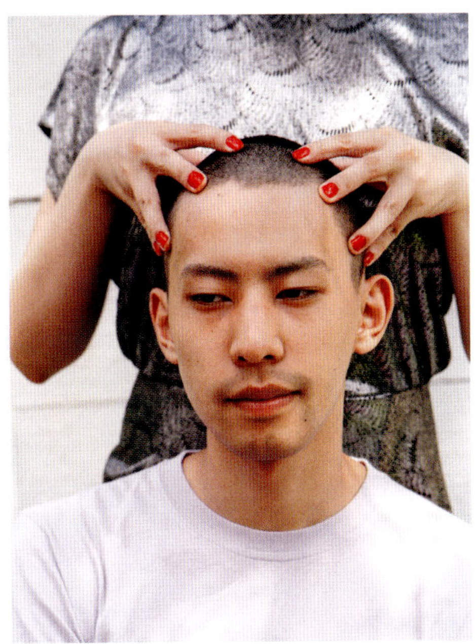

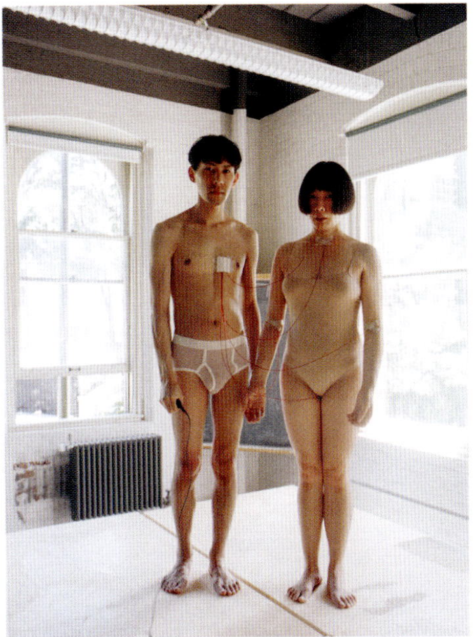

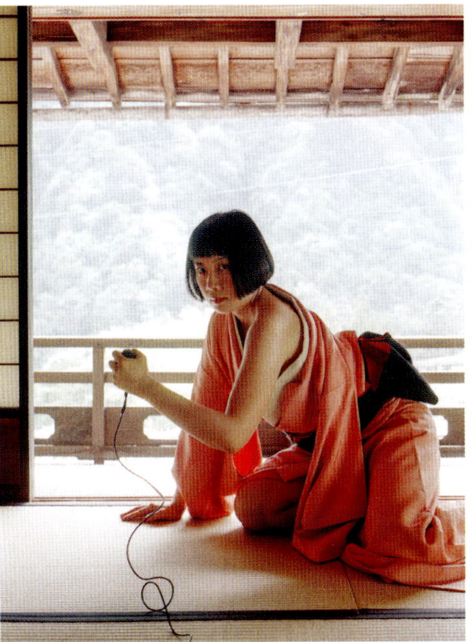

ABOVE LEFT: FIG. 159 Pixy Liao, *Mind-control is a woman's essential skill*, 2010

ABOVE CENTRE: FIG. 160 Pixy Liao, *We are connected*, 2015

ABOVE RIGHT: FIG. 161 Pixy Liao, *The woman who clicks the shutter*, 2018

subvert conventional representations of heterosexual relationships and challenge traditional notions of masculinity, Liao refuses to label her work as feminist art. Examples from her ongoing series *Experimental Relationship*, begun in 2007, demonstrate her evolving interrogation of relationships and sexuality, bodies and genders, and adulthood. *Mind-control is a woman's essential skill* (2010; FIG. 159) encapsulates the reversal of traditional heterosexual power dynamics as well as the tongue-in-cheek humour in Liao's (self-)portraits of Moro. Her pristinely manicured, red-painted fingernails gently and yet firmly grip the top of his shaved head, in a way that is both menacing and suggestive. *We are connected* (2015; FIG. 160) is a direct reference to Mexican artist Frida Kahlo's *The Two Fridas* (1939). Instead of the double self-portrait of the original—with one Kahlo dressed in a European style and the other in a traditional Tehuana outfit, suggesting the artist's different personalities—the two figures in Liao's photograph are Moro and Liao herself, stripped down to their underwear while holding hands like the two Fridas. Their open 'hearts' are connected by blood lines representing the commonality between two clearly separate identities. Liao sometimes features Moro by himself, but rarely appears on her own in her work. An exception is *The woman who clicks the shutter* (2018; FIG. 161). Set in a traditional Japanese domestic setting, the image is based on a 1970s Japanese sexploitation film called *Sex and Fury* by Suzuki Norifumi. Self-consciously revealing herself, Liao holds the camera's remote shutter release instead of a katana (a type of Japanese sword) while commanding the composition and the viewer's attention.

In their work, Akutagawa, Malani, and Liao address women as subjects *and* subjectivities. These artists take on the troubling dynamics and structures of power that continue to exist between genders to expose, parody, subvert, or bypass them. We might also see these artists as pointed ripostes to Picasso, the archetypal modern artist who is also an archetypal heterosexual man of potent virility, about whom one of his descendants said: 'He submitted [his women] to his animal sexuality, tamed them, bewitched them, ingested them, and crushed them onto his canvas ... After he had spent many nights extracting their essence, once they were bled dry, he would dispose of them.'[52] The women discussed in this section are confronting and contesting this vision of the male artist. Their work foregrounds female creative agency and empowerment while demonstrating an approach to art that grapples with history and myth without relying on tropes of dominance.

Departure

Living in Shanghai in the early 1980s, Cai Guo-Qiang (born 1957) began exploring alternative methods and materials for art-making that also resonated with Chinese traditions. He soon became interested in gunpowder. The small explosions he produced on flat substrates left residues and textures that he could not fully control. These chance results appealed to Cai. He felt that using gunpowder helped him to 'supplement the expression of the oil painting, adding a material richness and deliberately producing a seemingly profound sense of mystery'.[53] *Gunpowder Drawing No. 8-A5* (1988; FIG. 162) is one of the earliest examples of Cai's gunpowder works still in existence, made just before the artist began embarking on his spectacular daytime pyrotechnic displays. The composition, resulting from a combination of acrylic and gunpowder, features a central mass surrounded by a concentric frame, radiating lines, and spheres of charred areas, giving the whole canvas the impression of an aerial view of a distant, arid planet. Harnessing the alchemical transformation of materials into art itself, Cai's painting collapses destruction and creation into one. The artist's groundbreaking method is a late twentieth-century rejoinder to the destruction-as-creation that was Picasso's and Georges Braque's Cubism at the beginning of the century (see, for example, FIG. 33). Both Picasso's Cubism and Cai's gunpowder drawings redefine the role of the flat surface as a space for representation; and just as Cubism marked an unprecedented departure from this centuries-old tradition, so do Cai's drawings. These two artistic revolutions bookend the trajectory of modern art in the twentieth century.

If gunpowder for Cai is a substance representing ancient Chinese civilisation brought to the present to help remake the art of our time, Haegue Yang (born 1971) is interested in the material culture of our own epoch. One of the signature compositional objects Yang has used since the mid-2000s is the clothing rack on casters, the central element of an increasingly anthropomorphic—and then post-human—body of sculpture. Her sculptural trio *Totem Robots*, consisting of *Totem Robot – Forward*, *Totem Robot – Askew*, and *Totem Robot – Sidewise* (2010; FIG. 163), exemplifies her exuberant combinations, seemingly instinctive and simultaneously precise, of sundry, off-the-shelf items from discount stores. Pieces of stationery, beauty aids, and kitchen utensils hang cheek-by-jowl with such natural or handmade things as pine cones and knitting yarn, everything hung on electrical cords, rendering a drawing in space punctuated by lightbulbs. The sculptures are both 'totems', conjurers of spirits and ancestors out of quotidian materials, and homespun, low-tech robots cobbled together from the stuff of a household in a post-apocalyptic world. Yang exhibits a Midas-like ability to transform the banal into the human, as Picasso did with *The Bathers* (1956; FIG. 164) and *The Woman with the Stroller* (1950; FIG. 68), made out of ignoble pieces of wood and remnants of ordinary objects. But Picasso was sourcing materials from the flotsam and jetsam of his immediate environment, notably his studio and the garden of Villa La Californie, his residence in Cannes. Diasporic and nomadic, residing both in her home city of Seoul and in her adopted city of Berlin, and constantly travelling for research and work, Yang instead scavenges materials from much further afield, guided by an insatiable curiosity

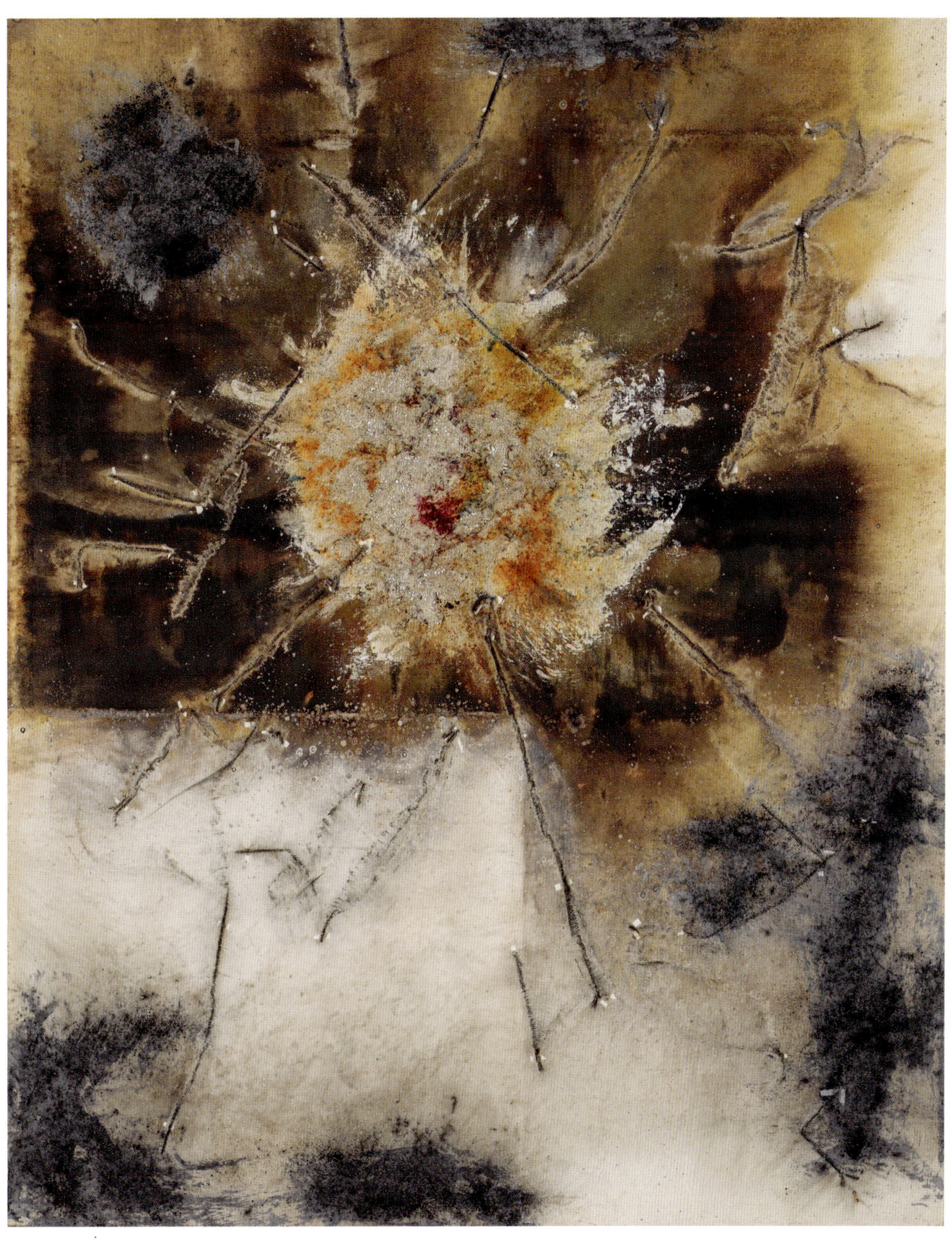

FIG. 162 Cai Guo-Qiang, *Gunpowder Drawing No. 8 A5*, 1988

OVERLEAF: FIG. 163 Haegue Yang, *Totem Robots* (from left): *Totem Robot – Forward*, *Totem Robot – Askew*, and *Totem Robot – Sidewise*, 2010

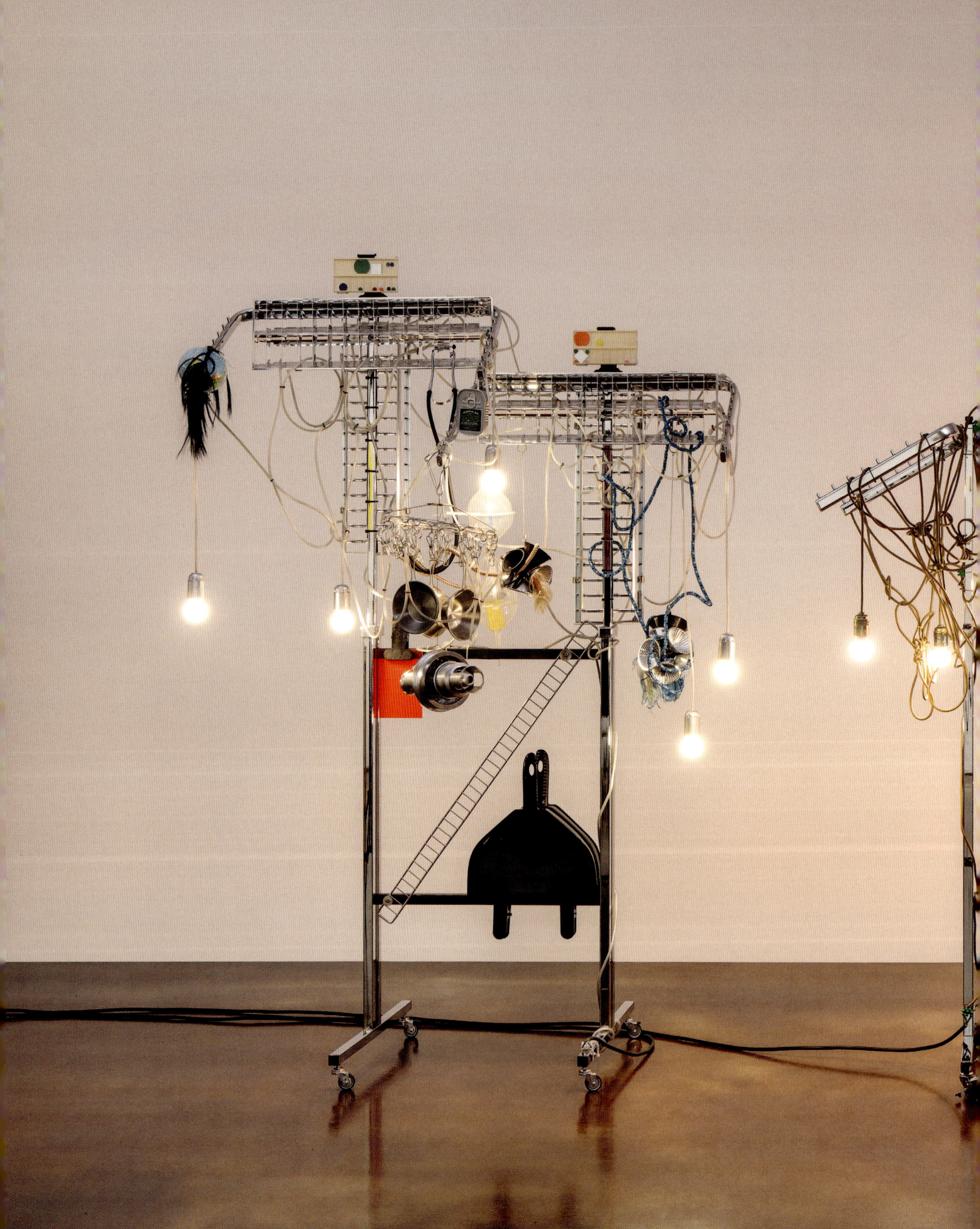

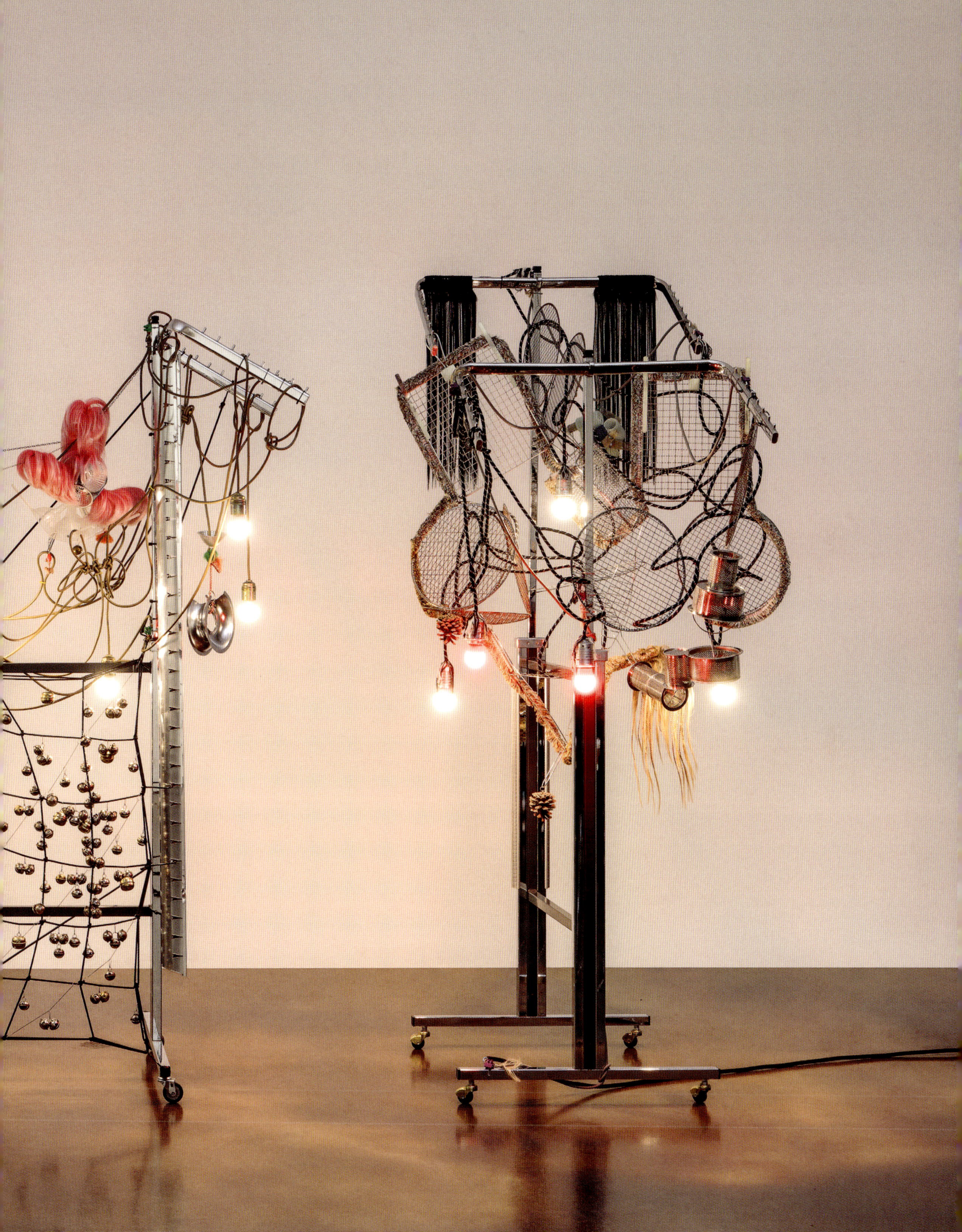

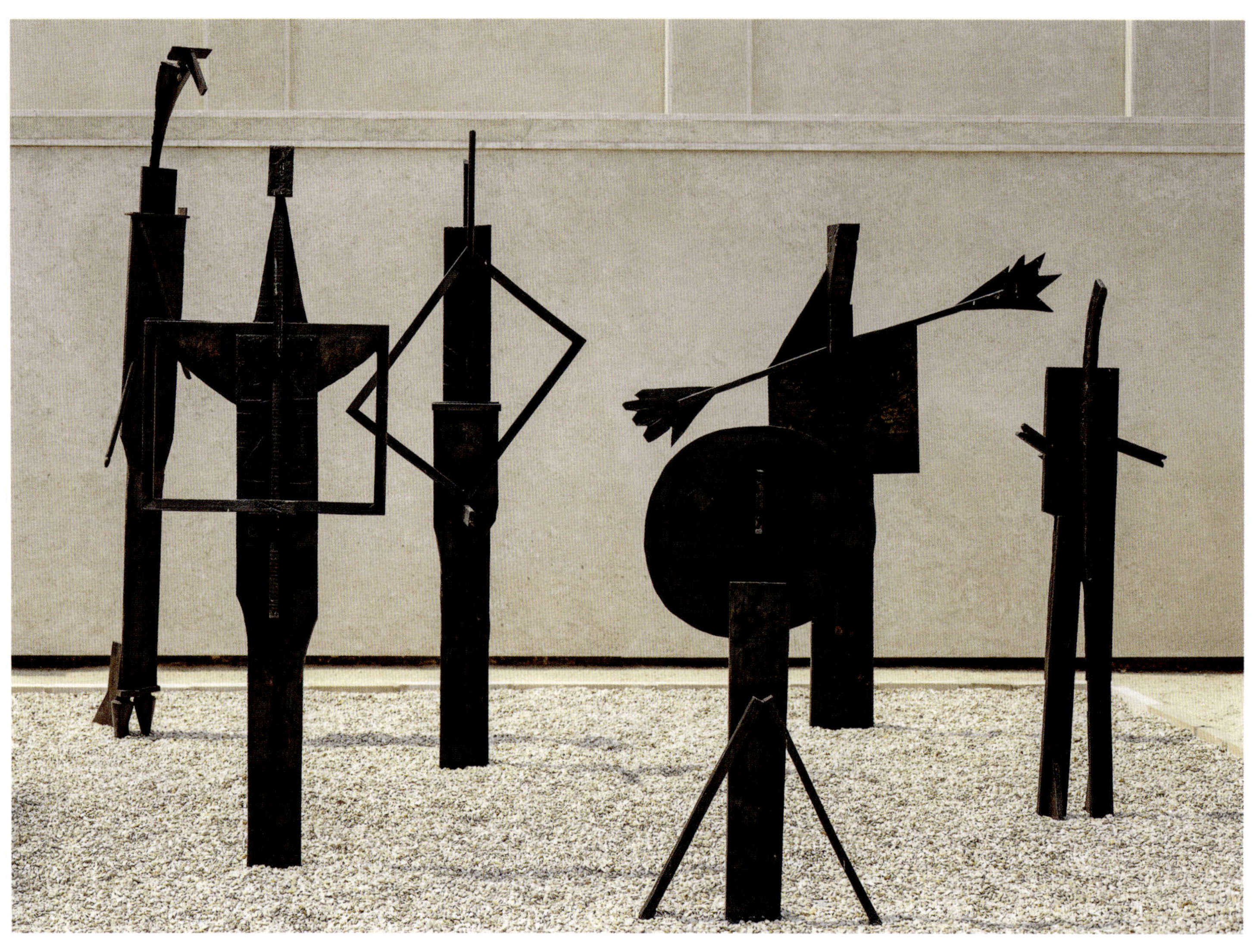

FIG. 164 *The Bathers*, 1956

for new encounters with cultures, familiar and strange. For artists who have deliberately decided to dislocate themselves and be rooted in multiple places, it is not an option to make art only out of the proximate and the familiar.

Isolated in Berlin during the early days of the Covid-19 pandemic in 2020, Simon Fujiwara (born 1982) began reflecting in new ways on the meaning of identity, the main subject of his work over the years. It soon led to the creation of a cartoon character named Who the Bær. Dressed in denim and with a golden heart, the gender-fluid character is also called, simply, 'Who'. In the artist's words, '"Who" is a "radical" proposition [that moves] through the world as a kind of protest—not a protest that is saying "no" to everything but one that says "yes" to everything. "Who" is everything and nothing, and in this sense, it is a philosophical proposition disguised as a silly, lovable cartoon bear.'[54] Vaguely resembling Mickey Mouse and Winnie the Pooh, and equipped with a ludicrously long, dribbling tongue inspired by the same anatomical feature of the Malayan sun bear, Who has been rampaging through art history, colonising and cannibalising a host of masters and masterpieces. No one seems off-limits, from Degas to Hokusai, Van Gogh to Warhol, and Picasso is no exception. Since conceiving of Who, Fujiwara has created more than two dozen works remaking Picasso's well-known classics. *Who vs Who vs Who? (A Picture of a Massacre)* (2024; FIG. 165) and *Decolonize Demoiselles de Who?* (2023), for instance, riff on Picasso's *Massacre in Korea* and *Les Demoiselles d'Avignon*, respectively. Fujiwara's updates have the women and children of the former holding up a small image of *Guernica* against a marauding pack of men, a horse, and others in a complexly meta picture-within-a-picture-about-other-pictures, and the audacious prostitutes of the latter decapitating their own heads (which are now masks of Who, not appropriated African masks). Like Tanaami Keiichi's ongoing marathon of remaking Picasso classics, Fujiwara's series was instigated by the pandemic. Yet both artists have established distinct relationships with the modern master. For Tanaami, Picasso is the incomparable signifier of art, as well as of life, which he endlessly resignifies with his own signifiers. Fujiwara's Who is blatantly promiscuous; Picasso masterpieces are no different from works by other artists, and they are all there for ravenous consumption. In the process, any connoisseurial differences are deleted, and the notion of mastery is demolished.

IN CLOSING

So where does this leave us? Asia—or Asian art and visual culture, and certain events in Asia, to be precise—appeared like shooting stars in the vast firmament of Picasso's art and life. In concluding this essay, proving how relevant or consequential Asia was to Picasso, and vice versa, is not as important as questioning the monumentality of such paradigms and archetypes as 'Asia' and 'Picasso'. Annie Cohen-Solal has recently reminded us that Picasso, the towering figure of modern art, was far from invulnerable and remained a 'foreigner' in his adopted country of France, where he spent the majority of his life. During the interwar years, which were marked by 'economic crisis and vague, successive xenophobia',[55] he was affected by the closure of his dedicated, long-time dealer Daniel-Henry Kahnweiler's gallery and needed to find new alliances, such as that with Sergei Diaghilev of the Ballets Russes. He could not be above working for the aristocracy as a decorator. He may be the *sui generis* modern artist of the twentieth century, but he was not immune to the need for artistic and cultural friendships, political alliances (such as the Spanish Republic cause), and institutional advocacy for his importance (Barr and MoMA, more than any others).[56] Such processes are the means by which all artists are made and become part of history.

Picasso may be thought of as the 'original' par excellence to this day, with successive generations of artists falling under his influence and struggling to follow and translate, or to resist. In his celebrated essay 'The Task of the Translator' (1923), Walter Benjamin writes: 'While content and language form a certain unity in the original, like a fruit and its skin, the language of the translation envelopes its content like a royal robe with ample folds. For it signifies a more exalted language than its own and thus remains unsuited to its content, overpowering and alien.'[57] 'Overpowering and alien' is a perfect description of Picasso's appropriation—translation—of African masks in *Les Demoiselles d'Avignon*, as well as of the legacy of his art. Without rejecting wholesale the paradigmatic and archetypal status Picasso continues to hold in the field of global art in the twenty-first century, we would all benefit from understanding his art in historically specific and contingent terms. He was a European artist—or, to be more precise, Spanish, and an essentially late nineteenth- and early twentieth-century artist, according to the trenchant description by John Berger[58]—who was shaped by Western metropolitan culture and imperialist expansion, the subsequent structural collapse of this technologised civilisation, and the recovery and renewal that followed. This historical trajectory had global consequences, and the contexts in which artists around the world live and work, including in Asia, are inextricably linked with Picasso's own.

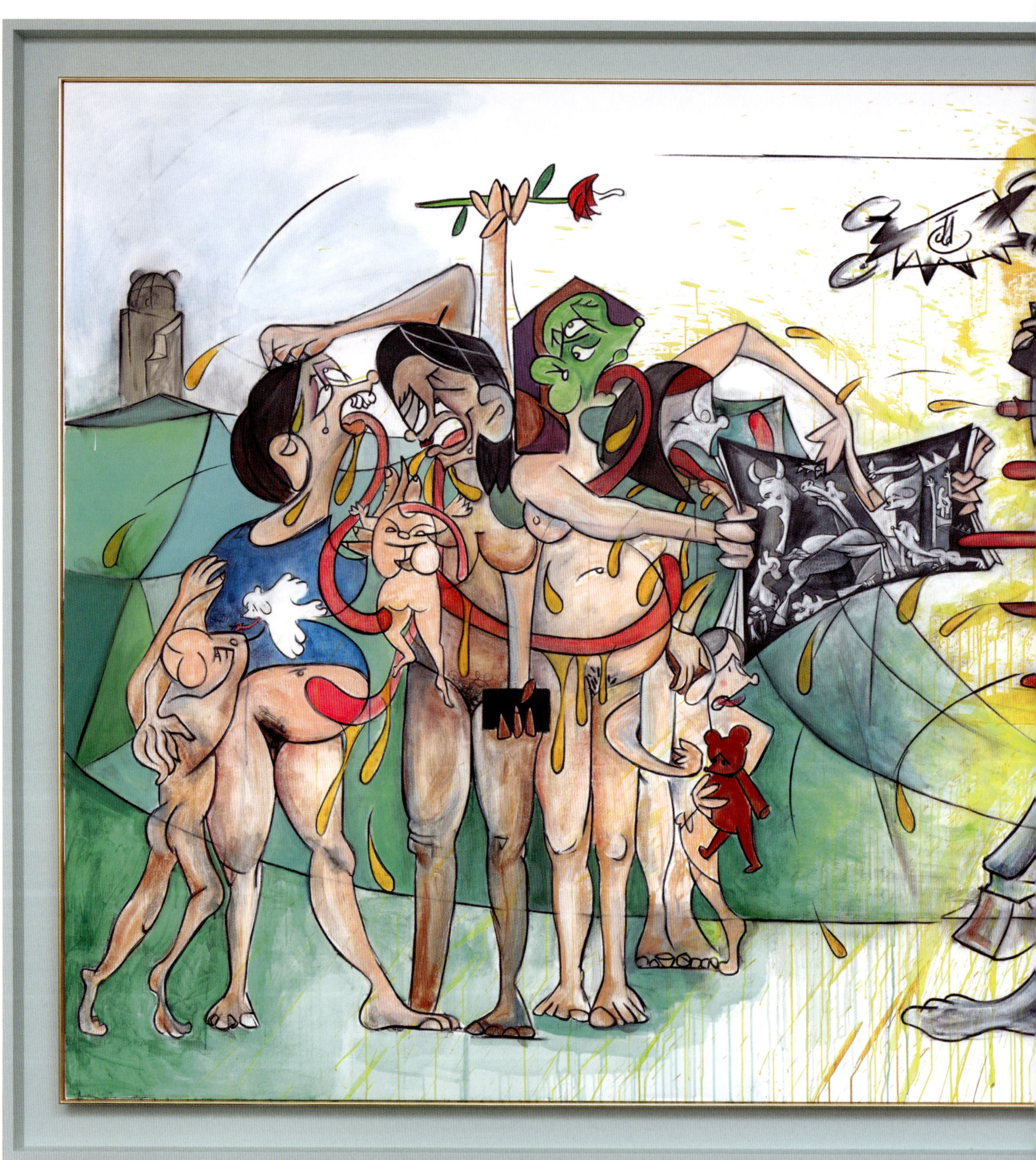

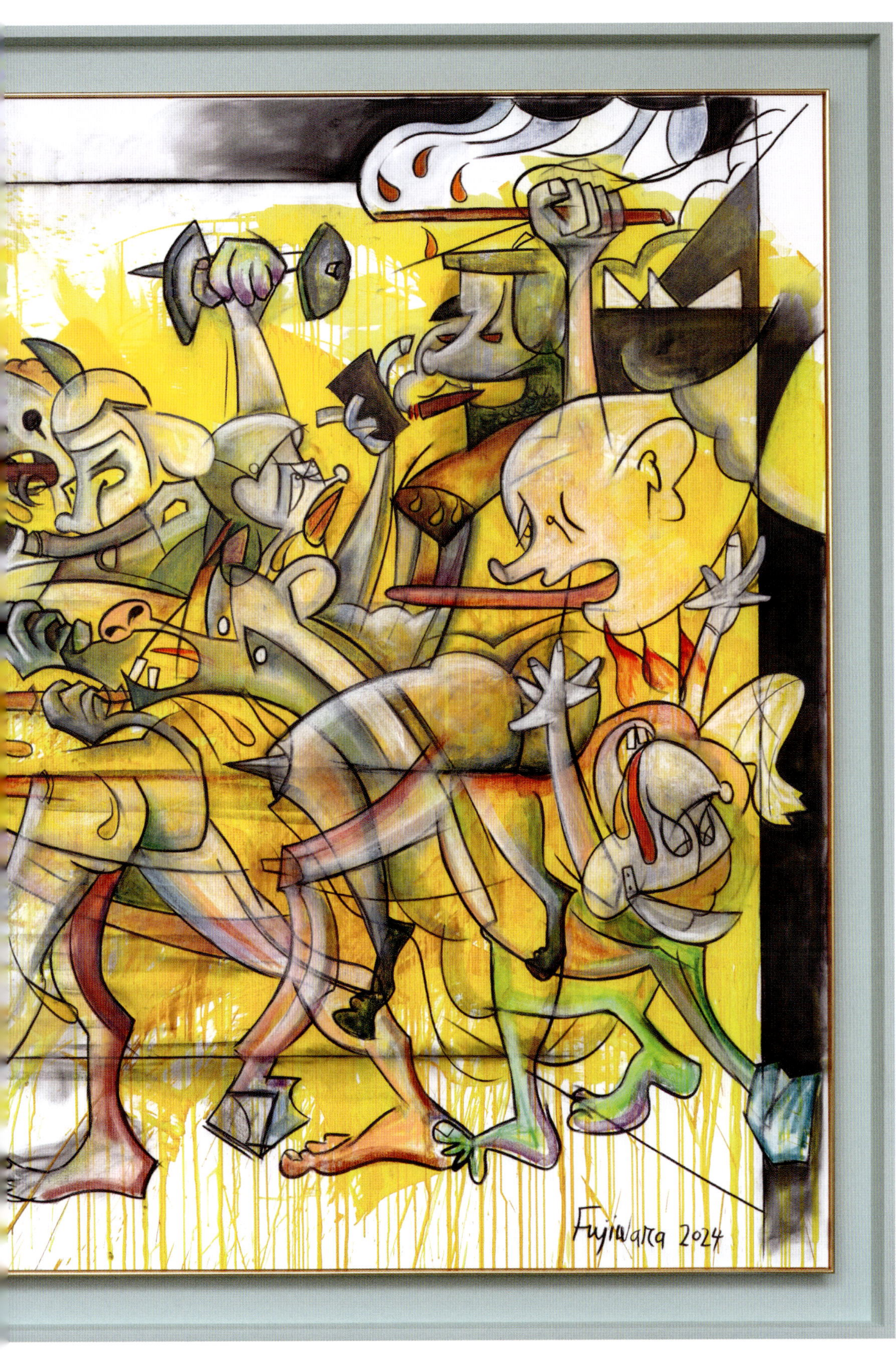

FIG. 165 Simon Fujiwara, *Who vs Who vs Who? (A Picture of a Massacre)*, 2024

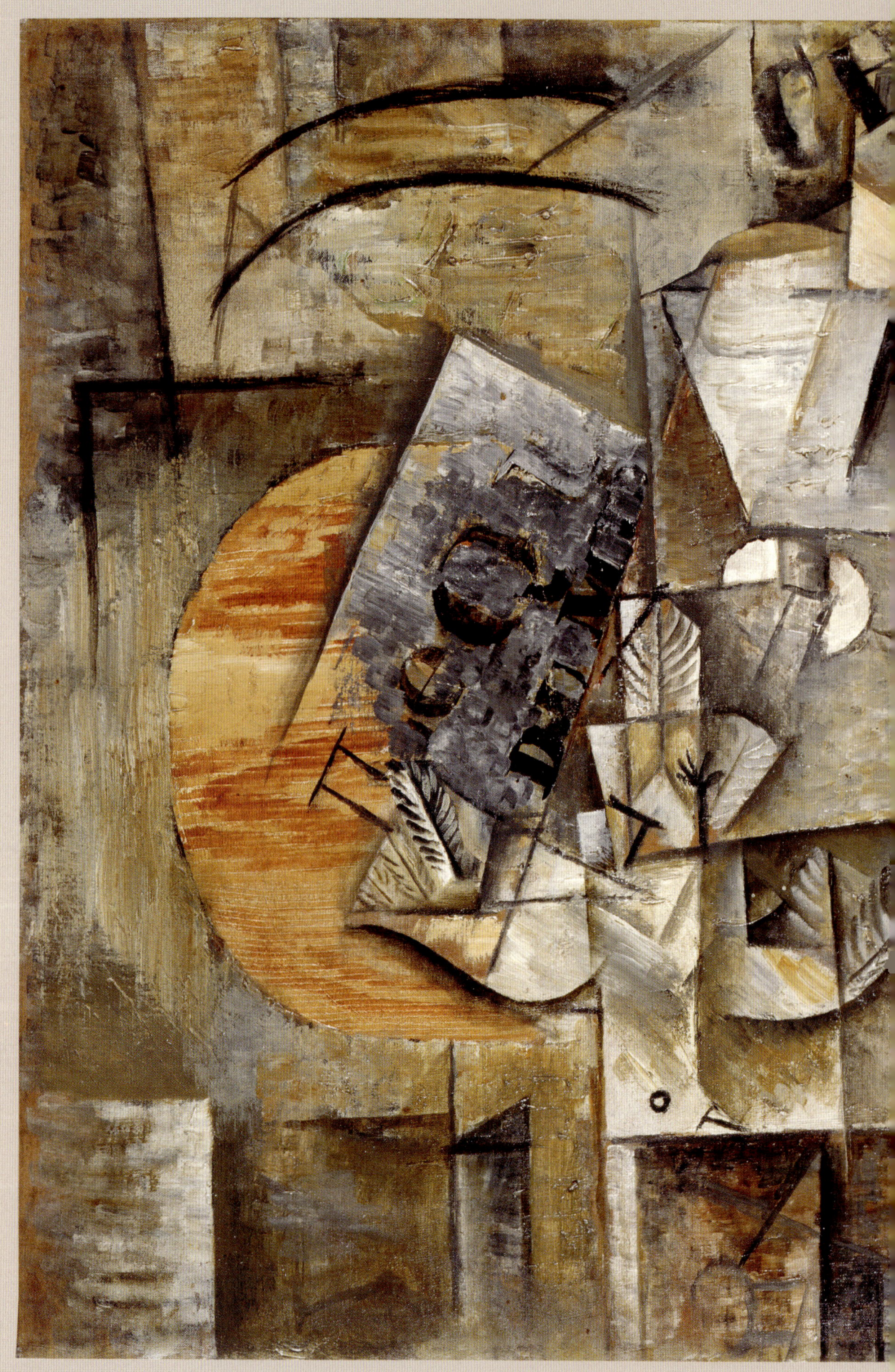

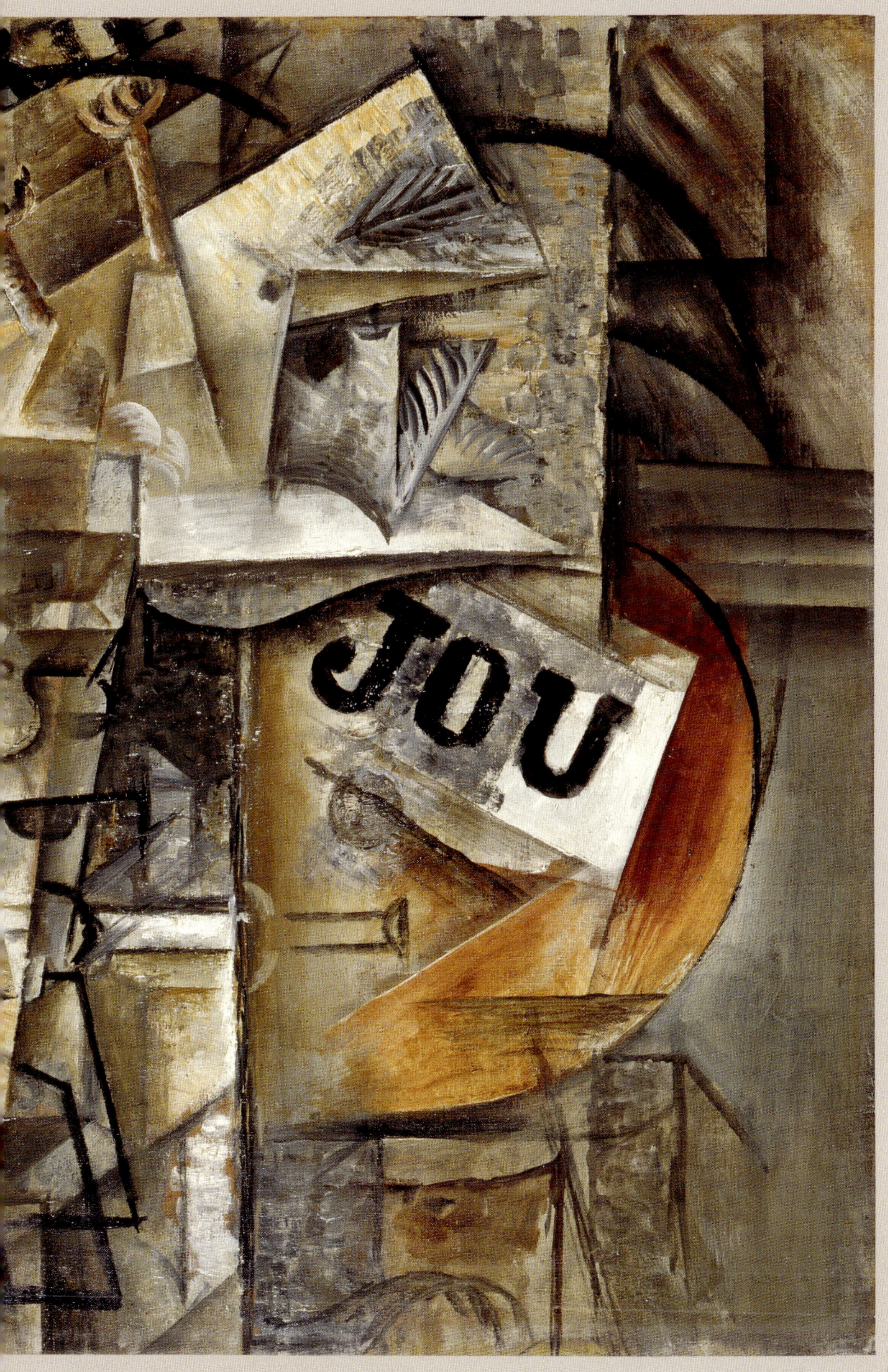
JOU

PICASSO AND ASIA:

A VISUAL CHRONOLOGY

Hester Chan

1800s

One's traditionalism is another's modernism.

Eugene Wang, Abby Aldrich Rockefeller Professor of Asian Art in the Department of History of Art and Architecture at Harvard University

1881

Pablo Picasso is born on 25 October in Málaga, Spain

He is the first child of art teacher José Ruiz y Blasco (1838–1913) and homemaker María Picasso López (1855–1939); later, he becomes brother to two sisters, María Dolores ('Lola') and María de la Concepción ('Conchita').

BELOW: Pablo Picasso at the age of seven, with his four-year-old sister Lola in Málaga, Spain, ca.1888

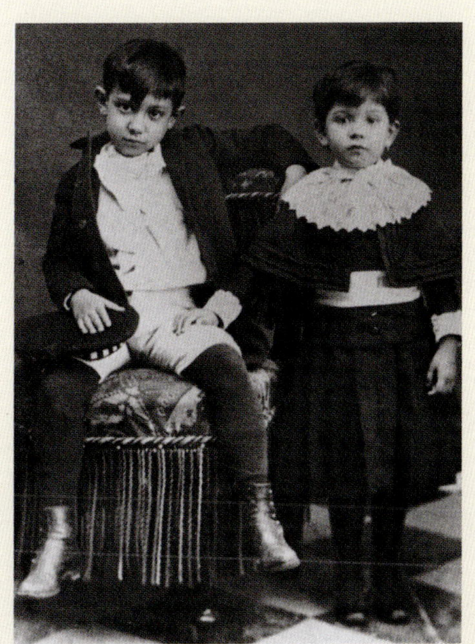

1896

The Tokyo School of Fine Arts establishes the first department of Western painting (*yōga*) in Japan

Following the 1868 Meiji Restoration, the Tokyo School of Fine Arts (established 1887, now Tokyo University of the Arts) introduced classes in Western painting (*yōga*), with a dedicated department founded nine years later. Japanese artists educated in Paris were selected for teaching positions.

The department was led by Kuroda Seiki (1866–1924, active in Paris 1884–1893), founder of the Hakuba-kai, or White Horse Society (active 1896–1911).

BELOW: Hakuba-kai (White Horse Society), Paris, 1900. Front: Iwamura Tōru; centre (from left): Kume Keiichirō, Kuroda Seiki, Gōda Kiyoshi; back (from left): Sano Akira, Wada Eisaku, Okada Saburōsuke, Shōdai Tameshige

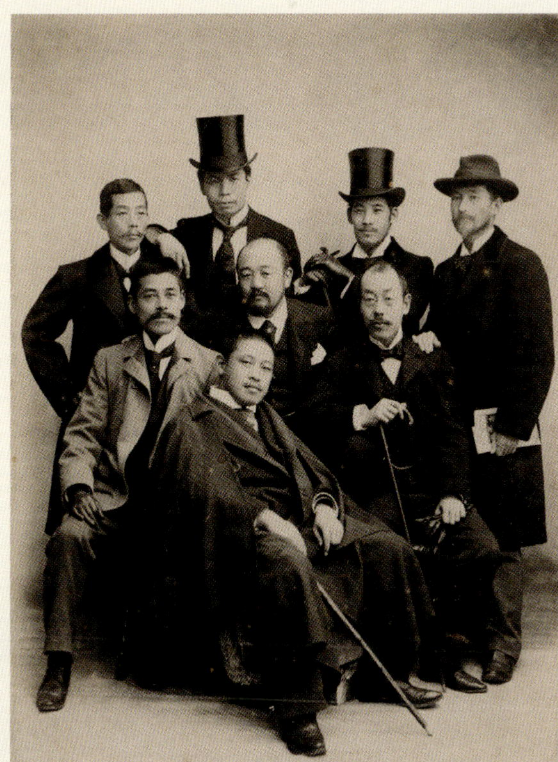

1900s

1900

Japan joins the fine arts section of the Exposition Universelle in Paris
Previous editions of the world's fair in Europe saw art from Japan categorised as decorative arts. This year, Japanese artworks hang in the fine arts section of the Grand Palais' South Wing. Kuroda Seiki submits five paintings, including *Lakeside* (1897) and *Wisdom, Impression, Sentiment* (1899). He receives the silver medal.

RIGHT: Study for *Last Moments*, 1899
BELOW: Kuroda Seiki, *Lakeside*, 1897

Picasso's painting *Last Moments* (1899) is selected for the Spanish pavilion at the Exposition Universelle in Paris[1]
At the age of nineteen, Picasso departs his native Spain for the first time and arrives in Paris in the middle of October.

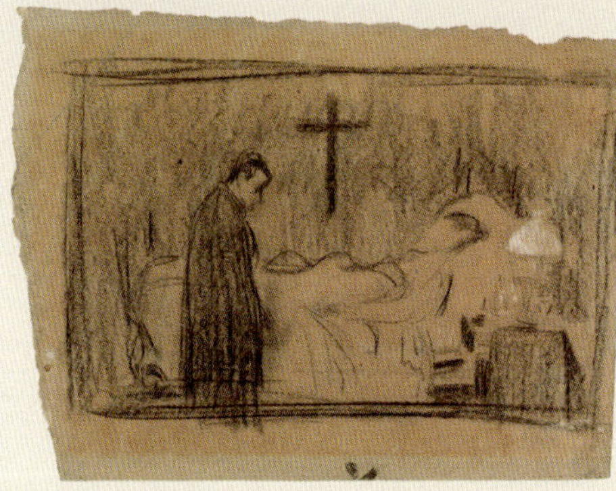

1900

Picasso produces sketches and a poster depicting Japanese actress and dancer Sada Yacco performing at the Loie Fuller Theatre in Paris
Le Théâtre reports of a major attraction at the Exposition Universelle in Paris: the Kawakami troupe from Japan featuring former geisha Sada Yacco (1871–1946). After a much lauded tour of the United States, the troupe staged productions in Paris, including *The Geisha and the Knight*, *The Loyalist*, and *The Inspired Sculpture*. The last of these is a kabuki-inspired adaptation of the popular stage comedy *Pygmalion and Galatea*.

BELOW: Illustration of Sada Yacco, based on a photograph by Paul Nadar, on the cover of French periodical *Le Théâtre*, no. 44, 11 October 1900

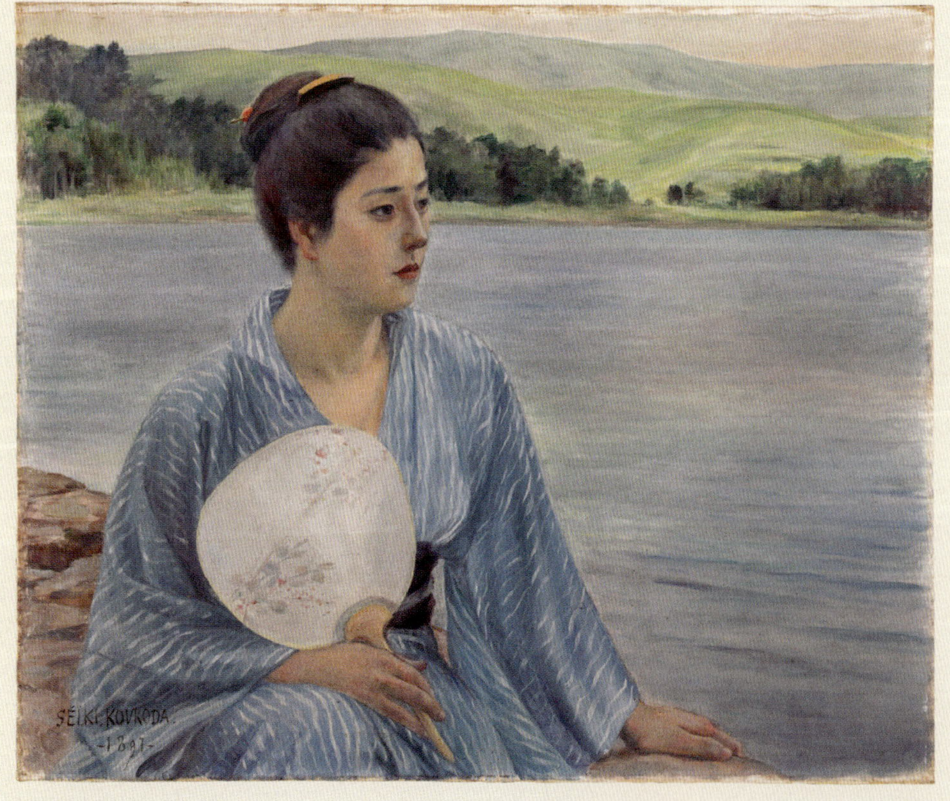

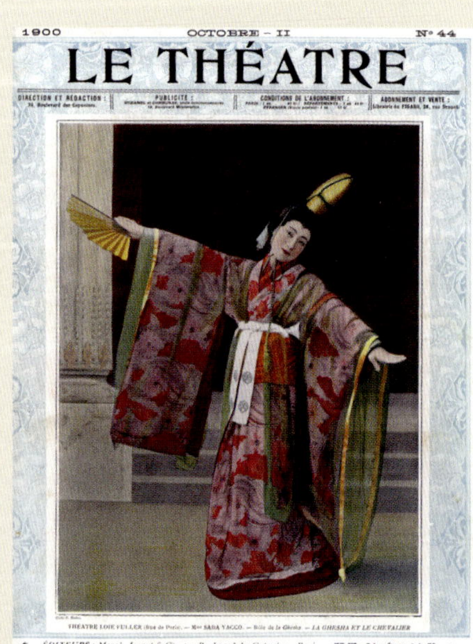

1900 OCTOBRE – II Nº 44

LE THÉATRE

DIRECTION ET RÉDACTION : | PUBLICITÉ : | CONDITIONS DE L'ABONNEMENT : | ABONNEMENT ET VENTE :

THÉATRE LOIE FULLER (Rue de Paris). — Mme SADA YACCO. — Rôle de la Ghesha. — LA GHESHA ET LE CHEVALIER

ÉDITEURS : Manzi, Joyant & Cie, 24, Boulevard des Capucines, Paris. — PRIX NET : 2 fr. ; Étranger, 2 fr. 50

Commissioned by American-French pioneer of modern dance Loie Fuller (1862–1928), Picasso creates a placard for the performances. The original poster design and several expressive sketches of Sada Yacco still exist but were never used.[2]

BELOW: Picasso's poster design of Sada Yacco, ca.1901

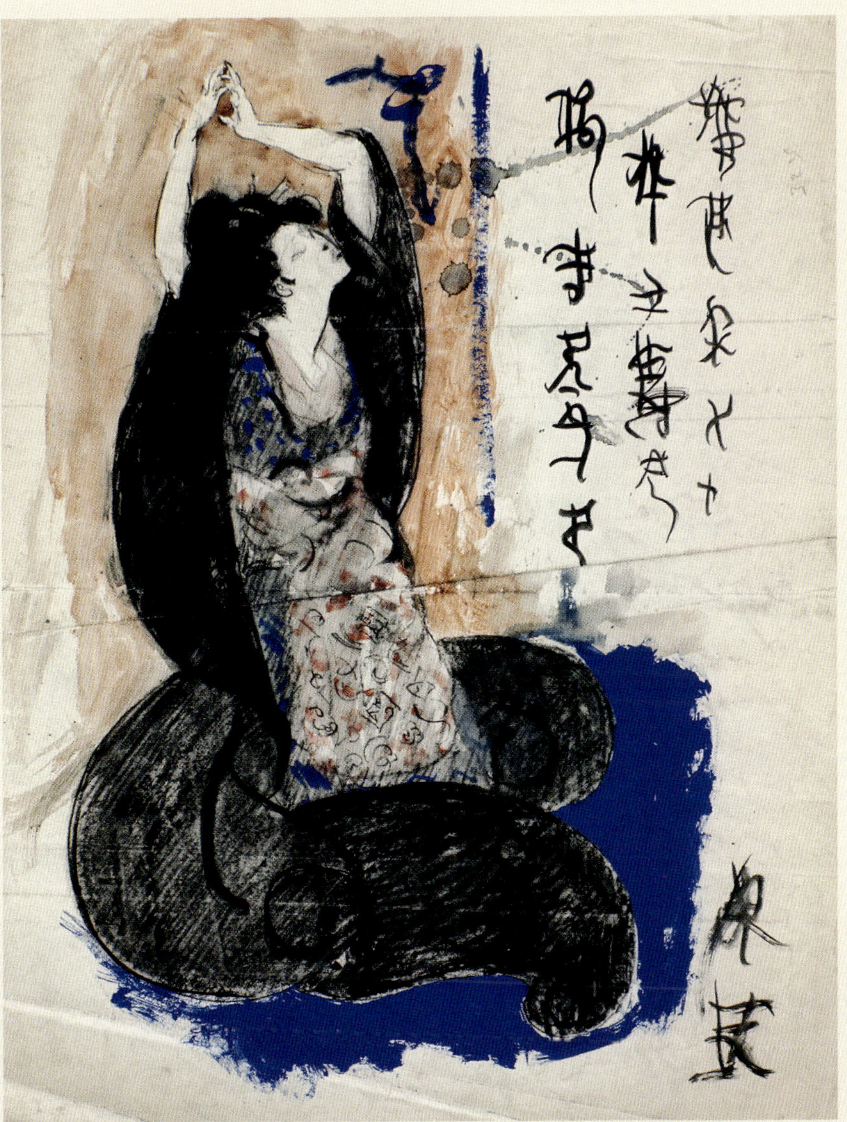

1900

Heightened tensions over the Boxer Rebellion in China lead to unrest at the Chinese pavilion during the Exposition Universelle in Paris

In protest at the privileges offered to foreign governments under the Qing dynasty, the Boxers, warriors from rural and impoverished districts in China, hold the international community members in Peking (now Beijing) under siege, resulting in fatalities. Agitated by the news of this tense political situation, bystanders attack a parade organised by the Chinese pavilion at the Exposition Universelle.[3]

BELOW: China Palace in Trocadéro Park, Paris, 1900

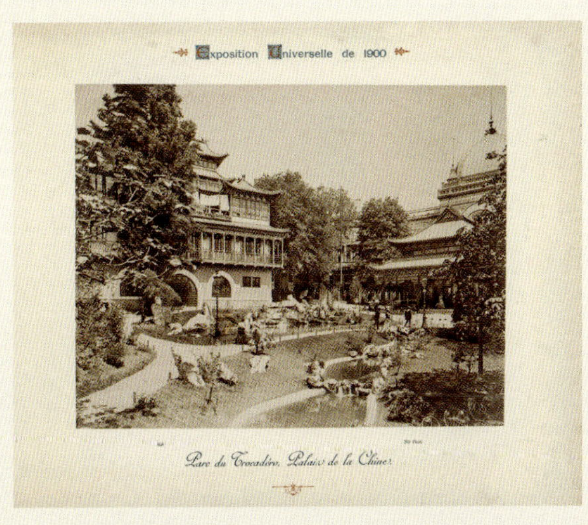

1905

The Reform Movement in China encourages cultural exchange
At the turn of the nineteenth century Western-style education replaces the Imperial examination system following similar pedagogical developments in Japan during the Meiji period. These changes signal the end of China's two-millennia-old dynastic rule.[4] China's Ministry of Education implements overseas study grants that allow Chinese students to receive Western academic training in oil painting, drawing, and the plastic arts in France or Japan. On the students' return to China, the new techniques and concepts they had learned would enrich the calligraphy and ink traditions, forming a solid foundation for the development of Chinese art over the first half of the twentieth century.[5]

BELOW: Coverage of works of art by Chinese students exhibited in Tokyo, published in *Liangyou* (The Young Companion), no. 91, 1 August 1934

中國留日學生美展出品

Works of Art by Chinese Students in Japan Exhibited at Tokyo

The exhibition room.

Nude. (By S. Cheng) — Portrait. (By W. F. Wang)
Mural decoration. (By T. P. Wang) — Nude. (By H. C. King)
The guitar. (By K. K. Lu)
Street scene. (By C. C. Zee) — Portrait. (By S. Y. Oo)
The violinist. (By S. Liu) — Landscape. (By H. T. Kong)
Peppets. (By K. Cheng)
Chinese landscape painting (by T. S. Mou)
Seals. (Carved by M. J. Wang)

1905

Picasso encounters Asian art in the Leo and Gertrude Stein collection
Between 1904 and 1909 Picasso lives with French model and muse Fernande Olivier (born Amélie Lang, 1881–1966) at the Bateau-Lavoir, a collection of studios housing artists, writers, and poets from various European countries. Regulars include Romanian sculptor Constantin Brâncuși, Italian painter Amedeo Modigliani, Dutch-German artist couple Kees and Guus van Dongen, Spanish artist Juan Gris, and French poet Max Jacob. Recalling this period, Olivier described how she and Picasso discovered new cultural expressions when visiting American writers and collectors Gertrude Stein (1874–1946) and Leo Stein (1872–1947). The Steins 'had a very important collection of Chinese and Japanese prints, which were extremely beautiful. If one felt bored one could always retire into a corner and sitting comfortably in an arm-chair forget oneself in contemplation of these masterpieces.'[6]

BELOW: Gertrude and Leo Stein's studio at 27 rue de Fleurus, Paris, ca.1905. Among two paintings by Paul Gauguin—*Three Tahitian Women Against a Yellow Background* (State Hermitage Museum; left) and *Sunflowers* (Bührle Collection; right)—are a selection of Japanese prints

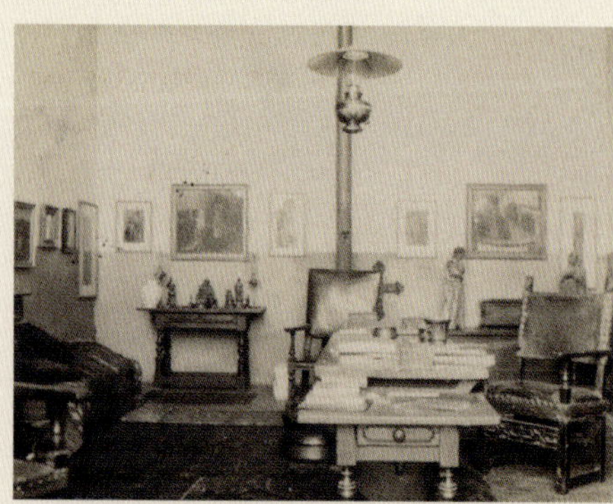

1907

Picasso's Chinese landscape

Among his sketches for *Les Demoiselles d'Avignon* (1907), the artist creates a Chinese-inspired scene with faux-Chinese calligraphic characters in the top left-hand corner. The sketch is reminiscent of a work from the Song dynasty, *Spring Mountains and Auspicious Pines*, attributed to Mi Fu (1051–1107).

BELOW: Chinese-inspired landscape by Picasso from the artist's sketchbook, 1907

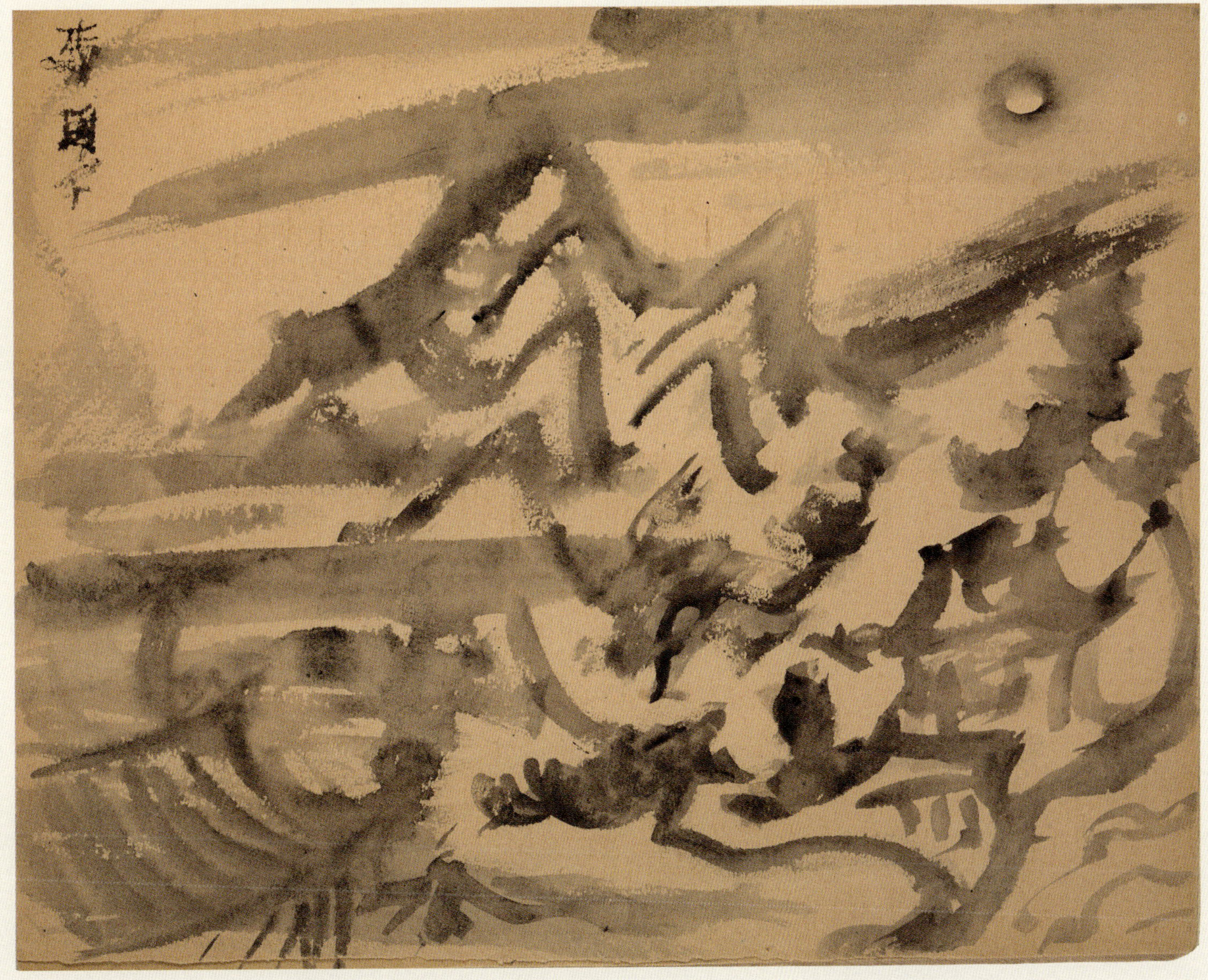

1908

Picasso studies ancient and non-Western art in museum collections in Paris
Picasso encounters the Iberian sculpture excavated in Andalusia at the Louvre, as well as cultural artefacts taken from French colonies in Africa and Oceania on display in ethnographic museums. Of his visits to the Musée d'Ethnographie du Trocadéro (now Musée de l'Homme), the artist once exclaimed: 'The masks weren't just like any other pieces of sculpture. Not at all. They were magic things ... They were against everything—against unknown, threatening spirits. I always looked at fetishes. I understood; I too am against everything.'[7]

The artist finds his revolutionary language in the tradition of the 'other' and starts to adopt the visual attributes of artefacts, particularly masks, in his drawings and canvases, creating a radical proto-Cubist language.

BELOW: Picasso in his studio with a collection of African art in the background, photographed at Bateau-Lavoir, 13 Place Émile Goudeau, Montmartre, 1908

1913

School of Paris: Foujita and Picasso
Japanese artist Léonard Tsuguharu Foujita (1886–1968) visits Picasso's studio the day after his arrival in Paris.[8] Of this encounter, Foujita writes: 'As soon as I got back from Picasso's, I went home and threw all my colours and painting materials on the floor. It was only the second day of my arrival in Paris, and already I was trying to forget all the techniques I'd learned in Japan, from how to hold a palette to how to wash brushes.'[9]

Foujita would continue to develop his signature style of figurative painting. For the Japanese, his works would firmly belong to the genre of Western painting; for Europeans, Foujita would exemplify a refined Japanese *nihonga*-style painting, wholly new and exciting. In the next two decades he would become the most important Asian artist working in the West during the twentieth century, joining Picasso as one of the prominent figures associated with the School of Paris.

RIGHT: *Woman with a Mandolin*, 1909
BELOW: Léonard Tsuguharu Foujita, *Self-Portrait*, 1936

First Japanese publication to reproduce a Picasso painting
Japanese art journal *Bijutsu shinpō* reproduces Picasso's Cubist painting *Woman with Mandolin* (1909). The work is accompanied by an essay by art critic Kinoshita Mokutarō (1885–1945) widely regarded as the first published introduction of Picasso to readers in Asia.[10]

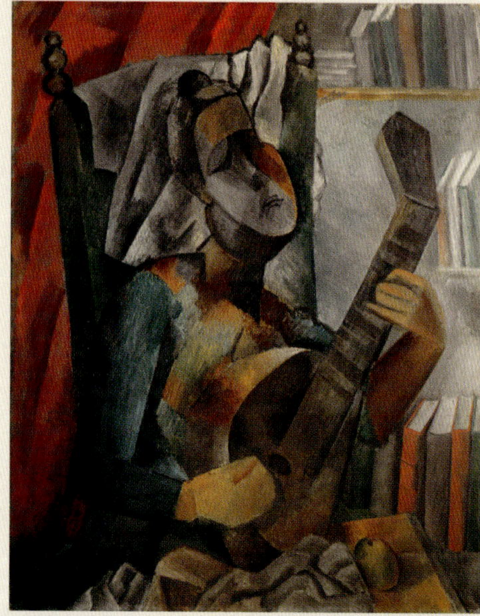

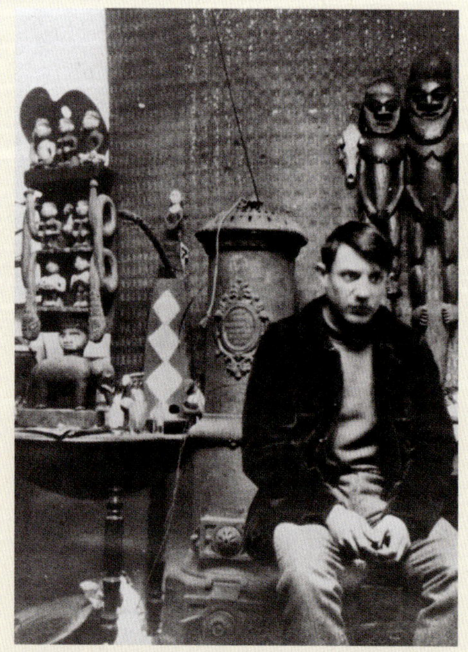

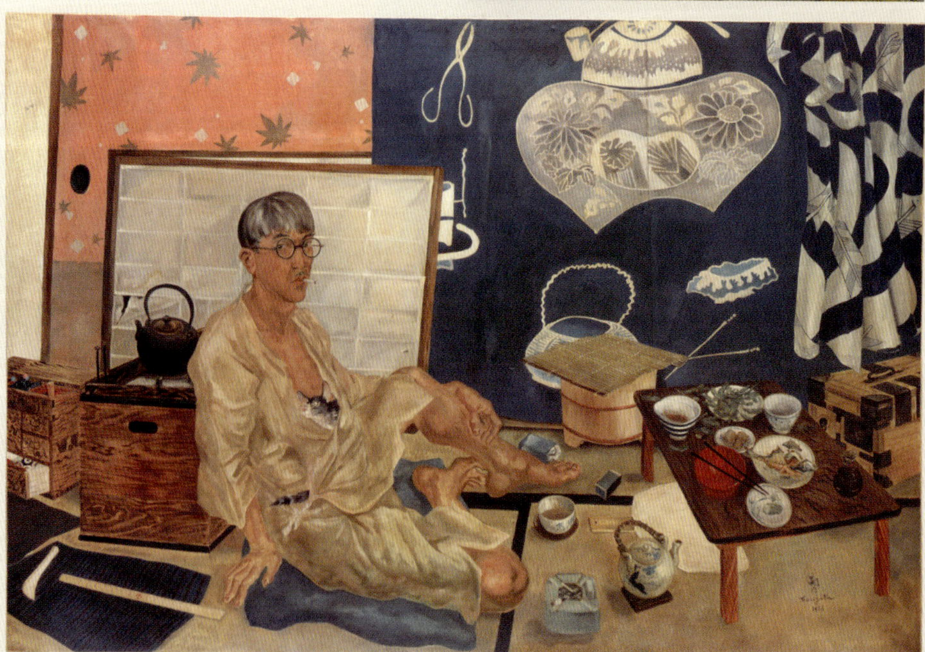

1915

Writers on the resonances between East and West
On the critical reception of Cubism in Asia, Japanese art historian Morita Kamenosuke (1883–1966) points to the influence of Asian art in the latest current of Western painting, stating that, 'Western painting became extremely Oriental, that is to say more and more subjective.'[11]

Arthur Jerome Eddy (1859–1920), a maverick collector of modern art from the United States, subscribes to a similar idea. In *Cubists and Post-Impressionism*, he critically observes how Cubism and 'the very high aesthetic value of drawing and painting in planes, and with small regard to the so-called laws of perspective, is illustrated in the rare beauty of Chinese and Japanese paintings'.[12]

Chinese educational reformer Cai Yuanpei (1868–1940), an early proponent of modern art movements, writes about his European tour (1907–1915), during which time he met Cubists Juan Gris and Max Jacob, and visited Picasso in his studio.[13] Cai describes how Picasso's creative distortion of nature echoes the work of the Northern Song dynasty poet and calligrapher Su Dongpo (Su Shi, 1037–1101),[14] whose revolutionary idea that painting was not representation but expression became one of the fundamental principles in literati aesthetics.[15]

1917

The Chinese Conjuror and Surrealism
Picasso creates the costumes and stage design for the ballet *Parade* (1917). Produced by Sergei Diaghilev, the larger-than-life Ballet Russes impresario, it is choreographed by Léonide Massine. One of the main parts is the Chinese Conjurer. The motifs used in Picasso's red, gold, and black design are Oriental stereotypes popularised by magician-conjurers active in Paris around the beginning of the twentieth century. The production debuts in May at the Théâtre du Châtelet in Paris. French poet Guillaume Apollinaire describes the performance as '*une sorte de surréalisme*', coining a term that would later encompass an art movement.[16]

BELOW: Costume design for the Chinese Conjuror by Pablo Picasso for the ballet *Parade*, 1917

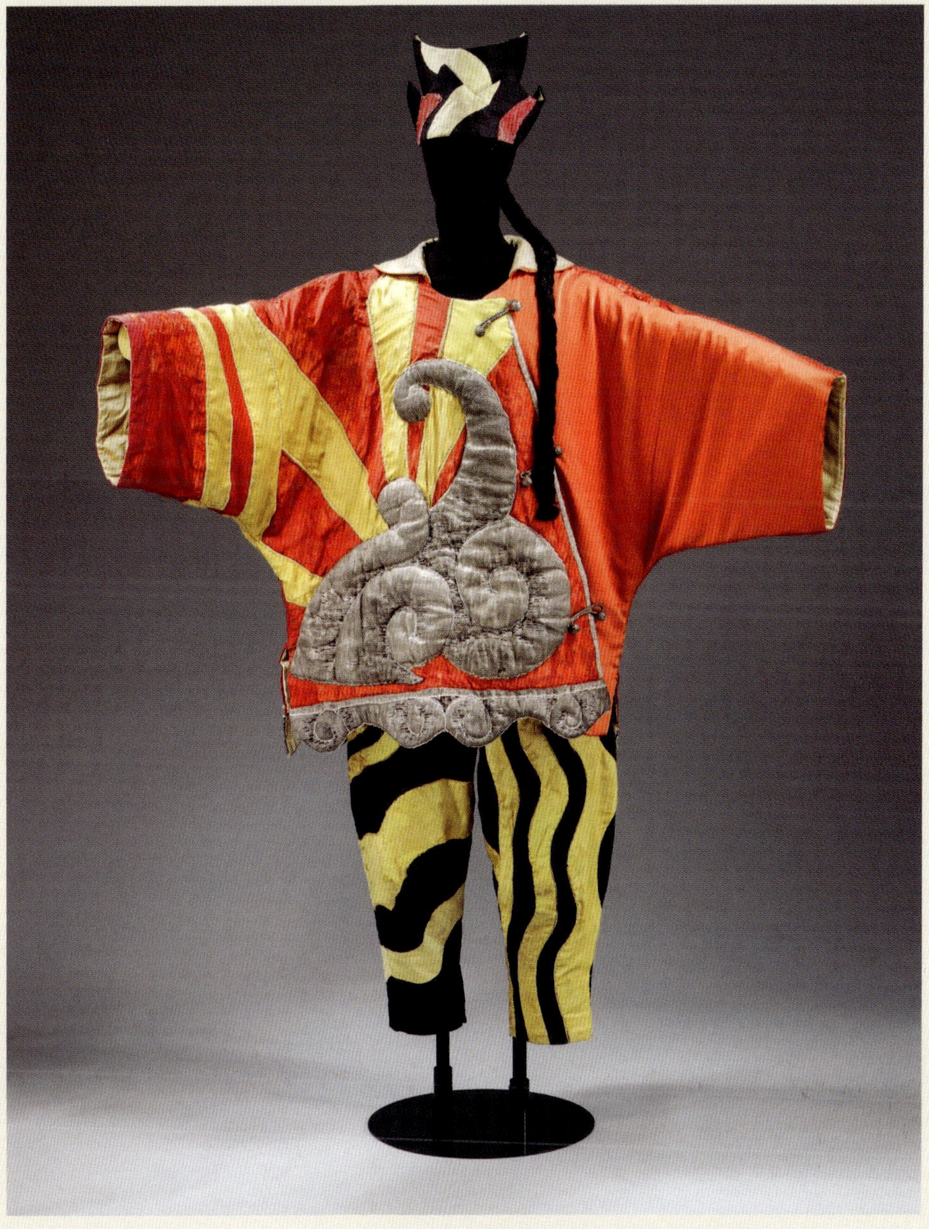

1918

Picasso and Cubism inscribed into modern Chinese art education

With the educational reform movement came the widespread distribution of Chinese textbooks. The art-history book series approved by the Republic of China's Ministry of Education, titled *Meishu shi* (Art History) from 1917 and *Meishu shi cankao shu* (Art History Reference Book) from 1918, became the gold standard in teaching materials. Authored by artist Jiang Danshu (1885–1962) and published by Shanghai Commercial Press, this series introduced the most important artists and artistic movements from China and abroad.

The entry on Cubism reads:

A new movement has emerged in Paris. This movement opposes the emphasis that impressionism and neo-impressionism give to light and colour; instead, Cubism explores the volume of images. Its aim is to express a sense of volume in the picture plane. Both the lines and the planes are represented cubically, creating interlocking structures that are hard to distinguish from one another and do not resemble natural appearances. At first glance, they seem quite unserious, but of late their ideas have been gradually accepted by scholars. The modern painter Pablo Picasso, a Spaniard living in Paris, is the leader of this school.[17]

1919

First Picasso exhibition in China

Five works by Picasso made between 1912 and 1914, during his Synthetic Cubist period, are shown at *An Exhibition of Modern European Painting* in Tianjin, northern China.[18] Cai Yuanpei had acquired the works directly from Picasso in 1915. Of the papier collé *Table with Guitar and Fruit Bowl in Front of a Window* (1912), Cai writes: 'In this still life, Picasso not merely deformed reality, like Zhu Da and Shi Tao, he literally tore it to pieces and reassembled it in a new way, with such sobriety and purity that unforeseen effects came about. The forms look as if cut out by a fret saw.'[19]

BELOW: *Guitar on a Table*, 1912, a similar work to *Table with Guitar and Fruit Bowl in Front of a Window* (1912), current location unknown

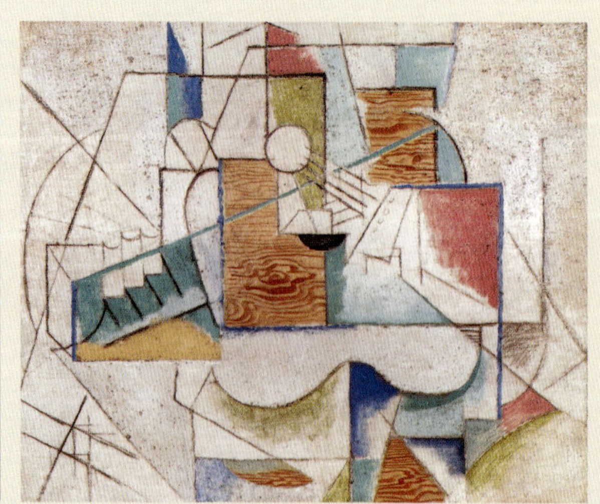

1922

An Indian Cubist

Stella Kramrisch (1896–1993), curator of the fourteenth annual exhibition of the Indian Society of Oriental Art, describes Bengal painter Gaganendranath Tagore (1867–1938) as an 'Indian Cubist'. One of the first Indian artists to respond to the Analytical Cubism of Picasso and Braque, Gaganendranath turned to Cubism to definitively break with the past, using the style as a building block to develop a new visual language.[20]

OPPOSITE: Illustrated postcard from Gaganendranath Tagore to Roop Krishna, Esq., ca.1920–1925. The message (verso) reads: 'My dear Roop, many thanks for your kind greetings for the new year ... I am practising Cubism and this is the result. Yours affl. G.Tagore', dated 17 April

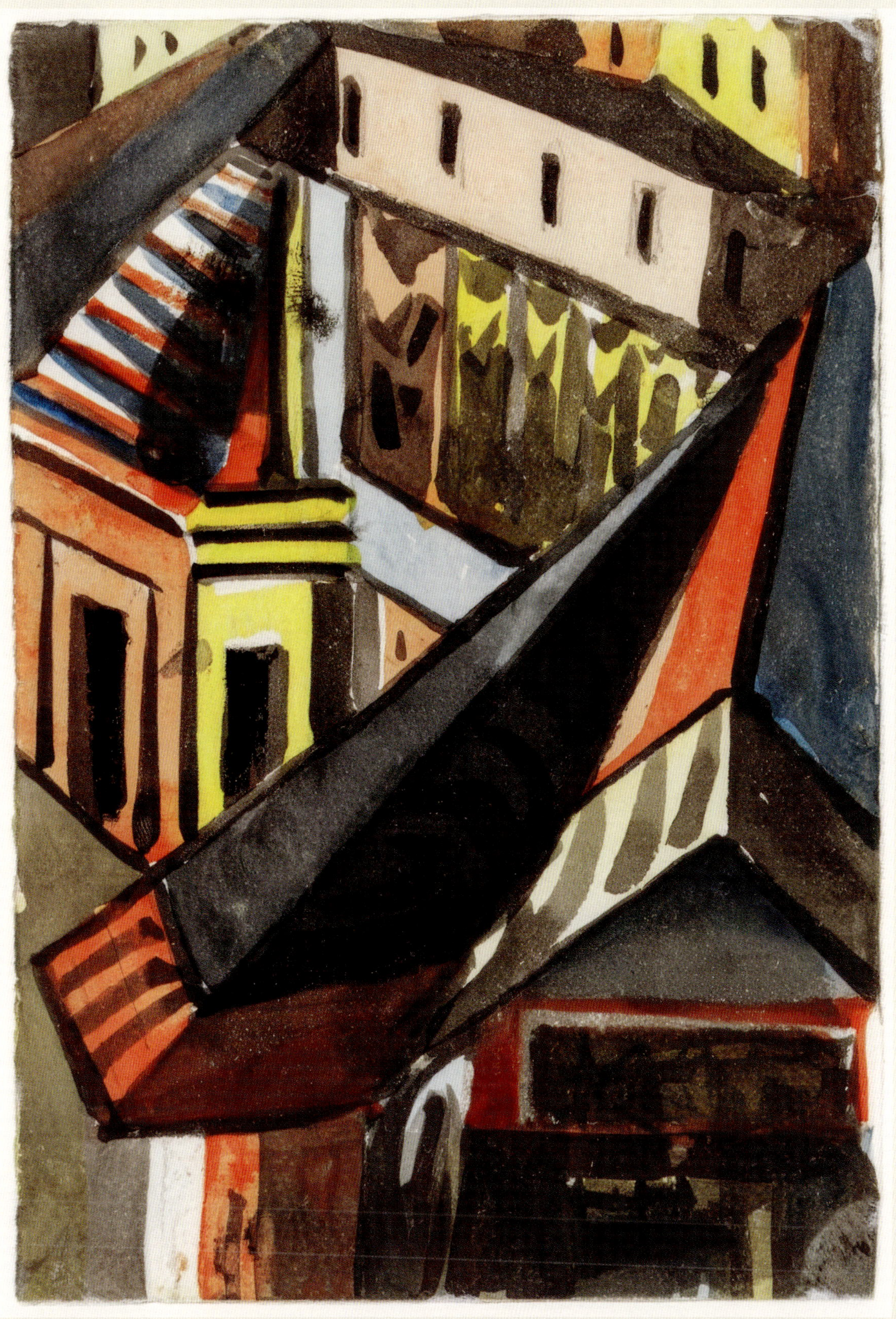

1923

Paintings by Picasso, Braque, and Lhote enter the 10th Nika-kai Annual Exhibition in Osaka, Japan
Organised in response to the traditional Bunten (an annual exhibition sponsored by the Japanese Ministry of Education, Science, Sports, and Culture), an exhibition produced by the artists of the Nika-kai, also known as the Second Section Association, features new directions in Western-style painting from such European schools as Fauvism, Cubism, and Futurism. Exemplifying a more radical agenda than that of past Western-style painting societies in Japan, the Nika-kai paired Cubist works from Europe with works by Japanese artists.

BELOW: Koga Harue, *Woman Divers*, 1923

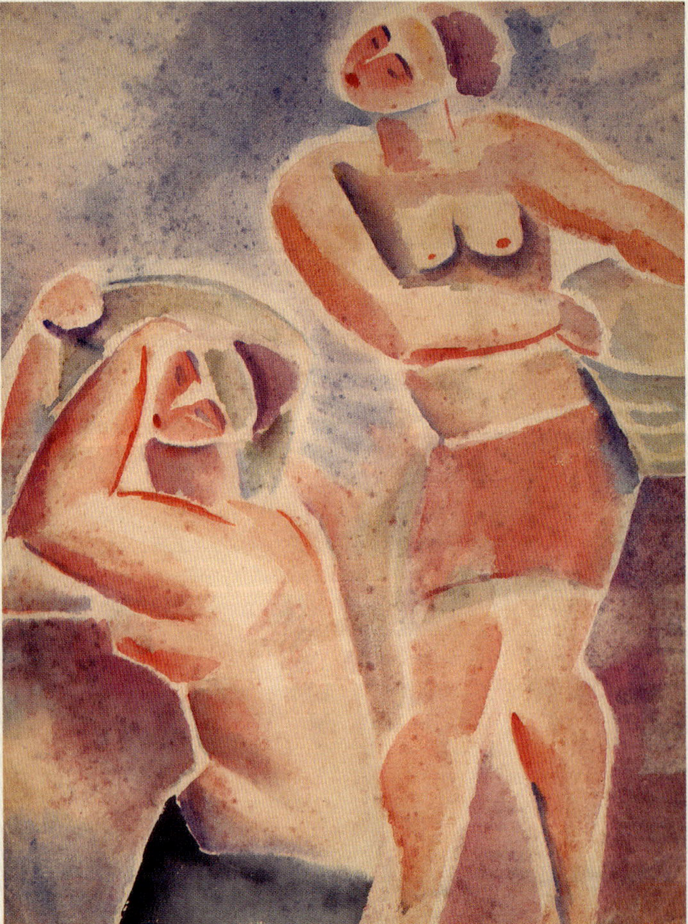

1925

First Japanese monograph dedicated to Picasso published in avant-garde art journal, *Mizue*
Nakada Sadanosuke (1888–1970, active in Paris in 1919) surveys the artist's development from his early works in 1895 to the Neoclassical paintings of 1923. In 1938 the author updates his essay to include Picasso's oeuvre up to and including 1937.[21]

BELOW: Nakada Sadanosuke, *Pikaso*, first published in *Mizue*, 1925, reissued and published in *Seiyō Bijutsu Bunko*, no. 18, 1938

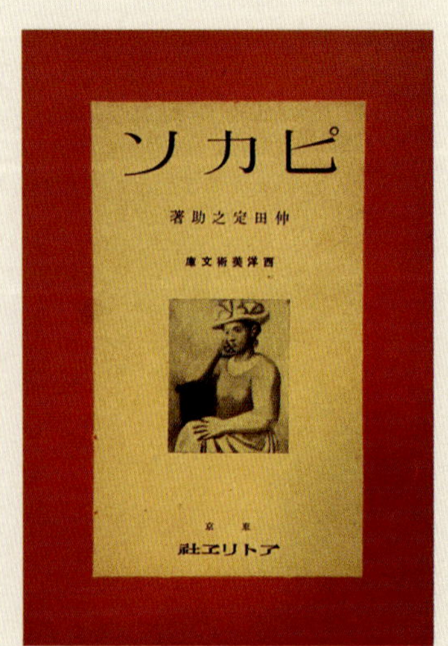

1926

Reconciliation of Eastern and Western art
Lin Fengmian (1900–1991, student in France 1918–1921), principal at the National College of Art in Beijing, publishes 'Dongxi yishu zhi qiantu' (The Future of Eastern and Western Art). He sets out his understanding of Eastern and Western art and proposes to reconcile both histories. Lin states: 'If we want to revive Chinese art, on the one hand we should inject the fundaments of Western art based on historical concepts and, on the other hand, sort out Chinese traditional art to contribute to the world.'[22]

1928

The Storm Society and the Western painting revolution
Mother and Son (1928), a work by Pang Hiunkin (1906–1985, educated in France 1925–1929), attests to Picasso's influence on young painters in Paris. Enrolled at the Paris Académie de la Grande Chaumière in the Montparnasse area, Pang returned to Shanghai in 1930 to form the Storm Society with fellow artist Ni Yide (1901–1970, student in Japan 1927–1928).[23] The Storm Society was the first Western painting collective in China to issue a manifesto. It was penned by Ni, who became an important voice for modern art in China, calling for art theory to advance alongside visual innovation.[24]

National Academy of Arts founded in Hangzhou
Supported by Cai Yuanpei, Lin Fengmian establishes the National Academy of Art (now the China Academy of Art) in Hangzhou. As in Japan, the departments of Western art are led by artists who have studied overseas. Among them is painter Fang Ganmin (1906–1984, educated in France 1926–1929), who would teach the next generation of Chinese modern masters: Zao Wou-Ki (1920–2013), Chu Teh-Chun (1920–2014), and Wu Guanzhong (1919–2010).[25]

BELOW: Pang Hiunkin, *Mother and Son*, 1928

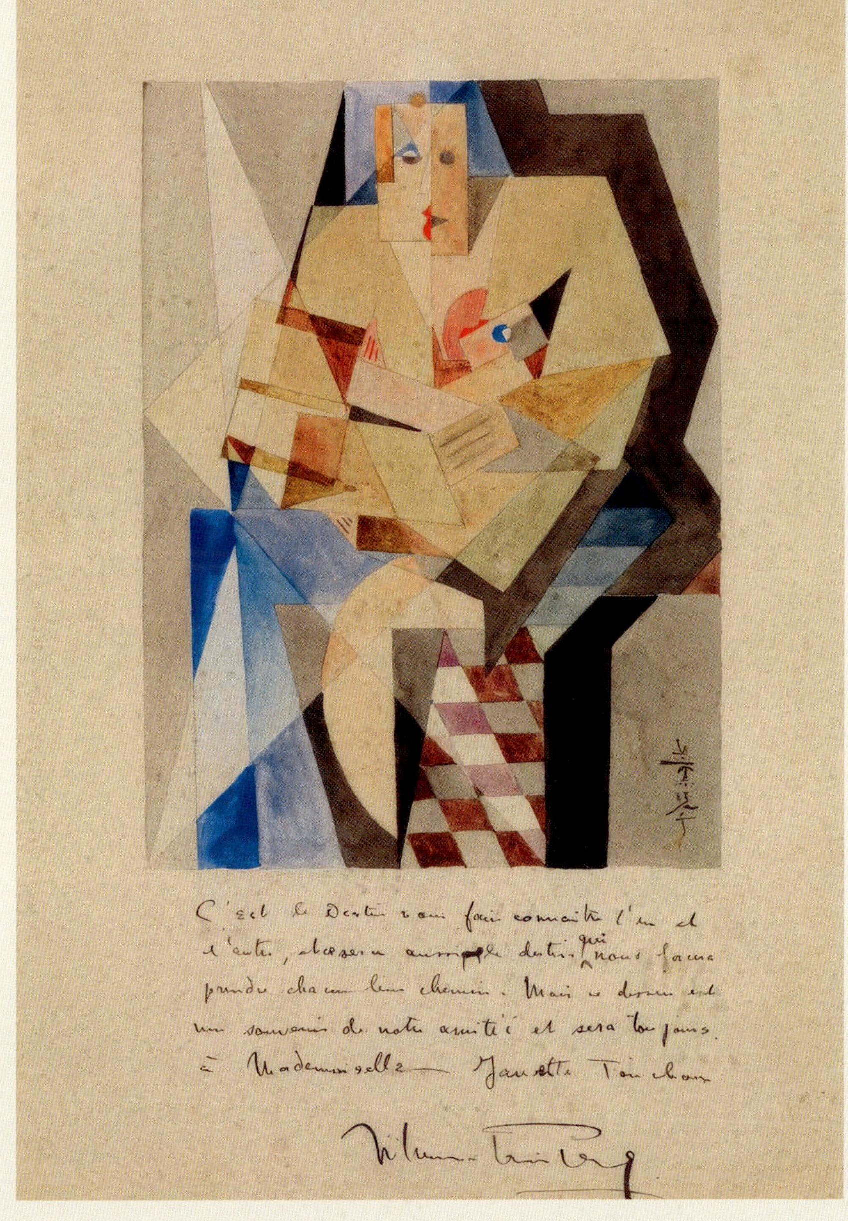

1929

Sri Lankan painter George Keyt quotes Picasso

By the late 1920s, George Keyt (1901–1993) was familiar with Picasso's Cubist works through reproductions published in the French art journal *Cahiers d'art* by art critic Christian Zervos (1889–1970). Keyt combines traditional South Asian fresco methods from the Ajanta Caves and Sigiriya with Cubist experimentations with the pictorial plane. With a clear awareness of Western art principles as presented through Matisse and Picasso, Keyt portrays gods from Hindu and Buddhist mythology, as well as ordinary people in their day-to-day surroundings.[26]

BELOW: George Keyt, *Triptych*, 1929

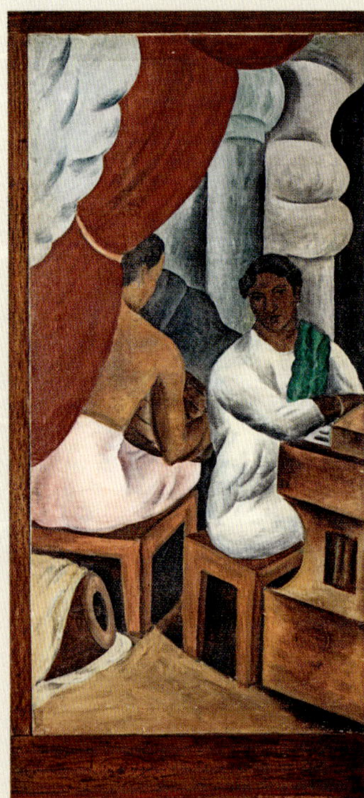
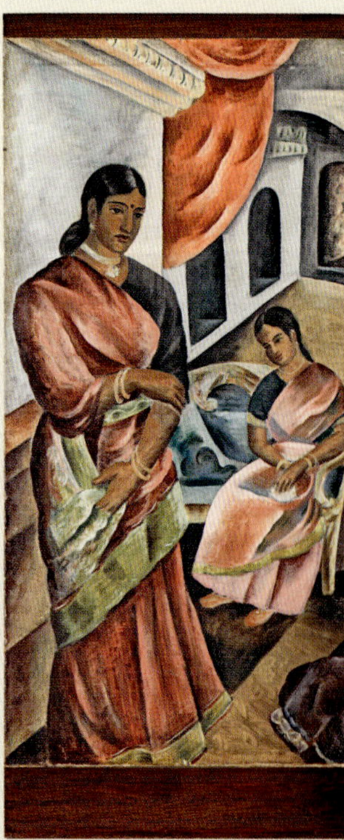
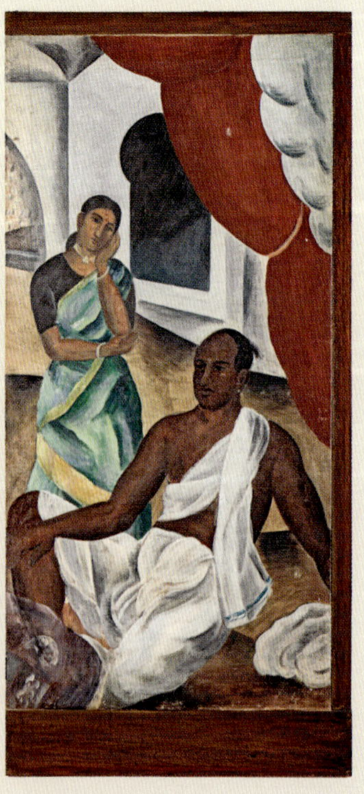

1930

Picasso explained through Chinese ink tradition

For the benefit of Chinese literati and students, cartoonist and writer Feng Zikai (1898–1975) publishes an essay in which he employs literati painter analogies to explain the stylistic qualities of three of the most famous European painters of the twentieth century. In Feng's telling, the expressive strokes of Yan Zhenqing (709–785) evoke the work of Cézanne; Dong Qichang (1555–1636), famous for his cursive style, is reminiscent of Matisse; and the playful freehand script of Zhang Xu (Tang dynasty) is as virtuous as that of Picasso.[27]

1932

Writers on Picasso's breakthrough moments

Members of the Storm Society organise the first public exhibition in China to feature artworks by Chinese artists working in the styles of Fauvism, Cubism, Neoclassicism, and Surrealism. In a statement published in *Yishu Xunkan*, Pang Hiunkin invokes Picasso, saying that sometimes the true meaning of art cannot be explained.[28]

In 'Overview of Surrealism', published in *Wuhan wenyi* (Wuhan Literature and Art) in 1932, Ni Yide divides Surrealism into four factions: Max Ernst, Giorgio de Chirico, Joan Miró, and Georges Braque together with Pablo Picasso. Of the last of these, Ni refers to Surrealist tendencies to 'transform realistic shapes' instead of André Breton's original statement that Picasso 'deceives appearance with reality'.[29]

Korean feminist writer Na Hyesuck (1896–1948, active in Europe 1927–1929) offers a different take on Picasso's breakthrough moment. Her first encounter with Cubism at the Salon d'Automne leads her to remark how 'Cubism's point of invention is that art is not artificial but scientific. It tries to paint movement with lines and colours. The Cubist painting is thus filled with convergence of colours, movements and compositions ... Cubism seeks to construct art based on all knowledge.'[30]

BELOW: 'Exhibition Announcement of Storm Society Paintings', *Shidai* (Modern Miscellany) 5, no. 1 (1933): 15–16

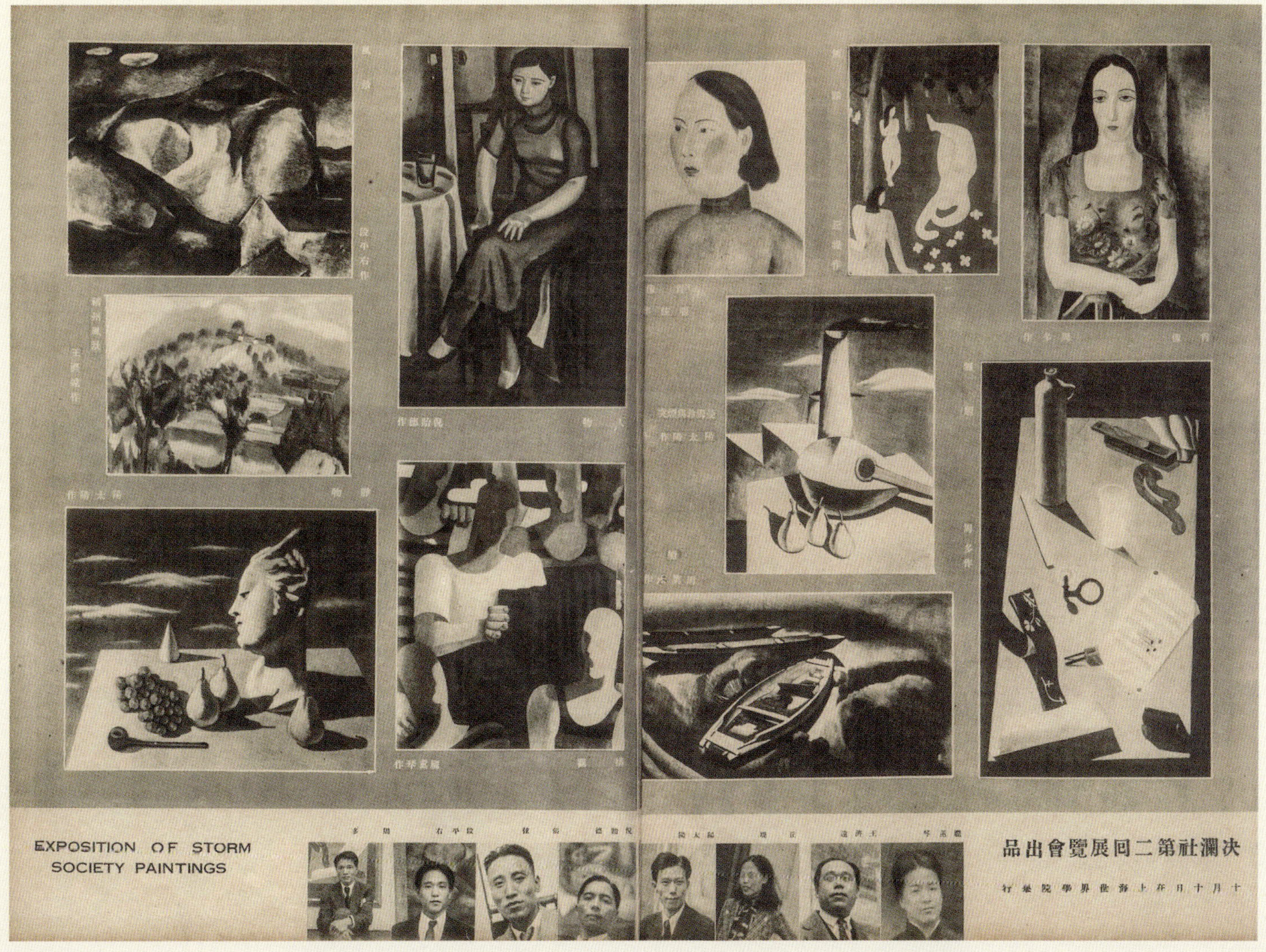

1933

Revolutionary China in Paris
Following an exhibition of Chinese ink paintings at the Musée du Jeu de Paume, curated by Xu Beihong (1895–1953, active in Europe 1919–1927), an exhibition showing a different China opens at Galerie Billiet-Pierre Vorms, a stone's throw from Picasso's studio on rue de la Boétie. *Peintres et graveurs de la Chine révolutionnaire* (Paintings and Prints of Revolutionary China) features fourteen oil paintings and fifty-eight woodcut prints. Co-organised by Lu Xun (1881–1936), a leading modern writer whom Mao Zedong honoured as 'the sage of China', and Soong Ching-ling (1893–1981), otherwise known as Madame Sun Yat-sen, the exhibition reveals a transforming China, an outward-looking nation that is closely aligned with the modern art movement.[31]

1938

Discovering tradition through the path of modernism
Cuban painter Wifredo Lam (1902–1982) visits Picasso in Paris for the first of many meetings.[32] The older artist takes Lam under his wing, jokingly calling him his 'Cuban cousin'. Lam stated that Picasso's art carried the 'presence of the aesthetic and spirit of African art', a cultural reference that, up to that point, Lam himself had never contemplated in his own art practice, despite his mixed cultural heritage as the child of a Cantonese father, Lam Yam, and an Afro-Cuban mother, Ana Serafina Castilla.

In May, two Picasso paintings are displayed at an exhibition of European modern art in Batavia (now Jakarta), Indonesia. The works are on loan from the collection of Pierre Alexandre Regnault, a Dutch entrepreneur active in Surabaya, Batavia, Semarang, and Singapore. One visitor to the exhibition is the artist Sindudarsono Sudjojono (1913–1985), who would establish the Union of Indonesian Painters (PERSAGI) the following October.[33]

Appealing to a national identity, Sudjojono called on Indonesian artists to paint the 'visible soul' of the nation and to address the social reality of the people. He sought to create a distinct form of modern art, stating: 'we will use [Europeans'] works as a landmark ... not only to enable artists to become artistic, but also to become as artistically conscious as Indonesia was before in the past.'[34]

BELOW: Wifredo Lam, *The Awakening I*, 1938

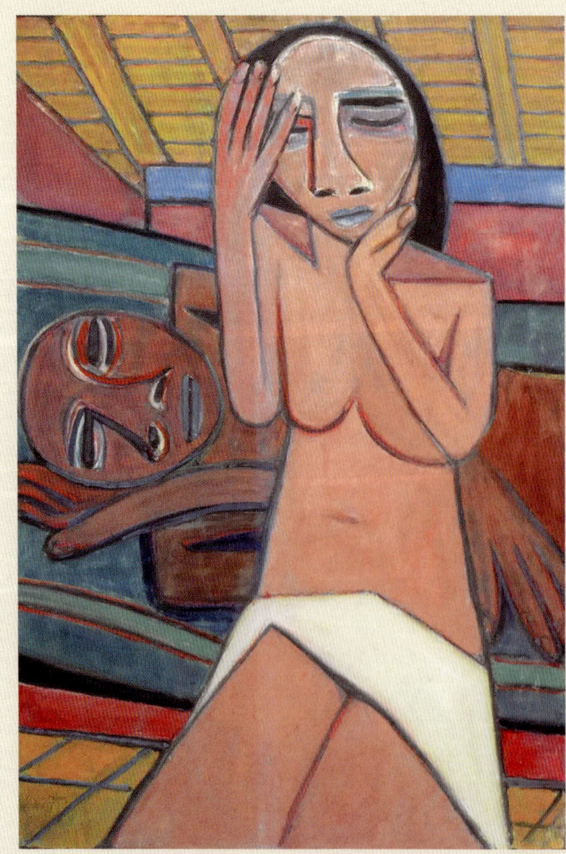

1944

On 4 October, Picasso joins the French Communist Party
After the liberation of Paris, the left-wing newspaper *L'Humanité* announces that Picasso has joined the French Communist Party, quoting the artist's statement: 'Now I found my true home.'[35]

1945

Chinese painter Sanyu defends Picasso

French Chinese artist Sanyu (1895–1966, educated in Japan 1918–1919, active in France) publishes 'Opinions d'un peintre chinois sur Picasso' (Opinions of a Chinese Painter on Picasso) in *Le Parisien libéré* on 19 January. He praises the Spaniard's art using an analogy of technological advancement.

To the eyes of this time, perhaps Picasso may appear shy. Remember when the railways appeared, we were frightened by this new phenomenon, and thought we would have to build ramparts along the railway tracks to protect residents from this madness! It was feared that travellers would die of suffocation in the airless tunnels! But don't worry, Picasso is not a public danger. Let's not build walls around Picasso.

1946

Picasso joke appears in China

Bright Weekly publishes a short story titled 'Picasso Complains that the Thief Is Stupid', demonstrating how Picasso jokes transcended language and cultural barriers.

One day, the house of famous Spanish painter Pablo Picasso was broken into. The burglars rummaged through chests and cupboards, making a complete mess of the house. They scattered paperwork all over the floor, and even shot a hole in the artist's desk. 'Did the robbers take anything of value?' asked [a] friend. 'Just a few shirts', the painter replied. 'Thank heavens, so why are you so angry?' 'I'm angry because they were too stupid to take my paintings!'[36]

1947

First exhibition of drawings and ceramics by Picasso in Bombay, India

The exhibition's organiser, Ebrahim Alkazi (1925–2020), was a pioneering theatre director who would become a powerful supporter of the Bombay Progressive Artists' Group. F. N. Souza (1924–2002) and M. F. Husain (1915–2011), both members of the group, were operating in a raw style evocative of Picasso's visual language.[37]

BELOW:
M. F. Husain, set design for *Murder in the Cathedral* by T. S. Eliot, dir. E. Alkazi, Theatre Group, Bombay, 1953

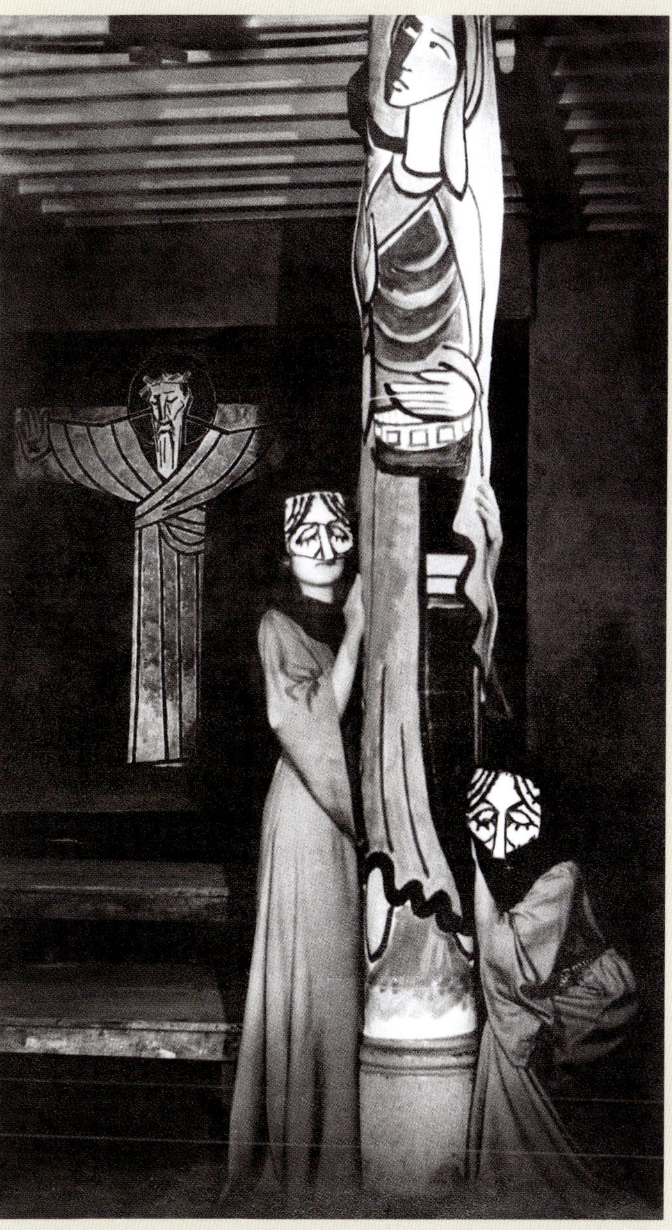

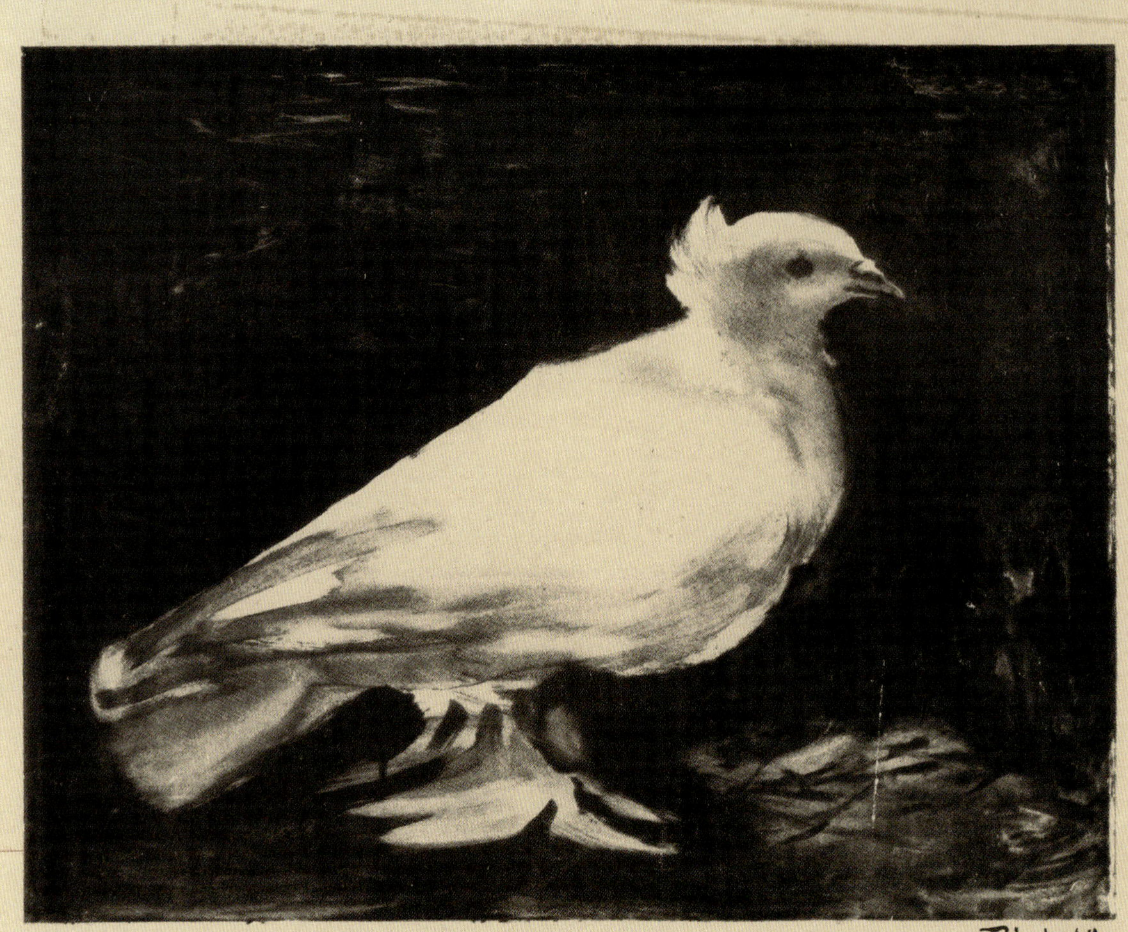
CONGRÈS MONDIAL
DES PARTISANS
DE LA PAIX
SALLE PLEYEL
20·21·22 ET 23 AVRIL 1949
PARIS
MOURLOT_IMP. PARIS

1949

Dove of peace
In the spring French poet and Communist Party member Louis Aragon (1897–1982) visits Picasso's studio and chooses a lithograph by the artist depicting a dove to become the poster for the First International Peace Congress to be held in Paris.[38]

La colombe (1949) was the first of several dove variations by Picasso to serve as emblems for world peace. The dove symbol would spread globally at an astonishing rate of transmission.

Reporting from the Chinese Conference for the Defence of World Peace in Beijing in October 1949, the *People's Daily* gives an account of the stage setting, remarking that 'portraits of Stalin and Mao Zedong hung above the dais, while Picasso's famous dove emanated a radiant light of peace'.[39] In a 1950 column, the paper reports on Picasso's next offering for the World Peace Council:

Last April, Picasso made a large painting for the first World Peace Council. He used a tranquil and pure dove to express millions of people's simple dignity and their wish to achieve world peace. This year, he painted another dove, this time with its wings spread in flight for the second World Peace Council in Warsaw. This dove symbolises peace advancing, the progress and victories that humanity has achieved, as well as the victories it will win in the future.[40]

Picasso won the 1950 World Peace Prize for his commitment to peace. In 1951 Soong Ching-ling would receive the Stalin International Peace Prize standing under Picasso's *Dove in Flight* (1950). Upon her death in May 1981, Madame Sun Yat-sen would receive the exclusive accolade of 'Honorary President of the People's Republic of China' from the Standing Committee of the National People's Congress (NPC Standing Committee), the only person to receive this honorary title.

LEFT: Picasso's *La colombe* (1949) becomes a symbol of peace, depicted on the poster for the First International Peace Congress in Paris, 1949

1950

Cubism in the Philippines
Filipino painter Vicente Silva Manansala (1910–1981) receives a nine-month scholarship to study at the École des Beaux-Arts in Paris. Upon his return to Manila, Manansala introduces Transparent Cubism,[41] a style of Cubism that splits the picture plane, as seen in Picasso's Analytical Cubism, and takes inspiration from the late-stage experimentation with glass-stained windows of Manansala's former mentor, Fernand Léger (1881–1955), arriving at a localised Cubism comprising diaphanous colour fields and illusionary spatial depth.

1951

Picasso's reception in Asia

Following the outbreak of the Korean War, Picasso responds with *Massacre in Korea* (1951; FIG. 97), a painting denouncing America's military intervention in the country. The painting is shown for the first time in Paris at the Salon de Mai and receives a lukewarm reception, not unlike the initial response to *Guernica* (FIG. 77) in 1937. *Massacre in Korea* also fails to garner approval from the Communist Party, which championed Socialist Realism in art. Of this experience, Picasso stated: 'I myself have begun to see it for what it is, and I know why it met with surprise: I had not done *Guernica* over again—which was what people were expecting.'[42]

In Japan, Picasso exhibitions are held at the Takashimaya department stores in Tokyo and Osaka from August to November. In a letter sent to the artist on 15 July 1952 from Tokyo, Kichihei Tsumugiya and Masaji Urazawa write: 'Your popularity in Japan is so great that the exhibition of your works drew huge crowds. After the exhibition, Picasso-style drawings became all the rage in Japan.'[43]

BELOW: *Picasso* exhibition poster, Takashimaya Department Store, Tokyo, 1951

1952

Picasso's dove in post-war Asia

The Asia and Pacific Rim Peace Conference takes place in Beijing, attracting more than 470 peace activists representing almost 50 nations, with a quarter coming from South and Southeast Asia.[44] On the front page of the *People's Daily* is a reproduction of Picasso's *Dove in Flight* (1950), published together with an interpretation that lauds the dove's 'familiar style that warms the hearts and souls of all who love peace'. The text continues:

However, this dove spreads its wings wider, its feathers are richer and fuller, and it is flying toward even higher reaches. The whole image of the dove clearly lets us know that the bird is younger, overflowing with limitless vitality. This image is a powerful expression of how, on the foundation of the continuous progress and victories that the world peace movement has already earned, the movement of peoples fighting for and defending peace will only develop further into a new phase and win even greater victories through this World Peace Council. With the support of all who love peace, this dove will courageously fly higher and higher.[45]

BELOW: Picasso's *Dove in Flight* (1950) decorates the Asia and Pacific Rim Peace Conference in Beijing, October 1952
OPPOSITE: Picasso's dove referenced on the cover of *Manhua Monthly*, no. 32, July 1953

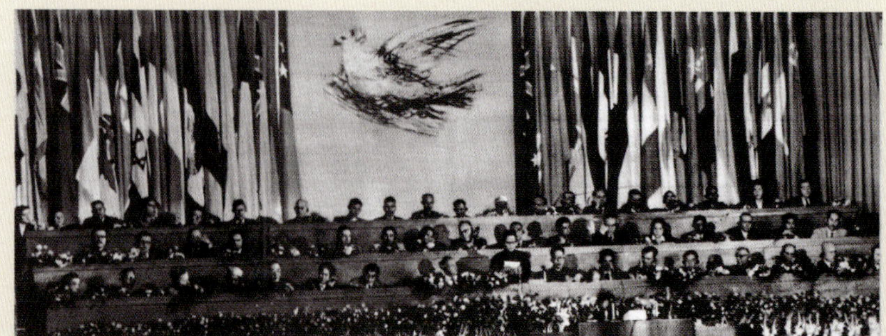

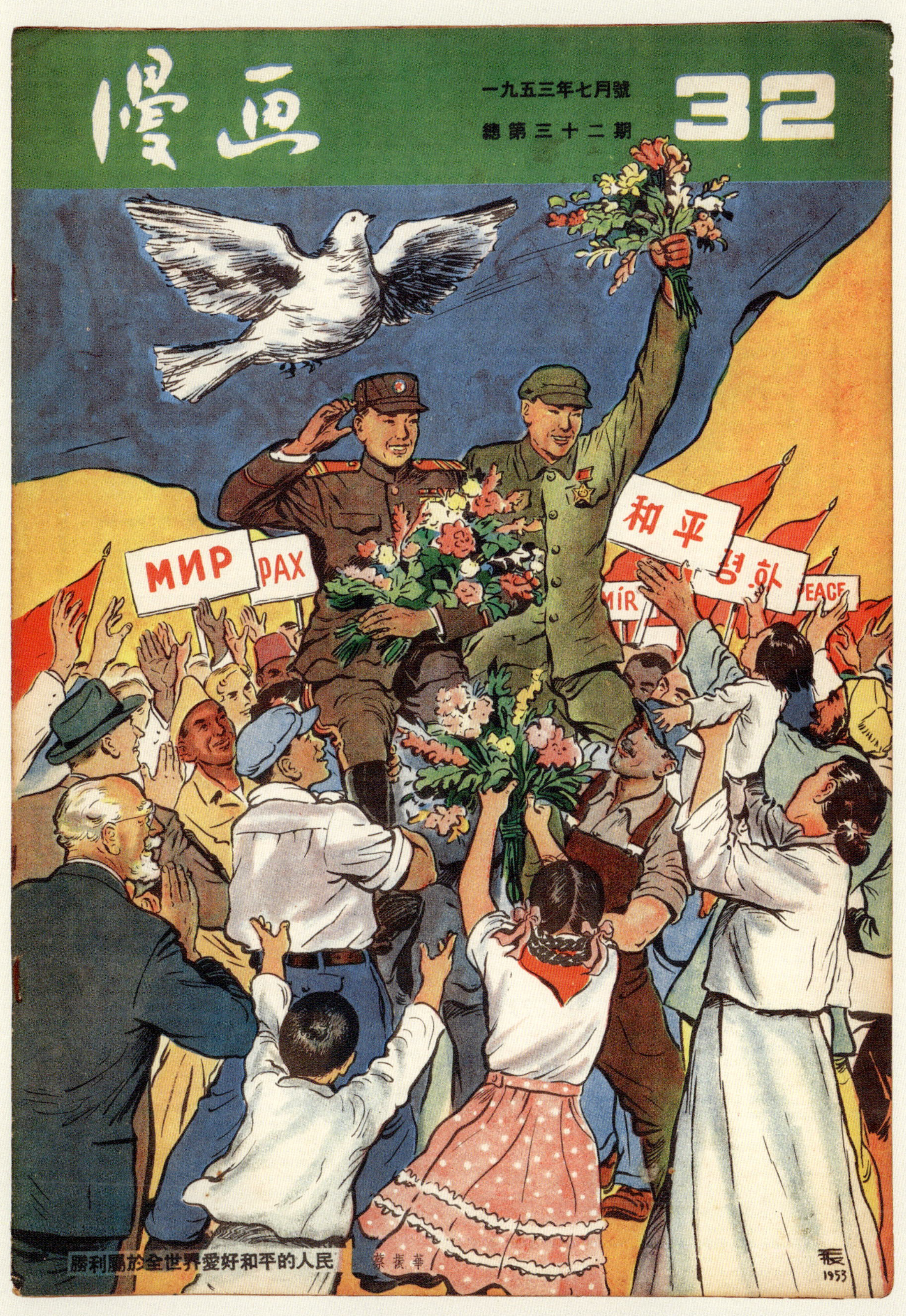
漫画
一九五三年七月號
總第三十二期
32
МИР
PAX
和平
평화
MÍR
PEACE
勝利屬於全世界愛好和平的人民
蔡振華
1953

1954

Picasso imagines himself as a Chinese painter
French poet Claude Roy (1915–1997) quotes Picasso in a reference to Chinese calligraphy:

If I'd been born Chinese, I wouldn't be a painter, but a writer. I would write my painting.[46]

1956

Qi Baishi prints gifted to Picasso
Zhang Ding (1917–2010), an artist and the designer of the Chinese national emblem (1949),[47] arrives in France as a member of a Chinese cultural delegation. Zhang serves as the chief architect of the Chinese pavilion at the Foire de Paris and travels to the south of France to visit Picasso, where he presents the Spaniard with a suite of lithographs by the 'People's Artist', Qi Baishi (1864–1957).[48] In return, Picasso gives Zhang a copy of Jean Cassou's monograph *Picasso*, drawing a dove of peace on it and writing his name in Chinese ideograms. Recalling this meeting, Zhang said:

It was afternoon when we arrived at Picasso's studio, which was a villa by the sea. Picasso had finished his midday nap, and he came downstairs to welcome us enthusiastically. He first gave us a tour of his studio ... All the studio walls were completely covered with new works. One can imagine that all his attention, thoughts, feelings, inspirations, and even his life itself were invested in the world of art. His shocking artistic labor and exuberant energy were truly admirable.[49]

Meeting of modern masters: Zhang Daqian and Picasso
In July, on the occasion of his monographic exhibition at the Musée d'art moderne in Paris, Chinese painter Zhang Daqian (1899–1983) recalls making several attempts to obtain an introduction to Picasso. Accompanied by Xu Wenbo (1926–2010), Zhang finally receives an invitation to visit the artist at his summer home, Villa La Californie, in the south of France. Among the gifts he brings for the Spanish artist are a collection of reproductions, two catalogues and two exhibition posters from Zhang's exhibition in Paris, and six ink brushes.

Zhang reported of that visit that Picasso showed him a sketchbook containing ink drawings of insects and plants, asking Zhang to critique his work.[50] Later, Zhang would be hailed the 'Picasso of China'.[51]

BELOW, LEFT: Zhang Daqian and Picasso at the artist's residence Villa La Californie, Cannes, 1956
BELOW: Qi Baishi, drawing from *Album of Insects and Plants*, 1943
OPPOSITE: Pablo Picasso, *Branch with Insect* (17.6.1956 II), from the artist's sketchbook *La Californie*, 9 March 1956–17 June 1956

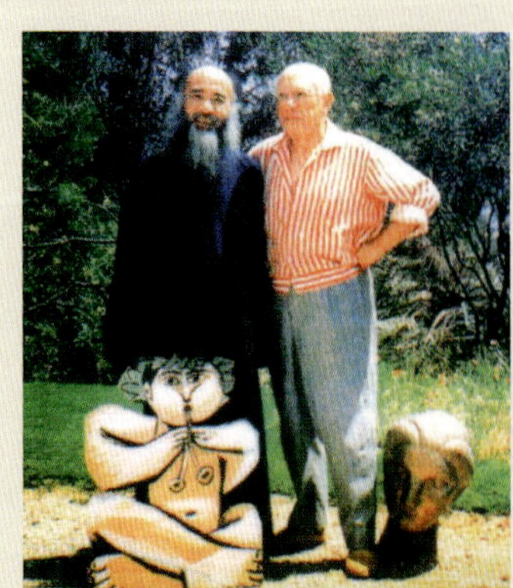

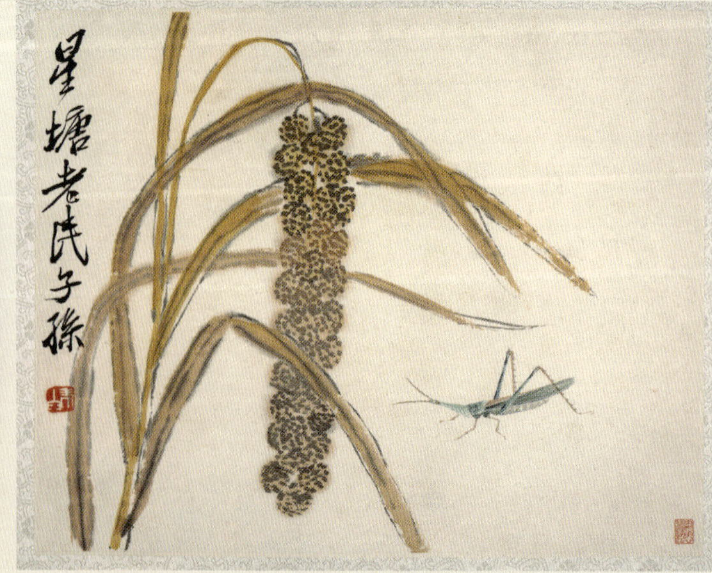

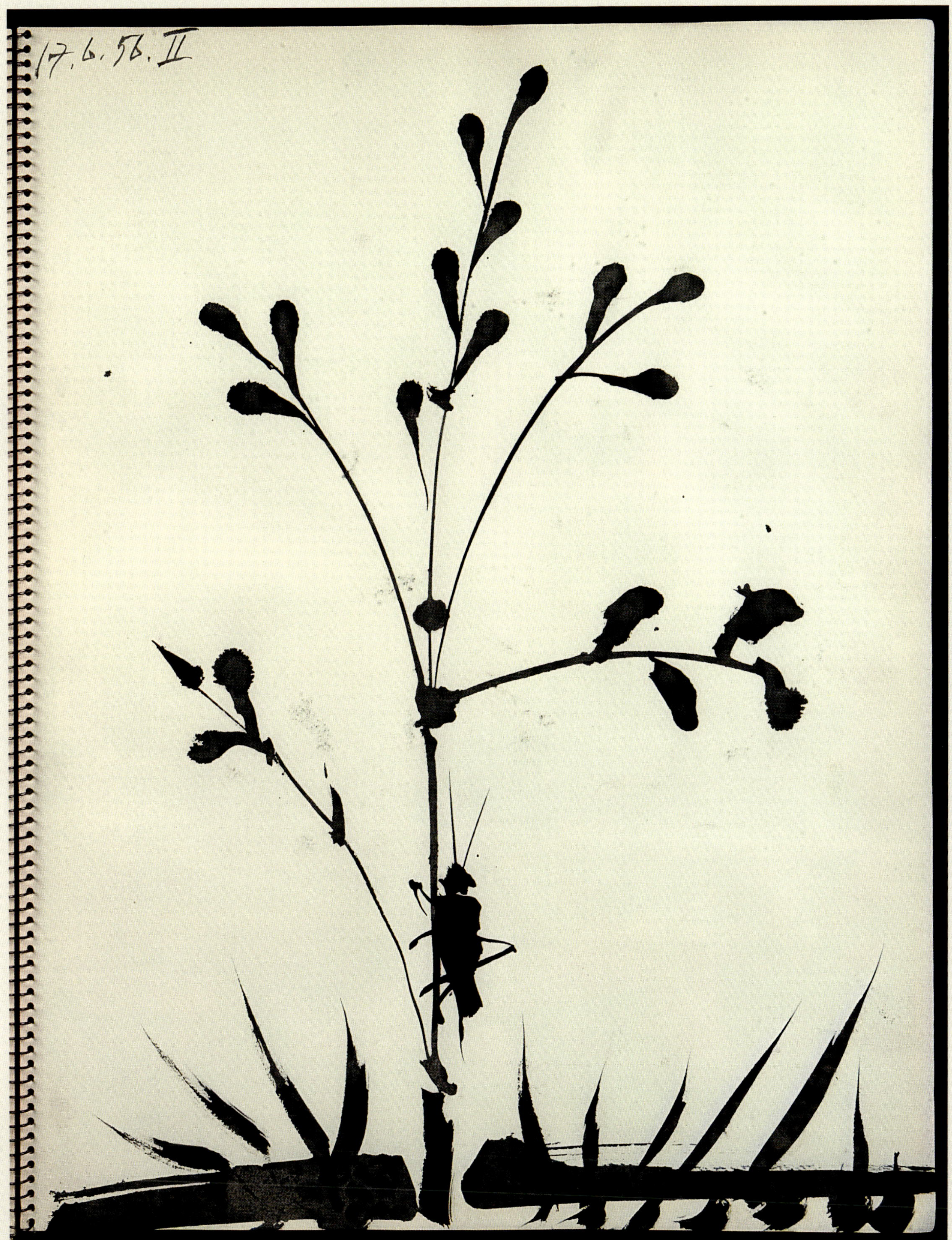
17.6.56.II

1961

Celebration of Picasso's eightieth birthday

French magazine *La nouvelle critique* dedicates an issue to the artist, inviting representatives of different countries to reflect on Picasso's meaning to their region. According to most of the accounts of representatives from South and Southeast Asia, Picasso entered the national consciousness only in the mid-twentieth century. By then, the artist was an established figure. Om Prakash Arya connects the artist's revolutionary questioning of the pictorial tradition with the Indian independence movement's reckoning with the colonial establishment. Other contributions are received from Yoshitomo Takeuchi (Japan); Captain Cong-Lé (Laos); Guo Moruo, chairman of the China Federation of Literary and Art Circles; and none other than Ho Chi Minh, who sends the artist his best wishes.[52]

1964

Picasso's post-war and political works in Japan

The largest Picasso retrospective in Asia to date, with 170 works created between 1899 and 1963, opens at the National Museum of Modern Art in Tokyo, later touring to Kyoto and Nagoya. The museum's curator-in-chief, Honma Masayoshi, believes the works of the *Guernica* period and after hold most appeal for Japanese art lovers, many of whom were deeply affected by the anger and intensity of Picasso's anti-war paintings.[53]

BELOW: Brian Brake, installation view of Picasso's *The Bathers* (1956) at the National Museum of Modern Art, Tokyo, 1964

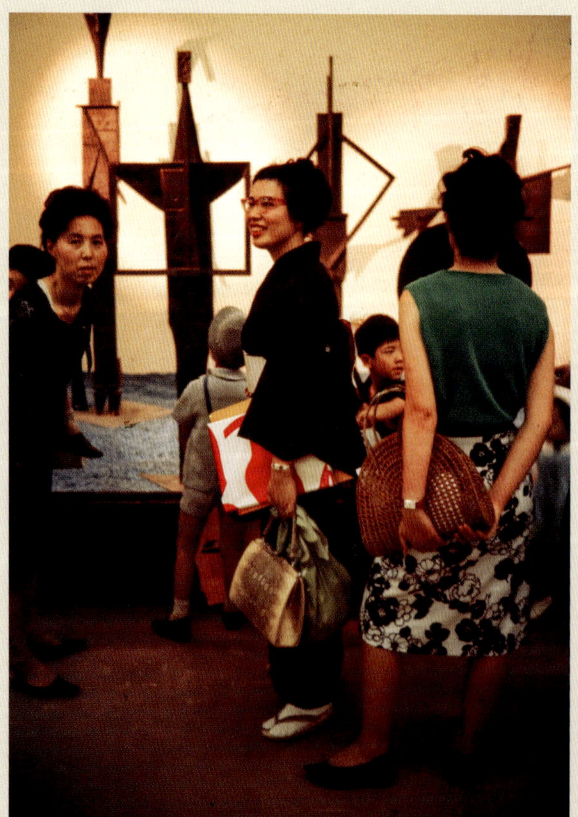

1965

Life with Picasso

Françoise Gilot publishes her memoir, *Life with Picasso*. She reveals the artist's awareness of literati principles, quoting Picasso's own words: 'We always had the idea that we were realists, but in the sense of the Chinese who said, "I don't imitate nature; I work like her".'[54] Later, in *Picasso's Mask,* André Malraux recalls the Spaniard explaining Chinese proverbs to him: 'you know the Chinese proverbs. One of them says the best thing I ever heard about painting: "We must not imitate life; we must work as life does".'[55]

British art critic and novelist John Berger (1926–2017) asks a critical question: what if Picasso had left Europe?

He might have visited India, Indonesia, China, Mexico, or West Africa. Perhaps he would have gone no farther than the first place. I have no idea which country or continent he would have chosen. Nor am I suggesting that he would necessarily have settled outside Europe. I am suggesting that outside Europe he would have found his work. His unusual speed of assimilation, the complex cross-breeding of his own cultural heritage, the intense physical basis of his art, the debt of his most personal style to non-European traditions of painting and sculpture, his newly acquired political convictions, the very nature of his genius as we have examined it in this essay – all would have specially qualified him to become the artist of the emerging world, challenging the hegemony of Europe.[56]

1966

Picasso and the modern art movement denounced in China

With the start of the Cultural Revolution, the *People's Daily* publishes 'Zhou Yang's "Liberalisation" Poisoned the Central Academy of Fine Arts', an article submitted by the revolutionary professors and students of the academy's Department of Printmaking. The text accuses the head of cultural affairs, Zhou Yang (1908–1989), of implementing a capitalist dictatorship within the academy. The article denounces Western artists as 'poisonous weeds that no one previously dared to bring forward, were all worshiped as fresh flowers', naming Picasso as one of these artists: 'In the studios of the Department of Printmaking, they were openly trafficking in Matisse, Picasso, and Fauvist art. A small salon was established outside the studio that took as its model the bourgeois, degenerate artists of the twentieth century.'[57]

1968

Cubist legacy in India

In February, Ratan Parimoo (born 1936), an art historian and co-founder of the experimental Baroda Group, addresses Picasso and Cubism in a speech at the First Indian Triennale, held at the Lalit Kala Akademi, New Delhi. He draws attention to the 'characteristics of synthetic phase of Cubism, such as dividing the picture surface in flat overlapping planes, and combining more than one viewpoint in a figure, to similar elements found in (ancient) Egyptian painting, (12th-century) Gothic and (17th-century) Rajput and Mughal painting and even in certain Indian sculptures'. Parimoo goes further to distinguish the different role that Cubism played for the development of modern Indian painting: rather than building upon what Cubism meant for the West, 'instead for Indian painters Cubism was a ready-made language from which borrowings could be freely made. Thus, the question would not be the Indian contribution to Cubism, or Indian version of Cubism but rather what kind of borrowings were made and what was done with such borrowings.'[58]

BELOW: Members of the Baroda Group at the Fine Arts College, Baroda, Gujarat, India, 1956. Posing with their works (clockwise from top right): Feroz Katpitia, Jyoti Bhatt, Prafull Dave, Triloke Kaul, Prabha Dongre, Kumud Patel, G. R. Santosh, Ratan Parimoo, Shanti Dave, and Raghav Kaneria

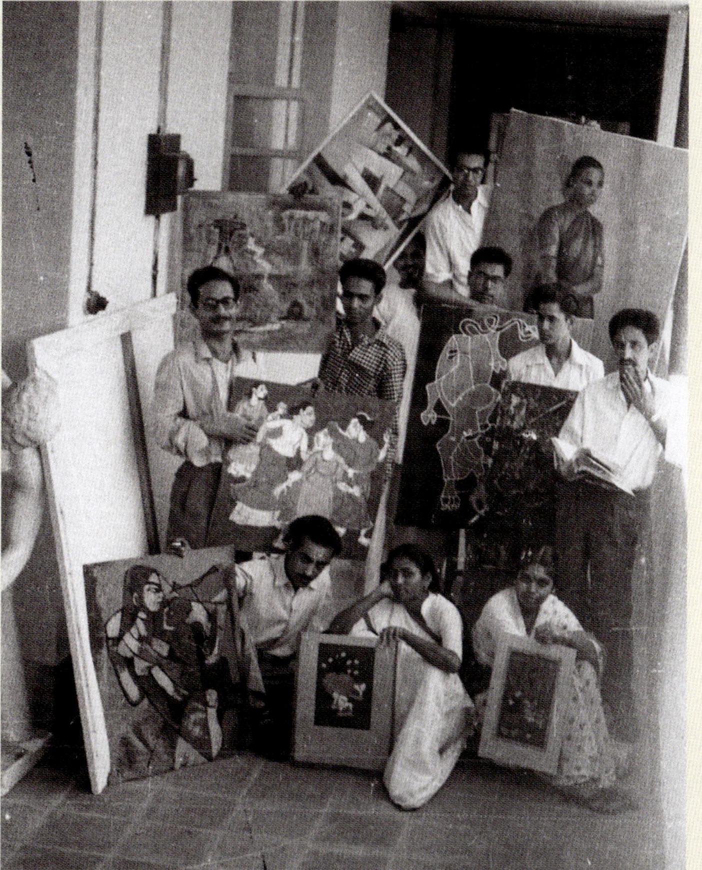

1973

Picasso dies on 8 April in Mougins, France

Artist and scholar K. G. Subramanyan (1924–2016) gives a radio eulogy for Picasso on All India Radio. He lauds the Spaniard as

a compulsive artist; any tool or concept that came handy was enough for him; in fact, he was from the beginning a versatile adventurer with other people's tools; of Toulouse Lautrec, of Puvis de Chavannes, of El Greco in his early work, of various traditional art phases later … The dimensional variety on today's art scene and the creative adventurism of today's artist is a great deal due to [Cubism's] liberating influence. It held in embryo various possibilities of visual exploration which others have pushed since to their logical extremes.[59]

1974

Picasso exhibition in Hong Kong

Curated by John Warner (1927–2021), *Picasso Original Prints 1959–1969* opens at the City Museum and Art Gallery in Hong Kong. Works are loaned from the collection of the Bibliothèque nationale de France. Scottish-born Hong Kong art critic and curator Nigel Cameron (1920–2017) pens a moving review of the exhibition, titled 'Picasso Comes Alive'. He shares his experience of re-engaging with Picasso's canonical works, many of which he last saw in his youth in Europe, now seen in the fresh context of Asia.

BELOW: *Picasso Original Prints 1959–1969* exhibition poster, City Museum and Art Gallery (now Hong Kong Museum of Art), 1974

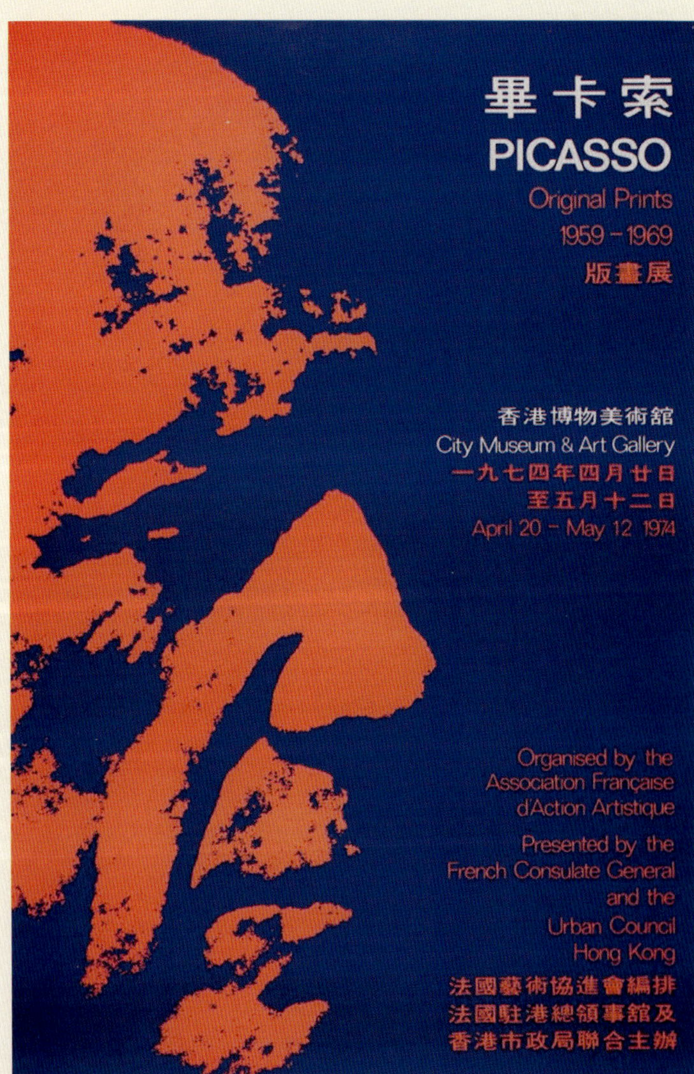

1979

Picasso and the modern art movement resurrected in China

In September the Stars Group (active in Beijing 1979–1983) mount an unauthorised outdoor exhibition next to the National Art Museum of China. More than 150 works by 23 artists are displayed on trees and metal gates. The action demanded artistic freedom with a slogan that harked back to the pacifist icons of a previous generation:

Käthe Kollwitz is our banner; Pablo Picasso is our pioneer.[60]

Picasso, vilified during the Cultural Revolution, once again becomes an inspiring figure for Chinese artists. Li Xianting (born 1949) writes that young artists 'want to be like Picasso, exploring endless horizons'.[61]

BELOW: Liu Heung Shing, *China After Mao—Wang Keping Demands Freedom For Art, Beijing*, 1979

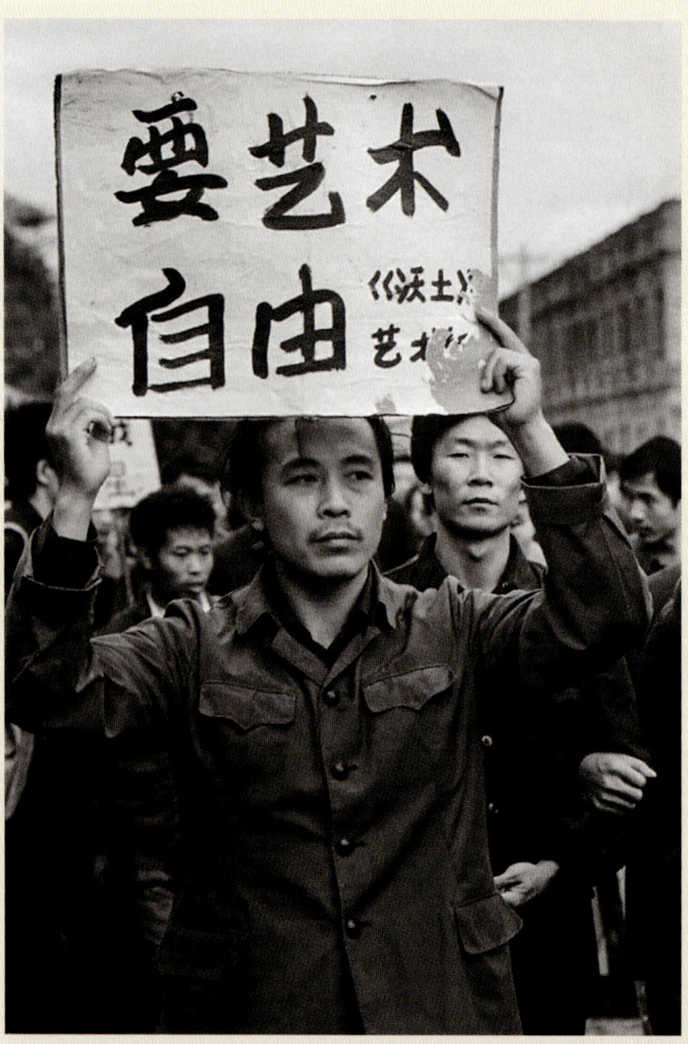

1980

Picasso's dove

The 19 June issue of *People's Daily* includes a poem by Zou Difan (1917–1995) that refers to the symbolic qualities of Picasso's dove:

The dove of peace is a symbol of revisionism.
Is revisionism tantamount to peace?
To care only for your braised beef and potatoes
is truly detestable,
is there a need to exterminate the doves too?
Ah, the white-jade dove,
the silver-gray dove,
fly!
Under Picasso's brush,
you inhabit our fontanelles
and fly forth from our skulls.
I know peace has a pair of wings:
with two stable and united wings,
it feeds the siren's power,
the crops' whey,
the rustling of schoolbooks ...
Fly, fly dove
Peace, peace ...[62]

1981

What Picasso means to Japan

Celebrating Picasso's centenary at UNESCO,[63] Japanese art historian Yoshiaki Tōno (1930–2005) reflects on Picasso's significance to Japan:

While passionate exchanges took place between Picasso and Mediterranean cultures, in Japan the impact was not the same. Did he sense Japanese civilization through Toulouse-Lautrec? Nothing brings him closer to this country. Violence. Sensuality, an interest in fauna in Picasso, delicacy, eroticism, a taste for flowers in Far Eastern artists. The infatuation with Picasso in Japan dates from the post-war period. He became a beacon, a pilot, a symbol of freedom for artists, and his influence was very strong.[64]

1982

***Picasso Intime* opens in Hong Kong**

The Hong Kong Museum of Art presents *Picasso Intime* featuring eighty-six works drawn from the collection of Maya Ruiz-Picasso, daughter of Picasso and Marie-Thérèse Walter. The exhibition includes a selection of paintings, watercolours, sculptures, and ceramics, as well as personal letters, and photographs dating from the 1930s to the 1950s.

BELOW: Inaugural ceremony of *Picasso Intime*, Hong Kong Museum of Art, 1982

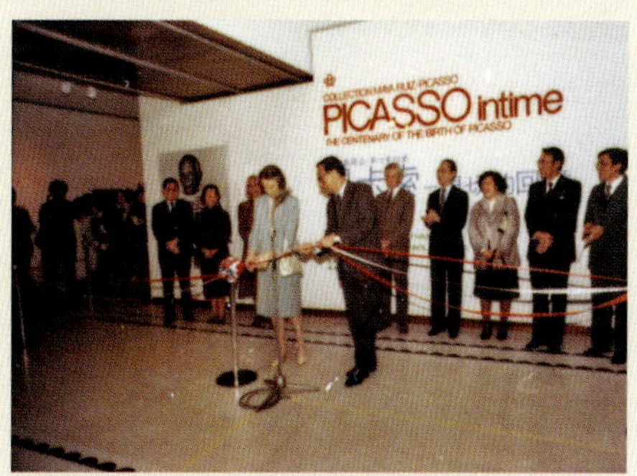

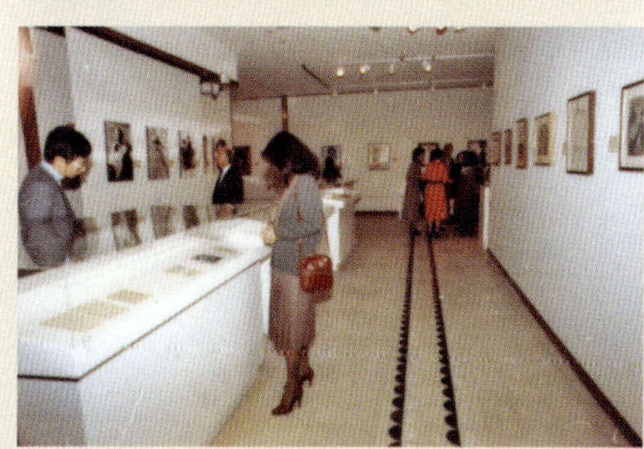

1982

Luis Chan (1905–1995), a self-taught artist from Hong Kong, works as a legal stenographer during the day and creates posters for the Hong Kong Star Ferry Corporation in the evening. With the money he earns from these commissions, he buys copies of various international art journals, such as *The Studio*, *ARTnews*, *Art in America*, and the Swiss publication *Art International*. Attentively studying, copying, and modifying the illustrations in these magazines, Chan effectively advances his grasp of twentieth-century Western art history.[65] The reproduction of Picasso's *Sleeping Woman on Red Cushion (Marie-Thérèse)* published in an exhibition catalogue becomes a playground for Chan's whimsical doodles.

RIGHT: *Sleeping Woman on Red Cushion (Marie-Thérèse)*, 1932
BELOW: Luis Chan, drawing on top of *Sleeping Woman on Red Cushion (Marie-Thérèse)* (1932) by Pablo Picasso, ca.1982

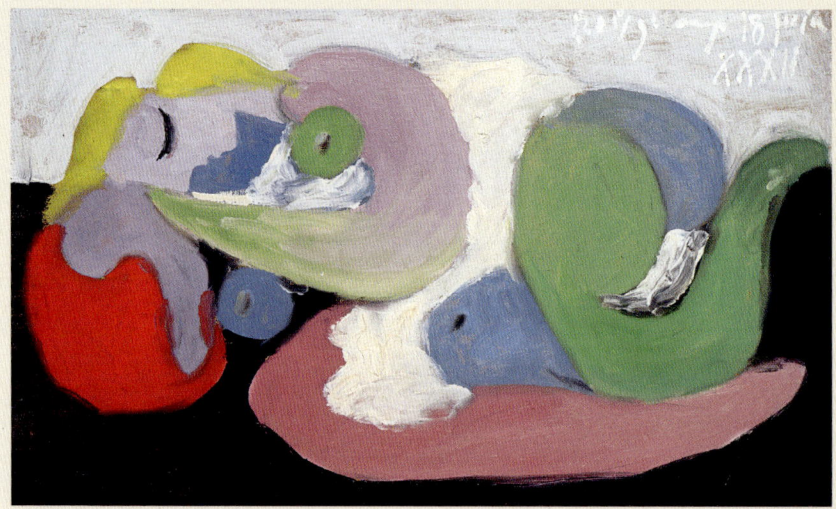

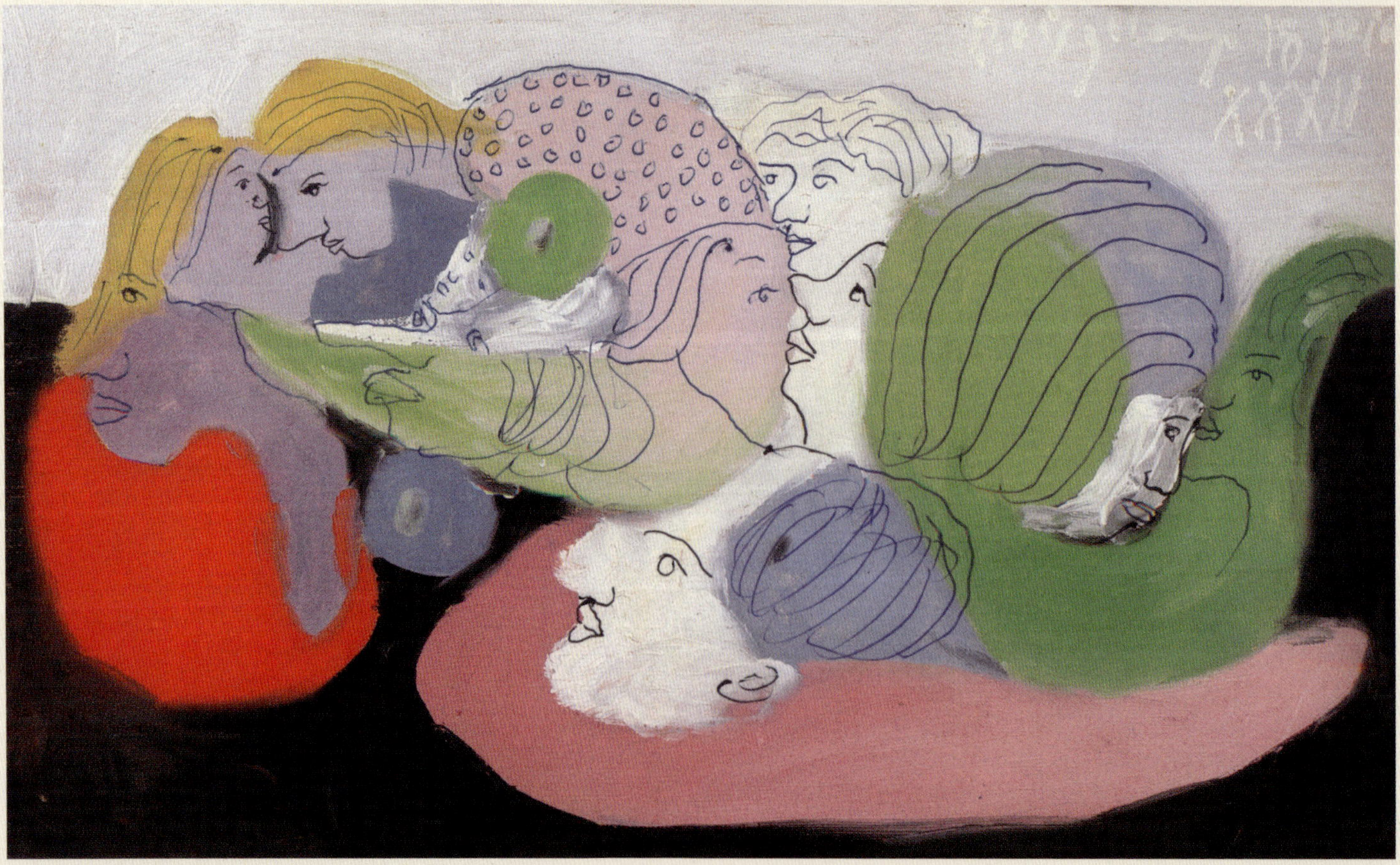

1983

Picasso diplomacy

The National Art Museum of China in Beijing opens *Picasso* in May during a state visit from French president François Mitterrand (in office May 1981–May 1995). The exhibition features thirty-three works made by Picasso between 1904 and 1970. *South China Morning Post* correspondent Victoria Graham reports that, on one particular Sunday, the exhibition receives 15,000 visitors.

1984

First dedicated Picasso exhibition space in Asia

Hakone Open Air Museum opens the Picasso Pavilion, a permanent exhibition space dedicated to the museum's collection of 319 works by the Spanish master.

BELOW: *Picasso Pavilion poster,* Hakone Open Air Museum, Japan, 1984

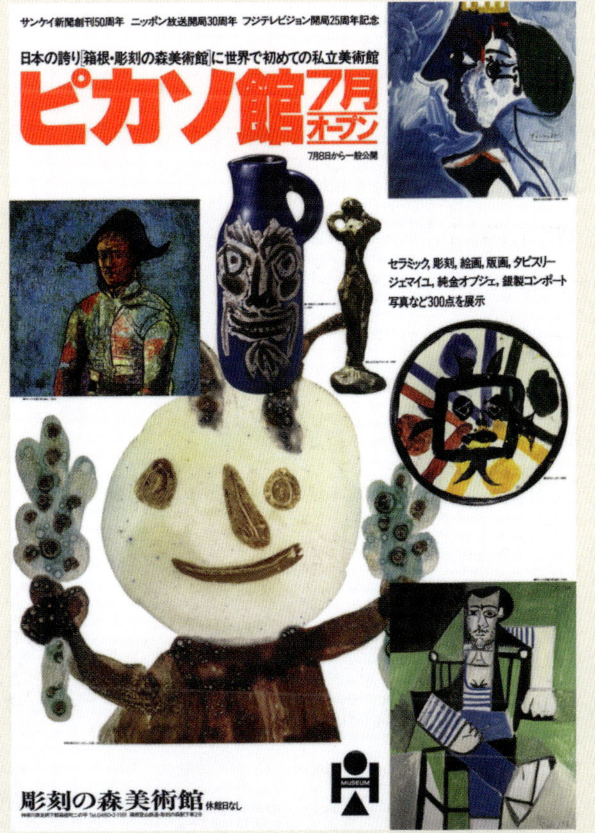

1985

Feminist critique of Picasso

Filipina terracotta artist Julie Lluch (born 1946) exhibits *Picasso y Yo* (ca.1985), a colourful terracotta sculpture echoing Picasso's harlequin and *saltimbanque* motifs. Lluch presents a feminist response to the subject of domestic struggle. The work is displayed as part of the group exhibition *Five Artists in March* at the Pinaglabanan Galleries, San Juan City, Philippines, curated by Nilo Ilarde and Roberto Chabet.

BELOW: Julie Lluch, *Picasso y Yo*, ca.1985

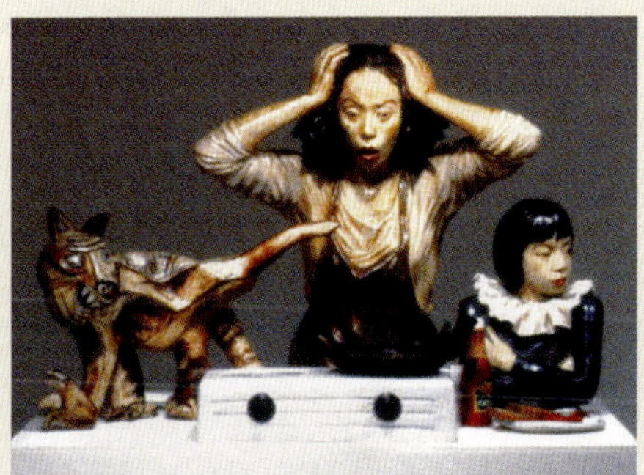

2000s

1996

Gift of Picasso to China
On 27 March, German philanthropists and collectors Peter Ludwig (1925–1996) and Irene Ludwig (1927–2010) donate eighty-nine artworks to the National Art Museum of China, including three paintings (1970s) and one ink drawing, *Figures* (1960s), by Picasso. The donation establishes the first public Western art collection in China.

BELOW: German federal president Roman Herzog and collector Irene Ludwig with Jiang Zemin, president of the People's Republic of China, in front of two Picasso paintings, *Infantryman with a Bird* (1972; left) and *Man and Woman by a Flower Vase* (1970; right)

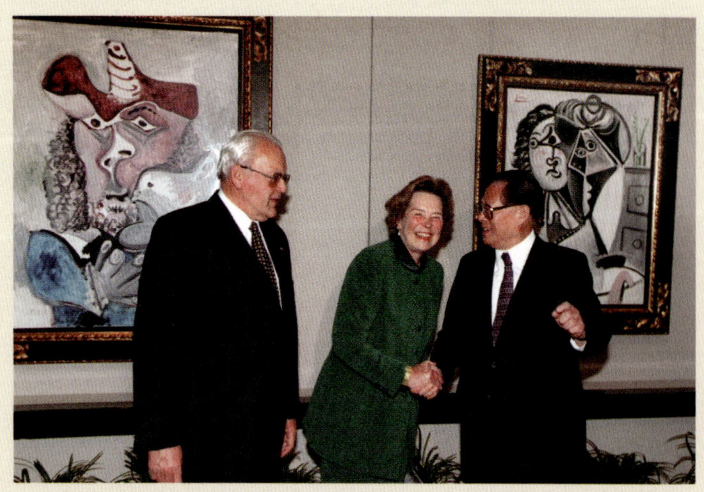

2001

First museum retrospective of Picasso in India
On 14 December, the first public Picasso exhibition in India opens at the National Gallery of Modern Art in New Delhi. Curated by Musée national Picasso-Paris, *Picasso: Metamorphoses 1900–1972* brings together 122 works from several French lenders. The exhibition is the result of a cultural exchange between France and India initiated by French president Jacques Chirac (in office May 1995–May 2007) and prime ministers Inder Kumar Gujral (in office April 1997–March 1998) and Kocheril Raman Narayanan (in office July 1997–July 2002).

Mumbai-born curator Zasha Colah remembers:

The Picasso exhibition, despite Picasso no longer being perceived as avant-garde, became a catalyst for avant-garde conversations in India. The exhibition took up every floor of the museum, with paintings, sculptures, and drawing series from all his periods. There were two reading areas set up at the different landings amid the exhibition. Artists were coming from nearby towns and villages, and sleeping rough at night, and then returning every morning to the exhibition to read the books for the whole duration of the exhibition.[66]

BELOW: Inaugural ceremony tour of *Picasso: Metamorphoses 1900–1972* at the National Gallery of Modern Art, New Delhi, 2001, with Picasso's *The Goat* (1950) in the foreground

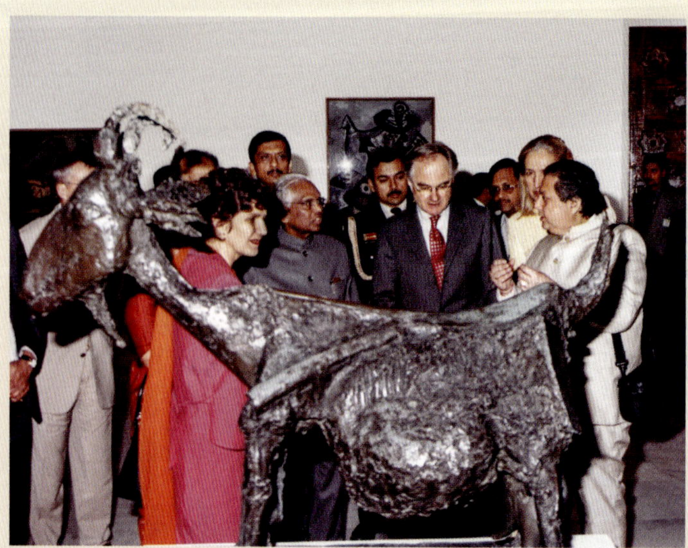

Speaking at the time of the exhibition, Professor Shukla Sawant of the School of Arts and Aesthetics at the Jawaharlal Nehru University says:

A Picasso exhibition is crucial at this juncture when there is a debate arising out of appropriation of images. For instance, when a European artist looks at other visual languages as resource, he is said to be inspired. In the case of, say, an Indian artist being influenced, he is said to be copying. Picasso highlights the different ways of looking. These are issues central to 20th century history of art. Other younger generation artists ... feel that Picasso is still relevant. None of these artists have seen the Picasso show yet, but have seen enough of his art in museums abroad. They are turned on by his energy, his honesty with material, his experiments with installations, assemblages and inventiveness.[67]

2011

Picasso exhibition at the China pavilion, Shanghai
More than a century after *Last Moments* (1899) was shown at the 1900 Exposition Universelle in Paris, the Spanish master once again returns to a world's fair setting. The exhibition of his work, organised by the Musée national Picasso-Paris, takes place at the China pavilion on the former site of the 2010 Shanghai World Expo from 18 October 2011 to 12 January 2012, as well as in Taipei and Hong Kong. On display are forty-eight paintings, seven prints, seven sculptures, and fifty photographs.

BELOW: Docent tour of Picasso's *Seated Woman in a Red Armchair* (1932) on display at the China pavilion, Shanghai, 2011

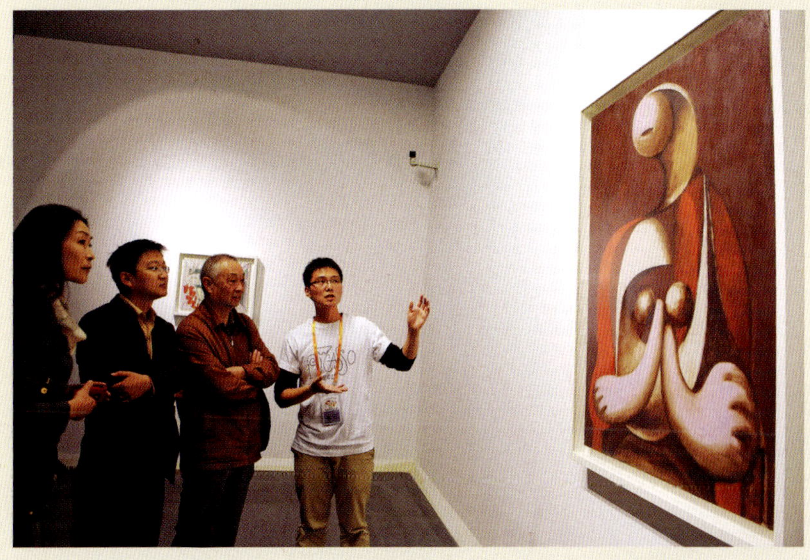

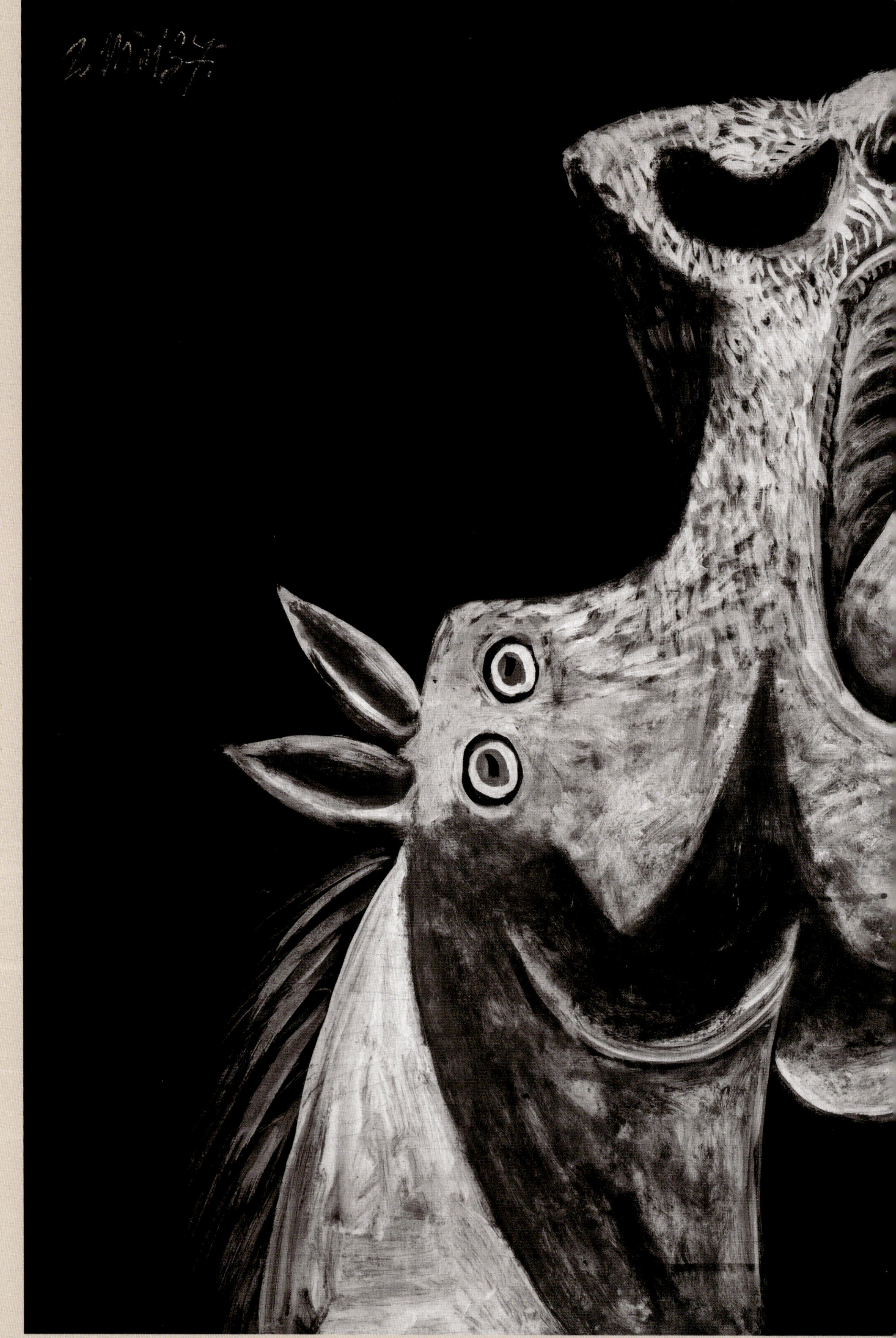

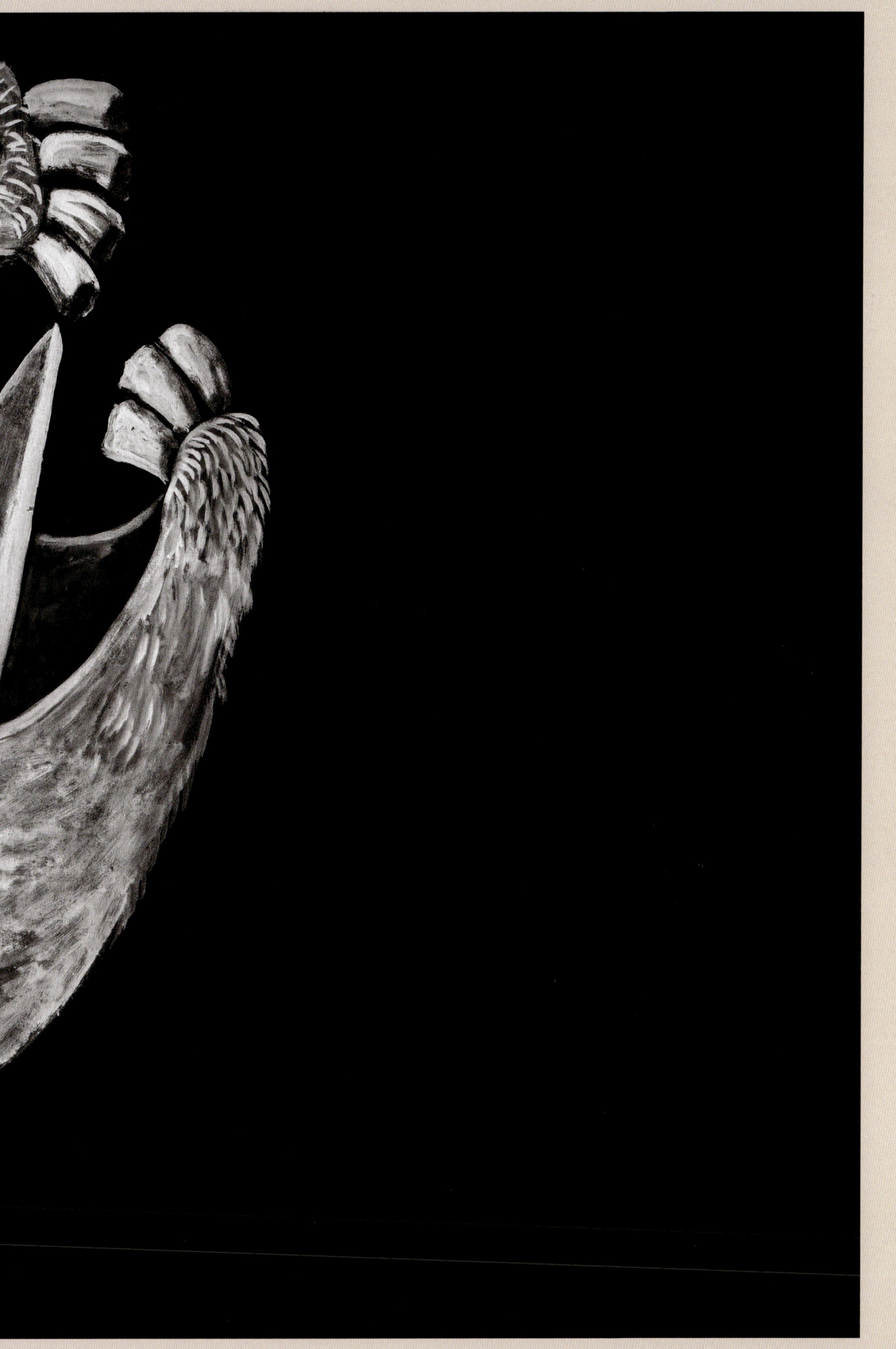

Notes

Invention of a Myth
François Dareau

1 Ernst Kris and Otto Kurz, *Legend, Myth, and Magic in the Image of the Artist* (New Haven and London: Yale University Press, 1979), 132.
2 Roland Barthes, *Mythologies* (Paris: Éditions du Seuil, 1957; edn 2014), 212. Unless noted otherwise, all translations from non-English-language sources are the author's own.
3 Sophie Calle, *Picalso* (Paris: Atelier EXB, 2023), 29.
4 '"Chinese Picasso" painting sells for record £2.6m', *BBC*, 23 May 2019, https://www.bbc.com/news/uk-england-berkshire-48381609, accessed 13 June 2024.
5 Judith Gogny-Goubert, 'Le Picasso de la gastronomie espagnole s'installe à la Maison Delano, à Paris', *Gala*, 2 May 2023, https://www.gala.fr/lifestyle/le-picasso-de-la-gastronomie-espagnole-sinstalle-a-la-maison-delano_519057, accessed 13 June 2024.
6 'Le FBI recherche les victimes du "Picasso des tueurs en série"', *Le Parisien*, 14 February 2019, https://www.leparisien.fr/faits-divers/le-fbi-recherche-les-victimes-du-picasso-des-tueurs-en-serie-14-02-2019-8011695.php, accessed 13 June 2024.
7 Pierre Bourdieu, 'L'illusion biographique', *Actes de la recherche en sciences sociales* 62–63 (June 1986): 69.
8 Alain Robbe-Grillet, *Le miroir qui revient* (Paris: Éditions de Minuit, 1984), 208. Quoted in Bourdieu, 'L'illusion biographique', 70.
9 Jean-Benoît Puech, 'La création biographique', in *L'auteur: Entre biographie et mythographie* (Pessac: Presses Universitaires de Bordeaux, 2002), 45.
10 Pablo Picasso, quoted in Brassaï, *Conversations with Picasso* (Chicago and London: University of Chicago Press, 1999), 93.
11 This would lead art historians Laurence Bertrand Dorléac and Androula Michaël to assert that '[Picasso] is presented as all-powerful over the world and as the conscious, diabolical founder of his own myth, whereas it was rather that he displayed a great social but empirical imagination, using circumstances and navigating by sight.' Laurence Bertrand Dorléac and Androula Michaël, *Picasso: L'objet du mythe* (Paris: École Nationale Supérieure des Beaux-Arts de Paris, 2005), 8.
12 Pablo Picasso, quoted in Christian Zervos, 'Conversation avec Picasso', *Cahiers d'art*, nos 7–10 (1935): 173.
13 'Like most painters, [Picasso] has little to say and is unable to clearly formulate his thoughts. His statements are made up of negations, wisecracks, pithy formulas.' Waldemar George, *L'art vivant*, August 1930, reproduced in *La critique hostile à Picasso* (Paris: Éditions Jannink, 2000), n.p.
14 Pablo Picasso, quoted in Àngel Ferran, 'Conversa amb Picasso', *La Publicitat*, Barcelona, 19 October 1926, reproduced in Marie-Laure Bernadac and Androula Michaël, eds, *Picasso: Propos sur l'art* (Paris: Gallimard, 1998), 26.
15 The writer Paul Léautaud, who took part in the articles' publication, evoked his encounter with a panicked art critic: 'Is there a new piece by Fernande Olivier? Does she mention me? What does she say?' Adolphe Basler, quoted in Paul Léautaud, *Journal littéraire*, vol. 9 (Paris: Mercure de France, 1960): 55.
16 'Quand on fumait l'opium près de Van Dongen et de Picasso', *Comœdia*, Paris, 3 May 1931, 3.
17 Fernande Olivier, *Picasso et ses amis* (Paris: Pygmalion, 2001), 84.
18 'Le tribunal refuse à Picasso l'autorisation de faire saisir le livre de Françoise Gilot', *Le Monde*, 15 April 1965, https://www.lemonde.fr/archives/article/1965/04/15/le-tribunal-refuse-a-picasso-l-autorisation-de-faire-saisir-le-livre-de-francoise-gilot_2182833_1819218.html, accessed 13 June 2024.
19 Françoise Gilot and Carlton Lake, *Life with Picasso* (London: Virago Press, 1990), 95.
20 'Le tribunal refuse à Picasso l'autorisation de faire saisir le livre de Françoise Gilot'.
21 In contrast to Picasso's portraits of men, whose subjects are named in the paintings' titles, his portraits of women rarely reveal the model's identity. There are, of course, a few notable exceptions, such as *Olga in an Armchair* (*Olga dans un fauteuil*; 1918), the title of which was *Portrait de Madame Picasso* during the artist's first retrospective, which took place in Paris in 1932. When Fernande Olivier published her story and in turn became a known figure in the Picasso narrative, the titles of some of the artworks in which her features can be seen mentioned her name. Beginning in the 1950s, when the artist married Jacqueline Roque, several of the portraits he produced at that time bore her first name.
22 Walter met Picasso in 1927 when she was seventeen years old. Together they had a daughter, Maya, who was born in 1935.
23 Pablo Picasso, quoted in Brassaï, *Conversations with Picasso*, 133.
24 Laurence Madeline, *Marie-Thérèse Walter et Pablo Picasso: Biographie d'une relation* (Paris: Nouvelles Éditions Scala, 2022), 576.
25 This is the approach that Dora Maar shared with Roland Penrose when he interviewed her in 1955 for his monograph on Picasso. See Elizabeth Cowling, *Visiting Picasso: The Notebooks and Letters of Roland Penrose* (London: Thames & Hudson, 2006), 132.
26 A few recent examples: in 2018 the American television series *Genius*, which traces the life of influential figures of the twentieth century, devoted its second season to Picasso, played by Antonio Banderas; the following year the exhibition *Picasso, Birth of a Genius* opened in Beijing, exploring the first three decades of his artistic activity.
27 Salvador Dalí, quoted in Pierre Cabanne, *Le siècle de Picasso 4: La gloire et la solitude, 1955–1973* (Paris: Gallimard, 1992), 704.
28 Wifredo Lam, *L'Humanité*, 10 April 1973, quoted in Marie-Sophie Carron, 'Fortune nécrologique de Picasso: Le mythe et l'homme', unpublished master's thesis, Université Panthéon-Sorbonne, Paris, 1983, 148.
29 Werner Schmalenbach, 'Nachruf auf Picasso', *Die Zeit*, 13 April 1973, reproduced in *Pablo Picasso* (Paris: Galerie Gmurzynska), 1983, 50–51.
30 Kris and Kurz, *Legend, Myth, and Magic in the Image of the Artist*, 13.
31 *Ibid.*, 28.
32 Max Jacob, 'Souvenirs sur Picasso contés par Max Jacob', *Cahiers d'art*, no. 6 (1927): 199.
33 John Richardson, *A Life of Picasso* (New York: Random House, 1991), 49.
34 Linda Nochlin, *Why Have There Been No Great Women Artists?* (London: Thames & Hudson, 2021), 38.
35 It remains difficult to prove that Picasso could have seen or been inspired by the work of Velázquez, as the portrait has always been in private collections.
36 For example, the lineage from the *Venus* of Giorgione to that of Titian, all the way to Manet's *Olympia* (1863).
37 In particular, this recalls Picasso's handwritten words in a notebook: 'Painting is stronger than me; it makes me do what it wants' (27 March 1963).
38 Despite a lukewarm performance at the box office, the film was presented in competition at the 1956 Cannes Film Festival, where it won the Special Jury Prize.
39 'The *Mystère of Picasso* is the mystery of life, which is to say, in romantic aesthetics, the mystery of genius.' C. F. B. Miller, *Radical Picasso: The Use Value of Genius* (Oakland: University of California Press, 2021), 221.
40 *The Mystery of Picasso* (1956), directed by Henri-Georges Clouzot, 78 mins.
41 Douglas Cooper, 'Courrier des lecteurs', *Connaissance des arts*, no. 257 (July 1973).
42 Alexander Sturgis et al., *Rebels and Martyrs: The Image of the Artist in the Nineteenth Century* (London: National Gallery, 2006), 89.
43 Michael Wilson, 'Rebels and Martyrs', in Sturgis et al., *Rebels and Martyrs*, 7.

44 Marilyn Ruth Brown, 'Vagabonds, chiffonniers, saltimbanques et autres marginaux', in Sylvain Amic, ed., *Bohèmes* (Paris: Réunion des Musées Nationaux, 2012), 45.
45 Pablo Picasso, quoted in Daniel-Henry Kahnweiler, '29 bis, rue d'Astorg, 2 décembre 1933', *Entretiens avec Picasso*, 1956, reproduced in Bernadac and Michaël, *Picasso: Propos sur l'art*, 75.
46 Max Raphael, *Proudhon, Marx, Picasso: Trois études sur la sociologie de l'art* (Paris: Éditions Excelsior, 1933), 200.
47 Linda Nochlin, 'The Vanishing Brothel', *London Review of Books* 19, no. 5 (6 March 1997), https://www.lrb.co.uk/the-paper/v19/n05/linda-nochlin/the-vanishing-brothel, accessed 13 June 2024.
48 Claire Le Thomas, *Racines populaires du cubisme* (Dijon: Presses du Réel, 2016).
49 The classical notion of the artist as magician is generally based on the artist's mastery of *trompe l'œil* and their skill in fooling the viewer. We find several expressions of this idea, with Pliny recounting how the grapes painted by Zeuxis were pecked at by swallows, or Vasari relating that, when Titian placed a portrait of the pope in front of a window, passers-by confused it with the real pontiff. Cocteau's story updates this myth by anchoring it no longer in the perfect imitation of nature but in the artist's ability to transform reality.
50 Jean Cocteau, *Picasso* (Paris: L'École des Loisirs, 1996), 105.
51 Christian Zervos grouped together certain works from this period in a 1938 article in *Cahiers d'art* titled 'Tableaux magiques de Picasso' (Magical Paintings by Picasso).
52 Cocteau, *Picasso*, 68–69.
53 Pablo Picasso, quoted in 'Pablo Picasso: "Si une machine enregistrait ce que je pense pendant que je peins ..."', *Le Monde*, 28 September 1960, https://www.lemonde.fr/archives/article/1960/09/28/si-une-machine-enregistrait-ce-que-je-pense-pendant-que-je-peins_2108023_1819218.html, accessed 13 June 2024.
54 Pablo Picasso, quoted in Zervos, 'Conversation avec Picasso', 176.
55 Gelett Burgess, 'The Wild Men of Paris', *Architectural Record* (May 1910): 408.
56 Pablo Picasso, quoted in Gilot and Lake, *Life with Picasso*, 248–249.
57 *Ibid.*, 248.
58 Umberto Eco, ed., *Histoire de la laideur* (Paris: Flammarion, 2007), 365.
59 Pierre Cabanne, *Le scandale dans l'art* (Paris: Éditions de la Différence, 2007), 129–130.
60 Jean-Marie Touratier, *Mauvais sang: Les nazis et l'art dégénéré* (Paris: Éditions Galilée, 2018).
61 Rosenberg excoriated Cubism and the following period, the 1920s, in extremely violent terms: 'What Picasso still shamefacedly concealed behind geometric artifices, appeared openly after the world war with arrogant boldness. The bastard claimed to represent in his bastard miscarriages produced by spiritual syphilis, an infantilism as the expression of the soul.' Alfred Rosenberg, *Le mythe du XXème siècle* (Paris: Éditions Avalon, 1986), 280, quoted in Touratier, *Mauvais sang*, 58.
62 Stéphane Guégan, 'Le temps et l'art de l'ambiguïté', in *Picasso: Au cœur des ténèbres (1939–1945)* (Paris: In Fine éditions d'art, 2019), 48–49.
63 Michel Leiris, 'L'exposition à la galerie Louise Leiris', 1945, reproduced in *Écrits sur l'art* (Paris: CNRS Éditions, 2011), 315.
64 Kris and Kurz, *Legend, Myth, and Magic in the Image of the Artist*, 90.
65 The biblical story of the Tower of Babel is a famous example of this. According to Genesis, humans attempted to build a city that would reach up to heaven. God then decided to confuse their language so that they could no longer understand one another, putting an end to the construction.
66 With the notable exception of a few slender sculptures carved in wood.
67 Pablo Picasso, quoted in Gilot and Lake, *Life with Picasso*, 43.
68 Carol Duncan, 'Virility and Domination in Early Twentieth-Century Vanguard Painting', in *Feminism and Art History* (New York: Harper & Row, 1982), 306.
69 Pablo Picasso, quoted in Dor de la Souchère, *Picasso à Antibes* (Paris: Hazan, 1960), 62.
70 Siri Hustvedt, *A Woman Looking at Men Looking at Women: Essays on Art, Sex, and the Mind* (New York: Simon & Schuster, 2016), 10.
71 Emilia Philippot and François Dareau, *Picasso: Figures* (Rome: MondoMostre, 2021).
72 Madeline, *Marie-Thérèse Walter et Pablo Picasso.*
73 The exhibition *It's Pablo-matic*, held at the Brooklyn Museum in 2023, addressed the complex issues of misogyny, artistic canons, and the figure of the 'genius'. Press reactions were mixed, demonstrating that the subject remains hotly debated.
74 Miller, *Radical Picasso*, 211.
75 From 31 January to 2 July 2023. It took place after another large-scale retrospective at the New Museum in New York City in 2022.
76 Miller, *Radical Picasso*, 23.

The author would like to thank Lucas Belloc, Juliette Degennes, and Léa Delplanque for their invaluable help.

Remaking Picasso for Asia
Doryun Chong

1 Janet Fluegel and William Rubin, eds, *Pablo Picasso: A Retrospective* (New York: Museum of Modern Art, 1980), 383.
2 Picasso had made references to David earlier, as exemplified by *Woman with a Stiletto* (1931; FIG. 19), an update on David's *The Death of Marat* (1793) through the introduction—among other additions—of the murderous Charlotte Corday, missing in the Neoclassical original.
3 Fluegel and Rubin, *Pablo Picasso: A Retrospective*, 382.
4 *Ibid.*, 383.
5 Kirsten Hoving Keen, 'Picasso's Communist Interlude: The Murals of "War" and "Peace"', *Burlington Magazine* 122, no. 928 (July 1980): 464.
6 *Ibid.*, 464, 467. The observation of Picasso's unusually obedient reaction to the French Communist Party's expectation was made by Pierre Daix, a biographer of Picasso and a fellow party member.
7 Keen, 'Picasso's Communist Interlude', 467.
8 See Annie Cohen-Solal, *Picasso the Foreigner: An Artist in France, 1900–1973* (New York: Farrar, Straus & Giroux, 2023), and Annie Cohen-Solal, ed., *Picasso, L'Étranger* (Paris: Fayard, 2021).
9 Kim In-hye, 'Picasso: Reception in Asian Countries in [the] 1940s–1950s', in Furuichi Yasuko, ed., *Cubism in Asia: Unbounded Dialogues* (Tokyo: National Museum of Modern Art, Tokyo, 2005), 244.
10 *Ibid.*
11 Needless to say, Asia is a huge area comprising a variety of regions. This book and this essay focus primarily on East Asia, including Greater China, Japan, and Korea, with occasional references to South and Southeast Asia. There are several other works and events in Picasso's oeuvre and biography that instantiate his other connections to Asia. See 'Picasso and Asia: A Visual Chronology' in this volume.
12 Gertrude Stein, *The Autobiography of Alice B. Toklas* (New York: Harcourt, Brace and Company, 1933), 56. *Ukiyo-e* (literally, 'pictures of the floating world') are woodblock prints that were widely distributed and hugely popular during the Edo period, from the seventeenth to the nineteenth centuries.
13 Fernande Olivier, *Picasso and His Friends* (London: Heinemann, 1964), 89.
14 Pablo Picasso, quoted in Guillaume Apollinaire, 'Propos de Pablo Picasso', in Pierre Caizergues and Hélène Shekel, eds, *Picasso/Apollinaire: Correspondance* (Paris: Gallimard, 1992), 201, 203. Unless noted otherwise, all translations from non-English-language sources are the author's own.
15 Malén Gual, 'Dialogue with Japanese Art', in *Secret Images: Picasso and the Japanese Erotic Print* (Barcelona: Museo Picasso Barcelona; London: Thames & Hudson, 2010), 80.
16 These events include the 1888 Barcelona Universal Exposition and, in Paris, the Expositions Universelle of 1889 and 1900.
17 Gual, 'Dialogue with Japanese Art', 83.
18 *Shunga* is a genre of erotic or pornographic *ukiyo-e*. 'Shun', the Sino-Japanese word for spring, is a euphemism commonly used for copulation.
19 The École de Paris, or School of Paris, became a collective term for non-French artists who had settled in the art metropolis in the interwar years. American art critic Harold Rosenberg observed that 'in the School of Paris, belonging to no one country, but world-wide and world timed and pertinent everywhere, the mind of the twentieth century projected itself into possibilities that will occupy mankind during many cycles of social adventures to come.' Harold Rosenberg, 'The Fall of Paris', *Partisan Review* 7, no. 6 (December 1940): 440–448.
20 Mark O'Neill, 'Zhang Daqian: The Chinese Picasso', *Macao*, 10 July 2010, https://macaomagazine.net/zhang-daqian-the-chinese-picasso/, accessed 2 March 2024.
21 During most of the Edo period (1603–1868), under the rule of the Tokugawa shogunate, Japan was closed to the rest of the world in order to curb Western colonial and religious infiltration. This national policy, which was later called *sakoku* (closed or locked country), came to an end in 1853–1854, when US Navy Commodore Matthew Perry used warships to force the country to open its ports and begin trading with the United States. A decade and a half later a group of young samurai began a movement to strengthen their nation, now open to foreign forces and influences, by restoring supreme political authority to the emperor, who had been marginalised during the Edo period. The political revolution of 1868, known as the Meiji Restoration, ended the Edo period and marked the beginning of modern Japan.
22 See Herbert Mitgang, 'When Picasso Spooked the F.B.I.', *New York Times*, 11 November 1990, https://www.nytimes.com/1990/11/11/arts/art-when-picasso-spooked-the-fbi.html, accessed 6 June 2024.
23 Ai Zhongxin, 'Zhu bijiasuo bashi dashou' (Happy Eightieth Birthday to Picasso), *Meishu* no. 5 (1961): 45–46.
24 The retrospective was presented at the National Museum of Modern Art, Tokyo, from 23 May to 5 July, followed by a tour to the National Museum of Modern Art, Kyoto (10 July to 2 August), and Aichi Prefecture Museum of Art (7 to 18 August).
25 Inada Seisuke, Director, National Museum of Modern Art, Tokyo, and Ueda Tsunetaka, President, Mainichi Newspapers, foreword to *Pablo Picasso Exhibition: Japan 1964* (Tokyo: Mainichi Newspapers, 1964), 9.
26 Alfred H. Barr, 'Introduction', in *Pablo Picasso Exhibition*, 23.
27 Daniel-Henry Kahnweiler, 'Introduction', in *Pablo Picasso Exhibition*, 18–19.
28 Commemorating the fiftieth anniversary of his death, in 1973, 'Picasso Celebration 1973–2023' brought together fifty exhibitions and events between 2022 and 2024 in Spain and France, as well as internationally; see https://celebracionpicasso.es/en, accessed 7 June 2024.
29 David Hockney, quoted in 'Chronology', *The David Hockney Foundation*, https://www.

thedavidhockneyfoundation.org/chronology/2003, accessed 7 June 2024.

30 Major exhibitions about the growing and continuing impact of Picasso's historic and ongoing legacy include *Picasso and American Art* at the Whitney Museum of American Art, New York (2006); *Post-Picasso: Contemporary Reactions* at the Museu Picasso Barcelona (2014); *Picasso.mania* at the Grand Palais, Paris (2015); and *The Echo of Picasso* at the Museo Picasso Málaga (2023).

31 One notable exhibition in this regard was *It's Pablo-matic: Picasso According to Hannah Gadsby*, held at the Brooklyn Museum, New York, in 2023. Officially a part of 'Picasso Celebration 1973–2023' and realised in collaboration with the Musée national Picasso-Paris, the exhibition was 'co-curated' by Gadsby, the Australian comic whose live stand-up special *Nanette* became a smash hit on Netflix upon its release in 2018. Gadsby calls Picasso a misogynist in the film.

32 For example, the UCCA Center for Contemporary Art, Beijing, staged *Picasso: Birth of a Genius* in 2019, while the Hangaram Art Museum in Seoul opened *Picasso, Into the Myth* in 2021.

33 Still the most important exhibition in this regard is the landmark project *Magiciens de la terre* (1989), curated by Jean-Hubert Martin and presented at the Centre Georges Pompidou and the Grand halle de la Vilette in Paris.

34 The work is part of a series of artist portraits by Zeng. Other artists he has painted include Monet, Van Gogh, Lucien Freud, and Francis Bacon.

35 In *Listening to Stone: The Art and Life of Isamu Noguchi* (New York: Farrar, Straus & Giroux, 2016), 96, Hayden Herrera writes: 'In *Leda*, a subject that had also inspired Brâncuși, a biomorphic figure (highly abstracted in a way that recalls Arp and Picasso) reels backward in shock at her ravishment by an invisible swan. The metal rods penetrating the sheet metal, and indeed the way the whole "figure" penetrates a tilted sheet metal ring, might also allude to the sexual encounter taking place.'

36 *Ibid.*, 223.

37 Max-Pol Fouchet, *Wifredo Lam* (Barcelona: Ediciones Polígrafa), 1989, 112.

38 Marie Sarré, 'Wifredo Lam (1902–1982)', in Didier Ottinger, ed., *The Picasso Century* (Melbourne: Council of Trustees of the National Gallery of Victoria, 2022), 61.

39 John Yau, 'Please Wait by the Coatroom: Wifredo Lam in the Museum of Modern Art', *Arts Magazine* 63, no. 4 (December 1988): 56–59. Reprinted in Catherine David, ed., *The EY Exhibition: Wifredo Lam* (London: Tate Publishing, 2016), 191.

40 *Ibid.*, 194.

41 Michel Leiris, *Wifredo Lam* (Brussels: Didier Devillez Editor, 1997), 36, quoted in Sarré, 'Wifredo Lam (1902–1982)', 282.

42 Introducing a recent exhibition aptly titled *The Echo of Picasso*, the show's curator, Éric Troncy, wrote: 'The title chosen for this exhibition ... seems to me to do justice to a project whose aim is precisely to show how the oeuvre of Picasso "resounds" with an echo, sometimes deafening and sometimes fainter, in contemporary ears. Whether contemporary with Picasso himself or subsequent to his demise, every period has found new echoes, again and again and for all sorts of reasons, in keeping with the thoughts proposed to us by artists.' Éric Troncy, ed., *The Echo of Picasso* (Málaga: Museo Picasso Málaga, 2023), 22.

43 Under the leadership and tutelage of Lui Shou-kwan, a new generation of artists drew inspiration from the modern Chinese ink painting of the Lingnan School, as well as from such modern Western art movements as Abstract Expressionism. The group included other respected figures, such as Liu Kuo-sung and Wucius Wong.

44 Pi Li, 'Fang Lijun', in Pi Li, ed., *Chinese Art Since 1970: The M+ Sigg Collection* (London: Thames & Hudson in association with M+, 2021), 122.

45 Troncy, *Echo of Picasso*, 22.

46 Pablo Picasso, quoted in Claire Dederer, *Monsters: A Fan's Dilemma* (New York: Knopf Doubleday, 2023), 95.

47 Dora Maar, quoted in *ibid.*

48 Perhaps still the most representative example of a critically feminist reading of Picasso's life is *Picasso: Creator and Destroyer* by Arianna Huffington (New York: Simon & Schuster, 1988). See also note 31, above.

49 See Dederer, *Monsters.*

50 Born Yamada Saori, Akutagawa adopted her husband's family name when she married composer Akutagawa Yasushi in 1946. They divorced in 1958. In 1961 she married architect Madokoro Yukio and was known by her second husband's family name until her death in 1966.

51 Nalini Malani, 'Cassandra', in Nalini Malani and Robert Storr, *Nalini Malani: Listening to the Shades* (New York: Charta & Arario, 2008), n.p.

52 Marina Picasso, quoted in Alan Riding, 'Grandpa Picasso: Terribly Famous, Not Terribly Nice', *New York Times*, 24 November 2001, https://www.nytimes.com/2001/11/24/books/grandpa-picasso-terribly-famous-not-terribly-nice.html, accessed 7 June 2024.

53 Chia Chi Jason Wang, 'A Passage Blown Between Space and Time: On the Art of Cai Guo Qiang', in Yao Chao, ed., *Cai Guo-Qiang: Hanging Out in the Museum* (Taipei: Taipei Fine Arts Museum 2009), 29.

54 Simon Fujiwara, quoted in Kim Jaeseok and Cho Jae Hee, eds, *Simon Fujiwara* (Seoul: Gallery Hyundai, 2023), 9.

55 Cohen-Solal, *Picasso, L'Etranger*, 16.

56 *Ibid.*, 111.

57 Walter Benjamin, 'The Task of the Translator', in Marcus Bullock and Michael W. Jennings, eds, *Selected Writings, Volume 1: 1913–1926* (Cambridge, MA, and London: Belknap Press), 258.

58 John Berger, *The Success and Failure of Picasso* (New York: Knopf Doubleday, 1993), 3–132.

Picasso and Asia: A Visual Chronology
Hester Chan

Epigraph: Eugene Wang, 'Sketch Conceptualism as Modernist Contingency', in Maxwell Hearn and Judith G. Smith, eds, *Chinese Art: Modern Expressions* (New York: Metropolitan Museum of Art, 2001), 103.

1 *Last Moments* was discovered underneath another Picasso painting, *La vie* (1903), from the Blue Period. The work is in the collection of the Cleveland Museum of Art. *Cleveland Art*, January/February 2014.

2 See Yoko Chiba, 'Sada Yacco and Kawakami: Performers of Japonisme', *Modern Drama* 35 (1992), 35–53; Elizabeth Emery, 'Appropriating Japonisme at the 1900 Exposition: Sada Yacco, Loie Fuller, and the "Geishas" of *Le Panorama du Tour du Monde*', *Dix-Neuf* 24, nos 2–3 (2020): 221–244; Tara Rodman, 'A Modernist Audience: The Kawakami Troupe, Matsuki Bunkio, and Boston Japonisme', *Theatre Journal* 65, no. 4 (2013): 489–505; Stanca Scholz-Cionca, 'Japanesque Shows for Western Markets: Loie Fuller and Japanese Theatre Tours through Europe (1900–08)', *Journal of Global Theatre History* 1, no. 1 (2016): 46–61.

3 Sylvain Ageorges, *Sur les traces des Exposition universelles 1855–1937* (Paris: Parigramme, 2006), 116–117.

4 See Yan Fengqiao, 'Modernization of Chinese Higher Education and Impact from Japan', *RIHE International Seminar Reports*, no. 26 (2022): 23–39.

5 Yang Yang, 'What Did the Chinese Artists Do in France? Story of Pioneering: Chinese Artists in France and Modern Chinese Art (1911–1949)', *Art Exchange* 1 (2019), https://www.cflac.org.cn/ArtExchange/ysjlzz/ysjl2019/201912/t20191210_465106.htm, accessed 27 November 2024.

6 Fernande Olivier, *Picasso and His Friends* (London: Heinemann, 1964), 89.

7 Pablo Picasso, quoted in André Malraux, *Picasso's Mask* (New York: Da Capo Press, 1994), 10–11.

8 Sylvie Buisson and Dominique Buisson, *La vie et l'oeuvre de Léonard-Tsuguharu Foujita* (Paris: ACR Éditions, 1987), 33–35.

9 Léonard Tsuguharu Foujita, quoted in Sylvie Buisson, *Foujita et ses amis du Montparnasse* (Paris: Éditions Alternatives, 2010), 46–47.

10 Kinoshita Mokutarō, 'Yōga ni okeru hishizenshugiteki keikō' (Non-Naturalistic Tendencies in Western Painting), *Bijutsu shinpō* 12, no. 4 (1913): 7–8; 12, no. 5 (1913): 2–8; 12, no. 8 (1913): 22–23.

11 Morita Kamenosuke, 'Taisei gakai shin'undō no keika oyobi Kyubizumu: Tsukeri sono hihyō (jō shōzen)', *Bijutsu shinpō* 14, no. 4 (1915): 7–11, in Inaga Shigemi, 'Between Revolutionary and Oriental Sage: Paul Cézanne in Japan', *Japan Review* 28 (2015): 133–172.

12 Arthur Jerome Eddy, *Cubists and Post-Impressionism* (Chicago: A. C. McClung, 1914), 79.

13 Michael Sullivan, *Art and Artists of Twentieth-Century China* (Berkeley: University of California Press, 1996), 65.

14 Hans van der Meyden, 'Early Picassos in the Collection of Mr. Chen Qinghua in Suzhou', *Apollo*, December 1986, 555.

15 Susan Bush, *The Chinese Literati on Painting: Su Shih (1037–1101) to Tung Ch'ich'ang (1555–1636)* (Hong Kong: Hong Kong University Press, 2012), 1, 29–32.

16 Francis Steegmuller, *Cocteau: A Biography* (Boston: Little, Brown, 1970), 182, 513.

17 Jiang Danshu, *Art History Reference Book*, vol. 2 (Shanghai: Shanghai Commercial Press, 1918), 29, quoted in Wu Xueshan, 'Picasso in China: 1817–2019', in *Picasso: Birth of a Genius* (Beijing: UCCA Center for Contemporary Art and Culture and Art Publishing House, 2019), 24.

18 Van der Meyden, 'Early Picassos', 556.

19 *Ibid.*, 555–557. Zhu Da, also known as Bada Shanren (1626–1705), was a late Ming/early Qing poet and painter, studied and copied by Zhang Daqian. Shi Tao (1642–1707) was a Qing dynasty landscape painter and calligraphist famed for breaking with tradition.

20 See Ratan Parimoo, *Art of Three Tagores: From Revival to Modernity* (New Delhi: Kumar Gallery, 2011); Don J. Cohn, 'Postcolonial Personalities: The Primitivist, the Mystic, the Cubist and the Martyr', *ArtAsiaPacific* 65 (2009), 162–163; Partha Mitter, *The Triumph of Modernism: India's Artists and the Avant-garde, 1922–47* (Chicago: University of Chicago Press, 2007); Stella Kramrisch, 'Indian Art and Europe', *Rupam* 11 (1922), 81–86.

21 Nakada Sadanosuke, *Pikaso, Mizue* (1925), reissued as *Seiyô Bijutsu Bunko No.18, Pikaso* (Tokyo: Atelier-sha, 1938).

22 Lin Fengmian, 'The Future of Eastern and Western Art', *Oriental Journal* 23, no. 10 (1926): 10.

23 'Chronology', *Pang Hiunkin*, n.d., https://www.panghiunkin.org/chronology.php?lang=en#close, accessed 27 November 2024.

24 Lauren Walden, 'Surrealism in Chinese Periodicals: Hedonism, Horror, and Shanghai's Former French Concession', *Dada/Surrealism* 24 (April 2023), 6.

25 Kuiyi Shen, 'The Lure of the West: Modern Chinese Oil Painting', in Julia F. Andrews and Kuiyi Shen, eds, *A Century in Crisis: Modernity and Tradition in the Art of Twentieth-Century China* (New York: Solomon R. Guggenheim Museum, 1998), 177.

26 Tim Scott, 'George Keyt of Sri Lanka and Picasso of France', transcript of lecture given at the HNB Auditorium, Colombo, 26 January 2012, reproduced in the 36th edition of the monthly lecture series of the National Trust of Sri Lanka.

27 Feng Zikai, *Xiyang hua pai shi'er jiang* (Twelve Lectures on Western Painting) (Shanghai: Kai Ming Shu Dian, 1930), 163.

28 Preface, *L'Art* 1, no. 2 (September 1932): 10–11.

29 See Lauren Walden, 'Surrealism in Chinese Periodicals: Hedonism, Horror and Shanghai's Former French Concession', *Dada/Surrealism* 24 (2023): 6–7.
30 Na's essay, 'The Lives of Parisian Artists and Models', published in *Samcheonli* in March 1932, provides an insightful account of a two-year art study trip around Europe, as quoted from Kim Youngna, 'Cubism in Korea', in Yasuko Furuichi, ed., *Cubism in Asia: Unbounded Dialogues* (Tokyo: National Museum of Modern Art, Tokyo, and Japan Foundation, 2005), 189.
31 Gloria Davies, *Lu Xun's Revolution: Writing in a Time of Violence* (Cambridge, MA: Harvard University Press, 2013).
32 Lam received a letter of introduction from Spanish sculptor Manolo (Manuel Hugué). See Lou Laurin-Lam, *Wifredo Lam Catalogue Raisonné of the Painted Work, Vol. I: 1923–1960* (Lausanne: Acatos, 1996); Catherine David, ed., *The EY Exhibition: Wifredo Lam* (London: Tate Publishing, 2016), 205.
33 The acronym PERSAGI stands for Persatuan Ahli Ahli Gambar Indonesia (Union of Indonesian Painters).
34 Tom van den Berge, 'Picasso in the Tropics: European Modern Painting in Indonesia, 1920–1957', in Susie Protschky and Tom van den Berge, eds, *Modern Times in Southeast Asia: 1920s–1970s* (Leiden: Brill, 2018), 87–113; Sindudarsono Sudjojono, 'We Know Where We Will Be Taking Indonesian Art. Southeast of Now', *Directions in Contemporary Modern Art in Asia* 1, no. 2 (1948): 159–164.
35 Marcel Cachin, 'Picasso a apporté son adhésion au parti de la renaissance française', *L'Humanité*, 5 October 1944.
36 'Picasso Complains that the Thief Is Stupid', *Bright Weekly* 2, no. 1 (1946).
37 Kim Inhye, 'Picasso: Reception in Asian Countries in 1940s–1950s', trans. Yun Heejin, in *Cubism in Asia: Unbounded Dialogues* (Singapore: Singapore Art Museum, 2006), 160.
38 Pierre Daix, *Le siècle de Picasso 2. La guerre, Le parti, La gloire, L'homme seul (1937–1973)* (Paris: Denoël, 1975), 180.
39 Zhang Pei, 'Long Live the Eastern Fortress of Peace! Report on China's Conference for the Protection of World Peace', *People's Daily*, 4 October 1949, 3, quoted in Wu Xueshan, 'Picasso in China: 1817–2019', in *Picasso: Birth of a Genius*, 31.
40 'Bijiasuo de xin xianli: heping gezi zai feixiang' (Picasso's New Offering: The Peace Dove in Flight), *People's Daily*, 17 November 1950.
41 Helena Čapková, 'The Japanese Cubist Body: Mapping Modern Experience in the Pre-WWII Japanese Artistic Network', *ARS* 47 (2014): 125.
42 Gertje Utley, *Picasso: The Communist Years* (New Haven and London: Yale University Press, 2000), 238.
43 Correspondence from Hiraga Kamesky to Pablo Picasso, 15 July 1952, 515AP/C/1953, Pablo Picasso Fonds, Musée national Picasso-Paris.
44 Rachel Leow, 'A Missing Peace', in 'Other Bandungs: Afro-Asian Internationalism in the Early Cold War', special issue, *Journal of World History* 30, nos 1–2 (June 2019): 24.
45 *People's Daily*, 14 December 1952.
46 'Si j'étais né chinois, je ne serais pas peintre, mais écrivain. J'écrirais mes tableaux.' Claude Roy, *La guerre et la paix* (Paris: Cercle d'art, 1954), 43.
47 Chen Chiyu, 'The Combination of Chinese and Western Influences on Chinese Modern Ink Painting with Lin Fengmian, Zhang Ding and Wu Guanzhong as Examples', *Art of the Orient* 2 (2013): 173.
48 In 1953 Qi Baishi was given the title 'People's Artist' by the Central Cultural Ministry of the People's Republic of China.
49 Li Zhaozhong, 'The Stones of Another Mountain: Zhang Ding and Picasso', *Masterpieces Review*, no. 3 (2016): 130, quoted in Wu Xueshan, 'Picasso in China: 1817–2019', in *Picasso: Birth of a Genius*, 21.
50 Xie Jiaxiao, 'Zhang Daqian and Picasso', *Panorama Magazine*, no. 21 (1 August 1975): 14–20.
51 'Zhang Daqian, the Picasso of China', *Sing Tao Evening Post*, 27 May 1968.
52 'Picasso numéro spéciale', special issue, *La nouvelle critique*, no. 130 (November 1961).
53 'Big Picasso Show to Open in Tokyo; $10 Million Exhibit Begins Today—170 Works Listed', *New York Times*, 23 May 1964.
54 Françoise Gilot, *Life with Picasso* (London: Virago, 1990), 70.
55 André Malraux, *Picasso's Mask* (New York: Holt, Rinehart & Winston), 1976, 65.
56 John Berger, *The Success and Failure of Picasso* (London: Penguin, 2018), 120.
57 'Zhou Yang's "Liberalization" Poisoned the Central Academy', *People's Daily*, 16 July 1966, quoted in Wu Xueshan, 'Picasso in China: 1817–2019', in *Picasso: Birth of a Genius*, 35–36.
58 Ratan Parimoo, 'Cubism, World Art and Indian Art', 1968, transcript of keynote speech delivered at a seminar organised by the Lalit Kala Akademi at the 1st Indian Triennale in February 1968. The transcript was later published in the New Delhi journal *Roop Lekha* in 1972 and in the *Times of India* on 23 July the same year.
59 Typed manuscript of a talk delivered by artist K. G. Subramanyan on All India Radio in 1973. The transcript was published under the title 'Picasso and Modern Art' in vol. 22 of *Nandan* magazine (Kala Bhavana, Visva Bharati University, Santiniketan) in 2002.
60 Wang Keping, quoted in Li Xianting, 'On the "Stars Exhibition"', *Meishu* no. 3 (1980), 9.
61 Li Xianting, 'On the "Stars Exhibition"', 9.
62 Zou Difan, 'Dove', *People's Daily*, 19 June 1980, quoted in Wu Xueshan, 'Picasso in China: 1817–2019', in *Picasso: Birth of a Genius*, 37.
63 Raoul Jean Moulin, 'Picasso, 1881–1981: celebración del centenario de su nacimiento.' Paper presented at 'Symposium on Tribute to Picasso', Paris, 1981.
64 Jeanine Warnod, 'Picasso: l'héritier de toutes les cultures', *Le Figaro*, 29 October 1981.
65 Joyce Hei-ting Wong, 'All the World's a Stage: Modernity and Urban Drama in the Art of Luis Chan', in Joyce Hei-ting Wong, ed., *All the World's a Stage: The Art of Luis Chan* (Hong Kong: Hong Kong Arts Centre, 2022), 23.
66 Zasha Colah, quoted in Reema Gehi, 'How Avant-garde Conversations around Picasso's NGMA Exhibit Inspired the Mumbai Mulgi', *Hindustan Times*, 10 September 2023.
67 Shukla Sawant, quoted in Ella Dutta, 'Critics Miss Blue and Rose on Picasso's Palette', *Telegraph India*, 15 December 2001.

Select Bibliography

Ageorges, Sylvain. *Sur les traces des Exposition universelles Paris, 1855–1937*. Paris: Parigramme, 2006.
Ai Zhongxin, ed. 'Congratulations on Picasso's 80th Birthday (Zhu bijiasuo bashi da shou)'. *Meishu* no. 5 (1961): 45–46.
Andrews, Julia Frances, and Shen Kuiyi. *A Century in Crisis: Modernity and Tradition in the Art of Twentieth-Century China*. New York: Solomon R. Guggenheim Museum, 1998.
Berger, John. *The Success and Failure of Picasso*. New York: Knopf Doubleday, 1993; London: Penguin, 2018.
Bernadac, Marie-Laure, and Androula Michael, eds. *Picasso: Propos sur l'art*. Paris: Gallimard, 1998.
Birnbaum, Phyllis. *Glory in a Line: A Life of Foujita – The Artist Caught Between East & West*. New York: Farrar, Straus & Giroux, 2007.
Bourdieu, Pierre. 'L'illusion biographique'. *Actes de la recherche en sciences sociales* 62–63 (June 1986): 69–72.
Brassaï. *Conversations with Picasso*. Translated by Jane Marie Todd. Chicago and London: University of Chicago Press, 1999.
Buisson, Sylvie. *Foujita et ses amis du Montparnasse*. Paris: Éditions Alternatives, 2010.
Buisson, Sylvie, and Dominique Buisson. *La vie et l'œuvre de Léonard-Tsuguharu Foujita*. Paris: ACR Éditions, 1987.
Burgess, Gelett. 'The Wild Men of Paris'. *Architectural Record* (May 1910): 401–414.
Bush, Susan. *The Chinese Literati on Painting: Su Shih (1037–1101) to Tung Ch'i-ch'ang (1555–1636)*. Hong Kong: Hong Kong University Press, 2012.
Cabanne, Pierre. *Le scandale dans l'art*. Paris: Éditions de la Différence, 2007.
——. *Le siècle de Picasso 2: La guerre, le parti, la gloire, l'homme seul (1937–1973)*. Paris: Denoël, 1975.
——. *Le siècle de Picasso 4: La gloire et la solitude (1955–1973)*. Paris: Gallimard, 1992.
Caizergues, Pierre, and Hélène Seckel, eds. *Picasso/Apollinaire: Correspondance*. Paris: Gallimard, 1992.
Calle, Sophie. *Picalso*. Paris: Atelier EXB, 2023.
Caws, Mary Ann. *Pablo Picasso*. London: Reaktion, 2005.
Chen Chiyu. 'The Combination of Chinese and Western Influences on Chinese Modern Ink Painting with Lin Fengmian, Zhang Ding and Wu Guanzhong as Examples'. *Art of the Orient* 2, no. 1 (1 January 2013): 165–188.
Cocteau, Jean. *Picasso*. Paris: L'École des Loisirs, 1996.
Cohen-Solal, Annie. *Picasso: L'Étranger*. Translated by Sam Taylor. Paris: Éditions Fayard, 2021.
——. *Picasso the Foreigner: An Artist in France, 1900–1973*. Translated by Sam Taylor. New York: Farrar, Straus & Giroux, 2023.
Davies, Gloria. *Lu Xun's Revolution: Writing in a Time of Violence*. Cambridge, MA: Harvard University Press, 2013.
Dederer, Claire. *Monsters: A Fan's Dilemma*. New York: Knopf Doubleday, 2023.
Duncan, Carol. 'Virility and Domination in Early Twentieth-Century Vanguard Painting'. In *Feminism and Art History*, edited by Norma Broude and Mary D. Garrard, 293–313. New York: Harper & Row, 1982.
Eco, Umberto, ed. *Histoire de la laideur*. Paris: Flammarion, 2007.
Fluegel, Janet, and William Rubin, eds. *Pablo Picasso: A Retrospective*. New York: Museum of Modern Art, 1980.
Furuichi Yasuko, ed. *Cubism in Asia: Unbounded Dialogues*. Tokyo: National Museum of Modern Art, Tokyo, 2005.
Gilot, Françoise, and Carlton Lake. *Life with Picasso*. London: Virago Press, 1990.
——. *Vivre avec Picasso*. Paris: Calmann-Lévy, 1965.
Guégan, Stéphane. 'Le temps et l'art de l'ambiguïté'. In *Picasso: Au cœur des ténèbres (1939–1945)*, 48–49. Paris: In Fine éditions d'art, 2019.
Hearn, Maxwell K., and Judith G. Smith, eds. *Chinese Art: Modern Expressions*. New York: Metropolitan Museum of Art, 2001.
Herrera, Hayden. *Listening to Stone: The Art and Life of Isamu Noguchi*. New York: Farrar, Straus & Giroux, 2016.
Huffington, Arianna. *Picasso: Creator and Destroyer*. New York: Simon & Schuster, 1988.
Hustvedt, Siri. *A Woman Looking at Men Looking at Women: Essays on Art, Sex, and the Mind*. New York: Simon & Schuster, 2016.
Inada Seisuke and Ueda Tsunetaka. *Pablo Picasso Exhibition–Japan 1964*. Tokyo: Mainichi Newspapers, 1964.
Keen, Kirsten Hoving. 'Picasso's Communist Interlude: The Murals of "War" and "Peace"'. *Burlington Magazine* 122, no. 928 (July 1980): 464–470.
Kim Jaeseok and Cho Jae Hee, eds. *Simon Fujiwara*. Seoul: Gallery Hyundai, 2023.
Kris, Ernst, and Otto Kurz. *Legend, Myth, and Magic in the Image of the Artist: A Historical Experiment*. New Haven and London: Yale University Press, 1979.
Le Thomas, Claire. *Racines populaires du cubisme*. Dijon: Presses du Réel, 2016.
Léautaud, Paul. *Journal littéraire* VIII. Paris: Mercure de France, 1960.
Leiris, Michel. *Wifredo Lam*. Brussels: Didier Devillez Editor, 1997.
——. *Écrits sur l'art*. Paris: CNRS Éditions, 2011.
Madeline, Laurence. *Marie-Thérèse Walter et Pablo Picasso – Biographie d'une relation*. Paris: Nouvelles Éditions Scala, 2022.
Malraux, André. *La tête d'obsidienne*. Paris: Gallimard, 1974.
——. *Picasso's Mask*. New York: Da Capo Press, 1994.
Miller, C. F. B. *Radical Picasso: The Use Value of Genius*. Oakland: University of California Press, 2021.
Mitter, Partha. *The Triumph of Modernism: India's Artists and the Avant-Garde, 1922–1947*. London: Reaktion, 2007.
Nakada Sadanosuke. *Pikaso*. Tokyo: Seiyô Bijutsu Bunko, 36, Atelier-Sha, 1938.
Nochlin, Linda. 'The Vanishing Brothel'. *London Review of Books* 19, no. 5 (6 March 1997), https://www.lrb.co.uk/the-paper/v19/n05/linda-nochlin/the-vanishing-brothel.
——. *Why Have There Been No Great Women Artists?* London: Thames & Hudson, 2021.
Olivier, Fernande. *Picasso et ses amis*. Paris: Pygmalion, 2001.
Ottinger, Didier, ed. *The Picasso Century*. Melbourne: Council of Trustees of the National Gallery of Victoria, 2022.
Parimoo, Ratan. *Art of Three Tagores: From Revival to Modernity*. New Delhi: Kumar Gallery, 2011.
Philippot, Emilia, and François Dareau. *Picasso. Figures*. Rome: MondoMostre, 2021.
Philippot, Emilia, and Wu Xueshan. *Picasso: Birth of a Genius*. Beijing: UCCA Center for Contemporary Art and Culture and Art Publishing House, 2019.
Pi Li, ed. *Chinese Art Since 1970: The M+ Sigg Collection*. Hong Kong: M+ and Thames & Hudson, 2021.
Picasso Exhibition Catalogue Editorial Committee et al., eds. *Picasso: Pablo Picasso Exhibition–Japan, 1964*. Tokyo: National Museum of Modern Art, Tokyo, 1964.
Protschky, Susie, and Tom van den Berge, eds. *Modern Times in Southeast Asia, 1920s–1970s*. Leiden: Brill, 2018.
Puech, Jean-Benoît. 'La création biographique'. In *L'Auteur: Entre biographie et mythographie*, edited by Robert Dion and Frances Fortier, 43–57. Pessac: Presses Universitaires de Bordeaux, 2002.
Raphael, Max. *Proudhon, Marx, Picasso: Trois études sur la sociologie de l'art*. Paris: Éditions Excelsior, 1933.
Richardson, John. *A Life of Picasso: 1881–1906*. New York: Random House, 1991.
Robbe-Grillet, Alain. *Le miroir qui revient*. Paris: Éditions de Minuit, 1984.
Rosenberg, Harold. 'On the Fall of Paris'. *Partisan Review* 7, no. 6 (December 1940): 440–448.
Roy, Claude. *La guerre et la paix*. Paris: Éditions Cercle d'art, 1954.

Scott, Tim. 'George Keyt of Sri Lanka and Picasso of France'. Thirty-sixth lecture in the *Monthly Lecture* series organised by the National Trust of Sri Lanka in Colombo, 26 January 2011.
Secret Images: Picasso and the Japanese Erotic Print. Barcelona: Museo Picasso Barcelona; London: Thames & Hudson, 2010.
Souchère, Dor de la. *Picasso à Antibes.* Paris: Hazan, 1960.
Stein, Gertrude. *The Autobiography of Alice B. Toklas.* New York: Harcourt, Brace and Company, 1933.
Storr, Robert. *Nalini Malani: Listening to the Shades.* New York: Charta & Arario, 2008.
Sturgis, Alexander. *Rebels and Martyrs: The Image of the Artist in the Nineteenth Century.* London: National Gallery, 2006.
Sullivan, Michael. *Art and Artists of Twentieth-Century China.* Berkeley: University of California Press, 1996.
Touratier, Jean-Marie. *Mauvais sang: Les nazis et l'art dégénéré.* Paris: Éditions Galilée, 2018.
Troncy, Éric, ed. *The Echo of Picasso.* Málaga: Museo Picasso Málaga, 2023.
Utley, Gertje R. *Picasso: The Communist Years.* New Haven and London: Yale University Press, 2000.
Wong, Joyce Hei-ting. *All the World's A Stage: The Art of Luis Chan.* Hong Kong: Hong Kong Arts Centre, 2022.
Yau, John. 'Please Wait by the Coatroom: Wifredo Lam in the Museum of Modern Art'. *Arts Magazine* 63, no. 4 (December 1988): 56–59. Reprinted in *The EY Exhibition: Wifredo Lam*, edited by Catherine David, 191–194. London: Tate Publishing, 2016.
Zervos, Christian. 'Conversation avec Picasso'. *Cahiers d'art* X, no. 7–10 (1935): 173–178.

List of Illustrations

Unless stated otherwise,
all works are by Pablo Picasso.

Page 2
Lucien Clergue
Pablo Picasso standing in front of Massacre in Korea *and ceramic elements on the floor at La Californie, Cannes November 4, 1955*
1955
Gelatin silver print, 30.5 × 24.2 cm
Musée national Picasso-Paris
APPH440

Page 6
Yan Pei-Ming
Young Picasso and His Sister—Permanent Rose (detail)
2024
Oil on canvas, 200 × 200 cm
Photo: Clérin-Morin

Page 8
Yan Pei-Ming
Young Picasso and His Sister—Permanent Rose
2024
Oil on canvas, approx. 200 × 370 cm (overall)
Photo: Clérin-Morin

Pages 10–11
Lee Mingwei
Installation view of *Guernica in Sand*, Martin Gropius Bau, Berlin, 2020
Photo: Laura Fiorio

Page 14
Studies
Paris, 1920
Oil on canvas, 100 × 81 cm
Musée national Picasso-Paris
MP65

Page 16, top right
Portrait of Fernande Olivier in the workshop of the sculptor Ignacio Pinazo Martínez at the Bateau-Lavoir, Paris, 1908
Musée national Picasso-Paris
FPPH147

Page 16, bottom left
Lee Miller
Françoise Gilot drawing in La Galloise's room, Vallauris
1953
Gelatin silver print, 10.3 × 11.1 cm
Musée national Picasso-Paris
APPH4383

Page 17
I, Picasso
1901
Oil on canvas, 73.5 × 60.5 cm
Private collection

Page 18
Gertrude Stein
1905–1906
Oil on canvas, 100 × 81.3 cm
Metropolitan Museum of Art, New York

Page 19
Picasso on the cover of *Life International* 31, no. 10, 1961

Page 20
Robert Doisneau
Picasso at the table with buns for fingers at La Galloise, Vallauris, in September 1952
1952
Gelatin silver print, 23.4 × 17.7 cm
Musée national Picasso-Paris
MPPH594

Page 21
Portrait of Marie-Thérèse
6 January 1937
Oil on canvas, 100 × 81 cm
Musée national Picasso-Paris
MP159
Page 22
The archives upon arrival at Musée national Picasso-Paris, 1992
Photo: Laurence Berthon-Marceillac

Page 23
Seated Woman with Arms Crossed
Le Tremblay-sur-Mauldre, 1937
Oil on canvas, 81 × 60 cm
Musée national Picasso-Paris
MP162

Page 24
Science and Charity
Barcelona, 1897
Oil on canvas, 197.5 × 250 cm
Museu Picasso de Barcelona

Page 25
José Ruiz Blasco, Father of the Artist
A Coruña, 1895
Oil on canvas, 52.2 × 32.3 cm
Musée national Picasso-Paris
MP2021-2

Page 26
Diego Velázquez
Young Woman
ca.1650
Oil on canvas, 65 × 51 cm
Private collection

Page 27
The Barefoot Girl
A Coruña, early 1895
Oil on canvas, 75 × 50 cm
Musée national Picasso-Paris
MP2

Page 29
Man with a Cap
A Coruña, early 1895
Oil on canvas, 72.5 × 50 cm
Musée national Picasso-Paris
MP1

Page 30
The Le Nain Brothers
The Happy Family or The Return from Baptism
1642
Oil on canvas, 61 × 78 cm
Musée du Louvre, Paris

Page 31
Return from the Baptism after Le Nain
Montrouge, autumn 1917
Oil on canvas, 162 × 118 cm
Musée national Picasso-Paris
MP56

Page 32
Jacques-Louis David
The Death of Marat
1793
Oil on canvas, 165 × 128 cm
Royal Museums of Fine Arts of Belgium, Brussels

Page 33
Woman with a Stiletto
Paris, 19–25 December 1931
Oil on canvas, 46.5 × 61.5 cm
Musée national Picasso-Paris
MP136

Page 34
Diego Velázquez
Las Meninas
1656
Oil on canvas, 320.3 × 279.1 cm
Museo Nacional del Prado, Madrid

Page 35
Las Meninas
Cannes, 1957
Oil on canvas, 161 × 129 cm
Museu Picasso de Barcelona

Page 36
Édouard Manet
Le déjeuner sur l'herbe
1863
Oil on canvas, 207 × 265 cm
Musée d'Orsay, Paris

Page 37
The Luncheon on the Grass after Manet
Mougins, 12 July 1961
Oil on canvas, 81 × 99.8 cm
Musée national Picasso-Paris
MP216

Page 38
Eugène Delacroix
Women of Algiers in their Apartment
1834
Oil on canvas, 180 × 229 cm
Musée du Louvre, Paris

Page 39
Women of Algiers after Delacroix. VIII
Paris, 31 January 1955
Sugar-lift aquatint, scraper, and burin on copper, 32.9 × 43.5 cm
Musée national Picasso-Paris
MP3022

Page 40
Nicolas Poussin
The Abduction of the Sabine Women
ca.1633–1634
Oil on canvas, 154.6 × 209.9 cm
Metropolitan Museum of Art, New York

Page 41
The Abduction of the Sabine Women
Mougins, 4–8 November 1962
Oil on canvas, 97 × 130 cm
Centre Pompidou, Paris

Page 42, top left
Picasso drawing with a felt-tip pen in the documentary *The Mystery of Picasso* directed by Henri-Georges Clouzot, Victorine studio, Nice, 1955
Gelatin silver print, 18.1 × 13.2 cm
Musée national Picasso-Paris
APPH15223

Page 42, bottom right
Installation view of *Picasso 1970–1972, 201 paintings*, May 23 to September 23, 1973, Palais des Papes, Avignon, France

Page 43
Couple
Mougins, 1970–1971
Oil on plywood, 163.5 × 131.5 cm
Musée national Picasso-Paris
MP1990-41

Page 44
The Old Man
Mougins, 25 September 1970
Oil on canvas, 194 × 130 cm
Musée national Picasso-Paris
MP1990-38

Page 45
The Matador
Mougins, 4 October 1970
Oil on canvas, 145.5 × 114 cm
Musée national Picasso-Paris
MP223

Page 47
Sacré-Cœur
Paris, winter 1909–1910
Oil on canvas, 92.5 × 65 cm
Musée national Picasso-Paris
MP30

Page 48
Le Moulin de la Galette
Paris, November 1900
Oil on canvas, 89.7 × 116.8 cm
Solomon R. Guggenheim Museum, New York

Page 49
At the Moulin Rouge (The Japanese Divan)
1901
Oil on board, 69.5 × 53.7 cm
Private collection

Page 50, top
Edvard Munch
Self-Portrait in Hell
1903
Oil on canvas, 82 × 66 cm
Munch Museum, Oslo

Page 50, bottom
Picasso Room at the Trubetskoy Palace, 1914
Pushkin State Museum of Fine Arts, Moscow
Photo: Pavel Orlov

Page 51
Self-Portrait
Paris, 1901
Oil on canvas, 81 × 60 cm
Musée national Picasso-Paris
MP4

Page 53
Portrait of a Man
Paris and Barcelona, winter 1902–1903
Oil on canvas, 92.5 × 65 cm
Musée national Picasso-Paris
MP5

Page 54
David Douglas Duncan
Pigeons in Picasso's living room and studio of La Californie, Cannes, April 1959
1959
Gelatin silver print
Musée national Picasso-Paris

Page 55
Melancholy Woman
1902
Oil on canvas, 100 × 69.2 cm
Detroit Institute of Arts, Bequest of Robert H. Tannahill, 70.190

Page 56
The Tragedy
Barcelona, 1903
Oil on wood, 105.3 × 69 cm
National Gallery of Art, Washington DC

Page 57
Acrobat on a Ball
1905
Oil on canvas, 147 × 95 cm
Pushkin State Museum of Fine Arts, Moscow

Page 58
Lady with a Fan
1905
Oil on canvas, 100.3 × 81 cm
National Gallery of Art, Washington DC

Page 59
The Blind Man's Meal
1903
Oil on canvas, 95.3 × 94.6 cm
Metropolitan Museum of Art, New York

Page 61
Les Demoiselles d'Avignon
Paris, June–July 1907
Oil on canvas, 243.9 × 233.7 cm
Museum of Modern Art, New York

Page 62
Daniel-Henry Kahnweiler
Autumn 1910
Oil on canvas, 100.4 × 72.4 cm
Art Institute of Chicago

Page 63, left
Man with a Mandolin
Paris, autumn 1911
Oil on canvas, 162 × 71 cm
Musée national Picasso-Paris
MP35

Page 63, right
Man with a Guitar
Paris, autumn 1911
Oil on canvas, 154 × 77.5 cm
Musée national Picasso-Paris
MP34

Page 64
Still Life: 'Job'
Paris, 1916
Oil and sand on canvas, 43.2 × 34.9 cm
Museum of Modern Art, New York

Page 65
Still Life with Chair Caning
Paris, spring 1912
Oil and oilcloth on canvas framed with rope, 29 × 37 cm
Musée national Picasso-Paris
MP36

Page 66
Marcel Duchamp
Bicycle Wheel
1913/1964
Metal and painted wood, 126.5 × 31.5 × 63.5 cm
Centre Pompidou, Paris

Page 67
Eva Hesse
Ennead
1966
Acrylic, papier-mâché, plastic, plywood, and string, 243.8 × 99.1 × 43.2 cm
Institute of Contemporary Art, Boston

Page 68
Violin and Music Sheet
Paris, autumn 1912
Coloured paper, music score, and wrapping paper cut and glued on cardboard, 78 × 63.5 cm
Musée national Picasso-Paris
MP368

Page 69
Glass of Absinthe
1914
Painted bronze with absinthe spoon, 22.5 × 12.1 × 8.6 cm
Philadelphia Museum of Art

Page 70
Object with Palm Leaf
Juan-les-Pins, 27 August 1930
Tinted sand, organic matter, cardboard, and nails glued and sewn on the reverse of canvas and stretcher, 25 × 33 × 4.5 cm
Musée national Picasso-Paris
MP129

Page 71
Landscape with Boats
Juan-les-Pins, 28 August 1930
Tinted sand, organic matter, cardboard, and miniature boats glued and sewn on the reverse of canvas and stretcher, 26 × 36 × 7.5 cm
Musée national Picasso-Paris
MP130

Page 72
Composition with Glove
Juan-les-Pins, 22 August 1930
Sand tinted in places on back of canvas and frame, glove, cardboard, and plants glued and sewn on canvas, 27.5 × 35.5 × 8 cm
Musée national Picasso-Paris
MP123

Page 73
Figure and Profile
Paris, 1928
Oil on canvas, 72 × 60 cm
Musée national Picasso-Paris
MP103

Page 74
Large Nude in a Red Armchair
Paris, 5 May 1929
Oil on canvas, 195 × 129 cm
Musée national Picasso-Paris
MP113

Page 75
The Acrobat
Paris, 18 January 1930
Oil on canvas, 162 × 130 cm
Musée national Picasso-Paris
MP120

Page 76
Bottle of Bass, Glass, and Newspaper
Paris, spring 1914
Cut and painted tinplate, sand, wire, and paper, 20 × 14 × 8.5 cm
Musée national Picasso-Paris
MP249

Page 77, bottom left
Head of a Bull
Paris, spring 1942
Saddle and handlebars (leather and metal), 33.5 × 43.5 × 19 cm
Musée national Picasso-Paris
MP330

Page 77, top right
Guitar
Paris, spring 1926
Ropes, newspaper, mop, and nails on painted canvas, 96 × 130 cm
Musée national Picasso-Paris
MP87

Page 78
Iron statue of Ebo, god of war, at the Musée d'Ethnographie du Trocadéro
1895
Musée du quai Branly – Jacques Chirac, Paris

Page 79
Head of a Woman
Paris, 1929–1930
Iron, sheet metal, painted springs, and strainers, 100 × 37 × 59 cm
Musée national Picasso-Paris
MP270

Page 80
Little Girl Jumping Rope
Vallauris, 1950
Plaster, wicker basket, cake tin, shoes, wood, iron, and ceramic, 152 × 65 × 66 cm
Musée national Picasso-Paris
MP336

Page 81
The Woman with the Stroller
Vallauris, 1950
Bronze, 203 × 145 × 61 cm
Musée national Picasso-Paris
MP337

Page 82
Plate with a Knife, Fork, Apple Cut in Two and Peel
Vallauris, 1947–1948
White clay with brushed slip glaze, 4.5 × 33 × 33 cm
Musée national Picasso-Paris
MP3687

Page 83
Owl with a Woman's Head
Vallauris, 1951–27 February 1953
White clay with slip glaze and pastel, 33.5 × 34.5 × 24 cm
Musée national Picasso-Paris
MP346

Page 84
Goat Skull, Bottle, and Candle
Paris, 25 March 1952
Oil on canvas, 89 × 116 cm
Musée national Picasso-Paris
MP206

Page 85
Foundry: C. Valsuani
Goat Skull, Bottle, and Candle
Vallauris, 1951–1953
Painted bronze, 79 × 93 × 54 cm
Musée national Picasso-Paris
MP341

Page 87
Jug Painted with Fauns
Vallauris, ca.1951
Red clay with slip glaze, 26 × 22.5 × 16 cm
Musée national Picasso-Paris
MP3723

Page 88
The Sideboard at Vauvenargues
Cannes-Vauvenargues, 23 March 1959–23 January 1960
Oil on canvas, 195 × 280 cm
Musée national Picasso-Paris
MP214

Page 89
Portrait of Nusch Eluard
Paris, autumn 1937
Oil on canvas, 92 × 65 cm
Musée national Picasso-Paris
MP1990-19

Page 90
Costume design by Picasso for the ballet *Parade*, worn by dancer Maximillian Statkiewicz in the role of 'The Manager from New York'
1917

Pages 92–93
Guernica
Paris, 1 May–4 June 1937
Oil on canvas, 349.3 × 776.6 cm
Museo Nacional Centro de Arte Reina Sofía, Madrid

Page 94
Head of a Woman
Dinard, summer 1922
Chalk on paper, 107.6 × 72.1 cm
Metropolitan Museum of Art, New York

Page 95
Young Sculptor Finishing a Plaster
Paris, 23 March 1933
Etching on copper, 34.7 × 26 cm
Musée national Picasso-Paris
MP2588

Page 96
Sculptures *Bust of a Woman* and *Head of a Woman* in the Boisgeloup studio, Gisors, 1931
Musée national Picasso-Paris
Photo: Boris Kochno

Page 97
Sculptor and His Self-Portrait Serving as a Pedestal for the Head of Marie-Thérèse
Paris, 26 March 1933
Etching on copper, 44.5 × 33.4 cm
Musée national Picasso-Paris
MP1982-107

Page 98
The Dream
1932
Oil on canvas, 130 × 97 cm
Private collection

Page 99
Large Still Life with Pedestal Table
Paris, 11 March 1931
Oil on canvas, 195 × 130.5 cm
Musée national Picasso-Paris
MP134

Page 100, top
Jean-Léon Gérôme
Pygmalion and Galatea
ca.1890
Oil on canvas, 88.9 × 68.6 cm
Metropolitan Museum of Art, New York

Page 100, bottom
Auguste Rodin
Pygmalion and Galatea
Modelled 1889, carved ca.1908–1909
Marble, 97.2 × 88.9 × 76.2 cm
Metropolitan Museum of Art, New York

Page 101
The Sculptor
Paris, 7 December 1931
Oil on plywood, 128.5 × 96 cm
Musée national Picasso-Paris
MP135

Page 102
Blind Minotaur Guided through a Starry Night by Marie-Thérèse with a Pigeon
Paris, 3 December 1934–1 January 1935
Aquatint treated with a scraper and drypoint on copper, 31.8 × 45.4 cm
Musée national Picasso-Paris
MP2701

Page 103
Dora Maar
Self-Portrait
1935
Autochrome, 18 × 13 cm
Centre Pompidou, Paris

Pages 104–105
Dora and the Minotaur
Mougins, 5 September 1936
Graphite pencil, coloured pencils, ink, and scratchings on paper, 40.5 × 73.5 cm
Musée national Picasso-Paris
MP1998-308

Page 106
Portrait of Dora Maar
Paris, 1937
Oil on canvas, 92 × 65 cm
Musée national Picasso-Paris
MP158

Page 107
Portrait of Dora Maar
Paris, 23 November 1937
Oil on canvas, 55.3 × 46.3 cm
Musée national Picasso-Paris
MP166

Page 108
Nessus and Déjanire
Juan-les-Pins, 12 September 1920
Ink on folded linen-textured woven paper, 21.3 × 27.5 cm
Musée national Picasso-Paris
MP935

Page 109
Faith Ringgold
Picasso's Studio
1991
Acrylic on canvas; printed and tie-dyed fabric, 185.4 × 172.7 cm
Worcester Art Museum, Massachusetts

Pages 110–111
Jaune Quick-to-See Smith
Trade Canoe for Don Quixote
2004
Acrylic, pencil, charcoal, and oil on canvas, 152.4 × 508 cm
Denver Art Museum

Page 111, top
Anti-Iraq War protest in New York City, 2003
Photo: Gregory Sholette

Page 111, bottom
Maria Llopis and her students at the Picasso Museum in Barcelona, 2021
Photo: Ismael Llopis

Page 112
Woman's Head (Fernande)
Paris, 1909–1910
Oil on canvas, 60 × 50 cm
Museo Nacional Centro de Arte Reina Sofía, Madrid

Page 113
Tanaami Keiichi
Pleasure of Picasso—Mother and Child No.653
2023
Acrylic on canvas, 41 × 31.8 × 2 cm
M+, Hong Kong

Pages 116–117
Massacre in Korea
Vallauris, 18 January 1951
Oil on plywood, 110 × 210 cm
Musée national Picasso-Paris
MP203

Page 118, top
Jacques-Louis David
Oath of the Horatii
1784
Oil on canvas, 330 × 425 cm
Musée du Louvre, Paris

Page 118, bottom
Jacques-Louis David
The Intervention of the Sabine Women
1799
Oil on canvas, 385 × 522 cm
Musée du Louvre, Paris

Page 119, top
Francisco Goya
The Third of May 1808
1814
Oil on canvas, 268 × 347 cm
Museo Nacional del Prado, Madrid

Page 119, bottom
Édouard Manet
The Execution of Emperor Maximilian
1868–1869
Oil on canvas, 252 × 302 cm
Kunsthalle Mannheim

Page 120
The Charnel House
Paris, 1944–1945
Oil and charcoal on canvas, 199.8 × 250.1 cm
Museum of Modern Art, New York

Page 121
Dove in Flight
Vallauris, 9 July 1950
Lithograph on ivory wove paper, 56.5 × 76.2 cm
Art Institute of Chicago

Page 123
The Dancer Sada Yacco
1900–1901
Pastel, crayon, and ink on paper, 37.1 × 25.5 cm
Private Collection, courtesy of Ward Moretti Ltd

Page 124, top
Raphael and the Fornarina. XX: The Pope Leaves
Mougins, 1968
Etching on copper printed on Rives vellum paper 14.8 × 20.9 cm
Museu Picasso de Barcelona

Page 124, bottom
Katsukawa Shunchō
Couple Sheltering Behind a Shōji Door
1789–1801
Colour woodblock print, 21.7 × 32.5 cm
Private collection

Page 125, top left
Léonard Tsuguharu Foujita
Fujita, Reclining Nude with Toile de Jouy
1922
Oil, ink, charcoal, and pencil on canvas, 130 × 195 cm
Musée d'Art Moderne de Paris

Page 125, bottom left
Zhang Daqian
Lady Holding a Fan
1944
Ink and colour on paper, 128.8 × 65.7 cm
Hong Kong Museum of Art

Page 125, bottom right
Pablo Picasso and Zhang Daqian at Villa La Californie, Cannes, 1956

Page 126, left
Lin Fengmian
Composition
ca.1934
Oil on canvas

Page 126, right
Fang Ganmin
Melody in Autumn
1933
Oil on canvas

Page 127
Lin Fengmian
Still Life
1952
Oil on canvas, 68 × 68.5 cm

Page 128, left
Tōgō Seiji
Playing the Contrabass
1915
Oil on canvas, 153 × 75.4 cm
Sompo Museum of Art, Tokyo

Page 128, top right
Kawaguchi Kigai
Still Life, Mandolin
1927–1931
Oil on canvas, 116.6 × 81.5 cm
National Museum of Modern Art, Tokyo

Page 128, bottom right
Sakata Kazuo
Cubistic Figure
1925
Oil on canvas, 90 × 65.1 cm
Okayama Prefectural Museum of Art

Page 129, left
Yorozu Tetsugorō
Self-Portrait with Red Eyes
1912–1913
Oil on canvas, 60.7 × 45.5 cm
Iwate Museum of Art

Page 129, right
Yorozu Tetsugorō
Leaning Woman
1917
Oil on canvas, 162.5 × 112.5 cm
National Museum of Modern Art, Tokyo

Page 130
Exhibition view of Jacqueline de la Baume Dürrbach's *Guernica (Tapestry after Pablo Picasso)* (1955) at *Picasso: Guernica*, National Museum of Western Art, Tokyo, 1962

Page 133
David Hockney
The Massacre and the Problems of Depiction
2003
Watercolour on paper, 143.5 × 183.5 cm
David Hockney Foundation

Page 134, top
Jasper Johns
Untitled
1990
Oil on canvas, 80 × 104.2 cm
Private collection

Page 134, bottom
George Condo
Spanish Head Composition
1988
Oil and collage on paper mounted on canvas, 299.7 × 248.9 cm
Museum of Modern Art, New York

Page 135, top left
Maurizio Cattelan
Untitled
1998
Chromogenic print, 183 × 228.6 cm
Fundación Almine y Bernard Ruiz-Picasso

Page 135, top right
Jean-Michel Basquiat
Untitled (Pablo Picasso)
1984
Oil, acrylic, and oil sticks on metal, 90.5 × 90. 5 cm
Private collection

Page 135, bottom right
Robert Colescott
Les Demoiselles d'Alabama: Vestidas
1985
Acrylic on canvas, 233.6 × 233.6 cm
Seattle Art Museum

Page 136
Atul Dodiya
Lamentation
1997
Oil, acrylic, and marble dust on canvas, 177 × 244 cm
RPG Collection

Page 137
Yokoo Tadanori
Marriage of Sympathetic and Parasympathetic Nerves
1991
Acrylic on canvas, 162 × 130.3 cm
Private collection

Page 138
Chéri Samba
What Future For Our Art? (1/3)
1997
Acrylic and glitter on canvas, 131 × 195 cm
The Jean Pigozzi African Art Collection

Page 139
Zeng Fanzhi
Picasso
2011
Oil on canvas, 180 × 150 cm
Collection of the artist

Page 141
Zeng Fanzhi
Picasso
2012
Oil on canvas, 180 × 150 cm
Private collection

Page 142
Yasumasa Morimura
A Requiem: Theater of Creativity / Self-Portrait as Pablo Picasso
2010
Gelatin silver print, 120 × 90 cm
M+, Hong Kong

Page 143
Yasumasa Morimura
Portrait (Futago)
1989
Chromogenic print, gel medium, 210 × 300 cm
Mori Art Museum, Tokyo

Page 144
Mother and Child (First Steps)
Paris, 21 May 1943; revised summer 1943
Oil on canvas, 130.2 × 97.1 cm
Yale University Art Gallery, New Haven
Gift of Stephen Carlton Clark, B.A. 1903

Page 145
Tanaami Keiichi
Pleasure of Picasso–Mother and Child 0221
2020
Acrylic on canvas, 30 × 30 × 3.7 cm
M+, Hong Kong. Gift of Keiichi Tanaami and Shinji Nanzuka

Page 146, bottom left
Tanaami Keiichi
Pleasure of Picasso–Mother and Child No.379
2020–2022
Acrylic on canvas, 41 × 31.8 × 2 cm
M+, Hong Kong

Page 146, top right
Tanaami Keiichi
Pleasure of Picasso–Mother and Child No.057
2020–2021
Acrylic on canvas, 41 × 31.8 × 2 cm
M+, Hong Kong

Page 147, left
Isamu Noguchi
Leda
1928
Aluminium bronze, brass, and marble, 59.4 × 30.2 × 32.1 cm; base: 2.9 × 38.1 × 38.1 cm
Isamu Noguchi Foundation and Garden Museum

Page 147, right
Constantin Brâncuși
Bird in Space
1932–1940
Brass, 151 × 21.6 × 16.5 cm
Solomon R. Guggenheim Foundation Peggy Guggenheim Collection, Venice, 1976

Page 148
Isamu Noguchi
Figure
1945
Tennessee marble, 152.4 × 54.3 × 34.3 cm
Image: ©INFGM

Page 149
Isamu Noguchi
Strange Bird
1945/1971
Brushed bronze, 141 × 54 × 51 cm
M+, Hong Kong
2020.288

Page 150
Figure
Paris, autumn 1927
Oil on plywood, 129 × 96 cm
Musée national Picasso-Paris
MP101

Page 151
Figures by the Sea
Paris, 12 January 1931
Oil on canvas, 130 × 195 cm
Musée national Picasso-Paris
MP131

Page 152
Wifredo Lam
The Jungle
1943
Gouache on paper on canvas, 239.4 × 229.9 cm
Museum of Modern Art, New York

Page 154
Guang Tingbo
I Graze Horse for My Motherland
1973
Oil on canvas, 127.5 × 249 cm
M+ Sigg Collection, Hong Kong. By donation
2012.380

Page 155, top left
Zheng Ziyan
Self-Portrait
1978
Oil on canvas, 34.6 × 27.7 × 2 cm
M+, Hong Kong
2017.176

Page 155, bottom left
Shi Zhenyu
Drunk
1974
Oil on canvas on masonite, 75 × 66.7 × 4.3 cm
M+, Hong Kong
2017.183

Page 155, bottom right
Wang Aihe
Portrait of Zhang Wei
1974
Oil on canvas, 37.7 × 27.3 cm
M+, Hong Kong
2016.807

Page 156
Wei Hai
Lady in Blue and Cloves
1975
Oil on canvas, 134.4 × 62 × 3.7 cm
M+, Hong Kong
2017.181

Page 157
Celestina (Woman with a Cloudy Eye)
Barcelona, March 1904
Oil on canvas, 74.5 × 58.5 cm
Musée national Picasso-Paris
MP1989-5

Page 158
Luis Chan
Cubist Sea Shore
1959
Oil on board, 40.5 × 51 cm
M+, Hong Kong

Page 159
Luis Chan
Joy of Life
1969
Acrylic on paper, 102 × 152 cm
M+, Hong Kong

Page 161
Firenze Lai
The Bone Setting Clinic
2012
Acrylic on canvas, 32.7 × 28.6 × 2 cm
M+, Hong Kong
2012.1620

Page 162
Irene Chou
Portrait #2
1970s
Ink and colour on paper, 217.5 × 107.9 cm
M+, Hong Kong
2012.1638

Page 163
Irene Chou
Untitled
1970s
Ink on paper, 91 × 91 cm
M+, Hong Kong. Gift of the Yiqingzhai Collection

Page 164
Feng Guodong
Body
1978
Oil on canvas, 76.5 × 108.5 × 3.5 cm
M+, Hong Kong
2018.1132

Page 166
Gu Dexin
B24
1983
Oil on canvas, 108 × 88 cm
M+, Hong Kong. Gift of Yang Bin and Yan Qing

Page 167
Fang Lijun
1995.2
1995
Oil on canvas, 250 × 180 cm
M+ Sigg Collection, Hong Kong. By donation
2012.322

Page 169
Madokoro (Akutagawa) Saori
God of Spring
1954
Dyed linen, 89.6 × 130.3 cm
M+, Hong Kong
2022.65

Page 170
Nalini Malani
In Search of Vanished Blood
2012
Single-channel digital video projection (colour, sound), duration: 11 min. 24 sec.
M+, Hong Kong. Gift of an anonymous donor, 2018
2019.528

Page 171, left
Pixy Liao
Mind-control is a woman's essential skill
2010
Inkjet print, 50 × 37.5 cm
M+, Hong Kong
2023.112

Page 171, centre
Pixy Liao
We are connected
2015
Inkjet print, 100 × 75 cm
M+, Hong Kong
2023.115

Page 171, right
Pixy Liao
The woman who clicks the shutter
2018
Inkjet print, 100 × 75 cm
M+, Hong Kong
2023.116

Page 173
Cai Guo-Qiang
Gunpowder Drawing No. 8-A5
1988
Gunpowder and acrylic on canvas, 226 × 180 × 6 cm
M+, Hong Kong
2016.716

Pages 174–175, left to right
Haegue Yang
Totem Robots: Totem Robot – Forward
2010
Clothing rack, casters, light bulbs, cable, zip ties, terminal strips, metal chains, metal rings, stainless steel hanging garment dryer, aluminium reflector, dustpan, sierra cup, plastic funnels, tin can, darklight louvre, price sign, felt, mirror, plexiglass, plexiglass stick, metal rack grid, hair rollers, sink strainers, clamp, hairpieces, mini globe, and stethoscope, 199 × 130 × 80 cm

Totem Robots: Totem Robot – Askew
2010
Clothing rack, casters, light bulbs, cable, zip ties, terminal strips, metal hangers, plastic funnels, elastic net, bells, float, aluminium reflector, darklight louvre, metal rings, metal chains, paper clips, rubber toy animal, hair rollers, and hairpieces, 190 × 130 × 75 cm

Totem Robots: Totem Robot – Sidewise
2010
Clothing rack, casters, light bulbs, cable, zip ties, terminal strips, grill grid, paint grid, sink strainer, metal rings, metal chains, spectacle frame, fringe, knitting yarn, hairpieces, hair rollers, bells, pine cone, seashells, and tea strainer, 188 × 107 × 102 cm

Courtesy of the artist's collection
Photo: Chunho An

Page 176
Foundry: C. Valsuani
The Bathers
Cannes, summer 1956
Bronze, dimensions variable
Musée national Picasso-Paris
MP352–MP357

Pages 178–179
Simon Fujiwara
Who vs Who vs Who? (A Picture of a Massacre)
2024
Acrylic, charcoal, and pastel on canvas, 247.2 × 427.2 × 8.2 cm (framed)
M+, Hong Kong

Pages 180–181
Dead Birds
Sorgues, summer 1912
Oil on canvas, 46 × 65 cm
Museo Nacional Centro de Arte Reina Sofía, Madrid
Legado Douglas Cooper, 1995

Page 183, left
Portrait of Picasso and his sister Lola in Málaga, Spain, ca.1888
Musée national Picasso-Paris

Page 183, right
Hakuba-kai (White Horse Society), Paris, 1900
Front: Iwamura Tōru; centre (from left): Kume Keiichirō, Kuroda Seiki, Gōda Kiyoshi; back (from left): Sano Akira, Wada Eisaku, Okada Saburōsuke, Shōdai Tameshige

Page 184, top
Study for Last Moments
Barcelona, 1899
Charcoal, chalk, and black pencil on paper, 29.7 × 39.7 cm
Museu Picasso de Barcelona

Page 184, bottom left
Kuroda Seiki
Lakeside
1897
Oil on canvas, 69 × 84.7 cm
Kuroda Memorial Hall, Tokyo

Page 184, bottom right
Illustration of Sada Yacco, based on a photograph by Paul Nadar, on the cover of French serial *Le Théâtre*, no. 44, 11 October 1900

Page 185, left
Poster design of Sada Yacco
ca.1901
Gouache and Indian ink on paper
Succession Picasso

Page 185, right
Trocadéro Park, China Palace
1900
Petit Palais, Musée des beaux-arts de la ville de Paris
Photo: Neurdein Frères

Page 186, left
Coverage of works of art by Chinese students exhibited in Tokyo, published in *Liangyou* (The Young Companion), no. 91, 1 August 1934

Page 186, right
Gertrude and Leo Stein's studio at 27 rue de Fleurus, Paris, ca.1905. Among two paintings by Paul Gauguin—*Three Tahitian Women Against a Yellow Background* (State Hermitage Museum; left) and *Sunflowers* (Bührle Collection; right)—are a selection of Japanese prints
Beinecke Rare Book & Manuscript Library, Yale University, New Haven

Page 187
Chinese-inspired landscape by Picasso from the artist's sketchbook
Paris, end of June–beginning of July 1907
Musée national Picasso-Paris
MP1990-96.08r

Page 188, left
Picasso in his studio with a collection of African art in the background, photographed at Bateau-Lavoir, 13 Place Émile Goudeau, Montmartre, 1908
Musée national Picasso-Paris
Photo: Madeleine Coursaget

Page 188, top right
Woman with a Mandolin
1909
Oil on canvas, 92 × 73 cm
State Hermitage Museum, St Petersburg

Page 188, bottom right
Léonard Tsuguharu Foujita
Self-Portrait
1936
Oil on canvas, 43 × 64 cm
Masakichi Hirano Art Foundation

Page 189
Costume design by Pablo Picasso for the ballet *Parade*, worn by the 'Chinese Conjuror', 1917
Victoria and Albert Museum, London

Page 190
Guitar on a Table
Paris, autumn 1912
Oil, sand, and charcoal on canvas, 51.1 × 61.6 cm
Collection of Hood Museum of Art, Dartmouth. Gift of Nelson A. Rockefeller, class of 1930

Page 191
Illustrated postcard from Gaganendranath Tagore to Roop Krishna Esq, ca.1920–1925. The message (verso) reads: 'My dear Roop, many thanks for your kind greetings for the new year ... I am practising Cubism and this is the result. Yours affl. G.Tagore.'
Dated 17 April
V&A Collection, London

Page 192, left
Koga Harue
Woman Divers
1923
Watercolour and pencil on paper, 50.4 × 38.1 cm
National Museum of Modern Art, Tokyo

Page 192, right
Nakada Sadanosuke
Pikaso
First published in *Mizue*, 1925, reissued and published in *Seiyō Bijutsu Bunko*, no. 18, 1938

Page 193
Pang Hiunkin
Mother and Son
1928
Watercolour on paper, 36 × 26.5 cm
Private collection

Page 194
George Keyt
Triptych
1929
Oil on canvas, approx. 172 × 228 cm (overall)
Kiran Nadar Museum of Art, New Delhi

Page 195
'Exhibition announcement of Storm Society Paintings', *Shidai* (Modern Miscellany) 5, no. 1, 1933: 15–16. Courtesy of Pang Hiunkin Archives, Li Ching Cultural and Educational Foundation

Page 196
Wifredo Lam
The Awakening I
1938
Gouache on paper mounted on canvas, 100 × 71 cm
Private collection

Page 197
M. F. Husain
Set design for *Murder in the Cathedral* by T. S. Eliot, dir. E. Alkazi, Theatre Group, Bombay, 1953
Dimensions and medium unverifiable

Page 198
Picasso's *La colombe* becomes a symbol of peace, depicted on the poster for the First International Peace Congress in Paris, 1949
Mourlot Editions, Paris

Page 200, left
Picasso exhibition poster, Takashimaya Department Store, Tokyo, 1951

Page 200, right
Picasso's *Dove in Flight* (1950) decorates the Asia and Pacific Rim Peace Conference in Beijing, October 1952

Page 201
Picasso's dove referenced on the cover of *Manhua Monthly*, no. 32, July 1953
M+, Hong Kong
CL.2017.4.23

Page 202, left
Zhang Daqian and Picasso at the artist's residence Villa La Californie, Cannes, 1956
Museum of Sichuan

Page 202, right
Qi Baishi
Drawing from *Album of Insects and Plants*
1943
Ink on paper, 25.7 × 34.3 cm
Metropolitan Museum of Art, New York

Page 203
Branch with Insect (17.6.1956 II) by Picasso from the artist's sketchbook *La Californie*
9 March 1956–17 June 1956
Ink on paper
Fundación Almine y Bernard Ruiz Picasso, Madrid

Page 204
Installation shot of Picasso's *The Bathers* (1956) at the National Museum of Modern Art, Tokyo, 1964
Museum of New Zealand Te Papa Tongarewa
Photo: Brian Brake

Page 205
Members of the Baroda Group at the Fine Arts College, Baroda, Gujarat, India, 1956. Posing with their works (clockwise from top right): Feroz Katpitia, Jyoti Bhatt, Prafull Dave, Triloke Kaul, Prabha Dongre, Kumud Patel, G. R. Santosh, Ratan Parimoo, Shanti Dave, and Raghav Kaneria
Photo: Asia Art Archive/Jyoti Bhatt Archive

Page 206, left
Picasso Original Prints 1959–1969 exhibition poster, City Museum and Art Gallery (now Hong Kong Museum of Art), 1974
M+, Hong Kong
2019.19

Page 206, right
Liu Heung Shing
China After Mao—Wang Keping Demands Freedom for Art, Beijing
1979
Inkjet print, 68.7 × 58.7 cm
M+, Hong Kong
2012.2094

Page 207, top
Inaugural ceremony of *Picasso Intime*, Hong Kong Museum of Art, 1982
Photo: Ha Bik Chuen
M+, Hong Kong

Page 207, bottom
Inaugural ceremony of *Picasso Intime*, Hong Kong Museum of Art, 1982
Photo: Ha Bik Chuen
M+, Hong Kong

Page 208, top
Sleeping Woman on Red Cushion (Marie-Thérèse)
1932
Private collection

Page 208, bottom
Luis Chan
Drawing on top of *Sleeping Woman on Red Cushion (Marie-Thérèse)* by Pablo Picasso
ca.1982

Page 209, left
Picasso Pavilion poster
1984
Hakone Open Air Museum, Japan

Page 209, right
Julie Lluch
Picasso y Yo
ca.1985
Terracotta and acrylic
Gilda Cordero-Fernando Collection

Page 210, left
German federal president Roman Herzog and collector Irene Ludwig with Jiang Zemin, president of the People's Republic of China, in front of two Picasso paintings, *Infantryman with a Bird* (1972) and *Man and Woman by a Flower Vase* (1970). Ludwig Museum for International Art/National Art Museum of China, Beijing. Photo: Martin Athenstädt/picture alliance via Getty Images

Page 210, right
Inaugural ceremony tour of *Picasso: Metamorphoses 1900–1972* at the National Gallery of Modern Art, New Delhi, 2002, with Picasso's *The Goat* (1950) in the foreground
Photo: National Gallery of Modern Art, New Delhi, India

Page 211
Docent tour of Picasso's *Woman Seated in a Red Armchair* (1932) on display at the China Pavilion, Shanghai, 2011
Photo: © ChinaImages via Depositphotos

Pages 212–213
Horse Head. Sketch for *Guernica*
Paris, 2 May 1937
Oil on canvas, 65 × 92 cm
Museo Nacional Centro de Arte Reina Sofía, Madrid
Legado Picasso, 1981

Artists' Biographies

Cai Guo-Qiang
born 1957, Fujian

Best known for his explosive gunpowder events, Cai Guo-Qiang has undertaken an artistic journey that has brought him from his home in Quanzhou to Japan and later to the United States. Drawing on a variety of sources for inspiration, such as humanity's relationship to the planet, his childhood surrounded by the sound of cannon and fireworks, as well as motifs and themes from Chinese culture and mythology, his practice encompasses various mediums, from painting to installation to performance art, as well as curatorial projects and collaborations. Among the first contemporary Chinese artists to break into not only the international art scene but also mainstream consciousness, Cai's works have been featured in major international exhibitions and events, most notably the 2008 Beijing Olympics.

—

Luis Chan
born 1905, Panama; died 1995, Hong Kong

Luis Chan was born in Panama but moved to Hong Kong at the age of 5, where he stayed for the rest of his life and established himself as one of the most vibrant portraitists of life in the city. Largely self-taught from books, magazine subscriptions, and an art degree by post, Chan's artworks resist easy definition, negotiating the languages of Western modernism and Hong Kong's New Ink Movement to depict characters and creatures simultaneously appropriated from his daily life, the everyday lives of people around him, and his imagination. Chan was a well-regarded figure in both the English- and Cantonese-speaking circles of Hong Kong's art community from the 1930s until his death in 1995, playing the roles of artist, writer, critic, curator, and teacher. His eccentric, psychedelic, and ever-changing styles and techniques have cemented his place as one of the founders of modern art in the city.

—

Irene Chou
born 1924, Shanghai; died 2011, Australia

Irene Chou is considered one of the most accomplished and idiosyncratic artists of the New Ink Movement in Hong Kong. After a progressive upbringing in Shanghai, she moved to Hong Kong in 1949 where she studied with second-generation Lingnan School painter Zhao Shao'ang, among other ink masters. In 1968 she joined the New Ink Movement, led by her mentor Lui Shou-kwan. Departing from the naturalistic styles of her male counterparts, including Lui, Chou developed an unprecedented visual language of her own. She painted organic, bodily forms, depicting a world of biomorphic elements that draw from the natural, sensual world but are clearly not of it. A practitioner of meditation and qigong, she maintained a lifelong interest in the relationship between the individual and the universe, often describing her works as portraits of the universe of her mind.

—

Jacqueline de la Baume Dürrbach
1920–1990, France

Jacqueline de la Baume Dürrbach was a French master weaver who created her own works as well as tapestry translations of major Cubist works. She created life-sized interpretations of Pablo Picasso's paintings, including *Guernica* (1937) in 1955 and *Les Demoiselles d'Avignon* (1907) in 1958. One of her *Guernica* tapestries has been hanging in the headquarters of the United Nations in New York City almost continuously since 1985. Because she modified the original compositions by simplifying or changing colours to suit the medium of tapestry, Dürrbach's works could be controversial. However, Picasso was satisfied with the tapestry recreations of his work, going so far as to display the *Les Demoiselles d'Avignon* tapestry at his studio at Villa La Californie. He considered Dürrbach's version 'far better than the original'.

—

Fang Ganmin
1906–1984, Zhejiang

Fang Ganmin was among one of the first generation of Chinese painters who trained abroad in France. After studying art in Shanghai in 1924, he attended the École des Beaux-Arts de Paris beginning in 1927. Two years later he returned to China to become an educator, bringing back the oil painting techniques and the modernist art styles he had learned from his time overseas. He formed part of the cohort of French-trained artists and academics who would go on to hold key positions at various major Chinese arts institutions. His paintings reflect the influence of Cubism and other styles he had encountered during his studies, but many of these works were destroyed when modernist art fell out of favour before and during the Cultural Revolution. Among his students are important figures of modern Chinese painting, such as Zao Wou-Ki (1920–2013), Chu Teh-Chun (1920–2014), and Wu Guanzhong (1919–2010).

—

Fang Lijun
born 1963, Hebei

The work of Fang Lijun exemplifies the contemporary art movement Cynical Realism. Best known for his woodblock prints and paintings depicting bald figures, his visual language suggests the disillusionment of Chinese society following the 1989 Tiananmen Square incident. The artist's compositions often feature impersonal, monumental heads in the foreground and ominous figures in the background, conveying a sense of ambivalence towards individual freedom and collectivism.

—

Feng Guodong
born 1948, Hebei; died 2005, Beijing

Working in a wide range of mediums, Feng Guodong produced a body of work characterised by unconventional techniques, distinctive colour palettes, and a unique visual language. Initially self-taught, he was later selected by his unit at the factory where he worked to take the fine art training course at the Beijing Working People's Cultural Palace. It was there he met Wang Luyan (born 1956) and other artists who played an important role in the '85 New Wave movement. Affiliated with the No Name Group, Feng made reference to the intuitive styles of Impressionists and Post-Impressionists in his paintings. Later in life he turned to assemblage and sculpture. Despite his renown, Feng was never swayed by the expectations of the state or the market, winning the respect of his peers and younger artists, and remaining an influence on many Chinese artists to this day.

—

Léonard Tsuguharu Foujita
born 1886, Japan; died 1968, Switzerland

Léonard Tsuguharu Foujita was a Japanese artist best known for figurative watercolours that combined *nihonga* (Japanese painting) and *ukiyo-e* (woodblock) aesthetics and techniques with the sights, subjects, and motifs common in his adoptive country of France. It was this unique and eclectic style that distinguished him as a major figure in the School of Paris and one of the best-known Asian artists from the time, drawing the attention of Pablo Picasso, Henri Matisse (1869–1954), and Amedeo Modigliani (1884–1920), among others. Having been a student of Seiki Kuroda (1866–1924) before his departure to France, Foujita returned in Japan in 1933 but never settled down, returning to France in 1950, later taking French nationality and converting to Catholicism.

—

Simon Fujiwara
born 1982, United Kingdom

Born to a British mother and Japanese father, Simon Fujiwara spent his youth living in Japan, Spain, and the United Kingdom. This multitude of different perspectives informs his work, which often comments on the fashioning of the self, the power of the popular image, and manifests in painting, video installations, and performative lectures. In 2021 Fujiwara's ideas culminated in the *Who the Bær* series, in which the artist interrogates our relationship to art-historical images through the mediation of a cartoon character, Who the Bær.

—

Gu Dexin
born 1962, Beijing

Gu Dexin was a principal representative of China's '85 New Wave movement despite being a self-taught artist. His works vary in scale and materials, from modest Surrealist watercolours to monumental installations using unconventional materials such as molten plastic, raw meat, and fruit. One of the first Chinese contemporary artists to be shown overseas, Gu was included in the seminal *Magiciens de la terre* at Centre Pompidou in Paris in 1989, alongside other major artists such as Huang Yong Ping (1954–2019) and Yang Jiechang (born 1956). Most of his artworks are without title or the date of their creation, reflecting the artist's desire to leave interpretation to the viewer. Becoming increasingly frustrated with the art world, Gu withdrew from the scene for good after his final exhibition in 2009.

—

Kawaguchi Kigai
1892–1966, Japan

Kawaguchi Kigai was a *yōga* painter who was among the Japanese artists who studied in France in the 1920s. At twenty he moved to Tokyo to study painting, and later participated in the 4th Nika Exhibition. In 1919 he moved to France and trained in Paris under Fernand Léger (1881–1955) alongside fellow Japanese artist Sakata Kazuo. Kigai also studied under André Lhote (1885–1962). Upon his return to Japan, he won the Nika Award at the 16th Nika Exhibition. He continued participating in group exhibitions and became a member of various art associations, later experimenting with abstraction in response to trends from post-war Europe.

—

Kuroda Seiki
1866–1924, Japan

Kuroda Seiki was considered one of the leaders of the Western style of Japanese painting at the turn of the twentieth century. Having initially travelled to Paris to study law in 1884, he developed an interest in art and later switched to studying painting full time. It was during his time in France that he gained experience with en plein air painting and Impressionism. He returned to Japan almost a decade later, making use of his new skills to depict the sights and scenes of his home country. He was an educator in institutions such as the Tokyo School of Fine Arts, founding their *yōga* (Japanese Western-style painting) department in 1896, becoming a major influence on the next generation of artists in Japan as one of the leaders of the Hakuba-kai art society. Later, he helped establish the first government-sponsored art exhibition, the *Bunten*. In 1910 he became the first *yōga* painter in the Japanese Imperial Court.

—

Firenze Lai
born 1984, Hong Kong

Firenze Lai is best known for what she calls 'situation portraits', paintings that depict isolated figures in what seem to be everyday scenarios. Based on the artist's observations of daily life and how bodies react to their surroundings, the paintings evoke states of psychological distress through gestural brushwork and distorted compositions. Lai's expressive and spontaneous use of colour and line lend her anonymous subjects a sense of inner life, allowing the viewer to identify with or project onto them. Perhaps inspired by her life in Hong Kong, Lai's introspective works reflect a sense of alienation and anxiety experienced by those living in fast-paced and dense urban environments.

—

Wifredo Lam
born 1902, Cuba; died 1982, France

Wifredo Lam, whom Pablo Picasso once claimed was his long-lost Cuban cousin, was raised by a Chinese father and an Afro-Cuban mother of Spanish descent. At age twenty-one Lam left for Madrid to continue his art studies, staying there until the end of the Spanish Civil War, during which he fought on the side of the Republicans against Franco. He later moved to Paris and befriended Picasso, who was a great admirer of his work and introduced him to his circle of artists, writers, and art dealers. Lam returned to Cuba in 1940, where he developed his signature style of magical surrealism and found inspiration in Santería, an Afro-Caribbean religion that joins together the cultural practices of traditional Yoruba religion from West Africa and Roman Catholicism. His later body of works often featured Santería motifs such as birds, dragons, and a horse-headed woman.

—

Lee Mingwei
born 1964, Taiwan

Lee Mingwei is internationally recognised for his participatory installations that foreground the human experience and our desire for connectedness. Educated in Taiwan and the United States, Lee forms part of a generation of artists in the 1990s who began to incorporate elements of participation into their art. Drawing upon his own life and everyday activities to create works that transcend cultural and political boundaries, Lee's works are best known for enabling strangers to interact with each other and engage with concepts of intimacy, reciprocity, and ephemerality.

—

Pixy Liao
born 1979, Shanghai

Pixy Liao's staged photographs offer intimate portraits of her evolving relationship with Moro, her Japanese university classmate-turned-partner and collaborator. Through her practice, such as in her signature photography series *Experimental Relationship* (2007–present) and *For Your Eyes Only* (2012–present), Liao depicts herself as the more dominant partner, casting her muse Moro in a more submissive role. By subverting stereotypes of heteronormative dynamics and ideas of artist and muse, she is able to examine the different forms relationships can take and explore societal and cultural norms.

—

Lin Fengmian
born 1900, Guangdong; died 1991, Hong Kong

Lin Fengmian is widely considered a pioneer of modern Chinese art for his role in reforming Chinese arts education, as well as for his painting practice, which used mainly Expressionist techniques to depict Chinese subjects. He left for France in 1919, and in 1921 began training in the atelier of Fernand Cormon (1845–1924), who had also taught artists including Vincent van Gogh (1853–1890) and Henri Matisse (1869–1954). During his time in Europe, Lin encountered Fauvism, Post-Impressionism, and Cubism—avant-garde styles that would later inform his own artwork. Returning to China in 1928, he founded what is now the China Academy of Art in Hangzhou, teaching alongside fellow French-trained Chinese artists such as Fang Ganmin (1906–1984), and was responsible for nurturing artists including Zao Wou-Ki (1920–2013) and Wu Guanzhong (1919–2010). Both followed his example and travelled to France for further study. Lin settled in Hong Kong in the 1970s and continued to paint for the rest of his life.

—

Julie Lluch
born 1946, Philippines

Julie Lluch is one of the most prolific terracotta ceramists in the Philippines. In a distinctive Surrealist style, she renders portraits of family and friends set in domestic scenes that reveal a commitment to addressing social issues, feminism, sexual freedom, and justice in her home country. During the 1980s Lluch focused on major figures in Western art history, appropriating works by Pablo Picasso and Paul Cézanne (1839–1906). Her lived experiences as a woman continue to inform her work to this day.

—

Madokoro (Akutagawa) Saori
1924–1966, Japan

Best known for her depictions of figures from Japanese creation mythology, Madokoro (Akutagawa) Saori was one of the few women active in the art scene of post-war Japan who took on these grand narrative topics. Her inspirations were Mexican muralism, European modernism, and the folklore of her home country. Most distinctively working in a textile dye and batik medium, commonly associated with crafts and women, Madokoro received a newcomer award from the Nika Association in 1955. In the 1960s Madokoro travelled and exhibited extensively, relocated and studied oil painting in New York, and participated in exhibitions alongside other Japanese artists, among them Yayoi Kusama.

—

Nalini Malani
born 1946, British India (now Pakistan)

Nalini Malani has distinguished herself as a trailblazer of experimental video art, and her long and prolific career spans film, installation, and painting. Informed by the early experience of being displaced in post-partition India, her works continually examine the ways political conflicts and social structures affect women and other marginalised communities. The artist layers motifs from folklore, classical literature, and personal narratives into multimedia works. While making reference to figures from ancient mythology, she often undercuts their conventional readings through surreal imagery and visual techniques, complicating their histories and navigating difficult themes of violence, repression, and politics.

—

Vicente Silva Manansala
1910–1981, Philippines

Vicente Silva Manansala adapted Western styles to develop Transparent Cubism, his own visual language which rendered paint layered in translucent surfaces and planes. Drawing inspiration from folk art, urban and rural life, as well as the social fabric in post-war Philippines, his figurative paintings responded to lived cultural experiences. Having studied fine arts in the Philippines, he received various scholarships which allowed him to study in Canada in 1949 and in France the following year, where he trained under Fernand Léger (1881–1955). At the forefront of the modernist movement in his home country, Manansala brought the topic of national identity to the wider consciousness and became a major influence on his contemporaries in the Philippines.

—

Yasumasa Morimura
born 1951, Japan

Using elaborate props, costumes, and make-up, Yasumasa Morimura creates photographic self-portraits that recreate famous paintings, such as Vincent van Gogh's *Self-Portrait* (1889), and iconic depictions of celebrities including Marilyn Monroe. His career took off during the era of Japan's bubble economy, when collecting Western art, particularly Impressionist works, was seen as a sign of affluence. Through drag and re-enactment, Morimura inserts himself into the Western-centric art canon and popular visual culture to explore how ideas of gender, race, and art history are constructed.

—

No Name Group
1974–1981, Beijing

Formed in Beijing during the early 1970s amid the Cultural Revolution, the No Name Group consisted of a group of artists who sought to make art that did not follow the state-endorsed propagandist visual language of Socialist Realism. Their subjects included landscape and scenes of everyday life, as well as depictions of each other. Members of the group, who were mostly self-taught, painted clandestinely, either working exclusively indoors or at remote locations to avoid arousing suspicion from the authorities. Many of this cohort later became renowned artists and academics in their own right, such as Ma Kelu (born 1954), who has been exhibited internationally since the 1980s, or Wang Aihe (born 1954), who is currently a professor at the University of Hong Kong. Others in the group include Zheng Ziyan (born 1951), Shi Zhenyu (born 1946), Tian Shuying (born 1955), Yang Yushu (born 1944), and Zhang Wei (born 1952).

—

Isamu Noguchi
1904–1988, United States

Isamu Noguchi was a prominent figure of international modernism with an expansive practice across art, design, and landscape architecture. While known for his Surrealist-influenced biomorphic sculptures, Noguchi was equally noted for his iconic design objects. Despite his use of industrial materials such as steel, he was often inspired by flowers, birds, and natural landscapes. Noguchi's tireless exploration of synthesis between Japanese tradition and Western modernism propelled close collaborations with luminaries across cultural disciplines, including Constantin Brâncuși (1876–1957), Buckminster Fuller (1895–1983), and Qi Baishi (1864–1957).

—

Pang Hiunkin
born 1906, Jiangsu; died 1985, Beijing

Pang Hiunkin co-founded the Storm Society in 1931 with artist and writer Ni Yide. The pioneering group advocated modern forms of artistic expression and opposed the conservative ideas and attitudes to painting which were prevalent in China at the time. Though he was interested in calligraphy and traditional ink painting in his early years, his mother encouraged him to pursue a robust education in the arts in France. He left China to study abroad in 1925, quickly developing friendships with the wave of Chinese art students who had already arrived in Paris, such as Sanyu (1901–1966) and Lin Fengmian (1900–1991). Five years later he returned to his home country with the intent to modernise the Chinese art community. He took on teaching roles, contributed to magazines, and continued his artistic exploration, blending oil painting techniques with Chinese subject matter. Alongside his fellow classmates from Paris, Pang would become one of the crucial figures in the development of modern Chinese art.

—

Faith Ringgold
1930–2024, United States

Growing up in the aftermath of the Harlem Renaissance, Faith Ringgold was a painter and mixed media sculptor who is also celebrated for her signature narrative quilts which explore the Black American experience and comment on issues of racism, sexism, and history. Her *French Collection* (1991–1997) series of paintings on quilts responds to the predominantly white and male canon of art history by illustrating a revisionist narrative of modernist art in the 1920s. Intertwined with her artistic practice was her activism, and she spent much of her career advocating for the inclusion of work by Black artists and women in art institutions.

—

Sakata Kazuo
1889–1956, Japan

Best known for his Cubist painting style, Sakata Kazuo had initially hoped to become a doctor, like his father, but decided to become an artist instead. At twenty-five he moved to Tokyo to study art, and in 1921 travelled to Paris to further his studies. He exhibited extensively during his decade in France, studying under artists such as André Lhote (1885–1962) and Fernand Léger (1881–1955) alongside fellow Japanese artist Kawaguchi Kigai. Upon his return to Japan in 1933, he set up a studio in his home prefecture, Okayama, creating abstract paintings inspired by Cubism. After the Second World War he founded and led the Avant-Garde Okayama art group.

—

Gaganendranath Tagore
1867–1938, British India

Gaganendranath Tagore was one of the first Indian artists to respond to the Cubism of Pablo Picasso and Georges Braque (1882–1963). Unlike his younger brother Abanindranath Tagore (1871–1951), who was the founder of the Bengal school of art, precursor to modern Indian painting, Gaganendranath followed Western Cubism. To him, Cubism as a Western art movement opposed traditional hegemony and therein Gaganendranath found his new identity, one that decidedly broke with the colonial past. He was dubbed 'an Indian Cubist', and produced paintings that drew from multiple perspectives, as well as South Asian cultural heritage.

—

Tanaami Keiichi
1936–2024, Japan

Tanaami Keiichi was a prolific Japanese graphic designer, artist, and animator whose practice spanned from the 1960s to the end of his life. Tanaami was nine years old when his home city of Tokyo was bombed during the Second World War in 1945, an experience that would later feature repeatedly in his work, through such images as American bomber planes, searchlights in the sky, and cities in a sea of fire. Growing up in post-war Japan also exposed him to American popular culture, psychedelic aesthetics, and Pop Art. He freely appropriated these sources and quickly gained recognition for his works of fine art, animation, and magazine covers, as well as collaborations with commercial brands. Unable to resume work on his projects during the pandemic in 2020, Tanaami turned to replicating and adapting paintings by Pablo Picasso, to date creating more than 400 versions.

—

Tōgō Seiji
1897–1978, Japan

Tōgō Seiji was celebrated for the distinctive style of his oil paintings depicting women. He held his first solo exhibition at age eighteen and in the next year won an award from the Nika Association, an art society formed in opposition to the Hakuba-kai art society and government-favoured styles of painting. From 1921 to 1928 he studied in France, where he was able to engage more deeply with arts movements such as Futurism, Cubism, and Surrealism, which he had already begun to encounter in Japan. Upon returning to his home country, he continued to evolve as an artist. Taking inspiration from modernist styles, Tōgō created not just oil paintings but also illustrations, book covers, and murals. In the 1960s he began to travel abroad frequently to participate in exhibitions for the Nika Association, often finding inspiration for his own art in the places he visited.

—

Yan Pei-Ming
born 1960, Shanghai

Fascinated by European classical painting, Yan Pei-Ming left China at the age of nineteen to study at the École des Beaux-Arts in Dijon. His visual vocabulary often includes raw and powerful colours presented in monumental formats. In 1990, he obtained French nationality and bought his first studio in Dijon. Frequently focusing on human subjects, his practice questions the complex and contradictory nature of being. More recently, Yan has confronted masters from the past by interpreting classic masterpieces, making use of a more subtle pictorial approach.

—

Haegue Yang
born 1971, South Korea

Spanning a vast array of media—from collage and kinetic sculpture to room-sized installations—Haegue Yang's work links disparate histories and traditions in a visual idiom that is her own. She draws on a variety of craft techniques and materials, including drying racks, Venetian blinds, *hanji* paper, and artificial straw, each carrying its own cultural connotations. Through multisensory environments that extend perception beyond sight, Yang's immersive experiences explore themes of labour, migration, and displacement. She serves as Vice-Rector of the Städelschule in Frankfurt am Main, where she graduated as Meisterschüler in 1999.

—

Yorozu Tetsugorō
1885–1927, Japan

Yorozu Tetsugorō was among the first generation of painters to introduce avant-garde art styles into *yōga* (Japanese Western-style painting). Having initially taught himself watercolour, he later attended meetings of the Hakuba-kai art society and began studying at the Tokyo Fine Arts School in 1907. Except for a brief stay in the United States in 1906, Yorozu did not travel overseas, but was aware of art movements abroad. His graduation work, titled *Nude Beauty* (1912), was one of the earliest examples of Japanese Fauvism, gaining him critical acclaim. He returned to his home in Iwate Prefecture in the mid-1910s and continued his practice, moving away from his previous Fauvist- and post-Impressionist–inspired style to experiment with Cubism. In 1919 he moved to Kanagawa Prefecture for health reasons, remaining active in various arts circles and expanding his art style to include Japanese literati painting and *nihonga* until his death.

—

Zhang Daqian
born 1899, Sichuan; died 1983, Taipei

Considered one of the great Chinese artists of the twentieth century, Zhang Daqian developed a versatile artistic language that spanned traditional Chinese *guohua* and combined the style with Western Abstract Expressionism. For his vibrant ink portraits, landscapes, and depictions of flowers and birds, Zhang drew inspiration from a wide variety of subjects around him. By his early twenties he was already well known among a circle of famous calligraphers and painters. He left China in the early 1950s and lived in Argentina, Brazil, the United States, and other countries. His famed encounter with Pablo Picasso, in 1956 in France, was touted as a meeting between the pinnacles of art in the East and West. In the late 1970s Zhang settled in Taipei, where he lived for the remainder of his life.

Picture Credits

Every effort has been made to appropriately credit the images included in this publication. Page numbers are given in **bold**.

l = left; r = right; t=top; b = bottom; c = centre

Front cover, 142, 143 © Yasumasa Morimura. Image courtesy of the artist; **2** © *Pablo Picasso devant* Massacre en Corée *et des éléments de céramique au sol de La Californie, Cannes, 4 novembre 1955*, Atelier Lucien Clergue, Saif, 2025. Image: © GrandPalaisRmn (Musée national Picasso-Paris)/Adrien Didierjean; **6, 8** © Yan Pei-Ming/ADAGP, Paris – SACK, Seoul, 2024. Photo: Clérin-Morin. Image courtesy of Atelier YAN Pei-Ming; **10–11** Courtesy of the artist and LEE Studio. Image: © Laura Fiorio; **14, 19, 21, 37, 39, 42b, 43, 63l, 63r, 68, 72, 73, 75, 77t, 80, 81, 82, 87, 89, 97, 99, 101, 104–105, 187** © Succession Picasso 2025. Image: © GrandPalaisRmn (musée national Picasso-Paris)/Adrien Didierjean; **16t, 188lb** © Succession Picasso 2025. Image: ©GrandPalaisRmn (musée national Picasso-Paris)/Madeleine Coursaget; **16b** © Lee Miller Archives, England 2024. All rights reserved. www.leemiller.co.uk. Image: © GrandPalaisRmn (Musée national Picasso-Paris)/image GrandPalaisRmn; **17, 98** © Succession Picasso 2025. Image: Art Resource, NY; **18, 59, 94** © Succession Picasso 2025. Image © The Metropolitan Museum of Art. Image source: Art Resource, NY; **20, back cover** © Robert Doisneau/Gamma-Legends via Getty Images; **22** © Succession Picasso 2025. Image: © GrandPalaisRmn (musée national Picasso-Paris)/Franck Raux. Author Rights: © Laurence Marceillac; **23, 31, 33, 45, 47, 51, 53, 65, 70, 71, 74, 77b, 79, 83, 84, 85, 88, 102, 106, 107, 108, 116–117, 150, 151, 157** © Succession Picasso 2025. Image: © GrandPalaisRmn (musée national Picasso-Paris)/Mathieu Rabeau; **24, 35, 124t, 184t** © Succession Picasso 2025. Image courtesy of Museu Picasso, Barcelona. Photo: Fotogasull; **25** © Succession Picasso 2025. Image: © GrandPalaisRmn (musée national Picasso-Paris)/ Rachel Prat; **26** Image: © ARTGEN/Alamy Stock Photo; **27, 29, 76** © Succession Picasso 2025. Image: © GrandPalaisRmn (musée national Picasso-Paris)/Adrien Didierjean/Mathieu Rabeau; **30** Image: © GrandPalaisRmn (musée du Louvre)/Jean-Gilles Berizzi; **32** © Photo Josse/ Scala, Florence; **34** Image: © Museo Nacional del Prado, Dist. GrandPalaisRmn/image du Prado; **36** Image © GrandPalaisRmn (musée d'Orsay)/Hervé Lewandowski; **38** Image: © GrandPalaisRmn (musée du Louvre)/Franck Raux; **40** Image: © The Metropolitan Museum of Art. Image source: Art Resource, NY; **41** © Succession Picasso 2025. Image: © Centre Pompidou, MNAM-CCI, Dist. GrandPalaisRmn/ Christian Bahier/Philippe Migeat; **42l** © Succession Picasso 2025/© All rights reserved. Image © GrandPalaisRmn (Musée national Picasso-Paris)/Mathieu Rabeau; **44** © Succession Picasso 2025. Image: © GrandPalaisRmn (musée national Picasso-Paris)/René-Gabriel Ojeda; **48** © Succession Picasso 2025. Image: The Solomon R. Guggenheim Foundation/Art Resource, NY; **49** © Succession Picasso 2025. Image: Private Collection Christie's Images/ © Succession Picasso/DACS, London 2024/ Bridgeman Images; **50t** Image: © Munchmuseet/ Juri Kobayashi. Image Number: MM.M.00591; **50b** © Fine Art Images/Heritage Images; **54** © David Douglas Duncan/© Succession Picasso 2025. © GrandPalaisRmn (musée national Picasso-Paris)/image GrandPalaisRmn; **55** © Succession Picasso 2025. Image: © Detroit Institute of Arts/© Succession Picasso/DACS, London 2024/ Bridgeman Images; **56, 58** © Succession Picasso 2025. Image courtesy of National Gallery of Art, Washington; **57** © Succession Picasso 2025. Image: 2024 © Photo Scala, Florence; **61, 64, 90, 120, 198** © Succession Picasso 2025. Photo: © Digital image, The Museum of Modern Art, New York/Scala, Florence; **62** © Succession Picasso 2025. Image: The Art Institute of Chicago/Art Resource, NY; **66** © Association Marcel Duchamp/ADAGP, Paris – SACK, Seoul, 2024. Image: © Centre Pompidou, MNAM-CCI, Dist. GrandPalaisRmn/Christian Bahier/Philippe Migeat; **67** © The Estate of Eva Hesse. Courtesy Hauser & Wirth; **69** © Succession Picasso 2025. Image: © The Philadelphia Museum of Art, Dist. GrandPalaisRmn/image Philadelphia Museum of Art; **78** Image: © musée du quai Branly – Jacques Chirac, Dist. GrandPalaisRmn; **92–93** © Succession Picasso 2025. Image: bpk/Alfredo Dagli Orti; **95** © Succession Picasso 2025. Image: © GrandPalaisRmn (musée national Picasso-Paris)/Gabriel de Carvalho **96** © Succession Picasso 2025/© All rights reserved. Image: © GrandPalaisRmn (musée national Picasso-Paris)/image GrandPalaisRmn; **100t** Image: The Metropolitan Museum of Art, New York, Gift of Louis C. Raegner, 1927; **100b** Image: The Metropolitan Museum of Art, New York, Gift of Thomas F. Ryan, in memory of William M. Laffan, 1910; **103** © Dora Maar/ADAGP, Paris – SACK, Seoul, 2024. Image: © Centre Pompidou, MNAM-CCI, Dist. GrandPalaisRmn; **109** © 2024 Anyone Can Fly Foundation/Artists Rights Society (ARS), New York. Image: Worcester Art Museum, Massachusetts, USA, Worcester Art Museum/Charlotte E. W. Buffington Fund/ Bridgeman Images; **110–111** © Jaune Quick-to-See-Smith and courtesy Garth Greenan Gallery,

New York. Photography courtesy Denver Art Museum; **111t** Image courtesy of Gregory Sholette; **111b** Photo: Ismael Llopis; **112, 180–181** © Succession Picasso 2025. Image: Photographic Archives Museo Nacional Centro de Arte Reina Sofía; **113, 145, 146t, 146b** © Keiichi Tanaami. Image courtesy of NANZUKA; **118t** Image: © GrandPalaisRmn (musée du Louvre)/ Gérard Blot/Christian Jean; **118b** Image: © GrandPalaisRmn (musée du Louvre)/René-Gabriel Ojeda; **119t** Image: © Museo Nacional del Prado, Dist. GrandPalaisRmn/image du Prado; **119b** Photo: © Kunsthalle Mannheim/Kathrin Schwab; **121** © Succession Picasso 2025. Image: The Art Institute of Chicago/Art Resource, NY; **123** © Succession Picasso 2025. Image © Ward Moretti Ltd; **124b** Image: © M+, Hong Kong; **125t** © Foujita Foundation/ADAGP, Paris – SACK, Seoul, 2024. Image: © GrandPalaisRmn/Agence Bulloz; **125c** Image supplied by the Hong Kong Museum of Art; **125b** © All rights reserved. Image source: https://auction.artron.net/paimai-art5014101032; **126l, 127** © Lin Fengmian; **126r** © Fang Ganmin; **128l** © Sompo Museum of Art, 24018. Image courtesy of Sompo Museum of Art; **128t** © Kigai Kawaguchi. Photo: MOMAT/ DNPartcom; **128b** Image courtesy of Okayama Prefectural Museum of Art; **129l** Image courtesy of Iwate Museum of Art; **129r, 192l** Photo: MOMAT/DNPartcom; **130** Jacqueline de la Baume-Dürrbach © Succession Picasso 2025. Photo: Marcel Coen. Archives de Marseille (82 Fl); **133** © David Hockney. Photo by Richard Schmidt. The David Hockney Foundation; **134t** © 2024 Jasper Johns/Licensed by VAGA at Artists Rights Society (ARS), NY. Image: Private Collection Christie's Images/Bridgeman Images; **134b** © 2024 George Condo/Artists Rights Society (ARS), New York. Photo: © Digital image, The Museum of Modern Art, New York/Scala, Florence; **135l** Image courtesy of Maurizio Cattelan and Fundación Almine y Bernard Ruiz-Picasso, Madrid © Philippe D. Photography; **135tr** © Estate of Jean-Michel Basquiat. Licensed by Artestar, New York. **135b** © Robert Colescott. Photo: Nathaniel Wilson; **136** © Atul Dodiya. Image courtesy of Chemould Prescott Road and the artist; **137** © Tadanori Yokoo. Image courtesy of the artist; **138** © Chéri Samba. Courtesy Galerie Magnin-A, Photo: Maurice Aeschimann. Image courtesy of The Jean Pigozzi African Art Collection; **139, 141** © 2024 Zeng Fanzhi; **144** © Succession Picasso 2025. Image: Yale University Art Gallery. Gift of Stephen Carlton Clark, B.A. 1903; **147l** © 2024 The Isamu Noguchi Foundation and Garden Museum, New York/Artists Rights Society (ARS), New York. Photo: Kevin Noble. Image courtesy of Isamu Noguchi Foundation and Garden Museum, New York; **147r** © Succession Brâncuși – All rights reserved ADAGP, Paris – SACK, Seoul, 2024. Image: Peggy Guggenheim Collection, Venice (Solomon R. Guggenheim Foundation, New York); **148** © 2024 The Isamu Noguchi Foundation and Garden Museum, New York/ Artists Rights Society (ARS), New York. Photo: Walter J. Russell. Image courtesy of The Isamu Noguchi Foundation and Garden Museum, New York; **149** © 2024 The Isamu Noguchi Foundation and Garden Museum, New York/Artists Rights Society (ARS), New York. Photo: Dan Leung © M+, Hong Kong; **152** © Wifredo Lam/ADAGP, Paris – SACK, Seoul, 2024. Image: Digital image, The Museum of Modern Art, New York/Scala, Florence; **154** © Guang Tingbo; **155t, 156** © Zheng Ziyan; **155b** © Shi Zhenyu; **155r** © Wang Aihe; **158, 159, 208b** © Luis Trust. Image courtesy of Hanart TZ Gallery; **161** © Firenze Lai; **162, 163** © Catherine Yang; **164** © Feng Xi; **166** © Gu Dexin. Image source: Fondation Guy et Myriam Ullens; **167** © Fang Lijun; **169** © Saori Akutagawa. Image courtesy of NUKAGA GALLERY; **170** © Nalini Malani. Courtesy Galerie Lelong & Co.; **171l, 171c, 171r** © Pixy Liao. Image courtesy of the artist and Blindspot Gallery; **173** © Cai Guo-Qiang; **174–175** Haegue Yang, Photo: Chunho An. Image courtesy of the artist; **176, 183l** © Succession Picasso 2025. Image: © GrandPalaisRmn (musée national Picasso-Paris)/image GrandPalaisRmn; **178–179** © Simon Fujiwara. Photo: © Ludger Paffrath. Image courtesy of Esther Schipper; **183r** © All rights reserved. Image approved by The Tokyo National Research Institute for Cultural Properties (TOBUNKEN); **184bl** Image source: ColBase: Integrated Collections Database of the National Institutes for Cultural Heritage, Japan (https://colbase.nich.go.jp/collection_items/ tnm/KU-a117); **184br** Image courtesy of Mary Evans Picture Library; **185l** © Succession Picasso 2025. Image: © All Rights Reserved; **185r** Image source: Museum of Fine Arts of the City of Paris; **186l** © All rights reserved. Image source: *Liangyou* (The Young Companion), no. 91, 1 August 1934; **186r** © All rights reserved. Image courtesy of Beinecke Rare Book and Manuscript Library. With thanks to the Gertrude Stein and Alice B. Toklas Estate; **188tr** © Succession Picasso 2025. Image: Photo Scala, Florence; **188br** © Foujita Foundation/ADAGP, Paris – SACK, Seoul, 2024. Image courtesy of Masakichi Hirano Art Foundation; **189** © Succession Picasso 2025. Image: © Victoria and Albert Museum, London; **190** © Succession Picasso 2025. Image courtesy of Hood Museum of Art; **191** Image: © Victoria and Albert Museum, London; **192r** © All rights reserved. Photo: M+, Hong Kong; **193, 195** Courtesy of The Pang Hiunkin [Pang Xunqin] Archives at The Liching Cultural and Educational Foundation; **194** © George Keyt; **196** © Wifredo Lam/ADAGP, Paris – SACK, Seoul, 2024. Image courtesy of the Artist Estate; **197** © Alkazi Theatre Archives; **200l** © Succession Picasso 2025; **200r** Image source: China Pictorial. October 1952; **201** © All rights reserved. Image: © M+, Hong Kong; **202l** Image courtesy of Macao Museum of Art; **202r** © Qi Baishi. Image: © The Metropolitan Museum of Art. Image source: Art Resource, NY; **203** © Succession Picasso 2025. Fundación Almine y Bernard Ruiz-Picasso, Madrid © FABA Photo: Marc Domage; **204** Photograph by Brian Brake, Museum of New Zealand Te Papa Tongarewa, negative number CT.035276; **205** Image courtesy of Jyoti Bhatt and Asia Art Archive; **206l** Image supplied by the Hong Kong Museum of Art; **206r** © M+ Hong Kong; **207t, 207b** Ha Bik Chuen Archive. Image courtesy of the Ha Family and Asia Art Archive; **208t** © Succession Picasso 2025. © Private Collection: Photo Robert McKeever; **209l** © Succession Picasso 2025. Image courtesy of The Hakone Open-Air Museum; **209r** © Julie Lluch Dalena; **210l** picture alliance/Contributor via Getty Images; **210r** Photo: © National Gallery of Modern Art; **211** Photo: © ChinaImages via Depositphotos; **212–213** © Succession Picasso 2025. Image: Album/Scala, Florence.

Index

Page numbers in *italic* refer to the illustrations

D

E

F

G

H

I

J

K

L

M

N

O

P

Q

R

S

T

U

V

W

X

Y

Z

First published in the United Kingdom in 2025 by Thames & Hudson Ltd, 181A High Holborn, London WC1V 7QX, in collaboration with M+, West Kowloon Cultural District, 38 Museum Drive, Kowloon, Hong Kong

First published in the United States of America in 2025 by Thames & Hudson Inc., 500 Fifth Avenue, New York, New York 10110

Published on the occasion of the exhibition *The Hong Kong Jockey Club Series: Picasso/Asia—A Conversation* at M+, Hong Kong, 15 March to 13 July 2025. The exhibition is co-organised by M+ and Musée national Picasso-Paris, and co-presented with the French May Arts Festival. It is the opening programme of the French May Arts Festival 2025. The exhibition is generously supported by the following sponsors:

Co-organisers

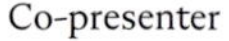

Co-presenter

Title sponsor

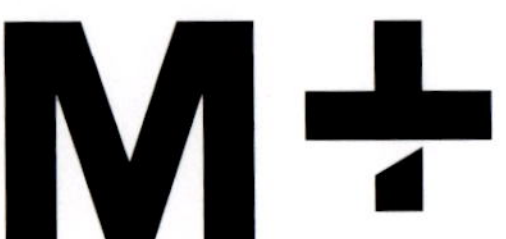

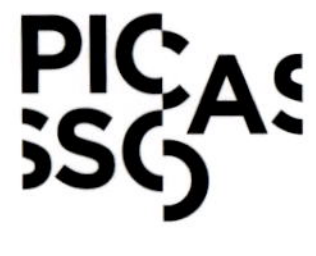

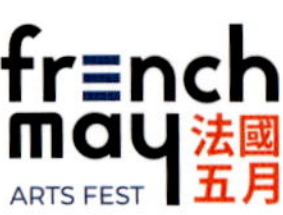

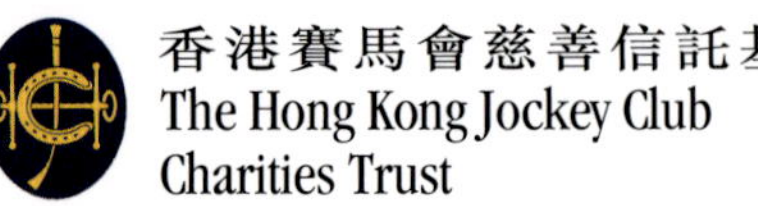

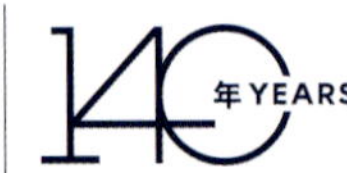

Major sponsors

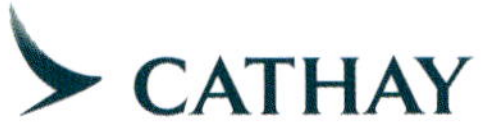

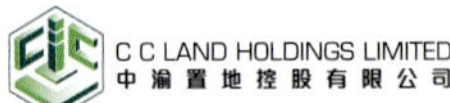

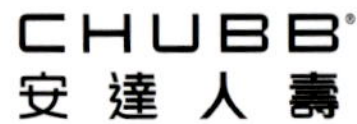

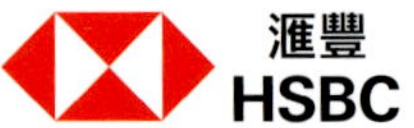

Project grant

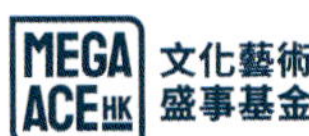

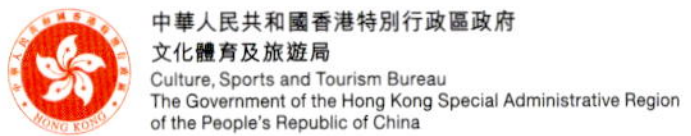

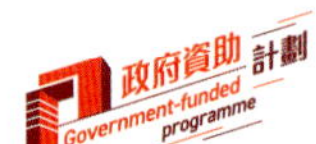

Editors: Doryun Chong, François Dareau
Assistant editor: Hester Chan
Project editor: William Smith
English editing: Patrick Rhine, Jacqueline Leung
Chinese editing: Lam Lap Wai, Zhong Yuling, Or Ka Uen
Editorial assistants: Annessa Chan, Angela Liu
Translation: Cecilia Kwan, Erica Leung, Winny Leung
Publishing management: Patrick Rhine, Juliet Cheung, Sasha Anderson
Rights and reproductions: Jacqueline Chan
Cover and interior layout design: Peter Dawson, Johanne Lian Olsen
Chinese typesetting: HATO

British Library Cataloguing-in-Publication Data
A catalogue record for this book is available from the British Library

Library of Congress Control Number 2024952497

ISBN 978-0-500-48114-1

Impression 01

Printed and bound in Hong Kong by 1010 Printing International Ltd

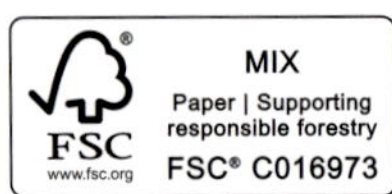

Front cover
Yasumasa Morimura, *A Requiem: Theater of Creativity / Self-Portrait as Pablo Picasso*, 2010 (see page 142)

Back cover
Robert Doisneau, *Picasso at the table with buns for fingers at La Galloise, Vallauris, in September 1952*, 1952 (see page 20)

Page 2
Lucien Clergue, *Pablo Picasso standing in front of* Massacre in Korea *and ceramic elements on the floor at Villa La Californie, Cannes, 4 November 1955*, 1955

Pages 112–113
Left: *Woman's Head (Fernande)*, 1909–1910
Right: Tanaami Keiichi, *Pleasure of Picasso—Mother and Child No.653*, 2023

Pages 180–181
Dead Birds, 1912

Pages 212–213
Horse Head. Sketch for *Guernica*, 1937